GROC'S CANDID GUIDE TO
THE CYCLADES ISLANDS
including
SYROS, MYKONOS, PAROS, NAXOS, IOS, SANTORINI, AMORGOS, ASTIPALAIA, TINOS ANDROS, SIKINOS, FOLEGANDROS, MILOS, SIPHNOS, SERIFOS, KITHNOS & KEA
with Excursion details to
DELOS, ANTIPAROS, ANAFI, DONOUSSA, KOUFONISSI, SHINOUSSA, IRAKLIA, KIMOLOS.
As well as
ATHENS CITY, PIRAEUS & THE MAINLAND PORTS
of
RAFINA & LAVRIO
for the package, villa, back-packer &
ferry-boating holiday maker,
whether travelling by air, car, coach or train.

by
Geoffrey O'Connell

Willowbridge Publishers
introduce to readers of GROC's Candid Guides

TRAVELSURANCE

A comprehensive holiday insurance plan that 'gives cover that many other policies do not reach' . . .

In addition to the more usual cover offered by other policies the **TRAVELSURANCE HOLIDAY PLAN** includes (where medically necessary).

(1) Fly-home repatriation by air ambulance.

(2) Inter-island travel costs for pregnant women.

Additionally personal accident and medical & emergency expenses EVEN while hiring a bicycle, scooter or car.

An example premium per person for Greece for 10 - 17 days is £13.40. Cover is arranged with Lloyds Underwriters.

For an application form please complete the section below and forward

To Willowbridge Enterprises, Willowbridge, Stoke Rd, Bletchley, Milton Keynes, Bucks.

Please forward me   *(block capitals please)*

Mr/Mrs/Miss . . . . Age . . . .

of . . . .

. . . .

a **TRAVELSURANCE** application form.

Date of commencement of holiday . . . . Duration . . . .

Signature. . . . . Date. . . . .

CONTENTS

ILLUSTRATIONS

Please do not forget that prices are given as a guide only especially restaurant and accommodation costs which are subject to fluctuation, almost always upwards. In the last year or so transport costs, especially ferry-boat fees have also escalated dramatically but the increased value of other currencies to the Greek drachmae has compensated, to some extent, for these seemingly inexorably rising charges.

The series is entering its fourth year of publication and I would appreciate continuing to hear from holidaymakers and travellers who have any additions or corrections to bring to my attention. As in the past, all correspondence (except that addressed 'Dear filth' or similar endearments) will be answered.

I hope readers will excuse the odd errors that creep (well gallop) into the welter of detailed information included in the body text. We manage, in order to keep the volumes as up to date as possible, to cut the period down from inception to publication to some five months which does result in the occasional slip up ...

INTRODUCTION

This volume is the fourth in the popular and proven series of GROC's Candid Greek Island Guides. The rationale, the *raison d'etre* behind their production is to treat each island grouping on an individual and comprehensive basis, rather than attempt overall coverage of the 100 or so islands usually described in one volume. This obviates attempting to do justice, to, say, Ios in amongst an aggregation of many other, often disparate, islands.

Due to the vast distances involved very few, if any, vacationers can possibly visit more than a number of islands in any one particular group, even if spending as much as four weeks in Greece.

It is important for package and villa holiday-makers to have an unbiased and relevant description of their planned holiday surroundings, rather than the usual extravagant hyperbole of the glossy sales brochure. It is vital for back-packers and ferry-boat travellers to have detailed and accurate information at their finger tips, on arrival. With these differing requirements in mind, factual, 'straight-from-the-shoulder' location reports have been combined with detailed plans of the major port, town and/or city of each island in the group as well as topographical island maps.

Amongst the guides on offer there are a number of books dealing with Ancient and Modern Greece, its mythology and history; there are a number of thumb-nail travel guides and there are some worthy if skimpy and or rather out-of-date guide books. Unfortunately they do not necessarily assuage the various travellers differing requirements which include speedy and accurate identification of one's position on arrival; the location of accommodation and the whereabouts of banks, post office and tourist offices. Additional requisites are a swift and easy to read resumé of the town's main locations, cafes, tavernas and restaurants; detailed local bus and ferry timetables as well as a full island narrative. Once the traveller has settled in, then and only then can they start to feel at ease, making their own finds and discoveries.

I have chosen to omit lengthy accounts of the relevant, fabulous Greek mythology and history. These aspects of Greece are, for the serious student, very ably related by authors far more erudite than myself. Moreover, most islands have a semi-official tourist guide translated into English, and for that matter, French, German and Scandinavian, which are well worth the 150 to 300 drachmae (drs) they cost. They are usually extremely informative and rather well produced, with excellent colour photographs. Admittedly the English translation might seem a little quaint (try to read Greek, let alone translate it), and the maps are often unreliable.

Each new edition is revised but follows the now well tried formula. Part One deals with the preliminaries and describes in detail the different aspects of travelling and enjoying to the full the unforgettable experience of a Greek Island holiday. Part Two gives a full and thoroughly redrafted account of Athens, still the hub for Greek island travel, and the relevant mainland ports for connections to the islands. Part Three introduces the Cyclades islands, followed by a detailed description of each island, the layout being designed to facilitate quick and easy reference.

The exchange rate has fluctuated quite violently in recent years and up-to-date information must be sought prior to departure. For instance at the time of writing the final draft, the rate to the English pound (£) was hovering about 218 drs and to the American dollar ($) some 153 drs but prices are subject to fluctuation, usually upward. Annual price increases vary between some 10-20% but fortunately the drachma devalues by approximately the same amount.

1

Recommendations and personalities are almost always based on personal observation and experience occasionally emphasised by the discerning comments of readers or colleagues and may well not only change from year to year but be subject to different interpretation by other observers.

For 1985 and future years some of the accommodation and eating places that are recommended in the Candid Guides may display a specially produced decal, to help readers identify the various establishments.

Enjoy yourselves and *Ya Sou* (welcome).

ACKNOWLEDGMENTS

Every year the list of those to be formally thanked grows and this edition shows no dimunition in their number which has forced the original brief entry from the inside front cover to an inside page.

There are those numerous friends and confidants we meet on passage and who, in the main, remain unnamed.

Rosemary who accompanies me, adding her often unwanted, uninformed comments and asides (and may well not be taken again!), requires especial thanks for unrelieved, unstinting (well amost unstinting) support despite being dragged from this or that sunkissed beach.

Although receiving reward, other than in heaven, some of those who assisted me in the production of this edition require specific acknowledgment for effort far beyond the siren call of vulgar remuneration! These worthies include Linda Fehrenbach, Graham Bishop, Ted Spittles, Elizabeth, and Barbara of The Monitor.

Lastly I must admonish Richard Joseph for ever encouraging and cajoling me to scribble.

Geoffrey O'Connell 1986

PART ONE

1 Packing, insurance, medical matters, climatic conditions, conversion tables & a starter course in Greek

Leisure nourishes the body and the mind is also fed thereby: on the other hand, immoderate labour exhausts both. *Ovid.*

Vacationing anywhere on an organised tour allows a certain amount of latitude regarding the amount of luggage packed, as this method of holiday does not preclude taking fairly substantial suitcases. On the other hand, ferry-boating and back-packing restricts the amount a traveller is able to carry and the means of conveyance. The usual method is to utilise back-packs and/or roll-bags, both of which are more suitable than suitcases for this mode of travel. The choice between roll-bags and back-packs does not only depend on which are the most commodious, for at the height of the season it can be advantageous to be distinguishable from the hordes of other back-packers. To promote the chances of being offered a room, the selection of roll-bags may help disassociation from the more hippy of 'genus rucksacker'. If roll-bags are selected they should include shoulder straps which help alleviate the discomfort experienced when searching out accommodation on hot afternoons with arms just stretching and stretching and stretching. In the highly populous, oversubscribed months of July and August, it is advisable to pack a thin, foam bedroll and lightweight sleeping bag, just in case accommodation cannot be located on the occasional night.

Unless camping out, I do not think a sweater is necessary between the months of May and September. A desert jacket or lightweight anorak is a better proposition and a stout pair of sandals or training shoes are mandatory, especially if very much walking is contemplated. Leave out the evening suit and cocktail dresses, as the Greeks are very informal, instead take loose-fitting, casual clothes, and do not forget sunglasses and a floppy hat.

Should there be any doubt about the electric supply (and you shave) include a pack of disposable razors. Ladies might consider acquiring one of the small gas cylinder, portable hair-curlers. Take along a supply of toilet rolls. They are useful for tasks other than that with which they are usually associated, including mopping up spilt liquid, wiping off plates, and blowing one's nose. Do not forget some washing powder, clothes pegs, string for a line, and a few wire hangers to hook up washing.

If travelling to any extent, it is advisable to pack a few plastic, sealed-lid, liquid containers, a plate and a cup, as well as a knife and fork, condiments, an all-purpose cutting/slicing/carving knife and a combination bottle and tin opener. These all facilitate economical dining whilst on the move as food and drink, when available on ferry-boats and trains, can be comparatively expensive. Camping out will require these elementary items to be augmented with simple cooking equipment.

Mosquito coils can be bought in Greece but a preferable gadget is a small, 2 prong electric heater on which a wafer thin tablet is placed. This device can be purchased locally for some 500 drs and comes complete with a pack of the capsules. One trade name is *Doker Mat* and almost every room has a suitable electric point. The odourless vapour given off, harmless to humans, certainly sorts out the mosquitoes. Mark you we did hear of a tourist who purchased one and swore by its efficacy not even aware it was necessary to place a tablet in position. . .

Consider packing a pair of tweezers, some plasters, calamine lotion, after-sun and insect cream, as well as a bottle of aspirin in addition to any pharmaceuticals usually required. It is worth noting that sun oil and small packets of soap powder are now cheaper in Greece than much of Europe whilst, shampoo and toothpaste cost about the same. Including a small phial of disinfectant has merit, but it is best not to leave the liquid in the original glass bottle. Should it break, the disinfectant and glass mingled with clothing can prove not only messy but also leaves a distinctive and lingering odour. Kaolin and morphine is a very reliable stomach settler. Greek chemists dispense medicines and prescriptions that only a doctor would be able to mete out in many other Western European countries, so, prior to summoning a doctor, try the local pharmacy.

Insurance & medical matters

While touching upon medical matters, a national of an EEC country, should extend their states National Health cover. United Kingdom residents should contact the local *Department of Health and Social Security* requesting form number *E111 UK*. When completed, and returned, this will result in a *Certificate of Entitlement to Benefits in Kind during a stay in a Member State*. Well, that's super! In short, it entitles a person to medical treatment in other EEC countries. Do not only rely on this prop, but seriously consider taking out a holiday insurance policy, covering loss of baggage and money, personal accident and medical expenses, cancellation of the holiday and personal liability. Check the exclusion clauses carefully. It is no good imagining one is covered for 'this or that' only to discover the insurance company has craftily excluded claims under a particular section. Should you intend to hire a scooter ensure this form of 'activity' is comprehensively insured. Rather than rely on the rather inadequate standard insurance cover offered by many tour companies, it is best to approach a specialist insurance broker. For instance, bearing in mind the rather rudimentary treatment offered by the average Greek island hospital, it is almost obligatory to include *Fly-Home Medicare* cover in any policy. A couple of illustrative homilies might reinforce the argument. Firstly the Greek hospital system expects the patients family to minister and feed the inmate out of hours. This can result in holiday companions having to camp out in the ward for the duration of any internment. Perhaps more thought-provoking is the home-spun belief that a patient is best left the first night to survive, if it is God's will, and to pass on if it is not! A number of years hearing of the unfortunate experiences of friends and readers, who failed to act on the advice given herein, as well as the inordinate difficulties I have experienced in arranging cover for myself, has prompted me to offer readers an all embracing travel insurance scheme. Details are to be found on Page iii. **DON'T DELAY, ACT NOW.**

Most rooms do not have rubbish containers so include some plastic bin liners which are very useful for packing food as well as storing dirty washing. A universal sink plug is almost a necessity. Many Greek sinks do not have one, but as the water usually drains away very slowly this could be considered an academic point.

Take along a pack of cards, and enough paperback reading to while away sunbathing sojourns and long journeys. Playing cards are subject to a government tax, which makes their price exorbitant and books are expensive but some shops and lodgings operate a book-swop scheme.

Many flights, buses, ferry-boats and train journeys start off early in the morning so a small battery-operated alarm clock may well help to save sleepless, fretful nights. A small hand or wrist compass can be an enormous help orientating in towns and if room and weight allow, a torch is a useful addition to the inventory.

Do not forget your passport which is absolutely essential to (1) enter Greece, (2) book into most hotels, pensions or camp-sites, (3) change money and (4) hire a scooter or car.

In the larger, more popular tourist orientated resorts Diners and American Express (Amex) credit cards are accepted. Personal cheques may be changed as long as accompanied by a Eurocheque bank card. Americans can use an Amex credit card at their overseas offices to change personal cheques up to $1000. They may, by prior arrangement, have cable transfers made to overseas banks, allowing 24 hrs from the moment their home bank receives specific instructions. It is wise to detail credit card, traveller's cheques and airline ticket numbers and keep the list separately from the aforementioned items, in case they should be mislaid. This is a piece of advice I always give but rarely, if ever, carry out myself.

Visitors are only allowed to import 3000 drs of Greek currency (in notes) and the balance required must be in traveller's cheques and/or foreign currency. It used to be 1500 drs but the decline in the value of the Greek drachma has resulted in the readjustment. With only 3000 drs in hand it is often necessary to change currency quite quickly. One problem, to bear in mind, is that arrival may be at the weekend, or the banks will be on strike, which in recent summers has become quite a common occurrence.

Imported spirits are comparatively expensive (except on some of the duty free Dodecanese islands) but the duty free allowance, that can be taken into Greece, is up to one and a half litres of alcohol. So if a whisky or gin drinker, and partial to an evening sundowner, acquire a bottle or two before arrival. Cigars are difficult to buy on the islands, so it may well be advantageous to take along the 75 that can be imported. Note the above only applies to fellow members of the EEC. Allowances for travellers from other countries are 1 litre of alcohol and 50 cigars.

Camera buffs should take as much film as possible as it is more costly in Greece than in most Western European countries.

Officially, the Cyclades has some 3000 hours of sunshine per year, out of an approximate, possible 4250. The prevailing summer wind is the northerly *Meltemi* which can blow very strongly, day in day out. The months of July and August are usually dry and very hot for 24 hours a day. The sea in April is perhaps a little cool for swimming, but May and June are marvellous months, as are September and October.

For the statistically minded

The monthly average temperatures of Naxos island are

		Jan	Feb	Mar	Apr	May	June	July	Aug	Sept	Oct	Nov	Dec
Average monthly air temperature.	C°	12½	12½	13½	16	19½	23	25	25	23	20	17	14
	F°	54	54	56	61	67	74	77	77	73	68	62	57
Sea surface temperature (at 1400 hrs).	C°	15	15	15	17	19	22	24	23½	23	20	17½	15½
	F°	59	59	59	62	66	72	75	74	73	68	63	60

The best time of the year to holiday

The above chart indicates that the best months are May, June, September and October, July and August probably being too hot. Additionally, the most crowded months when accommodation is at a premium, are also July and August and the first two weeks of September. Taking everything into account, it does not need an Einstein to work out the most favourable period to take a vacation.

Conversion tables & equivalents

Units	Approximate Conversion	Equivalent
Miles to kilometres	Divide by 5, multiply by 8	5 miles = 8 km
Kilometres to miles	Divide by 8, multiply by 5	
Feet to metres	Divide by 10, multiply by 3	10 ft = 3 m
Metres to feet	Divide by 3, multiply by 10	
Inches to centimetres	Divide by 2, multiply by 5	1 inch = 2.5 cm
Centimetres to inches	Divide by 5, multiply by 2	
Fahrenheit to centigrade	Deduct 32, divide by 9 and multiply by 5	77°F = 25°C
Centigrade to fahrenheit	Divide by 5, multiply by 9 and add 32	

Gallons to litres	Divide by 2, multiply by 9	2 gal = 9 litres
Litres to gallons	Divide by 9, multiply by 2	

Note: 1 pint = 0.6 of a litre and 1 litre = 1.8 pints.

Pounds (weight) to kilos	Divide by 11, multiply by 5	5 k = 11 lb
Kilos to pounds	Divide by 5, multiply by 11	

Note: 16 oz = 1 lb; 1000 g = 1 kg and 100 g = 3.5 oz.

Tyre pressures
Pounds per square inch to kilogrammes per square centimetre.

lb/sq. in.	kg/cm	lb/sq. in.	kg/cm
10	0.7	26	1.8
15	1.1	28	2.0
20	1.4	30	2.1
24	1.7	40	2.8

The Greeks use the metric system but most unreasonably sell liquid (i.e. wine, spirits and beer) by weight. Take my word for it, a 640 g bottle of wine is approximately 0.7 of a litre or 1.1 pints. Proprietory wines such as *Demestika* are sold in bottles holding as much as 950 g, which is 1000 ml or 1¾ pints and represents very good value.

Electric points in the larger towns, smarter hotels and holiday resorts are 220 volts AC and will power any American or British appliance. Older buildings in out of the way places might still have 110 DC supply. Remote pensions may not have any electricity, other than that supplied by a generator and even then the rooms might not be wired up. More correctly they may well be wired but not connected.

Greek time is 2 hours ahead of GMT, as it is during British Summer Time and 7 hours ahead of United States Eastern Time. That is except for a short period when the Greek clocks are corrected for their Winter at the end of September, some weeks ahead of United Kingdom alteration.

Basics & Essentials of the language

These notes and subsequent 'Useful Greek' at the relevant chapter endings are not, nor could be, intended to substitute for a formal phrase book, or two. Accent marks have been omitted.

Whilst in the United Kingdom it is worth noting that the British Broadcasting Co, Marylebone High St, London W1M 4AA have produced an excellent book, *Greek Language and People*, accompanied by a cassette and a record.

For the less committed a very useful pocket sized phrase book that I always have to hand is *The Greek Travelmate* by Richard Drew Publishing, Glasgow at a cost of £1.00.

The alphabet		**Sounds like**
Capitals	**Lower case**	
A	α	Alpha
B	β	Veeta
Γ	γ	Ghama
Δ	δ	Dhelta
E	ε	Epsilon
Z	ζ	Zeeta
H	η	Eeta
Θ	θ	Theeta
I	ι	Yiota
K	κ	Kapa
Λ	λ	Lamtha
M	μ	Mee
N	ν	Nee

Ξ	ξ	Ksee
O	o	Omikron
Π	π	Pee
P	ρ	Roh
Σ	σ	Sighma
T	τ	Taf
Υ	υ	Eepsilon
Φ	φ	Fee
X	χ	Chi
Ψ	ψ	Psi
Ω	ω	Omegha

Groupings

αι	'e' as in let
αυ	'av/af' as in have/haff
ει/οι	'ee' as in seen
εν	'ev/ef' as in ever/effort
ον	'oo' as in toot
γγ	'ng' as in ring
γκ	At the beginning of a word 'g' as in go
γχ	'nks' as in rinks
μπ	'b' as in beer
ντ	At the beginning of a word 'd' as in deer
	In the middle of a word 'nd' as in send
τζ	'ds' as in deeds

Useful Greek

English	Greek	Sounds like
Hello/goodbye	Τεια σου	Yia soo (informal singular said with a smile)
Good morning/day	Καλημερα	Kalimera
Good afternoon/evening	Καλησπερα	Kalispera (formal)
Good night	Καληνχτα	Kalinikta
See you later	Θα σε δω αργοτερα	Tha se thoargotera
See you tomorrow	Θα σε δω αυριο	Tha se tho avrio
Yes	Ναι	Ne (accompanied by a downwards and sideways nod of the head)
No	Οχι	Ochi (accompanied by an upward movement of the head, heavenwards and with a closing of the eyes)
Please	Παραχαλω	Parakalo
Thank you	(Σας) Ευχαριστω	(sas) Efkaristo
No, thanks	Οχι ευχαριστιεδ	Ochi, efkaristies
Thank you very much	Ευχαριστωπολυ	Efkaristo poli
After which the reply may well be	Παραχαλω	Thank you (and please)
Do you speak English?	Μιλατε Αγγλικα	Milahteh anglikah
How do you say...	Πωδ λενε...	Pos lene...
... in Greek?	...στα Ελληνικα	...sta Ellinika
What is this called?	Πωδ το λενε	Pos to lene
I do not understand	Δεν καταλαβαινω	Then katahlavehno
Could you speak more slowly (slower?)	Μπορετε να μηλατε πιο αργα	Borete na melatee peo seegha (arga)
Could you write it down	Μπορειτε νο μον το γραψετε	Boreete na moo to grapsete

7

NUMBERS

One	Ενα	enna
Two	Δυο	thio
Three	Τρια	triah
Four	Τεσσερα	tessehra
Five	Πεντε	pendhe
Six	Εξι	exhee
Seven	Επτα	eptah
Eight	Οκτω	ockto
Nine	Εννεα	ennea
Ten	Δεκα	thecca
Eleven	Εντεκα	endekha
Twelve	Δωδεκα	thiodhehka
Thirteen	Δεκατρια	thehka triah
Fourteen	Δεκατεσσερα	thehka tessehra
Fifteen	Δεκαπεντε	thehka pendhe
Sixteen	Δεκαεζι	theaexhee
Seventeen	Δεκαεπτα	thehkaeptah
Eighteen	Δεκαοκτω	thehkaockto
Nineteen	Δεκαεννεα	thehkaennea
Twenty	Εικοσι	eckossee
Twenty-one	Εικοσι ενα	eckossee enna
Twenty-two	Εικοσι δυο	eckossee thio
Thirty	Τριαντα	treandah
Forty	Σαραντα	sarandah
Fifty	Πενηντα	penindah
Sixty	Εζηντα	exhindah
Seventy	Εβδομηντα	evthomendah
Eighty	Ογδοντα	ogthondah
Ninety	Ενενητα	eneendah
One hundred	Εκατο	eckato
One hundred and one	Εκατον ενα	eckaton enna
Two hundred	Διακοσια	theeakossia
One thousand	Χιλια	kheelia
Two thousand	Δυοχιλιαδεζ	thio kheelia

2 Getting to & from the Cyclades, Athens & the mainland ports

If all the year were playing holidays, to sport would be as tedious as to work.

William Shakespeare

To start this chapter off, a word of introductory warning. Whatever form of travel is utilised, do not pack any money or travellers cheques in luggage that will have to be stowed away. The year before last, almost unbelievably, we met a young lady who had at the last moment, prior to checking-in at the airport, stuffed some drachmae notes in a zipped side pocket of one of her suitcases. On arrival in Greece, surprise, surprise she was minus the money.

BY AIR

Scheduled flights For the Cyclades it is necessary to fly direct to Athens East (international) airport, transferring by bus to Athens West (domestic) airport and then, by Olympic Airways, on to the islands of Milos, Mykonos, Paros or Santorini. Note both international and domestic Olympic flights use the West airport.

From the United Kingdom Heathrow to Athens (3¾ hours): daily, non-stop British Airways, Olympic and others.
Scheduled air-fare options include: 1st class return, economy, special economy and APEX (Advanced Purchase Excursion Fare), which is the cheapest scheduled fare.

Charter flights, package tours Some package tour operators keep a number of seats available on each flight for, what is in effect, a charter flight. A nominal charge is made for accommodation (which need not be taken up), the cost being included in the return air-fare. These seats are substantially cheaper than the scheduled APEX fares. Apart from the relatively low price, the normal two week holiday period can be extended by a further week or weeks for a small surcharge. There is a wide variety of United Kingdom departure airports, including Birmingham, Gatwick and Manchester, arriving at Athens. As one correspondent has pointed out, the frequency of charter flights tails off dramatically between October and March as does the choice of airport departure points. Do not forget this when contemplating an out-of-season holiday.

To ascertain what is on offer, scan the travel section of the Sunday papers, as well as the weekly magazine *Time Out* and, possibly, *Private Eye*. There are many varied package tours with a number of the large tour operators and the smaller, more personal, companies, offering a bewildering array of multi-centre, fly-drive, budget-bed, self catering and personally tailored holidays, in addition to the more usual hotel accommodation.

Exceptionally reasonable charter flights, with the necessary accommodation vouchers, are available through *Owners Abroad Ltd*, Ilford, who also have offices in Manchester, Birmingham, and Glasgow. Example fares and routes for 1986 include:

Two week return fares		Low season	Mid-season	High season
Athens leaving Gatwick Thursday, Friday, Sunday	From	£105.75	£124.75	£137.75
Athens leaving Manchester Thursday, Sunday	From	£118.75	£135.75	£149.75

These rates are subject to surcharges and airport taxes. The fares for three or four weeks are those above plus £20 and for five to six weeks, an additional 50 per cent is charged. Note that the extra weeks allowed for charter flights to Greece are restricted to six, not twelve weeks.

Perhaps the least expensive flights available are **Courier Flights** from *INFLIGHT COURIER, 7 - 9 Heath Rd, The Quadrant, Weybridge, Surrey KT13 8SX. Tel (0932) 57455/ 56.* These scheduled seats start off at about £69 return for the low season period BUT passengers can only take a maximum of 10 kg of hand-luggage. One holdall measuring no more than 1 ft x 2 ft — no other baggage.

Olympic Airways subsidiary, *Allsun Holidays* has taken up the challenge and offers selected island-hopping-holidays which include valid accommodation vouchers. This innovation includes the flight to Athens and then on to the Cyclades islands of Mykonos, Naxos, Paros, Antiparos, Ios, Santorini, Milos, Siphnos, Kimilos, Andros or Tinos. Olympic Airways has joined the charter flight fray with their *Love-A-Fare* service. (Yes love-a-fare!), the London to Athens return fare costing £159. The booking must be made at least one month in advance and allows a maximum of four weeks stay. There are Olympic offices in London as well as Manchester, Birmingham and Glasgow.

Companies offering interesting and slightly off-beat holidays include the *Aegina Club Ltd*, and *Ramblers Holidays.* Aegina have a wide range of holidays including tours, three different locations in up to three weeks, and additionally will tailor a programme to fit in with client's requirements. *Ramblers*, as would be imagined, include in their programme walking holidays based on a number of locations with half-board accommodation. More conventional offerings in smaller, more personal hotels, pensions and tavernas at more economical rates than the larger tour companies are available from *Simply Simon* who place at the holiday-makers disposal a variety of the more popular Cycladean islands. Their brochure is, refreshingly, almost completely four square.

Students
Students under 26 years of age (oh to be 26 again) should consider contacting *World-Wide Student Travel* who market a number of inexpensive charter flights. Students of any age or scholars under 22 years of age (whatever mode of travel is planned) should take their *International Student Identity Card* (ISIC). This will ensure discounts are available whenever they are applicable, not only in respect of travel but also for entry to museums, archaeological sites and some forms of entertainment.

If under 26 years of age, but not a student, it may be worthwhile applying for membership of *The Federation of International Youth Travel Organization* (FIYTO) which guarantees youth discounts from some ferry and tour operators.

Scheduled flights
From the United States of America
Scheduled Olympic flights include departures from:
Atlanta (via John F Kennedy (JFK) airport, New York (N.Y.)): daily
Boston (via JFK or La Guardia, N.Y.): daily
Chicago (via JFK): daily
Dallas (via JFK): daily
Houston (via JFK): daily
Los Angeles (via JFK): daily
Miami (via JFK; 15 hours): daily
Minneapolis (via JFK): daily
New York (JFK approximately 10½ hours); daily direct
Norfolk (via JFK): daily except Saturday
Philadelphia (via JFK; about 11 hours): daily
Rochester (via JFK): daily
San Francisco (via JFK; about 14½ hours): daily
Seattle (via JFK or London): daily
Tampa (via JFK): daily
Washington DC (via JFK or La Guardia): daily
Note that flights via New York's John F Kennedy airport involve a change of plane from, or

to, a domestic American airline.

USA domestic airlines, including TWA also run a number of flights to Greece and the choice of air fares is bewildering including economy, first class return, super APEX, APEX, GIT, excursion, ABC, OTC, ITC, and others, wherein part package costs are incorporated.

Charter/standby flights & secondary airlines

As in the United Kingdom, scanning the Sunday national papers' travel section, including the *New York Times*, will disclose various companies offering package tours and charter flights. Another way to make the journey is to take a standby flight to London and then fly, train or bus on to Greece. Alternatively, there are a number of inexpensive, secondary airline companies offering flights to London and the major Western European capitals.

Useful agencies, especially for students, include *Let's Go Travel Services*.

From Canada Scheduled Olympic flights include departures from:
Montreal: twice weekly direct
or (via Amsterdam, JFK and or La Guardia, N.Y.): daily except Mondays
Toronto: twice weekly (via Montreal)
or (via Amsterdam, JFK and/or La Guardia N.Y.): daily except Monday and Friday
Winnipeg (via Amsterdam): Thursday and Sunday only
As for the USA, the above flights involve a change of airline and there is a choice of domestic and package flights and a wide range of differing fares.

Student agencies include *Canadian Universities Travel Service*.

From Australia There are Australian airline scheduled flights from Adelaide, Brisbane, Melbourne and Sydney to Athens. Regular as well as excursion fares and affinity groups.

From New Zealand There are no scheduled flights.
Various connections are available as well as regular and affinity fares.

From South Africa Scheduled Olympic flights include departures from:
Cape Town (via Johannesburg): Fridays and Saturdays only
Durban (via Johannesburg): Fridays and Saturdays only
Johannesburg: direct, Thursday, Friday, Saturday (up to the 2nd September) and Sunday.
Flights via Johannesburg involve a change of plane from, or to, a domestic airline.
South African airline flights from Johannesburg to Athens on regular, excursion and affinity fares.

From Ireland Scheduled Olympic flights from:
Dublin: daily via London which involves a change of airline
Irish airline flights from Dublin.

Note that when flying from Ireland, Australia, New Zealand, South Africa, Canada and the USA there are sometimes advantages in travelling via London or other European capitals on stop-over and taking inexpensive connection flights to Greece.

Scandinavia including:-
From Denmark Scheduled Olympic flights from:
Copenhagen (via Frankfurt): daily involving a change of aircraft as well as non-stop flights on Tuesday, Wednesday, Friday and Sunday.

From Sweden Scheduled Olympic flights from:
Stockholm (via Frankfurt): daily involving a change of aircraft.

Illustration 1

KEY
★ Change Train
▄▆ Ferry

RAIL ROUTES

From Norway Scheduled Olympic flights from:
Oslo (via Frankfurt): daily involving a change of aircraft. Contact SAS Airlines for Olympic Airways.

All the Scandinavian countries have a large choice of domestic and package flights with a selection of offerings.

AIRPORTS
United Kingdom Do not forget if staying in Greece longer than two weeks, the long-stay car parking fees are fairly expensive. The difficulty is that most charter flights leave and arrive at rather unsociable hours, so friends and family may not be too keen to act as a taxi service.

Athens Hellinikon airport is split into two parts, West (Olympic domestic and international flights) and East (foreign airlines). There are coaches to make the connection between the two airports, and Olympic buses to Athens centre as well as the city buses. At the domestic or Western airport, the city buses pull in alongside the terminal building. Across the road is a pleasant cafe/restaurant but the service becomes fairly chaotic when packed out. To the left of the cafe (facing) is a newspaper kiosk and further on, across a side road, a Post Office is hidden in the depths of the first building.

The Eastern airport is outwardly quite smart but can, in reality, become an expensive, very cramped and uncomfortable location if there are long delays. These can occur when, for instance, the air traffic controllers strike elsewhere in Europe. Remember when leaving Greece to have enough money and some food left for an enforced stay, as flight departures are consistently overdue and food and drink in the airport are costly. There are simply no facilities for an overnight sleep and the bench seats are very soon taken up. You have been warned.

BY TRAIN

From the United Kingdom & European countries Recommended only for train buffs and masochists but one of the alternative routes to be considered where a visitor intends to stay in Greece in excess of 6 weeks. The quickest journey of the three major scheduled overland routes takes about 60 hours, and a second-class return fare costs in the region of £215.00. One advantage is that you can break the journey along the route (a little difficult on an airline flight), and another is that it is possible to travel out on one route and back by an alternative track (if you will excuse the pun). It is important to take along basic provisions, toilet paper, and to wear old clothes.

A recent return to the 'day of the train' reinforced my general opinion and introductory remarks in respect of this particular method of travel, bringing sharply back into focus the disadvantages and rejoinders. The list of points to bear in mind, drawbacks and faults should be enough to deter any but the most determined.

Try not to have a query involving the overseas information desk at Victoria Station. The facility is undermanned and the wait to get to a counter averages ¾hr. The staff are very willing but it is of interest that they overcome the intricacies of the official British Rail European timetable ("it's all Greek to me guvnor") by overtly referring to the (infinitely) more manageable Thomas Cook publication. The channel crossing is often on craft that would not be pressed into service if we declared war on the Isle of Wight, the journey is too short for any cabins to be available, the duty free goods on offer are very limited and there are inordinate delays between train, boat and train.

The French trains that ply between the coast and Paris are of an excellent standard. Changing trains at the 'black hole' of the Gare de Nord, Paris sharply focuses travellers attention on a whole sub-culture of human beings who exist in and around a number of European railway stations. My favourite example of this little known branch of the human race is the 'bag-shuffler' — usually a middle-aged lady. The genus is initially recognisable by the multitudinous paper and plastic bags festooned about the person. Once at rest the contents are constantly and interminably shuffled from one bag to another, and back again, the ritual being accompanied by low muttering.

French railway stations which are heated to a gentle simmering have perfected a waiting room seating arrangement that precludes any but a drunk, contortionist stretching out for a nap. In common with most other railway stations food and drink are expensive and credit cards impossible to use even at the swanky station restaurants.

The Metro connection between the Gare de Nord and the Gare de Lyon is not straightforward and involves a walk. The Gare de Lyon springs a minor trap for the unwary in that the inter-continental trains depart from platforms reached by a long walk up the far left platform (facing the trains). Incidentally some of the French trains now resemble childrens rocket drawings.

The stations toilet facilities are miniscule and, other than use of the mens urinal and washbasin, are charged. Ladies have to pay about 2 Francs (F), a private closet costs 6F and a shower 12F. And do not imagine you will be able to sneak in for a crafty stand-up wash — the toilets are intently watched over.

Although it may appear to be an optional extra, it is mandatory to purchase a couchette ticket for the journey as will become apparent. It is also necessary to pack food and drink at least for the French part of the journey as usually there are no refreshment services. In Italy most trains are met at the various station stops by trolley pushing vendors of (expensive) sustenance.

Venice station is signed *St Lucia* and is most conveniently sited bang on the edge of a main canal waterfront with shops and restaurants to the left. Some of the cake shops sell slabs of pizza pie for about 800 Lira (L) which furnishes good stand-by nourishment. The scheduled stop-over here will have to be adjusted for any (inevitable) delay in arrival. Venice (on the outward journey) is the watershed where Greek and the occasional Yugoslavian carriages are coupled up and passengers can be guaranteed to encounter a number of nasties. These compartments are seedier and dirtier than their European counterparts, and the lavatories vary between bad to unspeakable. Faults include toilets that won't flush (sometimes appearing to fill up), Greek toilet paper (which apart from other deficiencies lacks body and through which fingers break), no toilet paper at all, no soap in the dispenser, no coat hooks, water taps that don't and the whole rather grimy.

From Venice the term 'Express' should be ignored as the train's progress becomes slower and slower and slower with long unscheduled stops and quite inordinate delays at the Yugoslavian frontiers. For the Yugoslavian part of the journey it is necessary to lock oneself into the couchette as some of the locals have an annoying habit of entering a compartment and determinedly looting tourists luggage. It is inadvisable to leave the train at Belgrade for a stop-over as the rooms offered to tourists are extremely expensive and it is almost impossible to renegotiate a couchette for the remainder of the onward journey. There are trolley attendants at the major Yugoslavian railway stations but the contents of the rolls proffered are of an interesting nature resembling biltong or hard-tak burgers. Certainly when poked by the enthusiastic vendors I'm sure their fingers buckle. Another item on offer are large cheese curd pies and a railway employee wanders round twice a day with a very large aluminium teapot ostensibly containing coffee. Nobody appears to be interested in payment in Yugoslavian dinars, but American dollars or English pounds sterling almost cause a purr of satisfaction. Fortunately the carriage retainer usually keeps a stache of alcoholic drinks for sale. An aside is that the Yugoslavians are obsessed by wheel-tapping and at all and every stop, almost at the drop of a sleeper, will appear and perform. Much of the journey after Belgrade is on a single line track and should, for instance, a cow break into a trot the animal might well overtake the train. At the frontier one is reminded of the rigours of the Eastern States and passengers are subjected to rigorous and lengthy baggage and papers check by a swamp of officials which include stern faced, unsmiling, gun-toting police.

In stark contrast the friendly Greek frontier town of Idomeni is a tonic. Even late at night the stations' bank is open as is the station taverna/snack-bar with a scattering of tables on the platform and a buzz of brightly lit noise and activity.

To avoid the Yugoslavian experience a very pleasant alternative is to take the train the length of Italy to Brindisi port and catch an international ferry-boat to the mainland Greek ports of Igoumenitsa or Patras. From Patras a bus or the train can be used to make the connection with Athens.

Brindisi (Italy), contains several traps for the unwary. Unfortunately the railway station and quay for the Italy-Greek ferry-boats are some 200 m apart, which on a hot day...

The railway station has no formal ticket office or barrier. It is only necessary to dismount, turn left along the platform, left again, along the concrete wall supporting the first floor concourse (which stretches over and above the platforms), across the railway lines and left again along the sterile dockland street to the ferry-boat complex. The road, hemmed in by a prefabricated wall on the right, curves parallel to the seawall on the left from which it is separated by a high chain link fence, a number of railway lines and a tarmacadam quay. But, before leaving the station, stop, for all the ticket offices and necessary officials are situated in the referred to upper storey buildings and in the 'Main St'. My favourite tour office is across the road from the station, alongside a bank on the corner formed by the 'Main St' and the 'ferry-boat' street. The staff are very helpful and most informative. Diagonally across the bottom of this end of the 'Main St' is a small tree edged square which, as it is well endowed with park benches, makes for an unofficial waiting room with travellers and back-packers occupying most of the available space. Do not forget when booking rail tickets to ask for Brindisi Maritime, the town railway station is some kilometres inland.

The international ferry-boats on this route are, in the main, luxurious, beautifully appointed and expensive. Possible trappings include a sea-water swimming pool, ladies hairdresser and beauty salon, a number of restaurants and a self service cafeteria, a coffee bar and a disco. Unfortunately the self-service meals are also outrageously expensive with, for instance, a meal for two of veal and potatoes, a spinach pie, lettuce salad and a ½ bottle of emasculated retsina costing about 1500 drs. Coffee 80 drs. Moral, try not to eat on board. A splendid 2 berth cabin with a generous en suite bathroom will set a traveller back some 4000 drs. Prices everywhere are in American dollars and the change desk even when on the Greece to Italy leg, will not change currency into Italian lira. . .?

Travellers under 26 years of age can take advantage of British Rail's Inter-Rail pass while Americans and Canadians may obtain a Eurorail pass prior to reaching Europe by applying to *Victoria Travel Centre*. There is also the Transalpino ticket available from their London office and all these offers hold out a substantial discount on standard train and ferry fares, but are subject to various terms and conditions. Certainly it must be borne in mind that the Greek railway system is not extensive and unless travelling in other European countries, a concessionary pass might not represent much of a saving. On the other hand discounts in respect of the Greek railways may include travel on the state railway buses (OSE).

Other cut-price student outfits offering train, coach and flights include *London Student Travel* and *Eurotrain*. Examples of the tickets, costs and conditions include:

Inter-Rail ticket	Under 26 years of age, valid one month, for use in 21 countries and also allows half-fare travel in the UK, on Sealink and B+I ships as well as P&O ferries via Southampton and Le Havre	from	£119

		Single	**Return**
Transalpino ticket	Under 26, valid for two months, allows stop-over en route to the destination. London to Athens via Brindisi or Yugoslavia	from £88.35	£169.60

Timetables & routes (Illustration 1)

This paragraph caused me as much work as whole chapters on other subjects. *British Rail*, whose timetable I had the greatest difficulty deciphering, and *Thomas Cook*, whose timetable I could understand, were both helpful.

Choice of routes include:

(1) London (Victoria Station), Dover (Western Docks), (jetfoil), Ostend, Brussels, Liege, Aachen, Cologne (change train, ¾ hr delay), Mainz, Mannheim, Ulm, Munich (change train ¾ hr delay), Salzburg, Jesenice, Ljubljana, Zagreb, Belgrade (Beograd), Skopje, Gevgelija, Idomeni, Thessaloniki to Athens.

An example: of the journey is as follows:

Departure: 1300 hrs, afternoon sea crossing, evening on the train, late night change of train at Cologne, night on the train, morning change of train at Munich, all day and night on the train arriving Athens very late some 2½ days later at 2314 hrs.

(2) London (Charing Cross/Waterloo East stations), Dover Hoverport, (hovercraft), Boulogne Hoverpoint, Paris (de Nord), change train (and station) to Paris (de Lyon), Strasbourg, Munich, Salzburg, Ljubljana, Zagreb, Belgrade (change train, 1¼ hrs delay), Thessaloniki to Athens.

An example:

Departure: 0955 hrs and arrive 2½ days later at 2315 hrs.

Second class single fares from £112.60 and return fare from £215.30.

(3) London (Victoria), Folkestone Harbour, (ferry-boat), Calais, Paris (de Nord), change train (and station) to Paris (de Lyon), Venice, Ljubljana, Zagreb, Belgrade, Thessaloniki to Athens.

An example:

Departure: 1415 hrs and arrive 2¾ days later at 0840 hrs.

(4) London (Liverpool St.), Harwich (Parkeston Quay), ferry-boat, Hook of Holland, Rotterdam, Eindhoven, Venlo, Cologne (change train), Mainz, Mannheim, Stuttgart, Ulm, Munich, Salzburg, Jesenice, Ljubljana, Zagreb, Belgrade, Nis, Skopje, Gevgelija, Idomeni, Thessaloniki to Athens.

An example:

Departure: 1940 hrs, night ferry crossing, change train at Cologne between 1048 and 1330 hrs, first and second nights on the train and arrive at Athens middle of the day at 1440 hrs.

An alternative is to take the more pleasurable train journey through Italy and make a ferry-boat connection to Greece.

(5) London (Victoria), Folkestone Harbour, Calais, Boulogne, Amiens, Paris (de Nord), change train and station to Paris (de Lyon), Dijon, Vallorbe, Lausanne, Brig, Domodossala, Milan (Central), Bologna, Rimini, Ancona, Pescara, Bari to Brindisi.

(5a) Brindisi to Patras sea crossing.

(5b) Patras to Athens.

An example:

Departure: 0958 hrs, day ferry crossing, change of train at Paris to the Parthenon Express, one night on the train and arrive at Brindisi at 1850 hrs. Embark on the ferry-boat, departing at 2000 hrs, night on the ferry-boat and disembark at 1300 hrs the next day. Take the coach to Athens arriving at 1600 hrs.

The second class single fare costs from £124.90.

On all these services children benefit from reduced fares, depending on their age. Couchettes and sleepers are usually available at extra cost and Jetfoil sea crossings are subject to a surcharge.

The above are only a guide and up-to-date details must be checked with the relevant offices.

Details of fares and timetables are available from *British Rail Continental Enquiries*. Should enquiries fail at that address try the *European Rail Passenger Office* or *The Hellenic State Railways (OSE)*. The most cogent, helpful and informative firm through whom to book rail travel must be *Victoria Travel Centre*. I have always found them to be extremely accommodating.

It is well worth contacting *Thomas Cook Ltd*, who have a very useful range of literature and timetables available from their Publications Department.

From the Continent & Scandinavia to Athens Pick up one of the above main lines by using the appropriate connections detailed in Illustration 1.

Departure terminals from Scandinavia include Helsinki (Finland), Oslo (Norway), Gothenburg, Malmo, Stockholm (Sweden), Fredrikshavn and Copenhagen (Denmark).

BY COACH

This means of travel is for the more hardy voyager and/or the young. If the description of the train journey has caused apprehension, the tales of passengers of the less luxurious coach companies will strike terror into the recipient. Common 'faults' include lack of 'wash and brush up' stops, smugglers, prolonged border custom investigations, last minute changes of route and breakdowns. All this is on top of the forced intimacy with a number of widely disparate companions, some wildly drunk, in cramped, uncomfortable surroundings.

For details of the scheduled *Euroways Supabus* apply c/o Victoria Coach Station or to the *National Express Company*. A single fare costs £62 and a return ticket £115. This through service takes 4 days plus, with no overnight layovers but short stops at Cologne, Frankfurt and Munich where there is a change of coach. Fares include ferry costs but exclude refreshments. Arrival and departure in Greece is at the Peloponissou Railway Station, Athens. The timetable is as follows:

Departure from London, Victoria Coach Station, Bay 20: Friday and Saturday at 2030 hrs arriving at 1100 hrs 4½ days later.

Return journey
Departure from Filellinon St, Syntagma Sq, Athens: Wednesday and Friday at 1300 hrs arriving London at 0800 hrs, 4 days later.

Express coach companies include *Consolas Travel*. This well-established company runs daily buses during the summer months, except Sunday, and single fares start at about £35 with a return ticket costing from £69. Other services are run by the various 'pirate' bus companies, the journey time is about the same and, again, prices, which may be slightly cheaper, do not include meals. On a number of islands, travel agents signs refer to the *Magic Bus*, or as a fellow traveller so aptly put it — *The Tragic Bus*, but the company that ran this renowned and infamous service perished some years ago. Imitators may well perpetuate the name.

In the United Kingdom it is advisable to obtain a copy of the weekly magazine *Time Out* wherein the various coach companies advertise. For return trips from Athens, check shop windows in Omonia Sq, the American Express office in Syntagma Sq, or the Students Union in Filellinon St, just off Syntagma Sq.

BY CAR (Illustration 2)

Usually only a worthwhile alternative method of travel if there are at least three adults and you are planning to stay for longer than three weeks, as the journey from England is about 1900 miles and will take approximately 50 hrs non-stop driving.

One of the shortest routes from the United Kingdom is via car-ferry to Ostend, (Belgium), on to Munich, Salzburg (Germany), Klagenfurt (Austria) and Ljubljana (Yugoslavia). There the Autoput E94 is used, on to Zagreb, Belgrade (Beograd) and Nis on the E5, where the E27 and E55 are taken via Skopje to the frontier town of Gevgelija/Evzonoi. Due to major rebuilding works, the Yugoslavian road between Zagreb and Nis can be subject to lengthy delays.

The main road, through Greece, to Athens via Pirgos, Larissa and Lamia, is good but the speed of lorries and their trailer units can be disquieting. Vehicles being overtaken are expected to move right over and tuck well into the hard shoulder. From Evzonoi to Athens via Thessaloniki is 340 miles (550 kms) and some of the major autoroute is a toll road.

Personally my own favourite choice of route involves crossing the Channel to Le Havre, cutting down through France, which holds few perils for the traveller, via Evreux, Chartres, Pithiviers, Montargis, Clamecy, Nevers, Lyon and Chambery to the Italian border at Modane. Here the faint-hearted can take the tunnel whilst the adventurous wind their way over the Col du Mont Cenis.

ROAD ROUTES

Illustration 2

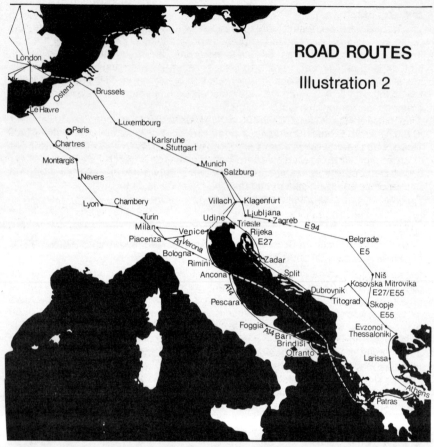

Once over the border into Italy, bypass Turin (Torino) and proceed to Piacenza, Brescia, Verona, Padua (Padova), Venice and cut up to Trieste.

I say bypass because the ordinary Italian roads are just 'neat aggravation' and the cities are impossible. Although motorways involve constant toll fees they are much quicker and less wearing on the nerves. Note that Italian petrol stations have a nasty habit of closing for the midday siesta between 1200 and 1500 hrs.

An alternative route is via Turin, Milan, Bergamo, Brescia, Verona and on to Trieste. This route leads around the southern edge of a few of the lakes in the area of Brescia. Excursions to Padua and Venice are obvious possibilities.

From Trieste the most scenic (and winding) route is to travel the Adriatic coast road via Rijeka, Zadar and Split to Dubrovnik. The lovely medieval inner city of Dubrovnik is well worth a visit. At Petrovac the pain starts and the road swings up to Titograd around to Kosovska Mitrovika, Pristina, Skopje and down to the border at Gevgelija. The stretch from Skopje to the Greek frontier can be rather unnerving. Sign-posting in Yugoslavia is usually very bad; always obtain petrol when the opportunity crops up and lastly but not least city lights are often turned out at night, making driving extremely hazardous. To save the journey from Petrovac, it is possible at the height of season to take a ferry from Dubrovnik or take the pretty coastal road on to the port of Bar and catch a boat to Igoumenitsa or Patras on the Greek mainland.

On the return journey it is possible to vary the route by driving across Greece to Igoumenitsa, catching a ferry-boat to Italy and driving along the Adriatic seaboard, but the northern coast of Italy is not very attractive.

Detailed road reports are available from the Automobile Association but I would like to stress that in the Yugoslavian mountains, especially after heavy rain, landslips can (no will) result in part of the road disappearing at the odd spot as well as the surface being littered with rocks. There you go!

General Vehicle & Personal Requirements

Documents required for travel in any European country include an *International Driving Licence*, and a *Carnet de Passages en Douanes* (both issued by the AA and valid for one year) as well as a *Green Insurance Card*. It is recommended to take the vehicle's registration documents as proof of ownership and the vehicle must have a nationality sticker of the approved pattern and design.

Particular countries' requirements include:

Italy Import allowances are as for Greece but the restriction on the importation of Italian currency equals about £100.

A recent requirement for all cars entering Italy is that they must possess both right and left hand, external driving mirrors.

Switzerland If intending to drive through Switzerland remember that the Swiss will require the vehicle and all the necessary documents to be absolutely correct. (They would). The authorities have a nasty habit of stopping vehicles some distance beyond the frontier posts.

Yugoslavia A valid passport is the only personal document required for citizens of, for example, Denmark, West Germany, Finland, Great Britain and Northern Ireland, Republic of Southern Ireland, Holland and Sweden. Americans and Canadians must have a visa and all formalities should be checked with the relevant Yugoslavian Tourist Office.

It is compulsory to carry a warning triangle, a first-aid kit in the vehicle and a set of replacement vehicle light bulbs. If you plan to travel during the winter it is advisable to check the special regulations governing the use of studded tyres. The use of spotlights is prohibited.

Visiting motorists cannot obtain fuel without petrol coupons, which are available at the frontier and, supposedly, from travel agents 'Kompas' or 'Putnik'. Carefully calculate the amount of coupons required for the journey and pay for them in foreign currency at the frontier as the rate allowed is very advantageous compared to that if the coupons are paid for in Yugoslavian dinars. Petrol stations can be far apart, closed or out of petrol, so fill up when possible.

Photographers are only allowed to import five rolls of film; drinkers a bottle of wine and a quarter litre of spirits and smokers 200 cigarettes or 50 cigars. Each person may bring in unlimited foreign currency but only 1500 dinars.

Fines are issued on the spot and the officer collecting the fine should issue an official receipt.

To obtain assistance in the case of accident or breakdown dial 987 and the 'SPI' will come to your assistance.

Greece It is compulsory to carry a first-aid kit as well as a fire extinguisher in a vehicle and failure to comply may result in a fine. It is also mandatory to carry a warning triangle and it is forbidden to carry petrol in cans. In Athens the police are empowered to confiscate and detain the numberplates of illegally parked vehicles.

The use of undipped headlights in towns is strictly prohibited.

Customs allow the importation of 200 cigarettes or 50 cigars, 1 litre of spirits or 2 litres of wine and only 3000 drs, but any amount of foreign currency. Visitors from the EEC may import 300 cigarettes or 75 cigars, 1½ litres of spirits or 4 litres of wine.

Speed Limits

See table below — all are standard legal limits which may be varied by signs.

	Built-up areas	Outside built-up areas	Motorways	Type of vehicle affected
Greece	31 mph (50 kph)	49 mph (80 kph)	62 mph (100 kph)	Private vehicles with or without trailers
Yugoslavia	37 mph (60 kph)	49 mph (80 kph) 62 mph* (100 kph)*	74 mph (120 kph)	Private vehicles without trailers

*Speed on dual carriageways.

BY FERRY-BOAT (Illustration 2)

Some of the descriptive matter under the heading **BY TRAIN** in this chapter refers to inter-country ferry-boat travel.

Due to the popularity of the ferry port of Brindisi travellers, at the height of the season, must be prepared for crowds, lengthy delays and the usual ferry-boat scrum (scrum not scum). Other irritants include the exasperating requirement to purchase an embarkation pass with the attendant formalities which include taking the pass to the police station on the second floor of the port office to have it punched! Oh, by the way, the distance between the railway station and the port is about 200 m and it is absolutely necessary to clock in at least 3 hrs before the ferries departure otherwise you may be 'scratched' from the fixture list, have to rebook and pay again. That is why the knowledgeable head for the other departure ports, more especially Otranto.

Great care must be taken when purchasing international ferry-boat tickets especially at Igoumenitsa. The competition is hot and tickets may well be sold below the published price. If so and you are amongst the 'lucky ones' do not count your drachmae until on board. The port officials check the tickets and if they find any that have been sold at a discount then they are confiscated and the purchaser made to buy replacements at the full price. Ouch!

See **Chapter 10 (Greek Mainland ports)** for particular details.

Do not forget that the availability of ferry-boat sailings must be continually checked as must airline and bus timetables. This is especially necessary during the months of October through to the beginning of May when the services are usually severely curtailed; so be warned.

Please refer to the individual mainland port and island chapters for full details of the inter-country ferry-boat timetables.

Useful names & addresses

The Automobile Association, Fanum House, Basingstoke, Hants RG21 2EA. Tel. (0256) 20123
The Greek National Tourist Organization, 195-197 Regent St., London W1R 8DL.
Tel. 01-734 5997
The Italian State Tourist Office, 1 Princes St., London W1R 7AR. Tel. 01-408 1245
The Yugoslav National Tourist Office, 143 Regent St., London W1R 8AE. Tel. 01-734 5243
British Rail Continental Enquiries, Sealink (UK) Limited, PO Box 29, London SW1V 1JX.
Tel. 01-834 2345
European Rail Passenger Office, Paddington Station, London W2 1HA. Tel. 01-723 7000
The Hellenic State Railways (OSE), 1-3 Karolou St., Athens, Greece. Tel. 01-5222-491
Thomas Cook Ltd, Publications Dept, PO Box 36, Thorpewood, Peterborough, PE3 6SB
Tel. 01-0733-63200

Other useful names & addresses mentioned in the text include:
Time Out, Southampton St., London. WC2E 7HD
Owners Abroad Ltd, Valentine House, Ilford Hill, Ilford, Essex IC1 2DG   Tel. 01-514 8844
Olympic Airways, 164 Piccadilly, London W1   Tel. 01-846 9080
Allsun Holidays, 164 Piccadilly, London W1   Tel. 01-846 9080
Aegina Club Ltd, 25A Hills Rd., Cambridge CB2 1NW.   Tel. 0223 63256
Ramblers Holidays, 13 Longcroft House, Fretherne Rd., Welwyn Garden City, Herts. AL8 6PQ.
     Tel. 07073 31133
Simply Simon Holidays Ltd, 1/45 Nevern Sq, London SW5 9PF   Tel. 01-373 1933
World Wide Student Travel, 38-39 Store St, London WC1E 7BZ.   Tel. 01-580 7733
Victoria Travel Centre, 52 Grosvenor Gdns., London SW1.   Tel. 01-730 8111
Transalpino, 214 Shaftesbury Ave., London WC2H 8EB.   Tel. 01-836 0087/8
London Student Travel (Tel. 01-730 4473) and **Eurotrain** (Tel. 01-730 6525) both at
     52 Grosvenor Gdns., London SW1N 0AG.
Euroways Supabus, c/o Victoria Coach Stn., London SW1.   Tel. 01-730 0202
     or c/o National Express Co.
     The Greek address is: 1 Karolou St., Athens.   Tel. 5240519/6
National Express Co, Westwood Garage, Margate Rd., Ramsgate CT12 6SL.   Tel. 0843 581333
Consolas Travel, 29-31 Euston Rd., London NW1.   Tel. 01-278 1931
     The Greek address is: 100 Eolou St., Athens.   Tel. 3219228

Amongst others, the agencies and offices listed above have, over the years, and in varying degrees, been helpful in the preparation of the guides and I would like to extend my sincere thanks to all those concerned. Some have proved more helpful than others!

Olympic Airways overseas office addresses are as follows:
America: 647 Fifth Ave., New York, NY 10022.   Tel. (0101-212)
     (Reservations) 838 3600
     (Ticket Office) 750 7933
Montreal: 200 McGill College Ave., Suite 1250 Montreal, Quebec.   Tel. 0101 514) 878 9691
Toronto: 80 Bloor St. West, Suite 406, Toronto.   Tel. (0101 416) 925 2272
Sydney: Suite 917, Australia Sq., Sydney, NSW 2000.   Tel. (01061 2) 241 1751
Johannesburg: Bank of Athens Buildings, 116 Marshall St, Johannesburg.   Tel. (01027 11) 836 5683
Denmark: 4 Jembadegade DK 1608, Copenhagen.   Tel. (010451) 126 100
Sweden: 44 Birger Jarlsqatan, 11429 Stockholm.   Tel. (010468) 101203

Other useful overseas names & addresses include:
Let's Go Travel Services, Harvard Student Agencies, Thayer Hall B, Harvard University, Cambridge. MA02138 USA.   Tel. 617 495 9649
Canadian Universities Travel Service, 44 George St, Toronto ONTM5S 2E4, Canada.   Tel. 979 2406
Automobile Association and Touring Club of Greece (ELPA), 2 Messogion Street, Athens.
     Tel. (01) 7791615
Italian Government Travel Office, 630 5th Ave, Suite 1565, New York, NY 10111.
     Tel. (0101-212) 245 4825
Greek National Tourist Organisation, 645 5th Ave, New York, NY 10022.
     (0101-212) 421 5777
     627 West 6th St, Los Angeles, CA 90017.   Tel. (0101-213) 626 6696
     168 North Michigan Ave, Chicago, IL 60601   Tel. (0101-312) 782 1084
     Suite 67, 2 Place Ville Marie, Esso Plaza, Montreal, Quebec H3B 2C9
Yugoslav State Tourist Office, 630 5th Ave, New York, NY 10111
     (0101-212) 757 2801

Ferry Lines — US Offices
Adriatica, 437 Madison Ave, New York   Tel. (0101-212) 838 2113
Chandris, 666 5th Ave, New York   Tel. (0101-212) 586 8370
Hellenic Mediterranean Lines, 200 Park Ave, New York   Tel. (0101-212) 697 4220
Karageorgis, 1350 Avenue of the Americas, New York   Tel. (0101-212) 582 3007

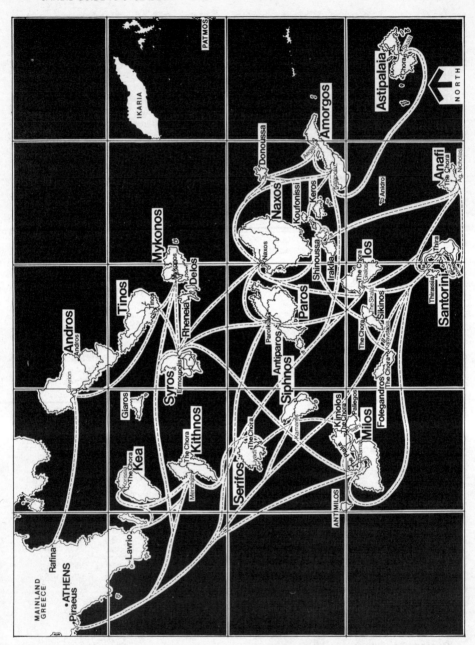

Illustration 3

3 Travel Between Athens & the Cyclades

I see land. I see the end of my labour. *Diogenes*

The Greek islands are very thick on the water, numbering between 1000 and 3000, depending upon which authority you wish to believe. Approximately 100 are inhabited of which some 24 are located in the Cyclades group of islands (Illustration 3). Historically, a specialised and efficient system of water-borne travel developed and in years gone by, the only way of setting foot on an island was to make for the relevant port and board a ferry-boat. The advent of international air flights direct to the larger islands, and the opening up of a number of airfields on the smaller islands (which must be regarded as a mixed blessing), has made it possible to fly to Athens and take a flight to the islands of Milos, Mykonos, Paros and Santorini.

BY AIR

It can prove difficult to purchase tickets on the spot, especially at the height of the tourist season, and it may be more convenient to book prior to departure, through the local Olympic office. Greeks utilise the services extensively, despite the extra cost of flying compared to other forms of travel which logically should discourage their use.

Travellers arriving in Athens other than by aircraft and wanting a domestic flight from the West airport can catch one of the Olympic coaches to the airport. These depart from the Olympic terminal and offices, 96-100 (Leoforos) Sygrou, between 0600 hrs and midnight and cost 45 drs compared to the 350/400 drs odd charged by a taxi. Relevant city buses are listed in Chapter 9 (Athens) in amongst the details of the bus timetable. An irate reader has taken me to task for not pointing out that approximately an hour must be allowed between catching the airline bus and the relevant plane check-in time.

Many travellers do not wish to stop over in Athens. If this is the case, and arriving other than on an Olympic flight, they can travel, directly after landing, to the domestic, West airport, using the connecting bus service.

The staff of Olympic, the Greek airline, are usually very helpful and their English good, although occasionally it is possible to fall foul of that sporadic Greek characteristic, intransigence. I remember arriving, heavily laden and tired, at the Olympic terminal offices about 1 am early one morning. On asking for advice about the location of any suitable hotel, I was politely directed, by the girl at the enquiries desk, to the Tourist police, which would have involved an uphill walk of at least a mile, weighed down by an assortment of bags. There was a hotel, in which we stayed, immediately around the corner from the terminal.

It is well worth considering utilising internal flights on one leg of a journey, if Athens is the point of arrival or departure. The extra cost of the flight, over and above the overland and ferry fares, must be balanced against the time element. For instance, Athens to Santorini by air takes some 40 mins whilst the ferry takes some 12 hours. One other advantage of domestic air travel is that the fares can be paid for by the use of American Express or Diners card, possibly saving precious drachmae, especially at the end of a holiday.

Cycladean Island airports Mykonos, Paros and Santorini are relatively sophisticated with Santorini now able to take the large jumbo jets but unlovely Milos airport does not let the side down.

Please refer to the Athens (Chapter 9) and the relevant island chapters for full details of airline timetables.

BY BUS

There are daily scheduled bus services to the mainland ports **(Chapter 10)** that connect by ferry-boat to the various Cyclades islands.

Please refer to the Chapter 9 (Athens) for full details of bus timetables.

BY FERRY-BOAT

In the following comments I am calling on my experience of travelling third and tourist class on any number of ferry-boats.

In general if sleeping arrangements are available they will be satisfactory if certain basic rules are followed. First claim a bunk by depositing luggage on the chosen berth, it will be quite safe as long as money and passports are removed. The position of a berth is important. Despite the labelling of 'Men' and 'Women' sleeping areas, a berth can usually be selected in either, but try to choose one adjacent to stern deck doors to ensure some ventilation. Due to the location of the third and tourist class accommodation it can get very hot and stuffy. Last tip is to lay a towel over plastic bunk covering, in order to alleviate what may well prove to be a sticky, uncomfortable night. The third class lavatories are often in an unsightly condition even prior to the craft's departure. To help enjoy reasonable surroundings and have the use of a shower, quietly trip into the next class and use their facilities (but don't tell everybody). Both the toilets and the showers suffer from the usual deficiencies listed under Greek bathrooms in Chapter 4, so be prepared.

Important points to take into account when inter-island ferry-boating include the following:

1. The ferries are owned by individual steamship companies and an employee of one Line will be unable or unwilling to give you information in respect of another company's timetable. Incidentally this individual ownership, can lead to a wide disparity in quality of service and general comfort.

2. The distances and voyage times are quite often lengthy and tiring. Additionally the duration of the passage sometimes, (no always), results in the timetable going to the wall with delays in scheduled departure times, on islands well into a ferry's voyage.

3. There are usually four basic fare classes: first, second, tourist and third/deck class. The published fares on scheduled ferries are government controlled and the third/deck class represents extremely good value. Ensure that you state the fare class you require. If you do not, you may well be sold a tourist instead of the cheaper deck class ticket. Note that there are a number of luxury ferries usually on a particular island-to-island journey, and tourist trip boats, on which charges are considerably higher. There are also hydrofoil 'Flying Dolphins', which result in journey times of under half those of the scheduled ferries but at approximately double the cost. Apart from the aforementioned four categories, there can be a variety of first- and second-class sleeping accommodation, including private and shared cabins.

4. Food and drink on the ferries used to be comparatively expensive, but price rises on the land have not been mirrored at sea. On the other hand the service is often discourteous and inefficient so it may be advantageous to pack provisions for a long voyage.

Wholesome and inexpensive ferry-boat picnic food includes: tomatoes, cucumber, bread, salami, ham, Sunfix orange juice and a bottle of wine (or two!). Take some bottled water. Greek chocolate (especially with nuts) is very good but does not keep well in the ambient daytime temperatures.

5. The state of the toilets and the lack of basic supplies makes it mandatory that one or two lavatory rolls are packed, easily to hand, as it were. The usual lack of washroom facilities commends the stowage of a pack of 'wipes'.

Quite frankly, on some occasions it will be necessary to stand on the rim of the toilet bowl as the only way of using the facility. Sorry!

6. Tickets should be purchased from a ticket agency prior to a voyage, as they can cost more when purchased on the boat. Ticket agency offices vary from 'the plush' to boxed-in back stairs, but check the scheduled prices and you should not go wrong. On the other hand be sure your list is up to date. In 1985 the prices went up twice by June and the last increase was 20%.

7. At the height of the season, the upper deck seats are extremely hot during the day and uncomfortably chilly at night. It is advisable to stake a claim to a seat fairly quickly, as the ferries are usually very crowded during the summer months.

8. Travellers should ensure they have a good, fat book and a pack of cards to while away the longer sea voyages. Despite the awesome beauty of the islands and the azure blue sea, there are often long, unbroken periods of Mediterranean passage to be endured, interrupted only by the occasional passing ship and the dramatic activity and ructions that take place during a port call.

9. Travellers sensitive to discordancy and who find disagreeable, a cacophany, a clamour of sound, may well find unacceptable the usual raucous mix experienced in the average 3rd class lounge. This is made up of two televisions, tuned to different programmes (the picture constantly flickering, suffering a snowstorm or horizontally high jumping in a series of flickering stills) accompanied by an overlaying wail of Greco-Turkish music piped over the ships tannoy system. Best to fly!

One delight is to keep a weather eye open and hope to observe some dolphins diving and leaping in the ship's wake. Their presence is often made discernible by the loud slapping noise they make when re-entering the water.

Ferry-boaters must take care when checking the connections, schedules and timetables as they can, no do, change during the year, especially outside the inclusive months of May to September, as well as from one year to another. So be warned!

Do not forget, when the information is at its most confusing, the Port police are totally reliable, but often a little short on English. Their offices are almost always on, or adjacent to, the quayside.

For some years the Government, in an effort to promote tourism to selected and usually 'backward' islands (whose the lucky ones) have offered free tickets during the out of season months. This offer usually ends on the 1st June (and may well start up in October) and Cycladean islands included in this ferry boat hand out include Amorgos, Donoussa, Koufonissi, Shinoussa and Iraklia. Tickets are certainly available on Naxos island.

Please refer to Chapter 10 (Mainland Ports) and island chapters for full details of ferry-boat timetables.

A few notes will not go amiss in respect of some of the various ferry-boats that ply the Cycladean seas.

Local craft are usually covered in the relevant island chapters and the most 'renowned', the **MV Marianna**, is detailed in **Chapter 15 (Naxos Island — See Ferry-Boats, A to Z)**.

The two most 'individual' inter-island craft must be the **MV Miaoulis** and the **MV Ios**. Both are skippered by 'distinctive' men. The captain of the **Miaoulis** sings his way round the Aegean piloting his eternally damp ship from one port to another with a certain wayward abandon. The 3rd class fare purchases a place on the seemingly always wet, open deck or forward, in a covered area (above the fish hold) that also runs with water. The seats are covered in clinging plastic and during the night time hours the crew vociferously argue away the voyage, sleeping during the day. The skipper of the **MV Ios** is rumoured to have been a destroyer captain and he certainly drives his small 'river-boat' in the same fashion. Even in middle May the craft is usually jam-packed, so goodness knows what matters are like at the height of the season. Overloading is occcasionally checked out by port officials. Passengers luggage is piled up below decks filling most of the lounge area.

The other side of the coin is represented by the excellent, well equipped car ferries

Lemnos, Naxos and **Santorini**. The **CF Lemnos** particularly springs to mind with a very good self-service cafeteria, air conditioning, clean lavatories and hot water.

CRUISE SHIPS

Fly/cruise packages on offer are usually rather up-market and in the main are based on seven days or multiples thereof. The cruise ships call in at selected islands for a part or full day, with excursions where applicable.

Other vacationers should note that the large influx of this genus of fun loving holiday-maker can have quite an impact on an island, and the cognoscenti normally vacate the particular port of call for that day.

GREEK ISLAND PLACE NAMES

This is probably the appropriate place to introduce the forever baffling problem which helps to bedevil the traveller — Greek place names. For instance, the island of Santorini is often designated Thira.

The reason for the apparently haphazard nomenclature lies in the long and complicated territorial ownership of Greece and its islands, more especially the islands. The base root may be Greek, Latin, Turkish or Venetian. Additionally the Greek language has three forms — Demotic (spoken), Katharevousa (literary) and Kathomiloumeni (compromise), of which the Demotic and Katharevousa have each been the offical linguistic style. Even as recently as 1967-74 the Colonels made Katharevousa once again the authorised form but Demotic is now the official language. Help!

Street names can be equally confusing and I have plumped for my personal choice and stated the alternatives, but where this is not possible, well, there you go! I mean how can Athens main square, Syntagma be spelt Syntagina, Sintagma or Syntagmatos?

Hotel and pension titles will also give rise to some frustration as can official guides using Greek script names, with two or three alternatives, including a similar meaning, Roman scripted appellation.

Street names are subject to some obscurity as the common noun Odhos (street) is often omitted, whilst Leoforos (avenue) and Plateia (square) are usually kept in the name. The prefix Saint of St. is variously written as Agios, Aghios, Ayios, Ag or Ai.

A *nome* approximates to a small English county, a number of which make up a province such as the *Peloponnese* or *Thessaly*.

At this stage, without apologies, I introduce my own definition to help identify an unspoilt, Greek town as follows: where the town's rubbish is collected by donkey, wooden panniers slung across its back, slowly wending its way up the hillside street, the driver, not in sight, probably languishing in a stray taverna.

Map nomenclature	Greek	Translation
Agios/Ag/Ayios/Aghios	Αγιου	Saint
Akra/Akrotiri	Ακρωτηρι	Cape/Headland
Ano	Ανω	Upper
Archeas/Oloyikos(horos)	Αρχαιοζ/Δογικοζ	Ancient (site)
Chora/Horo/Horio/Khorio	Χωριο	Village
Kato		Lower
Kolpos	Κολποδ	Gulf
Leoforos		Avenue
Limni	Διμνη	Lake/Marsh
Limin		Port harbour
Moni/Monastiri	Μοναστηρι	Monastery
Naos	Ναοζ	Temple
Nea/Neos	Νεο	New
Nissos		Island
Odhos/Odos	Δρομοξ	Street
Ormos		Bay

Oros		Mountain
Plateia	πλατεια	Square
Palios/Palaios	παλιοξ	Old
Potami	ποταμι	River
Spilia	Σπηλια	Cave
Vuno	**Βουνο**	Mountain

Useful Greek

English	Greek	Sounds like
Where is...	Που ειναι	Poo eene...
...the Olympic Airways office	τα γραφεια της Ολνμπιακης ζ	...ta grafia tis Olimbiakis
...the railway station	ο σιδηροδρουικοξ σταθμοξ	...sidheerothropikos stathmos
...the bus station	ο σταθμοξ των λεωφορεων	...stathmos ton leoforion
...the boat	το πλοιο	...to plio
...the nearest underground station	ο πλησιεστεροξ σταθμοξ του ηλεκτρικου	...o pleessiestehros stathmos too eelektrigoo
...the ticket office	το εκδοτηριο των ειοιτηριων	...to eckdhoterio ton essidirion
...the nearest travel agency	το πλησιεστεροξ πρακτορειον ταξιδιων	...to pleessiestehros praktorion taxidion
I'd like to reserve...	θελω να κρατησω	Thelo na kratiso...
...seat/seats on the	θεοη/ θσειδ λια	...these/thessis ghia
...to	για	...yia
...plane	αεροπλανο	...aeroplano
...train	τραινο	...treno
...bus	λεωφορειο	...leoforio
...ferry-boat	πλοιο	...plio
When does it leave/arrive	Ποτε φευγει/φθανει	Poteh fehvghi/fihanee
Is there...	Υπαρχει	Eebarhee...
...from here to	απ εδωστο	...abethosodo
...go to	στον	...ston
Where do I get off	Που κατεβαινομε	Poo katevenomhe
I want to go to	θελω να παω οτονς	Thelo na bao stoos...
I want to get off at	θελω να κατεβω στο	Thelo na katevo sto...
Will you tell me when to get off	Θα μον πτε πον να κατεβω	Thah moo peete poo nah kahlohvo
I want to go to...	θελω να παω οτονζ	Thelo na bao stoos
Stop here	Στοματα εδω	Stamata etho
How much is it	Ποσο ειναι	Posso eene
How much does it cost	Ποσο κανει η μεταρορα	Posso kano imedano
...to	στο	...sto
Do we call at	θα σταματησωμε στην	Tha stamadisomee stin

Signs often seen affixed to posts & doors

Greek	English
ΑΘ ΞΙΣ	ARRIVAL
ΑΝΑΧΩΡΗΣΙΣ	DEPARTURE
ΣΤΑΣΙΣ	BUS STOP
ΕΙΣΟΔΟΣ	ENTRANCE
ΕΞΟΔΟΣ	EXIT
ΚΕΝΤΡΟ	CENTRE (as in town centre)
ΕΙΣΟΔΟΣ ΕΛΕΥΘΕΡΑ	FREE ADMISSION
ΑΜΑΓΟΡΕΥΕΤΑΙ ΗΕΙΣΟΔΟΣ	NO ENTRANCE
ΕΙΣΙΤΗΡΙΑ	TICKET
ΠΡΟΣ ΤΑΣ ΑΠΟΒΑΘΡΑΣ	TO THE PLATFORMS
ΤΗΛΕΦΩΝΟΝ	TELEPHONE
ΑΝΔΡΩΝ	GENTLEMEN
ΓΥΝΑΙΚΩΝ	LADIES
ΑΠΑΓΟΡΕΤΕΤΑΙ ΤΟ ΚΑΠΝΗΣΜΑ	NO SMOKING

27

ΤΑΜΕΙΟΝ	CASH DESK
ΤΟΥΑΛΕΤΕΣ	TOILETS
ΑΝΟΙΚΤΟΝ	OPEN
ΚΛΕΙΣΤΟΝ	CLOSED
ΩΘΗΣΑΤΕ	PUSH
ΣΥΡΑΤΕ	PULL

4 Island Accommodation

How oft doth man by care oppressed, find in an inn a place of rest   Combe

Package, villa and tour organised holiday-makers will have accommodation arranged prior to arrival in Greece. If travelling around, then the most important matter is undoubtedly the procurement of lodgings, especially the first overnight stay on a new island or at an untried location.

The choice of accommodation is bewildering, varying from private houses (usually very clean but with basic bathroom facilities) to luxury class hotels able to hold their own with the most modern European counterpart. The deciding factor must be the budget and a person's sensibilities. My comments in respect of standards reflect comparisons with Western Europe establishments. Those referring to prices are usually in comparison with other Greek options. The standard of accommodation on the Cyclades naturally varies not only from island to island but from place to place. For instance, even amongst the long established tourist resorts of Mykonos, accommodation can range from the indecently plush to extremely simple island *pooms**.

Travellers stepping off a ferry-boat, will usually be part of a swarming throng made up of Greeks, tourists and back-packers engulfed by a quayside mass of Greeks, tourists and back-packers struggling to get aboard the ferry-boat. Visitors may well be approached by men, women and youngsters offering rooms. It is a matter of taking potluck there and then, or searching around the town oneself. The later in the day, the more advisable it is to take an offer, unseen. It is mandatory to establish the price, if the rooms are with or without shower and how far away they are located. It is unnerving to be 'picked up' and then commence on an ever-lengthening trudge through the back streets of a strange place, especially as Greek ideas of distance are rather optimistic.

Any accommodation usually calls for passports to be relinquished. A passport is also required to change money and to hire a car or a scooter, so it is a good idea, if married or travelling with friends, to have separate documents. Then, if necessary, one passport can be left at the abode and another kept for other purposes, as required.

Official sources and many guide-books lay much emphasis on the role of the Tourist police in finding accommodation, but this must not be relied upon as the offices may well be closed on arrival. Moreover recent changes in the structure of the various police forces is resulting in the once separate and independent Tourist police being integrated into the offices of the Town police. I regret that this may well be a very retrograde step. Such a pity that the Greeks, the innovators of this excellent service should now abandon the scheme, more especially in the light of the ever increasing numbers of tourists.

It can prove fruitful to enquire at a convenient taverna, which, more often than not, will result in an introduction to a room or pension owner. Failing that, they will usually send out for someone.

*A poom is a descriptive noun coined after sighting on Crete, some years ago, a crudely written sign that simply stated POOMS! The accommodation on offer was crude, low-ceilinged, raftered, earth-floored, windowless rooms simply equipped with a truckle bed and rickety oil-cloth covered washstand — very reminiscent of typical Cycladean cubicles of the 1950/60s period.

BEDROOMS

Greek bedrooms tend to be airy, whitewashed and sparsely furnished. The beds are often hard, as are the small pillows, and the unyielding mattresses may well be laid directly on to bed-boards and not springs.

It is advisable to inspect bedroom walls for blood-red splats of flattened, but once blood gorged, mosquitoes resulting from a previous occupant's night-time vigil. Well-designed rooms usually have a top-opening window screened off with gauze so that they can be left ajar without fear of incursions by winged creepy-crawlies. Where no gauze is in evidence, it is best to keep the windows tightly closed at night, however alien this may seem. Those not in possession of a proprietory repellent will have to reconcile themselves to a sleepless night, any tell-tale buzzing echoing in the ears indicating one has already been bitten. It is comparable to being attacked by Lilliputian Stuka night-fighters.

Hanging points are noticeable by their absence. Often there will be no wardrobe but if present there is every chance that there will be no hangers, not even the steel-wire type, and the doors may be missing. A rather idiosyncratic feature is that clothes hooks, when present, are often very inadequate, looking as if they have been designed, and are only suitable for, hanging coffee mugs by the handles.

Even more maligned and even more misunderstood than Greek food is

THE GREEK BATHROOM

I use the descriptive word bathroom, rather than refer simply to the toilets, because the total facility requires some elucidation. The following will not apply to luxury, A or B class hotels. Well, it should not!

The plumbing is quite often totally inadequate and instead of the separate wastes of the bath, shower and sink being plumbed into progressively larger soil pipes, thus achieving a 'venturi' effect, they are usually joined into a similar diameter tube to that of the individual pipes. This inevitably causes considerable back pressure with inescapable consequences. The toilet waste is almost always insufficient in size. Even normal, let alone excessive, use of toilet paper will result in dreadful things happening, not only to your bathroom, but probably to a number of bathrooms in the building, street and possibly the village. If this were not enough... the header tank usually does not deliver sufficient 'flush'. The Greeks have had, for many years, to be economic in the use of water and some islands ration it, turning off the supply for a number of hours per day, at the height of the summer.

Common faults are to find the lavatory without a seat; flooded to a depth of some inches; the bathroom light not working; no toilet roll; door locks not fitted; dirty WC pan and or any combination of the above. Furthermore, the wash basin may well be without a drain plug. Amongst other reasons, the lack of a plug is to stop flooding if a sink tap is accidently left turned on when the mains water is switched off, and not turned off when the water supply is resumed.

The most common type of en suite bathroom is an all purpose lavatory and shower room. Beware! The shower head, after years of research, is usually positioned in such a way as to not only shower the occupant but to drench the (amazingly) absorbent toilet roll, his or her clothes, towel and footwear. Incidentally the drain point is located to ensure that the bathroom is kept awash to a depth of between 1" and 3".

It is not unusual for there to be no hot water, even if a heating system is in evidence. Government energy conservation methods, the comparatively high cost of electricity and the use of moderately sized solar heating panels, all contribute to this state of affairs. Where solar panels are the means of heating the water, remember to beat the rush and shower as early as possible, for the water soon loses its heat. Why not share with a friend? If hot water is available, but it is not heated by solar energy, then it will be necessary to locate the relevant electric switch. This is usually a 4 way position ceramic knob hidden away behind a translucent panel door. On the other hand. . . .

One stipulation on water-short islands that really offends the West European (and North American?) sense of delicacy, is the oft present, hardly legible sign, requesting guests to put their 'papers' in the waste-bin supplied and not down the pan! I must own up to not always obeying this dictum and have had to make a hurried departure from an island, let alone a pension or village, when the consequences of my profligate use of toilet paper have become apparent.

Room charges are often increased by 50 to 100 drs per day for the use of a shower, but this will be detailed on the Government-controlled price list that should be displayed in every room, and is usually suspended on the back of the door.

THE BEACH
Some back-packing youngsters utilise the shore for their night's accommodation. In fact all island ferry-boaters must be prepared to consider the beach as a stand-by during the months of July and August in the more crowded locations although I have only had to spend one or two nights on the beach in the seven or eight years of island ferry-boating excursions. The weather could not be more ideal, the officials do not seem too fussed and may well direct you to a suitable spot. Beware of mosquitoes and tar.

CAMPING
In direct contrast to ad hoc sleeping out on the beach, camping, except on approved sites, is strictly forbidden, but the law is not always rigorously applied. The restriction comes about from a wish to improve general hygiene, to prohibit and discourage abuse of private property and as a precaution against forest fires. Usually the NTOG own the sites but there are some authorised, privately run camping grounds, which are price controlled. There are quite a few campsites on the Cyclades islands. A *Carnet-Camping International*, although not normally requested, affords campers world-wide, third-party liability cover and is available to United Kingdom residents from the AA and other similar organisations.

If moved on by any official for sleeping out on the beach or illegally camping, it is advisable not to argue and go quietly. The Greek police have fairly wide and autonomous powers and it is preferable not to upset them unnecessarily.

YOUTH HOSTELS (ΞΕΝΩΝΑΖ ΝΕΩΝ)
Establishments include the YMCA (**XAN**), YWCA (**XEN**) in Athens and the YHA in Athens.

Greek youth hostels are rather down at heel and tend to be operated in a somewhat slovenly manner. None of the old get-up-and-go familiar to some other countries members — morning ablutions in ice-cold water and placing used razor blades in disused tobacco tins nailed to the wall.

It is preferable to have current YHA membership, taking the Association's card along. Approximate prices per night at the YMCA and YWCA are 450 drs and in a Youth Hostel, 250 drs.

ROOMS (ΔΩΜΑΤΙΑ)
The story goes that as soon as a tourist steps off the ferry, he (or she)is surrounded by women crying **Rooms** (Dhomatio), and whoops, in minutes he is ensconced in some wonderful, Greek family's private home.

History may well have been like that, and in truth the ferries are still met at almost every island, the inhabitants offering not only rooms but pensions and the lower category hotels. Rooms are the cheapest accommodation, generally very clean and sometimes including the option of breakfast, which is ordinarily charged extra. Prices reflect an island's popularity and the season, but usually the mid-season cost will be between 700 and 1000 drs for a double room, depending upon the classification.

Apart from being approached leaving the ferry, the Tourist police would in the past advise of rooms to let but their role is being drastically reduced with their planned amalgamation with the Town police. Householders display the sign 'Ενοικαζονται δψματιοί, or simply 'Δωματια', when they have a room to rent. If the rooms are government approved and categorised, which they should be to be officially recognised, there will be a tariff, and they will be slightly more expensive than the free-lance householders. The Tourist police office will be signed 'ΤΟΥΡΙΣΤΙΚΗ ΑΣΤΥΝΟΜΙΑ', if at all (but their absorption into the other local police organisations will probably result in total emasculation).

A general point relates to a cautionary tale told to us by a delightful French couple. They were in the habit of replying to a room owners query as to how many nights they wished to stay by saying *"Tonight"*. One lady room owner interpreted this to mean two nights! Beware the inaccurate transcription.

PENSIONS (ΠΑΝΣΙΟΝ)

This type of lodging was a natural progression from **Rooms** and now represents the most easily found and reasonably priced accommodation on offer.

The older type of pension is rather reminiscent of those large Victorian English houses, split up into bed-sits. In the main though, they have been purpose built, usually during the Colonels' regime (1967-74) when government grants were freely available for the construction of tourist quarters. The owner often lives on one floor and acts as concierge. The rooms are functional and generally the guests on each level share a bathroom and shower and (a rather nice touch when provided) a communal refrigerator in which visitors can store their various provisions and drinks. Mid-season charges vary between 800 and 1200 drs for a double room.

Sometimes a breakfast of coffee, bread and jam, perhaps butter and a boiled egg, is available for about 150 drs and represents fair value compared with the cost of a cafe breakfast.

TAVERNAS (ΤΑΒΕΡΝΑ)

Tavernas are, first and foremost, eating places but some tavernas, especially those situated by, or near, beaches, have rooms available. The only drawback is that the more popular the taverna, the less likely guests are to get a full night's sleep, but of course the more involved they will be with the taverna's social life which will often continue on into the small hours.

HOTELS (ΞΕΝΟΔΟΧΕΙΟΝ)

Shades of difference and interpretation can be given to the nomenclature by variations of the bland, descriptive noun hotel. For instance ΞΝΟΔΟΧΕΙΟΝ ΥΠΝΟΥ indicates a hotel that does not serve meals and ΠΑΝΔΧΕΙΟΝ a low grade hotel.

Many back-packers will not consider hotels their first choice. The higher classification ones are more expensive than pensions and the lower grade hotels often cost the same, but may well be rather seedy and less desirable than the equivalent pension. Greek hotels are classified L (Luxury) A, B, C, D and E and the prices charged within these categories (except L) are controlled by the authorities.

It is unfortunately difficult to differentiate between hotels and their charges as each individual category is subject to fairly wide standards, and charges are subject to a multitude of possible percentage supplements and reductions as detailed below:

Shower extra (C, D and E hotels); number of days stayed less than three: plus 10 per cent; air conditioning extra (A and B hotels); out of season deduction (ask); high season extra: plus 20 per cent, ie the months of July, August and the first half of September; single occupancy: about 80 per cent of a double-room rate. The higher classification hotels may well insist on guests taking demi-pension terms, especially in high season. The following table must be treated as a guide only.

Class	Comments	Indicated mid-season double-bed price
L	All amenities and a very high standard and price. Probably at least one meal in addition to breakfast will have to be purchased. Very clean. Very hot water.	
A	High standard and price. Most rooms will have en suite shower or bath. Guests may well have to accept demi-pension terms. Clean. Hot water.	2500 drs
B	Good standard. Many rooms will have en suite shower or bath, clean, hot water.	2000 drs
C	Usually an older hotel. Faded elegance, shared bathroom, cleanish, possibly hot water.	1500 drs
D	Older hotel. Faded. Shared bathroom, which may well be 'interesting'. A shower, if available, will be an 'oxporionoo', and the water cold.	1000 drs
E	Old, faded and unclean. The whole stay will be an 'experience'. Only very cold water	750 drs

The prices indicated includes government taxes, service and room occupancy until noon.

THE XENIAS
Originally Government owned to ensure the availability of high-standard accommodation at important tourist centres but now often managed by private enterprise. Only A, B and C rated categories and they are of a better standard than hotels in a similar class.

FLATS & HOUSES
During the summer months this type of accommodation, referred to by travel agents and package tour operators as villas, is best booked prior to arriving in Greece. Not only will pre-booking be easier but, surprisingly, will prove cheaper than flying out and snooping around.

The winter is a different matter, but probably not within the scope of most of our readers.

Further useful names & addresses
The Youth Hostel Association, 14 Southampton St, London WC2E 7HY. Tel. 01-836 8541

Useful Greek

English	Greek	Sounds like
I want...	θελω	Thelo...
...a single room	ενα μονο δωματιο	...enna mono dhomatio
...a double room	ενα διπλο δωματιο	...enna thiplo dhomatio
...with a shower	με ντουζ	...me doosh
We would like a room	Θα θελαμε ενα δωματιο	Tha thelome ena dhomatio
for...	για	yia...
two/three days/a week/ until	δυο/τρεις μερεζ/μια εβδομαδα/μεχρι	thio/trees meres/meea evthomatha/ mekhri
Can you advise of another...	Ξερετε κανενα αλλο	Xerete kanena alo...
house with rooms	σπεετι με δωματιο	speeti meh dhomatio
pension	πανσιον	panseeon
inn	πανδοχειο	panthokheeo
hotel	ζενοδοχειο	ksenodhokheeo
youth hostel	ξενοναζ νεων	xenonas neon
How much is the room for a night?	Ποσο κανει το δωματιο για τη νυχτα	Poso kanee dho dhomatio yia ti neektah

That is too expensive	Εωαι πολυ ακριβα	Eene polee akriva
Have you anything cheaper?	Δεν εχετε αλλο πιο φθηνο	Dhen ekhete ahlo pio theeno
Is there...	Υπαρχει	Eeparkhee
a shower	ενα ντουζ	doosh
a refrigerator	ευα ψυγειο	psiyeeo
Where is the shower?	Που ειναι το ντουζ	Poo eene dho doosh
I have to leave...	Πρεπει να φυγω	Prebee na feegha...
today	σημερα	simera
tomorrow	αυριο	avrio
very early	Πολυ νωριζ	polee noris
Thank you for a	Ευχαριστω για την	Efkareesto gia tin
nice time	συμπαθτκοζωρα	simpathitikosora

5 Travelling around an island

A man is happier for life from having once made an agreeable tour   *Anon*

A few introductory remarks may well be apposite here in respect of holiday-makers' possessions and women in Greece. The matter will also be discussed elsewhere but it is not out of place to reiterate one or two points (Rosemary calls it 'carrying on').

Personal Possessions Do not leave airline tickets, money, travellers cheques and or passports behind at your accommodation. A man can quite easily acquire a wrist-strap handbag in which to conveniently carry these items. The danger does not, even today, lie with the Greeks, but with fellow tourists, down-and-outs and professional thieves working a territory.

Women There has been a movement towards the 'Spanish-costa' percentage ploy. Young Greek men, in the more popular tourist areas, have finally succumbed and will now sometimes try it on. It's up to you girls, there is no menace, only opportunities.

Now back to the main theme of the chapter but before expanding on the subject, a few words will not go amiss in respect of:-

Beaches Surprisingly, quite a few beaches are polluted in varying degrees, mainly by washed up plastic and some tar.

Jellyfish and sea urchins can occasionally be a problem in a particular bay, jellyfish increasingly so. One of my Mediterranean correspondents advises me that cures for the sting include, ammonia, urine (ugh) and a paste of meat tenderiser (it takes all sorts I suppose).

The biggest headache (literally) to a tourist is the sun, or more accurately, the heat of the sun at the height of the summer season. The Cyclades islands especially benefit from the relief of the prevailing wind, the Meltemi, but, to give an example of the extreme temperatures sometimes experienced, in Athens a few years ago birds were actually falling out of the trees, and they were the feathered variety. Every year dozens of holidaymakers are carted off, suffering from acute sunburn. A little often, (sun that is), must be the watchword.

It is very pleasant to observe more and more middle-aged Greek ladies taking to the sea, usually in an all enveloping black costume and a straw hat. Some to preserve their modesty, appear to swim in their everyday clothes

Despite the utterly reasonable condemnation of modern day advances in technology by us geriatrics, one amazing leap for all travelling and beach bound mankind is the Walk-Master personal stereo-cassettes. No more the strident, tinny beat of the transistor (or more commonly the 'Ghetto-Blaster'), now simply jigging silence of ear-muffed, face transfused youth. Splendid!

It may well be that you are a devoted sun worshipper and spend every available minute on the beach or terrace; if so do not read on. On the other hand if your interests range beyond the conversion of the sun's very strong rays into painful, peeling flesh and you wish to travel around an island, the question of modus operandi must be given some thought.

First, purchase an island map and one of the colourful and extremely informative tourist guides available on the larger islands. A rather incomplete map of the Cyclades and some island detail, that can be acquired prior to departure from the United Kingdom, is produced by the very helpful firm, **Clyde Surveys Ltd., Reform Rd., Maidenhead, Berks SL6 8BU. Tel. (0628) 21371**. The best, inexpensive, general map is printed in

Greece by Delta Publications

Then consider the alternative methods of travel and appraise their value to your circumstances.

On Foot Owing to the hilly terrain of the islands and the daytime heat encountered, you may well have enough walking to do without looking for trouble. A quick burst down to the local beach, taverna, shop or restaurant, and the resultant one hundred or so steps back up again, will often be quite enough to satiate any desire to go 'walkies'.

If you must, walking is often the only way to negotiate the more rugged donkey tracks and the minimum footwear required is a solid pair of sandals or 'trainers'.

Hitching The comparative paucity of privately owned cars makes hitch-hiking an unsatisfactory mode of travel. On the other hand, if striking out to get to, or return from, a particular village on a dead end road, most Greek drivers will stop when thumbed down. It will probably be a lift in the back of a Japanese pick-up truck, possibly sharing the space with some chickens, a goat or sheep or all three!

Donkey Although once a universal 'transportation module', now usually only available for hire on specific journey basis in particular locations. A personal prejudice is to consider donkey rides part of the unacceptable face of tourism added to which it is exorbitantly expensive.

Buses Buses are the universal method of travel in Greece, so the services are widespread if, naturally enough, a little Greek in operation. Generally they run approximately on time and the fares are, on the whole, extremely reasonable.

The trick is to find the square from which the buses depart, and then locate the ticket office. Here the timetable and fares structure will be stuck up in the window or on a wall, and tickets are pre-purchased. On some bus routes the fares are collected by a conductor, although this is unusual. Be available well prior to the scheduled departure times as buses have a 'nasty habit' of departing early. Ensure any luggage is placed in the correct storage department, otherwise it may go missing.

Buses are often crowded, especially if the journey coincides with a ferry-boat arrival. They are, with the taxi, the islanders main form of transportation, so expect fairly bulky loads and, occasionally, livestock to share the seats, storage racks and central aisle. A bus rarely leaves a potential client, they just encourage everyone in. The fun comes if the bus is not only 'sardine packed', but fares are collected by the conductor. Somehow he makes his way through, round and over the passengers. The timetables are usually scheduled so that a bus or buses await a ferry-boats arrival, except perhaps very early or late craft.

Do not fail to observe the decorations, festooned around and enveloping the driver. Often these displays resemble a shrine, which, taking account of the way some of the drivers propel their bus, is perhaps not so out of place. Finally, do have the right change, coins are always in short supply.

A critic recently took me to task for not stressing that the summer bus schedules detailed are the subject of severe curtailment, if not total termination, during the winter months from October through to May. So, smacked hand Geoffrey and readers please note.

Taxis Usually are very readily available, and can be remarkably modern and plush. On the other hand. . .

Ports and towns nearly always have a main square on which the taxis are ranked and very often they queue on the quayside to await a ferry-boat's arrival. Fares are governed by law and, at the main-rank, will be displayed giving examples of the cost to various destinations. The fares are reasonable by European standards, but it is essential to establish the cost prior to hiring a taxi.

It may come as a shock to have one's halting, pidgin Greek answered in 'pure' Australian or American. But this is not surprising when one considers that many island Greeks have spent their youth on merchant ships, or emigrated to the New World for 10 to 15 years. On their return home, with a relatively financially secure future, they have taken to taxi driving to supplement their income (and possibly to keep out of the little woman's way).

Bicycle, Moped, Scooter or Car Hire Be very careful to establish what (if any) insurance cover is included in the rental fee, and that the quoted hire charge includes the various compulsory taxes. On the whole, bicycles are very hard work and poor value in relation to, say, the cost of hiring a Lambretta or Vespa scooter — an option endorsed when the mountainous nature of most islands, and the midday heat is taken into consideration. The ubiquitous Italian models are being replaced by semi-automatic Japanese motorcycles. Although they do away with the necessity to fight the gears and clutch they are not entirely suited to transporting two heavyweights. I have had the frightening experience, when climbing a steep mountainside track, of the bike jumping out of gear, depositing my passenger and I on the ground and the scooter whirling round like a crazed mechanical catherine-wheel.

It is amazing how easy it is to get a good tan while scootering. The moderate island wind draws the sun's heat, the air is laden with the smell of wild sage and oleanders and with the sun on your back. . . marvellous!

Very rarely is a deposit requested when hiring a bike or motorbike but your passport may be retained. If not the number will be required, as may the sight of a driving licence or an International driving permit which can be acquired from a tourist's relevant national driving organisation, and is valid for a period of one year.

Always shop around to check out various companies' hire rates; the nearer to a port, town or city centre you are, the more expensive they will be. A small walk towards the unfashionable quarters can be very rewarding.

Take a close look over the chosen mode of transport before settling up, as maintenance of any mechanical unit in Greece is poor to non-existent. Bicycles and scooters, a few years old, will be 'pretty clapped out'. More especially check the brakes — you will need them and do not allow the hirer to fob you off without making sure there is a spare wheel. Increasingly, the owners of two wheeled vehicles are hiring out dubious looking crash helmets. Flash young Greek motobike riders usually wear their space age outfits on the handlebars.

A useful tip when hiring a scooter is to take along a towel. It doubles up as useful additional padding for the pillion passenger's bottom on rocky roads and saves sitting on painfully hot plastic seating if a hirer has forgotten to raise the squab when parked up. Sunglasses are necessary to protect a riders eyes from air-borne insects. Out of the height-of-season and early evening it can become very chilly so a sweater or jumper is a good idea and females may well require a head scarf, whatever the time of day or night.

Fuel is served in litres and five litres of two-stroke costs about 250 - 300 drs. Fill up as soon as possible, fuel stations are in fairly short supply outside the main towns.

Typical daily hire rates are, for a bicycle 150 drs, a scooter/Lambretta 600 to 1000 drs, and a car between 2000 and 3000 drs. More and more often car hire companies require a daily deposit, which can be as much as 5000 drs per day. Out of season and period hire can benefit from negotiation. Increasingly the gap between the scooter and the car is being filled with more sophisticated machinery which include moon-tyred and powerfully engined Japanese motorbikes and beach-buggies.

Several words of warning will not go amiss. Taking into account the state of the roads do not hire a two-wheeled conveyance if not thoroughly used to handling one. There are a number of very nasty accidents every year, involving tourists and hired scooters.

Additionally the combination of poor road surfaces and usually inadequate to non-existent lights should preclude any night time scootering. A hirer must ensure he (or she) is fully covered for medical insurance, including an unscheduled medi-care flight home, and check that a general policy does not exclude accidents incurred on hired transport. The glass fronted metal framed shrines mounted by the roadside are graphic reminders of a fatal accident at this or that spot. Incidentally, on a less macabre note, if the shrine is a memorial to a man, the picture and bottle usually present (more often than not of Sophia Loren and whisky) represent that person's favourite wishes. Back to finger-wagging. The importance of the correct holiday insurance cover cannot be over-stressed. The tribulations I have encountered in obtaining inclusive insurance combined with some readers disastrous experiences have resulted in the inclusion in the Guide of an all embracing scheme. This caveat should be coupled with the strictures in Chapter 1 drawing attention to the all-inclusive policy devised for readers of the *Candid Guides*, for details of which *See* Page iii. Enough said!

Another area that causes unpleasant disputes is the increasing habit of the hire companies to charge comparatively expensively for any damage incurred. Your detailed reasons for the causes of an accident, the damage and why it should not cost you anything inevitably falls on deaf ears. Furthermore it is no use threatening to involve the police as they will not be at all interested in the squabble.

Roads The main roads of most Cyclades islands are passable but metalled country lanes usually degenerate fairly alarmingly, becoming heavily rutted and cratered tracks. Much road building and reconstruction is under way. Beware as not all roads, indicated as being in existence on the official maps, are anything more than, at the best, donkey tracks and can be simply non-existent. Evidence of broken lines marking a road on the map must be interpreted as meaning there is no paved highway at all.

Useful Greek

English	Greek	Sounds like
Where can I hire a...	Που μπορω να νοικιασω ενα	Poo boro na neekeeaso enna...
...bicycle	ποδηλατο	...pothilato
...scooter	σκουτερ	...sckooter
...car	αυτοκινητο	...aftokinito
I'd like a...	Θα ηθελα ενα	Tha eethela enna...
I'd like it for...	Θα το ηθελα για	Tha dho eethela yia...
...a day	μια μερα	...mia mera
...days	μερες	...meres
...a week	μια εβδομαδα	...mia evthomadha
How much is it by the...	Ποσο κανει την	Poco kanoo tin...
...day	μερα	...mera
...week	εβδομαδα	...evthomadha
Does that include...	Συμπεριλαμβανονται σαντο	Simberitamvanonte safto
...mileage	τα χιλιομετρα	...tah hiliometra
...full insurance	μικτη ασφαλεια	...meektee asfaleah
I want some	Θελω	Thelo
...petrol (gas)	βενζινη	...vehnzini
...oil	λαδι	...lathi
...water	νερο	...nero
Fill it up	Γεμιστε το	Yemiste to
...litres of petrol (gas)	λιτρα βενξινηζ	...litra vehnzinis
How far is it to...	Ποσο απεχει	Poso abechee...
Which is the road for...	Ποιος ειναι ο δρομος λια	Pios eene o thromos yia
Where are we now	Που ειμαστε τωρα	Poo emaste tora
What is the name of this place	Πως ονομαξεται αυτο το μερος	Pos onomazete afto dho meros
Where is...	Που ειναι	Poo eene...

Road Signs

STOP	ΑΛΤ
NO ENTRY	ΑΠΑΓΟΡΕΥΕΤΑΙ Η ΕΙΣΟΔΟΣ
NO THROUGH ROAD	ΑΔΙΕΞΟΔΟΣ
DETOUR	ΠΑΡΑΚΑΜΠΤΗΡΙΟΣ
REDUCE SPEED	ΕΛΑΤΤΩΣΑΤΕ ΤΑΧΥΤΗΤΑΝ
NO WAITING	ΑΠΑΓΟΡΕΥΕΤΑΙ Η ΑΝΑΜΟΝΗ
ROAD REPAIRS	ΕΠΓΑ ΕΠΙ ΤΗΣ ΟΔΟΥ
BEWARE (Caution)	ΚΙΝΔΥΝΟΣ
NO OVERTAKING	ΑΠΓΟΡΕΥΕΤΑΙ ΤΟ ΠΡΟΣΠΕΡΑΣΜΑ
NO PARKING	ΑΠΑΓΟΡΕΥΕΤΑΙ Η ΣΤΑΘΜΕΥΣΙΣ

6 Island Food & Drink

Let us eat and drink for tomorrow we die. *Corinthians*

It is a pity that many tourists, prior to visiting Greece, have 'experienced' the offerings masquerading as Greek food served up at sundry restaurants in Europe and America. Greek food does not seem to cross its borders very well and probably it is impossible to recreate Greek cooking away from the homeland. Perhaps this is because the food and wine owe much of their taste to, and are in sympathy with, the very air laden with the scent of the flowers and herbs, the very water, clear and chill, the very soil of the plains and scrub-clad mountains, the ethereal and uncapturable quality that is Greece. Incidentally many critics woud say it was impossible to create Greek food, full stop, but be that as it may. . . Salad does not normally send me into ectasy but, after a few days in Greece, the very thought of a peasant salad consisting of endive leaves, sliced tomatoes and cucumber, black olives, olive oil and vinegar dressing all topped off with feta cheese and sprinkled with oregano, parsley or fennel, sends me salivating to the nearest taverna.

Admittedly, unless you are lucky enough to chance across an outstanding taverna, the majority are surprisingly unadventurous and the choice of menu limited.

Mind you there are one or two restaurants serving exciting and unusual meals if the spelling mistakes are ignored. For instance I have observed over the years the following no doubt appetising dishes:- *omeled, spachetti botonnaise, shrings salad, bowels entrails, lump cutlets, limp liver, mushed pot, schrimps, crambs, kid chops, grilled meat bolls, spar rips, wine vives, fiant oven, sward fish, pork shops, staffed vine leaves, wild greens, string queens, wildi cherry, bater honi, gregg goti(!)* and *Creek salad* — sounds interesting.

A FEW HINTS & TIPS

Do not insist upon butter, the Greek variant is not very tasty to the European palate, is expensive and in the heat tends to dissolve into greasy pools.

Sample the retsina wine and after a bottle or two a day for a few days there is every chance you will enjoy it. Moreover, retsina is beneficial (well that's what I tell myself), acting as a splendid anti-agent to the comparative oiliness of some of the food.

Bread will be automatically served with a meal — and charged for — if you do not indicate otherwise. It is very useful for mopping up any excessive olive oil and requires no butter to make it more greasy. It has become a noticeable, and regrettable, feature in recent years that the charge for bread has increased to between 10 and 20 drs per head and I have seen it as high as 30 drs. Naughty!

Greek food tends to be served on the 'cool' side and even if the meal started out hot, and by some mischance is speedily served, it will arrive on a thoroughly chilled plate.

The selection of both food and drink usually served up is, almost always, limited and unenterprising, unless you elect to frequent the more international restaurants (but why go to Greece?). On the other hand the choice of establishments in which to eat and/or drink is unlimited, in fact the profusion is such that it can prove very confusing. If in doubt about which particular restaurant or taverna to patronise, use the well tried principle of picking one frequented by the locals; it will inevitably serve good quality food at reasonable prices.

It is generally a waste of time to ask a Greek for guidance in selecting a good taverna or restaurant for, as he would not wish to offend anyone, he will be reluctant to give specific advice in case you might be dissatisfied.

Especially in the more rural areas, do not be shy, ask to look over the kitchen to see what's cooking. If denied this traditional right, be on your guard as the food may well be pre-cooked, tasteless and plastic, particularly if the various meals available are displayed in a neon-lit showcase.

Do not order the whole meal all at once as you would at home, for if you do it will be served simultaneously and/or in the wrong sequence. Order course by course and take your time, everyone else does. You are not being ignored if the waiter does not approach the table for anything up to 20 minutes, he is just taking his time and is probably over-worked. At first the blood pressure does tend to rise inexorably as the waiter, seemingly, continues to studiously disregard your presence. It makes a visitor's stay in Greece very much more enjoyable if all preconceived ideas of service can be forgotten. Lay back and settle into the glorious and indolent timelessness of the locals' way of life. If in a hurry, pay when the order arrives for if under the impression that it took a disproportionate time to be served, just wait until it comes to settling up. It will probably take twice as long to get the bill (*logaristhimo*), as it did to receive the food.

Fish, contrary to expectations, is very expensive, even in comparison with European prices, so you can imagine the disparity with the cost of other Greek food. When ordering fish, it is normal to select the choice from '*the ice*', and, fish being priced by weight, it will be put on the scales prior to cooking.

Price lists are mandatory for most drinking and eating places, stating the establishment's category and the price of every item served. Two prices are shown, the first being net is not really relevant, the second, showing the price you will actually be charged, includes service and taxes.

Food is natural and very rarely are canned or any frozen items used, even if available. When frozen foods are included in the meal the fact must be indicated on the menu by addition of the initials *KAT*. The olive oil used for cooking is excellent, as are the herbs and lemons, but it can take time to become accustomed to the different flavour imparted to food.

Before leaving the subject of hints and tips, remember that olive oil can be pressed into service for removing unwanted beach-tar from clothes.

A most enjoyable road, quayside or ferry-boat breakfast is to buy a large yoghurt and a small pot of honey, mix the honey into the yoghurt and then relish the bitter-sweet delight. If locally produced, natural yoghurt (usually stored in small, cool tubs and spooned into a container) cannot be purchased, the brand named *Total* is an adequate substitute being made from cow or sheep milk. I prefer the sheep derived product and, when words fail, break into a charade of 'baa-ing'. It keeps the other shoppers amused if nothing else. The succulent water melon, a common and inexpensive fruit, provides a juicy lunch-time refreshment.

Apart from waving the table-cloth in the air, or for that matter the table, it is usually to call '*parakalo*' (please). It is also permissible to say '*gkarson*' or simply waiter.

THE DRINKS

Non-alcoholic beverages Being a '*cafe*' (and '*taverna*') society, coffee is drunk at all times of the day and night. Greek coffee ('*kafe*') is in fact a left-over from the centuries long Turkish influence, being served without milk in small cups, always with a glass of deliciously cool water. Unless specified otherwise, it will come sickly sweet or *varigliko*. There are many variations but the three most usual are *sketto* (no sugar), *metrio* (medium) or *glyko* (sweet). Do not completely drain the cup, the bitter grains will choke you. Except in the most traditional establishments (*Kafeneions*), you can ask for *Nes-Kafe* or simply *Nes* which, as you would think, is an instant coffee but has a comparatively muddy taste. If you require milk with your coffee it is necessary to ask for *me ghala*. A most refreshing version is to have *Nes* chilled or *frappe*. French coffee (*ghaliko kafe*), served in a coffee pot with a separate jug of hot milk, espresso kafe and cappucino are found in the larger provincial cities, ports and international establishments. However, having made your detailed request, you may well receive any permutation of all the possibilities listed above, however carefully you think you have ordered.

Tea, (*tsai*), perhaps surprisingly, is quite freely available, made of course with the ubiquitous teabag, which is not so outrageous, since they have become so commonplace. In more out of the way places, you may be served herbal tea.

Purchasing bottled mineral waters is not always necessary as, generally, island water is superb. Should you wish to have some stashed away in the fridge, brand names include *Loutrakri*, *Nigita*, and *Sarizo*. Sprite is fizzy and Lemnada/Lemonatha a stillish lemonade. Orangeade (*portokaladha*), cherry soft drink (*visinatha*) and fruit juices are all palatable and sold, as often as not, under brand names, as is the universal *Koka-Kola*.

A word of warning emanates from a reader who reported that, in the very hot summer months, some youngsters drink nothing but sweet, fizzy beverages. This can result in mouth ulcers caused by fermenting sugar, so drink some water every day.

Alcoholic beverages
Generally sold by weight. Beer comes in 330g tins or 500g bottles (have the 500g, it is a good measure) and wine in 340 to 430g (half bottle), 680 to 730g (1.1 pints) and 950g (1¾ pints) bottles.

Greek brewed or bottled beers represent very good value except when served in cans, which are the export version and a 'rip off'. This European habit should be resisted for no other reason than it means the cost is almost doubled. Now that *Fix Hellas* is rarely available, due to the founder's death, the only other, widely available, bottled beers are *Amstel* and *Henninger*. Draught lager, is insidiously, creeping in to various resorts and should be avoided, not only for purist reasons, but because it is comparatively expensive as are the imported stronger bottled lagers. No names, no pack drill but *Carlsberg* is one that springs to mind. A small bottle of beer is *mikri bira* and a large one, *meghali bira.*

Wine Unresinated (*aretsinoto*) wine is European in style, palatable, and popular brands include red and white *Demestika* and *Cambas*. More refined palates will approve of the whites (aspro) and the reds (kokino) of Santorini island. Greek wine is not so much known for its quality but if quantity of brands can make up for this then Greece will not let you down.

Resinated wine is achieved, if you consider that to be the expression, by the barrels, in which the wine is to be fermented, being internally coated with pine-tree resin. The resultant liquid is referred to as retsina, most of which are white, with a kokkeneli or rosé version being available. Retsina is usually bottled, but in tavernas will quite often be served in a metal jug, or dispensed, for personal consumption, from large vats from sidestreet cellars, into any container you might like to use. The adjective 'open' is used to describe locally brewed retsina available on draught or more correctly from the barrel. Rumour has it that the younger retsinas are more easily palatable, but that is very much a matter of taste. A very good 'starter' kit is to drink a bottle or two of retsina twice a day for three or four days and if the pain goes. . .

Spirits & others As elsewhere in the world, if you stick to the national drinks they represent good value.

Ouzo, much maligned and blamed for other excesses, is, in reality, of the aniseed family of drinks (which include Ricard and Pernod) and, taken with water, is a splendid 'medicine'. *Ouzo* is traditionally served with *mezethes* (or *mezes*), the Greek equivalent of Spanish *tapas*, consisting of a small plate of, for instance, a slice of cheese, tomato, cucumber and possibly smoked eel, octopus and an olive. When served they are charged for, costing some 20 to 30 drs, but the tradition of offering them is disappearing in many tourist locations. If you specifically do not wish to be served *mezes* then the request is made '*ouzo sketto*'. *Raki* is a stronger alternative to *Ouzo*, often 'created' in Crete.

Greek *Metaxa* brandy, available in three, five and seven star quality, is very palatable but with a certain amount of 'body', whilst *Otys* brandy is smoother. Greek aperitifs include *Vermouth, Mastika* and *Citro.*

DRINKING PLACES

Prior to launching into the various branches of this subject, I am at a loss to understand why so many cafe-bar and taverna owners select chairs that are designed to cause the maximum discomfort, even suffering. Often too small for any but a very small bottom, too low and made up of wicker-work or rafia that painfully impresses the pattern on the sitters bare (sun-burnt?) thighs.

Kafeneion (ΚΑΦΕΝΙΟΝ) Greek cafe, serving only Turkish coffee. Very Greek, very masculine and I have never seen a woman in one. They are similar to a local working man's club, but with backgammon, worry beads and large open windows giving a dim view of the smoke-laden interior.

Ouzeries (ΟΥΞΕΡΙ) As above, but the house speciality is (well, well) *Ouzo*.

Cafe-bar (ΚΑΦΕ-ΜΠΑΡ) As above, but serving alcoholic beverages as well as coffee and women are to be seen.

Pavement cafes French in style, with outside tables and chairs sprawling over the road as well as the pavement. Inside, the locals will be chatting to each other in that peculiar Greek fashion, giving the impression that a full-blooded fight is about to break out at any moment. In reality, they are just good friends, chatting to each other over the noise of a televised football match, or watching some plastic, sickly American soap opera or ghastly English 'comic' programme with Greek subtitles. Open from mid-morning, through the day to one or two o'clock the next morning. Snacks and sweet cakes are usually available.

Drinks can always be obtained at a taverna or restaurant, but you may be expected to eat, so read on.

You can drink at hotel cocktail bars but why leave home!

EATING PLACES

At the cheapest end of the market, and more especially found in Athens, are pavement-mounted stands serving doughnut-shaped bread which give an inexpensive nibble.

Pistachio nut & ice cream vendors Respectively pushing their wheeled trolleys around the streets, selling a wide variety of nuts in paper bags for 10 drs or so and good value ice cream in a variety of flavours and prices.

Galaktopoleio (ΓΑΛΑΚΤΟΠΩΕΙΟ) A shop selling dairy products including milk (*gala*), butter, yoghurt (*yiaorti*), bread, honey, sometimes omelettes and fritters with honey (*loukoumades*). A traditional but more expensive alternative to a restaurant/bar in which to purchase breakfast.

Zacharoplasteion (ΖΑΧΑΡΟΠΛΑΣΤΕΙΟ) A shop specialising in pastries, cakes (*glyko*), chocolates (which are comparatively expensive) and soft drinks as well as, sometimes, a small selection of alcoholic drinks.

Galaktozacharoplasteion A combination of the two previously described establishments.

Snack bar (ΣΝΑΚ-ΜΠΑΡ, Souvlatzidika & Tyropitadika) Snack bars, not so numerous in the less touristy areas, and often restricted to one or two in the main town. They represent marvellous value for a stand-up snack and the most popular offering is *souvlaki* — pita bread (or a roll) filled with grilled meat or kebab, (*doner kebab* — slices off a rotating vertical spit of an upturned cone of meat also called '*giro*'), a slice of tomato, chopped onion and a dressing. Be careful, as souvlaki is not to be muddled with *souvlakia* which, when served at a snack bar, consists of pieces of lamb, pork or veal meat grilled on a wooden skewer and is indistinguishable from *Shish-Kebab*, or (guess what) a *souvlakia* when served at a sit-down meal where the metal skewered meat pieces are interspersed with vegetables. Other goodies include *tiropites* — hot flaky pastry pies filled with cream cheese; *boogatsa*

— a custard filled pastry, a wide variety of rolls and sandwiches (*sanduits*) with cheese, tomato, salami and other spiced meat fillings as well as toasted sandwiches (*tost*).

Pavement cafes Serve snacks and sweets.

Pizzerias Seem to be on the increase and are restaurants specialising in the imported Italian dish which prompts one to ask why not go to Italy. To be fair they usually represent very good value and a large serving will often feed two.

Tavernas (ΤΑΒΕΡΝΑ), Restaurants (ΕΣΤΙΑΤΟΡΙΟΝ), Rotisserie (ΨΥΣΤΕΡΙΑ) & Rural Centres (ΕΞΟΧΙΚΟΝ ΚΕΝΤΡΟΝ) Four variations on a theme. The traditional Greek taverna is a family concern, frequently only open in the evening. More often than not, the major part of the eating area is outside under a vine-covered patio, down the pavement and/or on a roof garden.

Restaurants tend to be more sophisticated, possibly open all day and night, but the definition between the two is rather blurred. The price lists may include a chancy English translation, the waiter might be smarter and the table cloth and napkins could well be linen, in place of the taverna's paper table covering and serviettes.

As tavernas often have a spit-roasting device tacked on, there is often little, discernible difference between a rotisserie and a taverna. A grilled meat restaurant may also be styled **ΨΗΣΤΑΡΙΑ**.

The rural centre is a mix of cafe-bar and taverna in, you've guessed it, a rural or seaside setting.

Fish tavernas (ΨΑΡΟΤΑΒΕΡΝΑ) Tavernas specialising in fish dishes.

Hotels (ΞΕΝΟΔΟΧΕΙΟΝ) ΞΕΝΟΔΟΧΕΙΟΝ ΥΠΝΟΥ is a hotel that does not serve food, **ΠΑΝΔΟΧΕΙΟΝ** a lower category hotel and Xenia, a Government-owned hotel.

The Xenia will be well run, the food and drink international, the menu will be in French and the prices will reflect all these 'attributes'.

An extremely unpleasant manifestation to old fogey's like me is illustrated by one or two menus spotted in the more 'international' locations, namely Greek bills of fare set out Chinese restaurant style. You know, set 'Meal A' for two, 'Meal B' for three and 'C' for four and more...!

THE FOOD
Some of the following represents a selection of the wide variety of food available.

Sample menu

Ψωμι (Psomi)	Bread
ΠΡΩΙΝΟ	BREAKFAST
Αυγα τηγανιτο με μπεικον και τοματα	Fried egg, bacon and tomato
Τοστ βουτυρο μαρμελαδα	Buttered toast and marmalade
Το προγευμα (to pro-ye-vma)	English (or American on some islands) breakfast
ΑΥΓΑ	EGGS
Μελατα	soft boiled
Σφικτα	hard boiled
Τηγανιτα	fried
Ποσσε	poached
ΤΟΣΤ ΣΑΝΤΟΥΙΤΣ	TOASTED SANDWICHES
Τοστ μετυρι	toasted cheese
Τοστ (με)Ζαμπον καιτυρι	toasted ham and cheese
Μπουρκερ	burger
Χα Μπουρκερ	hamburger
Τσισμπουρκερ	cheeseburger
Σαντουιτσ λουκανικο	hot dog
ΟΡΕΚΤΙΚΑ	APPETIZERS/HORS D'OEUVRES
Αυτξονγιεξ	anchovies

Ελιεζ	olives
Σαρδελλεζ	sardines
Σκορδαλιο	garlic dip
Τζατζικι	tzatziki (diced cucumber & garlic in yoghurt)
Ταραμοσαλατα	taramasalata (a fish roe pate)

ΣΟΥΠΕΣ — SOUPS

Σουπα φασωλια	bean
Αυγολεμονο	egg and lemon
Ψαροσουπα	fish
Κοτοσυπα	chicken
Ντοματοσουπα	tomato
Σουπα λαχανικων	vegetable

ΟΜΕΛΕΤΕΣ — OMELETTES

Ομελετα μπεικου	bacon
Ομελετα μπεικον τυρι τοματα	bacon, cheese and tomato
Ομελετα τυρι	cheese
Ομελετα ζαμπον	ham
Ομελετα συκωτα κια πουλιων	chicken liver

ΣΑΛΑΤΕΣ — SALADS

Ντοματα Σαλατα	tomato
Αγγουρι Σαλατα	cucumber
Αγγουοτοματα Σαλατα	tomato and cucumber
Χωριατικη	Greek peasant village salad

ΛΑΧΑΝΙΚΑ (ΛΑΔΕΡΑ)* — VEGETABLES

Πατατεζ	potatoes
Πατατεζ Τηγανιτεζ	chips (french fries)
φρεοκα φασολακια	green beans
Σπαραγκια	asparagus
Κολοκυθακια	courgettes
Σπανακι	spinach

*indicates cooked in oil.

Note various methods of cooking include:-
Baked — στο θουρνα; boiled — βραστα; creamed — με ασπρη σαλτσα; fried — τηγανιτα; grilled — στη σχαραρα; roasted — ψητα; spit roasted — σουβλας.

ΚΥΜΑΔΕΣ — MINCED MEATS

Μουσακαζ	moussaka
Ντοματεζ Γεμιστεζ	stuffed tomatoes (with rice or minced meat)
Κεφτεδεζ	meat balls
Ντολμαδακια	stuffed vine leaves (with rice or minced meat)
Πσπουτσακια	stuffed vegetable marrow (rice or meat)
Κανελονια	canelloni
Μακαρονια με κυμα	spaghetti bolognese (more correctly with mince)
Παστιτσιο	macaroni, mince and sauce
Σουβλακι	shish-kebab

PIZI — RICE

Πιλαφι	pilaff
Πιλαφι (με) γιαουρτι	with yoghurt
Πιλαφι συκωτακια	with liver
Σπανακοριζο	with spinach
Πιλαφι κυμα	with minced meat

ΠΟΥΛΕΡΙΚΑ — POULTRY

Κοτοπουλο	chicken, roasted
Ποδι κοταζ	leg of chicken
Στηθοζ κοταζ	chicken breast
Κοτοπουλο βραστο	boiled chicken

Ψητο κοτοπουλο στη σομβλα	spit-roasted chicken
ΚΡΕΑΣ	**MEAT**
Νεφρα	kidneys
Αρνι†	lamb†
Αρνιστεζ Μπριζολεζ	lamb chops
Παιδακια	lamb cutlets
Συκωτι	liver
Χοιρινο†	pork†
Χοιρινεζ Μπριζολεζ	pork chops
Λουκανικα	sausages
Μπιφτεκι	steak (beef)
Μοσχαρισιο	veal
Μοσχαρισιο Μπριζολεζ	veal chops
Μοσχαρι	grilled veal
Ψητο Μοσχαρακι	roast veal

†often with the prefix/suffix to indicated if roasted or grilled

ΨΑΡΙΑ	**FISH**
Σκουμπρι	mackerel
Σμναγριδα	red snapper
Μαριδεζ	whitebait
Οκταποδι	octopus
Καλαμαρια	squid
Μπαρμπουνι	red mullet
Κεφαλοζ	mullet
Λυθρινι	grey mullet
ΤΥΡΙΑ	**CHEESE**
φετα	feta (goat's-milk based)
Γραβιερα	gruyere-type cheese
Κασερι	cheddar-type (sheep's-milk based)
ΦΡΟΥΤΑ	**FRUITS**
Καρπουζι	water melon
Πεπονι	melon
Μηλα	apple
Πορτοκαλι	oranges
Σταφυλια	grapes
Κομποστα φρουτων	fruit compote
ΠΑΓΩΤΑ	**ICE-CREAM**
Σπεσιαλ	special
Παγωτο βανιλλια	vanilla
Παγωτο σοκολατα	chocolate
Παγωτο λεμονι	lemon
Υρανιτα	water ice
ΓΛΥΚΙΣΜΑΤΑ	**DESSERTS**
Κεικ	cake
ρουτοσαλατα	fruit salad
Κρεμα	milk pudding
Κρεμ καραμελ	cream caramel
Μπακλαβαζ	crisp pastry with nuts and syrup or honey
Καταιφι	fine shredded pastry with nuts and syrup or honey
Γαλακτομπουρεκο	fine crispy pastry with custard and syrup
Γιαουρτι	yoghurt
Μελι	honey
ΑΝΑΨΥΚΤΙΚΑ	**COLD DRINKS/SOFT DRINKS**
Πορτοκαλι	orange
Πορτοκαλαδα	orangeade
Λεμοναδα	lemonade made with lemon juice

Γκαζοζα (Gazozo)	fizzy lemonade
Μεταλλικο νερο	mineral water
Κοκα κολα	Coca-cola
Πεψι κολα	Pepsi-cola
Σεβεν-απ	Seven Up
Σοδα	soda
Τοη ικ	tonic
Νερο (Nero)	water
ΚΑφΕΔΕΣ	COFFEES
Ελληνικος (Καφεζ)	Greek coffee (sometimes called Turkish coffee ie Toupkikos **Καφε**)
σκετο (skehto)	no sugar
μετριο (metrio)	medium sweet
γλυκο (ghliko)	sweet (very)

(Unless stipulated it will turn up 'ghliko'. Do not drink before it has settled.

Νεζ καφε	Nescafé
Νεζ (με γαλα) (Nes me ghala)	Nescafé with milk
Εζπρεσσο	espresso
Καπουτσινο	cappucino
φραπε	chilled coffee is known as 'frappé'
Τσαι	tea
Σοκολατα γαλα⁻	chocolate milk
ΜΠΥΡΕΣ	BEERS
ΦΙΞ(ΕΛΛΑΣ) Μπυρα	Fix (Hellas) beer
φιαλν	bottle
κουτι	can
ΑΜΣΤΕΛ (Αμστελ)	Amstel
ΧΕΝΝΙΝΓΕΡ (Χεννινγκερ)	Henninger
	(300 g usually a can
	500 g usually a bottle)
ΠΟΤΑ	DRINKS
Ουζο	Ouzo
Κονιακ	Cognac
Μπραντυ	Brandy
Μεταξα	Metaxa
3 ΑΣΤ	3 star
5 ΑΣΤ	5 star
Ουισκυ	Whisky
Τςιν	Gin
Βοτκα	Vodka
Καμπαρι	Campari
Βερμουι	Vermouth
Μαρτινι	Martini
ΚΡΑΣΙΑ	WINES
Κοκκινο	red
Ασπρο	white
Ροζε Κοκκινελι	rosé
Σερο	dry
Υλυκο	sweet
Ρετοινα	resinated wine
e.g. θεοκρποξ	Theokritos
Αρετσινωτο	unresinated wine
e.g. Δεμεοτιχα	Demestica
	340 g is a ½ bottle
	680 g is a bottle
	950 g is a large bottle

Useful Greek

English	Greek	Sounds like
Have you a table for...	Εχετε ενα τραπεζι για	Echede enna trapezee ghia...
I'd like...	Θελω	Thelo...
We would like...	Θελουμε	Thelome...
a beer	μια μπυρα	meah beerah
a glass	ενα πορρι	ena poteeree
a carafe	μια καραφα	meea karafa
a small bottle	ενα μικρη μπουκαλι	ena mikri bookalee
a large bottle	ενα μεγαλη	ena meghali bookalee
bread	ψωμι	psomee
tea with milk	τσαι με γαλα	tsai me ghala
with lemon	τσαι με λεμονι	me lemoni
Turkish coffee (Greek)	Τουρκικο καφε	Toupkiko kafe
sweet	γλυκοζ	ghleekos
medium	μετριοζ	medreeo
bitter (no sugar)	πικρο	pikto
Black coffee	Nescafe χωριζ γαλα	Nescafé horis ghala
Coffee with milk	Nescafe με γαλα	Nescafé me ghala
a glass of water	ενα ποτηρι νερο	enna poteeree nero
a napkin	ενα πετσετα	enna petseta
an ashtray	ενα σταχτοδοχειο	enna stachdothocheeo
toothpick	μια οδοντογλυθιδα	mea odontoglifadha
the olive oil	η ελεολαδο	ee eleolatho
Where is the toilet?	Που ειναι η τουαλεττα	Poo eene i(ee) tooaleta?
What is this?	Τι ειναι αυτο	Ti ine afto
This is...	Αυτο ειναι	Afto eene
cold	κρυο	kreeo
bad	χαλασμενο	chalasmeno
stale	μπαγιατικο	bayhiatiko
undercooked	αψητο	apseeto
overcooked	παραβρασμενο	paravrasmeno
The bill please	Το λογαριασμο παρακαλω	To loghariasmo parakalo
How much is that?	Ποσο κανει αυτο	Poso kane afto?
That was an excellent meal	Περιφημο γευμα	Pereefimo yefma
We shall come again	Θα ζαναρθουμε	Tha xanarthoume

7 Shopping & Public Services

Let your purse be your master. *Proverb*

Purchasing items in Greece is still quite an art form or subject for a degree course. The difficulties have been compounded by the rest of the western world becoming nations of supermarket shoppers, whilst the Greeks have stayed traditionally and firmly with their individual shops, selling a fixed number of items and sometimes only one type of a product.

Shopping for a corkscrew, for instance, might well involve calling at two or three seemingly look-alike ironmongers, but, no, they each specialise in certain lines of goods and do not stock any items outside those prescribed, almost as if by holy writ.

Bakers usually have to be diligently searched for and when found are frequently located tucked away in or behind other shops. A pointer is that there is often a pile of blackened, twisted olive wood stacked up to one side of the entrance.

Cake shops (zacharoplasteion) may sell bottled mineral water (ask for a cold bottle).

The question of good and bad buys must be highly personal but the items listed below are highlighted on the basis of value for money and quality.

Clothing and accessories that are attractive and represent good value include embroidered peasant dresses, leather sandals, woven bags and furs. Day-to-day items that are inexpensive take in Greek cigarettes, drinks including ouzo, *Metaxa* brandy and selected island wines. Suitable gifts for family and friends include ceramic plates, sponges, Turkish delight, and worry beads (*komboloe*). Disproportionately expensive items include camera film, toiletries, books and playing cards.

Do not forget to compare prices and preferably shop in the streets and markets, not in airport and hotel concessionary shops which are often more expensive.

Try not to run short of change; everybody else does, including bus conductors, taxi drivers and shops.

Opening Hours Strict or old fashioned summer shop hours are:
Monday, Wednesday and Saturday: 0830-1400 hrs.
Tuesday, Thursday and Friday: 0830-1330 hrs & 1730-2030 hrs.

Generally shops in tourist areas, during the summer, are open Monday to Saturday from 0800-1300 hours, when they close until 1700 hours after which they open again until at least 2030 hours, if not 2200 hours. Sundays and Saints days are more indeterminate, but there will usually be a general shop open somewhere. In very popular tourist resorts and busy port shops are often open seven days a week.

Drink Available either in the markets from delicatessen meat/dairy counters or from 'off-licence'-type shops.

Smokers Imported French, English and American cigarettes are inexpensive, compared with European prices, at between 80 and 100 drs for a packet of 20. Greek cigarettes, which have a distinctive and different taste, are excellent. Try *Karellia*, which cost about 50 drs for a packet of 20 and note that the price is printed around the edge of the packet. Even Greek cigars are almost unheard of on the islands, while in Athens, they cost 5-10 drs and Dutch cigars work out at about, say, 20 drs each, so if a cigar-smoker, take along your holiday requirements.

Newspapers & Magazines The *Athens Daily News* and *Athens Daily Post* are both published in English. Overseas newspapers are available up to 24 hours behind the day of publication, but note that all printed matter is comparatively expensive.

Photography (Fotografion - ΦΩΤΟΓΡΑΦΕΙΟΝ) Travellers should bring their film with them if possible, being imported it is comparatively expensive. To counter the very bright sunlight, when using colour film, blue filters should be fitted to the lens.

Tourist Guides & Maps Shop around before purchasing, as the difference in price of the guides can be as much as 150 drs, ie. from 150-300 drs.

Some major ports and towns have one authentic, well stocked bookshop, more often than not a little off the town centre. The proprietor may well speak adequate English and will courteously answer most enquiries.

SHOPS

BAKERS & BREAD SHOPS (ΑΡΤΟΠΟΙΕΙΟΝ, ΑΡΤΟΠΩΛΕΙΟΝ or ΠΡΑΤΗΡΙΟΝ ΑΡΤΟΥ)
For some obscure reason bakers are nearly always difficult to locate, being hidden away, and bread shops are few and far between. Bakers may also sell cheese and meat pies. They are almost always closed on Sundays and all holidays despite their ovens often being used by the local community to cook the Sunday meal.

The method of purchasing bread can prove disconcerting, especially when sold by weight. Sometimes the purchaser selects the loaf and then pays but the most bewildering system is where it is necessary to pay first then collect the goods. Difficult if the shoppers level of Greek is limited to grunts, 'thank you' and 'please'!

Greek bread also has another parameter of measure, that is a graduation in hours — 1 hour, 4 hours and so on. After the period is up it is usually completely inedible, having transmogrified into a rock-like substance.

BUTCHER (ΚΡΕΟΠΩΛΕΙΟΝ) Similar to those at home but the cuts are quite different (surely the Common Market can legislate against this deviation!).

MARKETS The smaller ports and towns may have a market street and the larger municipalities often possess a market building, thronged with locals, where all the basic necessities can be procured inexpensively, with fruit and vegetable stalls interspaced by butchers and dairy delicatessen shops. During their opening hours, the proprietors are brought coffee and a glass of water by waiters carrying the cups and glasses, not on open trays, but in round aluminium salvers with a deep lip, held under a large ring handle, connected to the tray by three flat arms.

SUPERMARKETS (ΥΠΕΡΑΓΟΡΑ/ΣΟΥΠΕΡΜΑΡΚΕΤ) Very much on the increase and based on small-town, self-service stores but not to worry, they inherit all those delightful native Greek qualities including quiet chaos.

SPECIALITY SHOPS Found in some big towns and Athens. While pavement browsing, you will espy little basement shops, down a flight of steps, specialising, for instance, in dried fruit, beans, nuts and grains.

STREET KIOSKS (Periptero/ΠΕΡΙΠΤΕΡΟ) These unique, pagoda-like huts stay open remarkably long hours, often from early morning to after midnight and sell a wide range of goods including newspapers, magazines (surprisingly sometimes pornographic literature), postcards, tourist maps, postage stamps, sweets, chocolates, cigarettes, matches and cigars but not on the islands. *See* earlier comments. Additionally they form the outlet for the pay-phone system and, at the cost of 5 drs, a local call may be made. It is rather incongruous, to observe a Greek making a possibly important business call, in amongst a rack of papers and magazines, with a foreground of jostling pedestrians and a constant stream of noisy traffic in the background.

Alternate Ways of Shopping Then there are the other ways of shopping: from hand-carts, their street-vendor owners selling respectively nuts, ice creams, milk and yoghurt; the back of a donkey with vegetable-laden panniers or from two wheeled trailers drawn by fearsome sounding, agricultural rotovator power units, both with an enormous set of scales, swinging like a hangman's scaffold, from the back end, be it donkey or truck powered.

Frequently used shops include:

ΒΙΒΛΙΟΠΩΛΕΙΟΝ — Bookshop; **ΙΧΘΥΟΠΩΛΕΙΟΝ** — Fishmonger; **ΟΠΩΡΟΠΩΛΕΙΟΝ** — Greengrocer; **ΠΑΝΤΟΠΩΛΕΙΟΝ** — Grocer; **ΚΑΠΝΟΠΩΛΕΙΟΝ** — Tobacconist. You will note that the above have a similar ending and it is worth noting that all shop titles that terminate in 'ΠΩΛΕΙΟΝ/πωλειο' are selling something, if that's a help.

SERVICES

THE BANKS (ΤΡΑΠΕΖΑ) The minimum opening hours are 0800 to 1330 hrs, Monday to Thursday and 0800 to 1300 hrs on Friday. Some banks, in the most tourist ravaged spots, open on Saturday and a few on Sunday but smaller towns, villages or for that matter islands will not have a bank but occasionally a local money changer acting as agent for this or that national bank. Do not forget that a passport is usually required to change traveller's cheques. In the larger cities, personal cheques may be changed at a selected bank when backed by a Eurocheque or similar bank guarantee card. A small commission charge of between 50 and 100 drs is made whatever the size of the transaction. The service is generally discourteous and one employee will, reluctantly, speak English.

Make sure you select the correct bank to carry out a particular transaction (such as changing a personal cheque) Each bank displays a window sticker giving an indication of the tourist services carried out. There is nothing worse, after queuing for half an hour or so, than to be rudely told to go away. I once chose the wrong bank to change a personal cheque, only to receive a loud blast of abuse about some long-departed foreigner's bouncing cheque. Most embarrassing.

The larger hotels change traveller's cheques, but naturally enough at a disadvantageous rate compared with the banks.

Another interesting source of taking currency abroad for United Kingdom residents is to use National Giro Post Office cheques which can be cashed at any Post Office in Greece. This is a very useful wheeze especially on busy tourist islands where the foreign currency desk will be subject to long queues. Detailed arrangements have to be made with the International branch of Giro.

The basis of Greek currency is the drachma. This is nominally divided into 100 lepta and occasionally price lists show a price of, say, 62.60 drs. As prices are rounded up (or down), in practice, you will not encounter the lepta.

At the time of writing, the British pound sterling was worth approximately 210 drs and the US $ 143 drs (April 1986).

Notes are in denominations of 50, 100, 500, and 1000 drs and coins in denominations of 1 and 2 drs (bronze), 5, 10 and 20 and 50 drs (nickel). Do not run out of change, it is always in demand. Repetitious I know, but well worth remembering.

MUSEUMS The following is a mean average of the information to hand but each museum is likely to have its own particular pecularities. In the summer season (1st April - 31st October) they open daily 0845-1500/1900 hrs, Sundays and holidays 0930-1430/1530 hrs and are closed Mondays or Tuesdays. They are closed 1st January, 25th March, Good Friday, Easter holiday and 25th December. Admission costs range from free to 100/150 drs, whilst Sundays and holidays may well be free.

THE POST OFFICE (ΤΑΧΥΑΔΡΟΜΕΙΟΝ/ΕΛΤΑ) Stamps can be bought from kiosks and shops selling postcards as well as from Post Offices. Post boxes are scattered around, are usually painted yellow, are rather small in size and often difficult to find, being fixed, high up, on side-street walls.

Most major town Post Offices are modern and the service received, only slightly less rude than that handed out by bank staff.

When confronted by two letter-box openings, the inland service is marked Εχοτεβικοy and the overseas Εξοτερικοy. Letters can be sent for *poste-restante* collection, but a passport will be required. Post Offices are usually only open Monday to Friday between

0730-2030 hrs for stamps and registered mail, 0730-2000 hrs for poste-restante and 0730-1430 hrs for parcels.

Parcels have to be collected.

ΓΡΑΜΜΑΤΟΣΗΜΑ — stamps; ΔΕΜΑΤΑ — parcels.

TELEPHONE OFFICE (OTE) A separate organisation from the Post Office and to accomplish an overseas or long-distance call it is necessary to go to the OTE office. Here there are separate booths from which to make calls but busy offices will usually experience queues. The counter clerk will indicate which compartment is to be used and in a bank alongside him are mounted the instruments to meter the cost, payment being made after completion of the call. Ensure that the relevant meter is zeroed prior to making a connection. Opening days and hours vary enormously. Smaller offices may only open weekdays for say 7 hours between 0830-1530 hrs whilst the larger city offices may open 24 hours a day, seven days a week.

Overseas dialling codes		Inland services	
Australia	0061	Directory enquiries	131
Canada and USA	001	Provincial enquiries	132
New Zealand	0064	General information	134
South Africa	0027	Time	141
United Kingdom and Ireland	0044	Medical care	166
Other overseas countries	161	City Police	100
		Gendarmerie	109
		Fire	199
		Tourist police	171
		Roadside assistance	104
		Telegrams/cables	165

To dial England, drop the '0' from four figure codes, thus making a call to Portsmouth, for which the code is 0705, dial 0044 705 and then the number. Do not give up, keep dialling but slowly, and split the numbers up i.e. 00 44 705 ......

The internal service is both very good and reasonably priced. Local telephone calls cost 5 drs and can be made from some bars and the pavement kiosks (Periptero). The presence of a telephone will often be indicated by the sign ΕΔΩ ΤΗΛΕ ΦΝΕΙΤΕ, a blue background indicating a local phone, and an orange one an inter-city phone. Another sign εδω τηλεφωνειτε (the lower case equivalent), indicates 'telephone from here'. The method of operation is to insert the coin and dial. If you cannot make the connection place the receiver back on the cradle and the coin will be returned.

Telegrams may be sent from either the Post Office or the OTE.

Useful Greek

English	Greek	Sounds like
Where is...	Που ειναι	Poo enne...
Where is the nearest...	Που ειναι η πλησιεστερη	Poo eene dho bleesiesteri...
baker	ο φουρναρηζ/ψωμαζ/	foonaris/psomas/
	Αρτοποιειον	artopieon
bank	η τραπεζα	i(ee) trabeza
bookshop	το βιβλιοπωλειο	to vivleeobolieo
butchers shop	το χασαπιχο	o hasapiko
chemist shop	το φαρμακειο	to farmakio
dairy shop	το γαλακτοπωλειο	galaklopolieon
doctor	ο γιατροζ	o yiahtros
grocer	το μπακαληζ	to bakalis
hospital	το νοσοχομειο	to nosokomio
laundry	το πλυνη ριο	to plintireo
liquor store	το ποτοπωλειο	to potopolea
photographic shop	το φωτογραφειο	to fotoghrafeeo

post office	το ταχυδρομειο	to tahkethromeo
shoe repairer	το τσαγκαραδιχο	to tsangkaradiko
tailor	ο ραπτηζ	o raptis
Have you any...	Εχετε	Ekheteh...
Do you sell...	Πουλατε	Boulate...
How much is this...	Ποσο κανει αυτο	Posso kanee afto...
I want...	Θελω	Thelo...
half kilo/a kilo	ενα μισο κιλο/ενα κιλο	miso kilo/ena kilo
aspirin	η ασπιρινη	aspirini
apple(s)	το μηλο/μηλα	meelo/meela
banana(s)	η μπανανα/μπανανεζ	banana/bananes
bread	το ψωμι	psomee
butter	το βουτυρο	vutiro
cheese	το τυρι	tiree
cigarettes (filter tip)	το τσιγαρο (με φιλτρο)	to tsigharo (me filtro)
coffee	καφε	cafe
cotton wool	το βαμβαχι	to vambaki
crackers	τα κραχερζ	krackers
crisps	τσιπζ	tsseeps
cucumbers	το αγγουρι	anguree
disinfectant	το απολυμαντιχο	to apolimantiko
guide book	ο τουριστικοζ οδηγοζ	o touristikos odhigos
ham	το ξαμπον	zambon
ice cream	το παγωτο	paghoto
lemons	το λεμανια	lemonia
lettuce	το μαρουλι	to marooli
map	το χαρτηζ	o khartis
a box of matches	ενα χομτι οπιρτα	ena kuti spirta
milk	το γαλα	to ghalo
pate	πατε	pate
(ball point) pen	το μπιχ	to bikx
pencil	το μολυβι	to molivi
pepper	το πιπερι	to piperi
(safety) pin	μια παραμανα	mea paramana
potatoes	οι πατατεζ	patates
salad	η σαλατα	I salatah
salami	το σαλαμι	salahmi
sausages	το λουχανικα	lukahniko
soap	το σαπουνι	to sapooni
spaghetti	σπαγεττο	spayehto
string	ο σπαγγοζ	o spangos
sugar	η ζαχαρη	i zakhahree
tea	το τσαι	to tsai
tomatoes	η ντομφτεζ	domahdes
toothbrush	η οδοντοβουρτσα	odhondovourtsa
toothpaste	η οδοντοχρεμα	odhondokrema
writing paper	το χαρτι γραψιματοζ	to kharti grap-simatos

8 Greece: History, Mythology, Religion, Present-Day Greece, Greeks & their Holidays

All ancient histories, as one of our fine wits said, are but fables that have been accepted. *Voltaire*

Excavations have shown the presence of Palaeolithic man up to 100,000 years ago. Greece's history and mythology are, like the Greek language, formidable to say the least, with legend, myth, folk tales, fables and religious lore often inextricably mixed up. Archaeologists are now finding that some mythology is in fact based on historical fact. For instance the great Minoan civilisation centred on Crete, which may well have been the fabled Atlantis of pre-history, was mysteriously and suddenly destroyed. Recent, informed speculation leads to the conclusion that about 1700 BC a vast volcanic eruption, presumed to be centred on the island of Santorini (Thira) in the Cyclades, destroyed this flourishing and far reaching culture.

From then on Greeks fought Greeks, Phoenicians and Persians. Under Alexander the Great they conquered Egypt and vast tracts of Asia Minor. Then they in turn were conquered by the Romans. After the splitting of the Roman Empire into Western and Eastern Empires, the Greeks, with Constantinople as their capital, were ruled by the Eastern offshoot, only to fall into the hands of the Franks about AD 1200, then the Turks, with the Venetians, Genoese and finally the Turks ruling the islands.

In 1821 the War of Independence commenced, which eventually led to the setting up of a Parliamentary Republic in 1928. Incidentally, Thessaly, Crete and the Dodecanese islands remained under Turkish rule. By the time the Dodecanese had thrown out the Turks, the Italians had taken over. If you are now confused, give up, because it gets even more difficult to follow.

The Greek monarchy, which had come into being in 1833, and was related to the German Royal family, opted in 1913 to side with the Axis powers. The chief politician Eleftherios Venizelos, disagreed, was dismissed and set up a rival government, and the King, under Allied pressure, retired to Switzerland. After the war, the Turks and Greeks agreed, after some fairly bloody fighting to exchange a total of one and a half million people.

In 1936 a General Metaxas became dictator. He achieved immortal fame by booting out Mussolini's representative, when in 1940 Mussolini demanded permission for Italy's troops to traverse Greece, and received the famous *Ochi* (No). (This day has become a national festival known as *Ochi Day*, celebrated on 28th October). When the Italians demurred and marched on Greece, the Greeks reinforced their point by routing them, the Italians only being saved from total humiliation by the intervention of the Germans, who then occupied Greece for the duration of the Second World War. As German ascendancy declined, the Greek freedom fighters split into royalist and communist blocks and proceeded to knock as much stuffing out of each other as they had out of the Germans. After the end of hostilities, all the Italian-held Greek islands were reunited with mainland Greece.

Until the British intervention, followed by large injections of American money and weapons, it looked as if Greece would go behind the *Iron Curtain*. A second civil war broke out between 1947 and 1949 and this internal strife was reputed to have cost more Greek lives than were lost during the whole of the Second World War.

In 1951, Greece and Turkey became full members of NATO, but the issue of the ex-British colony of Cyprus was about to rear its ugly head, with the resultant, renewed estrangement between Greece and Turkey.

The various political manoeuvrings, the involvement of the Greek monarchy in domestic affairs and the worsening situation in Cyprus, led to the *coup d'état* by the **Colonels' Junta** in 1967, soon after which King Constantine II and his entourage fled to Italy. The Colonel's extremely repressive dictatorship was, seemingly, actively supported by the Americans and condoned by Britain. Popular country-wide feeling and, in particular, student uprisings between 1973-1974, initially put down in Athens by brutal tank attacks, led to the eventual collapse of the regime in 1974.

In the death-throes of their rule, the Colonels, using the Cyprus dream to distract the ordinary people's feeling of injustice, meddled and attempted to overthrow the vexatious priest, President Makarios. The net result was that the Turks invaded Cyprus and made an enforced divison of that unhappy, troubled island.

In 1974, Greece returned to republican democracy and in 1981 joined the EEC.

RELIGION

The Orthodox Church prevails everywhere but there are small pockets of Roman Catholicism and very minor enclaves of Turks on the Dodecanese and mainland western Thrace. The schism within the Holy Roman Empire, in 1054, caused the Catholic Church to be centred on Rome and the Orthodox Church on Constantinople.

The Turkish overlords encouraged the continuation of the indigenous church, probably to keep their bondsmen quiet, but it had the invaluable side effect of keeping alive Greek customs and traditions during the centuries of occupation.

The bewildering profusion of small churches, scattered 'indiscriminately' all over the islands, is not proof of the church's wealth, although the Greek people are not entirely convinced of that fact. It is evidence of the piety of the families or individuals who paid to have them erected, in the name of their selected patron saint, as thanksgiving for God's protection. The style of religious architecture changes between the island groups.

Many churches only have one service a year, on the name day of the particular patron saint, and this ceremony is named *Viorti* or *Panayieri*. It is well worth attending one of these self-indulgent, extravaganzas to observe and take part in Greek village, celebratory religious life and music. All-comers are welcome to the carnival festivities which include eating and dancing in, or adjacent to, the particular churchyard.

The words Byzantine and Byzantium crop up frequently with especial reference to churches and appertain to the period between the fourth and fourteenth centuries AD. During this epoch Greece was, at least nominally, under the control of Constantinople (Istanbul), which was built by the Emperor Constantine on the site of the old city of Byzantium.

Religious paintings executed on small wooden panels during this period are called *ikons*. Very, very few original ikons remain available for purchase, so beware if offered an apparent 'bargain'.

When visiting a church, you will observe pieces of shining, thin metal, placed haphazardly around or pinned to wooden carvings. These *tamata* or *exvotos* represent limbs or portions of the human body and are purchased by worshippers to be placed in the church as an offering, in the hope of an illness being cured and/or limbs healed.

GREEKS

In making assessment of the Greek people and their character, it must be remembered that, perhaps even more so than the Spaniards or the Portuguese, Greece has only recently emerged into the twentieth century. Unlike other newly discovered holiday countries, they have not, in the main, degraded or debased their principles or character, in the face of the on-rush of tourist wealth. For a people to have had so little as recently as the 1960s and to face so much demand for European necessities, would have strained a less hardy and well-balanced people.

Their recent emergence into the western world is well evidenced by the still partriarchal nature of Greek society supported, for instance, by the oft-seen spectacle of men lazing in the tavernas whilst their womenfolk work in the fields (and why not?)

Even the smallest village, on the remotest island, will usually have an English-speaking islander who has lived abroad, earning a living through seafaring, as a hotel waiter, or as a taxi driver. Thus, while making their escape from the comparative poverty at home, for a period of good earnings in the more lucrative world, a working knowledge of English, American (sic) or Australian (sic) will have been gained. Greek *strine*, or as usually contracted *grine*, simply has to be heard to be believed.

The greatest hurdle to understanding is undoubtedly the language barrier, especially if it is taken into account that the Greeks appear to have some difficulty with their own language in its various forms. Certainly, they seem, on occasions, not to understand each other and the subject matter has to be repeated a number of times. Perhaps that is the reason for all the shouting!

There can be no doubt that the traditional Greek welcome to the *xenos* or *singrafeus*, now increasingly becoming known as *touristas* has, naturally, become rather lukewarm in the more 'besieged' areas.

It is often difficult to reconcile the shrugged shoulders of a seemingly disinterested airline official or bus driver, with being stopped in the street by a gold-toothed, smiling Greek proffering some fruit. But remember the bus driver may realise the difficulty of overcoming the language barrier, it is very hot, he has been working long hours earning his living and you are on holiday.

Sometimes a drink appears mysteriously at your taverna table, the donor being indicated by a nod of the waiter's head but a word of warning here. Simply smile and accept the gift graciously. Any attempt to return the kindness by 'putting one in the stable' for your new found friend will only result in a 'who buys last' competition which you will lose. I know, I am speaking from battle-weary experience. A Greek may well be very welcoming and will occasionally invite you to his table, but do not expect more, they are reserved and have probably had previous experience of ungrateful, rude, overseas visitors.

To look over churches or monasteries visitors must ensure they are adequately covered, including legs and arms and should note that many religious establishments strictly apply the rules. It seems a pity for a tourist to have made a special excursion sometimes involving arduous walking, only to be turned away at the gate. Men must wear a shirt and trousers, not shorts, and women a modest blouse, a skirt and take a head scarf (as a back-stop).

Women tourists can travel quite freely in Greece without fear, except from other tourists. On the other hand females should not wear provocative attire or fail to wear sufficient clothing when coming into close social contact with Greek men, who might well be inflamed into action, or Greek women, whom it will offend. Certainly this was the case until very recently but the constant stream of 'available' young tourist ladies on the more popular islands, has resulted in the local lads taking a 'view', and a chance. It almost reminds one of the *Costa Brava* in the early 1960s. The disparate moral qualities of the native and tourist females is resulting in a conundrum for young Greek women. To compete for their men's affections they have had to loosen their principles with an unheard of and steadily increasing number of speedily arranged marriages, if you know what I mean.

Do not miss the Volta (**Βόλτα**), the traditional family evening walkabout in city, town or village square. Dressed for the event, an important part of the ritual is for the family to show off their marriageable daughters. Good fun and great watching, but the Greeks are rather protective of their family and all things Greek... you may comment favourably, but keep criticism to yourself.

It is interesting to speculate on the influence of the early Greek immigrants on American culture, especially when you consider the American habit of serving water with every meal, the ubiquitous hamburger, (which is surely a poorly reproduced and inferior *souvlaki*), and some of the official uniforms, more particularly the flat peaked hats of American postmen and policemen.

THE GREEK NATIONAL HOLIDAYS

Listed below are the national holidays and on these days many areas and islands hold festivals, but with a particular slant and emphasis.

1st January	New Year's Day/The Feast of Saint Basil
6th January	Epiphany/Blessing of the Waters — a cross is immersed in the sea, lake or river, during a religious ceremony
The period 27th Jan to 17 February	The Greek Carnival Season
25th March	The Greek National Anniversary/Independence Day
April — Movable days	Good Friday/Procession of the 'Epitaph'; Holy Week Saturday/Ceremony of the Resurrection; Easter Sunday/open air feasts
1st May	May/Labour Day/Feast of the Flowers
1st to 10th July	Greek Navy Week
15th August	Assumption Day/Festival of the Virgin Mary, especially on the Cycladian island of Tinos (beware travelling at this time anywhere in the area)
28th October	National Holiday/'Ochi' Day
24th December	Christmas Eve/carols evening
25th December	Christmas Day
26th December	St Stephen's Day
31st December	New Year's Eve/carols, festivals

In addition to these national days, each island has festivals and holidays particular to them which are listed individually under each island description. Moreover, many of the various island churches have only one service a year.

A word of warning to ferry-boat travellers will not go amiss here — DO NOT travel to an island immediately prior to one of these festivals NOR off the island immediately after the event. It will be almost impossible to do other than stand if one has not been trampled to death in the various stampedes off and on the boats.

9 ATHENS CITY (ATHINA, AΘHNAI)

There is no end to it in this city; wherever you set your foot, you encounter some memory of the past.   *Marcus Cicero.*

Tel. prefix 01

The capital of Greece and major city of Attica. Previously the springboard for travel to most of the Greek islands, but less so since a number of direct flights have become available. Experienced island travellers flying into Athens airport, often try to arrange their flight for an early morning arrival and head straight for either the West airport, Piraeus port, the railway station or bus terminal, so as to be able to get under way immediately.

ARRIVAL BY AIR
International flights other than Olympic Airways land at the

East airport
Public transport facilities include:

Bus No. 18:   East airport to Leoforos Amalias. Every 20 mins from 0600-2400 hrs. Fare 60 drs.

Bus No. 121:   East airport to Leoforos Olgas. 0650-2250 hrs. Fare 60 drs.

Bus No. 19:   East airport to Plateia Karaiskaki/Akti Tselepi, Piraeus port. Every hour from 0800-2000 hrs. Fare 60 drs.

Bus No. 101:   East airport via Leoforos Possidonos (coast road) to Klisovis/Theotoki St, Piraeus port. Every 20 mins from 0500-2245 hrs.

Domestic and all Olympic flights land at the

West airport
Public transport facilities include:

Bus No. 133:   West airport to Leoforos Square, Leoforos Amalias, Filellinon & Othonos Streets (Syntagma Sq). Every ½ hour from 0530-0030 hrs.

Bus No. 122:   West airport to Leoforos Olgas. Every 20 mins.

Buses No. 107: West airport via Leoforos Possidonos (coast road) to Klisovis St, Piraeus port.
 & 109:

In addition there are Olympic buses connecting West and East airports.

GENERAL (Illustrations 4 & 5)
Even if you are a European city dweller, Athens will come as a sociological and cultural shock to the system. In the summer it is a hot, dusty, dry, crowded, traffic-bound, exhaust polluted bedlam, but always friendly, cosmopolitan and ever on the move.

On arrival in Athens, and staying over, it is best to select the two main squares of Syntagma (*Tmr* 1.D/E4/5) and Omonia (*Tmr* 2.D3) as centres for the initial sally, and radiate out to the other squares or plateias.

There is no substitute for a city map which is issued free, yes free, from the Tourist Board desk in the National Bank of Greece on Syntagma Sq (*Tmr* 3.D/E4). *See* **NTOG — THE A to Z OF USEFUL INFORMATION (A to Z).**

Syntagma Square (Constitution or Parliament Square) (*Tmr* 1.D/E4/5) The airport and many other buses stop off here. It is the city centre with the most elite hotels, airline offices, international companies including the American Express headquarters, smart cafes and the Parliament building all circumscribing the central, sunken square. In the bottom right hand corner of the plateia, bounded by Odhos Othonos and Leoforos Amalias, there are some very clean, attendant minded toilets. There is a charge for the use of the squatties.

To orientate, the Parliament building and Monument to the Unknown Warrior lie to the east of the square. To the north-east, in the middle distance, is one of the twin hills of

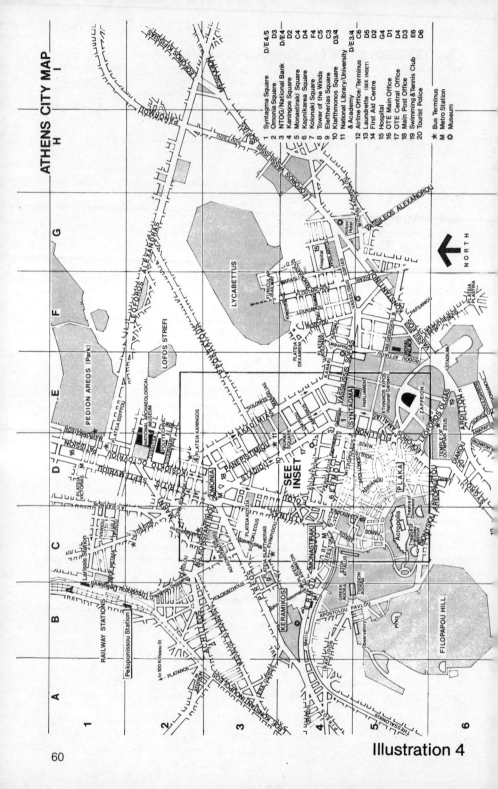

ATHENS CITY MAP

1 Syntagma Square — D/E4/5
2 Omonia Square — D3
3 NTOG/National Bank — D/E4
4 Kaningos Square — D2
5 Monastiraki Square — C4
6 Kapnikarea Square — D4
7 Kolonaki Square — F4
8 Tower of the Winds — C5
9 Eleftherias Square — C3
10 Klafthmonos Square — D3/4
11 National Library/University & Academy — D/E3,4
12 Airline Office/Terminus — C6
13 Laundrette [SEE INSET] — D5
14 First Aid Centre — D2
15 Hospital — G4
16 OTE Main Office — D1
17 OTE Central Office — D4
18 Main Post Office — D3
19 Swimming & Tennis Club — E6
20 Tourist Police — D6

★ Bus Terminus
M Metro Station
⊙ Museum

NORTH

60

Illustration 4

Athens, Mt Lycabettus (Lykavittos). The other hill is the Acropolis, to the south-west, and not now visible from Syntagma Sq. due to high-rise buildings. On the west side of the square are the offices of American Express and a battery of pavement cafes, with Ermou St leading due west to Monastiraki Sq. To the north are the two parallel, main avenues of Stadiou (a one-way street down to Syntagma) and Venizelou or Panepistimiou (a one-way street out of Syntagma) that both run due north-west to:

Omonia Square (Concorde or Harmony Square) (*Tmr* 2.D3) The Piccadilly Circus or Times Square of Athens but rather tatty really, with a constant stream of traffic bludgeoning its way round the large central island, which is crowned with an impressive fountain. Should you try to escape the human bustle on the pavements by stepping off into the kerbside, beware that you are not mown down by a bus, taxi or private car.

Constant activity night and day, with seemingly every nationality cheek by jowl, lends the square a cosmopolitan character all of its own. On every side there are hotels, varying from the downright seedy to the better-class tawdry, housed in rather undistinguished, 'neo city-municipal' style, nineteenth century buildings, almost unique to Athens.

Various underground train ontranoe/exits emerge around the square, similar to air raid shelters, spewing out and sucking in the metro travellers. The underground concourse has a Post office, telephones, a bank and, by the Dorou St entrance, a block of squatty toilets for which the attendant charges 5 drs for 2 sheets of paper.

Shops, cafes and booths fill the gaps between the hotels and the eight streets that converge on the square.

To the north-east side of Omonia, on the corner of Dorou St, is a taxi rank and beyond, on the right, a now rather squalid, covered arcade brimful of reasonably priced snack bars. Through this covered passage way, and turning to the left up 28 Ikosiokto Oktovriou (28th October St)/Patission St, and then right down Veranzerou St, leads to

Kaningos Square (*Tmr* 4.D2) Serves as a bus terminal for some routes.

To the south of Omonia Sq is Athinas St, the commercial thoroughfare of Athens. Here every conceivable item imaginable including ironmongery, tools, crockery and clothing can be purchased, and parallel to which, for half its length, runs Odhos Sokratous, the city street market during the day and the red-light area by night.

Athinas St drops due south to:

Monastiraki Square (*Tmr* 5.C4) This marks the northernmost edge of the area known as the Plaka (*Tmr* D5) bounded by Ermou St to the north, Filellinon St to the east, and to the south by the slopes of the Acropolis.

Many of the alleys in this area follow the course of the old Turkish streets, most of the houses are mid-nineteenth century and represent the 'Old Quarter'.

Climbing the twisting maze of streets and steps of the lower NE slopes of the Acropolis requires the stamina of a mountain goat. The almost primitive, island-village nature of some of the houses is very noticeable. This is due, it is said, to a Greek law passed after Independence to alleviate a housing shortage, and allowed anyone who could raise the roof of a dwelling between sunrise and sunset to finish and own the house. Some islanders from the Cyclades island of Anafi (Anaphe) were reputed to have been the first to benefit from this new law and others followed to specialise in restoration and rebuilding, thus bringing about a colony of expatriate islanders within the Plaka district.

From the south-west corner of Monastiraki Sq, Ifestou St and its associated byways house the **Flea Market**, which climaxes on Sunday into stall upon stall of junk, souvenirs, junk, hardware, junk, boots, junk, records, junk, clothes, junk, footwear, junk, pottery and junk. Where Ifestou becomes Astigos St, and curves round to join up with Ermou St, there are a couple of extensive second-hand bookshops with reasonably priced (for Greece that is), if battered, paperbacks for sale. From the south-east corner of Monastiraki, Pandrossou St, one of the only enduring reminders of the Turkish Bazaar, contains a better class of antique dealer, sandal and shoe makers, and pottery stores.

Due south of Monstiraki Sq is Odhos Areos, unfortunately the first 100 m or so of which is now host to a raggle-taggle band of European and Japanese drop-outs selling junk ie trinkets (not dope) from the pavement kerb. They seem to have driven out the original stallholders and shop keepers in this stretch. Climbing Odhos Areos skirts the Roman Agora, from which the various streets leading upwards, on ever upwards, contain a plethora of stalls and shops, specialising in leather goods, clothes and souvenirs. The further you climb, the cheaper the goods become. This interestingly enough does not apply to the tavernas and restaurants in the area, which seemingly become more expensive as one ascends.

The 'chatty' area known as the Plaka is 'littered' with eating places, a few good, some bad, some tourist rip-offs. The liveliest street in the Plaka is Odhos Kidathineon which is jam-packed with cafes, tavernas and restaurants and at night is bestrewn with music-playing layabouts, sorry students. The class, tone and price of the establishments improve as you progress north-eastwards. I have to admit to gently knocking the Plaka over the years but it must be acknowledged that the area offers the cheapest accommodation and eating places in Athens and generally appears to have been cleaned up in recent times.

From Monastiraki Sq, eastwards along Ermou St, the street is initially full of clothes and shoe shops. One third of the way to Syntagma Sq and Odhos Ermou opens out into a small square in which there is the lovely church of Kapnikarea (*Tmr* 6.D4). Continuing eastwards, the shops become smarter with a preponderance of fashion stores. Parallel to Ermou St is Odhos Ploutonos Nteka, which becomes Odhos Mitropoleos. Facing east, on the right, is the City's Greek Orthodox Cathedral, Great Mitropolis. The church was built about 1850 from the materials of 70 old churches, to the design of four different architects resulting, not unnaturally, in a building of a rather 'strange' appearance. Alongside and to the south is the diminutive medieval church, Little Mitropolis or Agios Eleftherios, dating back to at least the twelfth century but which has materials, reliefs and building blocks probably originating from the sixth century AD. A little further on is the intriguing and incongruous site of a small Byzantine church, built over and around by a modern office block, the columns of which tower above and beside the little church.

Leaving Syntagma Sq by the north-east corner, along Vassilissis Sofias, and turning left at Odhos Irodou Attikou, runs into:

Kolonaki Square (*Tmr* 7.F4) The most fashionable square in the most fashionable area of Athens, around which most of the foreign embassies are located. The British Council is located on the square, as are some relatively expensive cafes, restaurants and boutiques.

To the north of Kolonaki, across the pretty orange tree planted Dexameni Sq, is the southern-most edge of Mt Lycabettus (*Tmr* F/G3) and access to the summit can be made, on foot, by a number of steep paths. The main, stepped footpath is on up Loukianou St beyond Odhos Kleomenous. A little to the east, at the top of Ploutarchou St, which breaks into a sharply rising flight of steps, is the cable car funicular railway. This runs in a 700ft long tunnel, emerging near to the nineteenth-century chapel, which caps the fir-tree-covered mountain, alongside a modern and luxuriously expensive restaurant. There are also some excellent toilets. The railway service opens at 0845 hrs, shuts down at 0015 hrs and the trip costs 35 drs one-way and 65 drs for a return ticket. A more relaxed climb, passing the open air theatre, can be made from the north end of Lycabettus.

The top most part of the mountain where the funicular emerges is surprisingly small if not doll-like. The spectacular panorama that spreads out to the horizon, the stupendous views from far above the roar of the Athens traffic, is best seen in the early morning or late afternoon.

Leaving Plateia Kolonaki from the south corner and turning right at Vassilissis Sofias, brings one to the north corner of:

The National Garden (Ethnikos Kipos) (*Tmr* E5) Here peacocks, water fowl and songbirds blend with a profusion of shrubbery, subtropical trees, ornamental ponds, various busts and cafe tables through and around which thread neat gravel paths.

To the south of the gardens are the Zappeion Exhibition Halls. To the north-west, the Greek Parliament buildings, the old Royal Palace and the Tomb or Monument to the Unknown Warrior, guarded by the traditionally costumed **Evzones**, the Greek equivalent of the British palace guards (for more details of which *See* **Places of Interest (A to Z)**). South-east of the National Gardens is the Olympic Stadium erected in 1896 on the site of the original stadium, built in 330 BC, and situated in a valley of the Arditos Hills. South-west across Leoforos Olgas are the Olympic swimming pool, the Tennis and Athletic Club. To the west of these sporting facilities is the isolated gateway known as the Arch of Hadrian overlooking the busy traffic junction of Leoforos Olgas and Leoforos Amalias. Through the archway, the remains of the Temple of Olympian Zeus are outlined, 15 only of the original 104 Corinthian columns remaining.

Leaving Hadrian's Aroh, westwards along Odhos Dionysiou Areopagitou brings one to the south side of:

The Acropolis (Akropoli) (*Tmr* C5) A 10-acre rock rising 750 ft above the surrounding city and surmounted by the Parthenon Temple, built in approximately 450 BC, the Propylaia Gateway, the Temple to Athena Nike and the triple Temple of Erechtheion. Additionally, there has been added the modern Acropolis museum, discreetly tucked away almost out of sight.

At the bottom of the southern slope are the Theatres of Dionysos, originally said to seat up to 30,000 but more probably 17,000, and the smaller, second century AD, Odeion of Herodes Atticus, which has been restored and is used for plays and concerts during the summer festival.

The west slope leads to the Hill of Areopagos (Areios Pagos) where, in times of yore, a council of noble men dispensed supreme judgements. Across Apostolou Pavlou St lie the other tree-covered hills of Filopapou (Philopappos/Mouseion), or Hill of Muses, from whence the views are far-reaching and outstanding; Pnyx (Pnyka), where The Assembly once met and a son et lumière is now held, and the Asteroskopeion (Observatory), or the Hill of Nymphs, whereon stands, surprise, surprise, an observatory.

Descending from the Asteroskopeion towards and across Apostolou Pavlou St is:

The (Greek) Agora (*Tmr* B/C4) The gathering place from whence the Athenians would have approached the Acropolis. This market-place cum civic centre is now little more than rubble, but the glory that once was is recreated by a model.

Nearby the Temple of Hephaistos or Thission (Theseion) sits on a small hill overlooking the Agora and to one side is the recently reconstructed market-place, Stoa Attalus. The cost of this project was met from private donations raised by American citizens.

A short distance to the east of the Greek Agora is the site of:

The Roman Forum (or Agora) (*Tmr* C5) Close by is the Tower of the Winds (*Tmr* 8.C5), which remarkable octagonal tower, probably built in the first century BC, acted as a combination waterclock, sundial and weathervane. Early descriptions say the building was topped off with a bronze weathervane represented by the mythological Triton complete with a pronged trident. The carved eight gods of wind can be seen, as can traces of the corresponding sundials, but no interior mechanism remains and the building is now used as a store for various stone antiquities.

A short distance to the north-west is an area known as The Keramikos (*Tmr* B4), a cemetery or graveyard, containing the Street of the Tombs, a funeral avenue laid out about 400 BC.

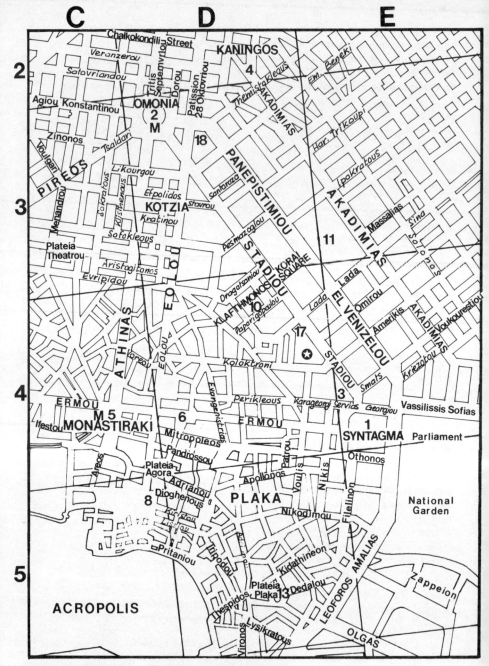

ATHENS CITY INSET

Illustration 5

In a north-easterly direction from Keramikos along Pireos St, via Eleftherias Sq bus terminal (*Tmr* 9.C3), turning right down Evripidou St, across Athinas and Eolou Streets, leads to:

Klafthmonos Square (Klathmonos) (*Tmr* 10.D3/4) Supposedly the most attractive Byzantine church in Athens, Aghii Theodori is positioned in the west corner of the square.

Looking north-east across Stadiou St, up Korai St (the site of another bus terminal), and across Panepistimiou Ave, reveals an imposing range of neo-classical buildings (*Tmr* 11.D/E3/4), fronted by laid-out gardens. These comprise the University flanked by, to the left (facing), the National Library, and to the right, the Academy. Behind and running parallel to Stadiou and Panepistimou, is Akadirnias St, on which is another major bus terminal. Just off Akadimias St, in Massalias St, is the Hellenic-American Union, many of whose facilities are open to the general public. These include an English and music library, as well as a cafeteria. In the summer a schedule of concerts and plays is staged in English.

North-west of Klafthmonos Sq, to the left of Eolou St, is:

Kotzia Square (*Tmr* D3) A very large plateia in which, on Sunday at least, there is a profusion of flower sellers' stalls.

Fokionos Negri Actually a street, if not more an avenue rather than a square. Rather distant, almost in the suburbs to the north, and usually just off the street plans of Athens. To reach it from Omonia Sq proceed up 28 (Ikosiokto) Oktovriou, which runs into Patission St, on past the National Archaeological Museum and Green Park (Pedion Areos), on the right, to where Agiou Meletiou St runs across Patission St. Fokionos Negri starts as a fairly small side-street to the right, but widens out into a tree-lined, short, squat avenue with a wide, spacious centre pedestrian way once gravelled and being extensively resurfaced in 1985. Supposedly the **Dolce Vita** or **Via Veneto** of Athens but not out of the ordinary if quiet wealth is normal. Extremely expensive cafes edge the square half way up on the right and it certainly becomes extremely lively after nightfall.

A number 5, 11, 12 or 13 trolley-bus, going north, will take you there.

THE ACCOMMODATION & EATING OUT

The Accommodation On the islands, pensions and (even) 'E' class hotels can be recommended, but in Athens I only include some 'B', 'C' and some better 'D' class hotels. There are a few reasonable Class 'E' hotels and good pensions but . . . .

On Adrianou St (*Tmr* D5) (Plaka district) there are a few very cheap dormitories and students' hostels, where a certain amount of roof-top sleeping is also allowed, costing upwards of 350 drs per night. Unless well off the main roads, a set of ear-muffs or plugs is almost obligatory to ensure a good night's sleep.

On a cautionary note, since the end of 1981 the Greek authorities have been closing a number of the more 'undesirable', unlicensed hotels, so your favourite over-night stop may no longer be in business.

Most of the Athenian hotel charges are priced at the 1985/86 rates which averaged out in 1985 as follows.

Class	Single	Double	
A	4000/4900 drs	5000/6200 drs	en suite bathroom
B	2500/3000 drs	3200/4000 drs	& breakfast included
C	1500/1900 drs	2400/3000 drs	sharing bathroom and
D	600/700 drs	900/1100 drs	room rate only

SYNTAGMA AREA (*Tmr* 1.D/E4/5)

Hotel Cleo (Cleopatra) (*Tmr* D4) (Class D) 3 Patrou St. Tel. 322-9053

Directions: Leaving Syntagma Sq, walk down Mitropoleos St, towards Monastiraki Sq and take the fourth turning left.

Well recommended if threadbare. Ground floor dormitory, free baggage store. Double rooms from 1150 drs.

NB. The owners also have a guest house nearby in 18 Apollonos St.

Pension John's Place (*Tmr* D4) (Class C) 5 Patrou St.　　　　　Tel. 322-9719
Directions: As for Hotel Cleo above.

Not surprisingly the affable old Papa is named John. Well kept, with singles from 650 drs and doubles from 800 drs rising to 900 drs and 1100 drs respectively, naturally sharing bathroom facilities.

George's Pension (*Tmr* D4) (Class B) 46 Nikis St.　　　　　Tel. 322-9569
Directions: As for Hotel Cleo, but take the first left-hand turning.

Recommended by four American Texas college girls, met on the train to Patras a few years ago and whose first stopover in Greece was this guest house. Shared bathroom and hot water in the evening, if you are quick. Doubles from 800 drs.

Hotel Kimon (*Tmr* D5) (Class D) 27 Apollonos　　　　　Tel. 323-5223
Directions: Mid-way on Apollonos St, one block down from Mitropoleos St.

Old but renovated. Single rooms sharing 560 drs increasing to 650 drs whilst double rooms start at 740 drs rising to 925 drs sharing a bathroom and 925 drs to 1110 drs en suite.

YMCA (XAN) (*Tmr* E4) 28 Omirou St.　　　　　Tel. 362-6970
Directions: North-east corner of Syntagma Sq up Panepistimiou St, third turning right and across Akadimias Avenue, on the right.

Institutional and not inexpensive accommodation costing some 550 drs for a single, and 900 drs for a double per night.

YWCA (XEN) (*Tmr* E4) 11 Amerikis St.　　　　　Tel. 362-4291
Directions: All as above but second turning off Panepistimiou St and on the left.

Self-service restaurant, hairdressing salon, library and laundry facilities.

OMONIA AREA (*Tmr* 2.D3) Any hotel or pension rooms facing Omonia square must be regarded as very noisy

Hotel Omonia (*Tmr* D3) (Class C) 4 Omonia Sq　　　　　Tel. 523-7210
Directions: Just stand in Omonia Sq and swivel on your heels, north side of the square.

The reception is on the first floor, as is a cafe-bar and terrace, overlooking the square and its action. Modern and 'worn' international look to the place. You may well have to take demi-pension terms. A double room en suite costs from 1300 drs, breakfast 150 drs and a meal from 600 drs.

Hotel Banghion (*Tmr* D3) (Class C) 18b Omonia Sq.　　　　　Tel. 324-2259
Directions: As for Hotel Omonia but south side of the square.

Elegant and ageing. From 1200 drs for a double room sharing a bathroom, increasing to 1450 drs, with breakfast available at 180 drs.

Hotel Carlton (*Tmr* D3) (Class C) 7 Omonia Sq.　　　　　Tel. 522-3201
Directions: As for Hotel Omonia.

Very Greek and old fashioned. Single rooms 900 drs and double rooms between 1st April - 31st December 1100 drs, both sharing a bathroom. Breakfast costs 200 drs.

Hotel Europa (*Tmr* D2) (Class C) 7 Veranzerou St.　　　　　Tel. 522-3081
Directions: North of Omonia Sq, the second main street up, lying east/west. This is very often listed as Chateaubriandou (Satovriandou) St but the local authorities either have, or have not, been notified of the change. The street is now a pedestrian precinct.

'Greek Provincial', the remarkably ancient lift of this hotel creaks its way up and down to the various floors. The rooms are adequate, even have a wardrobe and the floors are covered with brown linoleum. To use the shower the concierge must be asked for the relevant key in mime, if your Greek is sketchy, as the staff's knowledge of English is very limited. When produced, the key might well be adjudged large enough to open the doors of the **Bastille**. Weighed down by this instrument, the moment of truth is about to dawn, for when the door is opened, sheer disbelief may well be your first reaction, especially if it is your first stop off in Athens, as it was my own years ago. A cavernous and be-cobwebbed room reveals plumbing that beggars description. Enough to say the shower was most welcome, even if the lack of a point to anchor the shower head, whilst trying to soap oneself down, required interesting bodily contortions.

The single room rate is 600 drs while a double rises from 760 drs to 1000 drs.

Hotel Alma (*Tmr* 2.D2/3) (Class C) 5 Dorou   Tel. 524-0858
Directions: Dorou St runs north from the north-east corner of Omonia Sq.

Modern, the rooms with a verandah are on the seventh and eighth floors. From 1000 drs for a double room with breakfast costing 200 drs.

Hotel Parnon (*Tmr* D2) (Class C) 20 Tritis Septemvriou/21 Chalkokondili Tel. 523-5196
Directions: North of Omonia Sq on the junction of Tritis Septemvriou and Chalkokondili St.

Modern and noisy at 1300 drs for a double room with bath (April to October) and breakfast from 200 drs.

Hotel Eva (*Tmr* C2) (Class D) 31 Victoros Ougo   Tel. 522-3079
Directions: West of Omonia, parallel to and two blocks back from Ag Konstantinou.

Well recommended with single rooms from 760 drs and double rooms 1150 drs en suite. Breakfast 150 drs.

Hotel Marina (*Tmr* C3) (Class C) 13 Voulgari   Tel. 522-4769
Directions: South-west from Omonia along Odhos Pireos, 4th turning to the right.

Single rooms from 705 drs, double rooms 1010 drs sharing the bathroom and 970 drs and 1230 drs respectively en suite. Breakfast costs 150 drs.

Hotel Vienna (*Tmr* C3) (Class C) 20 Pireos   Tel. 524-9143
Directions: South-west off Omonia Sq.

New, clean and noisy, at about 1600 drs for a double in the early summer and breakfast 190 drs.

Hotel Athinea (*Tmr* C2) (Class C) 9 Vilara   Tel. 523-3884
Directions: Westwards on Ag Konstantinou and situated on one side of the small square of Agiou Konstantinou.

Old but beautifully positioned although cabaret night life can intrude. A restaurant and cake shop are close by as is a taxi rank. A single room starts at 1200 drs and a double 1600 drs en suite. Breakfast 200 drs.

Hotel Pythagorion (*Tmr* C2/3) (Class C) 28 Ag Konstantinou   Tel. 524-2811
Directions: West of Omonia Sq.

A single room from 1200 drs and a double room, both with bath from 1650 drs, breakfast is 140 drs and lunch/dinner from 450 drs.

Hotel Florida (*Tmr* C3) (Class C) 25 Menandrou   Tel. 522-3214
Directions: Third turning left, south-west along Pireos St.

Single rooms from 490/650 drs and doubles from 940 drs both without a bathroom, and en suite, 750 drs and 1150 drs respectively. Breakfast 150 drs.

Hotel Alcestis (Alkistis) (*Tmr* C3) (Class C) 18 Plateia Theatrou   Tel. 321-9811
Directions: Off Pireos St, either south down Sokratous or Menandrou St, and across Sofokleous St.

Despite its chromium-plated appearance, all glass and marble with a prairie-sized lobby awash with Americans, it is a Class C hotel in a commercial square. Popular, with double rooms from 1333 drs, breakfast 175 drs and lunch/dinner from 600 drs.

MONASTIRAKI AREA (*Tmr* 5.C4)

Hotel Tembi/Tempi (*Tmr* D4) (Class D) 29 Eolou (Aioulu/Aeolou)   Tel. 321-3175
Directions: A main street north of Ermou St, opposite the church of Ag Irini.

Pleasant rooms with singles sharing the bathroom starting at 500 drs and rising to 570 drs for the period 1st June - 30th September. Double rooms sharing cost from 750 drs and ensuite 880 drs advancing to 950 drs and 1100 drs respectively. Laundry facilities available.

Hotel Ideal (*Tmr* D4) (Class D) 39 Eolou/2 Voreou   Tel. 321-3195
Directions: On the left of Eolou walking up from Odhos Ermou and on the corner with Voreou St.

A perfect example of a weather-worn, 19th century Athens neo classical building complete with old fashioned metal and glass canopy entrance and matchbox sized wrought iron balconies. The accommodation lives up to all that the exterior promises. A telephone, TV room, bar and luggage is stored. The bathroom facililties are shared, with the basic single room rate 500 drs and double room 750 drs rising, for the period 16th June - 20th September, to 600 drs and 900 drs respectively.

Hotel Hermion (*Tmr* C/D4) (Class D) 66c Ermou St   Tel. 321-2753
Directions: East of Monastiraki adjacent to Kapnikarea Church and Sq.

Old but clean with the reception up the stairs. All rooms share bathrooms with the single rate starting off at 600 drs and the double rooms from 880 drs.

Hotel Attalos (*Tmr* C3/4) (Class C) 29 Athinas   Tel. 321-2801
Directions: North from Monastiraki Sq.

Recommended to us by a splendidly eccentric lady English artist who should know — she has been visiting Greece for some 20 years.

Between 16th March - 30th June singles 800 drs and doubles 1200 drs rising for the period 1st July - 30th September to 900 drs and 1500 drs. Breakfast costs 180 drs.

Hotel Cecil (*Tmr* C4) (Class D) 39 Athinas   Tel. 321-7079
Directions: North from Monastiraki Sq and two buildings up from the Kalamida St turning on the left-hand side. This is the other side of the road from a very small chapel, incongruously stuck on the pavement.

Clean looking with a single room costing 695 drs and a double 1048 drs. The bathrooms are shared.

PLAKA/METZ STADIUM AREAS (*Tmr* D5 & D/E6) The Plaka is rich in accommodation, as it is in most things.

Hotel Phaedra (*Tmr* D5) (Class D) 4 Adrianou/16 Herephontos   Tel. 323-8461
Directions: Situated close by a multi-junction of various streets including Lysikratous, Galanou, Adrianou and Herephontos, opposite the Byzantine church of Ag Aikaterini and its small, attractive gardens.

Pretty area by day, noisy by night. Family hotel with a ground-floor bar. Double rooms 1300 drs. Breakfast costs 130 drs.

Students' Inn (*Tmr* D5) 16 Kidathineon St.   Tel. 324-4808
Hostelish but recommended as good value with hot showers en tap (sorry) and an English-speaking owner. Roof top available as is a snack bar and the use of a washing machine. Clean with the basic double rooms complete with a rickety oil-cloth covered table and a mug costing 1000 drs.

Hotel Solonion (*Tmr* D5) (Class E) 11 Sp Tsagari/Dedalou   Tel. 322-0008
Directions: To the right of Kidathineon St, facing Syntagma Sq, between Dedalou St and Leoforos Amalias. Odhos Tsagari is a continuation of Asteriou St.

A pleasant, smiling Asian lady runs the old, faded but refurbished building. The accommodation is 'student provincial', the rooms being high ceilinged and the rather dodgy floor boards covered in brown linoleum. Hot water all day and on a fine day... you can espy the Acropolis. . . well a bit of it.

No singles, a double room sharing the bathroom costs 925 drs and en suite 1100 drs, 1st May - 31st October.

Close by the Hotel Solonion are the

Hotel Kekpoy (Cecrops) (*Tmr* D5) (Class D) 13 Tsagari   Tel. 322-3080
Directions: On the same side as the *Solonion* but a building or two towards Leoforos Amalias.

Similar to the *Solonion* with almost identical rates.

Hotel Phoebus (Fivos) (*Tmr* D5) (Class C) Asteriou/12 Peta   Tel. 322-0142
Directions: Back towards Kidathineon, on the corner of the Asteriou and Peta Streets.

Rather more up market that the 3 previously listed hotels. A double room en suite costs 1260 drs with the month of June - September rising to 1500 drs. Breakfast 160 drs.

A few side streets towards the Acropolis is the

Hotel Ava (*Tmr* D5) Lysikratous St
Directions: As above.

I have no personal experience but the establishment has been mentioned as a possibility.

New Clare's House (*Tmr* E6) (Class C Pension) 24 Sorvolou St   Tel. 922-2288
Directions: Rather uniquely, the owners have had a large compliments slip printed with a pen and ink drawing on the face, and on the reverse side, directions in Greek entitled:
Show this to the taxi driver.

This includes details of the location, south of the Stadium on Sorvolou St between Charvouri and Voulgareos Streets on the right, half-way down the reverse slope with the description **'white house with the green windows'**. From Syntagma take Leoforos Amalias, the main avenue south, and keep to the main avenues hugging the Temple of Olympian Zeus and along Odhos Diakou. Where Diakou makes a junction with Vouliagmenis and Ardittou Avenues, Odhos Anapavseos leads off in a south-east direction and Sorvolou St crescents off to the left. Trolley buses 2, 4, 11 & 12 will drop one off by the Stadium. It is quite a steep climb up Sorvolou St, which breaks into steps, to the pretty and highly recommended area of Metz (highly regarded by Athenians that is). Plus points are that the narrow nature of the lanes, which suddenly become steps, keeps the traffic down to a minimum and the height of the hill raises it above the general level of smog and pollution.

The pleasant flat fronted pension is on the right and has a marble floor entrance hall. Inside, off to the left is a large reception/lounge/bar/breakfast room and the right, the lift. The self assured, English speaking, owner presides from a large desk in the reception area and is warily helpful. The lady staff receptionists do not exactly go wild in an orgy of energy sapping activity, tending to indulge in a saturnalia of TV watching. Guests in the meantime can help themselves to bottles of beer (75 drs) and Coke from the bar and pay when convenient to them and the receptionist.

The nice double rooms share a red and black appointed bathroom with one other double room. Despite the self assured aura of excellence there are a collection of the usual faults — cracked loo seats, no hot water* (due to a plumbing fault we were airily advised), no locking mechanism on the lavatory door and the toilet had to be flushed by pulling a string. A double room and breakfast sets a guest back 1900 drs which at first and for that matter second impression appears on the expensive side. That is until it is realised that the 4th floor has a Common Room with balcony and a kitchen complete with cooker and a fridge. Added to this the 5th floor contains a laundry room with an iron and 2 roof-top clothes lines which facilities of course make a great deal of difference to the cost of a room.

The management create an atmosphere that will suit the young, very well behaved student and the older traveller but not exuberant rowdies as hands are smacked if guests lay around eating a snack on the front steps, hang washing out of the windows or make a noise especially between the hours of 1330 and 1700 hrs and after 2330 hrs. You know lights out boys and no smoking in the dorms. . .

Originally recommended by Alexis on the island of Kos but for 1986 is included in one or two of the smaller tour companies brochures for the Athens overnight stop.

*I must point out that Peter (an Aegean yachtsman who almost always spends some of the winter at **Clares**) insists that I include his disclaimer. He has never found the water anything but hot.

THISSION AREA (Thesion) (*Tmr* B/C4/5) First south-bound metro stop after Monastiraki and a much quieter area.

Hotel Phedias (*Tmr* B4) (Class C) 39 Apostoulou Pavlou　　　　　Tel. 345-9511
Directions: South of the metro station. Modern and friendly with double rooms from 1500 drs and breakfast 160 drs per head.

OLYMPIC OFFICE AREA (*Tmr* C6)
Hotel Karayannis (*Tmr* C6) (Class C) 94 Leoforos Sygrou　　　　　Tel. 921-5903
Directions: On the corner of Odhos Byzantiou and Leoforos Sygrou, opposite the side exit of the Olympic terminal office.

'Interesting', tatty and noisy, but very necessary, if travellers arrive really late at the terminal. Rooms facing the main road should be avoided. The Athenian traffic, which roars non-stop for a full 24 hours, appears to make the journey along Leoforos Sygrou, via the hotel's balconies, even three or four storeys up. Picturesque view of the Acropolis from the breakfast and bar roof-top terrace, even if it is through a maze of television aerials. Single rooms sharing the bathroom 1200 drs and a double room 1626 drs, with a double room en suite 1698 drs. Breakfast for one costs 190 drs.

Best to splash out for the en suite rooms as the Karayannis shared facilities are of the 'thought provoking' type with a number of the unique features detailed under the general description of bathrooms in the introductory chapters.

Whilst in this area it would be inappropriate not to mention the:

Cafe/Restaurant Behind the Olympic office.
Excellent service and snack bar food, reasonably priced. Closed on Sundays.

Youth Hostels (i.e. the official ones). I am never quite sure why overnighters use the Athens YHAs. Other accommodation is usually less expensive, cleaner and do away with the need to share dormitories. If you must, about 300 drs per person per night, including sheets.

(a) 57 Kypselis St and Agiou Meletiou 1　　　　　Tel. 822-5860
Area: Fokionos Negri, north Athens
Directions: Along 28 (Ikosiokto) Oktovriou/Patission Street from Omonia Sq beyond Pedion Areos Park to Ag Meletiou St. Turn right and follow until the junction with Kypselis St. Trolley-buses, No 3, 5, 11, 12 & 13.

(b) 1 Drossi St and Leoforos Alexandras 87 (*Tmr* G2)　　　　　Tel. 646-3669
Area: North-east Athens.
Directions: East of Pedion Aeros Park along Leoforos Alexandras almost until the junction with Ippokratous St. Odhos Drossi is on the left. Trolley-bus No 7 from Panepistiou or No 8 from Kanigos Sq or Akadimias St.

(c) 3 Hamilton St and 97 Patission St (*Tmr* D1)　　　　　Tel. 822-6425
Area: North Athens.
Directions: North from Omonia Sq along 28 (Ikosiokto) Oktovriou St as far as the top end of Pedion Areos Park. Hamilton St is on the left. Trolley-buses 2, 3, 4, 5, 11, 12 & 13.

If intending to stay at one of the Youth Hostels, it is favourite to go to the central office.

YHA Head Office (*Tmr* D3/4) 4 Dragatsaniou   Tel. 323-4107

Directions: The north side of Plateia Klafthmonos on the left hand side of Stadiou St.

Open Monday- Friday, 0900 - 1400 hrs and 1830 - 2030 hrs (but not Tuesday evening) and Saturday between 0900 - 1400 hrs. They advise of vacancies in the various youth hostels and issue international youth hostel cards.

LARISSIS STATION AREA (*Tmr* B/C1) *See* **Trains, A to Z.**

CAMPING Sample daily site charges per person vary between 170 - 210 drs and the hire of a tent between 150 - 185 drs.

Sites include the following:-

Distance from Athens	Site Name	Amenities
8 km	**Athens Camping,** 198 Athinon Ave. On the road to Dafni (due west of Athens). Tel. 581-4113	Open all year, 25 km from the sea. Bar, shop and showers
10 km	**Dafni Camping,** Dafni. On the Athens to Corinth National Road. Tel. 581-1562	Open all year. 5 km from the sea. Bar, shop, showers, disco and kitchen facilities

For the above: Bus 853 Athens - Elefsina departs Koumoundourou Sq/Deligeorgi St (*Tmr* C2/3) every 20 mins between 0510 - 2215 hrs.

14.5 km	**Patritsia,** Kato Kifissia, N. Athens. Tel. 801-1900	Open June - October. Bar, shop, showers, laundry and kitchen facilities
15 km	**Neo Evropaiko,** Nea Kifissia, N. Athens. Tel. 808-3482	Open April - October. 18 km from the sea. Bar, shop, showers, kitchen facilities and swimming pool
16 km	**Nea Kifissia,** Nea Kifissia, N. Athens. Tel. 801-0202	Open all year. 20 km from the sea. Bar, shop, showers, swimming pool and laundry
18 km	**Dionyssiotis,** Nea Kifissia, N. Athens. Tel. 807-1494	Open all year
25 km	**Papa Camping,** Zorgianni Ag Stefanos. Tel. 814-1446	Open June - September. 25 km from the sea. Laundry, bar and kitchen facilities

For the above (sited on or beside the Athens National Road, north to Lamia): Lamia bus from 260 Liossion St (*Tmr* C1/2), every hour from 0615 to 1915 and at 2030 hrs.

35 km	**Marathon Camping,** Kaminia, Marathon NE of Athens. Tel. 0294-55577	On a sandy beach. Open all year. Showers, bar, laundry, restaurant, shop, swimming pool (1½ km) and kitchen facilities
35 km	**Nea Makri,** 156 Marathonos Ave, Nea Makri. NE of Athens just south of Marathon. Tel. 0294-92719	Open April - October. 220 m from the sea. Sandy beach, laundry, bar and shop

For the above: The bus from Odhos Mavromateon, Plateia Egyptou (*Tmr* D1), every ½ hour from 0530 to 2200 hrs.

26 km	**Cococamp,** Rafina. East of Athens. Tel. 0294-23413	Open all year. On the beach, rocky coast. Laundry, bar, showers, kitchen facilities, shop and restaurant
29 km	**Kokkino Limanaki Camping,** Kokkino Limanaki, Rafina. Tel. 0294-26602	On the beach. Open April - October.
29 km	**Rafina Camping,** Rafina. East of Athens. Tel. 0294-23118	Open all year, 4 km from the sandy beach. Showers, bar, laundry, restaurant and shop

For the above: The Rafina bus from Mavromateon St, Plateia Egyptou (*Tmr* D1). Twenty-nine departures from 0550 to 2200 hrs.

20 km	**Voula Camping,** 2 Alkyonidon St, Voula. Just below Glyfada and the airport. Tel. 895-2712	Open all year. On the sandy beach. Showers, laundry, bar, shop and kitchen facilities
27 km	**Varkiza Beach Camping,** Varkiza. Coastal road Athens-Vouliagmenis-Sounion. Tel. 897-3613	Open all year. By a sandy beach. Bar, shop, laundry and kitchen facilities
60 km	**Sounion Camping,** Sounion. Tel. 0292-39358	Open all year. By a sandy beach. Bar, shop, laundry, kitchen facilities and a swimming pool
76 km	**Vakhos Camping,** Assimaki near Sounion. On the Sounion to Lavrion Road. Tel. 0292-39263	Open June - September. On the beach

For the above: Buses from Mavromateon St, Plateia Egyptou (*Tmr* D1) every hour from 0630 to 1730 hrs. Note to get to Vakhos Camping catch the Sounion bus via Markopoulon and Lavrion.

The Eating Out Where to dine out is a very personal choice and in a city the size of Athens there are so many restaurants and tavernas to choose from that only a few recommendations are made.

In general, steer clear of Luxury and Class A hotel dining rooms, restaurants offering international cuisine and tavernas with Greek music and/or dancing. They may be very good but will be expensive.

In Athens and the larger, more cosmopolitan, provincial cities, it is usual taverna practice to round up prices, which can prove a little disconcerting until you get used to the idea.

In despair it is noted that some restaurants and tavernas climbing the slopes of the Acropolis up Odhos Markou Avrilou, south of Eolou St, are allowing 'Chinese menu' style collective categories (A, B, C etc) to creep in to their Greek menu listings.

PLAKA AREA (*Tmr* D5) A glut of eating houses ranging from the very good and expensive, the very expensive and bad, to some inexpensive and very good.

Taverna Thespis 18 Thespidos St   Tel. 323-8242
Directions: Up a lane across the way from Kidathineon St, across the bottom or south east end of Adrianou St.

Recommended with friendly service and reasonably priced. The house retsina is served in metal jugs. A two-hour slap-up meal of souvlaki, Greek salad, fried zucchini, bread and two carafes of retsina totals some 1000 drs plus for two.

Plaka Village 28 Kidathineon
Directions: In the block edged by the streets of Adrianou and Kidathineon.

An excellent souvlaki-bar but (as is now prevalent in the Omonia Sq souvlaki arcade) to sit down costs an extra 16 drs per head. Price lists do not make this plain and the annoying habit can cause, at the least, irritation. A large bottle of beer costs 80 drs.

Gerani Ouzerie 14 Tripodou
Directions: Up the slope from the Thespidos/Kydathineon junction one to the left of Adrianou (facing Monastiraki Sq) and on the left. Distinguishing the establishment is not difficult as the 1st floor balcony is embellished with a large, stuffed bird and two large antique record player horns mounted on the wrought iron balustrade. The taverna, standing on its own evokes a provincial atmosphere and it is necessary to arrive early as it is well patronised by the locals.

Eden Taverna Flessa St
Directions: Off Adrianou St, almost opposite Odhos Nikodimou and on the left. Mentioned

because their menu includes many offerings that excellently cater (sorry) for vegetarian requirements.

Platanos Taverna 4 Dioghenous
Directions: Parallel to, but one down and to the top, Monastiraki end, of Adrianou St.
Conventional taverna serving inexpensive lunch and dinner. Closed Sundays.

Michiko Restaurant 27 Kidathineon
Directions: On the right beyond the junction with Asteriou St (in a north east direction towards Syntagma Sq) opposite a small square and church.
Japanese, if you must, and extremely expensive.

Xynou/Xynos 4 Arghelou Geronda (Angelou Geronta)
Directions: Left off Kidathineon St (facing Syntagma Sq).
One of the oldest and most reasonably priced tavernas in the Plaka, highly rated and well patronised by Athenians. Evenings only and closed on Sundays. A friend advises me that it is now almost obligatory to book in advance.

Plateia Agora, a lovely, elongated, chic Plaka Sq formed at the junction of the bottom of Eolou, the top of Adrianou and Kapnikareas Streets, spawns a number of cafe-bar restaurants. The include the *Possidion* and *Apollon*, the canopied chairs and tables of which edge the street all the way round the neat, paved plateia. There is a clean public lavatory at the top (Monastiraki) end. The *Apollon* has a particularly wide range of choice and one can sit at the comfortable tables for an hour or so over a coffee (84 drs), have a fried egg breakfast (220 drs) or a full blown meal. Hope your luck is in and the organ grinder wanders through.

STADIUM (PANGRATI) AREA (*Tmr* E/F6)
Karavitis Taverna (ΚΑΡΑΒΙΤΗΣ) 4 Pafsaniou (Paysanioy)
Directions: Beyond the Stadium (*Tmr* E/F6) going east (away from the Acropolis) along Vasileos Konstantinou, and Pafsaniou is 3rd turning to the right. The taverna is on the left.
A small, leafy tree shaded gravel square fronts the taverna which is so popular that there is an extension across the street through a pair of 'field gates'. Our friend Paul will probably berate me (more if he was not less of a gentleman) for listing this gem. Unknown to visitors but extremely popular with Athenians more especially those who, when college students, frequented this jewel in the Athens taverna crown as young men. A meal for 4 of a selection of dishes including lamb, beef in clay, giant haricot beans, garlic flavoured meat balls, greens, ztatziki, 2 plates of feta cheese, aubergines, courgettes, bread and 3 jugs of retsina from the barrel for some 1700 drs. Beat that, but some knowledge of Greek will help.

Also in this area is the

To Fanari (*Tmr* F6) Plastira Sq
Directions: South-east of the National Gardens, leaving the Stadium to the right, turn down Eratosthenous St from Vasileos Konstantinou to Plateia Plastira.
Very Greek and off the Plaka, Syntagma and Omonia Square 'tourist beat' and therefore comparatively inexpensive.

SYNTAGMA AREA (*Tmr* 1.D/E4/5)
Corfu Restaurant (*Tmr* E4) 6 Kriezotou St
Directions: North of Syntagma Sq and first turning right off Panepistimiou (Venizelou) St.
Extensive Greek and European dishes in a modern, friendly restaurant.

Delphi Restaurant (*Tmr* D4) 15 Nikis St
Directions: From the south-west corner of Syntagma Sq, east along Mitropoleos and the first turning left.

Modern, reasonably priced food and friendly. Extensive menu.

Sintrivani Restaurant (*Tmr* D/E5) 5 Filellinon St.
Directions: South-west corner of Syntagma Sq and due south.
Garden restaurant serving a traditional menu at reasonable prices.

Vassillis Restaurant (*Tmr* E4) 14A Voukourestiou
Directions: North of Syntagma Sq and the second turning off Panepistimiou St to the right along Odhos Smats and across Akadimias St.
Variety, in traditional surroundings.

Ideal Restaurant (*Tmr* D/E4) 46 Panepistimiou St
Directions: Proceed up Panepistimiou from the north-east corner of Syntagma Sq and the restaurant is on the right.
Good food at moderate prices.

YWCA 11 Amerikis St
Directions: North-west up either Stadiou or Panepistimiou St and second or third road to the right, depending which street is used.
Cafeteria — the food is inexpensive.

There are many cafes in or around Syntagma. Recommended but expensive are:

Brazilian Coffee Cafes
Two close by Syntagma Sq, one at the bottom of Stadiou St on the square and the other in Voukourestiou St, both serving coffee, tea, toast, butter and jam, breakfast, ice creams and pastries.

Zonar's 9 Panepistimiou (Venizelou)

OMONIA AREA (*Tmr* 2.D3)
Ellinikon (*Tmr* D2) On the corner of Dorou and Satovriandou Streets.
Directions: North of Omonia Sq along Dorou St and almost immediately on your left.
Good value, if a little showy.

Taverna Kostoyannus (*Tmr* E2) 37 Zaimi St
Directions: Leave Omonia northwards on 28 (Ikosiokto) Oktovriou, turn right at Odhos Stournara to the near side of the Polytechnic School, and Zaimi St is the second road along. The taverna is to the left approximately behind the National Archaeological Museum.
Satisfactory food and prices. Well recommended but, as in the case of many other Athenian tavernas, it is not open for lunch or on Sundays.

Snack Bars
Probably the most compact, reasonably priced 'offerings' in grubby surroundings lie in the arcade between Dorou St and 28 (Ikosiokto) Oktovriou, off Omonia Sq, wherein are situated cafes and stalls selling almost every variety of fast Greek convenience food. A 'standard' souvlaki costs 35 drs and a 'spezial' or de-luxe 50/55 drs BUT do not sit down unless you wish to be charged an extra 15 - 20 drs per head. A beer costs 55/65 drs.
Note the standard version is a preheated slab of meat and the 'spezial' the traditional giro meat-sliced offering.

Cafes
Everywhere of course, but on Omonia Sq, alongside Dorou St and adjacent to the Hotel Carlton, is a magnificent specimen of the traditional Kafeneion. Greek men sip coffee and tumble their worry beads, as they must have done since the turn of the century.

Flocas (*Tmr* D/E3/4) 4 Korai St
Directions: Half way down Panepistimiou St opposite the University.
Fair value, fast service for a range of dishes.

Odhos Sokratous south of Omonia Sq (parallel and west of Athinas St) is during the day

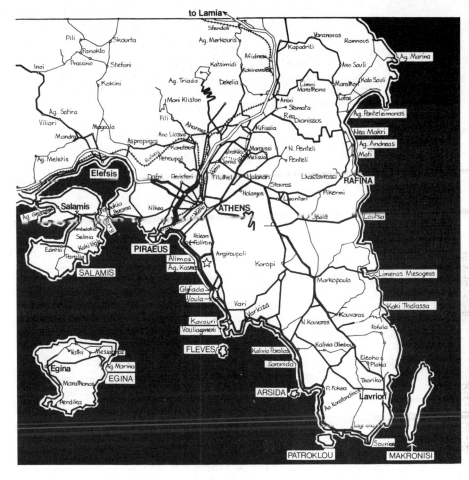

THE ENVIRONS OF ATHENS

Motorway
Road
Railway
Metro
☆ Airport

NORTH

Illustration 6

almost one great market, mainly meat. In amongst the stalls and counters are 3 inexpensive tavernas of some note.

LYCABETTUS (LYKAVITOS) AREA (*Tmr* F4)

Je Reviens Restaurant (*Tmr* F/G4/5) 49 Xenokratous St

Directions: North-east from Kolonaki Sq, up Patriachou Ioakim St to the junction with and left at Marasli St until it crosses Xenokratous St.

French food, creditable but "middlingly" expensive. Open midday and evenings.

L'Abreuvoir 51 Xenokratous St

Directions: As for *Je Reviens* as are the comments, but more expensive.

Al Convento Restaurant (*Tmr* G4) 4 Anapiron

Directions: North-east from Kolonaki Sq along Patriarchou Ioakim to Marasli St. Turn left and then right along Odhos Souidias and Anapiron St is nearly at the end.

Stage Coach Restaurant 14 Voukourestiou

Directions: From the north-west corner of Plateia Kolonaki, take Odhos Skoufa, which crosses Voukourestiou St.

Wild West in decor, air-conditioned, the food is American in style and content, and is not cheap with steaks as a house speciality. Why not go to the good old US of A? Lunch and evening meals, open 1200 to 1600 and 1900 to 0100 hrs.

THE A TO Z OF USEFUL INFORMATION

AIRLINE OFFICES & TERMINUS (*Tmr* 12.C6) Referred to in the introductory paragraphs as well as under **Accommodation**, the busy offices are to the left (facing Syntagma Sq), of the frantic Leoforos Sygrou. As with other Olympic facilities the office doubles as a terminus for airport buses arriving from and departing to East and West Airports.

AIRLINE TIMETABLES *See* **Chapter 3** for the islands described in this guide that are serviced from Athens and the individual islands for details of the actual timetables.

BANKS (Trapeza — ΤΡΑΠΕΖΑ) Normal opening times, 0900 to 1300 hrs, Monday-Friday. Do not forget to take your passport and note, that if a bank strike is under way (apparently becoming a natural part of the tourist season high-jinks) the National Bank in Syntagma Sq stays open and in business. However, it becomes more than usually crowded in these circumstances. Banks opening after normal hours include the:

National Bank of Greece (*Tmr* 3.D/E4) 2 Karageorgi Georgiou, Syntagma Sq

Open 0800 - 1300 and 1400 - 2100 hrs, Monday-Friday, 0800 - 2000 hrs Saturday and Sunday.

Ionian and Popular Bank (*Tmr* D/E4/5) 1 Mitropoleos St

Open 0800 - 1300 and 1400 - 1730 hrs, Monday-Saturday and 0900 - 1200 hrs, Sunday.

Commercial Bank of Greece (*Tmr* E4) 11 Panepistimiou (Venizelou)

Open 0800 - 1300 and 1400 - 1530 hrs, Monday-Saturday and 0900 - 1200 hrs, Sunday.

BEACHES Athens is not on a river or by the sea, so to enjoy a beach it is necessary to leave the main city and travel to those suburbs by the sea. Very often these beaches are operated under the aegis of the NTOG, or private enterprise in association with a hotel. The NTOG beaches usually have beach huts, cabins, tennis courts, a playground and catering facilities. Entrance charges vary from 25-100 drs.

There are beaches and/or swimming pools at

Paleon Faliron/Faliro	A seaside resort	Bus No. 126: Departs from Odhos Othonos, south side of Syntagma Sq (*Tmr* E5).

76

Alimos	NTOG beach	Bus No. 133: Departs from Odhos Othonos, south side of Syntagma Sq (*Tmr* E5).
Glyfada (Glifada)	A seaside resort	Bus No. 129: Departs from Leoforos Olgas, south side of the Zappeion Gdns (*Tmr* E5).
Voula	Class A NTOG beach	Bus No. 122: Departs from Leoforos Olgas, south side of the Zappeion Gdns (*Tmr* E5).
Voula	Class B NTOG beach	Bus No. 122.
Vouliagmeni	A luxury seaside resort and yacht marina. NTOG beach	Bus No. 118: Departs from Leoforos Olgas, south side of the Zappeion Gdns (*Tmr* E5).
Varkiza	A seaside resort and yacht marina. NTOG beach	Bus No. 115. Departs from Leoforos Olgas, south side of the Zappeion Gdns (*Tmr* E5).

There are other beaches all the way down to Cape Sounion (Sounio) via the coast road. Buses from 14 Mavromateon St (*Tmr* D/E1) (west of Pedion Areos Park, north of Omonia Sq). The Athens/Cape Sounion bus departs every hour from 0630 hrs and leaves Sounion for Athens every hour from 0800 - 1900 hrs, the one way fare costing about 250 drs and the journey takes 1½ hrs.

BOOKSELLERS Apart from the aforementioned Plaka **Flea Market** secondhand bookshops, there are three or four on Odhos Nikis (west of Syntagma Sq) and Odhos Amerikis (north-west of Syntagma Sq) as well as one on Lysikratous St (*Tmr* D5) opposite the small church. There is also a book trade stall on the Kidathineon St edge of the Plateia Plaka.

Of all the above it is perhaps invidious to select one but . . . .

The Compendium Bookshop (& Computors) 28 Nikis St   Tel. 3226931
Well recommended for a wide range of English language publications. The **Transalpino Travel** office is in the basement.

BREAD SHOPS
In the more popular shopping areas.

BUSES & TROLLEY BUSES These run variously between 0500 and 0030 (half an hour past midnight) and are usually crowded, but excellent value, fares costing between 10 and 20 drs Travel between 0500 and 0800 hrs is free.

BUSES The buses are blue (and green) and bus stops are marked Statis (ΣΤΑΣΙΣ).
Some one-man-operated buses are utilised and a few buses have an honesty box for fares.

TROLLEY-BUSES Yellow coloured vehicles and bus stops. Usually entered via the door at the rear marked Eisodos (ΣΙΣΟΔΟΣ), with the exit at the front, marked Exodus (ΕΞΟΔΟΣ).

Do have the correct money to hand as the driver and/or conductor may not have any change.

Major City Terminals & turn-round points† (see footnote page 79)
Kaningos Sq: (*Tmr* 4.D2) North-east of Omonia Sq
Korai Sq: (*Tmr* D3/4) Opposite the University between Stadiou and Panepistimiou Streets and Omonia and Syntagma Squares
Liossion St: (*Tmr* C1) North-west of Omonia Sq
Eleftherias Sq: (*Tmr* C3) North-west of Monastiraki Sq
Leoforos Olgas: (*Tmr* E5/6) South of the National Gardens
Mavromateon St†: (*Tmr* D/E1) West of Pedion Areos Park, north of Omonia Sq

Egyptou Place (Aigyptou/Egiptou): (*Tmr* D1) Just below the south-west corner of Pedion Areos Park, alongside 28 (Ikosiokto) Oktovriou

Agion Asomaton Place: (*Tmr* B4) West of Monastiraki Sq

Koumoundourou St: (*Tmr* C2/3) West of Omonia Sq, third turning right off Ag Konstantinou

† The tree shaded north-south street is lined with bus departure points. The Rafina bus leaves from about a third of the way up the street and the Lavrion bus from the square at the south end, on the junction with Leoforos Alexandras.

Trolley-buses timetables

Some major city routes include:

No. 1:   Plateia Attiki (metro station) (*Tmr* C1), Stathmos Larissis (railway station) (*Tmr* B/C1) Karaiskaki Place, Ag Konstantinou, Omonia Sq, Syntagma Sq, Kallithea suburb (SW Athens). Every 10 mins from 0505-2350 hrs.

No. 2:   Pangrati (*Tmr* F6), Leoforos Amalias (Central), Syntagma Sq, Omonia Sq, (28 Ikosiokto Oktovriou) Patission St, Kipseli (N Athens). From 0630-0020 hrs.

No. 10:   N Smirni (S Athens), Leoforos Sygrou, Leoforos Amalias, Syntagma Sq, Panepistimiou St, Korai St (*Tmr* D3/4) (opposite the University). From 0500-2345 hrs.

No. 12:   Leoforos Olgas (*Tmr* D/E5/6), Leoforos Amalias, Syntagma Sq, Omonia Sq, 28 Ikosiokto Oktovriou (Patission) St (N Athens). From 0630-2235 hrs.

Other routes covered by trolley-buses include:

No. 3:   Patissia to Erythrea (N to NNE Athens suburbs). From 0625-2230 hrs.

No. 4:   Odhos Kypselis (*Tmr* E1) (North of Pedion Areos park), Omonia Sq, Syntagma Sq, Leoforos Olgas to Ag Artemious (SSE Athens suburbs). From 0630-0020 hrs.

No. 5:   Patissia (N Athens suburb), Omonia Sq, Syntagma Sq, Filellinon St, Koukaki (S Athens suburb). From 0630-0015 hrs.

No. 6:   Ippokratous St (*Tmr* E3), Odhos Panepistimiou, Omonia Sq to N Filadelfia (N Athens suburbs). Every 10 mins from 0500 - 2320 hrs

No. 7:   Odhos Panepistimiou (*Tmr* D/E3/4), 28 Ikosiokto Oktovriou (Patission) St, to Leoforous Alexandras (N of Lycabettus). From 0630-0015 hrs.

No. 8:   Plateia Kaningos (*Tmr* D2), Odhos Akadimias, Vassilissis Sofias, Leoforos Alexandras, 28 Ikosiokto Oktovriou, (Patission) St. From 0630-0020 hrs.

No. 9:   Kypseli St (*Tmr* E1), 28 Ikosiokto Oktovriou (Patission) St, Stadiou St, Syntagma Sq, Petralona (W Athens suburb — far side of Filopapou). Every 10 mins from 0455 - 2345 hrs

No. 10:   Korai St (*Tmr* D3/4), Stadiou St, Syntagma Sq, Filellinon St, Leoforos Sygrou, Nea Smirni (S Athens suburb). Every 10 mins from 0500 - 2345 hrs

No. 11:   Koliatsou (NNE Athens suburb), 28 Ikosiokto Oktovriou (Patission) St, Stadiou St, Syntagma Sq, Filellinon St, Plastira Sq, Eftichidou St, N Pangrati (ESE Athens suburb). Every 5 mins from 0500 - 0010 hrs.

No. 13:   28 Ikosiokto Oktovriou (Patission) St, Akadimias St, Vassilissis Sofias, Plateia Papadiamantopoulou, Leoforos Kifissias, Neo Psychiko (NE Athens suburb). Every 10 mins from 0500-2400 hrs.

Buses Bus numbers are subject to a certain amount of confusion, but here goes! Some of the routes are as follows:

No. 022:   Kaningos Sq (*Tmr* D2), Akadimias, Kanari, Patriarchou Ioakim, Marasli, Genadiou St (SE Lycabettus). Every 10 mins from 0520 - 2330 hrs

No. 024:   Leoforos Amalias (*Tmr* D/E 5), Syntagma Sq, Panepistimiou St, Omonia Sq, Tritis Septemvriou, Stournari, Acharnon, Sourmeli, Liossion St. *NB This is the bus that delivers passengers to 260 Liossion St (Tmr C2), one of the main bus terminals.*

No. 040:   Filellinon St (Syntagma Sq), Leoforos Amalias, Leoforos Sygrou to Vassileos Konstantinou, Piraeus port. Every 10 mins, 24 hours a day. Green Bus.

No. 045:   Kaningos Sq (*Tmr* D2), Akadimias St, Vassilissis Sofias, Leoforos Kifissias to Kefalari and Politia (NE Athens suburb). Every 15 mins from 0600 - 0100 hrs

No. 049:   Athinas St (*Tmr* C/D3), (S of Omonia Sq), Sofokleous St, Pireos St, Sotiros St, Filonos St, to Plateia Themistokleous, Piraeus port. Every 10 mins, 24 hours a day. Green Bus.

No. 051:   Off Ag Konstantinou (*Tmr* C2/3), W of Omonia Sq, corner of Menandrou/Vitara Streets, Kolonou St, Platonos St (W Athens suburb). *NB This is the bus that connects to the 100 Kifissou St (Tmr A2), a main bus terminal.*

No. 115: Leoforos Olgas (*Tmr* E5/6), Leoforos Sygrou, Leoforos Possidonos (coast road) to Varkiza. Every 20 mins, 24 hours a day

No. 118: Leoforos Olgas (*Tmr* E5/6), Leoforos Sygrou, Leoforos Possidonos (coast road) to Vouliagmeni. Every 20 mins from 1245 - 2015 hrs

No. 122: Leoforos Olgas, Leoforos Sygrou, Leoforos Possidonos (coast road) to Voula. Every 20 mins from 0530 - 2400 hrs

No. 132: Othonos St (Syntagma Sq) (*Tmr* E5), Filellinon St, Leoforos Amalias, Leoforos Sygrou to Edem (SSE Athens suburb). Every 20 mins from 0530 - 1900 hrs

No. 224: Polygono (N Athens suburb), 28 Ikosiokto Oktovriou (Patission) St, Kaningos Sq, Vassilissis Sofias, Democratias St, (Kessariani, E Athens suburb). Every 20 mins from 0500 - 2400 hrs

No. 230: Ambelokipi (E Athens suburb), Leoforos Alexandras, Ippokratous St, Akadimias St, Syntagma Sq, Leoforos Amalias, Dionysiou Areopagitou St, Apostolou Pavlou, Thission. Every 10 mins from 0500 - 2320 hrs

No. 510: Kaningos Sq (*Tmr* D2), Akadimias St, Ippokratous St, Leoforos Alexandras, Leoforos Kifissias to Dionyssos (NE Athens suburb). Every 20 mins from 0530 - 2250 hrs

No. 527: Kaningos Sq (*Tmr* D2), Akadimias St, Leoforos Alexandras, Leoforos Kifissias to Amarousoion (NE Athens suburb). Every 15 mins from 0615 - 2215 hrs.

† The Athens-Attica bus services detailed above cover the city and its environs. The rest of Greece is served by:
1) KTEL: A pool of bus operators working through one company from two terminals: 260 Liossion St* and 100 Kifissou St**.
2) OSE (the State Railway Company) from an aggressive bus terminal alongside the main railway station of Stathmos Peloponissou. Apart from the domestic services, there is a terminal for other European capitals including Paris, Istanbul and Munich.

*Liossion St (*Tmr* D2) is to the east of Stathmos Peloponissou Railway Station. The terminus serves Halkida, Edipsos, Kimi, Delphi, Amfissa, Kamena Vourla, Larissa, Thiva, Trikala (Meteora) Livadia, Lamia. *See* the bus route No. 024 to get to the terminus.
**Kifissou St is to the west of Omonia Sq, beyond the 'steam railway' lines, across Leoforos Konstantinoupolos and up Odhos Platonos. The terminus serves Patras, Pirgos (Olympia), Nafplio (Mikines), Andritsena (Vasses), Kalamata, Sparti (Mistras), Githio (Diros), Tripolis, Messolongi, Igoumenitsa, Preveza, Ioanina, Corfu, Zakynthos, Cephalonia, Lefkas, Kozani, Kastoria, Florina, Grevena, Veria, Naoussa, Edessa, Seres, Kilkis, Kavala, Drama, Komotini, Korinthos, Kranidi, Xilokastro. *See* the bus route No. 051 to get to the terminus.

For any bus services connecting to the islands detailed in this guide, refer to the relevant Mainland Ports and Island chapters.

CAMPING *See* **Accommodation.**

CAR HIRE As any other capital city, numerous offices, the majority of which are lined up in the smarter areas and squares, such as Syntagma Sq and Leoforos Amalias. Typical is

Pappas, 44 Leoforos Amalias   Tel. 3220087

CAR REPAIR Help and advice can be obtained by contacting
The Automobile and Touring Club of Greece (ELPA) at 2 Messogion St (*Tmr* I3)   Tel. 779-1615.
For immediate, emergency attention dial 104.
    There are dozens of back-street car repairers, breakers and spare-part shops parallel to Leoforos Sygrou, in the area between the Olympic office and the Temple of Olympian Zeus.

CHEMIST *See* **Medical Care.**

CINEMAS There are a large number of out-door cinemas. Do not worry about a language barrier, the majority of the films have English dialogue with Greek subtitles.
    Aigli in the Zappeion is a must and is situated at the south end of the National Garden. Other cinemas are bunched together in Stadiou, Panepistimiou and 28 Ikosiokto Oktovriou (Patission) Streets.

CLUBS, BARS & DISCOS Why leave home? But if you must, there are enough to satiate the most voracious desires.

COMMERCIAL SHOPPING AREAS A very large street market ranges up Odhos Athinas (*Tmr* C3/4), Sokratous St and the associated side streets from Ermou St almost all the way up to Omonia Sq during the daylight hours. After dark the shutters are drawn down, the stalls canvassed over and the ladies of the night appear.

Plateia Kotzia (*Tmr* D3) spawns a flower market on Sundays whilst the Parliament Building side of Vassilissis Sofias (*Tmr* E4) is lined with smart flower stalls that open daily.

Monastiraki Sq (*Tmr* 5.C4) and the various streets that radiate off are abuzz, specialising in widely differing aspects of commercial and tourist trade. Odhos Areos contains a plethora of leather goods shops; the near end of Ifestou is edged by stall upon stall of junk and tourist 'omit-abilia' (the forgettable memorabilia); Pandrossou lane contains a better class of shop and stall selling sandals, pottery and smarter 'memorabilia' while the square itself has a number of hawkers and their handcarts.

The smart department stores are conveniently situated in or around Syntagma Sq, and the main streets that radiate off the square including Ermou, Stadiou and Panepistimiou.

DENTISTS & DOCTORS *See* **Medical Care.**

EMBASSIES

Australia: 15 Messogion Av.	Tel. 775-7650
Canada: 4 Ioannou Gennadiou St.	Tel. 723-9511
Great Britain: 1 Ploutarchou and Ypsilantou Sts.	Tel. 723-6211
Ireland: 7 Vassileos Konstantinou.	Tel. 723-2711
New Zealand: 15-17 An. Tsoha St.	Tel. 641-0311
South Africa: 124 Kifissias/Iatridou.	Tel. 692-2125
USA: 91 Vassilissis Sofias.	Tel. 721-2951
Denmark: 15 Philikis Etairias Sq.	Tel. 724-9315
Finland: 1 Eratosthenous and Vas Konstantinou Streets.	Tel. 751-5064
Norway: 7 Vassileos Konstantinou St.	Tel. 724-6173
Sweden: 7 Vassileos Konstantinou St.	Tel. 722-4504
Belgium: 3 Sekeri St.	Tel. 361-7886
France: 7 Vassilissis Sofias.	Tel. 361-1663
German Federal Republic: 3 Karaoli/Dimitriou Sts.	Tel. 36941
Netherlands: 5-7 Vassilissis Konstantinou	Tel. 723-9701

HAIRDRESSERS No problems with sufficient in the main shopping areas.

HOSPITALS *See* **Medical Care.**

LAUNDRETTES (*Tmr* 13.D5) There may be others but . . . this '**Self Service, The only Coin-Op in Athens**' is signposted from Kidathineon St (proceeding towards Syntagma Sq). At the far end of Plateia Plaka turn right down Angelou Geronda across Dedalou and the laundrette is on the right hand side. A machine load costs 200 drs, 9 mins of dryer 20 drs and powder 50 drs. In respect of the detergent, why not pop out to Kidathineon St and purchase a small packet of **Tide** for 38 drs. Open in the summer daily 0800-2100 hrs. Note that my lavatorial obsession would not be satisfied without mentioning that there is a public WC sited on Plateia Plaka.

LOST PROPERTY The main office is situated at 14 Messogion St (*Tmr* I2/3) Tel. 770-5771. But contact the relevant lost property office if you mislay anything, first asking the Tourist police for the correct address. Each form of transport has its own lost property office, as do the city authorities.

It is true to say that you are far more likely to 'lose' personal belongings to other tourists, than to Greeks.

LUGGAGE STORE A number of offices where one would expect them on Filellinon and Nikis Streets off Syntagma Sq. Charges from 50 drs per case per day.

MEDICAL CARE
Chemists/Pharmacies (Farmakio — ΦAPMAKEIO) Identified by a green or red cross on a white background. Normal opening hours and a rota operates to give a 'duty' chemist cover.

Dentists & Doctors Ask at the First Aid Centre for the address of the School of Dentistry where free treatment is available. Both Dentists and Doctors advertise widely and there is no shortage of practitioners.

First Aid Centre (KAT) 21 Tritis Septemvriou St (*Tmr* 14.D2), beyond the Chalkokondili turning, parallel to 28 Ikosiokto Oktovriou, and on the left. Tel. 150

Hospital (*Tmr* 15 G4)
Do not go direct to a hospital (first to GO!). No seriously folks, initially attend the First Aid Centre. If necessary they will direct a seriously ill patient to the correct destination.
Medical Emergency: Tel. 166

METRO/ELEKTRIKOS (HΣAM) The Athens underground or subway system, which operates underground in the heart of the city and over-ground for the rest of the journey. It is a simple one track layout from Kifissia (north-east Athens suburb) to Piraeus (south-west Athens port), and represents marvellous value with two rate fares of 20 and 40 drs. You must have the requisite coin to obtain a ticket from the machine prior to gaining access to the platforms.

Everyone is most helpful and will, if the ticket machine 'frightens' you, show how it should be operated. Beware, select the ticket value first, then put the coin in the slot (I think) and keep your ticket to hand in to the ticket collector at the journey's end. The service operates between 0505 and 0015 hrs and travel before 0800 hrs is free. Keep an eye out for the old-fashioned wooden carriages.

Station Stops There are 20 which include Kifissia (NE suburb), Stathmos Atiki (for the main railway stations), Plateia Victorias (N Athens), Omonia Sq, Monastiraki Sq (Plaka), Pl Thission (for the Acropolis) and (Piraeus) Port. From the outside, the Piraeus terminus is rather difficult to locate, the entrance being in the left-hand corner of what appears to be an oldish waterfront building.

MUSIC & DANCING See **Clubs, Bars & Discos.**

NTOG (EOT) The headquarters of the National Tourist Organisation (NTOG or in Greek, EOT — Ellinikos Organismos Tourismou — **EMHNIKOΣ OPΓANIΣMOΣ TOYPIΣMOY**) is on the 5th floor at 2 Amerikis St, near Syntagma Sq, but this office does not normally handle the usual tourist enquiries.

The Information desk, from whence maps and some advice, information folders, bus and boat schedules and hotel facts may be obtained, is situated just inside, on the left, of the foyer of the

National Bank of Greece (*Tmr* 3.D/E4) 2 Karageorgi Servias, Syntagma Sq
  Tel. 322-2545.

Do not hope to obtain anything other than the usual pamphlets, it would be unrealistic to expect personal attention from staff besieged by wave upon wave of tourists of every hue, race and colour. Open Monday - Saturday, 0800 - 2000 hrs.

A note of caution concerns the agencies inability to admit to their being any E class hotels.

There is also an office conveniently situated at the East Airport.

OPENING HOURS

(Summer months) These are only a guide-line and apply to Athens (as well as the larger cities).

Note that in country and village areas, it is more likely that shops will be open Monday-Saturday for over 12 hours a day, and on Sundays, holidays and Saints days, for a few hours either side of midday. The afternoon siesta will usually be taken between 1300/1400 hrs and 1500/1700 hrs.

Trade Stores & Chemists Monday, Wednesday and Saturday 0800-1430 hrs. Tuesday, Thursday and Friday 0800-1300 hrs and 1700-2030 hrs.

Food Stores Monday, Wednesday and Saturday 0800-1500 hrs. Tuesday, Thursday and Friday 0800-1400 hrs and 1730-2030 hrs.

Art & Gift Shops Weekdays 0800-2100 hrs. Sundays (Monastiraki area) 0930-1445 hrs.

Restaurants, Pastry Shops, Cafes & Dairy Shops Seven days a week.

Museums *See* the individual museums.

Public Services (including Banks) *See* the relevant subheading.

OTE There are OTE offices at 85, 28 Ikosiokto Oktovriou/Patission St (*Tmr* 16.D1) (open 24 hrs a day), 15 Stadiou St (*Tmr* 17.D4) (open Monday to Friday 0700-2400 hrs, Saturday and Sunday 0800-2400 hrs), 53 Solonos (*Tmr* E3/4) and 7 Kratinou (Plateia Kotzai) (*Tmr* D3) open between 0800 and 2200 hrs. There is also an office on Athinas St (*Tmr* C3).

PHARMACIES *See* **Medical Care.**

PLACES OF INTEREST

Parliament Building (*Tmr* E4/5) Syntagma Sq. The Greek equivalent of the British changing of the Guard at Buckingham Palace. The special guards are spectacularly outfitted with tasselled red caps, white shirts (blouses do I hear?), coloured waistcoats, a skirt, white tights, knee-garters and boots topped off with pom-poms. The ceremony is officially at 1100 hrs on Sunday morning but seems to kick off at about 1045 hrs. Incidentally there is a band thrown in for good measure.

Museums:

Seasons are split as follows: Winter: 1st November - 31st March; Summer: 1st April - 31st October.

Museums are closed on: 1st January, 25th March, Good Friday, Easter Day and Christmas Day.

Sunday hours are kept on Epiphany, Ash Monday, Easter Saturday, Easter Monday, 1st May, Whit Sunday, Assumption Day, 28th October and Boxing Day. They are only open in the mornings on Christmas Eve, New Year's Eve, 2nd January, Good Thursday and Easter Tuesday.

Museums are closed Tuesday (unless otherwise indicated), admission is in the main free on Sundays and students with cards will achieve a reduction in fees.

Acropolis (*Tmr* C5). The museum exhibits finds made on the site. Of especial interest are the sixth century BC statues of Korai women.

Entrance charges are included in the entrance fee to the Acropolis site, 250 drs per head. Summer: 0730 - 1930 hrs; Sunday and holidays 0800 - 1800 hrs.

The museum is open 0730 - 1930 hrs; Tuesdays 1100 - 1700 hrs; Sundays and holidays, 0800 - 1800 hrs.

Benaki (*Tmr* E/F4). On the corner of Vassilissis Sofias and Koubari (Koumbari) St, close by the Plateia Kolonaki. A very interesting variety of exhibits made up from private collections. Particularly diverting is a collection of national costumes.

Summer: daily 0830 - 1400 hrs. Entrance 100 drs.

Byzantine (*Tmr* F4/5) 22 Vassilissis Sofias. As you would think from the name — Byzantine art.
Summer: daily 0800 - 1900 hrs; Sunday and holidays, 0800 - 1800 hrs. Closed Mondays. Entrance 150 drs.

Goulandris, 13 Levidou St, Kifissia, N Athens. Natural history.
Summer: daily 0900 - 1300 and 1700 - 2000 hrs. Closed Fridays. Entrance 70 drs.

Kanelloupoulos (*Tmr* C5) On the corner of Theorias and Panos Sts, (Plaka). A smaller version of the Benaki Museum at the Monastiraki end of Adrianou St.
Summer: daily 0845 - 1500; Sunday and holidays 0930 - 1430 hrs. Entrance 100 drs which is charged Sundays and holidays.

Keramikos (*Tmr* B4), 148 Ermou St. Finds from Keramikos cemetery.
Summer: daily 0845 - 1500 hrs; Sunday and holidays, 0930 - 1430 hrs. The museum is closed Thursdays. Entrance to the site and museum 100 drs.

National Gallery & Alexandros Soutzos (*Tmr* F/G4/5), 46 Vassileos Konstantinou/ Sofias. Mainly 19th and 20th century Greek paintings.
Summer: 0900 - 1500 hrs; Sunday and holidays 1000 - 1400 hrs. Closed Mondays. Admission free.

National Historical & Ethnological (*Tmr* D4), Kolokotroni Square, off Stadiou St. Greek history and the War of Independence.
Summer: 0900 - 1400 hrs; Sunday and holidays 0900 - 1300 hrs. Closed Mondays. Entrance 100 drs, Thursday free.

National Archaeological (*Tmr* D/E2), 1 Tositsa St, off 28 Ikosiokto Oktovriou/Patission St. The largest and possibly the most important Greek museum, covering a wide variety of exhibits. A must if you are a museum buff.
Summer: 0800 - 1900 hrs; Sunday and holidays 0800 - 1800 hrs. Closed Mondays. Entrance 200 drs, includes entrance to the Santorini and Numismatic exhibitions (*See* below).

Numismatic In the same building as the National Archaeological. Displaying, as you would imagine, a collection of Greek coins, spanning the ages.
Summer: 0830 - 1330 hrs; Sunday and holidays 0900 - 1400 hrs.
Also housed in the same building are:
The Epigraphical Collection: Summer: 0830 - 1330 hrs; Sunday and holidays 0900 - 1400 hrs.
Santorini Exhibits: Summer: 0800 - 1900 hrs; Sunday and holidays 0800 - 1800 hrs. Closed Monday.
and
The Casts and Copies Exhibition: Summer: 0800 - 1900 hrs; Sunday and holidays 0800 - 1800 hrs.

Popular Art (*Tmr* D5), 17 Kidathineon St, The Plaka. Folk art, folklore and popular art.
Summer: 0845 - 1500 hrs; Sundays and holidays 0930 - 1430 hrs. Closed Mondays. Entrance free.

War (*Tmr* F4/5) 2 Rizari St, off Leoforos Vassilissis Sofias. Warfare exhibits covering a wide variety of subjects.
Summer: daily 0900 - 1400 hrs. Closed Mondays. Entrance free.

Theatres & Performances. For full, up to date details enquire at the **NTOG** office (*Tmr* 3.D/E4). They should be able to hand out a pamphlet giving a precise timetable for the year. As a guide the following are performed year in, year out:

Son et Lumière. From the Pnyx hill-side, a *Son et Lumière* features the Acropolis. The English performance starts at 2100 hrs every evening, except when the moon is full, and takes 45 minutes. There are French versions at 2200 hrs daily except Tuesdays and

Fridays when a German commentary is enacted. Tickets are available for 180 drs (students 70 drs) at the entrance of the church, Ag Dimitros Lombardiaris, on the way to the show. Catch a No. 230 bus along Dionysiou Areopagitou St, getting off one stop beyond the Odeion (Theatre) of Herodes Atticus and follow the sign-posted path on the left-hand side.

Athens Festival. Takes place in the restored and beautiful Odeion of Herodes Atticus, built in approximately AD 160 as a Roman theatre, seating about 5000 people and situated at the foot of the south-west corner of the Acropolis.

The festival lasts from early June to the middle of September, and consists of a series of plays, ballet, concerts and opera. The performances usually commence at 2100 hrs and tickets, which are on sale up to 10 days before the event, are obtainable from the Theatre or from the **Athens Festival booking office**, 4 Stadiou St, Tel. 322-1459.

Dora Stratou Theatre.A short stroll away on Mouseion or Hill of Muses. On the summit stands the Monument of the Filopapou (Philopappos) and nearby the Dora Stratou Theatre, where an internationally renowned troupe of folk dancers, dressed in traditional costumes, perform a series of Greek dances and songs. Performances here are timed to coincide with the ending of the Son et Lumière, on the Pynx. The show, produced between early May and the end of September, costs between 300 and 430 drs per head, starts at about 2215 hrs, lasts approximately one hour, and is worth a visit.

Lycabettus Theatre. On the north-east side of Lycabettus Hill (Lykavitos, Likavittos, Lykabettos, etc, etc). Concerts and theatrical performances take place in the hill-side open-air theatre between the middle of June and the first week of September from 2100 hrs. Tickets can be purchased from the theatre box office one hour before the event or from the **Athens Festival booking office** referred to above.

The Hellenic-American Union puts on a series of concerts and plays (*See* **Klafthmonos Sq.**in the introductory paragraphs).

POLICE *See* **Tourist Police.**

POST OFFICES (Tachidromio — ΤΑΧΙΔΡΟΜΕΙΟΝ) Weekday opening hours, as a guide, are 0800 to 1300 hrs.

The Central Post Office is at 100 Eolou St (*Tmr* 18.D3) close by Omonia Sq and is open Monday - Friday, 0730 - 2030 hrs and Saturday, 0730 - 1500 hrs.

Branch offices are situated on the corner of Othonos and Nikis Streets (Syntagma Sq); at the Omonia Sq underground in the Metro concourse and Dionysiou Areopagitou St on the corner of Tzireon St (*Tmr* D6).

The telephone and telegraph system is run by a separate state organisation. *See* **OTE.**

PHOTOGRAPHY (Fotografion - ΦΩΤΟΙΓΡΑΦΕΙΟΝ) If you require photographs for various membership cards, there is an instant photo-booth in the underground concourse beneath Omonia Sq (*Tmr* 2.D3).

SHOPPING HOURS *See* **Opening Hours.**

SPORTS FACILITIES

Golf. There is an 18 hole course, the **Glifada Golf Club** close by the East(ern) Airport. Changing rooms, restaurant and refreshment bar.

Swimming. There is a Swimming (and Tennis) Club on Leoforos Olgas (*Tmr* 19.E6), opposite the Zappeion Public Gardens.

The *Hilton Hotel* (*Tmr* G4) has a swimming pool but, if you are not staying there, it will cost the price of a (expensive) meal.
See **Beaches.**

Tennis. There are courts at all the NTOG beaches as well as at the Ag Kosmas athletics centre, close by the West airport.

TAXIS (TAΞI). Used extensively, although a little expensive, but the drivers are, now, generally without scruples. Fares are metered and are costed at about 20 drs per kilometre, but are subject to various surcharges including 10 drs for each piece of baggage, 5-10 drs for hours between midnight and 0600, 100 drs per hour of waiting time and 5 drs for picking up at, or delivering to, public transport facilities.

When standing at a taxi rank they must take your fare, but are not obliged to do so when cruising. The sign **EΛEYΘEPON** indicates they are free for hire.

TELEPHONE See **OTE.**

TOURIST OFFICE/AGENCIES See **NTOG** & **Travel Agents.**

TOURIST POLICE (*Tmr* 20 D6) I understand despite the reorganisation of the service that the Athens headquarters is to remain in operation. They are situated at 7 Sygrou (Leoforos Sygrou/Syngrou/Singrou Av). Open daily 0800 - 2100 hrs, Tel. 923-9224.
Tourist information in English is available from the Tourist police on the telephone, Tel. 171
There are also offices at **Larissis Railway Station**, open 0700 - 2300 hrs, Tel. 821-3574 and the **East Airport**, open 0600 - 2400 hrs, Tel. 981-4093.

TOILETS Apart from the various bus terminii and the railway stations there is a super public toilet on the south-east corner of Syntagma Sq as there is a pretty grim squatty in the Omonia Sq metro concourse.

The Plaka is well endowed with one at Plateia Plaka, (on Odhos Kidathineon) and another on the Plateia Agora at the other end of Odhos Adrianou. Visitors to Mt Lycabettus will not be caught short and the toilets are spotless.

TRAINS They arrive at (or depart from) either (a) Larissis Station (Stathmos No. 1) or (b) Peloponissou Station (Stathmos No. 2).

(a) Larissis Station (Stathmos No 1) (*Tmr* B/C1)   Tel. 821-3882
The main, more modern station of the two. Connections to the Western European services and the northern provinces of Central Greece, Thessaly, Macedonia and Thrace.

The National Bank of Greece has a branch in the station building open daily between 0800 - 2000 hrs. Through to the front of the station there is a pavement cafe-bar (a coffee 56 drs) and an elongated square, well more a widening of the road. With the station behind one there is to the right, across the concourse, on the corner, the:-

Hotel Lefkos Pirgos (Class E), 27 Neof. Metaxa/Stathos Larissis   Tel. 821-3765
Directions: As above.
Seedy looking with double rooms sharing a bathroom starting at 725 drs, rising to 930 drs.

Hotel Nana (Class C), 29 Neof. Metaxa   Tel. 884-2211
Directions: Alongside the *Hotel Lefkos Pirgos.*
Smarter, well it is C class, with the charges reflecting this eminence. A double room en suite starts off at 1575 drs but for the period between 16th March - 31st October this becomes 1945 drs.

Directly opposite the main station entrance is the
Hotel Oscar (Class B), 25 Samou/Filadelfias   Tel. 883-4215
Directions: As above.
I hardly dare detail the room rates which for a double kick off at 2515 drs rising to 2960 drs, en suite naturally.

Even early and late in the summer a number of the hardier stretch out on the pavements (and at the *Hotel Oscar's* rates I'm not surprised). Arrivals, even whilst on the train, are bombarded with offers of accommodation, so much so that the touts are a nuisance.

Buses: Trolley-bus No 1 pulls up to the right of the station as do the Nos 2 and 4. The fare to Syntagma Sq is 20 drs.

Advance Booking Office (*Tmr* D/E4)
81 Panepistimiou (Venizelou), opposite the University buildings.

(b) Peloponissou Station (Stathmos No 2) (*Tmr* B1/2)　　　　　Tel. 513-1601
The station for trains to the Peloponnese, the ferry connections for some of the Ionian islands and international ferries to Italy from Patras.

Advance Booking Office (*Tmr* C/D2/3) 18 Ag Konstantinou (Ay Konstandinou), west from Omonia Sq.

Tickets: (Peloponissou Station) The concept behind the acquisition of a ticket is similar to that of a lottery. On buying a ticket, a compartment seat is also allocated, and in theory this is a splendid scheme, but in practice the idea breaks down in a welter of bad-tempered arguments over whom is occupying whose seat. Manners and quaint old-fashioned habits of giving up one's seat to older people and ladies are best avoided. I write this from the bitter experience of offering my seat to elderly Greek ladies only for their husbands to immediately fill the vacant position. Not what one had in mind! Find your seat and stick to it like glue and if you have made a mistake feign madness, admit to being a foreigner, but do not budge.

The mechanics of buying a ticket takes place in organised bedlam. The ticket-office 'traps' open half an hour prior to the train's departure. Scenes reminiscent of a cup-final crowd develop, with prospective travellers pitching about within the barriers of the ticket hatch, and all this in the space of about 10 metres by 10 metres. To add to the difficulty, at Peloponissou Station, there are two hatch 'slots' and it is anybody's guess which one to select. It really is best to try and steal a march on this 'extra-curricula' activity, diving for a hatch whenever one opens up.

When booking a return journey train ticket to Europe and travelling via Italy ensure the ticket is from Patras, not Athens. (Yes Patras). Then purchase a separate Athens to Patras train ticket which will ensure a traveller gets a seat. A voyager boarding the train with an open ticket will almost surely have to stand for almost the whole of the 4 hour journey. Most Athens-Patras journeys seems to attract an 'Express' train surcharge of some 40 drs which is charged by the train ticket collector.

Incidentally, the general architecture of the Peloponissou building is delightful, especially the ceiling of the main booking-office hall, which is located centrally, under the main clock face. To the left, on entering the building, there is a glass-fronted information box with all the train times listed on the window. The staff manning this desk are extremely helpful and speak sufficient English to pose no problems in communication (the very opposite of the lack-lustre disinterest shown at the NTOG desk in the National Bank of Greece, on Syntagma Sq).

Trains General
Toilets. The station toilets usually, well always, lack toilet paper.

Sustenance (on the trains) An attendant brings inexpensive drinks and snacks around from time to time and, at major stations on the route, hot snacks are available from platform trolleys.

Railway Head Office (*Tmr* C2)
Hellenic Railways Organisation (OSE) 1-3 Karolou St.　　　　　Tel. 522-2491
　The far, west end of Ag Konstantinou from Omonia Sq.

Provisions. Shopping in the area of the railway stations is a bit of a task. A bread and a very good pie shop are located in an area to the east of the railway. From Larissis station wander off along Filadelfias into Livaniou or down Liossion St. From Peloponissou station walk down the station approach road southwards, over the railway bridge and up Mezonos or Favierou Streets.

Access to the stations

Bus/Trolley-bus. From the Airport, take the Olympic bus to the down-town terminal at 96-100 Leoforos Sygrou (which for 45 drs is extremely good value). Then catch a bus (Nos. 133, 040, 132, 155, 903 and 161 amongst others) from across the street to Syntagma Sq and a No. 1 trolley-bus to the station via Omonia Sq. It is also possible to walk west from Leoforos Sygrou to the parallel street of Odhos Dimitrakopoulou and catch a No. 1 trolley-bus all the way to the stations.

From Piraeus Port catch the No. 40 (green) bus on Leoforos Vassileos Konstantinou (parallel to the quay) to Syntagma Sq, or the No. 049 from Plateia Themistokleous to Athinas St, close by Omonia Sq.

Metro. The metro station for both railway stations is **ATIKI** from whence ('undergrounding' from the South) dismount and turn right down into the underpass to come out the far or west side of the station on Odhos Liossion. Turn left and walk to the large irregular Plateia Attikis (with the *Hotel Lydia* on the right) and proceed down Domokou St, the road that exits half right on the far side of the square and which spills into Plateia Deligiani edged by Stathmos Larissis. A more long-winded alternative is to take the metro to Omonia Sq, walk west along Ag Konstantinou to Karaiskaki Sq and then up Odhos Deligianni or catch a No. 1 trolley-bus.

Taxi.A taxi is a reasonable indulgence if in a hurry although it must be noted that in the crowded traffic conditions of Athens it can often be quicker to walk than catch a cab.

Station to Station. To get from one to the other, say Larissis to Peloponissou it is necessary to turn right out of the station and, after about 5 mins walk, turn right again over the bridge spanning the railway lines that angles back and round to the right onto the forecourt or plateia in front of Peloponissou. Almost, but not quite, adjacent as some guides put it, if 200 m on a very hot day, laden down with cases seems contiguous.

TRAIN TIMETABLES — Peloponissou Station It is easy to read the timetable and come to the conclusion that a large number of trains are leaving the station at the same time. On seeing the single-line track, a newcomer cannot be blamed for feeling apprehensive that it will prove difficult to select the correct carriages.

The mystification arises from the fact that the trains are detailed separately from Athens to Corinthos, Mikines, Argos, Tripolis, Pirgos and etc, etc. There is no mention that the railway line is a circular layout, with single trains circumscribing the route and that each place name is simply a stop on the journey.

Making changes for branch lines can be 'exciting'! Stations are labelled in demotic script and there is no understandable announcement from the guard, thus it is easy to fail to make an exit on cue!

Athens : (Stathmos Peloponissou)	Depart	0641, 0830, 1022, 1310, 1542, 2147 hrs
Patras Port :	Arrive	1058, 1215, 1459, 1700, 1959, 0203 hrs

Fares: Athens to Patras 390 drs.

TRAVEL AGENTS Tourist offices for tickets for almost anything to almost anywhere include:

ABC   59 Stadiou St. Tel. 321-1381

CHAT   4 Stadiou St. Tel. 322-2886
Key Tours 2 Ermou St. Tel. 323-3756
Viking*   3 Filellinon St. Tel. 322-9383
*Probably the agency most highly regarded by students for prices and variety.

International Student & Youth Travel Service (SYTS) 11 Nikis St.   Tel. 323-3767
For FIYTO membership. Second floor, open Monday - Friday 0830 - 1900 hrs and
Saturday from 0900 to 1400 hrs.

Filellinon and the parallel street of Odhos Nikis to the west of Syntagma Sq are jam
packed with tourist agencies and student organisations including one or two express
coach and train fare companies.

YOUTH HOSTEL ASSOCIATION *See* **Accommodation.**

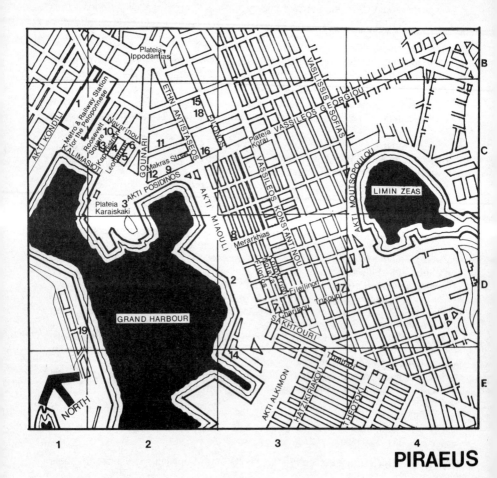

PIRAEUS

Illustration 7

10 PIRAEUS (PIREAS, PIREEFS) & OTHER MAINLAND PORTS

Fortune and hope farewell! I've found the port you've done with me; go now with others sport.

From a Greek epigram

Tel. prefix 01.

The Port of Athens (Illustrations 7, 8 & 9) and usual ferry-boat departure point for the Cyclades and, incidentally, most other Aegean islands. A confusing Town on first acquaintance, but fairly neat and tidy, very unlike the Piraeus portrayed in the film *Never on Sunday*. The bawdy seaport cafes, tavernas and seedy waterfront have been replaced by smart shipping offices, respectable banks and tree planted thoroughfares, squares and parks.

Arrival at Piraeus will usually be by Metro or bus if coming from inland, or by ferry-boat if arriving by sea. (Well, it would be a long tiring swim, wouldn't it?)

ARRIVAL BY METRO

Piraeus Metro Station (*Tmr* 1.C1/2), the end of the line, is hidden away in the corner of a large but rather inconspicuous building, flanked by Roosevelt Sq. It could well be a warehouse, an empty shell of an office block, in fact almost anything but a Metro terminus. Passengers emerge opposite the quayside, at the north end of the waterfront. If taking a Ferry almost immediately, it is probably best to turn right out of the entrance, follow the quay round to the left and fall into one of the three or so cafe bars on the right-hand side, making a temporary headquarters. The importance of establishing a shore-base, or bridgehead, will become increasingly apparent whilst attempts are made to locate the required ferry-boat departure point. To obtain tickets turn to the left (facing the harbour) out of the Metro station and follow the quayside. First major landmark is Karaiskaki (or Akti Tzelepi) Sq (*Tmr* C/D2), fronted by shipping office blocks, the left-hand one of which is surmounted by a neon **Coke** sign and another with the sign **Kaiser Henninger**. Proceed onwards with the seafront to the right and the quayside buildings across the road to the left, between the Streets of Gounari and Ethni Antistaseos (*Tmr* C2). The Port police are located in a quay shed and must be regarded as favourites to dispense fairly accurate information in respect of the Ferry-boats. Any information received is best tucked away for future comparison with the rest of the advice acquired.

ARRIVAL BY BUS

From Syntagma Sq, Athens, Bus No. 040 arrives at Korai Sq (*Tmr* C3). Well in truth that is rather simplistic. For a start the bus is absolutely crammed early morning and it can prove very difficult to know one's whereabouts which, as the bus hurtles on down Piraeus peninsula, does matter. The first marker is that at the port end of the ¾ hr journey the bus runs parallel to the Metro lines. The second is crossing a wide avenue at right angles (Leoforos Vassileos Georgiou) after which signs for the Archaeological Museum indicate it is time to bale out.

Back at Plateia Korai, north-west along Leoforos Vassileos Georgiou (Yeoryiou), leads to the Main (Grand or Central) Harbour (*Tmr* D2), south-east towards Limin Zeas (Pasalimani) (*Tmr* C/D4) and east towards Limin Mounikhias (Tourkolimano) (*Tmr* B5), the two small marina harbours.

From Omonia Sq, Athens, Bus No. 049 arrives at Ethni Antistaseos (*Tmr* C2); from the East airport, Bus No. 19 arrives at Karaiskaki Sq (*Tmr* C/D2), opposite Gounari St. Karaiskaki or Akti Tzelepi Square is a Main Bus terminal.

Another service (Bus No. 101) arrives at Theotoki St (*Tmr* E4/F3) from whence head towards Sakhtouri St and turn left in a northerly direction to reach the western end of the quay front

ARRIVAL BY FERRY-BOAT

Reorientate using the above information bearing in mind that ferries dock all the way round the Grand Harbour from the area of the Metro station (*Tmr* 1.C1/2) as far down as the Olympic office (*Tmr* 8.D3).

THE ACCOMMODATION & EATING OUT

The Accommodation General remarks as for Athens. Although I have never had to doss (or camp) out in Piraeus, I am advised that it is not to be recommended. There are just too many (desperate?) disparate characters wandering about

Close by the Metro Station.

Hotel Ionion (*Tmr* 4.C2) (Class C) 10 Kapodistrion   Tel. 417-0992
Directions: Turn left from the Metro station and/or Roosevelt Sq (*Fsw*) down the quay road, Kalimasioti St, and turn left at the first turning. The Hotel, half-way up on the right, is noticeable by the prominent sign promising **Family Hotel and from now on Economical Prices**. But is it with doubles from 1751 drs?

The Delfini (*Tmr* 5.C2) (Class C) 7, Leoharous St   Tel. 412-3512
Directions: As above, but the second turning left and doubles from 1700 drs.

Hotel Helektra (*Tmr* 6.C2) (Class E) 12 Navarinou   Tel. 417-7057
Directions: At the top of Leoharous St, turn right on to Navarinou St. The *Helektra* is at the end of the block.
During the season doubles sharing the bathroom cost 900 drs.

By following the quay road of Akti Posidinos round to the right, along the waterfront of Akti Miaouli, towards the Custom's House (*Tmr* 14.D/E3), close by the Church of Ag Nikoloas, leads to the bottom of Leoforos Charilaou Trikoupi (*Tmr* D3). This street runs south-east and is amply furnished with cheaper Hotels including the following:-

Capitol Hotel (*Tmr* 7.D3) (Class C) Ch. Trikoupi/147 Filonos Sts   Tel. 452-4911
Directions: As above.
A double en suite costs 1064 drs.

Glaros Hotel (Class C) 4 Ch. Trikoupi St   Tel. 452-7887
Double rooms start at 900 drs with breakfast costing 150 drs.

Serifos Hotel (Class C) 5 Ch. Trikoupi St   Tel. 452-4967
A double room en suite from 1060 drs.

Santorini Hotel (Class C) 6 Ch. Trikoupi St   Tel. 452-2147
Prices as for the *Serifos Hotel*.

Homeridion Hotel (Class B) 32 Ch. Trikoupi St   Tel. 451-9811
Rather expensive with a double room during the season costing 2900 drs.

Forming a junction with Leoforos Charilaou Trikoupi, to the left, is Notara St on which is sited the:-

Faros Hotel (Class D) 140 Notara St   Tel. 452-6317
Directions: As above.
More down-to-earth with a double room en suite from 930 drs.

Again at right angles to Leoforos Charilaou Trikoupi, is Koloktroni St on which are situated the following hotels:-

Park Hotel (Class B) 103 Kolokotroni St   Tel. 452-4611
Directions: As above.
Double rooms en suite from 2200 drs.

Aris Hotel (Class D) 117 Kolokotroni St   Tel. 452-0487
A double room sharing from 840 drs and en suite 1050 drs.

Leading off tò the left again, is Vassileos Konstantinou whereon:-

Noufara Hotel (Class B) 45 Vassileos Konstantinou   Tel. 411-5541
Doubles start at 2845 drs. (Phew!)

Savoy Hotel (Class B) 93 Vassileos Konstantinou   Tel. 413-1102
Guests will have to be flush with a double room costing 3050 drs.

From Vassileos Konstantinou, turn right or south-east off at Plateia Korai along Leoforos Vassileos Georgiou (Vassileos Yeoriou). To the left is the:-

Diogenis Hotel (Class B) 27 Leoforos Vassileos Georgiou   Tel. 412 5471
Directions: As above.
A few draohmae less than the *Savoy* at 2950 drs.

The Eating Out For eating out read the Athens comments as a general guide. Piraeus is not noted for outstanding rendezvous. There are numerous restaurants, tavernas and cafes along the quayside roads, as well as Akti Moutsopoulou (*Tmr* C3/D4) and Akti Koumoundourou (*Tmr* B5) encircling (respectively) the Zeas and Mounikhias harbours.

On Plateia Karaiskaki, a number of cafe-bar/restaurants stretch along the quay side of the large building that dominates the square. In 1985 a white van parked up, early in the day, on the edge of the square selling small pizza's and feta cheese pies for 60 drs from the back of the vehicle.

THE A TO Z OF USEFUL INFORMATION

AIRLINE OFFICE (*Tmr* 8.D3) The Olympic office is half-way down the esplanade of Akti Miaouli, on the junction with Odhos II Merarkhias.

BANKS The most impressive is a vast, imposing emporium situated opposite the corner of the Esplanade roads of Posidonos and Miaouli (*Tmr* 9.C2).

BEACHES Between Zeas and Mounikhias Harbours, opposite Stalida island. *See* **Athens, A to Z.**

BREAD SHOPS One on Roosevelt Sq (*Tmr* 10.C2) and another on Gournari St. (*Tmr* C2).

BUSES Two buses circulate around the peninsula of Piraeus. One from Roosevelt Sq to Limin Mounikhias and on to Neon Faliron and the other from Korai Sq (*Tmr* C3) via the Naval Cadets College to Limin Zeas.

COMMERCIAL SHOPPING AREA (*Tmr* 11.C2) There is a flourishing and busy Market area behind the Bank mentioned above and between the streets of Gounari and Ethni Antistaseos. There is an excellent Supermarket on the corner of Odhos Markras Stoas, if you cannot be bothered to visit the various shops and stalls of the market. Prices in Piraeus are generally higher than elsewhere.

FERRY-BOATS Most island ferry-boats leave from the area encompassed by Akti Kondili, to the north of the main harbour, Karaiskaki Sq, Akti Posidonos and Akti Miaouli, to the west of the Main Harbour. As a general rule the Aegean Ferries, including those heading for the Cyclades Islands, depart from the area of Karaiskaki Sq. International Ferries leave from the south or far end of the Akti Miaouli quay road.

See **Chapter 3** for ferry-boat connections to the Cyclades (Illustration 3) and the individual islands for details of the actual timetables.

FERRY-BOAT TICKET OFFICES Yes well, at least they lie extremely thick on the waterfront. It may well be best to purchase tickets prior to making enquiries about the exact location of the particular ferries' departure point. Any reference to the Ferry will only be written, and known about, in Greek. The ticket vendor will at least understand English, in direct contrast to everybody else including the Port police. Ticket sellers 'lie in wait' all the way down the quayside Streets of Kalimasioti and Akti Posidinos, that is, from the Metro station, past the Gounari St turning to the bottom of Ethni Antistaseos. They tend to refer to a ship's point of departure with an airy wave of the hand.

My two favourite offices lie at opposite ends of the spectrum, as it were.

Jannis Stoulis Travel (*Tmr* 12.C2) is situated on Gounari St. The owner, who wears a rather disinterested air, is extremely efficient and speaks three languages, including English.

His fast talking 'speedy Gonzales' counterpart occupies a wall-to-wall stairway on Kalimasioti St. (*Tmr* 13.C2). My regard for the latter operator may be coloured by the fact that he was the man who sold me my first ever Island ferry-boat ticket.

There are two offices on the harbour side of the building on Plateia Karaiskaki, beyond the cafes, and an enterprising vendor of tickets lurks from early morning amongst the ferry-boat stalls on Akti Posidinos.

When searching the quayside for the correct Ferry-boat, do not go beyond the Port Offices Custom House (*Tmr* 14/E3), towards the south end of the harbour, as these berths are for cruise ships only.

NTOG Somewhat inconveniently situated on Zeas Harbour (*Tmr* C4).

OTE (*Tmr* 15.C2) North of the Post Office.

PLACES OF INTEREST
Archaeological Museum (*Tmr* 17.D3) Situated between Filellinon and Leoforos Charilaou Trikoupi Sts and reopened in the last few years. Reportedly well laid out, with the exhibits easy to identify. Opening hours Monday to Saturday, 0830 to 1230 hrs and 1600 to 1830 hrs, Sunday from 0900 to 1500 hrs. Closed Tuesday. Admission is free on Sunday.

Ag Triada (*Tmr* 16.C2) The Cathedral was rebuilt in the early 1960s, having been destroyed in 1944. Distinctive, mosaic tile finish.

Zea Theatre Adjacent to the Archaeological Museum, the remains date from about the second century BC.

Limin Zeas (Pasalimani) (*Tmr* C/D4) This semi-circular harbour is of great antiquity. Now it shelters fishing boats and caiques, provides a yacht basin for larger modern yachts, is the location for the Naval Museum of Greece, contains a Flying Dolphin terminal as well as a base for yacht charterers. Excavations have shown that, in ancient times, several hundred boat sheds radiated out around the edge of the harbour housing the Triremes, the great, three-banked warships of antiquity.

The Naval Museum of Greece Adjacent to Zeas Harbour. Varied and interesting series of exhibits through the ages.

Limin Mounikhias (Tourkolimano or Mikroliamano) (*Tmr* B5) Continuing on round the coast cliff road from **Limin Zeas**, past the bathing beach (facing the tiny island of Stalida) and the Royal Yacht Club of Greece, leads to the renowned, chatty, picturesque and again semi-circular harbour of Mounikhias. From here racing yachts are believed to have departed for events in Saronikos Bay as far back as the 4th century BC, as they do now. The quayside is ringed with tavernas, cafes and restaurants forming a backcloth to the multi-coloured sails of the assembled yachts crowded into the harbour.

The Hill of Kastela overlooks the harbour and has a modern, open-air, marble amphitheatre, wherein theatre and dance displays are staged, more especially during the **Athens Festival.**

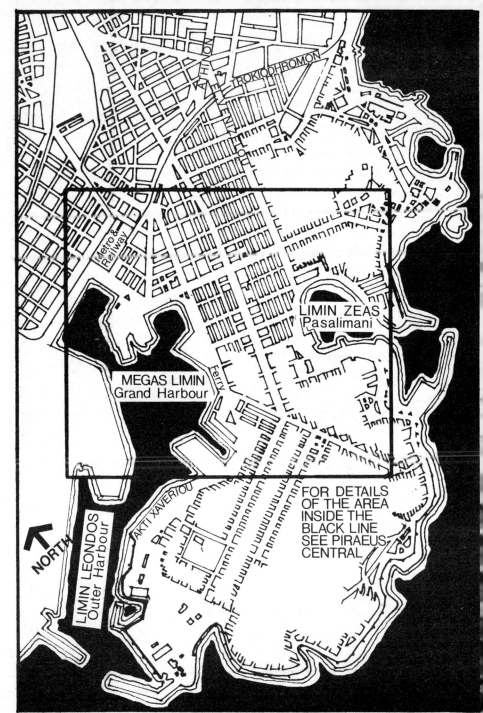

Illustration 8

Town of PIRAEUS

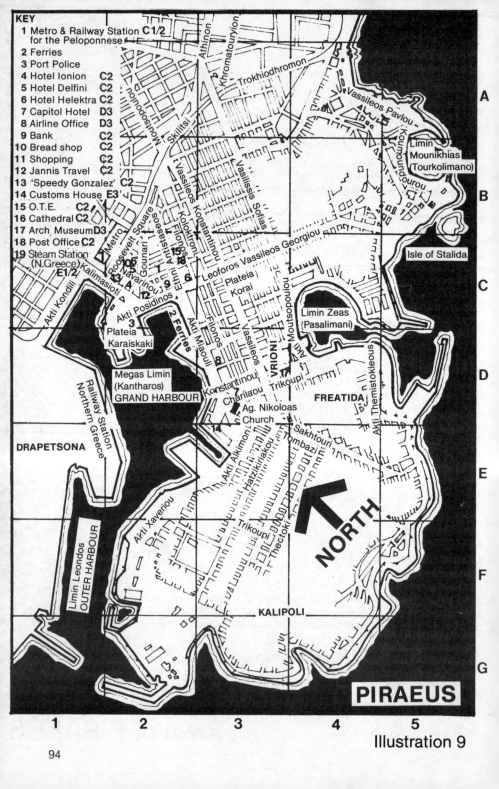

Illustration 9

94

Filonos Street (*Tmr* B/C2/3) The Soho of Piraeus, espousing the old **Never on Sunday** atmosphere of the town.

POLICE
Port   On the quay alongside Akti Posidinos
Tourist   On Akti Miaouli
Town   On Vassileos Konstantinou

POST OFFICE (*Tmr* 18.C2) On Filonos St, north-west of the Cathedral.

RAILWAY STATIONS
Metro/Underground (*Tmr* 1.C1/2). As described above.
'Steam' Station (*Tmr* 1.C1/2). For the Peloponnese is alongside and the far side of the Metro Station.
'Steam' Station (*Tmr* 19.E1/2). For Northern Greece and situated the other side of the Grand Harbour.

SHOP OPENING HOURS *See* **Athens.**

SWIMMING POOL Adjacent to **Limin Zeas** Harbour.

TELEPHONE NUMBERS & ADDRESSES
NTOG   Zeas Marina. Tel. 413-5716
Port authorities   Tel. 451-1311

Two other mainland Ports, Rafina and Lavrio, service Ferry-boats that make scheduled connections with various of the Cyclades islands and therefore require scrutiny. Unfortunately in order to connect between the two it is necessary to travel to Athens and then back out again.

RAFINA   Tel. prefix 0294
A noisy, clamorous, smelly, busy seaport, with an excellent bus service to Athens and the main Port for the islands of Andros and Tinos. This is important because it allows easy connection from the Cyclades Eastern wing into the mainstream of ferry-boat travel.

ARRIVAL BY BUS
The buses park up on the dual carriageway (*Tmr* 1.C4) that curves up from the large Ferry-boat quay (*Tmr* 2.D1/2). The Bus office is a small hut towards the top and on the right of this road (*Sbo*) with a timetable stuck up on the window.

ARRIVAL BY FERRY
There are Ferry-boats to Andros and Tinos and a height of season connection to Kea. *See* the individual islands for particulars.

The Ferry-boat quay (*Tmr* 2.D1/2) is at the bottom of the wide dual carriageway that climbs up to the Main Town Square. To the left the waterfront road follows the sea round but do not be side-tracked. Passengers disembarking at night and not prepared to travel on to Athens should make directly for one of the more easily accessible hotels.

The ferry-boat ticket offices are scattered about in amongst the restaurants and tavernas lining the road from the Ferry-boat quay.

THE ACCOMMODATION & EATING OUT
There are numerous restaurant/tavernas doing a roaring trade but accommodation is another matter.

The Accommodation
Hotel Korali (*Tmr* 3.B5/6) (Class D) 11 Plateia N Plastira   Tel. 22477
Directions: From the top of the dual carriageway, half-right across a small Square, and the

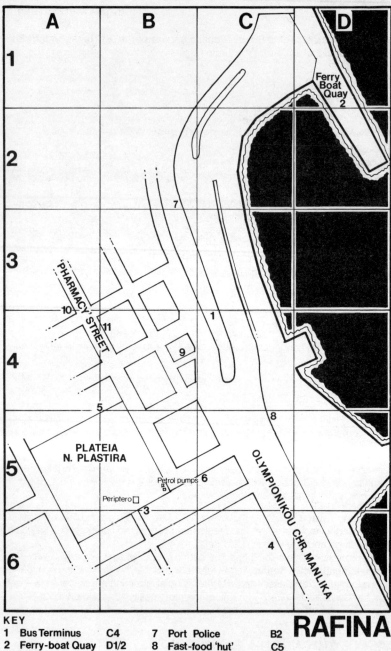

KEY

1	Bus Terminus	C4	7	Port Police	B2
2	Ferry-boat Quay	D1/2	8	Fast-food 'hut'	C5
3	Hotel Korali	B5/6	9	Tea Room & Pub	B4
4	Hotel Ina Marina	C6	10	Mykonos Disco Pub	A3/4
5	Hotel Rathina	A/B 4/5	11	Fruit & Vegetable Shop	B4
6	Hotel Kymata	C5			

RAFINA

Illustration 10

Hotel is on the left-hand side of the large pedestrian square (that now blocks off the old main street). A couple of Mobil petrol pumps are set on the far left corner of this Square.

A grey, urban, soulless, rather down-at-the-heel but clean 1920s establishment in front of which is a Periptero. The high ceilinged, linoleum floored rooms share the cavernous, massively equipped bathrooms. You know, cast iron cisterns, supported on very large cast iron brackets, 25mm pipes and mahogany lavatory seats. A single room costs 800 drs and a double 1150 drs. Madam does not live on the premises so if intending to leave early morning, pay up the night before departure.

Hotel Ina Marina (*Tmr* 4.C6) (Class C) Olympionikou Chr Manlika   Tel. 22215
Directions: From the top of the dual carriageway, keep along the avenue to the left and on the right. A double room costs about 1550 drs.

Hotel Rathina (*Tmr* 5.A/B4/5) (Class D) 2 Plateia N Plastira   Tel. 23460
Directions: Almost directly across the pedestrian way from the *Hotel Korali*
Greyer, scruffier and older than its counterpart across the way but cheaper with a double room, sharing the bathroom, costing 1000 drs.

Hotel Kymata (*Tmr* 6.C5) (Class D)   Tel. 23406
Directions: Before the *Hotel Korali* over a row of pizza-joints and rather difficult to spot. Similar prices and conditions to the *Korali*.

Camping Rafina
Directions: Oft referred to but is rather a long way (about 3¼ km) out of Rafina, on the Athens road.

The Eating Out Fish restaurants and tavernas with roof-top balconies, side-by-side up the right-hand side of the dual carriageway from the Ferry-boat quay as far as the Port police office (*Tmr* 7.B2). Apart from the mass of pizza eating places, the late night, hot-dog, soft drink hut (*Tmr* 8.C5) at the top of the dual carriageway might fill a nook or cranny.

Some might try the *Tea Room & Pub* (*Tmr* 9.B4) at the outset of and on the far right of the Plateia N. Plastira. Open between 0800 - 1200 hrs and 1900 - 2400 hrs. Others might be moved to visit the *Mykonos Disco Pub* (*Tmr* 10.A3/4). Oh goody, goody.

On 'Pharmacy' St, thus named due to the high proportion of these establishments, there is, on the right, a Fruit and Vegetable Shop (*Tmr* 11.B4).

Further along, the Main Avenue, or more correctly pedestrian way, of Plateia N. Plastira are the Banks and other public services.

LAVRIO (Lavrion)
A messy Town and savaged Port that probably once possessed a graceful Italianesque waterfront, the mute remains of which are represented by several crumbling 'neo municipal' buildings and a few tired, dusty palm trees.

The little harbour is host to a mix of speedboats and small commercial craft. Off the messy, quarried headland to the right is a stranded cargo ship that must have cut the corner rather too tightly. Offshore is the private island of Makranisos, mysteriously not included in the Cyclades.

ARRIVAL BY BUS
The Athens buses pull up on the edge of a large, grandiose park and inter-related maze of squares, interlaced by sweeping streets. There is a Bus office (*Tmr* 1.A4).

ARRIVAL BY FERRY
The shabby Ferry-boat quay (*Tmr* 2.E2/3) is shared with other commercial interests and the way along the finger pier is blocked by piles of 'this-and-that'. The small, dilapidated and crowded ticket office, converted from the remains of a concrete stucco restaurant, is surrounded by broken-down wire fences and crushed concrete posts. It services the one

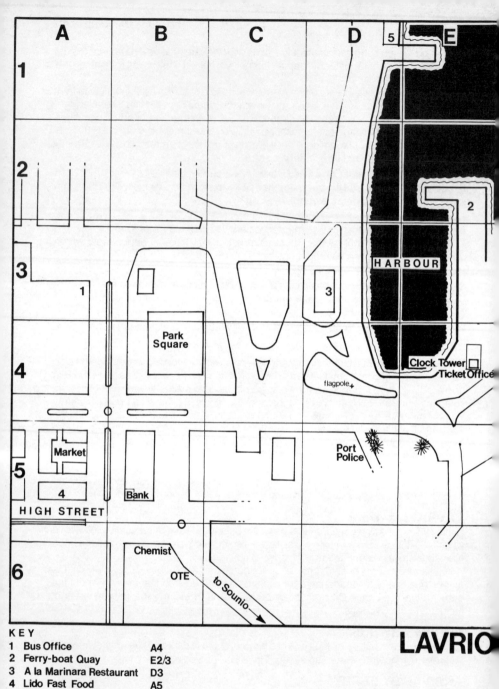

KEY

1	Bus Office	A4
2	Ferry-boat Quay	E2/3
3	A la Marinara Restaurant	D3
4	Lido Fast Food	A5
5	Café-bar To Moypagio	D1

Illustration 11

and only Ferry-boat, the **Ioulis Keas II**, sells a map and guide book of Kea island and opens about an hour prior to scheduled sailing times.

Note despite any advice, even from the main NTOG office in Athens, it is (or certainly was up to and including 1985) necessary to return to Lavrio to connect between Kea and Kithnos islands. This ferry does not go on from one to the other but makes a separate trip, via Lavrio.

Ferry-boat timetable
FB IOULIS KEAS II

Monday	1430 hrs	Kea
	1900 hrs	Kea
Tuesday	0830 hrs	Kithnos
	1800 hrs	Kea
Wednesday	0900 hrs	Kea
	1000 hrs	Kea
Thursday	0900 hrs	Kea
	1800 hrs	Kea
Friday	0815 hrs	Kithnos
	1430 hrs	Kea
	1900 hrs	Kea
Saturday	0830 hrs	Kea
	1230 hrs	Kithnos
	1900 hrs	Kea
Sunday	0830 hrs	Kea
	1700 hrs	Kea
	2115 hrs	Kea

One-way fare to Kea 430 drs & to Kithnos 650 drs; duration to Kea 2½ hrs & to Kithnos 4 hrs.

THE ACCOMMODATION & EATING OUT

The Accommodation Almost unbelievably not only could I not find anywhere, but even the official manual does not list accommodation. This may well not matter too much as Lavrio is not a place to stay.

The Eating Out A number of cafe-bars and taverna/restaurants. A very convenient establishment is the:-

A La Marinara (*Tmr* 3.D3)
Directions: On the edge of the harbour and a convenient spot to fritter away a few hours, being in sight of the Ferry-boat quay. Unfortunately most of the food is pre-packaged but the spaghetti bolognese (160 drs) is reasonably priced, as is a bottle of Amstel (65 drs).

On the way round from the Restaurant to the Ferry-boat quay is a pavement mounted shrine, close by which is a Meccano like, metal and wood trip boat jetty.

An inexpensive alternative, but horribly named cafe-bar is the:-

Lido Fast Food (*Tmr* 4.A5)
Directions: At the Ferry-boat end of the High St, close to the Sounio roundabout.

Perhaps Lavrio's saving grace is the small, lovely old Market behind the High St. A charming conglomeration of stalls set out in a cruciform with ancient night time lighting and a rather impressive donkey drinking trough.

Cafe-bar To Moypagio (*Tmr* 5.D1)
Directions: To the left-hand side of the harbour, facing the Ferry-boat quay with the Park behind one.

A small cafe-bar on the roadside with some convenient toilets.

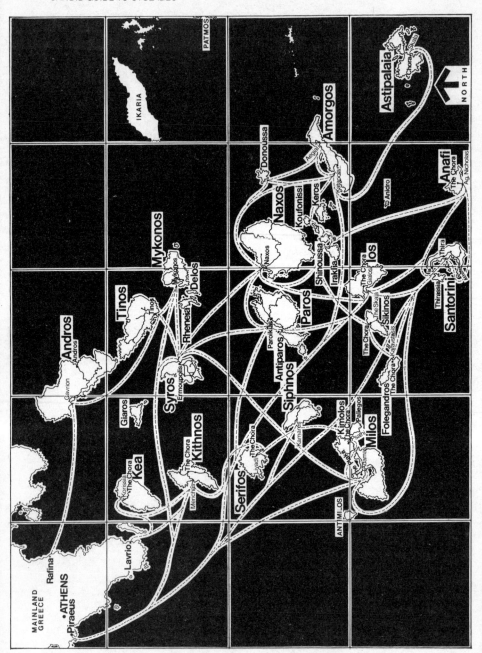

Illustration 12

11 INTRODUCTION TO THE CYCLADES ISLANDS (KIKLADES, KIKLADHES, KYKLADEN, ΚΥΚΛΑΔΕΣ)

A loosely knit scattering of some 24 inhabited islands set in the Aegean stretching south towards Crete, west beneath the island of Evia and east towards the island groupings that edge the Turkish mainland.

They range in size from large to tiny; verdant to arid; mountainous to gentle hills; beautiful to plain-featured and Western sophistication to *au naturel*. In fact the Cyclades offer almost every possible shade and hue of Greek island. Due to their variety, geographical spread and accessibility from the mainland port of Piraeus, they are very often the first islands to which a ferry-boat traveller aspires. This can be no bad choice for, to misquote Samuel Johnson, "a man who cannot find solace in the Cyclades will not find solace anywhere in Greece". Certainly there is a magic quality to the islands whether it is steaming past the rocky fastness of their perimeter or urgently bustling into port. Whether it is a cool, clear morning; a hot, motionless, steamy afternoon or, perchance, a deep purple night with the lights of other steamers and scattered island settlements winking in the distant darkness.

No two islands are the same but rarely are they so entirely different that each port of call will not recall both similarity and disimilarity to others in the chain. But two impressions amongst all others will surely prevail — the wind and the mountains. During the summer the gusts come and go, but from the middle of July to the middle of September, the **Meltemi** blows almost continuously from the north.

The almost impossible choice of islands on offer ranges from say Mykonos (once a haunt of the 'beautiful people' and now still chic but a holiday centre for homosexuals); Naxos (a wild mountainous north and gentle beach fringed south) to the simple, still comparatively untouched, charm of say Kimolos or Sikinos. The final selection can only depend on the travellers own sensibilities but whatever his or her fancy, the Cyclades will surely fulfil them all and the siren call will undoubtedly echo down over the years to return and return and . . .

It would be a travesty not to sound a warning note. The simple, naive, primitive Greece of 30 years ago (so appealing to voyagers in the past but born of grinding poverty) has all but disappeared. Mass tourism is not entirely to blame for once the decision had been made that the Greeks should be pitchforked into the 20th century then the curtain was slowly but surely rung down on the past, and rightly so. But all is not lost for the Greek people, in the main, retain their exuberance and simple charm in addition to which centuries old customs, ways and manners have not changed or disappeared altogether — 'Plus ca change, plus non ca change'.

The following chapters will, I trust, assist travellers planning to visit the Cyclades in the formulation of their arrangements. I hope they experience the same love affair that I have been privileged to enjoy over the years.

I have made a possibly controversial decision, which is to include Astipalaia in the Cyclades. I hope my reasons are sound but they are at least founded on practicality. Certainly Astipalaia is infinitely easier to reach from certain of the Cyclades islands than from the Dodecanese, with which it is usually bracketed. Additionally its geography and Chora* are distinctly Cycladean, rather than similar to any of the Dodecanese islands. I accept that Patmos (alone of the Dodecanese) has a Chora but very much a fortified monastery Chora, nothing like the typical Cycladean capital.

Main town or village of a Cycladean island usually separate from the port and ideally hill-top mounted.

The history of the islands bracketed together under the loose geographical ties of the Cyclades is, as elsewhere in Greece, confusing to say the least. Even the nomenclature and number of islands in the group has been the subject of much change and alteration over the years. Certainly by about 1000 BC, Ionians from the west coast of Greece had imposed their worship of Letos on Delos as well as imbued the island with various myths honouring Apollo. Thus for a time tiny Delos became the most important island in the whole Aegean. At about this time the Cyclades, or **Kyklos**, referred to the 12 or 15 islands circled around Delos but now refers to an administrative area including some 30 or so islands.

Settlement of the Cyclades can be traced as far back as the 7000 BC but the earliest, easily identifiable period of occupation is between 3000 - 2600 BC. An early attraction to outsiders was the volcanic mineral obsidian centred on Milos island. By about 2000 BC the Minoans of Crete were in command and had large settlements on the islands of Milos and Santorini. They were followed by the Mycenaeans, a Dark Age and then the Ionians. In their turn these invaders, in 490 BC, were routed by the Persians who were on their way to a naval punch-up with the City-State of Athens. This took place at Salamis and the Persians lost. Naturally the Athenians set up an Empire although they had the cunning to call it a League or Confederation. The Cycladian islands baulked against the regime but were bought back into line by Athens under the guise of a Second League. From then on times were turbulent with the Egyptian Ptolemies and others variously emerging winners until the Romans cropped up in 197 BC. They allowed the patriarchs of Rhodes island to run the show, taking the reins back again until their own empire broke up in AD 395. The Cycladians were then left to the ravages of various invading hordes. The Byzantine Empire, which remotely involved itself in the Cyclades, received a bloody nose in the early 1200s from Crusaders who, instead of sorting out the Arabs and Jerusalem, found an easier target in Constantinople which they laid waste. The Venetians who had been keeping a close eye on events took over the Cyclades as well as other bits of Greece including Crete, Rhodes, some of the Dodecanese and the Ionian islands. The Venetians parcelled up the various islands around their ruling families, one of whom, having taken the title of Duke of Naxos, sided with the Franks and managed to hang onto the island of Naxos until the 1560s, by which time most of the other islands had been lost to the Turks. The Venetians kept up a running battle with the Turks taking back this or that island until they irrevocably lost Crete to them in 1669. One outpost, Tinos remained in their hands until the early 1700s. In the meantime, during the middle 1600s, English ships captain adventurers, with letters of patent from Charles I, raided various Cycladean islands for antiquities. With the Turks firmly at the helm in the Aegean, a hundred years of peace ensued until the Russians and Turks pitched into each other in 1770. The Russians annexed numerous of the islands for the next five years after which the Turks took over again until 1821 when the Greeks kicked over the traces once and for all and painfully and slowly drove out their erstwhile overlords with the resultant formation of the Greek Independent State in 1832.

The principle religion is, naturally enough, Greek Orthodox but with Catholic enclaves left over from the Venetian occupation.

Before tackling the individual islands it is helpful to break them down into smaller geographical sections taking into account the ferry-boat lines of communication. The upshot is that they split into East and West chains with East and West wings. The East chain includes Syros, Mykonos, Paros, Naxos, Amorgos, Ios, and Santorini with the East wing taking in Andros and Tinos. The West chain incorporates Serifos, Siphnos and Milos with the West wing consisting of the islands of Kea and Kithnos. To these must be added the other islands and the various connections and excursions but at least this arrangement has enabled me to make a start.

The island chapters follow a format which has been devised and developed over the years to make the layout as easy as is possible, without losing the informative nature of the text. Each island is treated in a similar manner, giving the traveller easy identification of his immediate requirements. Below are detailed notes in respect of the few symbols occasionally used, and following that an alphabetical list of the islands included in my treatment of the Cyclades.

SYMBOLS Where inserted, a star system of rating indicates my judgment of an island, its accommodation and restaurant standards by the incorporation of one to five stars: 1 star signifies bad, 2 basic, 3 good, 4 very good and 5 excellent. I must admit the inclusion of ratings are carried out on idiosyncratic, whimsical grounds and are based purely on personal observation. For instance where an island or establishment receives a detailed critique I may consider that sufficient unto the day.... The absence of a star symbol or any mention at all has no detrimental significance, and might, for instance, indicate that I did not personally inspect the establishment. The text is faced by the relevant island, port and town maps with descriptions and text tied into the various island routes. The key *Tmr* is used as a map reference to aid easy location on port and town maps. Other keys used include *Sbo* or Sea behind one, *Fsw* or Facing seawards, *Fbqbo* or Ferry-boat quay behind one and OTT or Over The Top.

Island Name(s)	Capital	Ports (at which inter ferry-boats dock)	Ferry Connections (M = mainland)
Amorgos	Katapola	Katapola Aegiali	Aegiali (Amorgos) Katapola (Amorgos) Donoussa, Koufonissi, Shinoussa, Iraklia, Naxos, Astipalaia, Nisiros, Tilos, Simi, Rhodes, Kalimnos, Kos, Crete, Paros, Syros, Piraeus (M)
Anafi (Anaphi, Anaphe)	The Chora (Anafi)	Ag. Nicholas (Skala)	Santorini
Andros	Andros	Gavrion	Tinos, Syros, Mykonos, Rafina (M)
Antiparos	Antiparos (Kastro)		Excusion boats from Paros
Astipalaia (Astypalaia, Astypala, Asltipalea	Chora	Skala	See Amorgos
Delos (Dhilos, Dilos)			Excursion boats from Mykonos & Tinos
Donoussa (Dhenoussa, Dhonoussa, Donousa			See Amorgos
Folegandros (Pholegandros, Polycandros)	The Chora	Karavostasis	Ios, Santorini, Naxos, Paros, Syros, Sikinos, Piraeus (M)
Ios (Nios)	The Chora	Gialos	Naxos, Paros, Santorini, Mykonos, Folegandros, Sikinos, Siphnos, Serifos, Tinos, Piraeus (M)
Iraklia			See Amorgos
Kea (Tzia)	The Chora (Ioulis)	Korissia	Lavrio (M), Rafina (M)* *Height of season only?

Kimolos	The Chora (Kimilos)	Psathi	Pollonia (Milos), Adamas (Milos), Syros, Siphnos, Serifos, Kithnos, Ios, Santorini, Piraeus (M)
Kithnos (Kythnos, Thermia)	The Chora (Kithnos)	Merichas	Serifos, Siphnos, Milos, Kimolos, Syros, Lavrio (M), Piraeus (M)
Koufonissi (Koufonisia, Koufonisi)			*See* Amorgos
Milos (Melos, Milo)	The Plaka	Adamas	Kimolos, Siphnos, Serifos, Kithnos, Syros, Ios, Santorini, Piraeus (M)
Mykonos (Myconos, Mikonos, Miconos)	Mykonos	As capital	Tinos, Andros, Paros, Syros, Santorini, Rafina (M), Piraeus (M)
Naxos	Naxos	As capital	Ios, Paros, Santorini, Sikinos, Folegandros, Iraklia, Shinoussa, Koufonissi, Donoussa, Amorgos, Syros, Astipalaia, Piraeus (M)
Paros	Paroikias (Paros)	As capital	Naxos, Ios, Santorini, Anafi, Mykonos, Syros, Ikaria, Samos, Sikinos, Folegandros, Iraklia, Shinoussa, Koufonissi, Donoussa, Amorgos, Astipalaia, Nisiros, Kalymnos, Kos, Tilos, Simi, Rhodes, Karpathos, Kasos, Crete, Piraeus (M) Excursion boats to Antiparos, Siphnos
Santorini (Santorine, Thira, Thera)	Thira (Phira, Fira)	Thira, Ia, Athinos	Ios, Naxos, Paros, Sikinos, Folegandros, Siphnos, Serifos, Mykonos, Syros, Milos, Kithnos, Crete, Piraeus (M)
Serifos (Seriphos)	The Chora	Livadi	Siphnos, Ios, Santorini, Milos, Kimolos, Syros, Piraeus (M)
Shinoussa			*See* Amorgos
Sikinos	The Chora	The Skala (Aloproria)	Ios, Santorini, Folegandros, Paros, Syros, Naxos, Piraeus (M)
Siphnos (Sifnos)		Kamares	Serifos, Kithnos, Milos, Kimolos, Ios, Santorini, Syros, Piraeus (M) Excursion boats to Paros
Syros (Siros)	Ermoupolis	As capital	Paros, Ios, Santorini, Tinos, Mykonos, Andros, Naxos, Sikinos, Folegandros, Milos, Siphnos, Serifos, Kythnos, Ikaria, Samos, Iraklia, Shinoussa, Koufonissi, Donoussa, Amorgos, Astipalaia, Rafina (M), Piraeus (M)
Tinos	Tinos	As capital	Andros, Mykonos, Syros, Rafina (M), Piraeus (M) Excursion boats to Delos.

12 Syros (Siros, ΣΥΡΟΣ)
Cyclades Islands — Eastern chain

***

FIRST IMPRESSIONS
Grand churches and mansions; shuttered houses; paved roads; balconies; a rocky, bare island; large shipyard; no 'mama's' with rooms.

SPECIALITIES
Loukoumades (Turkish delight); nougat; octopus; Roman Catholicism.

RELIGIOUS HOLIDAYS & FESTIVALS
include: 24th September — the appearance of the Virgin Mary, Faneromenis Monastery (Catholic & Orthodox procession); 26th October — St Dimitrios Church; end of October/ early November — 'Apanosyria' festival, Ano Syros; 27th December — St Stephen, Gallisas. There are also Feasts at Kini and Finikas.

VITAL STATISTICS
Tel. prefix 0281. Syros, the legal and administrative centre of the Cyclades, is about 18 km from top to bottom and 10⅔ km wide with an area of 87 sq km. The population numbers about 19,000, two thirds of whom live in the main town and port of Ermoupolis and of that number some 1350 work in the shipyards.

HISTORY
Mentioned by Homer as 'abounding in pasture and wine, rich in sheep and corn'. Yes, well, not so now. The islands history mirrored that of the rest of the Cyclades until it came under the suzerainty of the Duke of Naxos in 1207. In this period the medieval town of Ano Syros was built and became a stronghold of the Roman Catholic faith brought to the island by Genoese and Venetian merchant colonists. This religious anomaly was supported by the King of France even during the Turkish rule.

The Russians interrupted the Turks occupation for four or five years when they captured the island in 1770, unfortunately plundering some antiquities which finished up in Leningrad museums. Under Turkish rule the islanders gained a rare number of concessions and flourished, which may well be one of the reasons that they did not physically join in the 1821 Independence uprising. Even during these uncertain times the French fleet kept a watching brief over the 5,000 or so Catholics. On the other hand the Syriots did help fund the struggle as well as taking in many thousands of refugees from other islands. They immediately set to and built the new town and port of Ermoupolis on the then undeveloped area between the hill, on which Ano Syros was built, and the sea's edge.

Despite, or perhaps because of the islands non-involvement in the War of Independence, Syros became the centre of the new States industrial and shipping thrust. The immense wealth and culture resulting from this prominence bequeathed some magnificent private and public buildings, a very grand plateia, Miaoulis Square, and a number of splendid churches. These have all contributed to the now present atmosphere of graceful, faded and long lost elegance in up-town Ermoupolis. The decline of coal vis-a-vis oil fired power resulted in transference, in the 1810s, first of the centre of shipping to Piraeus, the home port of Athens, followed by a slow run-down in industrial activity with the consequent closure of many of the cotton mills, tanneries, iron foundries, factories and

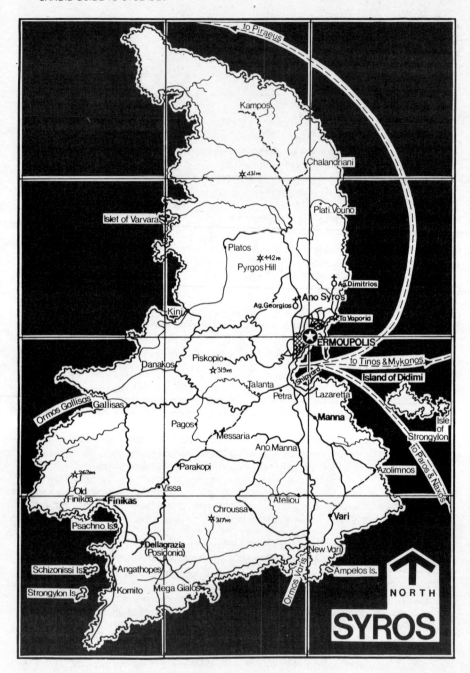

Illustration 13

warehouses. With a lot of Government encouragement the shipyard has remained active and prosperous.

GENERAL

Over the past 7 years little has changed and Syros remains quintessentially a Greek island with few publicised attractions for the tourist. Admittedly there are now a few more much needed hostelries but not a lot else has altered. It appears to be Central Government policy to keep the **NEORION** shipyard fully manned. Leisure activities and job opportunities including work in hotels, restaurants and all the associated services that could woo the workers away from the maritime industry are positively discouraged. Probably because of these strictures, Syros has retained much of the charm and essence of Greek island life which mass tourism has, elsewhere, ravaged and restructured.

So, why does Syros not receive more rave notices from travel writers, why does the average guide afford this pleasant refuge from the more characteristic Cycladean hurly-burly only a page? Surely it should rate as an appealing island at which to stop-off? Can it be that the lack of standard tourist pre-requisites — namely discos, international hotels, tavernas with 'traditional' Greek dancing, trip boats, excursion buses, jewellery & souvenir shops and 'Safari' evenings — has detracted from the island's native charm?

Of course there are shortcomings, including the lack of an adequate beach at Ermoupolis, the main port and town; the prices for accommodation and eating out are probably on the high side; water is in very short supply; mosquitoes can be a nuisance if the proper precautions are not observed; the bus service is adequate, but no more, and the night life in Ermoupolis is non-existent (goody). As against these possible deficiencies the **Ramblas** or **Volta** on the Port's main square is a nightly and colourful event; the island possesses in Γolias, probably the finest restaurant in the Greek islands; there are splendid beaches at Old Vari, Dellagrazia, Finikas, Gallisas and Kini all with accommodation to hand; there is a swinging disco at Gallisas and the island taxi service is excellent.

Incidentally the islanders are a colourful people and the 1985 hue was ochre.

ERMOUPOLIS: capital & main port (Illustration 14)

From a distance the twin hills overshadowing Ermoupolis, topped off with a Catholic cathedral to the left and a blue domed Orthodox church to the right, have an attractive look, even if the surrounding mountains are bare and unappealing.

On the approach to the bay of the Port, the islet of Didimi, often with a ship at anchor in the roads, has to be founded as does the southern headland of Lazaretta, once a quarantine stop (and of course the origin of our word Lazaretto). A closer inspection of the Port does not present a pretty sight. To the left (*sbo*) the curve of the bay is occupied with a shipyard, floating dock and other industrial workings and round to the far left, large oil storage tanks. If this were not enough the untidy Esplanade buildings and parallel side streets conceal the glory of the magnificent Main Square added to which the Venetian three or four storey homes of the Upper Town are hidden from view.

Referring back to my general definition of a Greek Town, the ports rubbish is bought down from the precipitous, stepped, upper levels (apparently battened to the hillsides) by donkeys with large, circular panniers strapped to their flanks. Naturally enough, I suppose, it is then tipped on to the quay front where the donkeys spread it about in their efforts to get a good meal. Later, much later, when the resultant mess is nicely churned up, the rubbish truck turns up.

The upper reaches of the Port are well worth exploring with old, paved roads and endless wide, arduous steps marching up the steep hillsides. Many of the houses are shuttered and in partial ruins. This seems a great pity but the old bogey of inheritance laws and bequests to religious houses does 'encourage' this wilful neglect.

The island is water-short and there is a desalination plant (that works) with a distribution office alongside *Yannis Guest House*. The outcome of this is that conservation includes

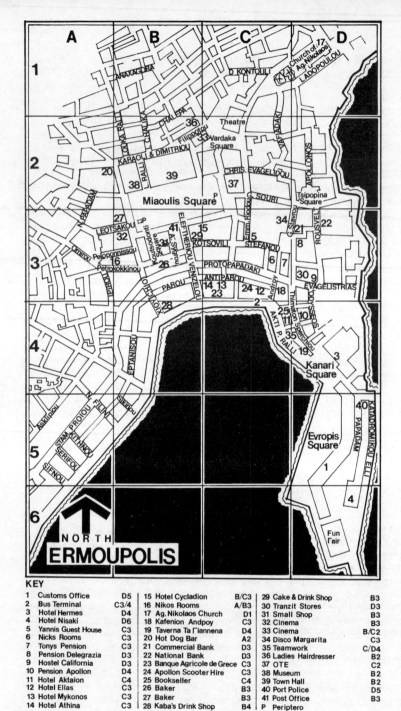

KEY

1	Customs Office	D5
2	Bus Terminal	C3/4
3	Hotel Hermes	D4
4	Hotel Nisaki	D6
5	Yannis Guest House	C3
6	Nicks Rooms	C3
7	Tonys Pension	C3
8	Pension Delegrazia	D3
9	Hostel California	D3
10	Pension Apollon	D4
11	Hotel Aktaion	C4
12	Hotel Ellas	C3
13	Hotel Mykonos	C3
14	Hotel Athina	C3
15	Hotel Cycladion	B/C3
16	Nikos Rooms	A/B3
17	Ag. Nikolaos Church	D1
18	Kafenion Andpoy	C3
19	Taverna Ta Γiannena	D4
20	Hot Dog Bar	A2
21	Commercial Bank	D3
22	National Bank	D3
23	Banque Agricole de Grece	C3
24	Apollon Scooter Hire	C3
25	Bookseller	C4
26	Baker	B3
27	Baker	B3
28	Kaba's Drink Shop	B4
29	Cake & Drink Shop	B3
30	Tranzit Stores	D3
31	Small Shop	B3
32	Cinema	B3
33	Cinema	B/C2
34	Disco Margarita	C3
35	Teamwork	C/D4
36	Ladies Hairdresser	B2
37	OTE	C2
38	Museum	B2
39	Town Hall	B2
40	Port Police	D5
41	Post Office	B3
P	Periptero	

Illustration 14

switching off the water during the day and a generally rather miserly attitude in respect of its use. Showers everywhere are charged as an extra, hot or cold, as is the utilisation of clothes washing machines. A relic of days of yore is the old boy whose large horse, bedecked with bells, pulls a large 4 wheeled cart supporting a big water tank decorated with 'murals'. The tap water can be very chalky and froths(!) so, on Syros, bottled water is a good buy.

ARRIVAL BY FERRY

A reliquiae of the once pivotal role of Syros and its continuing dominant administrative status is highlighted in the Island still remaining on many ferry-boat schedules. Despite this the leading position as the epicentre of the Cyclades has been taken over by Paros.

Ferries berth on the right-hand side of the Port, from close by the Customs office (*Tmr* 1.D5) down as far as the Bus terminal (*Tmr* 2.C3/4). The boats are met by owners of accommodation but to disembark it is first necessary to dodge the wild stampede of nougat-sellers. They wield very large, white linen wrapped baskets, and charge the ramps as they drop into place.

THE ACCOMMODATION & EATING OUT

The Accommodation Close by the ferry berths are the:-

Hotel Hermes (*Tmr* 3.D4) (Class B), Plateia Kanari   Tel. 28011
Directions: Across the Square from the middle of the quay on the right (*sbo*).

Pricey with double rooms sharing the bathroom costing from 1400 drs rising to 1600 drs and doubles en suite ranging between 1800 drs and 2100 drs.

Hotel Nisaki (*Tmr* 4.D6) (Class C) 2 E Papadam   Tel. 28200
Directions: Further towards the headland from the *Hotel Hermes*, close by the Fun-fair.

Usually block-booked by holiday-making Greeks with doubles starting at 1750 drs en suite.

Fortunately there is now more accommodation available than in the past when the availability of Rooms was a problem. Occasionally an island, for no particular reason, spawns an unusual manifestation, evolving peculiarities outside the main stream of development. For example Syros has remarkably few Pensions or Rooms but a disproportionate number of lodging or Guest-Houses. They are not an entirely suitable substitute, often being converted from large Victorian houses elementally divided up and with an atmosphere reminiscent of public school dormitories. Not that the next listed accommodation fits this genre.

Yannis Guest House (*Tmr* 5.C3) (Class B) 2 Emm Riodou   Tel. 28665
Directions: The entrance is in a side street off a 'back-street', three back and parallel to the waterfront towards the right or ferry-boat side of the port. There are wall mounted signs to some of the lodging houses but from the harbour turn left off the boat and keep on across the quay road, where it bends left by the Bus terminal, up the narrow lane. This leads past an alley on the left and on to the more substantial street of Protopapadaki (Σtam. Mpqioy). Either a left, right and left or straight across and left at No 14, *Nicks Rooms To Let* leads into the Street on the corner of which is Yannis.

The aged but clean, rambling old house with definite Simiot features has changed little over the last 6 or 7 years, experiencing only a minor adjustment in ownership. Originally a flower-power inspired dwelling, it still possesses innumerable notices stuck up all over the place including some advising of young Yannis's whereabouts. The main door is let into the side street wall of the building and entrance gives way to stone steps covered in by a glass sided conservatory entrance hall. A notice board has details of bus timetables, a sketch of the town and shopping information. Through the door at the top and the office is to the left and the dark main hall to the right. Yannis has added the house next door and the communal toilet/shower block, walled patio and gardens are down the steps past the office. Best not to be 'caught short' in the night as it is quite a stumble from the bedrooms including the short but steep flight of steps. A simple double room costs from 800 drs rising to 1100 drs with, if desired, continental breakfast charged at 170 drs and everything extra. A shower costs 60 drs, a machine full of clothing cycled by the pension staff works out at 600 drs. The 'Che-Guevarra' moustachioed proprietor can forget the original rate quoted and sometimes, half-heartedly, attempts to overcharge. This is perfectly understandable as the rates harden the later in the day that guests arrive. Room No 6 is one of two rooms with a double bed but kitchen smells tend to seep through the locked interconnecting door.

Nicks Rooms (*Tmr* 6.C3) No 14
Directions: As for *Yannis* above.
Comments as for all other Ermoupolis Guest-Houses.

Tonys Pension (*Tmr* 7.C3)
Directions: As for *Yannis*, but at Protopapadaki (Σtam Mpqioy) instead of crossing over, turn right up the street, take the next turning to the left and one up from the Dutch Consulate.

A worldly wise man in his 30s runs this well established Pension, but finds it difficult to get up in the mornings. Clean, airy, with a splendid, winding staircase and a Breakfast Room but only coffee is available despite the blurb. Book exchange. Double rooms from 800 drs.

Pension Delegrazia (*Tmr* 8.D3)
Directions: At the top of the same lane as *Tonys Pension* but on the other side of the road, across the street from the **Commercial Bank**. Comments as for the other Guest Houses.

Hostel California (*Tmr* 9.D3)
Directions: As for *Tonys Pension* but instead of turning off Protopapadaki continue on up and round following the left sweep of the road where it becomes Odhos Rousvelt. On the left, beyond the Catholic Church, Our Lady of Annunciation, on the other side of the road.

A newly acquired and recently converted grand old house run by relations of the owners of *Tonys Pension*. Don't miss the painted ceilings. The conversion has been hurriedly carried out. Soon after its opening in 1985, the shower head would only droop (a nut was missing) and the architect had omitted to put a drain in the floor of the toilet compartment containing the shower — result the floor swims. Ian, a Scots teacher has executed some splendid murals but I doubt if they will right any of the inadequacies. 'Canadian Costa', Tonys cousin and the young man of the family, is a pleasant, clean-cut young man and the establishment runs in a state of quiet, disorganised chaos. Lofty great rooms with a double room mid-season for 800 drs.

Pension Apollon (*Tmr* 10.D4) 8 Odysseos St.   Tel. 22158
Directions: From the right side of the harbour quay road (*Sbo*) an alley at right angles beside the *Hotel Aktaion* (*Tmr* 11.C4) leads to Odhos Thimaton Sperchiou across which another alley advances to a parallel street to the quay. The Pension, on the left, is operated by a piratical looking young partnership who also run Apollon Scooter Hire.

The large old house is just that little more run down and ethnic than its competitors at the same rates. . .

There are a number of 'Provincial' Hotels with shared bathrooms (unless stated otherwise) which require tracking down and include:-

Hotel Aktaion (*Tmr* 11.C4) (Class E) Akti P. Ralli   Tel. 22675
Directions: In the middle block immediately across the road from the Ferry-boat quay.

Doubles from 800 drs.

Hotel EλλαΣ (*Tmr* 12.C3) (Class E) Antiparou   Tel. 22519
Directions: Edging the Esplanade road across from the Bus terminal. The entrance is at the rear of the block facing the quay, next door to **Apollon Scooter Hire.** Doubles from 800drs.

Hotel Mykonos (*Tmr* 13.C3) (Class E) 18 Antiparou   Tel. 28346
Directions: Further along narrow Odhos Antiparou to the left (*Sbo*) in the next block.
    Doubles from 800 drs.

Pension Athina (*Tmr* 14.C3) (Class B)   Tel. 23600
Directions: Above the **Banque Agricole de Greece** on the Esplanade, entered at the back of the building from the alleyway Odhos Antiparou.
    Doubles from 1000 drs rising to 1200 drs and 1400 drs for the summer months.

Hotel Cycladikon (*Tmr* 15.B/C3) (Class C) Plateia Miaoulis   Tel. 22280
Directions: At the top of Odhos Eleftheriou Venizelou, facing the Square, and to the right, on the colonnaded pavement edging the square road. Signed *CENTRAL Rooms To Let.*
    Doubles from 850 drs.

Back to the Guest Houses and:-

Nikos Rooms (*Tmr* 16.A/B3) Odhos Petrokokkinou
Directions: At right angles to the Esplanade is Odhos Xioy, the Market Street, off which the third turning left angles away and the Rooms are on the right. 'Syros quaint' being chattily decorated with spidery red paint.
    The owner is often absent.

More up-market Hotels are represented by the following:-

Hotel Europe (Class C) 74 Stam Proiou   Tel. 28771
Directions: In the road above, one back and parallel to the down-town commercial quay away to the left of the harbour (*Sbo*). Some 200 m from the top of Market Street (Odhos Xioy), alongside the Chuch of the Assumption, and pleasantly situated overlooking the Bay although it does edge the Main Road out of Town. The view includes the Islet of Didimi with its lighthouse and often a tanker at anchor seemingly forever steaming around the headland. The building has a 1950s faded elegance and is constructed around a lovely courtyard. The rooms are carpeted and well appointed even if the carpet is rather faded and the walls show evidence of salt damp (where don't they).
    The pleasant double rooms en suite start at 1600 drs rising to 1800 drs. Run by the **Teamwork** (*Tmr* 35.C/D4) outfit and excellent value for Syros, that is if a traveller does not feel able to cope with the almost crude rusticity of most of the Guest Houses in town.

Two other excellent if very expensive establishments are situated up beyond the Church of Ag Nikolaos (*Tmr* 17.D1) on the east cliff of the town:-

Ipatia Guest House (Class A)   Tel. 23575
Directions: As above.
    Very well appointed but a double en suite costs 2450 drs and breakfast 150 drs.

Hotel Vourlis (Class A) 5 Mavrogordatou   Tel. 28440
Directions: From the *Ipatia Guest House* continue on up the cliff road for some 200 m and the Hotel is on the left. Unfortunately situated on a dangerous left bend about and around which there tends to be a lot of 'car hooter'.
    Normally totally outside the scope of this Guide Book but this luxury Hotel (well Pension actually) has been created from a splendidly proportioned 19th century mansion and both the public rooms and bedrooms are beautifully appointed and furnished.
    A single from 2500 drs and a double room from 3000 drs both, naturally, with en suite bathrooms. A Continental breakfast seems comparatively inexpensive at 170 drs.

The Eating Out Syros is remarkably short of above average tavernas and restaurants and prices are in the run-of-the-mill range. Mind you the main feature of an Ermoupolis evening is to sit at one of the numerous cafe-bars on the periphery of the Main Square and watch the colourful and extensive Ramblas which goes on for hours. In fact after nightfall Plateia Miaoulis resembles St Marcos in Venice and the most sought-after (and expensive) cafe-bars are those beneath the Museum and Town Hall. There are also a row of establishments on the road edging the Main Square, the most reasonable of which is probably the one beneath the *Central Rooms (Hotel Cycladikon)* (*Tmr* 15.B/C3) with a coffee for 50 drs and a bottle of beer 60 drs. The next door cafe-bar with an awning, covered chairs and tables terrace set up on the edge of the square alongside the Rotunda, is worth patronising with 2 beers, 2 Greek salads (admittedly small) and bread costing 320 drs.

At the far right hand corner the Taverna owner has set up a Heath Robinson charcoal grill from which, in the evenings, he serves up octupus portions accompanied by a glass of ouzo.

Another recommendation is:-

Kafenion Andpoy (*Tmr 18.C3*) *Odhos Andpoy*
Directions: In the narrow lane off the quay road opposite the Bus terminal. Beneath the sign **Breakfast, Fruit Juice, Toast** The entrance to the lane is barred to vehicles by bollards. Although favourably commended, this narrow fronted Kafenion/bar is possibly on the expensive side but serves up a good breakfast with fruit juice and toast just as the sign proclaims.

Towards the pier head, close by the *Hotel Hermes* is:-

Taverna Ta Γiannena (*Tmr* 19.D4)
Directions: As above.
Well patronised by Greeks, extremely convenient for the Ferries, with a varied menu but again not cheap. A plate of chips 55 drs, an unexceptional Greek salad 190 drs and 2 beers 134 drs. A noteworthy feature is that there is a 'trap' side window serving souvlakis costing 50 drs.

On the far left-hand side of Plateia Miaouli, beside a flight of steps is:-

'Hot Dog Bar' (*Tmr* 20.A2)
Directions: As above.
Very popular with the local lads. The hot-dogs are served in rolls but it seems a pity that the owner has not concentrated on the 'home-grown', infinitely preferable 'souvlaki with pita' but that's progress, isn't it?

Mind you when in the presence of a genius of the culinary craft, a wizard, an earth-bound God of cookery why look further? Many years ago after a vague recommendation we chanced upon a Taverna/Restaurant innocuously tucked away, high above the port. The self effacing owner and the pleasant but not outstanding surroundings did no more than prepare us for an average evening meal. As we sat down a crowd turned up from *Yannis Guest House* where we were also staying so we joined them. The meal that followed was sheer sorcery, and the company was good too. Course after course flowed across the table — hors-d'oeuvres, tiropites, pigeon breasts, cannelloni, roast rabbit and more, much more, with retsina and non resinated wine easing the melting food down our eager gullets.

At the time we postulated that it may have been a one-off affair, a matter of the locals being pampered. Certainly it did cross our minds that this standard was a bench-mark. (Incidentally thus spoilt we ferry-boated off on a four week sojourn and not surprisingly found no establishment to match this kitchen magic). Naturally, on our belated return to Syros, we could not wait to pay a return visit to:-

Γolias
Directions: From the left hand side of the Plateia Miaoulis (facing the Town Hall) start the quarter of an hour, 100+ steps climb up, ever up to the second metalled road at right angles (or 12th turning to the right from the square). From here a 100 m slightly downhill slope is followed by a left hand curve and *Γolias* is on the left, on the apex of the corner.

George Palamaros is a quiet almost shy man but the mark of a master craftsman in any trade is that they rarely appear to be at work and George is no exception. Very little is pre-cooked but the choice is very varied and interesting with a speciality of the day. Greed usually meant that our bill for two worked out at between 900 and 1000 drs but I should stress that less gluttonous diners could well knock some off this if (and this is a big if) they are able to resist the blandishments of his offerings. After a few meals sensibly selecting various items from the menu,why not entrust the evenings gourmet experience to George and his excellent assistants' gentle hands?. Simply request that they dish up what they consider to be appropriate. Don't worry George will patiently explain that if a particular dish is not satisfactory or to a person's liking then the offending item will unquestioningly be removed at no cost, or as he puts it "If you no like — give me back. No charge!"

Early in the summer George can serve up magnificent plates of mixed hors-d'oeuvres. Sample meals for two (eating like pigs) all with bread include the following: 1 fanta, 1 ouzo, jugs of retsina, tiropites, meat tubes in flaky pastry, Greek salad, tzatziki, cannellonis (a very long plateful) and a roll of pork for 1095 drs; one Greek salad, 3 bottles of retsina (I know, I know but it was a long, splendid evening) stuffed aubergines, lamb in oregano and roasted rabbit cost 1172 drs; a vast plate of salad and mixed vegetables, tzatziki, tiropites, meat rolls, 2 plates of kalamari and 2 bottles of retsina all for 1000 drs; hors-d'oeuvres with vegetables, cooked courgettes, tomatoes and feta, tzatziki, tiropites, beef pasta pot, dolmades, beetroot, spinach, fish and garlic sauce and retsina, 960 drs.

During the winter months he grills and roasts community lamb and the locals just shut down their kitchens and go to George's and I don't blame them. I realise it may sound as if I have shares in the restaurant or am a relation but I must assure readers that nothing could be further from the truth. But don't fail to bestow your custom and see if you agree.

THE A TO Z OF USEFUL INFORMATION
BANKS
The Commercial Bank (*Tmr* 21.D3) On Odhos G. Stavrou to the right of the harbour quay. The narrow lane (Odhos Andpoy), opposite the bus terminus, crosses the major Street of Protopapadaki and bends to the right where it joins two other streets forming an upside down 'Y'. Changes personal Eurocard backed cheques. Standard hours.

The National Bank (*Tmr* 22.D3) Along the lateral road from the **Commercial Bank** past the *Pension Delagrazia* and on Odhos Rousvelt/Kalomenopoulou.

Banque Agricole de Greece (*Tmr* 23.C3) On the Esplanade road Akth ΕθνικηΣ ΑντιΣταΣηΣ.

BEACHES The only 'nearly' beach is to the right of the town, up and beyond the twin spired and domed Church of Ag Nikolaos, keeping to the right. At the *Guest House Ipatia* turn right down the sloping, angled and stepped concrete pathway, that zig-zags down to sea-level. Here a rock edged concrete pathway, with small piers jutting into the sea, runs along the foot of the cliff face into which are set a few cave like store/dwellings. The path leads to a fairly large concrete jetty. Up against the cliff-side are the mute remains of the now derelict *Asteria Beach Bar*. Despite the sign **Dirty Waters to Swimming,** this delightful spot is used by the locals and cogniscent visitors to swim and sub-aqua.

There are narrow, stony pebbly beach coves behind the *Hotels Hermes* and *Nisaki*, which, despite their generally unsatisfactory nature, are often quite crowded. The sea is clean in stark contrast to the harbour which is murky. *See* EXCURSION TO AG DIMITRIOS CHURCH.

BICYCLE, SCOOTER & CAR HIRE There are a few firms renting scooters but none hiring out cars. This is not surprising as the road system is not extensive and the bus system is reasonable.

Apollon Scooter Hire (*Tmr* 24.C3) Odhos Antiparou   Tel. 26366
Up the lane Odhos Andpoy (what isn't?) opposite the Bus terminal, first turning on the left into the narrow lane that runs parallel to the Esplanade and one beyond the back entrance to the *Hotel EλλαΣ* on the left.

The proprietors are rather disinterested and hirers should ensure that the rate is fixed one day prior to the hire period. Haggle and they will drop about 200 drs to a daily rate of 1000 drs with further savings for 2-3 days hire.

There are mopeds for hire across from the Bus terminal (*Tmr* 2.C3/4) at a **Tour Office.**

BOOKSELLERS (*Tmr* 25.C4) On the Esplanade. An international newspaper shop with various language paperbacks in wire racks.

BREAD SHOPS One (*Tmr* 26.B3) on the main shopping Street, Odhos Protopapadaki, to the left of the High St (Odhos Eleftheriou Venizelou or Ermou). The bread is good quality and they also serve fresh cheese pies.

Another (*Tmr* 27.B3) opposite the Periptero at the left-hand bottom corner of the Main Square, Plateia Miaoulis (facing the Town Hall).

BUSES A widespread network covers the island and the summer season schedule is excellent. The terminus (*Tmr* 2.C3/4), or more accurately the 'park-up', is to the right of the harbour (*Sbo*). One at least of the buses is middlingly antique with a radiator grill resembling a Wurlitzer organ.

Bus timetable Note this is the basic, spring schedule.

Ermoupolis Town to Posidonia (Dellagrazia) Finikas, Gallisas, Talanta
Daily	0615 hrs	via Manna, Vari, Mega Gialos.
	0800 hrs	via Talanta, Gallisas, Finikas, Posidonia, Mega Gialos, Vari.
	0830 hrs	via Ano Manna, Parakopi, Finikas, Posidonia, Parakopi.
	1000 hrs	via Ano Manna, Parakopi, Posidonia, Finikas, Gallisas, Talanta.
	1130 hrs	via Ano Manna, Parakopi, Posidonia, Finikas, Gallisas, Talanta.
	1230 hrs	via Talanta, Gallisas, Finikas, Posidonia, Parakopi, Ano Manna.
	1345 hrs	via Ano Manna, Parakopi, Posidonia, Finikas, Gallisas, Talanta.
	1445 hrs	via Talanta, Gallisas, Finikas, Posidonia, Parakopi, Ano Manna.
	1600 hrs	via Ano Manna, Parakopi, Posidonia, Finikas, Vissa, Parakopi, Ano Manna.
	1745 hrs	via Talanta, Gallisas, Finikas, Posidonia, Parakopi, Ano Manna.
	1930 hrs	via Ano Manna, Parakopi, Finikas, Posidonia, Mega Gialos, Vari.

Ermoupolis Town to Manna, Vari, Mega Gialos.
Daily	0615 hrs	via Manna, Vari, Mega Gialos, Posidonia, Finikas, Gallisas, Talanta.
	0645 hrs	via Manna, Vari.
	1000 hrs	via Manna, Vari, Megas Gialos.
	1230 hrs	via Manna, Vari.
	1345 hrs	via Manna, Vari, Megas Gialos.
	1630 hrs	via Manna, Vari, Megas Gialos.

Ermoupolis Town to Kini
Daily   0700, 1400 hrs (via Piskopio).

Ermoupolis Town to Ano Syros
Daily   0745, 1030, 1130, 1230, 1345, 1600, 1830 hrs.

Ermoupolis Town to Manna, Vissa, Chroussa
Daily   0645, 1345 hrs

CHEMISTS *See* **Medical Care.**

COMMERCIAL SHOPPING AREA Not only is there a thriving Street Market that occupies the length of Odhos Xioy but a shop filled High St (Odhos Eleftheriou Venizelou or Ermou) and main shopping street Odhos Σtam Mpqioy or Protopadaki).

The market is a splendidly colourful affair and noteworthy must be the fish shop with a dinghy full of fish to the front of the stall. Particularly useful shops include:-

Nikas a well equipped, small supermarket with a range of meats on display located at the water-front end of the Market Street.

Kaba (*Tmr* 28.B4) an excellent wine, beer and spirits shop, some from the barrel, around the corner to the left from the quay end of the Market St.

A Cake and Drinks shop (*Tmr* 29.B3) on the right and Main Square end of the High Street. Sells cold bottled water and wedding dresses (if a client should so desire).

Tranzit Stores (*Tmr* 30.D3), a good general store with dairy products at the right-hand end of the main shopping street (*Sbo*).

A small shop (*Tmr* 31.B3) selling loose olives and cheeses situated in a little square off the bottom left of the Main Square, one turning prior to Odhos Xioy,

Close by Ag Nickolaos Church (*Tmr* 17.D1) there are grouped, on a corner of the tree filled, raised Square, a small Mini-Market and Grocers.

CINEMAS An open air Cinema (*Tmr* 32.B3) is located across the road from the bottom of the left-hand corner of the Main Square (facing the Town Hall). Another, an enclosed Cinema, (*Tmr* 33.B/C2) to the right and behind the same Town Hall, across the Square dominated by the supposed **La Scala** look-alike, the now neglected Apollon Theatre.

DOCTORS *See* **Medical Care.**

DISCOS
Disco Margarita (*Tmr* 34.C3) on the left of Odhos G. Stavrou.

EMBASSIES, CONSULATES & VICE-CONSULS I can only recall the Dutch Consulate next door to *Tonys Pension* (*Tmr* 7.C3).

FERRY-BOATS Syros is still nominally the epicentre of the Aegean ferry-boat system although for practical purposes **Paros** has now taken over this role. Notwithstanding this there are still a great number of cross connections made here. Naturally the build-up in the incidence ferry-boat sailings at the height of the summer affects the Syros listings more than most islands so I have attempted to present a 'middling' view. Ferries to and from Piraeus are boringly numerous. The trick of inter-island travel is to know about those Ferries that allow inter connection between the various Cycladean chains and wings (as outlined in Chapter 11). For instance a useful tip to remember is that there are frequent sailings from Mykonos to Tinos, Andros and Rafina (M) and that there are regular Syros-Mykonos connections. So rather than wait several days for a direct ship it is possible to change boat at Mykonos. Additionally there are 'Express' and small passenger boats, outside the scope of government controls, that also make various island scheduled journeys.

Ferry-boat timetable

Day	Departure time	Ferry-boat	Ports/Islands of Call
Monday	0020 hrs	Georgiou Express	Paros (0210 hrs), Ios (0610 hrs), Santorini† (0740 hrs)*

This schedule may include Sikinos and Folegandros.

	1215 hrs	Panagia Tinoy	Tinos (1315 hrs), Mykonos (1415 hrs), Tinos (1550 hrs) (M).
	1300 hrs	FB Eptanissos	Tinos (1435 hrs), Gavrio (Andros) (1645 hrs), Rafina (M 1930 hrs).
	1600 hrs	Georgiou Express	Piraeus (M 2020 hrs).
	1650 hrs	Panagia Tinoy	Piraeus (M 2100 hrs).
Tuesday	0745 hrs		Tinos, Andros, Rafina (M).
	1215 hrs	Naias II	Tinos (1315 hrs), Mykonos (1420 hrs), Tinos (1550 hrs).
	1245 hrs	Santorini	Paros, Naxos, Ios, Sikinos, Folegandros, Santorini†
	1300 hrs	Naxos	Naxos (1630 hrs).
	1650 hrs	Naias II	Piraeus (M 2100 hrs).
Wednesday	0400 hrs	Kimolos	Milos (0600 hrs), Siphnos (0800 hrs), Serifos (1200 hrs), Kithnos (1400 hrs), Piraeus (M 1700 hrs).
	1200 hrs	Ikaros	Evdilos (Ikaria), Karlovassi (Samos), Vathy (Samos).
	1200 hrs	Naxos	
	1200 hrs	Naxos	Piraeus (M 1730 hrs).
	1215 hrs	Panagia Tinoy	Tinos (1315 hrs), Mykonos (1415 hrs), Tinos (1550 hrs).
	1650 hrs	Panagia Tinoy	Piraeus (M 2100 hrs).
Thursday	1215 hrs	Naias II	Tinos (1315 hrs), Mykonos (1420 hrs), Tinos (1550 hrs).
	1650 hrs	Naias II	Piraeus (M 2100 hrs).
Friday	1200 hrs	Naxos	Piraeus (M 1730 hrs).
	1200 hrs	Lemnos	Paros, Naxos, Ios, Sikinos, Folegandros, Santorini† (and back on Saturday).
	1215 hrs	Panagia Tinoy	Tinos (1315 hrs), Mykonos (1415 hrs), Tinos (1550 hrs).
	1300 hrs	Limnos	Santorini (2300 hrs).
	1650 hrs	Panagia Tinoy	Piraeus (M 2100 hrs).
	2130 hrs	Georgiou Express	Mykonos (2230 hrs), Paros (0040 hrs**), Ios (0300 hrs**), Santorini (0430 hrs**).
**Next day.			
Saturday	1215 hrs	Naias II	Tinos (1315 hrs), Mykonos (1420 hrs), Tinos (1550 hrs).
	1635 hrs	Panagia Tinoy	Piraeus (M 2040 hrs).
	1650 hrs	Naias II	Piraeus (M 2100 hrs).
	1700 hrs	Lemnos	Piraeus (M 2100 hrs).
	2115 hrs	Nireus	Paros, Naxos, Iraklia, Schinoussa, Koufonissi, Aegiali (Amorgos), Katapola (Amorgos), Donoussa, Astipalaia.
Sunday	1215 hrs	Panagia Tinoy	Tinos (1315 hrs), Mykonos (1415 hrs), Tinos (1530 hrs).
	1630 hrs	Naias II	Piraeus (M 2040 hrs).
	1650 hrs	Panagia Tinoy	Piraeus (M 2040 hrs).

† *Santorini — the port of arrival is a mystery but almost always includes Athinos.* See **Santorini, Chapter 17.**
The fast 'Express catamaran' **Nearchos** *operates between Santorini and Crete and height-of-season also calls in at Syros and Mykonos.*

FERRY-BOAT TICKET OFFICES The quay-front buildings from Plateia Kanari on the right of the harbour (*Sbo*) all the way round to the High Street (Odhos Eleftheriou Venizelou) are sprinkled with ticket offices representing the various ferry-boat companies. To pick one or two would be invidious but naturally I will comment (as usual).

Syros Travel 18 Akti P. Ralli   Tel. 23338
Beneath the *Hotel Aktaion* (*Tmr* 11.C4). Mr Kouzoupis widely publicises the benefits of his office but in my opinion (and I can be wrong) negates all this self-acclaim with a cock-sure, 'wait-until-I'm-ready', attitude.

Customers do not have to put up with this though as other offices include one on the Esplanade between the *Hotel Mykonos* (*Tmr* 13.C3) and the **Banque Agricole de Greece** (*Tmr* 23.C3) which is run by a courteous and dignified old boy. He can well fulfill the same requirements and incidentally this firm is an agent for the successors to the Magic Bus (or as Ian the teacher so aptly put it the 'Tragic Bus') as well as representing the *Pension Athina.*

A very helpful office is that beneath the sign **Tourist Information Officer.-**

Teamwork (*Tmr* 35.C/D4) Akti P. Ralli   Tel. 23400
Run by the energetic Panayiotis Boudouris and his splendidly helpful and infinitely patient manager Andreas Kaloxylos (translated — 'Good wood'). Despite the fact that their office only represents one of the 'Express' boat services to Mykonos they will tirelessly answer all enquiries. Their office has flats and villas to let and represents the *Hotel Europe* which Mr Boudouris manages. Office hours are daily Monday to Friday 0830-1400 and 1630-2000 hrs, Saturdays closed and Sunday between 0900-1330 hrs.

HAIRDRESSERS Barbers (naturally) and a ladies hairdressers (*Tmr* 36.B2) on the right of the road between the old Theatre and the Church of Ag Nikolaos.

HOSPITAL *See* **Medical Care.**

LAUNDRETTE None, but 2 dry cleaner/laundries, one on Odhos Protopapadaki and the other close by on Odhos Andpoy.

MEDICAL CARE
Chemists & Pharmacies Numerous. Open shop hours but closed Saturday and Sundays. There is a night and weekend rota service for emergencies.

Dentists & Doctors There is a doctors name-plate on Odhos K. Stefanou close by *Yannis Guest House* (*Tmr* 5.C3) and a doctors surgery to the south of the Town where the quay and main roads merge.

Hospital The hospital is close by the doctors surgery on the roundabout, on the south side of the port, on the Main Road to Manna.

OPENING HOURS
Museum Daily (except Tuesday) 0900 - 1500 hrs; Sunday & holidays 1000 - 1430 hrs & Tuesdays closed.

Shops (in summer). Monday/Wednesday/Saturday 0800 - 1330 hrs; Tuesday/Thursday/Friday 0800 - 1330 hrs & 1700 - 2000 hrs.

NTOG None but *See* **Teamwork** (*Tmr* 35.C/D4), **Ferry-Boat Ticket Offices.**

OTE (*Tmr* 37.C2) On the right-hand top edge of Plateia Miaoulis.
Monday - Friday 0600 - 2400 hrs, weekends 0600 - 2300 hrs.

PETROL (GASOLINE) Several stations on the southern road out of Ermoupolis. Five litres (or just over 1 gallon) of petrol/oil (gasoline/oil) mix is rather expensive at 300 drs.

PHARMACIES *See* **Medical Care.**

PLACES OF INTEREST
Cathedrals & Churches

Church of Ag Nikolaos (*Tmr* 17.D1). A beautiful, twin spired Orthodox Church with a gold striped, blue domed roof in front of which is a raised, rectangular, tree planted garden. The road divides around the church which marks the start of the Old Quarter with an above average number of graceful balustraded, balconied mansions and known as **Ta Vaporia** or **The Ships**. The Church, named after the Patron Saint of sailors, has a monument to the Unknown Warrior carved by a well known Greek sculptor.

Some of the architecture in this area is fascinating as evidenced by No 28 Odhos Apollonos.

Two Churches (or more correctly one Church and a Cathedral) dominate Ermoupolis one each being mounted on top of the twin hills that tower over the port. On the left-hand hilltop is the old city of Ano Syros and the:-

Cathedral of St George A Roman Catholic Cathedral dating back to medieval times built in or, more correctly, on the town of Ano Syros which was founded in the 1300s. Most of the inhabitants of this fascinating settlement, only accessible to pedestrians, are the descendants of former merchant Catholic settlers. The religious tone was maintained initially by Capuchin and then Jesuit monks. The Capuchins founded a convent in 1535.

The right-hand hill of Vrontado is topped off by the:-

Church of Anastasis This Church embraces the Greek Orthodox faith and possesses some very fine, very old icons. There are wonderful views out over the sea and distant islands of Tinos, Delos and Mykonos.

To the left of the far side of the Plateia Miaouillis leads to lovely staircases of steps, some with self-rooting saplings scattered about and an Orthodox Church, beautifully draped with bougainvillea.

The house and shop lined streets in this area pleasantly wind down and around to the waterfront.

Cemetery, British On the road to Ano Syros, on the left beyond the Church of St Georgios, noticeable for its tall bell and clock tower. The cemetery is well maintained but kept locked. Of the 100 or so buried here, some 50 were victims of torpedo attacks on a British transport ship in the Aegean during the First World War.

Museum (*Tmr* 38.B2) To the left of the Town Hall (*Sbo*). Exhibits include items from surrounding islands but many Syriot island artefacts found their way into overseas museums.

Plateia Miaoulis (*Tmr* B2) Veritably a magnificent marble paved Square. The far side is edged by magnificent public buildings including the Museum, Town Hall and Library, in the basements of which are a row of smart cafe-bars, the tables and chairs of which are spread out beneath scattered trees and palms. An ideal position from which to view the evening entertainment — observing the endless and energetic Ramblas.

In contrast across the road from the near side of the Square are a row of seedy, colonnaded buildings, the ground floors of which are occupied by a number of cafe and restaurant bars. They have awning covered areas on the edge of the Square, to the right of the Statue of Admiral Miaoulis (a revolutionary hero) and the Rotunda bandstand.

Theatre (*Tmr* C2) I mention the Apollon Theatre as it is supposed to be modelled on the world famous La Scala in Milan and is purported, here and there, to still be putting on productions. The theatre may well be a miniature La Scala but certainly is rarely, if ever, open to the public. The forelorn, shuttered building, edged on one side with palm trees, now appears to be a repository for an assortment of junk.

Town Hall (*Tmr* 39.B2) This well proportioned, massive, neo-classical building dominates the Plateia Miaoulis. The central columned entrance is pleasantly balanced by corner towers.

POLICE
Port (*Tmr* 40.D5) Behind the quay front building edging the road, on the right of the harbour (*Sbo*).

Town In a narrow street off the near left edge of the Plateia Miaoulis. Their squad car and or Landrover often completely obstructs the roadway, but it is theirs I suppose!

POST OFFICE (*Tmr* 41.B3) On the left-hand corner of the High Street and Plateia Miaoulis. Normal hours.

TAXIS A very busy and well subscribed rank on the edge of Plateia Miaoulis — where else? The fare structure is detailed at the head of the line of affluent looking taxis which include numerous Mercedes.

TELEPHONE NUMBERS & ADDRESSES

Bus Terminus	Tel. 22575
Hospital	Tel. 22555
OTE	Tel. 24099
Police	Tel. 22610/22620
Post Office	Tel. 22590

TOILETS There is a vast, old fashioned and very clean facility to the right of the harbour, a few buildings down from the Customs office (*Tmr* 1.D5). To the left, men, to the right, ladies. An attendant oversees proceedings and sells the toilet paper. Another mens public lavatory is tucked away in a narrow alley behind the *Hotel Mykonos* (*Tmr* 13.C3). It certainly is public. . .

TRAVEL AGENTS *See* **Ferry-Boat Ticket Offices.**

EXCURSIONS TO ERMOUPOLIS TOWN SURROUNDS
Excursion to Ag Dimitrios (circa 2 km) From the upper port keep to the right
of Ag Nikolaos Church out along the cliff edge. Beyond the *Hotel Vourlis* there is a disco and a turning off to Ano Syros. Prior to reaching the Church a track leads down to a small shingle beach with two squatters cabins on the foreshore.

Ag Dimitrios is a colourful Church, built in the Byzantine style in the 1930s, close by the cliff-edge. The 'wedding cake', balustraded, arched, squared stonework with fiddly stone framed doors and windows is capped by the familiar, red tiled cupola with upturned edges. A pleasant picnic spot.

Excursion to Ano Syros It is possible to mount the hundreds of steps, starting out
from the left of the far top side of Plateia Miaoulis, leaving the large School on the right just behind and to one side of the Town Hall. But why not go by taxi or bus and save the exhausting climb that will take about an hour. Certainly the Medieval Town and its Roman Catholic Cathedral should be visited. (*See* **Places of Interest, A to Z**).

ROUTE ONE
To Kini & back to Ermoupolis via Posidonia (Dellagrazia) (35 km)
Whether leaving southwards from Ermoupolis by the high or low (quay) road they join at a roundabout to the south of the Port. The low or harbour road is remarkable for the fact that ships awaiting their turn at the repair yard are moored up in such a way as to tower over the street.

The first section of the road which circles the bottom of the bay is occupied by the shipyard and warehouses. Naturally it is not a particularly pretty sight, unless one is an industrial archaeologist with particular interest in the 19th century.

Keeping left on the main road leads to:–

MANNA (3 km from Ermoupolis Town) Not even a hamlet, or for that matter a particularly attractive site. The first 2 tavernas are divided from another taverna (set on a small boat quay) by the rocky foreshore. At each end is a stony cove if a visitor must swim here. There is a road, now surfaced, that reconnects farther on along with the main Manna to Vari road, but beware at the actual junction which can give a nasty moment due to the irregular surface.

VARI (NEW) (9 km from Ermoupolis Town) Pleasantly spread out and from whence the road wanders on to:–

OLD VARI (10 km from Ermoupolis Town) Most maps do not make a distinction but there certainly are two developments with the seaside Hamlet of Old Vari nestling at the end of Ormos Varis.

A pretty place to stay with a small, enclosed cove, the sandy beach of which has some rubbish on the foreshore. The left-hand headland is topped by an impressive, new, castellated mansion. Four tavernas edge the backshore which is planted with shady Arethemusa trees. One back from the shore road is the C class *Hotel Romantica* (Tel. 22704) with a double room en suite costing 1300 drs and the C class *Hotel Domenica* (Tel. 61216) edging the road down to the cove,with doubles from 1350 - 1550 drs.

To the far right of the bay (*Fsw*) a fishing fleet moors up. Despite the small, sandy cove sea-bed being weedy and the slight but pervading smell of diesel, the location is interestingly and squalidly attractive. The clean D class *Hotel Emily* (Tel. 61400), with a single room sharing the bathroom 660 drs and a double room 800 drs, en suite 1000 drs, edges the narrow beach. A bar/restaurant has a patio set into the sea.

The road, now mostly at or about sea level, skirts the indented rocky coves of this part of the coast and is lined with many new, Greek owned bungalows and chalets. The countryside is surprisingly well vegetated, similar to west Karpathos in the Dodecanese but with the difference that the road is in good condition.

The *Hotel Akrotira* is seemingly set down in the wilderness but is only 5 minutes walk from a very pleasant, sandy cove close by the Church of Ag Thekla (14 km from Ermoupolis Town). There is some kelp and at the far end caiques and benzinas are overlooked by the:–

Hotel Alexandra & Bar (Class C)   Tel. 42540
Directions: As above.

A double room en suite costs 1230 drs rising, for the months of July and August, to 1580 drs.

The other side of the peninsula headland is the '2 donkey droppings' hamlet of:–

MEGA GIALOS (14 km from Ermoupolis Town) A lot of villas being built.

POSIDONIA (Dellagrazia) (12 km from Ermoupolis Town) Confusingly known by both names. The colonial style Town is very interesting with some almost whimsical mansions enclosed with large railings and once owned by wealthy shipowners. The streets are gracefully tree-lined, all in amongst which new construction is underway. A definite aroma of money.

The bright blue Church, close by the junction with the Vissa road, is most unusual with the campanile separated from the main building, so much so that it forms a separate gateway.

The road cuts down to the coast on the left of a large bay. To the left a road, now paved, passes by a small, clean sandy beach with horizontal thin biscuit-like rocks in the shallows, all overlooked by the C class *Hotel Possidonion* (Tel. 42300). A double room en suite starts off at 1410 drs but rises steeply to 2060 drs for the period from 1st July to 10th September.

In the lee of the headland of Diakoftis is a caique harbour/cove beyond which a small army barracks and the other side, the very small seaside hamlet of :—

ANGATHOPES (14 km from Ermoupolis Town) Underrated. The locals have obviously made an effort with the sandy beach edged by spindly trees, and now cleaned up. Pleasant swimming with an islet close to the shore and, tucked into the crook of the headland, the low, rather ugly concrete box *Hotel Delagrazia*. Actually a B class pension (Tel. 42225). From Angathopes an unpaved track makes for a deserted spot place-named Komito on the maps. In reality this is simply where the path runs out on a relatively clean, shingly, sand and pebble beach with a few lumps of tar and backed by a thick grove of Arethemusa and Olive trees. No taverna or houses. On the headland to the left is a 'Dr No' house and, to seawards, a 'Dr No' island.

Back at the junction west of Posidonia, the right turning leads to :—

FINIKAS (12 km to Ermoupolis Town) In actuality the lovely family holiday location of Finikas and Posidonia almost run into each other. A curving, narrow tree-lined beach edges the bay hugging road. Hotels, bars, a Mini-Market, some *Rooms*, a benzina quay and *Finikas Furnishing Apartments* (sic).

Following the road round the bay leads shortly to :—

OLD FINIKAS A spacious fishing boat and caique quay complete with 2 shower-heads, all set in a rocky cove with a sliver of sand. The rustic taverna doubles up as a barbers.

On the outskirts of Finikas there is a petrol station and the main road leads inland towards Vissa. After about two thirds of a kilometre a left-hand turning proceeds northwards in the direction of :—

GALLISAS (9 km to Ermoupolis Town In the village, sited on a junction of the road from Finikas to Ermoupolis and the turning to the Ormos Gallisas, there are *Rooms* and innumerable Mini-Markets (well at least three).

The profusely bamboo groved, paved approach road to the bay passes the extremely smart looking C class *Hotel Francoise* (Tel. 42000). En suite singles 1000 drs and doubles 1350 drs, rising respectively to 1300 drs and 1600 drs (1st July and 10th September). There are also a Mini-Golf course (super!), shops, the Disco Aphroditi, *Rooms* and Villas to Let as well as a campsite.

The broad, large, curving, sandy beach is edged by tufted scrub. On the left, where the road runs out, is the *Green Dollars Bar* (yes Green Dollars) with unofficial camping in the garden grounds. The bar is the headquarters of the local hippy community that languishes hereabouts.

Further to the left is a benzina* quay and beyond that, set in the headland that blocks off this side of the bay, caves that are the repository for the 'great unwashed' that proliferate in the summer. The ranks of the hard-core unofficial residents, whose senior citizen is jewellery maker Alan (8 years on site), are swelled, if not swamped, by the summer influx of less dedicated migrants. Not one for the Mums and Dads.

Coninuing on the road back to Ermoupolis, after about 2 km a junction with the Kini road forks off to the left through the Village of Danakos and on to another fork. The left option leads down to:-

KINI (9 km from Ermoupolis Town) A pleasant settlement. The approach to the curving beach of sand laced with pebbles, is spanned by two 'laid back' tavernas. To the left (*Fsw*),

---

* *A benzina is a very small fishing boat*

over a small headland, is a sandy cove and to the right, the main body of the Village. Prior to the beach is the new, clean looking *Hotel Eλmiδa* opposite which, set back behind the railings, is a very smart Snack Bar with **Rooms** but they are very expensive with a double room mid-season costing 2400 drs. There are other **Rooms** including:-

49 Kini, Kini Beach   Tel. (an Ermoupolis No) 25632

Run by Marcos Kalogeras and his family, the rooms of this very clean, pleasant well presented set-up encircle a courtyard. The owner or a family member is present daily between 1400 - 2000 hrs. Doubles en suite 900 drs a night.

Several tavernas jut into the sea and to the far right is a fishing boat mole and moorings.

The road from Kini back to Ermoupolis Town winds pleasantly up on to the spine of the hills that dominate the skyline above the Port. The fork to the left up here blunders into the very large OTE installation.

Best to fork right and wander steeply down through beautifully rural countryside, past the turning to Piskopio, with, to the right, a deep meandering gorge spattered with farmsteads set in the steep sided defile.

ROUTE TWO

North of Ermoupolis Town and Ano Syros the surfaced road climbs out on to the dry, unwelcoming backbone of the mountain range that fills out this end of the Island and in reality leads nowhere. When the road surface breaks down, becoming a difficult, stony surface, a number of tracks and paths temptingly but rockily wander off. They appear to head off in the direction of tantalisingly glimpsed, distant sea bays but averagely these 'siren-calls' wind up in this or that farmyard and not hidden, undiscovered beaches.

13 Mykonos (Myconos, Mikonos, Miconos) & Delos (Dhilos, Dilos)
Cyclades Islands — Eastern chain

Straights   **
Gays   *****

FIRST IMPRESSIONS

Wind, rubbish; discos; youngsters (need only apply); tourists; numerous chapels; stone walls; stony countryside dotted with (ugly) modern Mykonos style buildings; wells; red as well as blue domed churches; wind-swept south coast; flies.

SPECIALITIES

Used to include almond sweet meats and Louza-seasoned and smoked rabbit meat (but these have probably been swept away on a tidal wave of tourism). Specialities still include hand-woven items encouraged by the same tidal wave; discos; tourist shops and tourists; Gays; boutiques and manganese ore.

RELIGIOUS HOLIDAYS & FESTIVALS

include: The usual National celebrations and festivities added to which are the 20th July — to celebrate the Prophet Elias; 15th August — Virgin Mary, Tourliani Monastery, Ano Mera; 29th August — St John the Baptist.

VITAL STATISTICS

Tel. prefix 0289. Some 18 km from west to east and 12½ km north to south with an area of about 75 sq km and a population of 4000.

HISTORY

Possibly due to the proximity of Delos, Mykonos does not receive many early historical mentions. The islanders gained infamy by siding (under coercion?) with the Persians during the wars with the Athenians between 500 BC and 480 BC. These culminated in the famous Greek victories on land at Marathon and at sea in the naval battle of Salamis. The island followed the historical path of a number of Cycladean islands joining, or being co-opted, into the Delian League organised by Athens and with the central funds originally 'banked' on Delos island. This arrangement hampered the Athenians ability to get their hands on the cash quickly enough so the Treasury was transferred to Athens in 450 BC. Oh ho, ho! After the eclipse of the Athenian empire and absorption into the Macedonian Kingdom, Mykonos followed the general drift of the regions with the Romans slowly gaining the ascendency from about the last century BC to the fourth century AD. As a result of the void created with the collapse of the Roman dominion there was a fair amount of piratical rape and pillage, although the Byzantine Empire was nominally in control.

The Venetians took over in the early 12th century but power was wrested from them in 1537 when the Turk Barbarossa invaded. During the Turkish occupation the islanders expanded their merchant fleets and piracy became an Island occupation, even an enterprise. Not only did the merchant marine increase the wealth but the merchants were also active in purchasing Aegean pirates booty. Nothing more than fences really!

It is said that no extensive fortifications were built on the Island, despite its pivotal position in the sea-lanes, due to its overall poverty. But this is not entirely consistent with the fact that in the 17th and 18th centuries the Island provisioned the various foreign naval

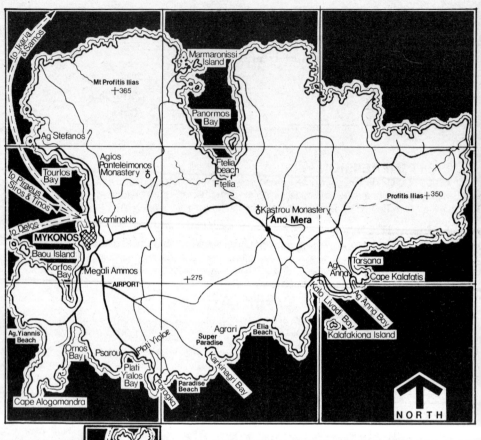

Island of MYKONOS

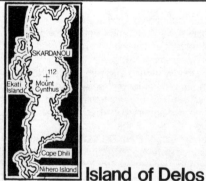

Island of Delos

Illustration 15

fleets that were very active in this area of the Aegean.

The particular skills and wealth attributable to all these activities were put to good use when the Mykoniots threw their energy into the Greek War of Independence (1821 - 1827), contributing some 22 ships armed with a total of 132 cannon. A heroine of the time was the no doubt indefatigable and remarkable woman, Manto Mavrogenous who helped organise the defence of the island against the subsequent Turkish reprisal raids.

The change in emphasis and direction of the shipping world resulted, here as elsewhere in the Aegean, in a general and steady decline in wealth and population, which trend reached its nadir by 1950. But, from the platform of being simply the stepping stone to the archaeological riches of the adjacent island of Delos, the naive, simple, white cubist simplicity of Mykonos Port and Chora, combined with some relatively far-flung but glorious sandy beaches, came to the attention of European sophisticates. They were followed by the rich, 'beautiful people'. They in their turn were succeeded by a train of vassals some of whom must have been hedonists of a particular bent as now the holiday-making, sun seekers that pack the island, appear to divide into two camps (sorry) — the sexually deviant and those who come to observe the phenomena. This of course, like many of my sweeping statements, is an over simplification and I would not wish to encompass, damn or mislead those hetrosexuals who are still attracted by the (now surely tarnished) magic still associated with the island.

GENERAL

Mykonos is a conundrum. Either you love it and your personality profile might suggest you are unmarried, in your middle 20s, love dressing up and are not an island aficionado or you will despise it. Scott Fitzgerald's hero in his book **The Great Gatsby** ghosted in and out of the 1920s 'beautiful people' who drove everywhere in large Cadillacs or Buicks. Those who visit Mykonos do so on crowded Ferry-boats or by aircraft. But is a more prosaic and egalitarian society than the privileged who originally discovered and patronised the Island in the early 1960s. Do not forget to pack your glad-rags, as the evenings in Mykonos Town are taken up with parading the quayside and guessing who might be straight — that is easier, there are less of them!

As the Greeks so nicely put it, "In the spring-time we inflate the island and tow it to its mooring place. At the onset of winter we deflate it and bring it back. . ."

MYKONOS: capital town & port (Ilustration 16)

One of the few island Cycladean Chora's set in comparatively low hills therefore not emulating most of its neighbours by marching up the contours of a steep hillside with the Town perched atop. In this respect Mykonos is similar to Paros but in comparison almost the whole town is a startlingly colourful, dazzlingly white and cubist Chora with a plethora of whitewashed lanes, steps and houses. The problem is that the street layout is inordinately complicated and it is extremely easy to get lost. Furthermore any resemblance between Mykonos and other Greek islands is purely coincidental. Seriously folks. . .

The Port area/harbour Esplanade is, in stark contrast to the Chora, disappointingly grubby and unattractive. Additionally the countryside is on the whole messy and indiscriminately peppered with what would appear to be a Mykoniot standard design 'prefab' villa, shaped in a blancmange mould.

ARRIVAL BY AIR

There are numerous domestic connections as well as some international flights daily. To reach Mykonos Town, about 3 km distant, the usual Olympic Bus drops clients off at the Airline office (*Tmr* 19.D2) for 45 drs or taxis cost 150 drs.

ARRIVAL BY FERRY

The Ferry-boat quay is set over to the far left of the harbour (*Sbo*) and is in fact a rather inconvenient distance to walk to the centre of the Town.

Mind you this is not the first hurdle to be crossed, for the hordes of disembarking travellers have to run the gauntlet of hordes of islanders frantically thrusting details of **Rooms**, Pensions and Hotels in their face. The potential clients are plucked at, pushed and jostled by the frenzied Room owners who unusually have pictures of their accommodation displayed on placards. Even early and late in the summer season this can prove quite a daunting prospect but I am assured by a tour guide girlfriend that the scenes in July and August are almost frightening.

To facilitate movement of clients and their baggage, Room owners bring up three wheeled trucks, more especially where the accommodation is out of town because the Chora is barred to traffic.

The Bus station for Ftelia Beach, Ano Mera, Kalafatis beach and Ag Stefanos is conveniently located on Odhos Polikandrioti (*Tmr* 1.D1), the road that connects the Ferry-boat quay to the broad Esplanade edging the main body of the Port. The other buses to, for instance, Ornos and Plati Yialos depart from an irregular Square (*Tmr* 2.C6) at the far end of the Chora, just off the 'ring road'. It is sign-posted throughout the Chora which is fortunate as until a visitor becomes accustomed to the maze-like convolutions of the Chora lane layout it can prove quite a tortuous business. Room owners from far afield push their guests on to the appropriate bus whilst the luggage follows on.

For those not 'captured' prior to getting off the quay, turn right with the sea to the right, past **The Pigeon Club**, an Archaeological Museum and a church. After some 200 m, the road curves sharp left away from the harbour. It is possible to wander off to the right down steps, leaving a block of buildings to the left, and regain the 'Beach Road' (Polikandrioti) or walk round the corner following the sweep of the road to the crossroads. Here turn right down the steep slope and along Odhos Polikandrioti. The crossroads are a messy affair with, on the left, a white building (with the standard rounded corners to the flat roof), terrace and stone wall enclosed yard festooned with signs variously proclaiming **STORK, STORK CLUB, STORK BAR DRINKS, ROOMS, KENTPON ΔΙΑΣΚΕΔΑΣΕΘΣ, AUTORENT MOTORBIKES, We rent Cars and Bikes at LOW PRICES, We Rent Bikes, MOTORBIKES FOR RENT HERE,** and *AUTO RENT A CAR*. If you should be in any doubt there are rooms, drinks, food and vehicle hire!

THE ACCOMMODATION & EATING OUT

The Accommodation The choice is to stay in the Chora, with all that entails, while the less trendy should consider heading for the country locations where it is quieter, easier to get personal washing done and usually cheaper. This of course is a comparative statement as **Rooms** in Mykonos Town are very expensive and in the country just costly.

In the Chora are the:-

Hotel Karboni (*Tmr* 3.C3) (Class D) Odhos Adronikou Matoyianni   Tel. 23127
Directions: From the Esplanade about midway round, turning off Plateia Manto Mavrogenous, between the shops of **Best Gold Store** and **Greek Light Jewellery**, is Odhos Adronikou-Matoyianni. This street is sprinkled with shops, restaurants, chemists and doctors. Beyond the Church, on the right, the building containing *Jimmys All Night Restaurant* and on the right.

Averagely expensive with a double room sharing a bathroom rising from 1100 drs to 1400 drs and en suite from 1500 drs to 2300 drs.

O Megas (Grocery Store) Odhos Adronikou-Matoyianni
Directions: One block back towards the harbour, on the same side of the Street. This Grocery Store has details of rooms both in the Chora and outside town.

Where Odhos Adronikou-Matoyianni makes a junction with Odhos Kalogera turn right and on the left is:-

Hotel Philippi (*Tmr* 4.C3/4) (Class D) 32 Kalogera St   Tel. 22294
Directions: As above.
   Lovely gardens with double rooms sharing the bathroom rising from 1100 drs to 1450 drs.

Further along, on the right is the:-
Hotel Zorzis (*Tmr* 5.C3) (Class C) Kalogera St   Tel. 22167
Directions: As above.
   'C' class and therefore commensurately even more expensive with double room rates starting off at 1200 drs.

Diagonally opposite is the:-
Hotel Marios (*Tmr* 6.C3) (Class C) 5 Kalogera St   Tel. 22704
Directions: As above but across the road.
   Rather less expensive than its other 'C' class rivals with doubles sharing the bathroom costing from 950 drs to 1365 drs and with an en suite bathroom from 1255 drs to 1850 drs.

Odhos Kalogera curves right into Odhos Dilou. A lane leads off to the left and on the left-hand corner is the:-
Hotel Maria (*Tmr* 7.C3) (Class D) 18 Kalogera St   Tel. 22317
Directions: As above.
   The prices are almost within reach with doubles sharing a bathroom rising from 950 drs to 1130 drs.

Back at the head of Odhos Dilou a sharp turning left wanders into Ag Gerasimou. By keeping left on to Odhos Meletopoulou and on the left, next door to a Chapel is:-
Rooms (*Tmr* 8.B4) Odhos Meletopoulou   Tel. 22731
Directions: As above.
   Nice looking two-storey house with courtyard, gardens and verandah. Usual rates.

Two other hotels worthy of a mention include the:-
Hotel Delfines (*Tmr* 9.D2) (Class D) Odhos Mavrogeni   Tel. 22292
Directions: Off up to the right from Plateia Manto Mavrogenous (*Tmr* C/D2) (*Sbo*) and on the right.
   A double room sharing the bathroom starts at 900 drs and rises to 1250 drs (July, August and early September).

Hotel Karbonaki (*Tmr* 10.D4) (Class D) 21 Panahrandou   Tel. 23127
Directions: Opposite the junction of Panahrandou and Filetairias Sts and is reached by proceeding up the aforementioned Odhos Adronikou-Matoyianni, crossing over Odhos Kalogera, jinking left after the *Restaurant Lotus* and right by *Vengera's Bar* leading into Panahrandou St. On the left, prior to Koutsomboles Church (the 4 churches in one). Sounds like a fizzy drink really.
   Single rooms sharing a bathroom from 1000 drs and doubles 1250 drs rising, for the months of July - September, to 1100 drs and 1400 drs. En suite rooms are 200/300 drs more expensive for a single room and 550/900 drs for a double room.

See **Paradise Beach** for details of the only official campsite.

The Tourist police (*Tmr* 13.B2), when open, are helpful and speak fair English. They have a list of most of the accommodation available and will place callers.

   Nancy, an American girlfriend, assures us that at the Hotel in which she stayed for almost a month, only she and the manager were 'straight', so bear in mind your preferences when selecting accommodation. A nod's as good as a wink. . .

The Eating Out Expensive, there is no other word for it, and generally small portions. Furthermore restaurants and tavernas fill up comparatively early due to the normal

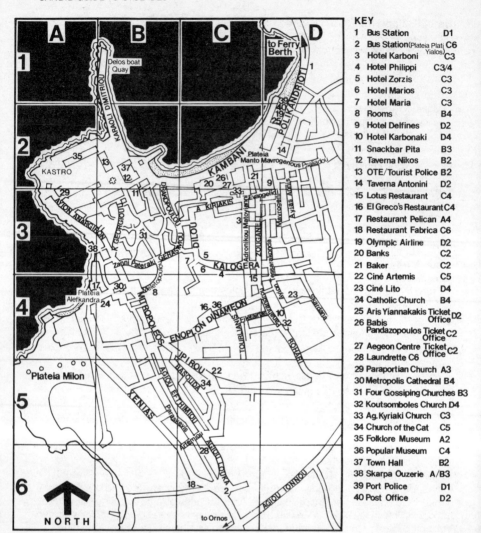

KEY

1 Bus Station — D1
2 Bus Station (Plateia Plati Yialos) — C6
3 Hotel Karboni — C3
4 Hotel Philippi — C3/4
5 Hotel Zorzis — C3
6 Hotel Marios — C3
7 Hotel Maria — C3
8 Rooms — B4
9 Hotel Delfines — D2
10 Hotel Karbonaki — D4
11 Snackbar Pita — B3
12 Taverna Nikos — B2
13 OTE/Tourist Police — B2
14 Taverna Antonini — D2
15 Lotus Restaurant — C4
16 El Greco's Restaurant — C4
17 Restaurant Pelican — A4
18 Restaurant Fabrica — C6
19 Olympic Airline — D2
20 Banks — C2
21 Baker — C2
22 Ciné Artemis — C5
23 Ciné Lito — D4
24 Catholic Church — B4
25 Aris Yiannakakis Ticket Office — D2
26 Babis Pandazopoulos Ticket Office — C2
27 Aegeon Centre Ticket Office — C2
28 Laundrette — C6
29 Paraportian Church — A3
30 Metropolis Cathedral — B4
31 Four Gossiping Churches — B3
32 Koutsomboles Church — D4
33 Ag. Kyriaki Church — C3
34 Church of the Cat — C5
35 Folklore Museum — A2
36 Popular Museum — C4
37 Town Hall — B2
38 Skarpa Ouzerie — A/B3
39 Port Police — D1
40 Post Office — D2

MYKONOS

Illustration 16

pressure of tourists being topped up with Cruise-Liner passengers.

Snackbar prices are on the other hand reasonable with a good souvlaki pita costing 50 drs. A particularly filling example is served up by a small Snack bar (*Tmr* 11.B3) 20 m down the alley alongside the shop of **Y. Voulgaris**. This is signposted **For Exchange National Bank of Greece** (but the bank has long moved away). The bar is at the end of a cul-de-sac on the left.

Further on down the alley and on the right is:-

Taverna Nikos (*Tmr* 12.B2)
Directions: As above or left at the tatty administration block housing the Tourist police and OTE (*Tmr* 13.B2), down the street and almost opposite a small Chapel.

Recommended and for Mykonos must rate very well but note the caveat 'for Mykonos'. There certainly is a fair selection on offer — including spinach and cheese pie at 100 drs, fried zucchini, and an assortment of salads including a Greek salad which is poor but only costs 100 drs. Main courses include the usual moussaka (200 drs), pastitso, stuffed tomatoes, meatballs, stuffed eggplant, all prices at 190 drs. Also on offer are roast beef (230 drs), 'succulent' roast lamb (320 drs) and various chops and steaks. A meal for 2 will set diners back about 950 drs including 2 bottles of retsina but note that only the large Cambas retsina is available costing 170 drs a bottle. The other wine offerings are damned expensive apart from a Rotunda also costing 170 drs. Oh where, oh where are the large Demestica's that used to cost 95 drs only five years ago but are now priced at about 170 drs. I must admit to often forgetting that the exchange rate has risen from about 112 drs to 170 drs against the English pound sterling in the same period!

Reputably the best taverna in town is:-

Taverna Antonini (*Tmr* 14.D2)
Directions: On the left of Plateia Manto Mavrogenous (*Sbo*). The Square with a railed off bust to the forefront, (celebrating the island's heroine), has the **Mad Club** on the left-hand corner, and blocking off the bottom side, the **Piano Club**. The Taverna is in the second block on the left edging the square. The tables are crammed on to the pavement and climb with the steps up into the building. Again not inexpensive with a meal for two of moussaka, 1 haricot beans, a Greek salad, half bottle of retsina and bread (40 drs) costing 950 drs. (Ouch!)

Lotus Restaurant (*Tmr* 15.C4)
Directions: On the main street of Adronikou-Matoyianni across Odhos Kalogera and on the left.

Narrow, bistro-ish, 'hole-in-the-wall' and serving good soups.

Continuing on into odhos Enoplon Dinameon which bends round to the right past the **Popular Museum** and on the right, opposite the **Three Wells** is:-

El Greco's (*Tmr* 16.C4)
Directions: As above.

Mouth-watering but pricey menu. This area is really bewitchingly lovely at night with electric lighting skilfully used to highlight the buildings, paved streets and surroundings.

One of the most picturesque locations must be that of the:-

Restaurant Pelican or **Alefkandra** (*Tmr* 17.A4)
Directions: From the OTE/Tourist police administration block (*Tmr* 13.B2), Odhos K. Georgouli winds towards the Plateia Milon (Windmill Sq). Halfway there and an area on the right contains a number of Churches past which leads to a scrubbly beach. *The Pelican* is on the right, at the start of a row of buildings that edge and jut out over the sea.

Splendidly situated but expensive.

Restaurant Fabrica (*Tmr* 18.C6)

Directions: On Xenias St which connects Plateia Milon and the Plati Yialos Bus terminal Sq, at the terminal end. Otherwise proceed from the Administration Block end of the harbour along Odhos K. Georgouli which jinks into Odhos Mitropoleos, thence into Ag Efthimiou, Ag Louka and the Plateia Plati Yialos Bus terminal. (*Tmr* 2.C6).

Good value.

THE A TO Z OF USEFUL INFORMATION

AIRLINE OFFICE & TERMINUS (*Tmr 19.D2*) In a block of buildings to the far right of the harbour. (*Fsw*), which also contains the ticket office of Aris Yiannakakis (*See* **Ferry-Boat Ticket Offices**), the Post Office and Port Authorities.

In common with all other Olympic offices, the staff display the signs of hardly controlled strain. This is brought on by the usual daily crop of tourists attempting to change their tickets, flying times and etc and etc. As this is a desperately busy office, even in May and October, the quiet chaos (often not so quiet) can be imagined!

Aircraft timetables

Mykonos to Athens (& vice-versa).

Up to seven flights a day until June when the number increases by some further four flights. One-way fare 2270 drs, duration 50 mins.

Mykonos to Iraklion (Crete)

Monday, Wednesday, Friday & Sunday	0840 hrs.
Tuesday, Thursday & Saturday	1310 hrs.
From 23rd June additionally Monday only	1525 hrs.

Return

Monday, Wednesday, Friday & Sunday	1040 hrs.
Tuesday, Thursday & Saturday	1440 hrs.

From 23rd June additionally

Tuesday, Wednesday, Saturday & Sunday	1320 hrs.
Tuesday, Thursday & Saturday	1445 hrs.
Monday	1655 hrs.

One-way fare 3000 drs, duration 1 hr 10 mins.

Mykonos to Rhodes island

Monday, Wednesday, Friday & Sunday	1310 hrs.
Tuesday, Thursday & Saturday	0840 hrs

Return

Monday, Wednesday, Friday & Sunday	1440 hrs.
Tuesday, Thursday & Saturday	1100 hrs.

One-way fare 3800 drs, duration 2 hrs.

Mykonos to Santorini (Thira) island

Daily	0840 hrs.

Return

Monday, Wednesday, Friday & Sunday	1140 hrs.
Tuesday, Thursday & Saturday	1220 hrs.

One-way fare 2690 drs, duration 1 hr 40 mins.

BANKS Two major banks almost side by side in the same building, central on the harbour Esplanade and next door to the Church of Ag Nicholas.

National & Commercial Banks (*Tmr* 20.C2) Only the usual banking hours, Monday to Friday. This is quite surprising considering the frantic internationalism of the Port with not only the 'resident' holiday-makers but seven or eight Cruise Liners a day plus Delos island visitors. There are straightforward facilities for travellers cheques in one or two of the **Ferry-Boat Ticket Offices.**

BEACHES To the right of the harbour (*Fsw*) there is a delightful, narrow, small, but very sandy beach beyond the Post Office building (*Tmr* D1) backed by Odhos Polikandrioti. At the height of the season it must be very, very crowded but early and late in the year has surprisingly few visitors.

Beneath Windmill Sq (*Tmr* A5) is a small, narrow but stony bit of scrubbly foreshore with some sand.

Towards the far end of the harbour wall, beyond the **Banks**, (*Tmr* 20.C2) a strip of sandy foreshore is used by local fishermen to beach their caiques and small benzinas but those keen enough could have a quick dip.

BICYCLE, SCOOTER & CAR HIRE 'Scooter Alley' (*Tmr* C6) is either side of the Ornos/ Psarou road on the edge of Town and is a rather messy area.

Ioannis Zouganelis   Tel. 23427
The last outfit on the right in the direction of Ornos.

Don't be put off by his 'more than usually' disinterested attitude. He is a straight-forward and honest chap but the rates are pretty horrific with the 24 hour hire of a scooter costing 1200 drs. Naturally 2 or 3 days brings the price down. Petrol (gasoline) costs 325 drs for 5 litres (just over one gallon of 2 stroke mix).

See **Arrival by Ferry** for another area of enquiry on the Ag Ioannou and Stefanou crossroads. Diagonally opposite this site, on the right of the slope down to the harbour beach road, is a **Rent A Car.**

BOOKSELLERS International papershop and paperbacks in Kambani St behind the **Banks** building. (I am aware that this is another Odhos Kambani!)

BREAD SHOPS
Mykonos Bakery (*Tmr* 21.C2) on the far corner of the large building on the right (*Sbo*) of Plateia Manto Mavrogenous.

BUSES A comprehensive service the timetable details of which are difficult to unearth although the Tourist police will advise. As discussed under **Arrival by Ferry**, there are two terminals,
1. Polikandrioti Beach road (*Tmr* 1.D1)
2. 'Plateia Plati Yialos' (*Tmr* 2.C6).

Bus timetable
1. Polikandrioti Beach road Terminal

Mykonos Town to Ano Mera & Kalafatis Beach
Daily   0700, 1015, 1215, 1400, 1700 hrs (Ano Mera only)

Mykonos Town to Ag Stefanos
No details

2. Plateia Plati Yialos Terminal

Mykonos Town to Plati Yialos & Psarou
Daily   0800, every hour on the hour to 2300 hrs

Mykonos Town to Ornos & Ag Yiannis Beach
Daily   0800, 1100 (Ag Yiannis), 1200, 1300 (Ag Yiannis),
                                          1500, 1700 (Ag Yiannis), 1900 (Ag Yiannis), 2100 hrs (Ag Yiannis)

CHEMISTS *See* **Medical Care.**

CINEMAS Two, the **Cine Artemis** (*Tmr* 22.C5) and **Cine Lito** (*Tmr* 23.D4).

COMMERCIAL SHOPPING AREA None, but there is nothing that cannot be purchased in the Chora stretching from one end of the almost circular harbour to the other. Naturally the internationalism of visitors, rather than Greek island requirements, is reflected in the number of shops selling jewellery, fur coats, knitwear, shoes, as well as boutiques, art, hair and beauty salons, picture galleries and fashion shops.

Most of the essential prerequisites can be found on the major streets of Adronikou-Matoyianni, Enoplon Dinameon, Mitropoleos, Ag Efthimiou and Ag Louka as well as the ancillary lanes of Kambani, A. Kiriakis, Evangelidi and Zouganeli.

DENTISTS *See* **Medical Care.**

DISCOS A profusion, probably more than on any other island, which speaks volumes. It is best to establish the particular bent, quirk and or character of this or that disco, it may well help to save everyone unnecessary embarrassment.

Establishments include:-

Apollo's Disco 2001 On Odhos Pasaliadou beside the **Piano Bar**, Plateia Manto Mavrogenous.

Baboulas Disco The Alefkandra Sq end of Odhos K. Georgouli.

Caprice Disco Bar In the same area as the *Restaurant Pelican* prior to Catholic Church (*Tmr* 24.B4) off Odhos K. Georgouli.

City Off K. Georgouli St.

Kastros Bar Classical music and comparative serenity. Close by the area known as Kastro, on the bluff beyond the Delos boat quay, overlooking the seafront at the top end of the Venice Quarter. They serve up their own version of Irish coffee which they imaginatively name —Kastro.

Mad Club Centrally situated on the corner of Plateia Manto Mavrogenous. Popular spot.

Pierros Disco Bar Opposite Ag Nicholas Church. The gayest bar in Town. Well I couldn't leave it out.

Pigeon House Club Ag Stefanou St, almost on the Ferry-boat quay.

Rainbow Disco Along Odhos K. Georgouli and at the start of Odhos Mitropoleos.

Remezzo On the junction formed by Ag Stefanou, Ag Ioannou and Polikandrioti Sts on the way to the Ferry-boat quay.

TKs At the commencement of Odhos K. Georgouli, behind the OTE/Tourist police administration block.

Yacht Club Well not really and the peaked cap, pressed slacks, 'yellow-wellie' brigade would go Wodehouse purple-faced at the very suggestion. Its only connection with a yacht must be the situation at the start of the Ferry-boat quay. Dancing, drinking (and debauchery) until the early morning hours.

And many, many more. . .

DOCTORS *See* **Medical Care.**

FERRY-BOATS Not a major ferry-boat axis but a very useful stop-off point from which to reach the Eastern wing of the Cyclades (the islands of Andros and Tinos); travel the East chain, to say Paros from whence there is a convenient local ferry connection with the Western chain island of Siphnos.

Ferry-boat timetables

Day	Departure time	Ferry-boat	Ports/Islands of Call
Daily	1450 hrs	Panagia Tinoy	Tinos, Piraeus (M. 2040 hrs)
	1415 hrs	Naias	Tinos, Piraeus (M. 2000 hrs)
Tuesday	0100 hrs	Atlas II	Tinos, Andros, Rafina (M)
Thursday	0100 hrs	Atlas II	Tinos, Andros, Rafina (M)
Friday	2230 hrs	Georgios Express	Paros, Ios, Santorini
Saturday	0100 hrs	Atlas II	Tinos, Andros, Rafina (M)
	1300 hrs	Atlas II	Tinos, Syros, Andros, Rafina (M)

See **MYKONOS EXCURSION** for Delos island connections.

FERRY-BOAT TICKET OFFICES A number of Esplanade offices but my own favourite is:-

Aris Yiannakakis (*Tmr* 25.D2) In the same block as the Post Office on the far right (*Fsw*). They are very helpful and lack that dismissive attitude cultivated here and there on the Greek islands.

Babis Pandazopoulos (*Tmr* 26.C2) The office is located on the Ferry-boat quay side of the Bank building.

Aegeon Centre (*Tmr* 27.C2) Adronikou-Matoyiani St towards the rear of the Bank building.

Sea and Sky Travel on Plateia Manto Mavrogenous.

HAIRDRESSERS A veritable plethora. In such a cosmopolitan spot it would be unendurable for the ladies to have to go without their weekly visit to the hairdressers surely! In any case 'the sea plays havoc with it . . !'

HOSPITAL *See* **Medical Care.**

LAUNDRETTE No 51 Ag Paraskevis (*Tmr* 28.C6). Just back from the Plateia Plati Yialos Bus terminal. Charges are 300 drs for a machine load, 500 drs for a full machine and the lady will iron as well.

Open daily 0900 - 1300/1800 - 2000 hrs and closed Sunday afternoon.

LUGGAGE STORE None, so almost everybody piles their cases and backpacks on and around the statue on Plateia Manto Mavrogenous.

MEDICAL CARE
Chemists Plentiful and often named 'Drug Stores'. Ugh.

Dentists Two officially listed— A Drakopoulou, Tel. 22503 and G Economou at Ornos, Tel. 22994.

Doctors A veritable rash of medical men including
Nikolos Michael, Odhos Adronikou-Matoyianni, Tel. 23026
Kourinis Loukianos, Adronikou-Matoyianni, Tel. 22588.

Hospital Last seen to the left of Adronikou-Matoyianni, after the crossroads with Odhos Kalogera (*Sbo*).

Pharmacies include Kousathanos, Markantonakis, and Stalnatopoulos. Usual weekday hours and closed weekends but a rota is in operation, the information about which is displayed in the various shop windows.

NTOG None. *See* **Tourist police.**

OPENING HOURS
Museums Daily 0900 - 1530 hrs, Sundays and holidays 1000 - 1500 hrs, closed Tuesday.

Shops A wider interpretation of the 'standard' shop hours with the more tourist orientated businesses staying open seven days a week, at least 12 hours a day.

OTE (*Tmr* 13.B2) In the same shabby block as the Tourist police. Daily 0730 - 2200 hrs, wekends 0730 - 1500 hrs.

PETROL (GASOLINE) There is a Petrol Station on the road to Ano Mera, close to the Town.

PLACES OF INTEREST
Cathedrals & Churches One informed source maintains that the building of the innumerable Churches and Chapels was funded from wealth accrued by fishing and piracy! Well, there you go.

Paraportian Church (*Tmr* 29.A3) A most unusual whitewashed structure cobbled together from four separate chapels over the centuries and situated on the Kastro bluff beyond the OTE/Tourist police offices.

Metropolis Cathedral (Tmr 30.B4) Orthodox.

Catholic Church (Tmr 24.B4) Blue domed and white walled.

'The Four Gossiping Churches' (Tmr 31.B3) Quaintly named, if nothing else, and straight down the lane from the OTE/Tourist police offices.

Koutsomboles Church (Tmr 32.D4) Known as the Four Churches. Why do they not also gossip?

Ag Kyriaki (Tmr 33.C3) Just off the Esplanade to the left of the **Bank** building *(Sbo)* and possessed of some very old icons.

Eklissoula Ton Ghatlou (Tmr 34.C5) More colloquially the Church of the Cat.

Museums

Archaeological On the eastern or Ferry-boat quay end of the Port. Five small rooms display, amongst other items, an unusual collection of ancient vases and pithoi between 2500 and 4500 years old including a 7th century BC pithoi with reliefs depicting the Trojan War, a selection of 1st and 2nd century BC funeral jewellery and headstones from close by Rheneia island, once the grave yard or Necropolis for adjacent Delos island, and a marble statue of Hercules.

Folklore Museum (Tmr 35.A2) At the other end of the harbour, on the sea-side of the OTE/ Tourist police building *(Tmr* 13.B2). A square, whitewashed 18th century mansion with contrasting wooden shutters and doors, an external staircase and a low, curved roof building butted on the side. Once owned by the Kyriazopoulos family and displaying memorabilia, artefacts, commemorative items, furniture, furnishings, utensils, books and documents of the past.

Mykonos Library (Tmr C2) To the rear of the **Bank** building, on the corner adjacent to Ag Kyriaki Church. A collection of Hellenistic coins and 18th/19th century seals.

Popular Museum (Tmr 36.C4) On Odhos Enoplon Dinameon prior to the **Three Wells** fountain. Local exhibits.

Popular Art Museum In the Galatis or Venetian Mansion.

Tria Pigadia or Three Wells *(Tmr* C4) Three carved fountain heads sited on the right of the picturesque Odhos Enoplon Dinameon from the direction of Odhos Adronikou-Matoyianni.

Harbour Esplanade & Chora The wide, curved, paved, traffic-less waterfront of the harbour, made up of the streets of Akti Kambani and Al Mavrogenous, from Plateia Manto Mavrogenous at the bottom (or east end) all the way round to the Town Hall *(Tmr* 37.B2) or north end. This is where the majority of the action takes place. Those that ceaselessly parade up and down being observed by the cafe-bar clients who endlessly watch them from the various establishments that sprawl across the wide thoroughfare. Participants vary from the outrageous to the 'my goodness' and beyond!.

The not particularly attractive waterfront, is edged by a harbour wall and narrow beach (off which moor up a wide selection of boats). On the other hand the Chora that stretches away from the Esplanade is startlingly, almost painfully beautiful. The 'doll-like' houses are festooned with flowers and plants, external steps, stairs and colourful balconies. They edge and spill out on to streets and lanes that vary from the wide to extremely narrow and the flags of which are picked out with whitewash, wandering and winding their way through the Town. Possibly prettiest at night when the darkness is brilliantly lit by dazzling bright, concealed electric lighting. The jostling crowds that throng the streets, bazaars, boutiques, bars, shops, tavernas and restaurants do so in surroundings of colourful vivid brightness, alluring shadows and purple darkness.

Particularly attractive spots include:-

Alefkandra (Tmr A/B4) Popularly known as the Venice Quarter, the houses of which unevenly edge the sea with their dissimilar railed and roofed balconies projecting over the water. At night the cafe-bars and tavernas at the *Skarpa Ouzerie (Tmr* 38.A/B3) end of the buildings throw out daubs, pools and splashes of luminescence in the shades of the enveloping night.

To the south and overlooking this beautiful spot is the:-

Plateia Milon (Tmr A5) Windmill Square on which the four 'dead' circular mill buildings (with their now forever still, projecting, circular sail frameworks) resemble silent, watchful Martian monsters temporarily halted in a terrestrial invasion.

Another sight that once had widespread fame is:-

Petros The Island pelican but not the original bird. None-the-less, the present incumbent has earned his share of popularity and interest although this has, naturally, waned somewhat. I say naturally because some of the specie of homo-sapiens would probably out do and up stage a pink elephant, even if one did appear on the waterfront.

Whilst on the subject of the pelican it reminds me of the rumour (only a rumour), that the original Petros took it upon himself to give up the delights of Mykonos and fly the nest, as it were, landing on Tinos. The Tiniots, unable to believe their luck, pampered the truant in an effort to keep him on the island ground-staff, claiming him as their own. The Mykoniots, when they discovered this underhand behaviour, took out a law suit to retrieve the miscreant. The elected judge, with the wisdom of Solomon, is said to have instructed the Mykonos fisherman, who was supposed to be the birds ex-keeper, to endure a mock savaging. On seeing his master being beaten the pelican went to the beleagured man's aid thus establishing, without doubt, his true home to which he was returned.

With the popularity of the Island in mind, it is not surprising that Mykonos is on the Cruise-Liner circuit. This naturally opens up the holiday sporting activities to include passenger spotting and watching.

An unfortunate side effect of their daily visitations is a further increase in the over-crowding, still higher prices and even less room at the inn's table.

POLICE
Port *(Tmr* 39.D1) At the Ferry-boat end of the harbour, at the far end of the building which contains the Post Office.

Tourist *(Tmr* 13.B2) Extremely helpful, pleasant and possessing a fair grasp of English. They have an extensive list of **Rooms** available and will place any enquirer. Incidentally their lists extend to ferry-boat and bus timetables. The office, which is open daily from 0800 to 1600 hrs, is in the same building as the OTE.

POST OFFICE *(Tmr* 40.D2) In a building that also houses the Port police and Olympic office.

TAXIS *(Tmr* C/D2) Plateia Manto Mavrogenous. A board advises the base line figures of the official tariffs including:
Mykonos Town to Ag (San) Stefanos from 130 drs; Tourlos 110 drs; Ano Mera 300 drs; Metaliou 500 drs; Kalafatis 480 drs; Plati Yialos 200 drs; Ornos 170 drs; Airport 150 drs; St John 220 drs.

Note that all sorts of extras are charged.

TELEPHONE NUMBERS & ADDRESSES

Bus Station	Tel. 23360
First Aid	Tel. 22274
OTE	Tel. 22499
Taxi rank	Tel. 22400
Tourist police	Tel. 22482

TOILETS Few facilities but there is one to the side of the OTE/Tourist police building (*Tmr* 13.B2). BUT lavatory paper costs 20 drs.

TRAVEL AGENTS *See* **Ferry-Boat Ticket Offices.**

ROUTE ONE
To Ag Stefanos (4 km) This route leads north from the Ferry-boat quay, edging the west coast line initially skirting an ugly quarry at Kaminakia.

TOURLOS (2 km from Mykonos Town) A broad bay with four coarse, sandy coves and some kelp. At the near end is the D class *Hotel Sunset* (Tel. 23013) also known as *Itiovassilema*. A single room 880 drs, a double room 1300 drs rising to 1100 drs and 1700 drs (July and August) all with en suite bathrooms. The *Sunset* is followed by *Pension Tourlas* with similar rates. At the far end is the *Pension & Restaurant Makis.*

AG STEFANOS (4 km from Mykonos Town) A chatty, busy, coarse sand beach, with the plush *Hotel Alkistes* marching up the hillside and three restaurants edging the backshore at the far end. Quite a lot of kelp and Ag Stefanos is on the flight path to the Airport!

ROUTE TWO
To Ano Mera (and beyond to Tarsana, Kalafatis &
Ag Anna Beaches) (8 km) The road climbs out of Mykonos Town through the messy outer ring of development past the petrol station and a car-breakers (yes a car-breaker). Frankly I don't find the Mykonos countryside at all attractive. It appears that the authorities exercise little control over house building as the landscape appears to be indiscriminately scattered with the standard Mykonos 'housepack' — a white cube with blancmange mould rounded roof edges and a decorative chimney. If a matchless example of my possible prejudice is required, beyond the turning off to the Monastery of Ag Panteleimonos, the town rubbish dump is possibly the most unattractive of its type that I have seen. The road edge containment is made up of a fence of beaten out and flattened rusty oildrums, discarded cookers and refrigerators.

Incidentally my obsession with 'dead buses' is satiated by an example way down in the fields to the left.

FTELIA BEACH (5 km from Mykonos Town) A turning off to the left and a bare kilometre down the steeply inclined road. This is initially surfaced but becomes a rough track that winds over messy scrub plain with car tyres scattered about. The large indented Bay of Panormos, skirted by many Chapels, is as attractive as the landward is unattractive. The right-hand side of the bay (*Fsw*) is mucky but to the left there is a very pleasant, clean, coarse sand beach, with some tar, sweeping round to the *Restaurant Ftelia* whose unattractive building is set into the hillside. Windsurfing.

It is thought provoking to realise that this area was the site of an ancient town and port.

ANO MERA (8 km from Mykonos Town) The rather confusing layout of this large, sleepy Village, dominated by the Monastery campanile, would appear to have simply happened but Ano Mera is one of the saving graces of the island.

On the approach, a sharp left winds off past Paleokastrou Monastery into a northern hinterland on the slopes of Mt Kourvousia. In actual fact Paleokastrou was a Convent or as the maps rather prettily put it a **Womens Monastery**.

Keeping to the left of the settlement along a wide, dusty track leads towards the beaches of Ag Anna, Kalaftis and Tarsana, of which more later.

Keeping to the right at the major fork gives way to two short roads, the low and the high, into the centre of the Village. The high road leads on to a large circular square, almost a roundabout, around which the Village is scattered.

At the far or east side of the Square is a Clinic and an Exchange Office, inside the entrance to which is a post box and opposite which is a Periptero with a telephone. There are 3 or 4 tavernas, a good bakery, a supermarket and a Public WC (or toilets for our American friends).

A number of the taverna signs are in English. My favourite watering-hole is the simple, long, single storey Kafenion/taverna at the west (or Mykonos Town) side of the Square. The patio is covered with a trellis bamboo roof, has two gum trees assisting the shading and a profusion of flowers. One of a number of signs and ice cream plaques announces **We serve Greek salads with Feta Cheese. . .** The elderly Mama has to move about from one end of the building to the other whilst cooking but she prepares a super meal from the simple bill of fare. A Greek salad large enough for two (160 drs), 2 omelettes (100 drs each), bread (15 drs) and a bottle of beer (60 drs), cost 435 drs, and this is Mykonos. A splendid find.

To the right (facing the Kafenion above or back towards Mykonos Town, if you will) is the:-

Tourliani Monastery A 16th century house of worship behind a fortified, very high wall above which peeps the campanile and rises a 'wedding-cake-stand' tower. The solid arched doorway let into the outer wall leads on to a spacious courtyard and, to one side of the cloistered perimeter, a simple two room museum.

Prior to leaving matters religious, as detailed above, the turning off to the left immediately prior to Ano Mera proceeds to the picturesque:-

Monastery of Paleokastrou (8½ km from Mykonos Town) More correctly a Nunnery or Convent and a place of quiet tranquility with a large tree dominating the flag-stoned courtyard from a branch of which is suspended a bell to summon the worthy.

For Elia Beach proceed across the Village leaving the roundabout to the right. It is possible to take the road signposted Ackari Beach (Agrari) but only if a traveller wishes to switch back up and over uncharted, unmade, wall-lined tracks for miles that double back towards the west. Otherwise it is necessary to turn left at the very expensive A class *Hotel Ano Mera*, a 'sore-thumb' construction that juts out of the bleak, stone walled surrounds, and rejoin the now long, wide downward track to:-

ELIA BEACH (8 km from Mykonos Town) Note that regular signposting runs out by the Hotel, reverting to red paint blobs and crude arrows. Steeply descending, the road passes on the left an interesting, unfinished, uninhabited building, styled on a windmill but with a large, stone, first storey patio. Possibly it was to be a night-spot. The lovely broad, coarse sand beach is set in a surrounding of hillsides. The foreshore is clean, even though some scattered kelp is piled up here and there. There are two tavernas to the left of the track down that runs out on the backshore of the beach. Many who stay in Mykonos Town travel out daily by taxi to enjoy the delights of this spot.

The bay of Kalo Livadi can also be reached from the indistinct network of lanes to the south of Ano Mera, as it can from the beaches of Tarsana and Ag Anna.

Returning to the Ano Mera 'by-pass', that is left at the fork at the onset of the village, leads eastwards whence, after another 2 km, a right hand turning bears off along an unsurfaced road to:-

TARSANA (12 km from Mykonos Town) The long, clean, coarse sand beach with some kelp, slowly curves around the very clear sea's edge of the bay. To the far left (*Fsw*) is the extremely expensive *Hotel Aphrodite* built in a series of cubes up the foothills of the backing hillside. The Hotel runs a cocktail bar (no hush my mouth), beach taverna distanced about 100 m in the small cliff edging the bay.

The Hotel serves up lunch-time meals from hay-boxes and pampered guests pick over this or that delicacy. Occasional and or casual visitors, are discouraged from bestowing their custom by being charged outrageous prices — that is outrageous to me — with a bottle of Carlsberg lager (and I wanted Amstel) costing 130 drs. There are a few pedaloes scattered about and bamboo beach sun umbrellas. On the way in, at the far right of the bay (*Fsw*) there are the twin peaks of Cape Kalafatis. The other side of the Cape is:-

AG ANNA (12 km from Mykonos Town) Not the Paradise beach Ag Anna, but a small bay and fine shingle beach, with a line of tar and some kelp, bordering the very clear sea. Rather ramshackle with, for instance, a lorry water tanker body abandoned on the backshore.

Both the above beaches are backed by gentle but unexciting, scrubby slopes but most importantly out of the height of season they are almost deserted.

Back on the Main Road it is really not worth going any further eastwards, although the oft mentioned Profitis Ilias, the highest island point at a lowly 351 m, is in this direction. The one or two beaches that can be spied way down on the right (or south coast) cannot be reached by road. Additionally the never-out-of-the-ordinary countryside becomes positively lunar with old quarry workings. The very eastern end of the island is uninhabited mountain moorland with the armed forces in occupation. Off shore is the Island of Dragonissi famed for its sea worked and shaped caves in which seals have their lodgings.

ROUTE THREE
To Psarou, Plati Yialos, Paradise & Super-Paradise Beaches (4 km) On a steep downward section of the road to Plati Yialos beach a backwards facing turning off to the right curves round to

PSAROU BEACH (4 km from Mykonos Town) The final, unsurfaced approach is through screens of bamboo petering out in the car park of *The Garden Restaurant*. The single-file footpath leads down the right-hand side of the Restaurant emerging on the extreme right-hand side of the beach (*Fsw*). The coarse sand beach is littered with straw sun umbrellas, and deck chairs; swing top litter bins are lined up but kelp is piled up on the seas edge. At the far end of the cove is a beach taverna. Water sports include para and wind-surfing and pedaloes. A smart feel and fairly crowded, even early and late in the year.

PLATI YIALOS BEACH (4 km from Mykonos Town) The surfaced road swoops steeply down besides the expensive C class *Hotels Petinos* and D class *Platy Gialos Beach* (Tel. 22913).

The thoroughfare peters out on a rough, small vehicle park at the extreme right of the lovely, narrow, curved, coarse sand beach set in a cove ending in a 'butterfly wing' of rocky outcrops at the far left-hand side. The near end of the beach is planted with beach umbrellas and deck chairs, the whole edged with bar/restaurants. An expensive feel, no water sports and crowded even early and late in the summer.

To the right around a low cliff edge is a jetty from which there are 'continuous' daily boat trips to Paragka, Paradise Beach (and Camping), Super Paradise Beach, Agrari and Elia beaches with a one-way fare to Paradise Beach costing 50 drs.

There are also excursions to Delos Island and Mykonos Caves (Dragonissa island). The first hotel on the way into the village has Greek dancing every Saturday night and despite the costly atmosphere to the place, a couple of frappe coffees only costs 112 drs.

Buses to Mykonos Town depart from 0810 hrs every hour until and including 2110 hrs, the last bus leaving at 2310 hrs. The bus stop, 200/300 m up the hill from the beach, is sign-posted.

There is a footpath from Plati Yialos to Paradise Beach, whereon nude bathing, and a difficult trek can be made to Super Paradise Beach where the majority of the more unnatural, beautiful young men sunbathe and disport themselves 'in the starkers'. Paradise Beach can be reached by track from a right hand spur off the Airport road. There is an official campsite (Tel. 22129) open from April to October.

ROUTE FOUR

Ornos & Ag Yiannis (4 kms) The road, almost for the whole of its length, borders the sea's edge. The initial part of the route passes through outer Mykonos Town with package tour hotels dotted about and a pleasant beach. About half way to Ornos, there is a development at:-

MEGALI AMMOS (1½ km from Mykonos Town) A splendid beach, edged by horizontal biscuit rock. To landward there are cubic condiminium chalet hotels set in the hillside, 1 cardinal red overlooked by blue coloured ones. There is a taverna at the Mykonos Town end of the beach.

The road curves to the right skirting the near side of Korfos Bay the beach of which is indescribably filthy being covered in all manner of rubbish and the backshore of which is used as a municipal civil engineering dump.

Not much further on along is a major fork in the road and if driving a scooter, beware as the surface here is very loose gravel. The left-hand turning snakes along to :-

ORNOS BEACH (3½ km from Mykonos Town) The road passes the *Hotel Asteri* on the right, **Rent-A-Car & Motor Byke** on the left and *Bistrot Boheme* on the right. The coarse sand beach, with some kelp, is edged by four taverna/beach restaurants as well as, to the left, the *Port Ornos Restaurant* and *Ornos Beach Hotel*, with some benzinas and powered motorboats anchored up. To the right are the condiminiums of the *Paralos Beach Hotel* and, at the far end, a Taverna with a painted fish fascia. They serve up, somewhat languidly, a reasonable range of middlingly expensive fare. Two large draught lagers cost 130 drs. Also on this portion of the beach are a few beach umbrellas.

Buses depart for Mykonos Town at 0810, 1120, 1210, 1320, 1510, 1720, 1920 and 2115 hrs and the one-way fare costs 30 drs.

Back at the fork in the road (incidentally around a cemetery) the right-hand route snakes up the hill bordering, on the right, what was obviously once planned as a village development. For instance there are neat signposts indicating the direction to this and that, one of which is for a supermarket. Forget it, there is no, repeat no, supermarket. Despite the winding nature of the road it follows the curve of the bay. On the last sharp right-hand bend a track sallys forth towards Cape Alogomandra, at the extreme tip of the Bay of Ornos, but peters out in another hill-bound discontinued development.

After the apex of the bend on the left is the:-

Pension Alefteria (Class E)   Tel. 23090
Directions: As above.

The good lady's card describes it as the *Hotel Koslas* but it is a Pension. Pleasantly situated, overlooking Ornos beach to which a convoluted track wanders down to the right-hand end of the beach. There is a bus stop right outside the door.

Mrs Theochari and her husband's English is limited but their daughter, a good looking, well-built lass in her late teens, has an excellent command of the language and will somewhat disinterestingly converse with foreign guests, when necessary. Breakfast if required is taken in the family kitchen off which the family bedrooms open out. A large double room with spacious en suite bathroom starts off at 1000 drs but naturally rises with the onset of summer.

Continuing on up the road leads over the hillside only to drop down the reverse side to:-

AG YIANNIS (4 km from Mykonos Town) A dramatic location with some development.

The rocky bay has a tiny beach of coarse sand, rocks and kelp. There are a few bamboo sun umbrellas, old pedaloes and one taverna to the left, beyond which are another two coves. But it is to the right of the bay that the eye is drawn where a small Chapel and stone jetty jut out into the sea, edged by a rocky hedland. There are a few caiques moored up. Unfortunately close up the scene is not as attractive. Some rock blasting has cleared a track round the headland, to the right of the Chapel but with little effect as it leads nowhere.

EXCURSION TO DELOS ISLAND (Dhilos, Dilos)

The sacred Island 'super-spot' of the Aegean and the envy of all the surrounding islands who would dearly love to have Delos as their own adjunct. Steal it, they would tow it away if they could. Tinos island ensures that it gets in on the act and runs pleasure cruises but Mykonos has the stranglehold on this most valuable tourist property.

Lizards everywhere and arid.

ARRIVAL BY CAIQUE Craft depart daily in the summer months from the quay close by the OTE/Tourist police offices (*Tmr* 13.B2) in Mykonos Town at 0830 - 0900 hrs and the trip takes some ½ hour. The round trip costs about 200 drs each and to go ashore costs another 100 drs. Some 3-4 hours is allowed onshore and the caiques and trip boats commence on the return journey from mid-day on. Tourists are not allowed (legally) to stay overnight or camp out and the *Xenia* is only for the use of bona-fide archaeologists.

Due to the complexities of the excavations it is preferable to join a guided party. The average visitor can only hope, in the short time available, to absorb part of the rarified atmosphere and wonder at the vast extent of the wild flower and weed bestrewn ruins in which nestle marvellous mosaics, terraces, cisterns and from which sprout rich outcrops of statues, stoas, columns, crepidoma, shrines and altars.

The amazing site includes a sacred harbour and lake, Temples to Apollo and the Athenian; Houses of the Naxians, Poseidoniasts, Cleopatra, Dionysos, Tritons, Masks and Dolphins; Sanctuaries, sacred ways, porticos, the Terrace of the Lions, the Theatre and Mt Kynthos.

A historical review shows that the island was occupied as long ago as 3000 BC and even before the arrival of the Ionians, in 1000 BC, was obviously a religious centre with a thriving port. The Ionians, in bringing the Mythological Cult of Leto, the mother of Artemis (or Diana) Goddess of hunting, woodlands and associated with fertility as well as being a Moon-Goddess and Apollo (God of music, poetry, archery, prophecy and healing) really gave an impetus to the island's sacred importance.

But as now, 'a good thing' was usually too much temptation for others to keep their 'sticky fingers' away from and it only took a few centuries for the Athenians to muscle in on the act. They joined the local Masons (well not really), more a United Nations of the Aegean, known as the Delian League, after Delos island where the central funds were deposited. In the meantime one Aegean bully-boy, Polykrates, tyrant of Samos and conqueror of the Cyclades, in an effort to impress the Gods, attached the larger, adjacent island of Rheneia to Delos by chains. These were stretched across the 1000 m channel separating the two, thus binding Rheneia to Delos, dedicating Rheneia to Apollo. Show-off!

After this unpleasant fellow's departure (522 BC), the Athenians got back to work with a will in the 'corridors of power'. Probably one of their chaps became Hon. Treasurer because lo and behold, in 454 BC, the funds were transferred to Athens for safe keeping. Oh yes! And when they got their hands on the money to what purpose do you think it was put? Beefing up the navy, building castles and fortifications? Oh no. One Perikles frittered the loot — sorry bank balance — on repairing damage incurred during Persian invasions and tarting up Athens. Well, well.

It was only a matter of a further few years of manoeuvring and disruptive activity (28 years actually) for the Athenians to convince the Islanders that Delos should be purified. This was actually the second ritual cleansing, one other having taken place in 543 BC. This time the proposed event was lent urgency due to the Athenians adjudging that an epidemic plaguing their city was due to the Gods' anger. It also had the effect of distancing the existing Delos residents from their ancestors thus breaking possible hereditary ties.

To propitiate the Gods, and loosen the Delians grip, not only was it decreed that all the tombs had to be removed to Rheneia island but that no further deaths or births could take place on Delos. Inhabitants would in future have to carry out these necessary bodily functions on Rheneia!

In an effort to rid themselves of the troublesome and despotic Athenians the Islanders appealed to the Spartans for support. When the Athenians heard of this they deported all the inhabitants in 422 BC and caused the leaders to be murdered. Once again the Athenians, suffering severe reversals in the Peloponnesian wars, agreed with the soothsayers and allowed the Islanders to return to Delos To show who was top dog Athens sent a delegation which landed on Rhoneia island from whence they threw across an olden-day, wooden equivalent of the modern day Bailey bridge, over which they marched in triumph. Known as putting a 'frightener on'.

Between about 404 and 394 BC, after the Athenians had been defeated by the Spartans, Delos revelled in a period of independence. This was followed by further interference from Athens until about 315 BC, when, with the Egyptians in charge of the Aegean, the island commenced probably its most prosperous era with the Romans appearing on the scene in about 250 BC. In 166 BC the Roman authorities let the Athenians loose, granted Free-Port status to the island in order to curb the power of Rhodes and turned a blind eye to the wholesale deportation of the Islanders once again. They must have felt like Yo-Yo's. Additionally the tenor of the great religious festivals was subtly altered and they became truly secular events, reminiscent of those epic Cecil B de Mille extravaganzas.

It is said that up to 10,000 slaves were sold every day of a festival. The decline, when it set in, was very rapid and began in 88 BC. Delos, caught up in the 'spin-off' of King Mithridates war against Rome, was sacked and razed to the ground, the Treasury robbed and the inhabitants murdered or taken into slavery.

Despite attempts to rebuild, repopulate, erect a fortification (in 66 BC) and resuscitate the flagging religious importance of the island, it was a down-hill slide. So much so that when the Athenians, in the 3rd century AD, attempted to sell the place off, there were no takers. Since this low point, over the centuries the island's visitors have been a mixture of shepherds, pirates and builders from Mykonos, Tinos and Syros who appropriated the basic building blocks. This fact is borne out when the plaster work is chipped off older buildings on the aforementioned islands and a block of ancient marble comes into view.

Naturally, the Venetians, Turks and British 'borrowed' a number of the more attractive statues, carvings and marbles. Finally, French archaeologists started the work in 1872 that still goes on today.

THE LAYOUT. The following brief discourse will not replace the services of a good guide or an extensive archaeological description, but here goes. The various sites are, in the main, identified.

From the modern day landing mole, with the ancient Sacred Harbour to the left and Commercial Harbour to the right, straight ahead is:–

The Agora (or Square) of the Competialists Competialists were Roman merchants, freed men and slaves, who worshipped the God of crossroads (Lares or Compita). The other merchants that traded here were formed into associations depending upon their religious affiliations including Apollo and Hermes to name but two. The Square also acted as a boundary between the Sacred area to the left, or north, and the commercial area to the right, or south.

To the left, from the Square, leads along the Sacred Way

with on the left-hand the:–

Stoa* of Philip Built by Phillip V of Macedon in 210 BC. 71 m by 11 m with 16 fluted Doric columns

*A portico, or as in this case, a roofed colonnade.

and on the right-hand the:-

South Stoa Erected in the 3rd century BC. 66 m by 13 m with 28 Doric columns, the rear of which was divided up into some 14 shops and through which was the:–

Agora of the Delians The path of the Sacred Way is impeded by the:–

Propylaea** of the Sanctuary of Apollo Built by the Athenians during the 2nd century BC and once packed with altars, temples and statues including the:–

**A gateway and or entrance to a temple

Oikos† of the Naxians A 6th century BC construction with central columns.

† A house

Temple 'C' To the right of the Naxian House and possibly dating back to the Mycenaean era.

Statue of Apollo Or the Collossus of the Naxians. Well, really only the base of what was once a very large Kouros‡ of the God and supposedly knocked of its perch by a giant bronze palm tree. The Venetians and others vandalised the marble statue and bits are exhibited here and there. Further along the now wide Sacred Way are, on the right, three temples

‡ A male statue

The Great Temple The Temple of the Delians on which construction started between 480 and 470 BC, at the outset of the Delian League, stopped when the 'naughty' Athenians transferred the funds back to Athens and only restarted in the 3rd century BC. The interior was divided into Pronaos (vestibules), Cella (the main body of the Temple) and the Opisthodomos ('the room at the rear' — often a strong-room).

The Temple of the Athenians Built about 425 BC, the Cella originally had seven statues mounted on a semi-circular pedestal

and

The Poros Temple Dating back to the 6th century BC, this Temple was the treasury of the Delian League until the funds were 'relocated' to Athens. In front of the temple are two bases and beyond the last temple an arc of five Treasuries or small Temples. In the same circular sweep arching back behind the **South Stoa**, are the remains of three buildings and to the east of which is the:–

Monument of the Bulls This 67 m long by 9 m wide building could well require renaming as it probably housed a trireme as a votive offering, celebrating victory in some ancient sea battle.

Across the Sacred Way from the three Temples are a scatter of temples edged by the:–

Stoa of the Naxians Built in the 6th century BC and forming the south-western boundary of the Sanctuary and which at its far (north) closes with the:–

Oikos of Hieropoieon & Andros. Houses dating back to the 6th century BC, to the right and north of which are the remains of an unremarkable Stoa alongside and around which was the:–

Sanctuary of Artemis In which is the Temple of Artemis, rebuilt three times on the same site, and north of which is the:–

Thesmophorion A 5th century BC Temple built in three sections, the centre one a courtyard and converted by early Christians into a place of worship. Close by, to the east, is the:–

Ekklesiasterion. So named because it was in this building that the Delos Council or Assembly met.

From here it is only a short skip and a jump to a building, originally an office and house, but into which, at a later date, the Romans built a Bath in the ruins.

Continuing in an easterly direction is the:–

Stoa of Antigonus. Marks the northerly edge of the Sanctuary. Built in the 3rd century BC and 120m in length. To either side there are extant the remains of a number of statue bases, buildings, sanctuaries, shops, fountains and tombs, the most thought provoking of which must be through the gateway in the north-east corner of the Sanctuary. The guide books coyly refer to the multilated statues as 'bases embellished. . .', 'marble phalli. . .' and 'marble bases designed to support statues. . .'. They mark the site of the:–

Sanctuary of Dionysos. The plain fact is that the remains are in fact 'ginormous' genitalia of which only the testicles and a stump remain. When complete they must have made a most interesting sight!

The gateway gives access to the:–

Museum. Naturally, the repository of the archaeological finds on both Delos and Rheneia. That is the finds that have not been appropriated by Athens (ever plunderers!).

North of the Sanctuary is the area surrounding the:–

Sacred Lake. Now devoid of water but as it was built sometime ago, I suppose that is acceptable — perhaps somebody removed the plug! The sacred nature is attributable to mythology and is the place where Leto gave birth to Apollo whilst clinging to a palm tree. Swans once graced the Holy water.

Alongside is the:–

Terrace of the Lions. From the original nine or so, some five magnificent specimens remain crouching. Originally a gift from the islanders of Naxos in the 7th century BC, one of the missing statues resides in Venice.

To the south of the Lake (in between the Stoa of Antigonos and the Lake) was the:–

Agora of the Italians.A largish, open courtyard, 110½ m by 69 m, once edged by marble columns and a colonnaded gallery and constructed by Italian merchants in about 110 BC. The exterior was circled by shops.

To the west are variously and in order, the Temple of Leto, Temple of the 12 Gods and the Stoa of Poseidon (probably a 2nd Century market hall).

To the north-west of the Lake is the:–

Institution of the Poseidoniasts of Berytos. That's a mouthful. Originally constructed by shippers and traders from Syria who were followers of a pagan god that they linked with Poseidon.

Other remains in this area include the House of Diadumenos, the House of Comedians, Granite Palaestra and the Lake House. Further to the north-east are the Gymnasium, Stadium, Xystos track, Stadium Quarter and the Synagogue.

Back, as they say, at the landing mole, and straight ahead (east) is the Theatre Quarter. This comparatively cramped residential area rises towards the Area of Sanctuaries through which the Theatre Road threads its way past, amongst others, the House of Cleopatra and Discourides, the House of Dionysos, and the House of the Trident. Other buildings of note (beyond the Theatre) include the Houses of the Dolphins and the Masks.

A number of these Houses possess outstanding mosaics whilst the street not unnaturally leads to the:–

Theatre. Rather a disappointment compared to other examples throughout Greece, but with splendid views. Built in the 3rd/2nd century BC with a capacity for about 5500 people. Perhaps the most interesting fact is that the theatre area was used to collect and distribute rain water to the adjacent and intriguing Theatre Cisterns which serviced some of the settlements water requirements.

Alongside the Theatre is a building possibly used as a Hotel. A path or Sacred Way climbs Mt. Kynthos (110m) from the area of the Museum past, on the left the:–

Sanctuaries of the Foreign Gods. These included Syrian and Egyptian sanctuaries.

Beyond, alongside and clustered about the Heraion are a Samothrakeion and three Serapeion shrines. Further on up the Mountain are various shrines and sanctuaries including the Grotto of Herakles (Hercules) formed by huge slabs of stone.

Possibly the most enchanting, dramatic and awe-inspiring of all the Greek archaeological sites.

14 Paros & Antiparos (Andiparos)
Cyclades Islands — Eastern chain

Paroikias Port ★★
Rest of the island ★★★

FIRST IMPRESSIONS
Travel agents/tourist offices; port bustle/ferry-boats; car hire; English; discos; self-service; Old Quarter; lack of mountains; cultivated countryside; indented coastline.

SPECIALITIES
Marble quarrying; a red wine; agriculture; cheapest postcards in the Cyclades (5 dr).

RELIGIOUS HOLIDAYS & FESTIVALS
include: July — Festival of fish and wine; 15th August — Fair and Festival of Panagia Ekatontapyliani, Paroikias; 23rd August — Festival, Naoussa; 24th September — Festival of Panagia Myrtidiotissa Thapsanon, Mt Ag Pantes.

VITAL STATISTICS
Tel prefix 0284. 21 km from north-east to south-west and 16½ km across totalling some 190 sq km in area. The population numbers about 7,000 of which some 3,000 live in and around the main Port, Town and Chora of Paroikias (Paros).

HISTORY
Apart from the usual Neolithic remains, Saliangos islet, north of Antiparos island in the narrowest point of the channel between the two islands, has revealed a complete Neolithic settlement dating from 4000 BC.

During the years 2000 - 1500 BC the island traded extensively with Crete. Conquest by the Ionians resulted in the arts flourishing and a great age of prosperity with colonies also being established on Thasos and on the Dalmation coast. Architochos, the poet who created **iambic** (pardon?) verse, achieved fame in both poetry and war, dying in a battle with the citizens of Naxos (654 BC), and was deified by Parians for some years.

The Island supported the Persians during the conflict with Athens — and after the Greek victory at Marathon (490 BC) were inevitably at the receiving end of a punitive raid instigated by Athens. They recruited one Miltiades to undertake the mission but he failed, incurring a wound from which he died while attempting to seize a holy relic, one of the objects necessary to ensure success. His son was left to pay the Athenians for the fine levied as a result of his fathers failure. Oh dear, the cost of the sins of the father did visit the son.

Island marble was exported far and wide for sculptures and building works and the affluence continued through to the period of domination by the Romans. The Island re-emerged into the spotlight of history with the establishment of the Church of Panagia Ekatontapyliani. The church was reputedly founded in the third century AD by St Helena (the mother of Constantine the Great, the Byzantine Emperor) whilst she was voyaging to the Holy Land, of which more later.

A savage raid by Arabs in the early 9th century left the island depopulated until the arrival of the Venetians in the early 1200s. During their rule castles were built at Paroikias, Naoussa and Kefalos. A couple of particularly devastating pirate raids resulted in the capital being relocated, for a time, at Kefalos. In 1537 the Turkish Admiral Barbarossa precipitated the beginning of the end for the Venetians with a savage attack resulting in the capture of the Island which finally came under direct Turkish administration in 1560.

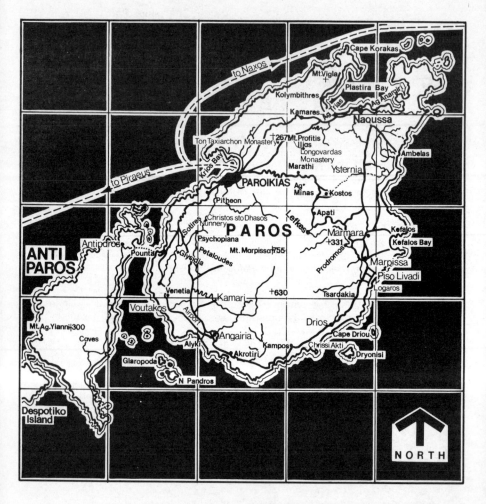

Islands of PAROS and ANTIPAROS

Illustration 17

On the other hand the Turks did not have it all their own way but unfortunately this led to the citizens of Paros being the losers in a number of Venetian reprisal raids. Despite the Turks reputation for savagery they were extremely liberal with respect to the Greeks religious freedom and some 30 monasteries were established during their occupation.

The Russo-Turkish War (1770-74) resulted in the arrival of the Russian fleet who anchored up at Baousa for a winter. After the War of Independence the Mykonos herione, Manto Mavrogenous settled on Paros.

GENERAL

Paros has been the destination for holidaymakers for many years and obviously has had to adapt to cope with the increasing summer hordes. An island can contend with quite large numbers of disparate, small groups of people but Paros has taken on board package tourists in very large numbers. They by their very composition and style of holidaymaking create, some would say, inordinate demands on the inhabitants and amenities more especially at Paroikias, the main Port and Chora. Easily visible manifestations include the high incidence of seaside hotels, car hire firms as well as restaurants offering *Meal A, Meal B* and so on. Surprisingly the Old Quarter, or Chora, of the Town remains almost untouched by the shallow impression a two week visitor can inflict. Furthermore the agricultural countryside, in which are set some attractive small villages, is absolutely delightful.

PAROIKIAS (Paros): capital town & main port (Illustration 18)

Low-lying and possibly the busiest Greek island Port in the Aegean. The Esplanade has lost the little charm it possessed. Even the picturesque windmill opposite the Ferry-boat quay, once occupied by the Tourist Police, now looks abject and forlorn in the surge of steamship passengers that ebbs and flows across the waterfront. Not all is dross though for the Old Quarter that lies behind the Esplanade is a lovely maze of lanes, alleys and steps. Naturally the intensive tourism has proved very penetrative but the infiltration is not as extensive and overpowering as on Mykonos, but should that be the yard-stick?

ARRIVAL BY AIR

The airfield at Alyki is almost the other side of the Island, some 12 km from Paroikias. It is experiencing a vigorous expansion with construction underway in 1985 to enable the airport to be able to accommodate larger aircraft.

ARRIVAL BY FERRY

Rarely can a Ferry-boat quay (*Tmr*1.D1) be so conveniently located, but then it needs to be in order to cope with the enormous inward and outward flow experienced due to the island's pivotal role in the ferry-boat system. Connections can be made from here with the Western chain (by small passenger ferries to Siphnos); Naxos for the far flung Eastern islands of Iraklia, Shinoussa, Koufonissi, Donoussa, Amorgos and Astipalaia, and Mykonos for the Eastern wing of islands (Andros and Tinos). Added to which it is on the main line route linking Syros, Ios and Santorini.

The number of passengers has necessitated the erection of large 'cages' in which those about to embark are kept penned while those disembarking make the short walk to the Esplanade roundabout at the end of the quay. Representatives of hotels and pensions and Room owners, both in and out of Town, clamour for clients, swarming over the disembarking passengers. Note that owners of the more desirable Chora accommodation do not have to bother to join in this scrum except at the very beginning and end of the summer season.

If by some mischance a traveller is not offered rooms, across the road, the other side of the roundabout and half-right (*Sbo*) opens out into a large park-like Square (Plateia Mavrogenous) on which is the office of the Tourist police (*Tmr* 2.D2). Note a dried up, concreted river-bed splits the area into two dissimilar sized portions.

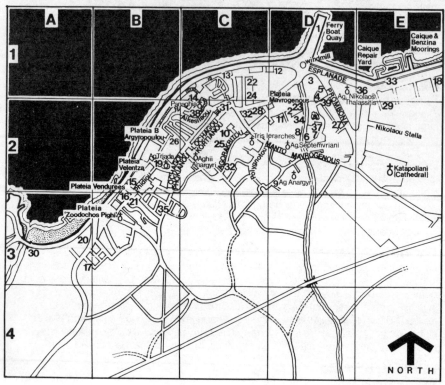

PAROIKIAS

NORTH

KEY

1 Ferry-boat Quay	D1	
2 Tourist Police	D2	
3 Paros Travel Agency	D1	
4 Hotel Kontes	D1	
5 ITS Travel Agency	D1	
6 Pension Constantine	D2	
7 Rooms	D2	
8 Rooms	D2	
9 Rooms	D2	
10 Rooms Mimikos	C2	
11 Hotel Georgy	D2	
12 OTE Office	D1	
13 Scopas Travel Agency	C1	

14 Rooms	C1/2
15 Rooms	B2
16 Rooms	B2/3
17 Rooms	A3
18 Rooms	E1
19 Taverna	B2
20 Restaurant Liminaki	A3
21 Nicks Hamburgers	B3
22 Special Soyvlaki	C1
23 Cyclades Tourist Agency	D2
24 Palm Tree Café	C1
25 To Tamarisk Restaurant	C2
26 May Tey Restaurant	B/C2

27 Olympic Airline Office	D2
28 National Bank	C2
29 Scooter Hire	E1/2
30 Rent a Car/Motorbike	A3
31 Bookshop	C2
32 Bakers	
33 Bus Terminal	E1
34 Supermarket	D2
35 Drop Art Gallery	B3
36 Public Toilets	E1
37 Laundry	D2
38 The Kastro	C2
39 Post Office	D1/2

Illustration 18

Leave **Paros Travel Agency** (*Tmr* 3.D1) and the river-bed to the left. Wandering across Plateia Mavrogenous towards the Chora will more often than not 'flush out' the offer of accommodation.

There is a signboard to the left of the **Paros Travel Agency** listing island hotels and telephone numbers.

To the left, (*Sbo*) along the waterfront hugging Esplanade leads to the newly developed part of Paroikias, which suburbs growth has been necessitated by the sharp increase in the number of package-holiday-makers. To the right the waterfront road bends around to the left and then curves slowly back, all the while edging the Old Quarter on the left, to which various steps and squares give access.

A number of 'in-the-know' backpackers, on landing, make straight for outlying seaside and inland locations, which might include Alyki, Piso Livadi or the small port of Naoussa.

THE ACCOMMODATION & EATING OUT

The Accommodation A plethora of hotels, a large number of which are tour-operator booked. There are plenty of D and E class establishments to go round, as there are pensions and *Rooms*, with the exception possibly of the height-of-the-season. But that is to be expected anywhere in the Aegean, let alone the Cyclades.

Note that the C class hotels are rather expensive.

Hotel Kontes (*Tmr* 4.D1) (Class D)   Tel. 21246
Directions: In the block of buildings, at the apex of the corner formed by Odhos (almost Leoforos) Prombona and the Square, half-left from the end of the Ferry-boat quay (*Sbo*). Rather masked by **Paros Travel Agency** (*Tmr* 3.D1) and to the right of the **ITS Travel Agency** (*Tmr* 5.D1). A noisy area.

A fairly modern building. Doubles sharing the bathroom, start at 900 drs and en suite from 1050 drs rising, for the period 16th June - 30th September, to 1150 drs and 1300 drs respectively. Single rooms start at 600 drs.

Pension — Constantine Passos (*Tmr* 6.D2)
Directions: Proceeding half-right as if towards Plateia Mavrogenous diagonally across the Esplanade roundabout, it is necessary to turn left before the concrete river-bed (either side of **Paros Travel**, (*Tmr* 3.D1). This opens out into an irregular shaped Platela with a colourful, low walled triangular garden in the centre, and bounded, on the right, by the river-bed. The far side is edged with two restaurants and a Dry Cleaners. Off the bottom left-hand side, a narrow street bends round to the right opening out into another irregular, oldish, small and slightly sunken square. The cracked and sunken surface appears to mask broken drains and when the summer is at its hottest the mosquitoes and smells prove interesting. *Mrs Passos's Pension* is at the far right-hand side.

The establishment is impersonal but the rooms are spacious, the shared bathrooms clean and well equipped, the water hot and there is a communal fridge on each landing. A double room starts at 800 drs. The bedroom doors tend to close with a hollow bang, day and night.

Rooms (*Tmr* 7.D2)
Directions: Next door and prior to *Constantine Passos* above. Same rates and comments regarding the surrounds.

Rooms (*Tmr* 8.D2)
Directions: Back at the 'river-bed' Plateia (*Tmr* D2), the dry concrete lined water-course is used as a pedestrian way and this accommodation is beyond the far right corner of the Square.

Double rooms from 800 drs.

Continuing on along the river-bed, it progresses to the main 'arterial' lane of Manto Mavrogenous that bridges the stream bed at right angles from which 'doo-hickey' steps climb. Turn right along Odhos Manto Mavrogenous and then quarter left along the narrow lane that branches off, leads across crossroads, past the Church of Ag Anargyri on the left and, just beyond the side turning on the right, is:-

Rooms (*Tmr* 9.D2)

Back at the river-bed, turn right along Odhos Manto Mavrogenous past the fountain of Mavrogenous 'A' and the Church of Ag Septemvriani on the right, two lanes and the Church of Tris Lerarches on the left. The next left turning, Odhos Agorakritou, is beneath a covered way and by keeping round to the right leads into a dead-end, small square, on the left of which is:-

Rooms Mimikos (*Tmr* 10.C2)
Directions: As above.
The usual rates with doubles from 800 drs.

Back at the main park-like Plateia Mavrogenous, and at the far left is the:-

Hotel Georgy (*Tmr* 11.D2) Plateia Mavrogenous   Tel. 21667
Directions: As above. The Hotel is over a Cafeteria and Travel Agent.
Expensive with double rooms en suite, up to 1st July, costing 1500 drs after which, until the end of September, they are priced at 2050 drs.

Proceeding across the centre of the Plateia, past the Banks on the left, along the street, over a crossroads which jinks around the excellent Grocery on the left, and on to Odhos Lochagou Kortianou. This 'main' lane parallels the Esplanade for a distance prior to curving round on to Plateia Velentza on the edge of the Esplanade.

Hotel Dina (*Tmr* B2) (Class E)   Tel. 21325
Directions: As above but on the slow right-hand curve in the street as it bends round to Velentza Sq prior to (another) Mavrogenous Fountain and the Church of Ag Triada on the other side of the street.
No singles and doubles sharing the bathrooms cost from 760 drs rising to 910 drs (July - September) and en suite 1150 drs and 1380 drs respectively.

Back on the Esplanade, proceeding southwards or to the right (*Sbo*) from the roundabout and beyond the OTE office (*Tmr* 12.D1) and a Chapel is the:-

Scopas Travel Agency (*Tmr* 13.C1)
Directions: As above and on the left (well it would have to be wouldn't it . .). Apart from the usual travel agency functions this cavernous office advertises **Rooms.**

In the Old Quarter, or Chora, amongst the Old Castle walls and Tower are two private houses offering accommodation:-

Rooms (*Tmr* 14.C1/2)
Directions: As the Esplanade road curves to the left beyond **Scoras Travel Agency** (*Tmr* 13.C1) and the second flight of steps climbs up into the Chora and leads to, on the right, a rectangular terrace (once a Temple). The narrow lane left or eastwards off the terrace and one of the **Rooms** is on the left. Further on down the alley and sharp right at the square (close by the Churches of Ag Aikaterini and Panaghia) along the lateral lane and the other **Rooms** is on the right. Both are 'town provincial' but beautifully positioned in a very lovely part of Paroikias Old Quarter. Doubles sharing the bathroom from 800 drs.

Further south along the Esplanade, beyond Plateia Velentza there are:-

Rooms (*Tmr* 15.B2)
Directions: As above, on the near corner of the next square, Plateia Vendurees, over a 'local' Kafenion.

Rooms (*Tmr* 16.B2/3)
Directions: As above but on the far side of the Plateia Vendurees in the first block over the *Pizzaria Europa,* next door to the *Souvlaki Asteras.*

The Esplanade runs into the long, rectangular Plateia 'Zoodochos Pighi'*, from which a street, that was or is a river-bed, winds obliquely off the far left-hand corner. Up the third lane to the left, on the right-hand side is:-

Rooms (*Tmr* 17.A3)
Directions: As above.

Back at the Ferry-boat quay roundabout, the new, broad, waterside Esplanade loops off on its slow semi-circular route round the bay in a north-easterly direction.

Rooms (*Tmr* 18.E1)
Directions: Alongside **Panos Rent-A-Car** on the right beyond some waste ground and opposite a caique repair yard and moorings.

Further on is:-

Rooms
Directions: Prior to the *Asterias Hotel* over the top of a **Rent-A-Car & Motorbyke** outfit.

Beyond the *Asterias Hotel* a rough track makes its way up the slope, there being a sign indicating that 60m up the path are:-

Rooms Icarus

From hereon, beyond the *Hotel Stella* is a veritable warren of package holiday hotels in almost every nook and cranny. The street rising gently off to the right between the *Hotel Zannet* and the *Taverna Katerina* leads on up past-

Rooms
Directions: As above.
   Three separate houses on the left.

Hotel Kyclades (Class C)   Tel. 22048
Directions: As above, on the right.
   Doubles en suite start at 1300 drs rising dramatically to 2050 drs (July and August).

Hotel Hellinikon (Class E)   Tel. 21429
Directions: As above, on the left.
   Doubles en suite start at 1150 drs rising to 1220 drs for mid season and 2050 drs for the height-of-the-season.

Still on the Esplanade road now edging a beach with a grove of trees and on the right is the:-

Hotel Argo (Class C)
Directions: Next door to the *Taverna Katerina.*
   Doubles en suite 1600 drs increasing to 2100 drs (1st July - 15th September).

Further on is the:-

Pension Piertzovani

followed by the:-

Hotel Livadia (Class D)   Tel. 21597
Directions: As above.
   Not quite as shown in some old photographs but was that ever thus. Doubles sharing a bathroom from 980 drs and en suite from 1430 drs.

Rooms Violetta, Rooms and:-

Camping Koula   Tel. 22082
Open from 1st June to 30th October and facilities include a restaurant, mini-market, bar, cooking facilities, hot water and a shower/toilet block. Shaded by trees but low lying.

*Not the official name I know, but any designation is better than none.

Hotel Alkion (Class C)   Tel. 21506
Directions: Beyond the campsite.

The classification is surprisingly high, probably because the sign for the Hotel is ancient! Doubles sharing the bathroom 1425 drs and en suite 1515 drs rising respectively to 2400 drs and 2670 drs (1st July - 15th September).

Beyond this hotel there is a signpost pointing down a track to the 'tucked-up':-

Rooms To Let Shower

From hereon the waterfront peters out only to stutter briefly into life again by another hotel.

Opposite a sliver of sandy beach (*See* **Beaches No 3 — A to Z**), is a fairly dead looking campsite:-

Paros Camping

I say 'dead' but even this lifeless barrack-like layout could conceivably be resurrected at the very height of season. That is if the usual Greek ability and ingenuity to resuscitate seemingly deceased hotels, pensions, tavernas, restaurants for the summer months, is anything to go by. I'm not sure that even their resourcefulness would not be taxed by this particular proposition but the Bar appears to be revived for the busiest months.

The Eating Out Naturally I should preface my remarks by advising readers that they are purely personal, sweeping, all-embracing observations but I am sure I do not need to reiterate these caveats. Perhaps it should be restated that I make judgements from a particularly opinionated point of view; that I am mean and greedy, and that one of the critera is comparison with that which is available within, in this instance, the other Cyclades islands. Having got that off my chest I must draw attention to the introductory remarks in which I commented on the manifestation of restaurants offering Chinese style Meal A, Meal B and so on. Paros proliferates an abnormally high incidence of 'low-life' eating places — self-service tat, fixed-menu tat and at the other end of the scale, the very expensive, complete with linen table-cloths, flowers and menus that often do not list prices. Where, oh where are the tavernas?

Well there is one left:-

Taverna (*Tmr* 19.B2)

Directions: From Plateia Velentza take the Main Street off the bottom left corner (*Sbo*), the first left and the establishment is on the first right-hand corner.

A small square building unfortunately bereft of a patio, terrace or garden but in a desert of gourmet emporiums. . . Perhaps on the pokey side with huge barrels in the rafters against the far wall. The portly proprietor (now possibly tourist-weary after years in the heat of the kitchen), his wife and son administer proceedings. The small number of chairs and tables fill up very quickly so arrive early. The usual pressures on the available space are exacerbated by one or two package holiday reps who bring along selected clients for an evening. 'Keep it under your hat — I'll show you a really local taverna'. The food is prepared daily so is fresh if a little on the oily side. Kalamari stew for 2 (400 drs), a Greek salad, 1 fassolakia freska, a plate of zucchini and potatoes, 2 retsina from the barrel and bread all for 825 drs. A less gargantuan meal of meat balls for one (that must indicate my trust in the taverna's kitchens, for normally I will not order meat balls), a plate of stuffed tomatoes, 1 ratatouille, a plate of chips, 2 jugs of retsina (well why not) and bread cost 575 drs. Excellent.

Now back to the 'norm'.

Recommended (that is recommended to me) was the:-

Restaurant Limanaki (*Tmr* 20.A3)

Directions: Towards the far south end of the Esplanade beyond Plateia 'Zoodochos Pighi' on the left opposite a tree-lined sand and shingle beach.

A sample of the offerings includes the set meal 'Todays Spesial (sic) of red mullet, Greece salat (sic), yoghurt garlic-tzatziki 390 drs'.

This particular stretch of waterfront all the way back to Plateia B Argyropoulou is knee-deep in this style of taverna/restaurant.

For those who relish hamburgers instead of the home grown souvlaki-pita then I suppose it is necessary to visit:-

Nick's Hamburgers (*Tmr* 21.B3) Plateia Vendurees
Directions: Bottom right-hand corner (*Sbo*).

Mincing(!) Nick Kossoudjis, a great self publicist, runs a very garish New York style, but one must admit, very professional burger-bar. Embellishments include personalised cartons for the chips and a loudspeaker system to call up clients numbers when an order is ready. Prices range from 95 drs for a Nickburger to 286 drs for a Special Supernik. Vegetarians may revel in an Organik sandwich. 'Dear Appolo. . .!

See **Commercial Shopping Area** for details of Nicks other (unrelated) activity —
Nicks Trading Post

Mention of the traditional souvlaki-pita thankfully leads me to the more traditional offerings of:-

Special - Sovvlaki (sic) — **'The best in Paros'** (*Tmr* 22.C1)
Directions: On the south-west or bottom right side (*F-bqbo*) of Plateia Mavrogenous.

I'm not sure that his claim is true and myself prefer the more modest:-

Souvlaki
Directions: Next door to **Cyclades Tourist Agency** (*Tmr* 23.D2) on the left flank of the Plateia Mavrogenous alongside the river-bed (almost diagonally opposite the Souvlaki Bar above).

This narrow fronted stall offers a variation on the souvlaki-pita that is becoming increasingly common. Clients are offered either the more traditional slices of meat, with pieces of tomato, onion, maybe a chip or two and some yoghurt wrapped in a pita costing between 50/55 drs or a slab of pre-cooked beefmeat (biltong?) wrapped in pita and costing about 45 drs.

On the same square is:-

Palm Tree Cafe (*Tmr* 24.C1)
Directions: On the far edge of Plateia Mavrogenous (*Sbo*). **The Commercial Bank** is on the corner, followed by the *Argonauta Restaurant* — linen table-cloths, no prices on the menu (a particular hate of mine this) and a smoothie proprietor who expresses the utmost surprise when a prospective client has the temerity to ask for a price list and then the *Palm Tree*.

Although self-service (another of the banes of my life) the system here is comprehensive, polite, quite reasonably priced and operates from morning through to late in the evening. Patronised by Greeks and usually very busy with a nice patio across the street on the edge of the park, a few seats on the pavement and ample room inside for chilly evenings. The range on offer encompasses breakfasts, cakes, snacks and light suppers. Coffee 52 drs, milk chocolate (goats) 54 drs, a plate of spaghetti bolognese 180 drs and so on.

Tommy's Peanut Shop
Directions: Beneath *Pebbles Bar,* which looks out over the south waterfront just prior to *Saloon d'Or,* on the edge of Plateia B. Argyropolou.

Run by a smiling, pleasant Canadian Greek with every conceivable type of nut and a good range of ice-creams available.

In the north-east 'package holiday' end of the harbour there are a number of acceptable taverna/restaurants of which I would select the:-

Taverna Katerina
A wide variety of food on offer at acceptable prices.

Not quite so far along the Esplanade, in fact in the **Rent A Car** stretch opposite the small caique moorings is

No 30 Cafe-Bar
An unusual, reasonably tasteful self-service cafe-bar that is open all night (0000 - 1200 hrs) but is closed for the rest of the day. Ideal for night owls and insomniacs.

There are, as advised, one or two very smart restaurants which are usually outside the scope of my research (and pocket) but this does not mean one or two should not be highlighted. They include:-

To Tamarisk (*Tmr* 25.C2) Odhos Agorakritou
Directions: In giving directions I may well commence from an easy starting point but naturally readers will, once their sense of direction and orientation has taken over, find simpler, shorter routes than I describe. From the Church of Panagia Katapoliani (*Tmr* E2) or from the river-bed pedestrian way, walk along Odhos Manto Mavrogenous in a northwesterly or right-hand direction (*Sbo*). Proceed past Mavrogenous Fountain 'A' and the Church of Ag Septemvriani on the right, two alleyways and the Church of Tris Lerarches on the left. The turning beneath an archway leads on to Odhos Agorakritou. The Taverna with very neat, tree planted gardens, is on the right.
    The menu includes 'Filet Mignon' which I'm sure is very nice but need I say more.

Also in this area, back a few metres and left into a 'Cul-de-sac Plateia' gives out to the rear entrance of a very, very smart restaurant. Staying on Odhos Manto Mavrogenous in the direction of the crossroads with Odhos Lochagou Kortianou passes the discreet front entrance. Credit cards accepted, candles in delicate lamp-holders, folded linen napkins — splendid, but outside the range of the book.

Two other very pleasant but very expensive restaurants that should be mentioned, but beyond my drachmae range, are:-

Kriako's Restaurant (*Tmr* B2) and **Creperie/Bistro Balcony**
both on Odhos Lochagou Kortianou.
Directions: At the Plateia Velentza end of this main thoroughfare on the right-hand curve, almost opposite the Church of Ag Triada.
    A Greek salad costs between 250/300 drs. No need to read on.

On the far left-hand corner of Plateia Mavrogenous (*F-bqbo*) there is a good **Zacharoplasteion** that serves up 'mentionable' pies.

Prior to *Kriako's* and the *Bistro Balcony*, an alley branches right off the connection of Odhos Lochagou Kortianou and Phokianou, opposite the Church of Taxiarchis leading to:-

May Tey Restaurant (*Tmr* 26.B/C2)
Directions: As above and on the left opposite an **Antique Carpet Shop** and the Church of Panagia Eleoussa.
    Surely incongruous and unnecessary, serving Oriental food in Western decor, brightly lit and stylish and not very Greek.

THE A TO Z OF USEFUL INFORMATION
AIRLINE OFFICES & TERMINUS (*Tmr* 27.D2) The Olympic office is at the far end of Odhos Prombona. Turn half-left from the Ferry-boat roundabout, and beyond the *Hotel Oasis* (C class), the Post Office, several rent-a-car outfits, the *Hotels Parko* (E class) and *Kypredi* (D class). Office hours 0800 - 1530 hrs weekdays only.

Aircraft timetables
Paros to Athens (& vice-versa)
A minimum of three flights a day

	0750, 1640, 1900 hrs
Tuesday, Thursday & Saturday	1040, 1345 hrs

Sunday	1345 hrs
Up to 30th April	
Daily	1830 hrs
From 1st May additionally	
Daily	1835 hrs
Tuesday, Thursday & Saturday	1615 hrs
From 23rd June additionally	
Tuesday, Thursday, Saturday & Sunday	1925 hrs

One-way fare 2540 drs, duration 50 mins.

Paros to Iraklion (Crete)

From 1st May	
Tuesday, Thursday & Saturday	1405 hrs
Return	
Tuesday, Thursday & Saturday	1510 hrs

One-way fare 3480 drs, duration 45 mins.

Paros to Rhodes island

Tuesday, Thursday, Saturday & Sunday	0835 hrs
Return	
Tuesday, Thursday, Saturday & Sunday	1215 hrs

One-way fare 3960 drs, duration 1 hr 10 mins.

BANKS

The National Bank (*Tmr* 28.C2) Far left-hand corner of Plateia Mavrogenous (*F-bqbo*). It is more than a pleasure to report that the service is swift and smiling. Travellers cheques as well as Eurocheque card backed personal cheques are cashed. Normal banking hours.

BEACHES Two or perhaps three small beaches — depending on how one regards the treatment of the north-east end of town.

Beach 1. To the south-west almost at the far end of the Esplanade opposite Plateia 'Zoodochos Pighi'. Not very large, being fairly narrow and of no great length, exposed to the sea but pleasantly tree-lined on the roadside edge. Sand mixed with shingle. A plus is that this end of the harbour is almost exclusively in the hands of the backpackers who stay in the Port and Chora quarters. Thus it is less crowded as distinct from the other two beaches at the north-east or package holiday end of the large curving bay which includes:-

Beach 2. Narrow, small, coarse sand mixed with shingle and copiously tree-lined. Beach beds cost 100 drs. Edged by the road across which are a stretch of taverna/restaurants and hotels, thus ensuring crowding with the sun worshippers overlaid by lots of jolly beach footballers.

Beach 3. The beach above runs out alongside a low retaining wall which meanders into a long but very narrow strip of scrappy sand and shingle sprinkled with occasional tar. Some tree cover with beach beds at the broader, near end and wind-surfing at the far, narrow end. The beach is, in the main, edged by the 'dead'(?) concrete barrack yard of *Camping Poros*.

BICYCLE, SCOOTER & CAR HIRE Beyond the Bus terminal, north-east from the Ferry-boat quay, are two **Rent-a-Car** firms, one of whom offers scooters (of which more later as the saying goes). The usual range of vehicles include the increasingly popular beach-buggies, that is popular only with the hirer. Another Rent-a-Car Street is Odhos Prombona that forms the right-hand side of a fairly large park.

The scooter hire situation is possibly the worst I have ever experienced. For instance the two Car Hire firms on the north-east esplanade each advertise along the lines of 'we have 90 scooters' with a few smart versions propped up across the road. In actuality they are simply fronting for a set-up at the back of the Town. I very nearly wrote 'set-down' for the 'disorganisation', is a wire-fenced, back street shambles. The compound contains quite possibly a 100 scooters parked up, but of this number about half are being repaired, a quarter are totally unfit to hire out and some are on hire, leaving about 6 'clapped out' units considered fit for use. The 'office' is a greasy lean-to, and the oily overall clad owners attempt to obtain payment in advance as well as a hirers passport. Tell them to forget it — one or the other. Rates tumble from a 1000 drs to 700 drs a day with some bargaining but carefully check the intended conveyance and insist upon the supply of a spare tyre and plug.

Not all is lost though as there are two 'independents'.

One (*Tmr* 29.E1/2), run by a less than enthusiastic proprietor, operates from a plot, tucked away down a cul-de-sac on the way to the north-east Esplanade, immediately prior to the Bus terminus (*Tmr* 32.E1).

The other is:-

Rent A Car/Motorbyke (*Tmr* 30.A3)
Directions: At the far south-west end of the Esplanade alongside **Disco 7** and edged by a dry river-bed on the right-hand side (*Sbo*).

The pleasant, committed, young proprietor speaks good English and although, or perhaps because, he is a small operator, hires out well maintained units, even if 1000 drs a day is more expensive than the other bandits — sorry firms.

BOOKSELLERS A well stocked shop (*Tmr* 31.C2) on the right of Odhos Lochagou Kortianou not far from the crossroads with Odhos Manto Mavrogenous.

BREAD SHOPS One bakery (*Tmr* 32.C2) on the left of the street off the far end of Plateia Mavrogenous, opposite the Commercial Bank. Another (*Tmr* 32.C2) on the back lane of Odhos Agorakritou, the other side of the road and beyond the *To Tamarisk Taverna* (for directional assistance *See* **Eating Out**) and yet another on the Commercial Street of Lachagou Phokianou towards Plateia Velentza, between a Supermarket and the *Hotel Dina.*

BUSES The Bus terminal (*Tmr* 32.E1) is located on the Esplanade about 200m to the left of the Ferry-boat quay. The Ticket Office is simply a shack immediately prior to the bus layby. Note that the owner of the Periptero close by speaks English and is very helpful.

Opposite is a **'Left-Luggage' Office** — open daily 0800 - 2000 hrs, with a charge of 50 drs per piece of luggage and 80 drs for 24 hr storage.

Bus timetable
Paroikias (Paros Port) to Alyki, Angairia
Daily   0700, 0750, 1100, 1300, 1400, 1600 hrs
Return journey
Daily   0725, 0815, 1125, 1330, 1430, 1630 hrs

Paroikias to Marmara, Marpissa, Piso Livadi, Logaras, Golden Beach, Drios
Daily   0800, 1000, 1100, 1200, 1300, 1400, 1500, 1600, 1800 hrs
Return journey
Daily   0725, 0900, 1100, 1200, 1300, 1500, 1600, 1700, 1900 hrs

Paroikias to Naoussa
Daily   0800, 0900, 1000, 1100, 1200, 1300, 1400, 1500, 1600, 1700, 1800, 2000 hrs
Return journey
Daily   0800, 0830, 0930, 1030, 1130, 1300, 1430, 1530, 1630, 1730, 1830, 2030 hrs

Paroikias to Pounta (Punta) (departure point for Antiparos island)
Daily   0730, 1000, 1200, 1400, 1600 hrs
Return journey
Daily   0800, 1015, 1215, 1415, 1615 hrs

There are also buses to Petaloudes (Valley of the Butterflies).
See ROUTE TWO for further details.

CHEMISTS *See* **Medical Care.**

CINEMAS At the north-eastern end of the Esplanade, prior to the beach a turning off to the right, alongside the *Hotel Stella*, advances to the **Cine Paros**. At the other end of the Esplanade, off Plateia 'Zoodochos Pighi', along the old river-bed Street at the far top left-hand corner and first left leads to **Cine Rex.**

COMMERCIAL SHOPPING AREA The Main or High St, Odos Lochagou Kortianou, starts from the far edge of Plateia Mavrogenous (*F.bqbo*), becomes Odhos Lochagou Phokianou that curves around on to Plateia Velentza and constitutes the Commercial Shopping Area. From start to finish, in a south-westerly direction, passes:-

Diplos Supermarket Excellent stock and inexpensive.

'Excellent Grocery' Well if they say so. . .

'The Tea Pot' A chic spice shop in a lane off to the left.

A Supermarket

There are, interspaced amongst the above, two bakers previously detailed and a number of fruit and vegetable shops.

Worth mentioning must be:-

Nicks Trading Post Plateia Vendurees

Directions: Almost alongside *Nicks Hamburger* joint (*Tmr* 21.B3, *See* **The Eating Out**), and run by our Fast-Food king.

Apart from an ill-assorted miscellany of car-boot type goods displayed in this unbelievably neat shop, Nick operates an extremely complicated Book Exchange and swop scheme. He will buy and sell almost anything.

There is a large Supermarket (*Tmr* 34.D2) on the edge of the Square to the left of the concreted river-bed (*F-bqbo*).

I do not often detail shops ranging from Art Galleries through Fur and Fashion to Jewellery Emporiums for a number of reasons. Not least of these is that they bear little relationship to the Greece I am trying to prise open for the reader. . . Apart from which they are not slow in coming forward in the normal course of events being more than a little publicity conscious. But I must mention:-

Drop Art Gallery (*Tmr* 35.B3)

Located along Odhos Lochagou Phokianou by proceeding straight on in a southerly direction, and not following the curve of the street round to the Plateia Velentza. The lane jinks past the Church of Ag Vithleem and the shop is in a slight recess on the right. My notes simply say 'everything for everybody's pocket'. Certainly some very inexpensive but tasteful prints which help fill the presents list without having to resort to the usual mass produced junk.

DENTISTS *See* **Medical Care.**

DISCOS Quite a number including a clutch at the far, south-west end of the Esplanade, beyond Plateia 'Zoodochos Pighi'. These include **Hesperedes**, the **Irish Bar**, **Disco 7** and **Easy Going** with **Disco Psarades** on Plateia B. Argyropoulou.

There are a number of extremely trendy and smart cocktail bars including *Pebbles* and *Statue*, close by the Old Quarter Castle, both looking out to sea. Habitat style slatted furniture and 1930s style cocktail glasses. Prices reflect these 'attributes'.

FERRY-BOATS A very, very busy port with possibly the largest number of island connections of any Aegean island.

Ferry-boat timetable

Day	Departure time	Ferry-boat	Ports/Islands of Call
Monday	0120 hrs	Georgios Express	Folegandros, Sikinos, Ios, Santorini†
	1420 hrs	Georgios Express	Syros, Piraeus (M.2020 hrs)
Tuesday	0100 hrs	Miaoulis	Aegiali (Amorgas), Katapola (Amorgas), Astipalaia, Nisiros
	1430 hrs	Naxos	Naxos
	1540 hrs	Aegeon	Ikaria, Samos
	1500 hrs*	Santorini	Naxos, Ios, Sikinos, Folegandros, Santorini†
	2300 hrs*	Nireus	Amorgos, Astipalaia, Kalimnos, Kos, Nisiros, Tilos, Simi, Rhodes, Karpathos, Kasos, Crete
Wednesday	1030 hrs	Naxos	Syros, Piraeus (M.1730 hrs)
	1330 hrs	Aegeon	Piraeus (M.1800 hrs)
	1335 hrs	Georgios Express	Naxos, Ios, Santorini†
	1400 hrs*	Lemnos	Naxos, Ios, Ia (Santorini), Athinos (Santorini)
	2330 hrs	Georgios Express	Piraeus (M.0515 hrs Thursday)
Thursday	1335 hrs	Georgios Express	Naxos, Ios, Santorini†
	1340 hrs*	Aegeon	Ikaria, Samos
	1430 hrs*	Naxos	Naxos, Iraklia, Shinoussa, Koufonissi, Amorgos
	1445 hrs*	Santorini	Naxos, Ios, Santorini†
	2330 hrs	Georgios Express	Piraeus (M.0515 hrs Friday)
Friday	1030 hrs	Naxos	Syros, Piraeus (M.1730 hrs)
	1400 hrs*	Limnos	Naxos, Ios, Ia (Santorini), Athinos (Santorini)
	1415 hrs	Aegeon	Piraeus (M.1900 hrs)
Saturday	0040 hrs	Georgios Express	Ios, Santorini†
	1215 hrs	Georgios Express	Piraeus (M.1730 hrs)
	1340 hrs	Aegeon	Ikaria, Samos
	1430 hrs	Naxos	Naxos
	1445 hrs*	Santorini	Naxos, Ia (Santorini), Santorini†
	2400 hrs	*See* Sunday	
Sunday	0000 hrs*	Miaoulis	Ios, Santorini,‡ Anafi
	0000 hrs*	Nireus	Naxos, Iraklia, Shinoussa, Koufonissi, Donoussa, Aegiali (Amorgos), Katapola (Amorgos), Astipalaia
	0120 hrs	Georgios Express	Naxos, Ios, Santorini†
	1030 hrs	Naxos	Piraeus (M.1730 hrs)
	1310 hrs	Georgios Express	Piraeus (M.1880 hrs)
	1400 hrs	Limnos	Naxos, Ios, Ia (Santorini) Athinos (Santorini)
	1415 hrs	Aegeon	Piraeus (M.1900 hrs)

Approximate time   †probably Athinos port   ‡quite possibly all 3 Santorini ports

In addition to the above

| Tuesday,
Wednesday,
Friday | 1150 hrs | MV Ios | Naxos, Mykonos |
| Saturday,
Sunday | 1810 hrs | MV Ios | Ios, Athinos (Santorini) |

Most important are the inter-island excursion boats connecting Paros and Siphnos which allows an excellent link between the East and West Cyclades island chains.

| Daily | 1100 hrs | MV Yiannis Latsos | Siphnos (1415 hrs) |
| | 1500 hrs | MV Magarita | Siphnos (1800 hrs) |

See **Pounta** for connections to Antiparos.

FERRY-BOAT TICKET OFFICES The activity generated at the few Paroikias Port ticket offices would turn many another, more leisurely, less active operator on other islands green, very green with envy. The prime location is occuped by:-

Paros Travel Agency (*Tmr* 3.D1) Immediately across from the Ferry boat quay, occupying an island site. Possibly the rudest most disinterested office it has been my wont to encounter but they do almost have a monopoly of the very busy trade.

A blackboard under the verandah advertises daily sailings with large boards on the outside of the office wall, indicating the weeks activity. The very speed of service can lead to mistakes so however poor the attention and however annoying it must be for the staff, insist your instructions are clearly understood prior to paying for tickets. Money will not be refunded for any incorrect or mistaken purchase. This caveat is not unique to this office but applies everywhere.

The Agency advertises a tourist bus trip 'Round of Paros by Bus Every Day'. The journey starts at 1000 hrs returning at 1700 hrs and costs 1000 drs. They also offer daily bus tours to Petaloudes (Butterfly Valley) at a cost of 300 drs (*See* ROUTE TWO).

ITS Travel Agency (*Tmr* 5.D1) To the left of **Paros Travel**. More polite but very tied up with the package holiday trade, acting as agents for **Sun-Med.**

Cyclades Tourist Agency (*Tmr* 23.D2) Past the Periptero on the far edge (*F-bqbo*) of the dry river-bed and sharp left along the low retaining wall. The problem is that **Paros Travel** has it almost entirely wrapped up.

Two other offices worthy of note are detailed under **Travel Agents.**

LAUNDRY There is a dry cleaners (*Tmr* 37.D2) on the Square to the left of the river-bed, close by the Ferry-boat quay.

LUGGAGE STORE *See* **Buses.**

MEDICAL CARE
Chemists & Pharmacies Not over many but located in and around Plateia Mavrogenous and along the High St, Odhos Lochagou Kortianou and Phokianou.

There is a good Pharmacy on the far edge of Plateia Mavrogenous close by the *Palm Tree Cafe* (*Tmr* 24.C1).

Clinic The telephone number is not in dispute (Tel 21235) but the location is a query. Officially opposite and across road from the Town public lavatory block (*Tmr* 36.E1) which is on the left edge of the park to the left of the Ferry-boat quay (*Sbo*). But. . .

Dentists Yes, reputedly a Mr N Kiriafanos (Tel 21552).

Doctors Dr Kebabis (Tel 21256).

NTOG None. *See* **Tourist Police.**

OPENING HOURS
Museums— Archaeological. Own up Geoffrey, I'm not sure but have a feeling it is open

every other day, usual hours.

Shops (Summer): Apart from the more conservative shops, as would be expected on a very tourist orientated island.

OTE (*Tmr* 12.D1) Keep right (*F-bqbo*) along the Esplanade in a south-west direction and almost immediately on the left. The rear of the office backs on to the edge of Plateia Mavrogenous.

Surprisingly small for such a busy, international island and not open at weekends or holidays — yet! Weekday hours 0730 - 2000 hrs.

PETROL (GASOLINE) A number of stations on the Naoussa road that climbs out of Port.

PLACES OF INTEREST
Cathedrals & Churches
The Cathedral Church of Panagia Ekatontapyliani (Katapoliani) (*Tmr* E2) Despite or perhaps because of the pre-publicity I regard the stories attached to the church far more interesting than the building itself. The text books display an alarming uniformity respecting the origins, reasons for the name and legends associated with the Church. The most recent research suggests that the Church is positioned on the site of a very early place of worship on which was built a Christian Church. This was added to over the centuries, with another 2 or 3 religious buildings tacked on to the original structure. Certainly in the 6th century AD a major tidy-up and rebuilding took place, incorporating the earlier works and slapping on the then fashionable domed basilica. Badly damaged in 1733 by earthquake, the structure was the subject of a considerable restoration in the early 1960s. The alternative name 'Katapoliani' is thought to be a derivation of the common-place Cycladean *Katapola* — or low ground.

Now to legend which postulated that the Church was founded in AD 326 by St Helena, the mother of Constantine the Great. 'Ekatontapyliani' is popularly supposed to refer to a 100 doors but reflection causes the windows to be counted in as well. Even so I doubt the addition. Perhaps the best story revolves around the architect/builder and 'legends' that the Master Builder employed an apprentice, one Ignatius to oversee the work. The beauty of the finished job so enraged his employer that, in a fit of jealous rage, he attempted to throw Ignatius off the roof. In a last, grasping hand-hold the apprentice seized the architect and they both plunged to their death on the patio below. Well there you go! Dress modestly — no shorts. Opening hours are 0800 hrs - 1200 hrs and 1600 hrs - 2000 hrs.

There are a clutch of 16th and 18th century churches in the area of the old Kastro. This sits atop the lowly hill now named after the fascinating colonnaded Church of Ag Konstantinos. Apart from these there are a number of enchanting, old churches scattered about the Town including:-

Church of Ag Nicholaos Thalassitis (*Tmr* D1) Small 17th century but now rather forlorn and isolated being situated on the broad pavement to the side of the Esplanade road, left of the Ferry-boat quay (*Sbo*).

From the Cathedral Church of Panagia Ekatontapylian (*Tmr* E2), the time-worn street of Manto Mavrogenous starts off by the School, opposite which are the:-

Church of Ag Nikolaos (1823) and the *Frangonastiro Monastery*, once a Capuchin order and built in the 18th century.

Further along on the right is the:-

Church of Ag Septemvriani Built in 1592 and possessing a pleasingly carved, stone door lintel.

On the left is the:-

Church of Tris Lerarches Dated 1695.

Beyond the turning left into Odhos Lochagou Kortianou, in the parallel lane, is the:-

Church of Ag Athanassios 1695.

On the right are the:-

Churches of Ag Onouphrios and **Ag Markos**

Where the two lanes join up again are the:-

Churches of Taxiarchis 1633, and *Ag Nikolaos* 1823.

On the bend round to Plateia Velentza is the:–

Church of Ag Triada

But this is only a sampling as there are more, many more for the aficionado.

Kastro (*Tmr* 38.C2) Very little is left of this 13th century Fort except a tower and a piece of wall which incorporates some rather strange, circular stones and blocks of varying thickness. The whole seems oddly incompatible which may be explained by the fact that the materials came from the ruins of the ancient Temple of Demeter. In the shadow of the wall is the tiny Church of Ag Anna.

Fountains The above mentioned lanes of Mantos Mavorgenous, Lochagou Kortianou and Phokianou have 'sprinkled' (sorry) along their length three lovely water fountains dedicated to the War of Independence heroine Manto Mavrogenous.

Museum Adjacent to the School playground across the way from the Cathedral Church of Ekatontapyliani (*Tmr* E2). A display of island finds, with one or two notable pieces.

POLICE

Tourist (*Tmr* 2.D2) Until quite recently their office was romantically located in the solitary windmill, a centre feature of the roundabout set in the Esplanade road. Now they are more prosaically situated on the left-hand edge of Plateia Mavrogenous up a flight of steps to the upper storey of the block, a few down from the office of **Cyclades Tourist Agency**. One feels that the service has been emasculated in the move and the romantic swagger, associated with the officers years ago, now replaced by a more sober, grey countenance. In the meantime the thatch of the now empty windmill is deteriorating. Still very helpful but of course normal office hours with a lunch time siesta.

POST OFFICE (*Tmr* 39.D1/2) On Odhos Prombona, diagonally off to the left towards the Church of Panaghia Ekatontapyliani, (*F-bqbo*). On the corner of the side-turning to the right down the side of the *Hotel Oasis*. One of the only places to buy stamps. This may sound an obvious statement but it is usually easy to purchase them at a number of other locations, including Peripteros, but not on Paros.

TAXIS The rank is close by the Periptero on the left side of the road that cuts diagonally across the Plateia Mavrogenous.

TELEPHONE NUMBERS & ADDRESSES

Clinic	Tel. 21235
Port police	Tel. 21240
Taxi tank	Tel. 21500
Tourist police	Tel. 21673
Town police	Tel. 22221

TOILETS A very smart, clean facility (*Tmr* 36.E1) to the left of the Ferry-boat quay (*Sbo*), beyond the small Church on the right-hand side of the Esplanade and right down the broad avenue flanking the park. An attendant in attendance (what else?) and clients have to pay for toilet paper.

TRAVEL AGENTS *See* **Ferry-Boat Ticket Offices** in addition to which there are:-

Polos Tours On the Esplanade to the right of the Ferry-boat quay (*Sbo*), alongside the

OTE office (*Tmr* 12.D1).

Handles international boat and plane travel. Considering their comparatively helpful attitude in comparison to one or two of the other offices, mores the pity that they are not involved in domestic business. They do act as agents for Apartments, Hotels and **Rooms**. Additionally they 'Fotocopy'.

Scopas Travel Agency (*Tmr* 13.C1) Further on along the south-west Esplanade, on the left — well to be on the right would involve getting very wet feet. An enterprising firm in a dark, deep-set office. Apart from travel excursions, they operate a baby sitting agency, book swop and have **Rooms** for rent on their books.

EXCURSION TO PAROIKIAS PORT SURROUNDS

Excursion to Krios Bay (3½ km) The cognoscenti tend to head out of the Port as fast as is possible and this is one convenient option.

The Krios beach water-taxi moors up to the left of the Ferry-boat quay (*Sbo*). For landlubbers the Esplanade road hugs the sea edge until the far end of Paroikias Bay. The now unsurfaced track winds around the deserted campsite over the hills and then turns towards

KRIOS BEACH A lovely sweeping bay with a sandy foreshore. The clean beach with an outcrop of pebbles, edges the gently shelving foreshore and crystal clear sea. The approach road forks right to a grove of trees in which is set building blocks of an erstwhile dream. The left fork high on the low hillside runs out above a small trip-boat pier. A small, clean beach is divided by the Disco-Bar terrace that juts into the sea with, to the right, a building in which are **Rooms** to let (1200 drs a double room per night) and to the left a Bar and Cafe-bar terrace. Both edge the waterfront. The Greek owners, in their middle 30's, operate the small cabin boat shuttle service to Paroikias Port. A find.

ROUTE ONE

To Naoussa (& beyond) (11 km) The Main Road leads off from the Park to the left of the Ferry-boat quay (*Sbo*) and divides around the slopes of Profitis Ilias about a kilometre out of town. The left-hand route proceeds via the village of Kamares whilst the right-hand fork passes on the left the:-

Monastery of Ton Taxiarchon Constructed in the 16/17th centuries with one or two icons in the Church and, on the right, a track to the

Monastery of Longovardas The whitewashed buildings built in 1638 surround the Church with cells all around the Cypress tree planted rectangle. There is a library.

The two roads join up again at the Village of:-

AGIA TRIAS (about 8 km from Paroikias Port) After another 1½ km the road joins the coast at Plastira Bay. There is a junction with an unmade track that angles off to the left, encircling the bay around to the north (for details *See* EXCURSIONS TO NAOUSSA PORT SURROUNDS). A few metres further along the Main Road, to the right, are the nicely laid out, if somewhat isolated *Bungalows Naoussa* followed by the smart *Hotel Ippokampous*.

From about this point there is a splendid panorama across the bay with a tiny Chapel capped Islet set in the Bay and the horn of the encircling peninsula of Mt Vigla forming the backcloth.

NAOUSSA (Naousa) (11 km from Paroikias Port) (Illustration 19) On the outskirts of Naoussa a junction is made with the Ambelas/Piso Livadi road. There is a fuel station, quite a lot of new development, including low rise flats, several restaurants and a few hotels.

The downhill section of the road passes a small cove and shingle beach with some **Rooms** splendidly sited on a small headland overlooking the foreshore. Proceeding to the centre of this very pleasant fishing village, a Greek St Ives, there are, on the right, some six houses with **Rooms.**

The heart of Naoussa is over the bridge that spans the wide, summer-dry river-bed although it is possible to use the concreted ford to the left of the bridge. Locals park their cars beneath the bridge for shade and the surfaced river-bed is used as a thoroughfare. The Port is formed by large rocky boulders and stretches around the small headland incorporating a ruined Venetian Castle and forming a U shaped caique harbour. The agreeably messy port quay and inner harbour has an intimate, friendly atmosphere with the far end of the quay, dominated by a small Chapel, edged by tavernas. The quay is, at the near end, lined with parked cars with two Churches at the far end and modern, tourist craft and yachts moored up. The concrete and paved surface is littered with nets spread out to dry and stowed nets in bulky bundles dotted about here and there. The small caique harbour is crowded in by an assorted collection of varying sized cubic buildings and by caiques which press up to the seawall.

An excellent spot to make for as soon as a visitor has landed at Paroikias but the knowledge has spread and the very lovely Port has a considerable band of followers, so much so that the local bus making the connection is usually very crowded, so be quick.

The tiny Old Quarter is a charming maze of lanes and alleys, down which the swallows swoop in a never ending display of aerial acrobatics.

THE ACCOMMODATION & EATING OUT

The Accommodation An adequate if not inexpensive mixture of **Rooms** and Hotels, but not many Pensions, and an abundance of Apartments.

On the road into the Port from Paroikias, apart from the aforementioned accommodation, there are:-

Rooms (*Tmr* 1.A2)
Directions: Above the *Restaurant Meltemi* to the left, prior to the main bridge and close by the seafront

By the roadside, on the right are the:-

Hotel Atlantis (*Tmr* 2.A3) (Class C)   Tel. 51209
Doubles en suite rising from 1100 drs to 1350 drs and for the months of July-September, 1830 drs.

Hotel Drossia (*Tmr* 3.A3) (Class D)   Tel. 51213
Doubles from about 1200 drs.

Hotel Madaki (*Tmr* 4.A3) (Class E)   Tel. 51475
Reasonably priced with doubles sharing starting at 540 drs and rising to 670 drs whilst en suite rooms cost from 850 drs to 1250 drs.

Once over the bridge the broad Main Street which doubles up as the Square, opens out to the right and on the edge of which is the:-

Hotel Aliprantis (*Tmr* 5.B3) (Class C)   Tel. 51571
Directions: As above, to right of centre.

Not outrageously expensive for such a prime location with en suite doubles starting at 1060 drs, rising to 1950 drs.

From the left-hand, far edge of the Square, just beyond **Gavalos Tours** (*Tmr* 6.B/C3) (of which more to follow), a lane curves away half-left beneath an archway. Beyond the Church of Ag Nikolaos Mostratou (on the right) Odhos Grammou is off to the left. Beyond *Quick Snacks — Spaper* (yes, Spaper) and the barbers shop **O Dimitris** there is:-

Rooms Sofia (*Tmr* 7.C3)

Back at the Main Square the High St curves off to the right gently up-hill between pleasantly tree-lined pavements and edged, for the first part, by tavernas. Towards the top

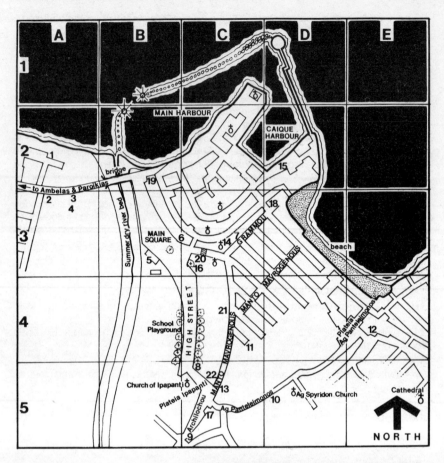

KEY

1	Rooms/Restaurant Meltemi	A2
2	Hotel Atlantis	A3
3	Hotel Drossia	A3
4	Hotel Madaki	A3
5	Hotel Aliprantis	B3
6	Gavalos Tours	B/C3
7	Rooms Sofia	C3
8	Rooms - A.N.Spirou	C4/5
9	Rooms	C5
10	Hotel Minoa	D5
11	Rooms	C4
12	Rooms	E4
13	Christos Taverna	C5
14	Quick Snacks	C3
15	National Bank	D2
16	Scooter hire	C3
17	Baker	C5
18	Grocer/Fruit Shop	D3
19	Chemists	B3
20	Clinic	C3
21	OTE	C4
22	Post Office	C5

NAOUSSA - Island of Paros

Illustration 19

end of the street, beyond the School playground on the right, and on the left is

(Scooter Rental &) Rooms — A.N. Spirou (*Tmr* 8.C4/5) (Class C)   Tel. 51366
A double room from 800 drs and apartments from 1000 drs, both of which represent good value.

From the head of the Street, the road bends to the left around the Church of Ipapanti on to Odhos Archilochou to the right. Beyond the Ice-Cream parlour sign is, on the left:-

Rooms (*Tmr* 9.C5)

From the junction of the High St, Odhos Archilochou and Odhos Manto Mavrogenous, the street of Ag Panteleimonos curves round encircling the top of the Port.

Hotel Minoa (*Tmr* 10.D5) (Class C)   Tel. 51309
Directions: As above and on the right, prior to Ag Spyridon Church.
Recommended to us as clean, serving up good meals and the en suite bedrooms having pleasant balconies. My notes also say wood/tiles/marble — sometimes, I wonder what I am on about? On the expensive side with single rooms rising from 920 drs to 1150 drs for the months of July - September. Double rooms cost 1610 and 1820 drs in the high season.

Odhos Manto Mavrogenous gently curves away to the left, back down towards the Port quay. The first right cul-de-sac gives access to:-

Rooms (*Tmr* 11.C4)
The situation is very beautiful but so it should be with a double room costing from 1180 drs.

Further up the hillside, towards the Cathedral (*Tmr* E5) and the windmills, are:-

Rooms (*Tmr* 12.E4)
Directions: On up a pace or two in the climb to the Cathedral from Plateia Ag Panteleimonos, a small square with a statue and garden.

Rooms
Directions: To the left of the Cathedral.

The Eating Out As detailed above the broad High St narrows down as it curves uphill, towards the Church of Ipapanti. At the widest it is lined both sides, with tree shaded tavernas.

Plateia Ipapanti is at the top of the High St to the left of Ipapanti Church. Across the road, to the left, is:-

Christos Taverna (*Tmr* 13.C5)
Directions: As above, next door to a water fountain.
Comes well recommended.

From the Main Square beneath the archway, and left down Odhos Grammou and on the left is:-

Quick Snacks — Spaper (sic) (*Tmr* 14.C3)
Directions: As above.
As could be expected a Snack-Bar with toasties and other hand-held munchies.

The main quay is edged by tavernas at the top or north end and the adjacent caique harbour is lined with cafe-bars and tavernas. Of these a very popular Cafe-bar is at the right (*Fsw*) or south side of the harbour, the seats and tables of which nestle up to the **National Bank** (*Tmr* 15.D2).

THE A TO Z OF USEFUL INFORMATION
BANKS
National Bank (*Tmr* 15.D2) On the right (*Fsw*) of the caique harbour. A very small branch only open the usual weekday hours.

BEACHES One to the west or left and the other to the right or south of the main quay. The former is more a disorganised, stony foreshore with odd boats upturned, keel to the sky, and trailers here and there. The latter, officially designated as the Town beach, is frankly disappointing. No, frankly it is more a disaster. It is fairly narrow, with the flanks edged by peeling and unpainted backs of buildings. The locals tend to dump their building materials here and there and, although it is sandy, it is also stone and rubbish littered with a resident clutch of domestic chickens that shelter in the shade of various bits of driftwood.

See also EXCURSIONS TO NAOUSSA PORT SURROUNDS

BICYCLE, SCOOTER & CAR HIRE The scooter hire companies include two (*Tmr* 16.C3 & 8.C4/5), one each end of the High Street, both on the left-hand side (*Sbo*). Average rates.

Cars are hired by **Gavalos Tours/Nissiotissa Tourist Bureau** (*Tmr* 6.B/C3). *See* **Travel Agents.**

BOOKSELLERS There is not an 'International' firm but **Gavalos Tours** (*Tmr* 6.B/C3) transacts book swop.

BREAD SHOP A baker (*Tmr* 17.C5) is tucked away behind the ice-cream sign on the left side of Odhos Archilochou on the far side of the Church of Ipapanti.

BUSES The terminal, more a turn round, is on the Main Square end of the High Street.

Bus timetable
See **Paroikias Port bus timetable.**

CHEMIST *See* **Medical Care.**

COMMERCIAL SHOPPING AREA None but the back lanes have a sprinkling of fruit and vegetable shops with a concentration in the area of the Caique Harbour. Close by, one particular grocer/fruit shop owner (*Tmr* 18.D3) takes his produce inside during the afternoon siesta — a sorry commentary on the light fingered tendencies of tourists.

There are two Peripteros on the Main Square.

DENTISTS
See **Medical Care.**

DISCOS Yes, **Disco Cave** up, beyond and behind the Cathedral.

DOCTORS *See* **Medical Care.**

FERRY-BOATS None, but trip-boats to other locations on Paros island and Mykonos island. Tickets and details from the usual offices (*See* **Travel Agents**).

HOSPITALS *See* **Medical Care.**

MEDICAL CARE
Chemists & Pharmacy (*Tmr* 19.B3) Immediately on the left of the Main Square.

Clinic (*Tmr* 20.C3) Whoopee, at the top, left-hand end of the Main Square (*Sbo*), in the fork of the roads.

OPENING HOURS *See* **Paroikias Port.**

OTE (*Tmr* 21.C4) On the right of Odhos Manto Mavrogenous, which lane runs approximately parallel to the curve of the High St. A very provincial, 'doo-hickey' office.

PETROL (GASOLINE) On the junction of the road to Ambelas and Paroikias.

POST OFFICE (*Tmr* 22.C5) Across the road from the Church of Ipapanti at the top end of the High Street.

TAXIS On the Main Square.

TELEPHONE NUMBERS & ADDRESSES

Clinic	Tel. 51216
Police	Tel. 51202
Post Office	Tel. 51425

TOILETS Yes, beyond the **National Bank** (*Tmr* 15.D2) on the mole leading out to the ruined Fort.

TRAVEL AGENTS
Gavalos Tours and or **Nissiotissa Tourist Office** (*Tmr* 6.B/C3)   Tel. 51480
Cathy and or Kostas serve up attentive assistance. The office is on the left of the Main Square. Services include booking hotel and room accommodation, apartments or bungalows, tours, trips and excursions, car-rental, ferry-boat tickets (domestic and international), left-luggage and ad infinitum as well as book swop.
     The other tourist office on the Main Square is:-

Katerina Simitzi   Tel. 51444
All as for Nissiotissa but for Cathy/Kostas read Katerina.

EXCURSIONS TO NAOUSSA PORT SURROUNDS
Excursion to the North Peninsula/Ormos Langeri (about 6 km) The
road curves around the back of the Port off the Ambelas junction to

AG ARGIRI (1 km from Naoussa Port) A sandy beach overlooked by the *Hotels Kalypso* (Class C, Tel 51488), and *Cavos* (Class C, Tel 51367), as well as the *Batistas* and *Ioli* Holiday Apartment blocks.
     The surfaced road runs out into track. Keep to the left or west side of the peninsula in the low-lying, softly undulating countryside amongst which are set the occasional apartment buildings for rent. Mind you they are rather out of the way.
     After about 3½ kms, a lump of land projecting into the bay is tenuously connected by a sandy causeway.
     At the northern end there is a lovely, sweeping, sandy beach backed by dunes and low, windswept trees.

Excursion to Kolymbithres Beach, Ag Giannis Detis & beyond
(7½ km) Back along the Paroikias road to the junction beyond *Naoussa Bungalows*. Here a wide, rough surfaced track forks off to the right curving around the rocky sea-shore of the bay.
Camping Naoussa
Directions: As above on the left.
     Well laid out, with shower block, reception, mini-market and bar. One has to consider the low-lying nature of the river and swampy surrounds and ponder about the possible mosquito problem.
The track now turns towards the sea and beach area known as

KOLYMBITHRES (3 km from Naoussa Port) Famed for the unusual wind and sea scoured rocks on the water's edge. The marshy land in this area has a sandy foreshore almost continuously washed over by the sea. The beaches are haphazardly barbed wired off and signposted private, apart from one public access also signed, as is 'Nudist Beach 3 km'.
     After the final right-hand curve of the Kolymbithres beach the route climbs into a rocky

hillside, with patchy development centred around an old farmstead and one taverna.

A kilometre or so further on and, to the right, is a 'bit of a beach' with the Port of Naoussa glittering white in the distance across the bay. This is followed by a surprisingly large caique repair yard on the foreshore, more a levelled area than a formal boat yard, in the lee of the very large Chapel of Ag Giannis Detis. The Chapel surmounts a headland beyond which is a small shady cove with a simple hut taverna. However idyllically quiet and deserted the spot seems out of the height of season, there are windsurfers stacked up. Additionally the Chapel sports a signboard requesting people not to sunbathe, and certainly not starkers, in the grounds of the chapel. To the left, across the narrow neck of the land hereabouts, the seascape is reminiscent of a rocky Guernsey inlet.

The small hut taverna is a little above a bare circular area, almost in the form of a roundabout, from which a track climbs away across craggy scenery to the lighthouse on Cape Korakas.

Excursion to Ambelas (4 km) The road from the outskirts of Naoussa forks after 1¼ km, the right hand to Piso Livadi and the left to

AMBELAS (4 km from Naoussa Port) This once charming fishing hamlet with a small taverna and pleasant beach, is now the proud possessor of several hotels and apartments including the C class *Hotel Ambelas* (Tel 51324) with doubles sharing the bathroom from 1000 drs rising to 1200 drs (July - August).

The Naoussa to Piso Livadi road (*See* ROUTE TWO) passes through rolling agricultural countryside with large enough fields for farming machinery to be utilised, rather than donkeys. There are Olive groves and Pine trees occasionally dotted about in clumps.

ROUTE TWO
From & back to Paroikias (a southern circular route) via Pounta, Alyki, Drios & Lefkes (47 km) From Paroikias Port the south
Esplanade road climbs up and around past the *Hotel Xenia*, interestingly incorporating an old windmill, making towards some popular beaches. The first signposted beach is a pleasant sandy cove which unfortunately breaks into shingly sand with some kelp and general rubbish scattered about. From hereabouts some of the more energetic sand-searchers walk up and along the hillside to the left (*Fsw*), climb over a stone wall by the red painted metal gates and down to a nice, sandy cove. Above this small bay and down below the main road is:-

Parasporos Camping (2½ km from Paroikias Town) Bar, restaurant and mini-market.

In this area, to the left of the main road, are the remains of the Asklipieion (shades of Kos?), an ancient Medical School. Pithion indicated on some maps is south of the Asklipieion across country and marks the site of an ancient temple.

At about 3 km a beefy sign points along a rough track to the right and offers much but...! This side route descends across country past the chapel of Ag Irini (4½ km from Paroikias Town). A lovely location with the island of Antiparos in the middle distance. The tree edged beach with some kelp degenerates into pebbles and then rocks. The track comes to an end in a forsaken farmyard by an almost entirely sea-swept, small, sandy cove edged by a stone wall and trees. There are a few benzinas to the right. Despite the invocations of those signs back on the main road, there are no surfboards or camping but there are manifestations of a bar in one of the outbuildings. More annoyingly there is no way through for wheeled transport and it is necessary to retrace ones footsteps or wheels as the case may be.

On the Main Road again, after about 4 km a fork in the road allows the left turn to lead through the village of Sotires and on to:-

PETALOUDES (8 km from Paroikias Town) Note that it is quicker and more direct to get to Petaloudes on the secondary road via the large Nunnery of Monastiri Christos sto Dhasos and the village of Psychopiana.

The luxuriantly vegetated valley, once part of the estate of a rich, landed Paros family, is thickly wooded and, vital to attract the butterflies and moths, has a constantly running stream. The situation brings to mind the more famous valley on Rhodes island. The best time of year is early summer. Despite the Bus Company running a service, **Paros Travel** in Paroikias operate tour buses daily, the round trip costing some 300 drs. Taxis charge about 550 drs and entrance to the Valley costs 30 drs.

Back on the Main Road, after some 5 kms, with Antiparos looming large, there is another fork in the road. The right hand turning leads down the fast and wide road to:-

POUNTA (Punda, Punta) (6 km from Paroikias Town) Yes, well! A rather Mexican hamlet. . . One very, very smart hotel on the right, a couple of tavernas, a cafe, *Bar Pounta* and a damned big quay.

The *raison d'etre* for the spot is the trip boat shuttle connections to and from the Island of Antiparos (*See* EXCURSION TO ANTIPAROS).

The Main Road parallels the coastline around to

ALYKI (12 km from Paroikias Town) Once an area of salt pans, some evidence of which remains, and a small fishing boat Port which happily is still sparsely developed. But the presence of vast and extensive earthworks being inflicted on the Airport about 1 km previous to the Port bodes ill. Ill not only for Alyki, but for all the seaside villages of the south, south-west and east of the island.

There are two hotels, a few cafe-bars, tavernas, several restaurants, a disco and a lovely tree-lined sandy beach. The cafe-bar Apollon, opposite which is a Periptero on the elbow of the beach, has **Rooms** from 1180 drs for a double room en suite although the owner 'depresses the price in September'. The *Hotel Afroditi* (well, really a B class Pension) charges 1100 drs for an en suite double which rate rises to 1290 drs (1st July - 15th September).

Do visit before the Airport enlargement is completed.

From Alyki to Drios the track is unsurfaced, routed fairly high up the hillside and passes through beautiful agricultural countryside above lovely coastal scenery inset by numerous small, sand and shingle coves. Beyond Kampos Village the track surface becomes really rough.

DRIOS (22 km from Paroikias Town) On the western approaches to this lovely, small village holiday resort, there are a couple of hotels as well as **Rooms**, and a track opposite them down to the sea. It is easy to drive past the main body of the hamlet which lies hidden to the right side of the road. The turning to the beach is posted close by *Cafe Lake* and some apartments. The faded sign points past a look-a-like English, tree-shaded village pond, alongside which the locals while away the day (and night) in the Kafenion under an awning of tree branches. The gently inclined lane down to the seafront, runs straight and true, hemmed in by high stone walls attractively tree and flower planted and, at the small, shingle sand beach, turns sharp left.

The high, steep retaining wall on the beach side of the road is planted with mature trees. Across the road in the angle of the bend in the road is the surprisingly large, barn-like, 'laid-back'

Restaurant Kyma

Accommodation available with a double room from 1000 drs. Two small omelettes, a Greek salad, 1 beer and bread cost 350 drs.

To the right (*Fsw*) back along the coast line are two low key hotels, one of them the *Avra*

(C Class) with a double room rising from 840 drs sharing a bathroom and 1050 drs en suite to 1080 drs and 1400 drs respectively.

On the left of the Quay Road, towards the small fishing boat mole used by a few benzinas and caiques, is the rather incongruous **Art Club**.

Close by, at Cape Driou, there is evidence of long established habitation for carved in the rocks are some ancient, ships slipways.

A little further along the Main Road the package holidaymakers needs have been thoughtfully catered for at:-

CHRISSI AKTI (23 km from Paroikias Port) Signposted imaginatively 'Golden' this and 'Golden' that, the track off the Main Road bends past, on the left, the bamboo shaded *Restaurant Zina* (smelling strongly of burnt cooking oil) and runs out on the backshore in between two hotel restaurants. By the way the beach really is 'Golden'.

A crudely painted signpost pointing to the left along the beautiful hard sandy beach proclaims *Apartments/Rooms*. In this direction there is also a taverna edging the backshore.

Beyond the hamlet of Tsardakia, a couple of turnings off, lead down to:-

LOGAROS (22 km* from Paroikias Town) A comparitively undeveloped and sparse settlement, spread along the narrow bay and lovely, sandy beach. There are a few **Rooms** and tavernas with a huddle at the tree-edged, right-hand end (*Fsw*), including the *Logaras Beach*.

Around the headland is the increasingly popular

PISO LIVADI (21 km from Paroikias Town) A pleasant, lively fishing port, which is at the moment holding off the ravages inflicted by organised holiday firms. One street in, one street out with a right angled waterfront. The short, narrow peninsular down-leg on the left-hand side (of the right-angle) is (*Fsw*) lined with a few 3 storey tavernas and hotels, backed by a steep hillside. It terminates in a concrete quay, beyond which a rocky breakwater curves into the sea. The right-hand side encompasses the beach which is edged by a few 2 storey taverna buildings with **Rooms** and then by the southward tree-lined road.

Many **Rooms** (the most inexpensive are up the hillside above the quay on the left-hand side), tavernas and restaurants as well as two travel agents, yacht charterer **Cymatour Tours**, a mini-market and 350m out on the Marpissa road, *Captain Kafkis Camping* Tel. 41479. Hotels include the C class *Leto*, (Tel. 41283), *Lodos* (Tel. 41218), *Pisso Livadi* (Tel. 41309), *Vicky* (Tel. 41333), and E class *Dimaras* (Tel. 41324), *Coralli* (Tel. 41289), and *Lena* (Tel. 41296). Double room rates range between 950 drs and 1300 drs for the E class establishments, except the *Coralli* which is in the C class price bracket of 1100 drs to 1500 drs.

Very reasonably priced **Rooms** are available over the *Restaurant Bolas*, with a double room costing, mid season, 1300 drs, including breakfast and most acceptably priced single rooms at the rear of the building from 600 drs. Food and drink in the Port is that 10 drs or so more expensive which is due as much to the presence of affluent yacht charterers, as it is to package holidaymakers.

The Information Office, on the left at the road junction entering from the Marpissa direction, is helpful and if the gentleman is not in his office he can usually be found lounging in one or other of the nearby tavernas.

The beach is sandy with some shingle but towards the far right-hand end there is more shingle and pebbles in the shallows and some kelp.

From Piso Livadi the road system in the region of the spread out villages of both Marpissa and Marmara is complicated and the signposting poor. Both date from early times and are endowed with a multiplicity of Churches. There is petrol at Marpissa and both have a road

*Note distances are now in a clockwise direction not counter-clockwise as heretofore.

down to the Bay of Kefalos on which there is now only a tiny scattered settlement on the left-hand side and a large headland to the right. The bay is truly dramatic but unfortunately the foreshore is pebbly.

The onset of the lovely cross-country mountain road, passing through fertile agricultural countryside, is marked by a large, untidy quarry at the roadside, near the Village of:-

PRODROMOS (14 km from Paroikias Town) Also known as Draghoulas. It is a very good example of a Cycladian fortified village with the outer walls of the perimeter houses forming a defensive rampart. The settlement is on a side road and entry is from an eastern direction via an arched gateway flanked by two Churches.

To the left of the main road's steep climb, way up on the left on the mountain crest, are a number of windmills, one or two of which are still working.

LEFKAS (10 km from Paroikias Town) A lovely mountain-side village to one side of the main road with a massive *Xenia Hotel*

From Lefkas the road, after Apati, by-passes Kostos and winds around to:

MARATHI (5 km from Paroikias Town) Famed for the marble quarries which date back to antiquity and are located on the Lefkas side of the hamlet, to the left in the direction of the small 17th century Monastery of Ag Minas. There are extensive underground workings with evidence of the old quarrying tools engraved in the rock.

EXCURSION TO ANTIPAROS ISLAND (Andiparos)

This small, unforgiving Island is 12 km from top to bottom and up to 6 km wide, with an area of about 40 sq km and a population numbering not quite 600.

Trip-boats run from Paroikias Port which have their schedules fixed to the side of the boat. The trip takes between ¾ and 1 hour.

The other departure point is Pounta on the west coast of the island from whence the short sea journey takes about 10 minutes. Rumour has it, most lyrically, that passengers wishing to cross over are supposed to open the small Chapel door to signal the Antiparos ferry-man. This may hold good for the winter months, but I suspect nowadays readers will find the Chapel door locked and or 'chapel door openers' will be charged with 'Intent to thieve'. Nowadays during the summer months the service shuttles backwards and forwards, rolling and pitching uncomfortably in the narrow channel.

There is only one settlement of any size, the fortified town of Antiparos, or Kastro, separated from the lagoon like ferry-boat quay, by a 5 minute walk. The island's hotels, pensions, rooms, restaurants, tavernas and Kafenions are gathered about the Quay, town and connecting road. Hotels include the C class *Chryssi Akti* (Tel. 61206) with doubles en suite rising from 1067 drs to 1515 drs, the D class *Anargyros* (Tel. 61204) from 1156 drs and the *Mantalena* (Tel. 61220) with a double room, sharing the bathroom, costing 756 drs and en suite 1067 drs increasing, for the period 21st June - 10th September, to 1156 drs and 1511 drs.

Additionally, there is signposted, the well laid-out campsite of *Camping Antiparos* (Tel. 61221), about a 10 minutes walk to the north of Antiparos Town close by a satisfactory beach. This end of the Island has a monopoly of the beaches within easy walking distance, there being 5 or 6.

Incidentally everything on the island is a walk or a boat trip including the

Cave of Antiparos The track from Town is in good condition but it is a 1½ - 2 hour tramp and on a hot day. . . The other method of getting there is by tripboat which costs 100 drs each way.

The Cave is sited close to the top of Mt Ag Yianni and the arduous climb from the docking area takes up to ½ hour. During the summer months donkeys can ease the slog at a cost of 200 drs, and a makeshift cafe looks after the inner man and or woman.

The cave's attractions are the stalactites and stalagmites, the fame of which has been well known for centuries. Bits of the calcified 'mites' are to be found not only on display on the island but it is suggested as far away as a Russian Museum which 'piracy' must date from their occupation in the 1770s. Entrance is alongside the small Chapel and modern day descent into the cave is made rather easier by the use of some 400 concrete steps, in place of the ropes that used to be the *modus operandi*.

For hundreds of years visitors have been 'carving' their names, one such dating back to the 14th century. Another inscription on a stalagmite engraved in 1673, records the use of the dank and dark antechamber as a place of worship and the particular stalagmite as an altar by a French ambassador to Turkey. To make this ceremony he transported not only his retinue but it is documented, some islanders making a total of about 500 celebrants. And they all had to be 'roped down'! It must of been quite a feat to organize this spectacular.

Apart from the graffiti and collectors depredations over the centuries it is said that during the Second World War, the Occupation Axis troops caused further damage with hand granades whilst flushing out Partisan Guerillas who used the Cave as a place of refuge.

15 Naxos
Cyclades Islands — Eastern chain

****

FIRST IMPRESSIONS
River-beds and waterfalls of Oieanders cascading down the mountain sides; lizards; donkeys and mules; eagles.

SPECIALITIES
Kitron liqueur (made from Lomon tree leaves); white Promponas wine; emery; Kouros.

RELIGIOUS HOLIDAYS & FESTIVALS
include: 10th February — Festival of St Charalampos, Angidia; 25th March — Festival of Evangelismou, Chalki; 23rd April — Festival of St George at Kinidaros & Potamia; Friday after Easter — Procession & pilgrimage of the Virgin of the Life-Giving Spring (Zoodochos Pigi), Koronos; 14th July — Religious procession and festival of St Nikadimos, Naxos Town; first week August — Festivals & folk dances (dating back to the pagan cult of Dionysus); 15th August — Assumption of the Virgin at Apipathos, Filoti, Faneromenis Monastery and Sangri.

VITAL STATISTICS
Tel. prefix 0285. The largest of the Cyclades, the Island is 32 kms long and 24½ kms wide, with an area of 428 sq km and total population of about 14,000, of which Naxos Town contains some 3,700.

HISTORY
Mentioned by Homer (Zia or Zeus Island), its mythological fame is due to Theseus, an Athenian hero and the slayer of the Minotaur, leaving his lover Ariadne on the island asleep. Ariadne, a Cretan princess and half-sister to the Minotaur, had aided Theseus by arming him with the ball of string that helped him defeat the mysteries of the labyrinth. For whatever reason she was abandoned, Dionysus (Bacchus, the god of wine) arrived on the scene and they fell in love and coupled — well they would, wouldn't they?

The Cretans were early inhabitants and by the 7th century BC Naxos marble was being sculpted for export far and wide, the Delos Lions being created here as were numerous Kouros (male statues).

The 6th century BC ushered in a period of great affluence but the silly islanders ruined this with internal strife which allowed one Lygdamis, universally named a tyrant, to slip in and take over in 535 BC. Some exiles encouraged the Persians to pitch for the island but they suffered a reverse which their fleet revenged in 490 BC, sacking the island. A few years later the Naxiots sneaked off 4 or 5 ships in support of the Greek navy, which 'whopped' the Persians at the sea battle of Salamis, in 480 BC. The Island joined the Delian League but on trying to opt out were taken over by Athens. After this Naxos was conspicuous by its absence from even the 'inside pages' of history, that is until the arrival of the Venetians, except for an entry recording that in the 1st Century AD the Apostle, St John of Patmos converted the inhabitants to Christianity.

Marco Sanudo, a Venetian, captured Naxos in 1207, left his Italian overlords in the lurch by putting himself under the patronage of the Franks and established a strong family dynasty that lasted for 359 years until the Turks captured the Island. The Russians briefly ousted the Turks for 4 years, between 1770-1774, when the former masters regained their possession until the Greek War of Independence (1821 - 1827) when Naxos joined the United Greece.

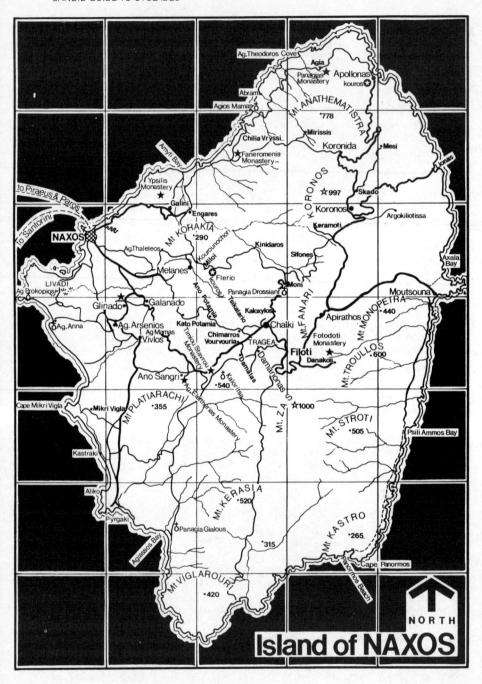

Island of NAXOS

NORTH

Illustration 20

GENERAL

The Island is probably overall one of the most attractive and beautiful of the Greek islands. I would rank it with my other favourites that include Lefkas and Ithaca (Ionian group) and Karpathos (Dodecanese). For instance Naxos harmoniously combines the majestic mountain beauty of Crete with the intensively cultivated agricultural plains and miles of sweeping golden sands of Rhodes. The northern part of the Island is green, verdant and very beautiful, with the summer-dry river-beds a riot of tumbling, flowering Oleander bushes. The high central plain centred around Chalki is mainly planted with large, prolific old Olive groves. In the drier, but still green, south-west, almost the whole length of the coast is golden beaches intermittently broken up by rocky headlands. The almost totally deserted south-east coast, rimmed by mountains, is a moorland vista edged by a rocky waters edge regularly, if widely, interspersed by delightful, sandy coves.

Long may Naxos and its amiable inhabitants prosper but hurry, an Airport is in the planning stages.

NAXOS: capital town & main port (Illustration 21)

Naxos Town is, at first glance, a busy commercial seaport with, tacked on the side as it were, a holiday resort round the corner. But it is not that simple, for behind the waterfront an extensive almost Medieval Old Quarter, of much greater complexity and interest than, say, Paros, stretches away up the hillside. Apart from size, one of the greatest differences between the two is that the Paros Chora is 'light and sun' whilst the Naxos Chora is darker and more secretive. No whitewash here, that is strictly for the tourists, but that is not to say that the Town, or the Island for that matter, has turned its face against the avalanche of visitors. Far from it, added to which the locals could not be more friendly. Certainly the variety of activity, the seclusion and traditional qualities of the Chora, combined with the comparitive proximity of a magnificent beach, must be enough to captivate even an aficionado Greek island traveller and halt any hasty retreat (or should it be advance) to a more far-flung location. Be that as it may. . .

ARRIVAL BY FERRY

More than adequate connections with the other islands and although not quite such an important terminus as say Paros, it is the springboard for the scattered Eastern Cycladic Islands of Iraklia, Schinoussa, Koufonissi, Donoussa, Amorgas and Astipalaia. The massive quay (*Tmr* A.2/3), on which passengers are corralled in roofed pens, merges with the Esplanade at the northern end. This is not inconvenient as the ferries are met by a respectable number of Room owners and the Bus terminal is at this end of the waterfront, on the expansive 'Bus Terminal Square'.

THE ACCOMMODATION & EATING OUT

The Accommodation Possibly no other Island Town is able to offer as much accommodation as Naxos but due to the maze-like nature of the Old Quarter to locate many of the **Rooms** requires diligence.

Hotel Proto (*Tmr* 1.B2) (Class D) 13, Protopapaki   Tel. 22394
Directions: Almost opposite the Ferry-boat quay, across the wide expanse of Esplanade, above a motorbike hire firm.

Doubles sharing a bathroom cost 710 drs a night rising to 860 drs (16th June - 15th September). Single room costs are 490 drs and 590 drs.

In the parallel street, one back from the Esplanade are the:-

Hotel Oceanis (*Tmr* 2.B1/2) (Class D) 11 Odhos Damirali   Tel. 22436
Directions: As above and at the north, top or left-hand end (*Fbqbo*), on the left-hand side.

Double room prices range from 1000 drs to 1300 drs.

Pension (*Tmr* 3.B2) Odhos Damirali
Directions: Almost behind the *Hotel Proto* on the same side as the *Oceanis* but about the centre of the street. A crudely painted sign with red lettering proclaims 'We Serve Coffee, Rooms, Hot Showers, Clothes Washed Here, Douche Chaud'. Run by a smiley-faced lady. Average rates.

Odhos Damirali runs into the main Galini road off which a right-hand fork, Odhos Neofytou, encircles the north side of the Town. The *Cafe-Bar Restaurant Elli* is close by the divergence of the ways.

Hotel Anna (*Tmr* 4.C/D2) (Class E) 58 Odhos Neophytou   Tel. 22475
Directions: As above and on the left about 200m along the gently curving, badly surfaced road of Down-Town Naxos. Really a 2 storey, low-rise Guest House with sea views. The old lady, of Romany appearance, oversees a spotless Pension, personalised with nice touches, and the lovely rooms have small, en suite bathrooms.

Rates for a double room range from 1100 drs to 1400 drs.

On the same side, a few metres further along behind Taxiarchis Church is the:-

Hotel Apollon (*Tmr* 5.D2) (Class C) 61 Odhos Neophytou   Tel. 22468
Double rooms sharing a bathroom cost 800 drs rising to 1000 drs (July-September).

Keeping round to the right up the narrow, rising lane forking left, and on the right, is:-

Pension Anna Maria (*Tmr* 6.D2)
Double room rates as for other Pensions.

Back on a Town circling lane, Odhos Mitropolitou Neophytou and a dirt track drops down and across some waste ground on which the odd hobbled cow, goat and or sheep are grazed. Behind, towering over and almost abutting a small Chapel is a modern block of Apartments with a distinctly unfinished look. None the less the left-hand building immediately to the rear of the Chapel belongs to:-

Aikaterini Lampri (*Tmr* 7.D3)   Tel. 23519
Directions: As above. The grown up children of Aikaterini meet the Ferries and lead 'Roomers' through the tortuous back streets, a route that can engender unworthy thoughts in respect of distance and destination.

The appearance of the rather dismal surroundings is little alleviated by the bare, concrete, 'tower-block' steps to the third floor, but all is well. The large rooms are obviously used by the family out of season and they are furnished with pieces that are Victorian in size and hue. The two (yes two) bathrooms on this floor are excellent and use of the kitchen is thrown in. Good value from between 700 and 1000 drs for a double room.

Although I could continue the circular theme the labyrinth nature of the back street layout makes description easier by dropping back to the waterfront. South or right (*F-bqbo*) alongside the Esplanade, past the *Cafeteria Pharos Elpidas* (*Tmr* 8.B2) and on the left is the Main Square, Plateia Prantouna (*Tmr* 9.B2), from which the convoluted Old Quarter radiates. Generally the Old Quarter, parallel to and above the Esplanade, is riddled with *Rooms* but one interesting example of the genus '*Hellene Domicilius*' is the:-

Hotel Dionyssos (*Tmr* 10.C2) (Class D) 110 Persefonis   Tel. 22331
Directions: From the Plateia Prantouna take Odhos Apollonos off the far right-hand corner and the third alley to the left. It is possible to follow the stencilled 'hand' but this is not an infallible method as the winter whitewashing tends to obscure some of the pointers.

In piratical days of yore, or possibly, and more accurately, Dickensian England, the less-than-winsome proprietor would have put one in mind of Fagin or the overseer of a boy chimney-sweep. The area is pleasant enough and the premises have a splendid rooftop terrace. Accommodation on offer starts with students tiered bunks in an arched, darkened cellar around which are dotted oilcloth covered, rickety card tables but for 200 drs a night

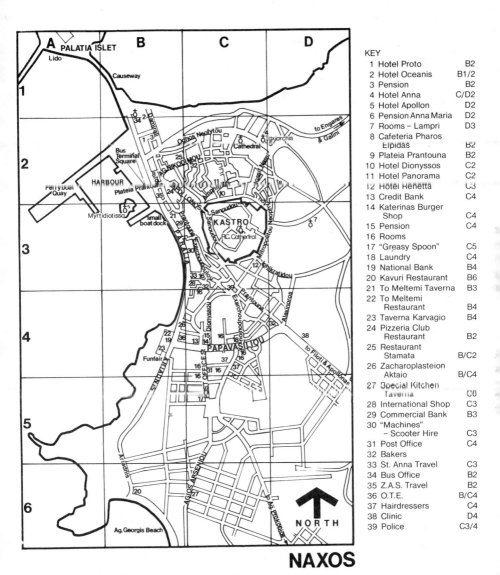

KEY

1	Hotel Proto	B2
2	Hotel Oceanis	B1/2
3	Pension	B2
4	Hotel Anna	C/D2
5	Hotel Apollon	D2
6	Pension Anna Maria	D2
7	Rooms – Lampri	D3
8	Cafeteria Pharos Elpidas	B2
9	Plateia Prantouna	B2
10	Hotel Dionyssos	C2
11	Hotel Panorama	C2
12	Hotel Renetta	C3
13	Credit Bank	C4
14	Katerinas Burger Shop	C4
15	Pension	C4
16	Rooms	
17	"Greasy Spoon"	C5
18	Laundry	C4
19	National Bank	B4
20	Kavuri Restaurant	B6
21	To Meltemi Taverna	B3
22	To Meltemi Restaurant	B4
23	Taverna Karvagio	B4
24	Pizzeria Club Restaurant	B2
25	Restaurant Stamata	B/C2
26	Zacharoplasteion Aktaio	B/C4
27	Special Kitchen Taverna	C6
28	International Shop	C3
29	Commercial Bank	B3
30	"Machines" – Scooter Hire	C3
31	Post Office	C4
32	Bakers	
33	St. Anna Travel	C3
34	Bus Office	B2
35	Z.A.S. Travel	B2
36	O.T.E.	B/C4
37	Hairdressers	C4
38	Clinic	D4
39	Police	C3/4

NAXOS

Illustration 21

what can a traveller expect? A double room sharing the bathroom kicks off from 600 drs whilst an en suite room starts at 700 drs. More a hostel than a hotel.

Fairly close by are the Hotels:-

Anixis (Class D) 330 Amphitritis   Tel. 22112
Directions: As above and on the corner of the Square.

Distinctly smarter than the 'Dinosaur', no hush my mouth, The *Dionyssos*, but then one pays for it with a double room sharing the bathroom costing a 1000 drs, rising to 1200 drs (1st June - 14th September), and en suite 1200 drs and 1600 drs respectively.

Panorama (*Tmr* 11.C2) (Class C) Amphitritis Kastro   Tel. 22330
Directions: As above but one block to the north.

Double rooms sharing the bathroom range between 1040 and 1300 drs and en suite 1100 and 1415 drs. The high season months are July and August.

From the *Hotel Dionyssos* (*Tmr* 10.C2) in a clockwise direction, Odhos Mitropolitou Neophytou circles the Kastro area of the Old Quarter. Beyond the junction with Odhos Iphikratidou is the:-

Hotel Renetta (*Tmr* 12.C3) (Class C)   Tel. 22952
The friendly, smiling proprietress Maria is active in procuring guests for her Hotel which is situated in this very attractive area of winding alleys and lanes. She will always stop likely looking travellers.

En suite double rooms rise from 1100 to 1500 drs.

To the south of the Esplanade the area either side of the Main Road out of Town (Odhos Papavasiliou), which rises up from the waterfront and takes a right dog-leg at the top of the hill, is rich in accommodation. Towards the Esplanade end of Odhos Papavasiliou, opposite 'Post Office St', a street flanked by on one corner the **Credit Bank** (*Tmr* 13.C4) and on the other *Katerinas Burger Shop*, (*Tmr* 14.C4) curves back towards the waterfront and on the right is a very big:-

Pension (*Tmr* 15.C4)
Directions: As above.

A large flight of stairs leads up to the first floor. The proprietor is often conspicuous by his absence and I have spent the odd hour or two trying to raise him, so renting a Room can prove tiresome. Maybe the loud gossip of 'meaningful' young American girls drowned out my door knocking and cries for attention. Prices are average.

Almost opposite, across the road there are **Rooms** and down the street on the right is the pricey *Hotel Aegean.*

More reasonably priced accommodation lurks either side of the 'Post Office' St (*Tmr* 16.C4 and *Tmr* 16.C4/5, over the *Greasy Spoon* (*Tmr* 17.C5, *See* **The Eating Out**), as it does in the area of the street opposite the Laundry (*Tmr* 18.C4).

At the Esplanade, by the **National Bank** (*Tmr* 19.B4), a narrow street to the left (*Fsw*) climbs up to level out in the area used as a Lorry Park and on towards the package tour end of Naxos Town. Beyond the low single storey *Hotel Ariadni*, scruffy Odhos Ariadnis drops down to the lovely sandy beach of Ag Georgios alongside the *Kavuri Restaurant* (*Tmr* 20.B6) at the start of a sweeping bay. Off to the left of Ariadnis St a grid layout of urban style roads give access to a litter of hotels most of which are block-booked by the tour companies. At the far end of the gently curving, sandy Ag Georgios beach is the *Cafe-Bar/Disco Flisvos* from which a 1000m track leads to:-

Camping Naxos   Tel. 23501
Directions: As above but due to the distance involved it is best to use the campsite bus which, as they do on many islands, meets the Ferry-boat arrivals.

All the usual facilities including hire of tents but a word of warning involves the general area which is towards the old salt flats or Alikes. The development in the surrounding area is rather shanty in nature in a low-lying land criss-crossed by stagnant drainage ditches with all the attendant problems of insects and unsatisfactory aromas.

In amongst all this nestles the C class *Hotel Naxos Beach.* Say no more!

The Eating Out The accommodation may be excellent but the establishments at which to 'scoff', fill the nose-bag or gourmandise are frankly, generally uninspiring. Furthermore some are subject to a malaise or affliction that brings me to boiling point, namely unpriced menus. It is not that there are less than a plethora of restaurants but on the whole they are uninspiring or have been lionised by and cater only for the more ample purses of German and Scandinavian package holiday tourists, hence, I suspect, the number of expensive and unpriced menus.

Further evidence of deviant trends is the number of the cafe-bars, tavernas and restaurants that line the Esplanade offering 'numbered' breakfasts listed 1, 2 & 3 and featured as 'English Scandinavian, Continental and Normal' fare, one even listing baked beans — how Greek! Oddly enough, for which blessings must be offered, this habit has not spread to mid-day or evening meals, only applying to breakfasts. Before leaving the subject I hope visitors will not patronise restaurants that eschew the legal requirement of displaying a controlled price list for surely it is an oversight . . . . .! One last and unusual point is that tomatoes are quite often in short supply both in the vegetable shops and eating houses. Perhaps the hotels scoop them all up.

Cafeteria Faros Elpidas (*Tmr* 8.B2)
Directions: From the Ferry-boat quay right and almost on the edge of the small Main Square, Plateia Prantouna. Run by Alpetha and her brother, whose father is the very friendly Demetrios who owns the bookshop at the far end of the Esplanade —of which more later.

Very friendly and good service with a range of breakfasts, cakes, pastries, ice-creams, and drinks. Breakfasts cost from 130 to 300 drs, a nescafe with milk 55 drs and an Amstel beer 66 drs.

To Meltemi Taverna (*Tmr* 21.B3)
Directions: On the left of the Esplanade, beyond the small boat quay and Periptero, in the block containing the **Commercial Bank.**

The waiter is a friendly man, if somewhat humourless, the patrons wife can be seen peeling vegetables during the day, the taverna has a pleasantly dark interior with a few tables on the narrow pavement as well as a number of tables and chairs beneath an awning, across the road, beside the waters edge. All augers well but the interesting if limited looking and reasonably priced menu is nearly always served up cold. A pity this as offerings include the ubiquitous moussaka (160 drs), spaghetti with mince (150 drs), stuffed tomatoes (160 drs), spinach, green beans, Greek salad (130 drs), a bottle of Amstel (60 drs), and a bottle of retsina (70 drs). The menu is a gem and includes 'fresh boutter', 'vegetabies', 'red mulled kilo', 'gigantes', 'marrovv augraten' and 'Ozo' may be mixed with 'Miner Waters'.

Confusingly there is another Taverna with a similar name:-

To Meltemi (*Tmr* 22.B4)
Directions: At the far, south end of the Esplanade behind or on the corner of the sea-side of the block containing the **National Bank** (*Tmr* 19.B4).

Not inexpensive and caters for and is popularly patronised by Dutch and German tour parties.

Further on, towards the Fun-fair, from this last *To Meltemi* is the:-

Taverna Karvagio (*Tmr* 23.B4)
The varied but expensive menu reads like that of an English Bistro. The items listed include 'country pot roast with herbs and noodles' 300 drs and 'Beef Stroganoff' 320 drs.

But back to saner 'troughs':-

Pizzeria Club Restaurant (*Tmr* 24.B2)
Directions: Off to the right of the Plateia Prantouna (*Sbo*) and on the left. A popular eating place with the chairs and tables on a raised patio. Inconveniently the shared toilet faces on to the patio added to which the door opens outwards. Due to the crush this results in those diners in the immediate area having to be constantly on the move.

The pizza's are big enough for two in many cases and a large meal of 1 (enormous) Pizza Naxos, a pork cutlet, a plate of zucchini and potatoes, Greek salad, bread and 2 bottles of retsina all for 925 drs.

Restaurant Stamata (*Tmr* 25.B/C2)
Directions: From the far left side of Plateia Prantouna (*Sbo*), Odhos Agios Nikodimou (the Old Market Street), curves sharply and gently climbs, passing beneath covered arches. On the left down some steps is a pleasant Square bounded by Churches on two sides. More interestingly perhaps, the Restaurant Square is also edged by a house from which an elderly, over-painted harridan hangs out of one of her upstairs windows engaging, well more haranguing, the occasional passer-by with conversation.

No retsina but a local Naxos white wine only costs 170 drs. A hot, appetising meal for two of kalamari (200 drs), stuffed tomatoes (100 drs), a plate of green beans, bread and a bottle of Promponas wine costs about 740 drs. Certainly one of the best eateries in town.

Close by is:-

Manolis Taverna
Directions: Further along Odhos Agios Nikodimou from *Restaurant Stamata* and jinking to the right and then left.

This is a reasonable priced Taverna with the garden on the left, a Chapel alongside, and the kitchen on the right of the narrow lane.

Zacharoplasteion Aktaio (*Tmr* 26.B/C4)
Directions: The far, south end of the Esplanade, beneath the *Hotel Koronis.*

'Cakes Made In Our Own Laboratories'. Well, well. Comfortable seats and well frequented by locals.

Beyond the **Rent-A-Car** firm alongside, is a:-

Souvlaki Pita Bar

Further on and left up Odhos Papavasiliou and (if you must), on the left is:-

Katerinas Burger Shop (*Tmr* 14.C4)
Across the road is the side turning of 'Post Office' St which, not surprisingly, leads past the **Post Office** and opens out on to a large, unequal sided Square formed by the various roads that branch off. On the right nearside is a:-

Cafe-Bar (*Tmr* 17.C5)
Directions: As above.

A small 'greasy-spoon' with **Rooms** above.

Across the Square, past a Church, behind which is a cemetery, and the main right fork of Odhos Agios Arseniou tumbles down the hillside towards Ag Georgios Beach. Diagonally across the road (well more a rectangle), from the **Disco/Medusa Funbar** and across from the *Hotel Iliovassilema* is the:-

'Special Kitchen' Taverna (*Tmr* 27.C6)
Directions: As above.

A family run establishment in a comparatively modern block, the ground floor of which is occupied by the Taverna but that somehow misses the 'sauce-boat'. Perhaps it is a lack of other than a contrived atmosphere, which may not be assisted by the unseemly haste with which a menu is slapped in customers hands — I am unable to pin-point the cause.

Certainly the food is rather 'pre-prepared' but is reasonably priced. A very large Greek salad, a plate of haricot beans, generous stuffed aubergine, a plate of stuffed tomatoes, zucchini and potatoes, bread and retsina from the barrel costs about 775 drs.

At the Town end of Agios Georgios Beach is the:-

Kavuri Restaurant (*Tmr* 20.B6)
More a Taverna but open during the day (so it's not a taverna!) and often with little choice left in the evening. A good selection when available at average prices.

For bathers the provision of showers is a noteworthy point.

Before leaving the subject one other establishment, a rather strange Store, rates a criticism

The International Shop (*Tmr* 28.C3)
Directions: Two thirds of the way round the Esplanade from the Ferry-boat quay, flanked by the **Santa Anna Travel Agency** and a Supermarket — of which more later.

The surly 'opportunist' owners sell a limited range of provisions during the day and incongruously the place doubles up in the evening as a Grill eating place. Neither disparate or expensive function is performed very well. *Rooms* over.

THE A TO Z OF USEFUL INFORMATION
BANKS
The Commercial Bank (*Tmr* 29.B3) On the Esplanade road a few yards down from the Port. Eurocheques cashed, normal banking hours.

BEACHES Not only does Naxos Town possess one of the finest beaches of any Cycladic island but the south-west coast of the island is almost one long, sandy beach.

At the north end of the Town either side of the causeway to Palatia islet, on which stands the reworked marble Gate of Apollo, are:-

Beach 1: On the left of the actual causeway. More a place for a quick dip but obviously favoured as a Lido for there are the remains (not Roman) of a faded, bamboo faced Beach Bar and changing rooms which like a moth flickers briefly but frantically to life at the height of the season.

Beach 2: To the right of the start of the causeway. A scrubbly bit of old beach. But do not be down-hearted for the jewel in Naxos's crown is:-

Beach 3: Agios Georgios Beach to the south-west of the Town, edged at the near end by the package holiday development. A long, curving, sandy bay with a gently shelving sea bottom and very clear water. The first tree-lined portion is dotted with tavernas. Between the *Kavuri Restaurant* and the **Disco Asteria**, a trio of bars are spaced around a patio, the middle one of which, the *Naxos Club* is run by a very pleasant, smiley lady. The first bit of foreshore is kelpy and the sea very shallow. The backshore to most of this extensive beach is rather scrubby and, in spite of signs forbidding the same, is used as a road by the locals. Half-way round there are pedaloes for hire and the **Disco Asteria**. The far end of the really attractive sweep of sand is marked by the *Cafe-Bar/Disco Flisvos* with its distinctive mock windmill but the bay magnificently curves on towards Cape Moungri.

BICYCLE, SCOOTER & CAR HIRE The hirers of scooters are wary men and bearing in mind the mountainous and large nature of the island, this is not surprising. Unless a Vespa or similar is in good condition it will not carry two on the more adventurous journeys. The balance of choice is weighted towards Jeep and Beach-buggy hire outfits. Fuel costs are about 75 drs a litre and a full Vespa scooter tank costs some 380 drs.

From the bottom of the Ferry-boat quay (*Tmr* B2), almost across the Esplanade beneath the *Hotel Proto* (*Tmr* 1.B2) is:-

The Jeep A smart office. At least the young man is brutally honest and admits his scooters will not carry a passenger, pleasantly recommending prospective clients to go elsewhere. Naturally he is more interested in hiring out Mini-Mokes, *et al*.

Maganari Next door to *Zacharoplasteion Aktaio* (*Tmr* 26.B/C4). Incidentally, hire rates for a Suzuki Jeep work out at about 8000 drs for 3 days with full insurance but the daily accident deposit has to be allowed for in any calculation.

The Esplanade has a number of outfits including:-

'Machines' (*Tmr* 30.C3) Once a garage, located beneath an Art Gallery.

Perhaps the most 'fertile ground' for scooters is in 'Post Office' St— in fact almost next door to the Post Office (*Tmr* 31.C4) where there are two firms side by side.

The first is run by a very honest and ingenuous man who hires out well maintained machines at about 1000 drs, which price can be negotiated down to 800 drs a day for 3 days.

Where 'Post Office' St breaks out into a large Square, there is a very smart:-

Rental Center — Rent a Jeep The plush surroundings would be more suitable to say Oxford Street.

Perhaps the firm offering 'Rent-a-Baggy' has it right!

BOOKSELLERS To the right-hand of the far side of Plateia Prantouna (*Tmr* 9.B2) and on the left is a good foreign language book and paper shop. From the Main Square, along the Esplanade towards the Ferry-boat quay, past *Faros Elpidas Cafeteria* (*Tmr* 8.B2), the 'Chora Cafe-Bar' and an alley-way and on the right is:-

Mr. Melissinos's A card, gift and dress shop of which naught, but he is the brother of George the author of the only Island Guide available which is naturally enough on sale here. The Guide is old fashioned in style, but the photographs are well worth the 170 drs purchase price. Mr. Melissinos also sells stamps.

A most interesting venue on Odhos Paralia, the Esplanade road, two narrow lanes beyond the **Commercial Bank** (*Tmr* 29.B3) is:-

Upstairs We Sell and Buy Used Books Upstairs it is, because, as with quite a lot of the Esplanade, the ground floor of the back of any building is the first floor of the front. The business sells jewellery and dresses but as the charming owner declares the books are his 'trap'. And what a trap with 3 full shelves each of English, French and German books.

Perhaps the most inviting book (and dress) shop is that run by the gentle and very pleasant Demetrios. He is father of the brother and sister who run *Faros Elpidas Cafeteria*, and his emporium is located beneath *Katerinas Burger Shop* (*Tmr* 14.C4). He sells dresses, maps and books including the beautifully produced Architectural Guides published by 'Melissa'. His English is good and the cellar shop is reached down a flight of steps, is distinguished by his habit of hanging dresses on the lintel of the door. He is contemplating selling up though, so in future years this delightful character may no longer be in evidence, which will be a great pity.

There is another **We Sell Used Books** in the Old Quarter, off to the right of Odhos Agios Nikodimou.

BREAD SHOPS In the Old Quarter, off to the right of Odhos Agios Nikodimou and on the left (*Tmr* 32.C2) just before *Manolis Taverna*.

Along the Esplanade, Odhos Paralia, close by **Santa Anna Travel** (*Tmr* 33.C3), stencilled signs on the walls lead the way up steep steps to a Bakery (*Tmr* 32.C/4) on the right of an irregular Square. There are also a couple of *Rooms* behind the aforementioned Travel Agency.

Another Baker (*Tmr* 32.D4) is located on the dog-leg of Odhos Papavasiliou, at the top of the steep rise from the waterfront, where Odhos Prantouna makes a junction with the Main Road.

BUSES The Bus office (*Tmr* 34.B2) is not quite where it is indicated on some island maps but a little to the north, beyond a small public garden, whilst the buses turn round and park up around this very large Square at the bottom of the Ferry-boat quay.

Bus timetable Please note these are the minimum schedules. During the height of summer, the frequency increases. For instance, Apollonas gets up to 4 buses a day.

Naxos Town to Apollonas (North coast)
Daily   0930 hrs
Return journey
Daily   1430 hrs
One-way fare 180 drs, duration 2½ hrs

Naxos Town to Koronida (Komiaki) (North island)
Daily   0930, 1300 hrs
Return journey
Daily   0700, 1500 hrs
One-way fare 140 drs

Naxos Town to Apirathos (Centre island)
Daily   0930, 1300 hrs
Return journey
Daily   0730, 0845, 1530 hrs
One-way fare 90 drs

Naxos Town to Chalki, Filoti (Centre island)
Daily   0930, 1100, 1200, 1300, 1700 hrs
Return journey
Daily   0700, 0745, 0900, 1545 hrs
One-way fare 65 drs

Naxos Town to Pyrgaki (South-west coast)
Daily   1000, 1400 hrs
Return journey
Daily   1030, 1430 hrs
One-way fare 70 drs

Naxos Town to Tripodes (Vivlos) (South-west island)
Daily   1100, 1300 hrs
Return journey
Daily   0730, 0845 hrs
One-way fare 35 drs

Naxos Town to Melanes (East of Naxos Town)
Daily   1430 hrs
Return journey
Daily   0700, 1500 hrs
One-way fare 35 drs

Naxos Town to Ag Anna (South-west coast)
Daily   1030, 1200, 1700 hrs
Return journey
Daily   1100, 1230, 1730 hrs
One-way fare 45 drs

There is also a connection of sorts to both Moutsouna (East coast) and Lionas (90 drs).

On Monday, Wednesday and Fridays only there are the following connections:-

Naxos Town to Kinidaros (Centre island)
            1200 hrs
Return journey
            0700 hrs
One-way fare 65 drs

Naxos Town to Potamia (Centre island)
    1430 hrs
Return journey
    0700 hrs
One-way fare 45 drs

Naxos Town to Galini (North-east of Naxos Town)
    0730, 1330 hrs
Return journey
    0800, 1400 hrs
One-way fare 30 drs

Naxos Town to Keramoti, Danakos (Centre island)
    1200 hrs
Return journey
    0700 hrs
One-way fare 115 drs.

CHEMISTS *See* **Medical Care.**

COMMERCIAL SHOPPING AREA The Chora or Old Quarter provides a splendid area for most shops which are interspersed along the narrow climbing, tumbling alleys of Odhos Agios Nikodimou and Odhos Apollonos both of which radiate off the Main Square, Plateia Prantouna. The usual fruit and vegetable shops with the occasional butcher. One particular shop that draws attention is the old man who sells sponges and decorative shells towards the far end of Odhos Agios Nikodimou.

On the left of Odhos Apollonos, as it climbs towards the Museum, is an imposing cavernous shop, advertising its activities 'We have Naxos Cheese, Honey, Wine'!

The Esplanade has a number of mini and supermarkets, the most comprehensive and reasonably priced of which is beyond the **Santa Anna Travel Agency** (from the Ferry-boat quay).

Recognizable by the turnstiles which are to aid the owners keep an eye on the customers. The store closes on Wednesday afternoon and all day Sunday. This reminds me to stress that Naxos has not allowed tourism to affect the old siesta habits after which many businesses do not re-open.

Most of the supermarkets display a most unwelcome sight, a silent comment on the habits of the more light-fingered holidaymakers, namely signs requesting tourists to leave all bags outside.

DENTISTS *See* **Medical Care.**

DISCOS *See* **Beaches.**

FERRY-BOATS A fairly busy port and importantly a stepping stone to the far Eastern Cycladian islands of Iraklia, Schinoussa, Koufonissi, Donoussa, Amorgos and Astipalaia. It should be noted that up to the 1st June and from about the middle to the end of September onwards there are a number of free passages to these islands (excluding Astipalaia).

Re-read the notes in Chapter 3 regarding the attributes and short-comings of the various inter-island ferries but note that the local Excursion Craft are covered under the particular island chapter.

Ferry-boat timetable

Day	Departure time	Ferry-boat	Ports/Islands of Call
Tuesday	1630 hrs*	Santorini	Ios, Sikinos, Folegandros, Santorini†
Wednesday	0930 hrs	Naxos	Paros, Piraeus (M. arrive 1730 hrs)
	1400 hrs*	Limnos	Ios, Ia (Santorini), Santorini†

	1500 hrs*	Georgios Express	Ios, Santorini†
	2215 hrs	Georgios Express	Paros, Piraeus, (M. arrive 0515 hrs next day)
Thursday	1435 hrs*	Georgios Express	Ios, Santorini†
	1530 hrs*	Santorini	Ios, Santorini†
	1600 hrs	Naxos	Iraklia, Schinoussa, Koufonissi, Donoussa, Amorgas‡
	2215 hrs	Georgios Express	Paros, Piraeus, (M. arrive 0515 hrs next day)
Friday	0930 hrs	Naxos	Paros, Syros, Piraeus, (M. arrive 1730 hrs)
	1400 hrs*	Limnos	Ios, Ia (Santorini), Santorini†
Saturday	1100 hrs	Georgios Express	Paros, Piraeus (M. arrive 1730 hrs)
	1045 hrs	Santorini	Ios, Santorini†
Sunday	0100 hrs*	Nireus (Miaoulis)	Iraklia, Schinoussa, Koufonissi, Donoussa, Aegiali (Amorgas), Katapola (Amorgas), Astypalaia
	0240 hrs	Georgios Express	Ios, Santorini†
	0930 hrs	Naxos	Paros, Piraeus, (M. arrive 1730 hrs)
	1150 hrs	Georgios Express	Paros, Piraeus, (M. arrive 1830 hrs)

*Approximate time   † Probably Athinos Port ‡ Probably both Aegiali and Katapola (in that order).

In addition to the above

| Tuesday, Wednesday, Friday, Saturday, Sunday | 1325 hrs | MV Ios | Mykonos |

| LOCAL | | | |
| Monday/Thursday & Sunday | 1000 hrs** | MV Marianna | Iraklia, Schinoussa, Koufonissi, Donoussa, Aegiali (Amorgas), Katapola (Amorgas) |

**Often up to ¾ hrs delay and docks at Katapola at approximately 1800 hrs.

The **MV Marianna** will require some dissertation here as being a local ferry it is not covered in Chapter 3, wherein the attributes and defects of the more 'International' of the boats are laid bare. The **Marianna**, metaphysically surely a relation of the **African Queen**, is a very small inter-island ferry-boat evocative of the 1950s, which was probably the last date the toilets were cleaned out. The comparatively high structure and upper deck result in the 'old bucket' rolling a bit even in a flat calm and once on the Donoussa leg she will lurch and pitch however settled the weather. The curvature of the deck, combined with the unsecured, rickety seats, makes for an interesting voyage in rolling seas and baggage should be securely located. The best seating position is on the top deck, back to the funnel. Due to the diminutive size of the vessel it is best to embark early to secure a seat for, apart from the decks, there is only one beneath deck cabin in which the Greek ladies gather to be ill, and that's before leaving port. As there is no galley it is necessary to take provisions for the voyage. Again because of the vessel's size it is much slower than the **Marianna's** modern counterparts. One last caveat is that rough weather results in the 'good-ship' delaying and or cancelling its departure.

FERRY-BOAT TICKET OFFICES A number of Ticket Agencies spread along the Esplanade but as on most islands one agency has cornered the market.

ZAS Travel (*Tmr* 35.B2)   Tel. 23330
Directions: Located beneath the Town Hall (ΔHMAPXEION), almost opposite the caique quay that forms the south-side of the harbour, to the right of Plateia Prantouna (*Sbo*).

A 'switched on', efficient staff runs this office which handles most ferries including the **MV Marianna** and change currency.

Two other ticket offices, more involved in trip boat and excursion traffic, are the:-

Santa Anna Travel Agency (*Tmr* 33.C3)
Directions: Two thirds of the way along the Esplanade from the Ferry-boat quay. Often does not open up in the evening.

Travel Centre of Naxos
Directions: Close to the OTE (*Tmr* 36.B/C4).

HAIRDRESSERS At least two ladies hairdressers (*Tmr* 37.C4), both accessible from the 'Post Office' St down the first left-hand turning (from the Port).

LAUNDRY Two, one on the left of Odhos Papavasiliou (*Tmr* 18.C4) and the other next door to the 1st Hairdresser above. Both advertise that they wash and press clothes.

LUGGAGE STORE On Odhos Damirali, opposite the *Hotel Oceanis* (*Tmr* 2.B1/2), which street runs parallel to the top or Ferry-boat quay end of the Esplanade.

MEDICAL CARE
Chemists & Pharmacies One, Nik Dellaroca, on the Town side of the 'Bus terminal Square' (*Tmr* B2) and another close by the OTE (*Tmr* 36.B/C4).

Clinic (*Tmr* 38.D4) To the left of the main Filoti road out of Naxos Town where it becomes industrial 'Down-Town'.

Dentists There are three listed, Bardanis (Tel 22317), Mamouzelos (Tel 22315) and Sofia Kritikou (Tel 23771).

Doctors Kastritsios (Tel 22308), Sofigitis (Tel 22302) and Venieris (Tel 22557).

NTOG None nor are there any Tourist police, which may be one of the reasons why some of the restaurants omit to display the legally required Controlled Price Lists.

OPENING HOURS
Museum *See* **Places of Interest** for the reasons I am not listing them.

Shops (summer) Despite the level of tourism most shops stick to the old traditions for details of which refer to **Chapter 7**.

OTE (*Tmr* 36.B/C4) At the far end of Odhos Paralia, the Esplanade road, just before the *Hotel Ermis*. Despite being the largest island in the Cyclades the office does not open over the weekend. Opening times Monday to Friday 0730 - 2200 hrs, closed weekends, 'High-Days' and holidays.

PETROL (GASOLINE) There are two petrol stations on the south-eastern outskirts of Naxos Town on the Filoti main road. There are several more up to 3 km further on the road to Galanado.

PLACES OF INTEREST
Cathedrals & Churches
The Church of Myrtidiotissa Possibly the first Church on the island seen by a visitor, as the little Chapel picturesquely sits on a tiny islet to one side of the Harbour.

There is a veritable clutch of Churches as well as the Orthodox Cathedral to the north of the Old Quarter (*Tmr* C2).

The Catholic Cathedral (*Tmr* C3) A lovely building with a boldly domed roof in the rather small, claustrophobic Kastro Square. It was originally built in the 13th century, 'restored' in the 16th/17th centuries and subsequently and recently restored back to the original! It is located at the centre of the old Kastro walls which are breached at the old gateways, but is not very well signposted.

The Kastro (Tmr C3) There is not a lot left and the only real evidence is the Venetian houses, many with heraldic devices that were built into the old walls forming a picturesque ring of Medieval buildings. Within these is a beautiful area, a jumble of paved streets, an ancient cistern, the Catholic Cathedral, the Museum, the Palace of Sanudo and other attractive buildings.

Chora The Old Quarter is quite extensive, radiating out from the epicentre of the steep hilltop Kastro, around which the lanes, alleys and arched walkways wind tortuously.

Unlike Mykonos and Paros, the Old Quarter does not have the feeling of being tarted up for the delectation of tourists. In fact the Administration appears to be actively discouraging sightseeing by continuously digging up various lanes.

Museum I will mention its physical presence, despite its being closed for a few years for renovation. It is rather tucked away but is reached by initially facing (*Sbo*), and then keeping round to the right of the Catholic Cathedral on the main Kastro walkway. The exhibits are rumoured to include jewellery, pottery and sculptures.

Close by is the one-time French Ursuline Convent.

Temple Prominent especially to Ferry-boat travellers. More a single remaining and standing gateway on Palatia islet, reputably of the Temple of Apollo, which was probably started in the 5th Century BC. Frankly the site is a rather messy scatter of discarded and fallen lumps of masonry, set amongst heather clumps, once enclosed in a now trampled wire fence with the occasional, defunct floodlight.

POLICE Rarely have I failed to pin-point the police but I can assure readers this is no Freudian slip. I must own up that I am not prepared to be dogmatic about the location of the office. With the general absorption of the Tourist police into the local service, the situation has become rather more muddled.

The police are certainly conspicuous by their retiring nature. On my last visit, although it was election night, with all the emotional build-up involved and the odd chap hurling the occasional stick of dynamite about in the direction of a politically dissenting fellow citizen, officers were rarely to be seen. Even on that exciting, tumultous evening they were only to be observed simply putting in place the night-time signs barring Esplanade traffic.

I do list the telephone number (*See* **Telephone Numbers & Addresses**) and, seriously folks, the office (*Tmr* 39.C3/4) used to be most easily reached by climbing Odhos Papavasiliou and turning left down Odhos Exarchopoulou, whence it was on the left, at a meeting of the ways.

POST OFFICE (*Tmr* 31.C4) On the left-hand side of the major side street, called for convenience sake 'Post Office' St, which is right off Odhos Papavasiliou (*Sbo*). Usual facilities and hours.

TAXIS No particular rank as they are located at a number of strategic points throughout the Town including the 'Bus Terminal Sq' (at the Ferry-boat quay end of the Esplanade), in the area of the junction of the Esplanade road and Odhos Papavasiliou and in and around the package holiday end of Town.

TELEPHONE NUMBERS & ADDRESSES

Clinic	Tel. 22346
Police	Tel. 22100
Taxis	Tel. 22444

Note Doctors and Dentists phone numbers are detailed under **Medical Care.**

TOILETS Off Prantouna Sq (*Tmr* 9.B2) and up Odhos Prantouna a few metres and on the left are the Municipal Lavatories, shower (hot water) and WC's. My notes simply read 'Richter scale 7'. Ugh! If the attendant is sought he may well direct clients to facilities that register an 'eye-watering state' reduced to 5. I'd better point out that for a 'pourboire' (or tip) the lavatory person ensures a better class of toilet compartment, nothing else.

TRAVEL AGENTS *See* **Ferry-Boat Ticket Offices.**

ROUTE ONE
To Apollonas via Galini and Abram (circa 30 km) Possibly, consistently
the prettiest route I have travelled on any Greek island with magnificent, majestic and
stunning scenery, even if the outset is rather inauspicious.

The Galini/Engares road heads off from the north end of the Esplanade keeping left at
the first fork, alongside the *Cafe-Bar Restaurant Elli*. The rough surfaced road rises quite
steeply past high-rise apartments leaving the Town ring-road to the right.

Naxos does not forego the right to site the Town rubbish dump in such a way as to make
a most unsightly mess and ensure the pollution of at least one bay. Well, there you
go!

GALINI (5 km from Naxos Town) A dirt road leads off to the defunct Monastery of
Ypsilis once converted into a Castle/Church.

Beyond the villages of Galini (6 km) and Engares (8 km) the road is unsurfaced. On the
left a lovely valley runs down to a large, shingly beach foreshore with a bamboo bestrewn,
shrub growing backshore. On the left (*Fsw*) is a narrow band of discontinuous small rocks
in the very clear sea. The other side of the small headland bifurcating the (river) valley, is a
lovely, small, very sandy beach, set alongside the translucent Aegean Sea. The backshore
is cluttered with storm-tossed rubbish in amongst the sand dunes, all overlooked by a few
unobtrusive houses built on the gentle hillsides.

This bay is followed by a very small U-shaped cove with a large Church by the road
junction. The shore of this lovely location is shingle and the sea bottom consists of weed
covered small rocks.

Beyond the bluff a larger bay marks the start of a rocky, low cliff edge stretching away in
the distance.

The road cuts slightly inland and passes over a bridge spanning a boulderous river bed,
attractively beflowered with Oleanders and during much of the summer, running with
water. Upstream of the bridge is a small waterfall.

The Monastery of Faneromenis (approx 14 km from Naxos Town) On the left, but
now no longer a working community and beyond which is the 'donkey dropping' hamlet
of:-

CHILIA VRYSSI (16 km from Naxos Town) From here a track leads down to a lovely,
small cove at the bottom of a valley cleft. This is followed by a large cove, the land behind
which is cultivated all the way down to the rocky foreshore.

After another kilometre or so on this marvellous, coast-hugging road, skirting the indented
shore-line at a height, and a track leads down to:-

ABRAM BEACH (20 km from Naxos Town) In the summer-time the river of this
agricultural valley is almost stagnant. On the left (*Fsw*), there is a small Chapel overlooking
the pebble beach with a sandy backshore from which rises up the hillside, in the style of a
large concrete steps the:-

Pension Efthinios   Tel. 22997
Directions: As above.

Mama Athena, who presides over the business, has a small amount of English —
enough to take a booking over the phone as long as a caller is explicit. She is very friendly
and will invite casual (but interested) callers in for a cup of Greek coffee, accompanied by
a cold glass of water. A simple, old fashioned room, costs between 800 and 1000 drs,
depending upon the time of year, but at the height of the season regulars are likely to
occupy most, if not all, of the available accommodation. An idyllic spot for 'the get away
from it all — I know this little spot. . .'

On this section of the road to Apollonas the air is rich with the mellifluous sounds of goat-
bells and the almost deafening, sawing of the grasshoppers. Another 3 km or so along the

'Main' road (okay a stony, rough track) and way down below is the small shingle/kelpy cove of Ag Theodoros in a beautifully poetic setting.

AGIA (25 km from Naxos Town) Another 'single donkey dropping' scattering of farmsteads, more a slight thickening out than a collection of buildings, adjacent to the Monastery of Panagias. The location is again perfectly lovely, high up on the mountain side overlooking a small indented bay in which are moored 2 or 3 fishing boats.

And thence (as they say) to:-

APOLLONAS (30 km from Naxos Town) A very lovely, sleepy, archetypal island fishing port and village on a bay sheltered by high mountain sides but which is, unfortunately, now the target for Excursion Buses, that roll in and out during the daylight hours. As on Simi island, in the Dodecanese, the moral is simple — hole up during the day and stay overnight!

The bay is split into two by a rocky projection, on which are built four changing rooms. To the right (FSW), is the main, wide, shingly beach, with some kelp, stretching away to the far edge of the bay. The Port is to the left with a small, very sandy beach. 'Nudism Forbidden' signs on both beaches and the sea is sparkingly clear.

The short paved quayside of the port (all other streets being rough surfaced), is edged with tavernas and restaurants, intermixed with and behind which, are **Rooms.**

For instance the last four taverna/restaurants prior to the fishing boat quay, have accommodation. The Hotels include the E class *Aegeon, Atlantis* and *Kouros*, two of which are set on the edge of the main beach. Room prices range from 800 - 1000 drs and Hotels between 900 and 1200 drs. Particularly recommended **Rooms** include *The Falcon* up the steps from the harbour wall that finish up on a small plateia overlooking the sea. A double room en suite costs 900 drs and they have one room with a kitchen attached for about 1000 drs. On this headland a French girl lets out a room with en suite bathroom, a fridge and balcony with views over the garden and the sea all for 700 drs.

Rumour, only rumour, has it that the reason that there is only a track down to the peculiar beige coloured *Kouras Hotel* is that Addonis and Marianna who run the accommodation, though both from the island weren't born and bred in Apollonas so the locals will not vote to build a road. . . . Above the rock that divides up the bay, is the path to the famous stone carved 'Kouros'. To the side of this track is the brand new *The Old House* with double rooms to rent. The shared bathroom has hot water and the cost varies between 900 drs and 1200 drs.

Of the waterfront tavernas, the third along, *Nikos* is very reasonably priced with 2 bacon omelettes (well salami really) and a beer costing 215 drs.

The mini-market is run by Costas who has lived in Camden Town, London for a time and he not only will help with information but runs a second-hand book trade. One of the partners in the gift shop, David, an Englishman, was proposing, in 1985, to open a disco. I wouldn't wish him ill in normal circumstances but it would be nice if he could change his mind, wouldn't it?

It is worth bearing in mind that Apollonas was rather remote and inaccessible until recent times and the inhabitants relaxed, 'laid-back' attitude reflects this isolation. For instance, the eating places quite often run out of this or that without being unduly concerned and it is necessary to accept what is on offer.

Bearing in mind the remarks about the beautifully clear sea I am reluctant to report on the Public Toilets, but there you go. At the end of the quay, around to the left an area has been surfaced on which the Tour-Buses park up and, at the far side, on the rocks is the toilet block. Unfortunately the builders decided that it would facilitiate drainage by simply building the squatties over the sea. . . . Added to which the facility is an eye-watering 'Richter scale 10'.

189

When the buses have all departed the locals occasionally stage a football match on the beach.

A short way, off the main road route to Naxos Town (via Filoti) is signposted the **Kouros of Apollonas**. This remarkable, but abandoned, incomplete marble figure, sculpted in about 650 BC and originally probably destined for Delos Island. It is approximately 10½ m in height and lies in a long deserted quarry. Close by and opposite to the quarry entrance, are the remains of the Venetian Fort of Kalogeros which either gave its name to the north-eastern region or (surprise, surprise), vise-versa.

ROUTE TWO
To Apollonas via Galanado, Chalki, Filoti and Apirathos (54 km)
The Main Road route to Apollonas is, at first, unremarkable passing through agricultural countryside until the lower foothills of the central mountain range. These uphills start after about 8 km close by the 8th century Ag Mamas down a path to the left, was once the Cathedral of Naxos and possessing some remarkable 7th century icons.

The road now slowly ascends to the hamlets of:-

SANGRI (10 km from Naxos Town) Kato Sangri has the remains of a Venetian Castle; Ano Sangri, the Monastery of Ag Eleftherios which became a secret School for Greek children during the Turkish Occupation and now houses a Folk Museum. There is also an ancient archaeological site and beyond, still on the main Chalki road, the 16th century Monastery of Timiou Stavrou and the 14th/15th century Church of Kaloritsa with a number of original frescoes.

Prior to Timiou Stavrou Monastery a dirt road heads south ending up at Ormos Agiassos and the Church Panagia Gialous almost in the centre of the beach. Here, as elsewhere on Naxos, there is an overseas development of Bungalows, to the right of the bay (*Fsw*). It is off the beaten track to anywhere, naturally enough I suppose as further travel in a southerly direction must necessitate an amphibious outfit. Pyrgaki is around a bluff to the right but only accessible on foot if you are very brave. The arid slopes of Mt Viglarouri blocks off travel to the left.

From the 'Sangri's' the road passes through Vourvouria to:-

CHALKI (Chalkio) (16 km from Naxos Town) This pretty Village is set at a high altitude, on a great plain of very old Olive trees. On the Filoti side of the Village both bread and petrol are available. There are a number of fortified tower-houses including the outstanding Pirgos Frangopoulou.

From Chalki radiate out a number of hamlets and interesting locations which include, from the north-west in an anticlockwise direction, Apano Kastro — a Venetian Castle; Tsikalario (Tsingalario) — ancient monuments; towards Damarionas — the 12th century Church of Panagia Protothroni with some restored frescoes; Kaloxylos — the highly rated Church of Ag Trias and towards Moni, the 8th century Church of Drossiani, from whence some of the more remarkable frescoes have been removed to Athens for 'safe keeping'.

From the enchanted Olive tree forests of the Plain of Tragea this route becomes truly dramatic with the craggy, towering mountains dwarfing the surrounding countryside and providing tremendous vistas. Still climbing the road passes through the Village of the island:-

FILOTI (19 km from Naxos Town) This unremarkable settlement does not appear to be all that loftily located, although situated well up on the flank of Mt Zas.

At about 22 km from Naxos Town a right-hand fork leads off to:-

DANAKOS (24 km from Naxos Town) Known for the fast flowing streams, which in years gone by powered a number of waterwheels, but renowned for the Byzantine sculptures of the Monastery of Fotodoti which is above the Village, to the north.

APIRATHOS (Apeiranthos) (27 km from Naxos Town)
The Village is quite pretty and was supposed to have originally been settled by Cretans.

To the right a badly potholed, winding road dramatically snakes and plunges down through the dry, Broom and Sage growing, mountain side. In the middle distance are the Islands of Makares and, behind them, Donoussa set in the sparkling cobalt sea. To the right, a gorge filled with a dry river bed flowing with Oleanders all the way to:-

MOUTSOUNA (39 km from Naxos Town) As with the other eastern coastal Village of Lionas and the workings riddling the surrounding mountain sides, the *raison d'etre* is, or more correctly was, the quarrying of Emery. The stone was bucketed down on aerial cableways to the surprisingly massive works and docking quays for outbound shipment. The Village is 'one-eyed' with a scruffy taverna to the left of the approach road. Beyond, on the waterside, are the deserted warehouses and workings associated with the quarry stone cable cars and two small Tramp Steamer quays (between which is a 'table-cloth' sized beach). Further on to the right is a small, sandy, shingle beach set in rocks.

Prior to Moutsouna, while still on the downward slope, and through a gateway to the left, a track makes across the neck of the headland to a large beach with groves of trees at either end.

From Moutsouna, an excursion on an excursion, is to take the track due south which edges the coastline from some 14 km. This jaunt is not for the faint-hearted, nor for those who like there to be a definite goal to any trip.

In the first kilometre, there are three small coves varying from pebble to fine shingle then, *en route*, a gate, yes a five bar gate, similar to those that shut off English fields, followed by various small coves. The wide track jolts on, with rocky coast to the left and mountain foothills to the right. The surrounds become sandy dunes with much moorland Gorse on the approach to:-

PSILI AMMOS (47 km from Naxos Town) A spread-out agricultural backyard through which the road bends and in which a surprising amount of private house development is taking place despite there being no apparent focal point or, for that matter, any trade being carried out. Beyond the hamlet is a big, sand dune backed beach.

From hereon the surface of the track becomes rougher and the width narrower, passing the occasionally lovely cove here and there, until the coastline proceeds to curve around Cape Panormos. Here the track becomes decidedly rough in patches struggling on to decant and run out in the lovely fastness of the small cove and beach of Panormos. A Church, a dwelling house, a fishing caique often moored up and nothing else. Additionally, whatever is written, maps may detail or you are told, this is the end of the road. Any further progress must be made on foot so do not plan to make a round trip of 'the junket'.

Back at Apirathos, north on the Main Road and, after another 5 km, a turning off to the left heads westwards on an unsurfaced (well all right), unmade road which proceeds through Sifones, past a 'T' junction connection to Moni and on to:-

KINIDAROS (16 km from Naxos Town) A very 'backyard' Village to the north of which the Church of Ag Artemios is built on or over the remains of a Temple to Diana.

Beyond Kinidaros, prior to the hamlet of Miloi, and to the left, is the area known as:-

FLERIO (9 km from Naxos Town) Here are ancient marble quarries and another **Kouros**. This is a later sculpting than the **Apollonas Kouros** and a mere 6.40 m in height.

Miloi is followed by the Village of:-

KOUROUNOCHORI (8 km from Naxos Town) Here are the remains of a Venetian Castle. From Kourounochori there is a choice of route via Engares or the village of Ag Thaleleos, with a 13th century Church of the same name.

Back on the Main Road, once again, and the next Village on the road to Apollonas is:-

KORONOS (36 km from Naxos Town) A stepped town scrabbling up the mountain sides and renowned for its Emery mines. A turning off to the right, ½ km prior to Koronos, proceeds east to the Village and Church of Argokiliotissa which on Easter Friday, plays host to hordes of worshippers.

From Koronos a side road to the right initially describes large loops, which increasingly tighten up, passing steeply down the mountain side, past evidence of extensive quarrying, to the erstwhile Port of:-

LIONAS (44 km from Naxos Town) The Oleander planted river-bed passes by two now 'dead' tavernas at the onset of the Village which is set in a steep sided gorge. The immediate central area is simply waste ground with the remnants of very large, old houses dotted about. A number of new, more humble dwellings are built into both sides of the gorge. The beach at the bottom of the Bay is made up of large pebbles washed over by the startlingly clear sea-water. This rather strange place does not go out of its way to encourage the casual tourist visitor.

From Koronos the Main Road passes through the 'one donkey-dropping' Village of Skado from whence an unmade track also connects with the coastal Village of Lionos BUT it does not join up with the surfaced road from Koronos, so beware!

KORONIDA (also known as Komiaka) (43 km from Naxos Town) Part of the road through Koronida becomes a rough track and the Village is noted, if for nothing else, for being the island village built at the highest altitude, some 700 m. Not unnaturally there are splendid views more especially as the mountains fall rapidly away to the coastal plain and the Port of Apollonas. The surrounding countryside is particularly lush and lovely, the road being shaded by bowers of trees and cleft by mountain streams. Apart from the distractions of the view, it is necessary for travellers to keep their wits about them for about halfway down the steep descent the road unexpectedly reverts to rough track for a stretch. Nasty.

ROUTE THREE
To Pyrgaki via Glinado, Vivlos (Tripodes) (21½ km) The first part of the
route in the direction of Galanado is as described under ROUTE TWO. Incidentally, whilst describing that route I did not draw attention to the large area of land bounded by the sea and the prominent rock headland known as Stelida and Livadi. Once an area of salt flats or 'Alikes', the flat land is intensively farmed, with bamboo fences dividing up the small individual plots of land. After 5½ km the right-hand turning off, should be followed to:-

GLINADO (6 km from Naxos Town) On the approach the 17th century Monastery Ag Saranta possesses some fine post-Byzantine icons.

AG ARSENIOS (8 km from Naxos Town) The friendly inhabitants of this small Village make up for any difficulties experienced in negotiating the lanes towards:-

AG ANNA (12 km from Naxos Town) The approach is through extensively cultivated land over a rough, narrow track tightly hemmed in by bamboo 'hedgerows' through which it seems unlikely that the bus could negotiate — but it does.

The lane widens out and spills on to the sandy, rather bedraggled, narrow waterfront. There is a large quay alongside which a converted but decrepit, listing and possibly abandoned landing craft is now berthed. Flanking the access road where the bus pulls up, are two 'lived-in' tavernas.

The middle 30s, bearded proprietor of the left-hand establishment, *The Gorgou Cafe-Restaurant* (*Fsw*), also owns the *Hotel/Pension Gorgona* to the rear. This accommodation is surprisingly smart and averagely priced with doubles en suite ranging from 870 to 1050 drs. Admittedly the 'garden' he proudly encompasses with an expansive wave of the hand is nothing more than a rather mangy patch of weeds in which the odd domestic animal grazes and snuffles. A note of warning regarding the oh-so affable proprietor is that, despite the official height-of-season-rate being 1050 drs, he does have a tendency to edge his prices up to the region of 1500 drs.

The curving, narrow, sandy foreshore, which doubles up as an 'Esplanade', stretches away to the right of the quay, all the way to Ag Prokopios. It is edged, here and there, by clumps of trees and in Ag Anna by rather seedy, low, shack-like buildings which include the business of **Santa Anna Travel Agency** and one set of *Rooms*. There are a total of five E class Hotels in and between Ag Prokopios and Ag Anna. The beach is rubbish littered here and there.

To the left of the quay (*Fsw*) the Bay curves quite sharply around to a low headland hill, topped by a small Chapel and which almost creates a lagoon, the beach of which is sandy, if messy. Walking to the left along the sandy track, over the base of the small dune headland, spills out on to the right-hand end of a great, sweeping sandy beach backed by tufted sand dunes in which are set clumps of low trees and Gorse. In the lee of the Chapel headland, in amongst the dunes thickly planted with marine Pines, a certain amount of illegal camping takes place. The conveniently located, if provincial *Taverna Paradiso*, with a tree-shaded patio, is well patronised by all and sundry. At the rear of the establishment are some old fashioned showers and toilets, which are put to extensive use, especially by the campers. Effectively the beach stretches all the way from Ag Prokopios in the north, as far as Pyrgaki, in the south-west, with the occasional headland protruding into the Aegean forming three great Bays sprinkled with the odd cove.

Back on the route to Pyrgaki, from Ag Arsenios the road rolls over the gently sloping countryside to:-

VIVLOS (also known as Tripodes) (9 km from Naxos Town) The question of the totally disparate names is all to do with the change in the agricultural emphasis of the village. The modern name is Tripodes, a now thriving agricultural community, but the old name stubbornly refuses to lie down and disappear, dating back to the days of yore when the village was famed for its wine.

Prior to the Village signposts invitingly lure the unwary voyager to turn off right towards the **Plaka Beach**. The thought is indeed beguiling but resist the temptation. . . . If the siren calls cannot be resisted it is necessary to take a right fork from the heights of Vivlos to join the detour to the broad, intensively worked agricultural plain which opens out below, bounded by a rocky outcrop to the right. Also to the right are the remains of a Medieval tower and the Church of Ag Mattheos built on earlier Christian ruins. In the distance is the shimmering outline of Paros Island. A ridged, concrete path leads down to the plain where an adventurer's problems really start. The landscape is criss-crossed with boulderous and rutted tracks most of which are hemmed in by high bamboos and thick vegetation, blocking out any possible sight of and clue how to reach the sea. Every so often a donkey, its load and owner pops out from this or that 'tunnel' with a friendly 'Yassas' only to disappear as suddenly. Best to approach this beach from the Agia Anna end, don't you know!

From Vivlos the next turning off after some 15 km is signposted to:-

CAPE MIKRI VIGLA (18 km from Naxos Town) The track wanders down to the coast passing through a farmstead and the backs of various dwellings through fenced fields.

The way forks with the right-hand turning making towards the north of the Cape. Here the once deserted, small, very sandy beach (coarse sand), cradled in the curve of the land bounded by upwards sweeping dunes and turquoise sea, is now backed by a new and imaginative development. Admittedly the concept is obviously highly professional, tasteful and up-market but none-the-less. . . .

The gently ascending, Gorse growing and spring-turf moorland that rises to the lighthouse topped cape, now has a monstrously large taverna plonked down to the left of the beach, but that's progress, isn't it? Interestingly enough, the area is obviously on an established goat and sheep herd walk and besides the taverna is a well with a sign in English 'This water is drinking. Please keep clean'. Some hope. These Cycladean wells are interesting in that instead of the more usual raised stone work of the neck, the top is almost flush with the ground and surrounded by a low walled catchment area. Part of this is compartmented off to keep an open drinking trough topped up and the rest of any overflow channelled back into the well.

South of the large headland of Mikri Vigla leads to the top end of a magnificent, huge, coarse sand sea-shore that sweeps all the way past Kastraki as far as Alyko. Some tar is in evidence and part of the shallow sea-bed is made up of horizontal slabs of biscuit rock. There is a small taverna conveniently tucked into the lee of the rocky headland.

KASTRAKI (17 km from Naxos Town) This hamlet edges the large beach described above and on the shore of which is plonked down, almost in the middle of nowhere, the rather 'doo-hickey' *Zorbas Taverna*. This provides a focal point of fun, lust — no hush my mouth, drinking, eating and basic accommodation at inexpensive prices.

ALYKO (19 km from Naxos Town) En route the road passes by large inland lagoons after which some chalet development but perhaps the most surprising site (and sight) is at a fork in the road at about 20 km. Well, more correctly, not actually at the fork but after a short drive. Take the right-hand turn, the surfaced road of which sweeps through a forlorn gate and collapsed gatepost, on to a large sand-duned headland. Over this is spread an enormous, unfinished and deserted development which basks in the sun overlooking a lovely cove and the sea to the south of the cape. Possibly this massive dream was embarked on during the Colonels regime, for locals reckon it demised some 15 years ago. Worth a visit if only to view a magnificent folly now only accommodating lizards and other lowly life forms.

The Main Road edges the rocky coastline which is broken up by three coves, the first two pebbly, the last smaller but sandy.

PYRGAKI (21½ km from Naxos Town) Here a very smart, multi-cellular Holiday Complex is set into the sloping, arid hillside. Braver inmates of this unnecessarily elaborate development for European 'fat-cats' brave the elements and wander the ½ km back up the road to the saving-grace, small, simple, roadside taverna. This Alice-Springs watering hole serves basic drinks and meals, set in a pleasantly tree-shaded yard across the tarmacadam from the sea. Super!

To expand on the three coves, the first at the Alyko end is large pebbles, somewhat rocky and backed by, across the road, a swamp. The second is pebbly with rocks some 50 m out to sea. The third, in the shadow of the referred to Complex, is beautiful sand. The whole bay of this sun drenched corner is clear and clean sea.

A nice note on which to end the description of this lovely island.

16 Ios (Nios)
Cyclades Islands — Eastern Chain

The young in heart ★★★★★
The rest of us ★★★

FIRST IMPRESSIONS
Sand, sea, sun, youngsters, fun, discos (almost synonymous aren't they?); wind; rubbish; only 3 settlements — the Port, Chora and Beach.

SPECIALITIES
Sand, sea, sun, youngsters, fun and discos — (no seriously folks); Homer; chapels; pasteli (sesame cake) and cheese.

RELIGIOUS HOLIDAYS & FESTIVALS
include: 22nd June — Festival of St John, Pyrgos; 2nd August — Festival of Ag Theodotis, Psathis Bay; 29th August — Feast and festival St John (Ag Yiannis), Kalamos Bay; 8th September —Feast and festival of the Virgin, Ag Theodotis, Theodotis Bay.

NB It has to be admitted that the information about which panayieri* is where and when and to whom is confusing, very confusing.

*Feast day

VITAL STATISTICS
Tel prefix 0286. The island is 18 km in length, up to 10 km wide with an area of about 105 sq km. Most of the 1,300 population live in or around the Chora and Gialos Port.

HISTORY
Follows the pattern of the other, adjacent islands having been colonised by the Ionians; became a member of the Delian League; endured Egyptian and then Roman rule and, in the Middle Ages, the omnipresent Dukes of Naxos. On the death of Nicolas II, one of the Dukes, a son, Marcos, assumed the mantle of suzerainity and built a now long lost Castle on 'Chora Hill'. He was an interesting fellow and to bolster the lack of native muscle, imported a number of Albanians.

In with general Cycladic history, the Turks took over in 1536/37. In 1558 the Turks razed the island and sold off those inhabitants they could lay their hands on. In 1579 the Turks decided to recolonize the Island, once again with Albanians. The present day historians fall over themselves to stress that these Albanians were totally Hellenized, being absorbed into the families of native Greeks, some of whom had remained undiscovered and others who struggled valiantly to return from far and near. Oh, well it wouldn't do to admit that Niots were anything but the 'true-blue' product, would it?

For a short time, as elsewhere, the Russians took over, in the 1770s. Later the islanders joined in the struggle for Independence joining the new Greek state in 1829. The Island spawned a hero in the fight for Independence, one Spiros Valetas — to whom a sculpture in the Chora. In the Second World War, Kostas Bouloubassis, who fought for the underground partisans in Athens, was discovered, tortured and executed —another sculpture.

Perhaps the most interesting historical event is the possibility that Homer, shipwrecked on his way from Samos to Athens, died and was buried on the Island. A Dutchman landed on Ios in the 1770s and, supposedly inspired by writings but more probably by rumour and legend, carried out excavations in the area of Plakotos, to the north of the Island.

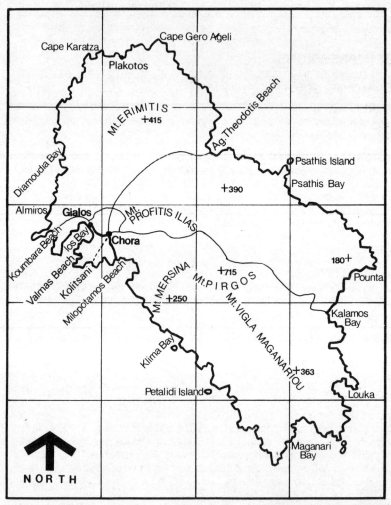

Island of IOS

Illustration 22

Perhaps in mind of the tourist trade to come, he supposedly found Homers grave, even down to a detailed inscription. Strangely the original headstone disappeared but perhaps our Dutchman dug up anothers tomb? Further the exact location as described by various authorities is the subject of some doubt. I must own up to not having made the pilgrimage so have to rely on others for the details. Some relate that is is on the northern slopes of Mt Pirgos but I am fairly certain it is on the northern slope of Mt Erimitis where a commemorative engraved stone has been erected. Interestingly it is postulated that the coast at Plakotos marks the spot where an ancient city was engulfed by the sea.

To a present day visitor it may well seem unbelievable that an earthquake in 1951 caused Gialos Port to be totally devastated. There was every chance that the Island would end up deserted if the lure of prosperity had not held the natives rooted to the spot by the trickle of overseas visitors that started in the 1960s and which later became a deluge. It is interesting to contemplate that in the 1970s most passengers had to be taken on and off the Ferry-boats by caique (as they still have to be to this day on neighbouring Sikinos) and even up until 1979/80 only one or two passenger boats docked each week.

GENERAL

The Ios of the 1960s 'flower-power' generation graduated through the 'great unwashed' of the 1970s to emerge in the 1980s still as a young peoples island, but that of the clean-cut, solid-limbed, college students.

The original dirt track from Gialos Port to Milopotamos Beach via the Chora, may have made way for a dusty but surfaced road; the bus may now turn round at Milopotamos Beach on a concrete pad rather than duck-boards; the majority of beach sleepers may have been herded into official campsites but the bedrock of a young peoples paradise remains. Admittedly the Port is better organised (and has expanded a little); the Chora has enlarged, but across the road from the Old Town and the buildings at Milopotamos Beach have increased but not a lot. What could ruin the magnificent sweep of this great sandy bay? Mosquitoes and rubbish may be an irritant but for the young hedonist the day-time lazing on the sun drenched beach, the early evening animation of cafe-bar conversation and the frenzy of dusk to dawn disco dancing proves an undiminished magnet. It is intriguing that despite the wordly-wise nature of much of the holiday-makers delights, there remains a charmingly naive quality to the atmosphere.

The older generations (those over 30 years of age!), perhaps seeking less active diversions, can rest assured that there are other, almost deserted, locations than those referred to above. Added to which, even Milopotamos Beach and its environs are almost deserted after the first ear-splitting crescendo of the disco's echoes through the Chora.

Ios is not only for the young with sex, sun, and souvlaki, in any order. The young in heart will also find the Island irresistibly and excitingly attractive. So the more mature traveller need not stay away and miss the undoubted charms of the sparse but lovely Island. An added advantage is that years of holiday-making by impecunious British summer visitors has held prices down to such an extent that, of the popular Cyclades islands, Ios is noticeably one of the least costly on which to stay. You note I write 'popular' for the less visited islands of say, Amorgos and Sikinos are even more reasonably priced.

GIALOS (Ormos Iou): the port (Illustration 23)

There are a number of Greek island ports at which the docking is even more exciting than usual and forever remains a magical moment. These include, at random, Vathi (Ithaca), Simi, Astipalaia, Siphnos and Ios Port.

Incoming boats breast the natural horns of land that seem to almost pinch off the entrance to the harbour bay. The neck of the entrance bends round to the right and on the elbow, there is the small, pretty Byzantine Church of Ag Irinis perched on a rocky outcrop. This Church is proclaimed by some as a classic example of its genre. The sturdy bell tower is pierced by the characteristic elongated, curved arches, the quintessential domed roof is topped off with a small cross and the cupola pierced by thin plates of rock forming steps (incidentally, giving it the appearance of a Second World War sea mine).

High above the Port the white cubes of the Chora peep out from around the sides of its hilltop fastness.

As in other Ios matters even the name of the Port is in some doubt. Certainly Gialos appears rather disembodied and disjointed but this is not surprising, considering that in the 1950s it was wiped out by an earthquake originated tidal wave.

ARRIVAL BY FERRY
Not quite the central terminus of the system, but a very important junction with connections to the most important islands and a stepping off stop for Sikinos and Folegandros.

The Ferry-boat quay and dock (*Tmr* 1.A4) is conveniently very central. Away to the left (*Sbo*) is the Port beach and a number of *Rooms*. Straight ahead is a clutch of hotels, travel agents, cafe-bars, tavernas and the Bus turn-round (*Tmr* 2.B4). From the Bus Square, steps and the Main Road sally forth to the Chora, both with a scattering of hotels and *Rooms*. To the right, round the dock, is a hotel, a couple of pensions and some *Rooms* within 200/300m. The boats are met by more than sufficient owners of accommodation from the Port, Chora and Milopotamos Beach, even late into the night.

THE ACCOMMODATION & EATING OUT
The Accommodation A reasonably wide choice of *Rooms* and Hotels (but few Pensions) including the following, listed in approximate order of distance from the Ferry-boat quay. A note here may help explain the omission of the usual garrulous and over-wordy description of this or that accommodation. I must own up to having a favourite establishment and, as on Syros in respect of eating out, I have indulged this whim (sounds nasty) over the years by simply heading for my particular 'Shangri-La'. For details *See* **Milopotamos Beach**.

A word of caution when approaching any hotel for rooms is to bear in mind that the Port hoteliers are rather particular (all right inhospitable) and amongst their proclivities is a reluctance to let a room for less than 2/3 nights. In direct contrast to 4 or 5 years ago, generally accommodation in the Port is expensive, especially the more obvious hotels and lodgings.

Hotel Fragakis (*Tmr* 3.A4) (Class C)   Tel 91231
Directions: In the block immediately in front of those disembarking from a Ferry-boat, alongside *Doras Bar*.

Rates for a double room en suite are in the region of 1500 drs rising to 1900 drs.

Hotel Acteon (*Tmr* 4.B4) (Class D)   Tel 91207
Directions: Over and above the offices of the **Acteon Travel** building blocking off the far side of the Port Square.

Single rooms start at 750 drs rising to 1055 drs (1st July - 15th September) whilst a double room starts at 1000 drs and peaks at 1320 drs.

Hotel Sea Breeze (*Tmr* 5.B4) (Class C)   Tel 91285
Directions: In the small lane to the left of the **Acteon** building (*F-bqbo*).

Doubles en suite, in line with other C class establishments, cost from 1314 drs to 1785 drs.

Hotel Armadoros (*Tmr* 6.C4) (Class C)   Tel 91201
Directions: From the Bus Square (more a mini-roundabout), the other side of **Acteon Travel**, a narrow lane cuts up beside the Baker, to the left of the garish *Ios Burger Self Service*. The smart *Armadoros* is on the right at the top of the lane.

Prior to June and after the 15th September, a single room costs 800 drs and a double en suite 1000 drs rising respectively to 1000 drs and 1200 drs in June and then to 1200 drs and 1575 drs per night.

Guest House (*Tmr* 7.B4)
Directions: On the way to the *Hotel Armadoros*, on the lane beside the bakery.

Closed except for the height of season with a double room sharing the bathroom at about 1000 drs.

Hotel Flisvos (*Tmr* 8.B5) (Class C)   Tel 91315
Directions: From the Bus Square around the corner of the dock to the right, opposite the private yacht moorings.

Single rooms en suite start at 1200 drs rising to 1500 drs (June- September) and double rooms en suite rise from 1500 drs to 1900 drs.

Further on, off the far corner of the dock to the right of **Frogs Rock Club**, a path followed by steps rising towards a converted windmill leads to the pleasantly situated:-

Poseidon Rooms (*Tmr* 9.B5)
Rates in line with top end of average.

Further on round the dock, on the other side from the Ferry-boat quay, behind **Skipper's Bar** are:-

Rooms (*Tmr* 10.A5)

Ios Camping   Tel 91329
Directions: Beyond the Port police office (*Tmr* 11.A5) and along some 50 m of Ag Irene beach. This is a narrow sliver of picturesque squalor on which a number of small boats are pulled up in various states of disrepair. Flotsam laps the waters edge and the campsite is on the left.

A reasonable, average site, but apart from convenience and proximity to the Ferry-boats, cannot compare less than favourably with the admirable *Camping Stars* at Milopotamos Beach.

Back at the Ferry-boat quay and away to the left (*Sbo*) is the Port beach — where some hardier souls stretch out for the night, and:-.

Hotel Korali (*Tmr* 12.A2) (Class C)   Tel 91272
Directions: Beyond the 'ranch like' **My Way Disco** and on the right, almost opposite the middle of the beach, which is tree-edged here.

Double room rates are average for a C class hotel.

Meltemi Rooms (*Tmr* 13.A2)
Directions: Positioned between the *Hotel Korali* and the *Restaurant/Taverna Aphroditi*. Fronted by a pleasant rose garden edging the road. The young girl of the house speaks English.

Excellent value and a very nice billet, with a double room sharing the bathroom costing 600 drs mid-season.

Hotel Mare-Monte (*Tmr* 14.A2) (Class C)   Tel 91564
Directions: Third building along from the *Meltemi Rooms*, that is past the *Aphroditi Taverna* and the *Marina Bistro.*

A double room en suite starts at 1600 drs and rises to 1950 drs (June -September). Single rooms en suite cost 1280 drs rising to 1560 drs.

Incidentally, at the far end of the beach, just before the track turns off to make the trek over the neck of land to Koumbara Beach, there are a number of very smarty accommodation cubes strung out at right-angles to the waterfront.

Whilst back at the Ferry-boat quay... from the Bus Square the one and only road makes off for the zig-zag up to the Chora. A hundred metres or so up the initially gentle incline and at the left-hand bend there is a choice of route. The road continues on to the left whilst almost straight ahead a broad, stepped, paved and well shaded path takes a more direct route to the Chora.

The Main Road can offer the:-

Pension Olga

and the

Homers Inn Hotel (*Tmr* 15.C/D1/2) (Class C)   Tel 91365
Directions: As above, on the left.

The cost of a double room en suite rises from 1590 drs to 1770 drs.

The Inn is followed by:-

Stelios Pension

The Steps are a more fruitful source of accommodation with two **Rooms** (*Tmr* 16.D3) on the right and the:-

Hotel Moschonas, No 662   Tel 91218
Directions: As above, on the left at a crook in the path. Provincial and more a pension than a hotel with a single-minded landlady.

Some rooms en suite, some sharing the bathroom, with double room rates starting at 700 drs. Emphatically disinterested in one night stands!

The Eating Out There are numerous mediocre cafe-bars, a number of bars, quite a few forgettable restaurants/tavernas and regrettably a rather garish hamburger joint. Far be it from me to crib, but on a general note it is a fact that the Ios Island Greek salad is a particularly poor thing there rarely being any olives nor for that matter onion or. . . .

The Baker (*Tmr* 17.B4) sells excellent doughnuts for 35 drs.

Probably the best value and neatest cafe-bar is the:-

New Corner (*Tmr* 18.B4)
Directions: Behind and to one side of **Acteon Travel**. Outside tables and chairs and despite the remarkable neatness and rather chic feel to the place, quite reasonably priced and justifiably popular. The service is slow, even by Greek standards and the proprietor is rather precious.

An order for two coffees results in a coffee pot, giving sufficient for three cups, all for 104 drs. Open 0800 - 1430 hrs and 1930 - 2400 hrs but during the closed hours the self-service bar, around the corner in the narrow alley on the left, ably fills in.

The only snag is that the *New Corner* is blinded from sight of the Ferry-boat quay.

The coffee served in the Snackbar alongside the front of **Acteon Travel** is perfectly foul.

Ios Burger Self-Service (*Tmr* 19.B4)
Directions: From the Bus Square, around to the right of the dock.

Disturbingly modern looking, with yellow signs. My prejudices might well be showing as it has to be admitted, that I favour neither hamburgers nor self-service! A large burger costs 125 drs.

Taverna Andreas (*Tmr* 20.B4)
Directions: On the left, at the start of the Main Road opposite the water fountain.

More a snackbar really with a reasonable priced if rather limited number of offerings.

Remmezo Cafe-Bar (*Tmr* 21.B5)
Directions: On the far side of the harbour from the Ferry-boat quay almost behind the pretentious *Skippers Bar.*

Chi-chi and on the expensive side.

Restaurant Fisherman
Directions: In the same block as *Remmezo's above.*

I cannot comment but have an hunch that it may be worth a whirl.

THE A TO Z OF USEFUL INFORMATION

BANKS

The National Bank (*Tmr* 22.B4) Boxed in between the Bakery and *Ios Burger*. It only throws open the doors for the months of June to September. Open the normal weekday hours.

See **Acteon Travel, Ferry-Boat Ticket Offices.**

BEACHES

Beach 1. Ag Irenes, on the right of the dock (*Sbo*). Really more a narrow foreshore, cluttered with small boats or benzinas in various states of decaying repair and littered with rubbish. Not recommended.

Beach 2. To reach Valmas beach skirt Ag Irenes beach described above and take the steps up to and then the track around the Chapel of Ag Irenes. The 20 minute walk on the stony path clings to the top of the cliff edge passing one or two pocket handkerchief sized plots of sand hemmed in by the sea washed rocks. The trek finishes up some way above the nearside of the small, sandy Valmas beach which is set in the cleft of a cove. On the opposite side is a cluster of buildings amongst which is a small, simple taverna. It is necessary to clamber down to the backshore of the quite steeply sloping and sharply narrowing beach on which are set two large wells. The chosen few, cogniscent regulars sunbathe in the nude lying just beyond the startlingly and appealingly clear sea-water.

The slow moving taverna owner can be difficult, or to put it more plainly, pretty awkward. The limited choice of drinks and Greek salad available are not inexpensive but then almost everything has to be transported by sea.

Very regular 'regulars', with some Greek, may possibly be able to rent a room to the side of the taverna, but only if the proprietor really takes to you — no promises.

Beach 3. The Port beach, round to the left (*Sbo*) from the Ferry-boat quay. The narrow beach is fine shingle backed by scrubby grass with two separate clumps of trees. The far end is tatty.

Beach 4. From the Port beach a rough, stony track winds to the left round the coastline of the bay and then up and over the neck of the rocky, scrub grass and low Gorse covered land separating Ormos Iou from Koumbara Beach.

Here, on the seaward side, is a small Chapel on the edge of a rocky bay. Beyond is a stony, sloping caique mole, a curving cove with a lovely, coarse sand beach. The stony backshore ends in a short isthmus with, at its extremity, a low rock islet seemingly sunbathing in the sparkling seawater. To the right of the neck of land there are a couple of very small, stony sand coves. Both the beach areas appear deserted but closer examination reveals that the stone cairns dotted about are the 'beach huts and rooms' of itinerant travellers. Overnight, unofficial campers also occupy the few low caves formed by overhanging rocks. The water is clean and crystal clear although there is some tar scattered about. Koumbara Beach is very quiet and the needs of the scattered population are catered for by one taverna with a large patio, across the track from the sea. On the sea side of the track is a small doorless shack-like building, with a filthy interior that was probably once a 'squatty'.

BICYCLE, SCOOTER & CAR HIRE None and quite rightly so as the only road is the short metalled road up to The Chora and on down to Milopatamos Beach. That is apart from the stony track across the island to Ag Theodotis (*See* **Places of Interest**). The one and only route is well serviced by an excellent bus service. *See* **The Chora.**

BOOKSELLERS A shop on the quay side of the Port Square doubles up as an international newspaper vendor, foreign language bookshop, small store and ferry-boat ticket office. The restless owner keeps a vigilant watch out for light fingered shoppers and browsers.

BREAD SHOPS One Bakery (*Tmr* 17.B4) on the far edge of the Bus Square. The shop also sells bottled water, honey and milk.

BUSES The buses park up on the Bus Sq (*Tmr* 2.B4) close to the dock, the furthest end from the Ferry-boat quay.

There are three buses for the one and only bus route from the Port to the Chora and on to Milopotamos Beach. They operate all day long between 0800 - 2300 hrs except Sundays when the timetable starts up at 0830 hrs. As a rough guide the buses depart every ½ hour on the hour and half-hour. The Port to Milopotamos Beach journey costs 30 drs and the drivers herald their arrival and departure with a blast of the horn.

CHEMISTS *See* **Medical Care.**

COMMERCIAL SHOPPING AREA None, not unnaturally, bearing in mind the small size of the Port. Facing the Ferry-boat quay is a Fruit Market (*Tmr* 23.A4), more a stall, positioned alongside a Supermarket. Various gift shops in the alley to the side of **Acteon Travel.**

DISCOS On yes. Ios must have nearly as many sophisticated discos as it has Chapels but from these few lines please do not misconstrue these comments. They are concentrated up in the Chora and need not impinge on those who do not wish them to encroach. The Ports only contribution to this concentrated cacophony is **My Way** (*Tmr* 24.B3), on the near edge of the Port beach. It only opens for the height of season months.

FERRY-BOATS Interestingly located almost at the epicentre of the Cyclades. Ios is not the busiest, nor the most important port of call but it is definitely near the top of the pile. Furthermore Ios is a very convenient stepping-off point for the islands of Sikinos and Folegandros as well as connecting with the Western chain of Milos, Serifos and Siphnos, the Eastern wing of Tinos and of course the pivotal islands of Paros, Naxos, Mykonos, Syros and Santorini.

Ferry-boat timetable

Day	Departure time	Ferry-boat	Ports/Islands of Call
Tuesday, Wednesday, Friday.	1000 hrs	Ios	Paros, Naxos, Mykonos
Saturday & Sunday	2020 hrs	Ios	Santorini (Athinos)
Monday	0600 hrs	Georgios Express	Santorini
	0900 hrs	Lemnos	Naxos, Paros, Piraeus
	0945 hrs	Georgios Express	Sikinos, Folegandros, Paros, Syros, Piraeus (M)
	1330 hrs	Megalohari	Santorini
	1600 hrs	Kimolos	Santorini
	1730 hrs	Megalohari	Paros, Mykonos
	2030 hrs	Kimolos	Siphnos, Serifos, Piraeus (M)
Tuesday	1330 hrs	Megalohari	Santorini
	1700 hrs	Lemnos	Santorini
	1800 hrs	Santorini	Sikinos, Folegandros, Santorini
	2030 hrs	Lemnos	Naxos, Paros, Piraeus (M)
Wednesday	1000 hrs	Megalohari	Paros, Mykonos, Tinos
	1630 hrs	Georgios Express	Santorini
	1700 hrs	Lemnos	Santorini
	2045 hrs	Georgios Express	Naxos, Paros, Piraeus (M)

Thursday	0900 hrs	Lemnos	Naxos, Paros, Piraeus (M)
	1330 hrs	Megalohari	Santorini
	1600 hrs	Kimolos	Santorini, Siphnos, Piraeus (M)
	1630 hrs	Georgios Express	Santorini
	1730 hrs	Megalohari	Paros, Mykonos
	2045 hrs	Georgios Express	Naxos, Paros, Piraeus (M)
Friday	1330 hrs	Megalohari	Santorini
	1800 hrs	Lemnos	Sikinos, Folegandros, Santorini
Saturday	0300 hrs	Georgios Express	Santorini
	0800 hrs	Lemnos	Tinos
	0945 hrs	Georgios Express	Naxos, Paros, Piraeus (M)
	1000 hrs	Megalohari	Paros, Mykonos, Tinos
	1045 hrs	Lemnos	Naxos, Paros, Syros, Piraeus (M)
	2030 hrs	Kimolos	Santorini
Sunday	0500 hrs	Georgios Express	Santorini
	0915 hrs	Kimolos	Milos, Siphnos, Serifos, Piraeus (M)
	0016 hrs	Georgios Express	Naxos, Paros, Piraeus (M)
	1700 hrs	Lemnos	Santorini

FERRY-BOAT TICKET OFFICES

Acteon Travel & Tours (*Tmr* 25.B4) Port Square   Tel 91207
Directions: Dominates the far or north end of the Port Square as should I suppose the 'Mr Big' of the business.

The office extends through the building from front to the back. The large, smart office fronting the Port Square deals with tours, change facilities, including foreign exchange and travellers cheques, bus tickets to various European capitals, has a phone and no end of information. The phone is very expensive to use at 4½ drs per unit compared to the usual 2.91 drs. They quote bus tickets to London (presumably from Athens), via Italy at 7000 drs. Other capitals on offer include Milan, Munich, Paris, Amsterdam, Brussels, Zurich and Frankfurt. Another useful service in the front office is a notice board for personal messages. It is a pity that both the youngster and baldish desk employees can be abrupt and rude. Is there a malaise that affects staff involved with money?

The jewel in this company's particular crown operates the 'hatch' at the rear facing the Bus Sq, alongside the *New Corner* Cafe-bar. I first met Andreas Vasillades many years ago when he fronted up the local Ferry-boat department in the main office, where he used to operate two visitors books, one for all and sundry and the other for the Irish! Pressures of space have resulted in his department moving to the rear where he dispenses tickets and information in a confident, quick-fire manner. Andreas now 50 years young is a 'smiley', Greek Cypriot with an acute sense of humour who well could be English, his mastery of the language is so complete. Probably a 'born again' character long before it became fashionable, Andreas will recall his waiter days in London when he was a fast moving, fast talking, hard living gambler. That is until his own 'Road to Damascus' when a steward on the fated **Cruise Liner Laconia**. On its maiden voyage, after an overhaul and change of name, the ship foundered in December 1963 off the island of Madeira and he survived his Atlantic dunking — after a number of acts of bravery saving passengers lives*. From then on Andreas became a reformed character or so he will tell you, but I'm not so sure with that twinkle in his eyes. He has developed a theory of longevity based on the necessity to take in copious amounts of water, to which he attributes his fitness of which he is so assured that he will throw out a running race challenge. If he has a tiny fault or two he is not as attentive a listener as perhaps he could be, and he tends to dissuade the more adventurous from visiting the smaller islands of Sikinos and Folegandros with dismissive, derogatory asides — Sikinos — "full of hippies, dirty, no money" (once true I suspect but

The story has been related by David Marchbanks in his book 'The Painted Ship' published in 1964.

now totally incorrect). Perhaps his remark in respect of the Ios Chora was particularly apt when, in answer to some question about the night life there, he snapped... "If you must go to that jungle". A man that it has been a pleasure to meet.

Incidentally, before completing this panegyric, the rear office offers a baggage store facility at 50 drs per piece per 12 hr period and sell the only usable island map available for about 60 drs. Tours on offer include the Ag Theodotis excursion (*See* EXCURSIONS TO GIALOS PORT SURROUNDS).

The front office is open seven days a week 0700 - 2230 hrs and the back hatch 0700 - 2100 hrs.

Kritikakis Travel Agency (*Tmr* 26.B4)   Tel 91254
Directions: The office is on the left of the alley that runs down the left-hand side of **Acteon** from the Port Square. This office sells tickets for another inter-island 'African Queen', the **MV Ios**, and the pleasure boat **Magaro** which plies back and forth to Maganari Beach (*See* EXCURSIONS TO GIALOS PORT SURROUNDS).

They are Olympic agents and change foreign money. **Kritikakis** also acts as an agent for a substitute ('Tragic') 'Magic Bus' service to London 7000 drs, Amsterdam 7000 drs, Paris 8000 drs, Milan and Venice 4500 drs.

Plakiotis Travel Agency (*Tmr* 27.B4/5)   Tel 91277
Directions: Around the dock and beyond the *Ios Burger* Cafe-bar. Perhaps the most interesting item about this agency is the little brochure they produce more especially the photograph on the inside front cover, above the thumbnail map of the Cyclades. The picture shows an old view of the harbour prior to the dock or Ferry-boat quay being built. This explains the now truncated, rather pathetic Ag Irenes beach, obviously once the far end of a much larger, sandy cove. Another plus is that the **Ios Club** musical programme is displayed on the notice board, a must this. For further details of which *See* the Chora, **Discos, A to Z.**

LUGGAGE STORE *See* **Acteon Travel, Ferry-Boat Ticket Offices.**

MEDICAL CARE Don't be ill in the Port — the only medical care available is in the Chora, about 1 km up the hill.

NTOG *See* the Chora.

OPENING HOURS Range from the traditional to tourist hours but the arrangements are muddied by Ferry-boat arrivals.

OTE *See* the Chora.

PLACES OF INTEREST Covered in the other headings.

POLICE *See* the Chora.

POST OFFICE *See* the Chora.

TAXIS Rumoured to lurk on the quay, but I cannot 'press a taramosalata to my heart'and own up to ever observing the rank. In any case the Bus service is so excellent, and the road system so minimal, that there is really no necessity to contemplate their use.

TELEPHONE NUMBERS & ADDRESSES *See* the Chora.

TOILETS A number of the older travel books refer to there being only one unusable, unflushable toilet. Despite this being blown up some years ago, it is still impossible to find any toilet facility, the desperate having to use those of an obliging cafe-bar or taverna. Whilst on this note in the area of the dock every now and then there is an 'interesting' but very distinctive aroma.

TRAVEL AGENTS *See* **Ferry-Boat Ticket Offices.**

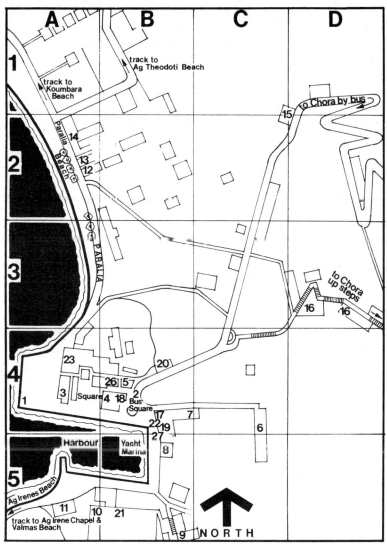

GIALOS

Illustration 23

EXCURSION TO GIALOS PORT SURROUNDS

Well not so much the exact surrounds (for which *See* **Beaches, A to Z**) but two locations that most logically fit the text are included here.

Excursion to Ag Theodoti Beach

The rough stone path, once only used by the devoted fun lovers for a particular panayieri, has been engineered sufficiently to accommodate a mid-summer daily 'Red-Bus' service. Incidentally, the state of the road is used as an excuse not to run the excursion until numbers make the trip financial feasible. Our old friends **Acteon** have cornered this particular commodity selling tickets from the 'rear hatch' '. . . for Peace and Nature Lovers. . . Huge Sandy Beach. . . Rooms and Restaurant . . Rooms. Indian Huts'. The one-way fare costs 150 drs for the 45 minute journey and a return ticket can be used whenever. Departures for the height of summer months are scheduled at 1000 hrs and 1200 hrs, returning at 1700 hrs and 1900 hrs. Huts and double rooms cost 700 drs a night.

Naturally the promotion of this large bay and valley has ensured that it can now hardly be an exclusive jewel of a find but that's life. . . despite the fact that its perfect for peace and nature lovers!

Excursion to Maganari Beach

Only accessible by trip boat. **Kritikakis Travel** office handles the pleasure boat **MV Margaro** which departs at 1000 hrs and returns at 1800 hrs. The 50 minute journey costs 500 drs for a return ticket. The story behind the original development here, the subsequent degeneration and the slow reversal of fortunes would make a story in itself. Enough to say that the Hotel, restaurant and disco are now operating correctly, if expensively.

For lovers of Natural History matters it is, or was, here (and Milopotamos Beach) that in the month of August the local cuttlefish made a lemming-like beach assault, throwing themselves out of the sea in order to lay their eggs. Doubtful now if at the height of season they would be able to find a decently clear bit of space on the packed beaches.

THE CHORA: capital town (Illustration 24)

Also known as 'the Village' or the 'Jungle', the Main Road bypasses the pretty, hill clambering Town. Buses decant travellers on a dusty, bedraggled Square to the right side with the Port behind one. On the right-hand edge of this Square is the rather unimposing, tired looking Town Hall (*Tmr* 1.B4) behind which, on a gently rising slope, the untidy overflow development of the Chora has had to take place.

From the Bus Square (*Tmr* 2.B3/4) the Chora is reached across a walled causeway that skirts the dusty recreation ground terminating at the imposing Cathedral Church of Evagelismos or Annunciation with its pretty, light blue domes. Behind the Cathedral is Ag Evagelismos Square (*Tmr* 3.B2/3) for which the Steps up from the Port also head, thus making it a good starting off point.

Even during daylight hours there is a thinly veiled suggestion of youthful, vibrant energy, a scarcely concealed warning of the frenetic activity that bursts asunder once darkness descends. An analogy might be a heavyweight champion weight-lifter who attempts to disguise his bulging muscles in a size too small, tight fitting 'T' shirt.

In the morning hours the majority of the Chora visitors sit around at the various cafe-bars, reminding one of a party of revellers who have been to a really excellent late night party— which is in fact almost to a man and woman what they are. Mid-day and afternoon, the sun worshippers tumble down to Milopotamos Beach to bathe away the excesses of the night before only, once resuscitated, to bundle back into the Chora to gather strength for another evening's assault on the auditory and pleasure senses. This movement of bodies resembles a mass migration. Even in the broad daylight almost every other doorway emits sound and light in varying degrees of mind-numbing intensity.

Oddly enough despite many of the ingredients that go to make up the Chora being those that should bring Greek island lovers out in a rash — and cause the very old to write letters to **The Times** — it is almost impossible not to be infected with the atmosphere generated. I realise that this is of course a contradiction in terms but there it is and this despite the inordinate number of fashion and jewellery shops, bars, discos and pubs that dominate the pretty rising and falling, swaying alleys and lanes. Oddly enough even in this 'jungle' it is only necessary to climb to the upper reaches of the village to slip gradually out of the 20th century into the Greece of old, with donkeys unexpectedly emerging from picturesque passageways.

The climb up the ever ascending alleys to the little Chapel that tops the wedding cake of a Town is particularly pleasant. (*See* **Places of Interest, A to Z**).

THE ACCOMMODATION & EATING OUT

The Accommodation The 'High Lane' half right and rising up from Ag Evagelismos Square (*Tmr* 3.B2/3) (Cathedral behind one) has **Rooms** signposted off all the way along its length but before proceeding in this direction there are:-

Rooms (*Tmr* 4.B2)
Directions: From Ag Evagelismos Sq (*Tmr* 3.B2/3), half-left up the cul-de-sac and on the right.

Proceeding up the 'High Lane', the first turning off, an acute angled left-hand lane, climbs high on to the hill above and overlooks the road down to the Port.

Papa Antonios Pension (*Tmr* 5.A2)   Tel 91309
Directions: As above and distinguishable from below, on the Main Road, by the large sign acclaiming 'Young Peoples Pension'.

A well-practiced proprietor runs a busy establishment that in its delights includes a common room/dining room, a dish-of-the-day costing between 150/200 drs, filtered coffee, 'very sexy (sic) ice cream', clothes washing for 100 drs and wide patios, edging the hillside from which there are splendid views.

Accommodation on offer includes a dormitory bed costing 350 drs per night. Rather incongruously for what is manifestly a student establishment, there are also some luxurious double bedrooms with en suite bathrooms and a private portion of the patio which cost 1500 drs a night. Lastly, but not least the height of Antonio's Pension on the hillside makes for a very cool location even in the hot summer months.

Incidentally, there are **Rooms** next door to *Papa Antonios.*

One other establishment in this rarified atmosphere was brought to our attention by 'Pamela', one of the regrettably diminishing number of great British characters that used to spread out over Europe in the heyday of the Empire. Her recommendation was:-

Dormitory Pension
Directions: Near and below the hill-topping Chapels of Ag Elephterio and the Christ of Castro. The patron Lefteris Platais, who speaks fluent French, and his wife Maroussais run the establishment. If you are into dormitory beds, it comes well recommended, and is inexpensive at 350 drs a night. The girls and boys are separated which of course may or may not suit everyone.

Hotel Philippou (*Tmr* 6.B2) (Class C)   Tel 91290
Directions: On the corner of Ag Evagelismos Square. The only Hotel in the Old Chora, the rest being on the opposite side of the Main Road.

No singles, with a double room en suite costing 1400 drs rising between 1st July—15th September to 1750 drs.

At the far top of the 'High Lane' and around to the left on Odhos Ano Piaza is:-

Rooms (*Tmr* 4.D1/2)
Directions: As above, opposite the **Orange Club.**

A double room sharing a bathroom costs 700 drs in mid-season.

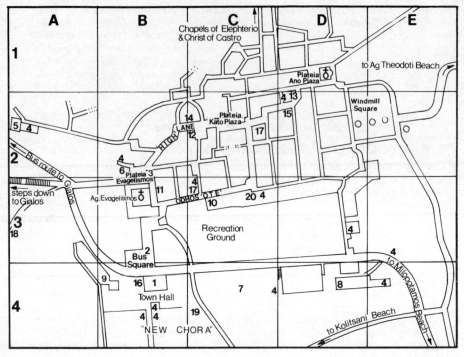

IOS CHORA

KEY
1 Town Hall   B4
2 Bus Square   B3/4
3 Plateia
   Evagelismos   B2/3
4 Rooms
5 Papa Antonios
   Pension   A2
6 Hotel Philippou   B2
7 Hotel Aphroditi   C4
8 Hotel Parthenon   D4
9 Olympic Flame...   D4
10 Restaurant
   Romantica   C3
11 Margarets   B3
12 Restaurant –
   Antonis   C2
13 Taverna   D1/2
14 National Bank   B/C2
15 Commercial Bank   D2
16 Scooter hire   B4
17 Bakers
18 Ios Club   A3
19 Grill House   C4
20 O.T.E.   C3

Illustration 24

Back at Ag Evagelismos Sq and edging round the Cathedral as if proceeding back to the Bus Sq, a lane (nicknamed 'Odhos OTE') runs parallel to the Main Road (in the direction of Milopotamos).

Rooms (*Tmr* 4.C3)
Directions: To the left, in the second block, to the side of the Baker.

Rooms (*Tmr* 4.C3)
Directions: As above, and on the far side of the OTE.

By carrying on along this lane, almost to the far end of the village, there is a turning to the right, which is in fact a track back to the Main Road.

Rooms (*Tmr* 4.D3)
Directions: As above and half-way along the track and on the left is a once magnificent old houco, the grounds of which the track circumambulates.

This ramshackle and 'provincial' establishment, next door to the School, lets out rudimentary double rooms, mid season for 811 drs sharing the distinctly antediluvian bathroom.

In the 'New Town', that is the modern day development behind the Town Hall (*Tmr* 1.B4) to the right of the main road (*Sbo*), there are a clutch of Hotels and **Rooms** to let including three separate houses.

Rooms (*Tmr* 4.B4)
Directions: Behind the Town Hall.

Hotel Aphroditi (*Tmr* 7.C4) (Class D)   Tel 91546
Directions: Right of the Main Road, further along from the Town Hall in the Milopotamos Beach direction.

Double rooms en suite cost between 1350 and 1760 drs (1st July - 15th September). Incidentally, single rooms are very pricey here, with the differential a mere 200 drs. So why not share with a friend?

Rooms (*Tmr* 4.C4)
Directions: To the right (Chora behind one) or nearside of the block containing a pharmacy, up a flight of steps.

Hotel Parthenon (*Tmr* 8.D4) (Class E)   Tel 91275
Directions: Still further along in the Milopotamos direction from the Town Hall, behind **Up Down** disco and alongside the **Disco PN**.

Single rooms en suite start off at 900 drs rising to 1150 drs (16th June - 15th September) while double rooms en suite cost 1100 drs rising to 1400 drs.

Rooms (*Tmr* 4.E4 & 4.E3)
Directions: One house the other side of the **Disco PN** and another the other side of the Main Road opposite to the street down from the *Hotel Parthenon*.

Near the magnificent 'old house' pension is a most unusual sign advertising a place to rest one's weary head, the **Okey Kokey Refrigerator Bar** Rooms and Flor (sic) to let. One does wonder, doesn't one?

The Eating Out Innumerable places to fill the inner man or woman but many are mainly memorable, simply for the awfulness of their nomenclature and or offerings. These must include:-

Olympic Flame Pizza Spaghetti (*Tmr* 9.B4)

and next door, the

Captains Table Offers 'Original English Fish And Chips'. Oh, goody!

Others in the 'table of dread' might embody the:-

Why Not? Pub The management extol the virtues of its Greek kitchen which incidentally serves up chicken curry, chilli con carne, Alfredos spaghetti (what?) and goulash. . . and 'low prises' (sic). It also proclaims in the publicity blurb that... 'in fact (it) has no equivalent anywhere else in the world' Yes, well, one can only agree, really.

Now for the recommendations:-

Romantica Zachar (*Tmr* 10.C3)
Directions: On 'Odhos OTE' on the same side as the OTE office, below street level.
Popular with good breakfasts and pizzas.

Margarets (*Tmr* 11.B3)
Directions: Back at the starting point of Plateia Ag Evagelismos (*Tmr* 3.B2/3) and on the narrow lane around the side of the Cathedral.

Recommended to us by Martin, an Irish tea-taster whose palette must be exceptional as we also found the small Cafe-bar excellent news. The only draw-back is that there is no patio but that is a small price to pay for good service, food and fair prices. Margaret, in her short chef's hat, and her husband are helpful and run a wholesome and neat place with wicker stools at the 'soda parlour' bench tables. They proudly advertise 'Everything is Home Made'. Surely it must be for the range of pies, which includes chicken, potato as well as spinach, are very good. For instance spinach pie costs 60 drs, a bottle of retsina 44 drs, a bottle of beer 53 drs, Nescafe 40 drs and tea 24 drs. Perhaps the remark that sums it all up was the Patron's "Everything special but the apple-pie is very special"!

Antonis Restaurant (*Tmr* 12.C2)
Directions: From Plateia Ag Evagelismos half-right along the 'High Lane' and on the right, on the corner of the first small Square, opposite the **National Bank of Greece**.

Although rather a 'barn of a place', not only do they serve souvlakis from a side window but they put on a very good value 'Special of the Day'. For example a plate of veal, potatoes, beans and carrots costs 280 drs, a beer 65 drs and a coffee 45 drs.

In the 'High Lane', prior to *Antonis Restaurant,* a cluster comprising the **Why Not? Pub**, **Kalimera** cocktail bar and **The Jazz Club** operate under an umbrella of self publicity if not the same management. Not loathe to hide their light under anything, they print a **Time Out** publicity hand-out which, in glowing terms, describes the wild, heart pumping, breathtaking delights available at their various establishments. These embrace a Video Cinema Bar serving cocktails including one named 'Orgasm' and another 'Foreplay' (I can only guess that the videos must be blue movies) and late night drinking at the **Kalimera** bar at which the delights include 'happenings' **The Jazz Club** not to be outdone describes itself as 'for those with the most refined taste in music' and not for those who enjoy 'unbearably loud disco for (all) sorts of Punk, Folk, Rock 'n Roll and New Wave Standards'. So there!

Two reasonably priced Tavernas are on opposite sides of the top of the 'High Lane' where it joins Ano Piaza alley.

Taverna (*Tmr* 13.D1/2)
Directions: The left hand establishment, as above and across the way from the **Orange Bar.**

Serves up a reasonably priced meal from a limited menu. Two vegetable soups (80 drs each and jolly good); a Greek salad (poor and 110 drs); a very large and very, very enjoyable Special Pizza (350 drs), bread and a bottle of retsina all for 704 drs. The young, serious countenanced son waits on the tables and the place gets deservedly busy.

THE A TO Z OF USEFUL INFORMATION
BANKS
The National Bank of Greece (*Tmr* 14.B/C2) On the left of the 'High Lane' close by the first small Square from Ag Evagelismos Square.

The Commercial Bank (*Tmr* 15.D2) The same 'High Lane' towards the far end, on the right. Accepts personal cheques, backed by a Eurocard.

Both only open the usual hours.

BEACHES In actual fact the magnificent Milopotamos Beach is no further away than many a Port beach..

Kolitsani Beach: A road starts out from opposite the **Fanari disco** which itself runs out on to the track leading off from behind the Town Hall (*Tmr* 1.B4). The walk takes about 15 minutes and the beach is pebbly and well sheltered. A half-hearted local keeps a caravan refreshment-bar open most afternoons.

BICYCLE, SCOOTER & CAR HIRE Oddly enough in the last few years a very 'laid-back' outfit (*Tmr* 16.B4) has opened up, hiring small mopeds at 200 drs a day with a significant reduction for a weeks hire at 700 drs. The hire charge includes the necessary propellant (okay fuel), which it should as there is nowhere really to go that the buses will not transport one efficiently, if crowdedly. The descriptive phrase, 'laid back', is more than a euphemism as the proprietor and his young assistant simply lie on the ground in the shade of a large Gum tree on the Port side of the Town Hall whilst awaiting the next client.

BOOKSELLERS On the right of the 'High Lane', about half-way along.

BREAD SHOPS There is a Baker/cake shop (*Tmr* 17.C2) beyond Plateia Kato Piaza, on the right and another (*Tmr* 17.B/C3) on the left of 'Odhos OTE', in the second block along from Plateia Ag Evagelismos.

BUSES Pull up, naturally enough I suppose, on Bus Square. The drivers use the occasion for a long-winded natter. (*See* **Gialos Bus timetable, A to Z**).

CHEMISTS *See* **Medical Care.**

COMMERCIAL SHOPPING CENTRE Based on the 'High Lane' and 'Odhos OTE' with almost the whole of the lower Chora a market place. A couple of shops deserve a mention. From 'Odhos OTE' an alley cuts off to the left by the bakers. At the top, on the edge of an irregular square there is a 'Tomato Juice' fruit shop with hairdressing going on. Strange! The other on the 'High Lane', opposite the **Commercial Bank** (*Tmr* 15.D2), is the small almost poky '**Nicolas Store Handicrafts**' at No 26. The very pleasant proprietor is most helpful and sells, at reasonable prices, some unusual and extremely nice tiles and cups with Ios scenes and characters. My favourite is one which depicts an old man wearing traditional clothes and footwear (the owners now deceased father).

DENTISTS *See* **Medical Care.**

DISCOS Almost a growth industry that is if there aren't already enough in the Chora. My informant Pamela's personal opinion is that:-

Homerscave on Ano Piaza Square is a good starting-off point to be followed after midnight by **Scorpions** to the right of the Milopotamos Road.

The Ios Club (*Tmr* 18.A3) So often loudly heralded events and or places are disappointing in actuality but not so the **Ios Club.** Approached by a track to the left of the steps down to the Port, the spectacular setting is high above and looks out over Ormos Iou towards Sikinos island. Within the high, roofless wall the layout is a small, informal rocky amphitheatre and entrance costs 50 drs per person. Clients are given a shell or bead which acts as a credit towards the cost of the first drink. For example, 2 people pay 100 drs to get in but the baubles reduce the price of an Export Henninger and orange juice to just 20 drs. To reinforce the impression that the club is not a rip off, should a spectator purchase another drink, they only charge 70 drs for a can of beer. I realise that if I was in a taverna and was even offered a can of beer I would probably break out in spots but this is a club.

In my enthusiasm I have not explained that for the hour or so spanning the setting of the sun, the club plays a programme of appropriate classical music. And there is no finer location in the Cyclades from which to watch the beauty of the setting sun. After the magic dying moments of the sunset, the music reverts to more popular beats.

Incidentally the town plans referring to the **Up Down disco** have incorrectly listed the title which posterity will be pleased to note is the **Upside Down.**

FERRY-BOAT TICKET OFFICES *See* **Travel Agents.**

HAIRDRESSERS At least a couple, one referred to under Commercial Shopping Area and another on Kato Piaza Square.

LAUNDRY Own up Geoffrey, you are pretty sure there is one but can only position it as in the 'New Town', that is in the area of the Town Hall side of the Main Road.

LUGGAGE STORE *See* **Acteon Tours, Gialos Port.**

MEDICAL CARE
Chemists & Pharmacies Only two specialist 'chappies' on the Island let alone the Chora. One on Odhos Ano Piaza (*Tmr* D1) almost opposite the **Orange Bar** and the other at the Milopotamos end of the Main Road, a 100 m along from the Town Hall.

Clinic *See* **Doctor.**

Dentists Not one, not two but three! Two are on the left of the lane up to *Papa Antonios* (*Tmr* 5.A2) and another behind the *Grill House* (*Tmr* 19.C4) on the road off to the right of the Main Road, next turning after the Town Hall.

Doctors Conveniently situated in the Town Hall (*Tmr* 1.B4). Did you know. . . doctors are drafted to the islands for a fixed period — a sort of punishment for all the money they will make in the years to come in the more lucrative suburbs of large Greek mainland towns. It is said of the present incumbent that he was posted to Ios years ago and, against the run of play, opted to stay on. But he is now, much to all and sundries consternation, rumoured to be considering departing for halycon fields — greener drachmae pastures.

NTOG None *See* **Police.**

OPENING HOURS Usual hours otherwise *See* **Gialos Port.**

OTE (*Tmr* 20.C3) Halfway along, on the right of 'Odhos OTE' that runs parallel to the Main Road, from alongside the Ag Evagelismos Cathedral. Flanked by **Kritikakis Tours** on the near side and **Rooms** on the far side. Only open weekdays between 0730 - 1510 hrs.

PETROL (GASOLINE) None.

PLACES OF INTEREST Yes well. In the welter of silence I found very comforting the remains of the old donkey driven water pump on the Milopotamos side of the Town Hall. The donkeys used to have to walk round and round a track circumscribing the well with a wooden shaft strapped to the animal and the other end hafted into a socket on top of the mechanical arrangement. Unusable now because a road has been constructed tight to one side of the well top but reassuring to see how 'chaps' used to have to survive. It gives one a warm glow to think of the tap at home, if you get my drift. The climb up to and the Chora hilltop are notable not only for the dramatic views, more especially of the Port area, but for the three churches. The approach is via

Churches & Cathedrals
Ag Gremmiotissa A pleasantl, flagstone yard surrounds the Church with an attractive Campanile and a solitary, rather lean, palm tree planted one side of the whitewash outlined courtyard. **Ag Gremmiotissa** is famed for its icon of the Virgin about which not unnaturally there is woven a fable. It appears that a devout Christian Cretan 'freedom

fighter' set afloat the icon and a lamp in order to save the holy relics from Turkish oppressors and which finished up on Ios. The natives put the seaborne icon in a local Chapel but after this and every other night it was found on the site where now stands the Church. Finally somebody twigged that it was best to let it stay where it finished up and built Ag Gremmiotissa, from whence it is supposed to be possible to see Crete but. . . .

Above Ag Gremmiotissa, on the way to the topmost Chapel is the:-

Church of Christ of Castro

and on the very highest rocky point, picked out in whitewash, is the:-

Chapel of Ag Elephterios Once well decorated by frescoes but both Elephterios and Castro have been allowed to fall into disrepair and the interiors are supposed to be ruined. The exteriors are almost 'panstick' thick with whitewash. One intriguing rumour is the one which suggests the existence of a tunnel from Elephterios to a safe haven some hours away. The builders would have required nuclear blasting to get through the rock or an act of God. Maybe. . . .

Windmill Square Once known as Platoia Plano or Upper Square and originally laid out with the circular paved winnowing groundworks. The three windmills now stand mutely silent on an unattractive raised area now flanked by two disco bars. Well that's progress, isn't it?

There are also rumours of a ruined 15th century Fort about 2½ hours walk from the Chora.

POLICE Their office is located in the Town Hall (*Tmr* 1.B4). Definitely a 9 to 5 'set of chaps' but that is Greek 9 to 5 which translated, gives hours of 0800 - 1200 and 1400 - 1800 hrs weekdays. At the height-of-the-summer-season there is weekend presence.

POST OFFICE In the multi-purpose Town Hall (*Tmr* 1.B4).

TAXIS *See* **Gialos Port.**

TELEPHONE NUMBERS & ADDRESSES

Doctor	Tel 91222
Police	Tel 91227

TOILETS An average facility up to the left from Kato Piaza Sq (*Tmr* C2) (approaching along the 'High Lane' from Plateia Ag Evagegelismos).

There is another Public Toilet to the Port side of the Town Hall (*Tmr* 1.B4).

TRAVEL AGENTS From Plateia Evagelismos up the 'High Lane' and immediately beyond Plateia Kato Piaza (*Tmr* C2) in the next building to the left is:-

Plakiotis Travel Change but not personal cheques.

Further on, beyond the next turning right, with one office on the right and one down the alley to the right and on the left, are the offices of:-

Acteon Travel Only pale shadows of the Gialos Port office.

Kritikakis Tours Alongside the OTE office (*Tmr* 20.C3)

MILOPOTAMOS: the beach (Illustration 25)

Simply one of the greatest sweeps of beach in the Cyclades. It has to be admitted that the magnificence of the 'spread' is accentuated by the approach, being from on high, as it were. Added to this the extraordinarily wide, long, slow curve of glorious sand is framed in a broad fertile plain bordered by a large range of mountains and to the seaward side by the rocky hillsides of the bay.

The road zig-zags down from the rocky promontory above the nearside of the bay, passing close to sea level, an imaginative, if somewhat 'OTT' mini-walled estate down below on a bluff. This house is complete with castellated walls and large statues of horses and figures, and is rumoured to be owned by a wealthy Frenchman. Also high above the beach is a small Chapel from the side of which almost every professional photographer takes a panoramic view of Milopatamos Beach.

The near, or Chora side, has experienced some amount of development in the last five or six years but the central plain and far end of the beach remain almost unchanged. Despite my obvious partiality I consider that Milopotamos Beach has actually improved during this period. Also on the credit side is that the most undesirable elements have been discouraged from camping out on the backshore.

It is pleasing to observe how much the donkey is still in evidence, here being utilised in their traditional role as pack-animals for the transport of goods to the far end of the beach. Unfortunately the other creature much in evidence is the mosquito.

I have indicated that I have a prejudice in respect of accommodation on los island and have to own up to landing and heading straight for the *Brothers Dracos Taverna.* This is admirably sited on the very nearest edge of this almost obscenely lovely, broad swathe of sandy beach that stretches on, for in excess of a kilometre, and edges a beautiful clear sea with solid sand bottom. Although during the months of June, July, August and September it has to be admitted that the foreshore does get almost jam-packed with sun worshippers, even at its most crowded the far end is almost always practically empty. But whatever the midday situation by late afternoon the beach empties as if all the day's visitors have been hoovered off. In general terms the far end of the beach is the preserve of the topless (and bottomless); as are the nearside slab rocks around to the right of the bay (*Fsw*). The middle ground is occupied by the Windsurf School and sand-seated, circled groups of folk-singing youngsters as well as almost every variety of game known to 'beach groupies'. The near end of the beach is more than often used by locals. At nights end there is even a man cleaning up the beach but, as with the rest of the Island, the rubbish is a problem. Here it is assiduously swept up, collected, packed in bins and plastic bags but then left where stacked only to be spread all over the place again. . . to be collected up all over again. . . .

Some things change. The rocky goat path from the area of the *Acropolis Hotel* has, at its lower end, become a wide, very steep, dusty swathe; the beach duck-boards that the bus used to turn, back and park up on have been replaced by a concrete pad and the hillside to the right of *Dracos Taverna* (*Fsw*) has become an extremely expensive, tasteful hotel complex climbing up the craggy hillside with a swimming pool (yes a swimming pool, beside this of all beaches). The unofficial campsite that used to lay out along the low concrete wall, now part collapsed, has been done away with and a shiny, new official camping site has sprung up to complement the original, now rather run-down facility half-way along the beach.

THE ACCOMMODATION & EATING OUT

The Accommodation I am of course blinkered but I must own up to heading straight for

The Brothers Draco Pension & Taverna (& Mini-Market)　　　　Tel 91243
Directions: Where the road runs out on the beach in the near right corner of the beach and bay.

A lovely mixture of taverna and pension, developed over the years first by Mother and Father, now run by their twin sons, George and Yianni and their wives with hindrance from the Grandchildren. The Grandparents still help in the taverna and run the mini-market (of which more later) although Papa is really only interested in his daily fishing expeditions on which the brothers alternate to help lay the nets. The side benefit is that family caught fresh fish are always on the menu and a little cheaper than elsewhere. The best positioned accommodation is the original line of first floor balcony rooms, complete with small en suite bathrooms that face out over the bay. This is not to say that time has not accentuated some of the usual 'Greek Room Idiosyncrasies' — no toilet roll; doors that shut and will not open; doors that will not shut; suspect drainage with the occasional concrete block or tile laid over long missing grilles of the access trap. I assume the contemporaneous lid is to seal off the smells as well as to stop clients tripping. But I carp. A double room ranges between 700 - 1000 drs.

The Dracos two patio terraces must be almost unrivalled for position and make a splendid location to have a meal or simply a drink or two (or three or four). The simple fare and insouciant service (okay, easy-going, still a euphemism for casual) has been given a bit of a shake-up by the splendid *Far Out* (for details of which read on). Enough to say that food and drink is available all day until late in the evening, from the almost self-service servery abutting the top patio. The pre-prepared trays of, for instance, stuffed tomatoes, moussaka, stuffed aubergines or spaghetti bolognese are best tackled as close to the time of preparation as is possible. In common with most Greek tavernas, the food can become 'tired' as the day wears on. That is certainly so, where and when the turnover is slow.

Naturally enough with Grandpapa's overriding piscatorial enthusiasm, fish is a speciality and the Brothers will select a reasonably priced dish for impecunious clients. Of course, as always, kalamares make an inexpensive choice. A meal for two of soup, poached fish with boiled potatoes, a Greek salad, a plate of chips, bread and 2 bottles of retsina for 795 drs, represents very good value. An evening's repast, including 2 glasses of brandy, 2 bottles of orange, 2 bottles of retsina, 2 kalamares, a plate of chips, 2 feta-less salads, bread and 2 coffees has to be good news at 915 drs.

Before leaving this particular laudatory eulogy the family has in recent years opened up a cellar-like mini-market beneath the lower of the two patios. This is quite in line with the Greek obsession for competing head-on with each other. When will the *Camping Stars Super-market* owner open up a taverna, or has he already? One certainty is that the Dracos shop is the cheapest in Milopotamos for many items and they also sell international newspapers at the height of the season. It is another sad marginalia to add that the family has found it necessary to erect a sign reading 'Shoplifters will be Prosecuted', the necessity for which is underlined by the spelling being correct! One Brother speaks excellent English, the other sufficient, but as I am totally incapable of sorting out which 'twin has the Toni...' it is no earthly use my identifying them. Enough to say that from the ever smiling Grandmama, dour Papa, the friendly, if sometimes preoccupied, twin Brothers to their wives and children, it is difficult to find a more genuine family.

After that fulsome testimonial... it is necessary to point out that there are other more than adequate establishments, including the *Hotel Galaxy* which I am fairly certain is package booked. But all is not lost.

Hotel (Nissos) Ios (Class D)   Tel 91306
Directions: To the waterfront side of *Camping Stars.*

The daily rate for a double room ranges from 850 drs to 950 drs for the months of July and August.

The Hotel Aegeon (Class E)   Tel 91392
Directions: To the left-hand of the road a 100 metres or so along the backshore and distinguished by an arched entrance to the grounds.

Doubles en suite from middle May to middle October from 840 drs with the high season months of July and August costing 970 drs.

Marcos Beach Hotel (Class E)   Tel — only an Athens number given
Directions: Behind and slightly to the right of the *Hotel Aegeon* (*Sbo*).

Reasonably priced single rooms costing en suite from 560 - 620 drs whilst double rooms en suite rise from 840 drs (1st May - 15th June), 970 drs (16th June - 25th August) to 900 drs (26th August - 31st October).

Attractively situated at the far end of the bay are the *Gorgona Hotel* which, unless I am very mistaken, is now closed and the:-

Dracos Restaurant

Distant cousins of our favourite Milopotamos family but there all resemblance ceases. The standard accommodation is at the reather sleazy end of the scale, as is the establishment, with a double room sharing the bathroom starting at 600 drs and en suite from 800 drs. But they also own, round to the right on the edge of the backshore, a very pleasant development of Cabin/Chalets with a two bed unit costing 1000 drs per night.

There is also a choice of two campsites:-

Camping Stars   Tel 91302

Directions: On the left of the Main Road some 50m before the beach edge. The entrance stands back from the road's edge. This is an excellent site, very well managed and smart as one would expect of the small, gold toothed, smiling proprietor who has owned the supermarket alongside for as long as I can remember.

It is a proud boast that there is 'Perpetual Hot Water' to service the high quality toilet block. The charge is 130 drs per head and tents are available for hire at 70 drs per day. The reception block has a bank of security lockers and a post box on the office wall. The other flank of the small square is taken up by a Restaurant/Cafe with steps to the fore.

The other (orginal site) is:-

Camping Souli   Tel. 91554

Directions: About halfway along the backshore, to the left of the road from the Chora.

The frankly rather tatty site, is located in a low-lying area which must be prone to mosquitoes. The proprietress is charming but *Camping Stars* must have knocked her trade more than a little. A night costs 100 - 130 drs and she hires tents when necessary. Facilities include a toilet block and reception.

Whilst on the bus from the Chora it is quite on the cards that likely looking passengers will be offered *Rooms* by the fullsome lady conductress or her colleagues. Her pension is located high up on the hillside, on the right-hand side of the road overlooking Milopotamos Beach, close by a Chapel and before the *Hotel Acropolis*. There is often a bus parked up on the large forecourt.

This newish building is kept spotless and a double room with bathroom costs from 800 drs a day.

The Pension Acropolis

Directions: Close to the edge of the drop into the sea on the hilltop overlooking the Beach. To the right of the road, just about where it starts to wind down to the nearside of the plain that backs the bay, and close by the small Chapel that is inevitably included in panoramic views of Milopotamos Beach. The entrance to the house is through a concrete arch.

Served only by its own generator, the rooms despite being wired up, do not always have electricity flowing, but paraffin lamps are supplied. The rooms are spacious with en suite bathrooms and the water is solar heated. Ground floor rooms almost all open out on to the large patio that surrounds the house. A clothes line is thoughtfully provided but beware, the high winds can blow washing straight over the cliffside. The pension overlooks the startling 'OTT' holiday home to which reference has previously been made. Despite the excellent position and friendly family the double room rate of 1200 drs seems rather exorbitant. A shame really, and this is the mid season charge.

It is to the front of the pension that a goat track scrambles down the rock hillside cutting out the circuitous road route to the beach.

The Eating Out A number of establishments have been covered in the descriptions of accommodation but these did not include the:-

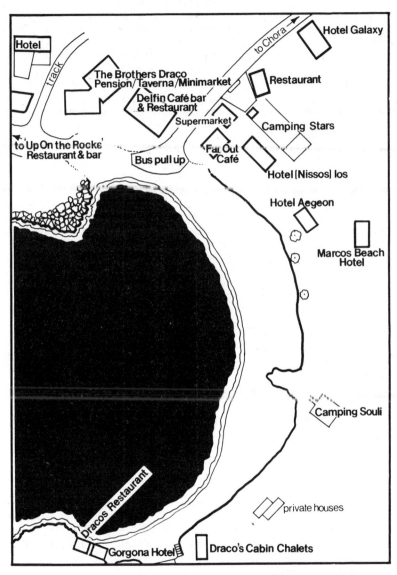

MILOPOTAMOS BEACH

Illustration 25

Delfin Cafe-Bar & Restaurant
Directions: Between the road and *Brothers Draco* and behind which is the *Hotel Delfini.*
Neat enough and, at the height of season, fills up as does everywhere in Milopotamos but at any other time it has to compete, in common with other eating establishments with the:-

Far Out Cafe
Directions: Flanks the left of the Chora road where it runs out on the beach.
The place almost defies description, and is probably the slickest operation I have encountered in Greece. The main body of the building, edging the very large terrace, houses the most incredible self-service operation I have ever seen. Not only is the choice imaginative but the standard of food is excellent, even if portions might be considered on the small side. The self-service even extends to the bread and the bottles of drinks that are stocked in a cold cabinet. There is a separate 'Tost Snack Bar' and service starts early morning with bacon and eggs available and terminates late at night, but the food often runs out early evening.

The terrace is crammed with youngsters of every shape, size, colour and creed and the loudspeakers belt out non-stop pop until the evening Video show. Yes, not one but 2 video shows a night, with one of the films being a full length feature. The massed audience simply sit goggle-eyed and glued to their seats with the velvet darkness of the night closed down round the patio, almost like a curtain.

Food on offer can include soup, egg meat-loaf, moussaka, stuffed tomatoes, pasta, macaroni pie, meat balls and rice, spaghetti bolognese, chicken, green beans, potatoes and tomatoes, potatoes and peas and Greek salad. Prices for a plate or helping include moussaka 180 drs, spaghetti with sauce 100 drs, spaghetti with meat sauce 180 drs, potatoes and zucchini 90 drs, bean soup 100 drs, rice 60 drs, stuffed tomatoes 180 drs and Greek salad 110 drs.

One other very useful service is a notice board for personal messages.
Another establishment is:-

Up On The Rocks
Directions: Along the wide track edging the right-hand side of the bay (*Fsw*) that starts out alongside the *Draco Brothers* taverna.
Once very popular and certainly spotlessly clean, the menu is limited and the prices average.

THE A TO Z OF USEFUL INFORMATION

BANKS None, it being necessary to pop up to the Chora.

BOOKSELLERS The excellent **Camping Stars Supermarket** stocks a good range of paperbacks and the *Draco Brothers* mini-market a number of international newspapers.

BREAD SHOPS No specific baker but the two shops above sell rolls and bread.

BUSES They pull up on the beach heralding both arrival and imminent departure by enthusiastic horn blowing. *See* **Gialos Port** for details of timetables.

CHEMISTS The shops sell the more mundane items, otherwise it is necessary to go to the Chora.

COMMERCIAL SHOPPING AREA Of course none but the merits of the **Draco Brothers Mini-Market** have already been discussed. **Camping Stars Supermarket** is a very well stocked shop with a wide range of goods. Another mute commentary on the light fingered nature of the tourists is that the proprietor's elderly parents are employed to watch over the stock displayed in front of the shop. There is now a third Mini-Market in the bowels of the *Hotel Delfini* behind the *Delfini Restaurant.* How on earth the Beach can support three shops I really don't know but the old habit of just not being able to resist rushing in whenever anyone else seems to be making an honest drachmae still thrives.

DISCOS Apart from **Far Out's** non-stop clamour nearly all the discos are concentrated in or around the Chora.

MEDICAL CARE *See* the Chora.

TOILETS There is no public block and it is necessary to use the relevant 'offices' of the various restaurants/tavernas/cafe-bars. **Far Out** has a very accessible facility.

TRAVEL AGENTS Surprisingly two offices (but they only open up for the months of June through to early October) which include:-

Acteon Tours: Positioned on the corner of the **Far Out** and **Kritikakis Travel** Alongside the third mini-market, in the basement of the *Hotel Delfini.*

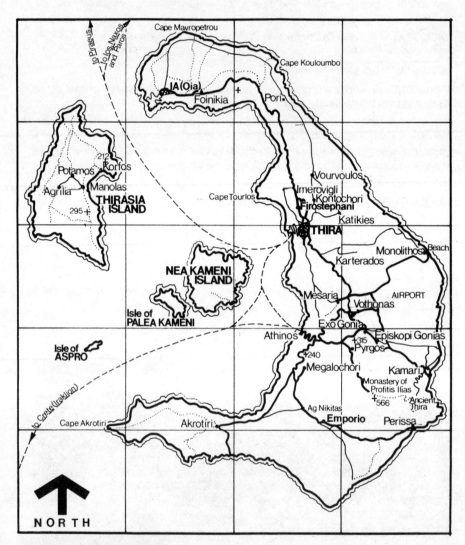

SANTORINI

Illustration 26

17 Santorini (Santorine, Thira, Thera) & Anafi
Cyclades Islands — Eastern chain

Visually	★★★★★
Otherwise	★★★

FIRST IMPRESSIONS
Stunningly dramatic coastline; country lanes; churches; barrel roofs; donkeys; happy pcoplo; cruioe linero; duty free shops.

SPECIALITIES
Stunningly dramatic coastline and cruise liners; wine; tomatoes; export of pumice stone, china clay and rock soil for cement making; breakfast (Thira Town).

RELIGIOUS HOLIDAYS & FESTIVALS
include: 23rd May — Feast, Karterados; 19th-20th July — Festival, Profitas Ilias; 15th August — Feast, Episkopi (Mesa) Gonia; 1st September — Feast, Thira; 20th October — Festival Ag Artemiou Church, Thira; 26th October — Festival, Ag Dimitriou, Karterados.

VITAL STATISTICS
Tel prefix 0286. The island, shaped like a half saucer (or a foetal old man in the moon) is up to 17 km long, between 1¼ and 12 kms across and has an area of 75 sq km, with a population of 6,500 of which approximately 1,500 live in Thira, the capital.

HISTORY
A couple of fundamental differences from the Cycladean islands 'norm' include the Cretan or more correctly the Minoan 'connection', that ended rather dramatically in about 1520 BC, and the more than usually Machiavellian and multifarious infighting and coups of the Venetian ruling families.

The Minoan link and other interwoven items have fostered the possibility that Santorini was part of the lost city of Atlantis, popularised in the writings of Plato and Egyptian papyrists. Perhaps it was geological justice that the island originally formed by volcanic activity some 20-25,000 years ago, should be blown in half by an enormous eruption circa 1600 BC. It is postulated that the tidal waves resulting from this cataclysmic eruption almost completely destroyed the ancient Minoan civilisation. Not that this was to be the last volcanic acitivity experienced by the island. In fact the present day complex of five islands owes its form to a series of volcanic activity right up to 1950. After the 'big bang' the islands of Santorini, Thirasia and Aspronissi and an enormous bay or 'caldera' were in position. Explosions, eruptions and discharges over the years eventually formed the other offshore islands of Nea and Palia Kameni. Two particular periods of activity merit a mention. The first in 1650 lasted for several months and created an islet 7 km off the eastern shore, the shock waves of which were recorded as being heard in Chios, flooding Ios and Sikinos, causing havoc on the shores of Crete and 'filling the farms of Santorini with sea'. Now known as the Kouloumbos reef it lies about 18½ m beneath the sea's surface. The other event was as recent as 1925, when an island appeared above the surface which finally enlarged the existing Nea Kameni. The island of Nea Kameni was associated with vampires, so much so that the Greeks had a saying similar to our '...coals to Newcastle', or don't bring a vampire to Nea Kameni, there are enough already.

Another item of note is Medieval and perhaps owes its inclusion to my sense of the unusual (or my unusual senses!). It appears that the Turks at some stage granted governorship of a group of Cyclades islands, including Santorini, to a Jew, one Joseph Nazi!

GENERAL

Extremely tourist-popular islands usually have their charms diminished to the point of vanishing as in the case of say Kos (Dodecanese) and Mykonos (Cyclades). There is always an exception to the rule and Santorini is that exception. Despite 20 years of Cruise Liner visits, the serried ranks of backpackers and, in recent years, swarms of packaged holidaymakers, the sheer beauty, the stunning visual effects of the cliff-hanging towns, the loveliness of the countryside and the undiminished friendliness of the people continue to triumph. Santorini still weaves its magic charms even around hardened travellers who should be innured to any island's wiles. If natural beauty were not enough, fate decreed that the dice should, perhaps unfairly, be further loaded in Santorini's favour, with the comparitively recent discovery of perhaps the most interesting of all such archaeological digs, the Akrotiri excavations.

Mind you how long Santorini can rise above the hordes of visitors is difficult to foresee now that the airfield can take fully fledged jumbo-jets.

Santorini is a humid island (as is Mykonos) and is supposed to be 'good for the skin, bad for the bones'. The prevailing wind is so strong and water so short that the vines grow low to the ground, nourished on humidity.

Out of line with the general format adopted it will make descriptions easier if the introduction is modified to allow for the unusual complications caused by there being three main ports of call, all on the west coast. They include Ia (Oia) in the north, Thira (Phira, Fira), the capital, in the centre of the crescent shaped island circling the east of the enormous caldera, and Athinos (Athinios, Athiniou) to the south. The traditional Ports of Ia and Thira have now largely been superseded by the new port of Athinos where the larger ferries almost always call. The smaller Ferry-boats often make the older ports their docking point but difficulties are caused by Ferries sometimes berthing at one, two or all three. Those steeped in the general vagaries of the ferry-boat system will need no assuring that the operators make the most of this additional obstacle and maximise the uncertainties that are already the lot of the hapless traveller. To the disorientated, identification of the Ports will help. Ia and Thira are ostensibly similar, with the small and pretty facilities nestling at the bottom of volcanic cliffs but the relative position of the Islands of Thirasia and Nea Kameni helps detection as does the reminder that only Thira has a cable car. The Port of Athinos is a large, comparitively modern quay about which there is nothing quaint.

When Ferries call in at Ia and or Thira it is quite common for passengers to be transferred to 'bum' or passage boats, even the small **MV Ios** transferring its clients in this fashion.

THIRA (Phira, Fira): capital & port (Illustration 27)

Possibly one of the most amazingly and breathtakingly situated capital Towns not only in the Cyclades but in most of Greece. The rambling, brilliant white buildings with the occasional blue dome standing out, skirt and range up and down the multi-coloured and layered cliff-edge. The impact is quite staggering and it is no coincidence that so much publicity material, so many Guide Books and travel brochures feature a picture of the view from the Town looking out to sea. Unfortunately this riveting beauty has resulted in a surfeit of tourism, some of which is represented by a rarified species, that rather narrow band of visitors carried to the island by Cruise Liners which moor up at the foot of the cliff-face and disembark their clientele into ships boats.

For many years the only way up to the top of the cliff was via a steep, zig-zagging path with 550/650 steps. A band of donkey men had a monopoly on the route but those brave enough to shoulder aside the massed barricades of skittish donkey flesh, faced a 25/30

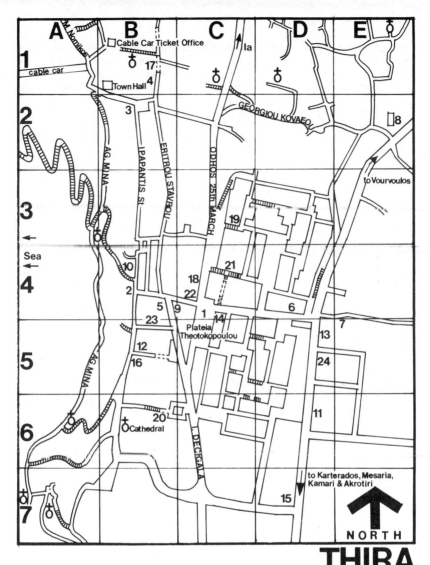

THIRA

NORTH

Illustration 27

minute climb. Those who gave in to their vaguely menacing presence had to fork out about 250/300 drs. Some years ago the muleteers agreed to allow an erosion of their monopoly with the installation of the cable car as long as they received a share of the 'take'. In 1985 the owners of the Funicular omitted to pay over the 'brigands protection money' which resulted in the donkey men (and their donkeys?) occupying the premises until the funds were made available.

The affluent Liner clientele, emanating an aura of wealth, have resulted in the streets lining and parallel to the top of the cliff, being jammed with sleek boutiques, jewellery and gift shops, the windows of which shriek with inducements to pay by credit card. No junk here, only top quality goods for the predominantly elderly, prosperous and often ridiculously clothed dilettantes.

The oft repeated GROC adage in respect of Ports on the Cruise Liner schedule, to vacate town when the ships moor up does assume that there are days of respite. Not so here, for as many as 6 or 7 call in for a Port stop each and every day.

ARRIVAL BY (ISLAND) BUS
With larger and larger inter-island ferries coming into service it is likely that visitors will disembark at Athinos (*See* **Arrival by Ferry**) and catch the bus from the Port to Thira Bus Square (*Tmr* 1.C4/5), Plateia Theotopkopulou. Compared to the patina of quiet wealth overlaying the cliff edge streets, the Bus Square is rather more downbeat, well sordid. Apart from the summer time heat, the sheer volume of buses and passengers could well melt the concrete. The Square has a number of travel offices around the edge including **Domigos** and **Pelikan Tours** as well as stalls and shops selling almost everything from pizzas to postcards. There is a bus timetable on the south side of the Square and the buses are met by Room offering mamas.

ARRIVAL BY FERRY — Athinos (Athinios, Athiniou)
Most ferries dock at the new Port of Athinos sometimes also calling in at the Thira Town landing stage which has 3 tavernas and the usual cluster of buildings.

Athinos is (yes is) a very large concrete quay edged by unattractive concrete faced restaurant/cafe-bars with plenty of signs advertising the various business's wares. These include an 'Official Exchange' over the patio of the *Restaurant Volcano*. There is a small stall which is very useful for a snatched cup of coffee but plastic cups are order of the day — perhaps they lost too many china ones?

A swarm of hotel buses line up to meet disembarking clients and, if everything is in order, there will be several island buses waiting. Destinations include Thira (of course), Kamari and Akrotiri. Even in early and late summer the buses get very crowded and it is advantageous for ferry-boat travellers to be as close to first off as is possible. Despite patrons being packed in like sardines, fares are collected by a conductor who has to climb over the passengers. The fare to Thira Town is 75 drs per head.

The Ferries are also met by Room owners from the various parts of the Island who, when they have bagged a client or two, stuff them on the particular bus, often with one of their children to act as guide. It can be somewhat disconcerting and, if not 'selected', my advice is to head for Karterados, for which reasons *See* ROUTE ONE.

If arrival is disconcerting, departure is downright disquieting. Apart from, or because of, the uncertainty of the Ferry-boats Port or Ports of departure, it may well be necessary to catch a bus to make the connection (and Santorini island is often an early morning call). Furthermore the Ferries, especially the smaller craft, may well be overbooked which will not matter as long as port officials do not decide to have a head-count. On my last trip our friend Georgio of **Nomikos Travel**, who had arranged to deliver us to Athinos, casually informed us that it would be possible to board the ferry at Thira Port but ... the boat was rumoured to be 30 passengers over the limit. As it was docking at Athinos Port first, perhaps it would be best to board the craft there. 'You bet your sweet ... it was'! Tickets should be purchased the day before a planned sailing, which might ensure a place, added to which there are no, repeat no, ticket offices or sales at Athinos.

Extra buses are usually laid on to meet the Ferries and they start operating from Thira Town as early as 0600 hrs. If it is necessary to catch a taxi, the fare from Thira to Athinos cost about 500 drs.

Some camp out on the stony foreshore round a rock or two to the south of the quay, which might become compulsory if arriving very late at Athinos.

Ferry-boat timetable

Day	Departure time	Ferry-boat	Ports/Islands of Call
Monday	0730 hrs	Limnos	Ioo, Naxos, Paros, Piraeus (M)*
	0800 hrs	Georgios Express	Ios, Sikinos, Folegandros, Paros, Syros, Piraeus (M)
	1900 hrs	Kimolos	Ios, Siphnos, Serifos, Piraeus (M)
Tuesday	0800 hrs	Ios	Ios, Naxos, Paros, Mykonos
	1730 hrs	Portokalis Ilios	Iraklion (Crete)*
Wednesday	0715 hrs	Santorini	Ios, Sikinos, Folegandros, Naxos, Paros, Syros, Piraeus (M)
	0800 hrs	Mecaloxari	Ios, Paros, Mykonos, Tinos†
	1045 hrs	Nearxos	Ios, Mykonos
	1800 hrs	Nearxos	Iraklion (Crete)*
Thursday	0730 hrs	Limnos	Ios, Naxos, Paros, Piraeus (M)
	0830 hrs	Georgios Express	Ios, Paros, Naxos, Piraeus (M)
	1730 hrs	Portokalis Ilios	Iraklion, (Crete)*
Friday	0715 hrs	Santorini	Ios, Naxos, Paros, Piraeus (M)
	0800 hrs	Ios	Ios, Naxos, Paros, Mykonos
Saturday	0800 hrs	Mecaloxari	Ios, Paros, Mykonos, Tinos†
	0730 hrs	Limnos	Ios, Sikinos, Folegandros, Naxos, Paros, Syros, Piraeus (M)
	1400 hrs	Miaoulis	Ios, Paros, Mykonos, Piraeus (M)*†
	1045 hrs	Nearxos	Ios, Mykonos, Syros
	1730 hrs	Portokalis Ilios	Iraklion (Crete)*
	1800 hrs	Nearxos	Iraklion (Crete)*
Sunday	0715 hrs	Santorini	Ios, Naxos, Paros, Piraeus (M)*
	0800 hrs	Kimolos	Ios, Kimolos, Milos, Siphnos, Serifos, Kithnos, Piraeus (M)
	0800 hrs	Ios	Ios, Naxos, Paros, Mykonos†
	0830 hrs	Georgios Express	Ios, Naxos, Paros, Piraeus (M)*
	1730 hrs	Portokalis Ilios	Iraklion (Crete)*

*Definitely from Athinos Port
†Calls at both Thira Town and Athinos Ports
*† Thira Town Port

But check and double check.

THE ACCOMMODATION & EATING OUT

The Accommodation A wide range of Hotels, Pensions and **Rooms** with prices on the high side in addition to which the Town fills up early as most tourists head for Thira. I would not stay here but then it could be argued that I consider Karterados the centre of the island! (*See* ROUTE ONE).

The cliff-edge hotels are fearsomely expensive apart from the:-

Hotel Lucas (*Tmr* 2.B4) (Class D) Old Port Steps   Tel 22480
Directions: On the left of the steps down to the Old Port.

Comparatively inexpensive considering the location but the donkey droppings deposited on the steps to the Port ensure a healthy insect population. A single room sharing the bathroom costs 700 drs and en suite 900 drs with a double room 1000 drs and 1600 drs respectively.

From the top of the Old Port Steps, follow the pebbled, rising Ipapantis St which is hedged in with expensive tourist shops, towards the cable-car station. At the Archaeological Museum (*Tmr* 3.B2) it is possible to turn left or right. Both routes have a few **Rooms** signed. The left lane passes the Town Hall and then right along Odhos M Nomikos to the Funicular ticket office. The right-hand turning and then left (in effect completing the other side of the Square), leads up the narrow Odhos Eritrou Stavrou and, after a roofed-in section, a left-hand turn on to Agios Ioannis advances to the head of the cable-car. This route leads past a Tourist Office, the *Asimina Hotel and Pension* and, on the left of Odhos Eritrou Stavrou, the:-

Kamares Youth Hostel (*Tmr* 4.B1) Odhos Eritrou Stavrou
Not really a 'Youth Hostel', more a (highly recommended) hostel. The dormitory rooms, in which a bed costs 250 drs, fill up very early in the day due to the establishments popularity (and cheapness?). A few paces beyond the *Kamares Youth Hostel* is a local Museum collection in a rather splendid building.

By keeping on in a northerly direction towards the suburb called Firostephani beyond the cable-car and the Town becomes Greek again with, on the left, houses here and there signed unsafe where they have started to slide down the multi-brown coloured volcanic cliff-face. **Rooms**, pensions and tavernas are scattered about and their distance from the centre of Thira is reflected in the more reasonable room rates. (*See* **The Eating Out** for a recommended taverna in Firostephani).

The other Youth Hostel (the official one), is to the right, about 350 m up the Main Road north of Thira Town from the Bus Square The signs loudly herald that this is the authorised establishment. A dormitory bed costs 225 drs.

In fact the road to Ia as far as Firostephani, which is now really part of Thira, is crammed with **Rooms**, Pensions and Hotels which include the *Margarita* (Class E), a double room with en suite bathroom costs 1800 drs; *Aphroditi* (Class E) doubles en suite 1490 drs; *Thira* (Class E), doubles sharing 1120 drs and the *Kafieries* (Class E) a double sharing 1350 drs.

Another rich and very convenient vein of **Rooms**, generally 'ethnic and provincial' in style, is in the large square of buildings in the centre of the Town formed by the main roads. The area, laced with alleys, is immediately behind and down from the Bus Square (*Tmr* 1.C4/5).

Hotels and Pensions close by include:-

Hotel Tataki (*Tmr* 5.B4) (Class D) M Danezi   Tel 22389
Directions: Up the lane (with **Pelikan Tours** on the corner), to the right of the Bus Square (*Tmr* 1.C4/5) (**Domigos Tours** behind one) and on the left. 'We have heating and hot showers in the rooms'. God knows why the heating?

A double in this busy commercial area of town costs 1700 drs.

Hotel Lignos (*Tmr* 6.D4)
Directions: Down the Main Street from the bottom right-hand corner of the Bus Square (**Domigos Tours** behind one) and on the left, at the junction with the Vourvoulos/Akrotiri road.

A double room en suite costs about 1550 drs.

Hotel Antonia Roussou (*Tmr* 7.E4/5)
Directions: From the *Hotel Lignos* (*Tmr* 6.D4), almost directly across the Main Road to the left of the **Self Service Store/bakery.**

Doubles en suite 1350 drs.

There are also **Rooms** in the row of buildings in which the **Olympic office** is located on the far (or east side) of the Akrotiri road (from the Bus Square).

Hotel Therassia (*Tmr* 8.E2)
Directions: Still from the *Hotel Lignos* (*Tmr* 6.D4), turn left along the Vourvoulos road and on the left.

Double rooms sharing a bathroom cost about 1050 drs and en suite 1250 drs.

To end the accommodation paragraph it is enough to repeat that I would advise visitors to stay in Karterados but I must admit to being biased.

The Eating Out Yes, well! When a Town harbours establishments such as the **Paradise Video - Music Club** which serves 'Sangria Cup'. . . then the portents for the inner man, or woman, are not good. Added to this prices are generally expensive. But all is not lost.

The Pleasure (*Tmr* 9.B/C4) Odhos M Danezi
Directions: From the Bus Square (*Tmr* 1.C4/5) up the right-hand lane, on the corner of which is the **Pelikan Tours**, and half-way up on the left.

Not the smartest cafe-bar I know and, as is often the case in Thira, due to the wind, no patio. In fact possibly rather 'doo-hickey'* but this simple, home-spun, cafe-bar, masquerading as a restaurant, is excellent value. A smiley, middle-aged Mama makes breakfast a speciality and the 'Nes' served here is the best and cheapest I have had anywhere in Greece. A breakfast of eggs and bacon costs 80 drs, a tea 30 drs, a Nescafe with milk 38 drs, yoghurt and honey 80 drs, rice pudding 40 drs and a beer 64 drs. After breakfast time Mama flicks over the price board to reveal the daytime drinks prices.

*This is an Irish colloquialism indicating lack of sophistication despite contrary indications in 'Partridge's Dictionary of Slang'

Cheek by jowl, next door, is:-

Petros
A pleasant, covered in and elongated alleyway establishment but smarter and more expensive.

Restaurant Helidoni
Directions: Across the street, down some steps.

Not exactly my prime choice but a 'greasy' spit-roast outfit serving a reasonably priced menu (for Santorini that is). A Greek salad costs 150 drs.

The really expensive offerings can be found on the cliff top road and on the upper part of the Old Port Steps. The *Kastro Cocktail Bar and Restaurant* opposite the cable-car building is a good example of this genre.

Nicks (Nicholas) Taverna (*Tmr* 10.B4)
Directions: Descending the Old Port Steps and on the right.

The view is magnificent, the prices seem reasonable but the food is not. The Greek salad wasn't; if they were baby kalamares, I'd hate to see or eat mature ones; the bread that was offered was stale; the ratatouille was good; the moussaka acceptable and the red wine tasty but expensive. A meal for two will cost some 900 drs. Let us hope the taverna across the steps opens up again.

Incidentally there is little retsina available on Santorini but *See* Kartarados for an amusing little tale.

Taverna Roussos
Directions: It is necessary to walk up to Firostephani to locate this blue painted taverna, about two buildings before the Church. But arrive early as the locals know about it and eat here. How unreasonable. Comes highly recommended so all should be well. Mr Roussos also owns the *Hotel Galini* but Room rates are on the expensive side.

THE A TO Z OF USEFUL INFORMATION

AIRLINE OFFICE & TERMINUS (*Tmr* 11.D6) Down the road from the bottom right-hand corner of the Bus Square (*Tmr* 1.C4/5) (**Domigos Tours** behind one), right at the junction of the Vourvoulos/Aktotiri road and on the left. Santorini makes a surprisingly wide number of inter-island connections, but the services are so popular with the locals that it is difficult to get a seat.

Aircraft timetables

Santorini to Athens

Daily	0740, 1850 hrs
Tuesday	1140 hrs
From 23rd June additionally	
Thursday, Friday	1050 hrs
Saturday	1555 hrs

Return journey

Daily	0620, 1730 hrs
Tuesday	1020 hrs
From 23rd June additionally	
Thursday, Friday	0930 hrs
Saturday	1435 hrs

One-way fare 2690 drs, duration 40 minutes.

Santorini to Crete (Iraklion)

Monday, Wednesday, Friday, Sunday	0940 hrs

Return journey

Monday, Wednesday, Friday, Sunday	1040 hrs

One-way fare 2080 drs, duration 40 minutes.

Santorini to Mykonos

Monday, Wednesday, Friday, Sunday	1140 hrs
Tuesday, Thursday, Saturday	1220 hrs

Return journey

Daily	0840 hrs

One-way fare 1800 drs, duration 40 minutes.

Santorini to Rhodes

Tuesday, Thursday, Saturday	0940 hrs

Return journey

Tuesday, Thursday, Saturday	1100 hrs

One-way fare 3030 drs, duration 1 hr.

BANKS

The National Bank (*Tmr* 12.B5) Off to the right of a path connecting the angled 'Taxi St' (Odhos I Decigala) and the Esplanade (Odhos Ipapantis). There is a separate change office behind the main building alongside a vine covered patio/garden with seats. Normal weekday hours but long queues form every day.

BEACHES Not surprisingly, mindful of the geographical nature of the Town's position, none.

BICYCLE, SCOOTER & CAR HIRE The majority of the firms are located either side of the main road to Ia from the Bus Square. The average island scooter hire fee is about 1200 drs daily including fuel but Vespas in Thira average 1100 drs and can be found as low as 1000 drs per day.

BOOKSELLERS There is a shop selling overseas magazines on the far side of the Bus Square (*Tmr* 1.C4/5) (**Domigos Tours** behind one).

BREAD SHOPS A Bakery in the **Self Service** (*Tmr* 13.D5) adjacent to **Nomikos Travel** on the Vourvoulos/Akrotiri road down from the Bus Square.

BUSES Pull up on the Plateia Theotokopoulou or Bus Square (*Tmr* 1.C4/5).

Bus timetable
Thira Town to Ia (Oia)
Daily	0900, 1100, 1200, 1300, 1400, 1600, 1730, 1830, 2030 hrs
Return journey	
Daily	0730, 0930, 1130, 1230, 1330, 1430, 1700, 1800, 2000 hrs
One-way fare 55 drs.	

Thira Town to Kamari
Daily	0700, 0800, 0900, 1000, & then every ½ hr to 1800, 1900, 2000, 2100 hrs
Return journey	
As above.	

Thira Town to Perissa
Daily	0800, 0915, 1030, 1200, 1300, 1400, 1600, 1800, 1930, 2100 hrs
Sunday/holidays	0800, 1000, 1200, 1400, 1600, 1800, 2000 hrs
Return journey	
As above.	

Thira Town to Akrotiri
Daily	0830, 0930, 1030, 1130, 1230, 1345, 1530, 1750, 2000 hrs
Sunday/holidays	0815, 1130, 1445, 1800 hrs
Return journey	
Daily	0730, 0900, 1000, 1100, 1200, 1300, 1500, 1720, 1900 hrs

CABLE CAR (*Tmr* B1) Saves donkey haggling or walking. A one-way trip costs 300 drs.

CHEMISTS *See* **Medical Care.**

COMMERCIAL SHOPPING AREA None although the narrow lane, second right off Odhos M Danezi (from the Bus Square (*Tmr* 1.C4/5) is lined with vegetable stalls. As already discussed the Esplanade cliff-top Street, Odhos Ipapantis, is jammed with high quality gift, boutique and jewellery shops (very Greek Island, don't you know!). Hereabouts a drink shop attempted to overcharge me 20 drs on a 150 drs bottle of brandy, possibly only the fourth time in seven years that a similar occurrence has happened. The Bus Square is lined by stalls, shops and travel offices selling everything from pizzas to tour tickets. There is a dentist and a Periptero at each side of the Square. Odhos Erythrou Stavrou, one back and parallel to Odhos Ipapantis, is initially lined with gift and tourist shops.

DENTISTS & DOCTORS *See* **Medical Care.**

DISCOS Yes, a number including **Disco Forum** close by the Bus Square.

FERRY-BOATS & FERRY-BOAT TIMETABLES *See* **Athinos & Introduction.**

FERRY-BOAT TICKET OFFICES *See* **Travel Agents.**

HAIRDRESSERS Oddly enough, for an island with this level of high-spending visitors, none that I could say I bumped into. Possibly one may be hiding its light. It is more likely, as with other services not available (ie NTOG, Tourist police) or for which there is restricted provision (OTE), that the Cruise-Liners fulfil all their clients necessary requirements.

HOSPITAL *See* **Medical Care.**

LUGGAGE STORE Domigos Tours (*Tmr* 14.C4/5), on the Bus Square takes in bags at 50 drs a piece.

MEDICAL CARE
Chemists & Pharmacies A number including one on the Main Road down from the bottom right-hand corner of the Bus Square (**Domigos Tours** behind one). A rota is operated out of hours.

Clinic (*Tmr* 15.D7) On the corner formed by the one-way system on the Akrotiri road, to the south end of the Town.

Dentist One on the Bus Square (*Tmr* 1.C4/5).

NTOG None, which is surprising for an island of this pivotal importance. *See* Ia.

OTE (*Tmr* 16.B5) On the Esplanade, Odhos Ipapantis, towards the Cathedral. Only open Monday - Friday 0730 - 2200 hrs.

PETROL (GASOLINE) There is a station on the Akrotiri Road out of the Town.

PHARMACIES *See* **Medical Care.**

PLACES OF INTEREST Who needs anything more than the position! To supplement this there are an Archaeological (*Tmr* 3.B2) and Local Museum (*Tmr* 17.B1).

The Local Museum is open Monday to Friday 0845 - 1500 hrs (closed Tuesday) and Saturday/Sunday 0930 - 1430 hrs.

The travel agents have packaged a number of Excursions including boat trips to the Volcano on Nea Kameni Island. I am assured by participants that the round-the-island coach trip is good value.

POLICE
Port (*Tmr* 18.C4) On the Ia side of the Bus Square on Odhos 25th March.

Town Police (*Tmr* 19.C3) On the right 10/20 m along the Ia road from the Bus Square.

Note there is no Tourist police office.

POST OFFICE (*Tmr* 20.B6) On the 'Taxi St' of Odhos I Decigala.

TAXIS Line up along Odhos I Decigala. The street rises quite steeply so the taxis rank from the top backwards — Irish I know but.... The phone is at the corner of the fork where I Decigala angles off and up from the approach to the Bus Square. The taxis pull up in the queue at the front and then as cabs depart from the back, take the handbrake off and roll backwards to the 'front' of the rank. Sample fares include Thira Town to Ia 350 drs and to Athinos Port 500 drs.

TELEPHONE NUMBERS & ADDRESSES
Clinic		Tel 22237
Taxis	I Decigala	Tel 22492
Town police		Tel 22649

TOILETS (*Tmr* 21.C4) There is a public toilet down to the right from the Main Road to Ia, almost opposite the Port police office (*Tmr* 18.C4).

TRAVEL AGENTS Naturally I suppose, a fair number. As always I must bow to prejudice and eulogise in respect of the firm that I consider gives the best service, **Nomikos Travel.** Prior to so doing, I should mention,

Domigos Tours (*Tmr* 14.C4/5)
Directions: On the main Bus Square.

Helpful and impersonal, but the human traffic is overwhelming.

Pelikan Travel (*Tmr* 22.C4)
Directions: On the right-hand corner of the Bus Square (**Domigos Tours** behind one).

Atlantis Tours
Directions: On the west side of the Bus Square (*Tmr* 1.C4/5).

Kameria Travel (*Tmr* 23.B4)
Directions: The first street, off to the left of Odhos I Decigala prior to the *Hotel Theoxenia*. Possibly the oldest agency but now rather 'tired'. The dynamic duo, Georgio and Gisella who used to be the driving force, have departed and set up on their own. Thus my favourite, my considered recommendation must be:-

Nomikos Travel (*Tmr* 24.D5)
Directions: Down the Main Street from the Bus Square. At the junction with the Vourvoulos/Akrotiri road turn right and the office is on the left prior to the **Olympic Airways** office. Gisella, Georgio's wife (yes they once of **Kameria**), runs this office. Delightful girl and American by birth she can prove rather prickly at first but is excellent news and an infinite source of knowledge. For more chit-chat and information, *See* Karterados, ROUTE ONE.

ROUTE ONE
To Akrotiri via Karterados & Mesaria (14 km) A gently downwards sloping road, lined with shady trees, passes a petrol station to the right, a rather untidy car breakers and repair workshop to the left. After about 1½ km alongside a bus stop and the rather surprisingly named *Restaurant Sweet Home Zofos,* there is a turning off to the left to:-

KARTERADOS (2 km from Thira Town) The poorly surfaced side road drifts by a 'dead' bus to the left, sloping and gently winding through the surrounding vine fields. On the left is the:-

Hotel Cyclades (Class D)   Tel 22948
A neat, two storey building with double rooms en suite starting at 1180 drs rising to 1475 drs (1st May - 20th September).
   Almost opposite this hotel, across the field is *Rent Rooms.* Another 100 m on and the first Village Square is reached. There, on the left is:-

Rooms to Let/Pension Prekas   Tel 22586
Directions: As above, prior to the *Taverna Glaros.*
   Doubles from 900 - 1200 drs.

Edging the other side of the road is the:-

Hotel Oyannis, H Tatakis
Double rooms range between 1200 and 1600 drs. The 'Council have thoughtfully installed an orange coloured, pedal operated, rubbish bin (against the Hotel's wall) which is planted with pot plants!
   On the far side of the *Hotel Tatakis* is:-

Nomikos Travel
The young Georgio and Gisella left another travel and tour office to do their own thing in 1983. For all travellers that can only be considered a splendid decision. Gisella runs the Thira Town office, Georgio, the Karterados operation and at the height of the season they open up in Perissa. Their helpfulness and knowledge is almost unequalled in my experience and generally no enquiry or subject, however abstruse is outside their polite attention. I hesitate to refer to Georgio as a 'Mr Fixit', for that is a descriptive term I usually reserve for rather less principled individuals, but I am unsure if there is anything he would not be able to arrange, given time. Most important, the motivation is not simply profit but a burning desire to ensure that as many holiday-makers as possible leave Santorini

satisfied customers. A tall order, but if it were left to Georgio he would give it a whirl.

The offices have lists of accommodation as well as bus and ferry-boat timetables and Georgio will make every effort to ensure clients get on the correct Ferry. The offices stay open between 0830 - 2100 hrs and the staff are themselves proficient in English and almost as supportive as the proprietors, if that is possible. They thoughtfully provide a public telephone in the corner of the office for general use.

After that fulsome panegyric back to business. . . .

On the left, the other side of the *Glaros Taverna*, another Square opens out, the circumference of which is lined by a small travel office with scooters for hire, (**Halaris Travel Tourist Office & Information**), *Taverna Coral No 2* and *Taverna Neraida*, in front of which is a monument. This last establishment hires out scooters and has Greek dancing on Wednesday nights.

I am informed that Halaris (the scooter man) started up at the same time as Nomikos opened their office. Nomikos stuck to travel and Halaris to scooter hire until he went into travel. . . . Naturally **Nomikos Travel** now operates scooter hire.

Before passing on, the *Taverna/Restaurants, Coral* and *Neraida* serve a fair meal with kalamares, fassolakia freska, Greek salad, chips and a large retsina for two costing about 750 drs.

Beyond the *Taverna Neraida*, the Main Street falls away to the left on to another large, dusty Square, the far side of which is a small General Store and, alongside the local telephone office, the:-

Hotel Gina (Class E)   Tel 22834
Doubles en suite start at 1300 drs rising to 1600 drs (July - September).

There are **Rooms** on the periphery of this Square. From the far left-hand corner a wide track makes off towards the coast (of which more under Monolithos) edging a small ravine and passing three magnificent Churches below road level, one of which sports a Feast Day on the 23rd May. Beyond the *Hotel Gina* there is a scooter outfit hidden away around to the right but this may well be the repair depot for the 'front line' boys. Around to the left, down from the edge of this third Plateia and up again the other side of a gulch is *Pension Nickle*

Back at the second Square, with *Taverna Neraida* on the left, a lane opposite leads away to the right past the:-

Kafenion Astron
Directions: As above and on the right.

For those tempted to eschew the smarter tourist tavernas this small Kafenion must seem a heaven-sent opportunity to mix in with the locals. This motivation is strengthened when one finds out that Mama prepares 'a meal of the day'. The Kafenion only sports a narrow concrete verandah and sustenance is served inside. Our one and only visit brought forth a rather cold, greasy kalamares and rice stew, a so-so Greek salad, bread and in place of retsina, a murky white 'moonshine', open retsina. Mama almost sat over us to ensure we finished off the liquid and ate all our food up, like good tourists, including the squids eyes. (Oh dear). The cost for two including coffee was a rather steep 750 drs. That wine lived with me for a few days. Perhaps it would be more correct to write that Mama brews a dish of yesterday?

Carrying on along beyond the Kafenion and the lane jinks left and then right past several 'dead' buses on the left and behind which, across some waste land, are two buidings with **Rooms**. The lane becomes an alley, passes a well stocked General Store on the right, dropping downhill and curving left to a fork. At this junction to the right proceeds back up to the Main Road whilst towards the left descends in a narrow, wall enclosed cleft. Beyond the single campanile of a simple Church, reached through a wicket gate, and on the right is the:-

Rooms Kavalari   Tel 23067

Mr and Mrs Kavalari, with the assistance of their charming daughters, are very eager to please and guests may well be greeted with a glass of very cold water and a plate of sweets.

Pleasant rooms with a balcony and shared bathroom which exhibits a few of the usual small defects but the water is hot as long as the relevant electric switch is turned on. The cost of a double room starts at 700 drs. Incidentally the family live in a home let into the hillside behind the main accommodation block. This strange feature is repeated down the lane with the pueblo-style, white painted buildings in front of and let into the rock face.

This lane is decorated (as are some of those in Ia), with flower outlines painted on the paving stones. As it descends it becomes overgrown and runs out eventually in a series of cliff cave donkey stables let into the low hillside. Before reaching the end, about 60 m beyond *Kavalari Rooms*, on the left is a path that leads to another **Rooms**.

The Village has a number of examples of the unusual barrel-vaulted roofs, rarely seen elsewhere on the Cyclades, and obviously adopted to help combat earthquake tremors. Here as elsewhere on the Island the Churches have separate campaniles (similar to those on the Ionian islands) but which are attached at the roof of the main building.

I realise I might appear to have spent a disproportionate amount of time on such a small Village but it is only 20 minutes walk uphill to Thira Town, there is a regular bus service and the villagers have, without formal permission, carved a 2½ km roadway eastwards to Takki Beach which is, in effect, the far left-hand end (*Fsw*) of Monolithos Beach. A very thought provoking alternative to the Main Town in which to make one's base.

The Main Road continues to descend to:-

MESARIA (4 km from Thira Town) The Village is up to the right, the Main Road passing through a large tree shaded crossroads on the edge of which is a sandy, low wall enclosed square or plateia. The buses stop here.

The road to the 'Chora' runs up a dry river-bed, dividing around a football ground. There are two or three lovely, old, semi-derelict mansions in the upper reaches of the meandering village and a number of the distinctive barrel roofed buildings.

Straddling the crossroads are a few shops, a mini-supermarket, a tour office, a couple of restaurants and hotels. Bread is distributed from the baker in the Upper Village. Mesaria seems some way out of Thira Town for a base, compared to say Karterados, and most of the hotels are expensive. Standing on the approach to the crossroads from the Thira Town direction, and on the right are the:-

Hotel Artemidoros (Class C)   Tel 22502

Single rooms are only available with en suite bathroom starting at 1180 drs rising to 1535 drs (July - September). Double rooms sharing the bathroom cost 1180 drs and 1535 drs while en suite range from 1445 drs to 1885 drs.

Hotel Andreas (Class E)   Tel 22501

Single rooms sharing the bathroom rise from 600 drs to 800 drs (June - September) and doubles, 800 drs to 1000 drs.

These two hotels are followed by the *Kanal Pub* and **Santorini Rent-A-Car** on the corner.

On the village leg (or right at the crossroads) is the *Restaurant Mario* and the other side of the Plateia, a small cafe which is convenient for waiting bus passengers.

Straight on (in the Akrotiri direction) and on the right are the:-

Hotel Loizos (Class C)   Tel 22359

All rooms have en suite bathrooms with singles costing 1280 drs and 1680 drs (1st July - 15th September) and doubles 1600 drs and 2040 drs respectively.

Hotel Apollon (Class D)   Tel 22906

Rooms are complete with bathrooms, single rooms rising from 1100 drs to 1280 drs (July-

August) and doubles 1230 drs to 1600 drs.

Across on the other side of the road is the office of **Kritikakis Tours** and the

Hotel Messaria (Class E)   Tel 22594
Single rooms have en suite bathrooms and are charged at 900 drs rising to 1100 drs
(June- September). Double rooms sharing the bathroom start at 1000 drs and rise to 1300
drs while en suite cost 1100 drs and 1400 drs.

In the ground floor of the *Hotel Messaria* is a **Kameria Tours** office and a mini-market
with a public telephone. There is a cafe and the *Hotel Margariti* on the corner of the turning
to:-

MONOLITHOS (7 km from Thira Town) The road down to the coast passes a turning off
to Episkopi (or Mesa) Gonias and Kamari and has to divert around a very large extension
to the Airport which now almost fills the Gonias Valley. Older maps detail the road
ploughing straight on in an easterly direction but if it did the likelihood is that travellers
would be crushed beneath the landing wheels of one of the 'big boys' that land with
regularity. The road bends round a Chapel let into a singular, large rock outcrop and down
to the right-hand edge of a black sand beach. Yes, fine, black sand forms the broad beach
enclosed by rocky moles in to which the sea rolls. The foreshore is kelpy for a metre or so
then the sea is very clear. As with other black sand beaches the surface at mid-day is
almost impossible to walk on with bare feet. Nude bathing but goodness knows what that
does to the skin.

Not much of a village but the broad backshore is rimmed by groves of Arethemusa
trees, beneath which the locals park their cars. This is backed by a dusty, packed earth
wasteground on the far edge from the sea of which are two tavernas set in amongst other
jumbled buildings and power cable posts. The far Taverna sports a distinctly rickety
shower head. Incidentally a gang of 'chaps', complete with wheelbarrow, keep the beach
clear of sea-borne debris.

To the left (*Fsw*) is a bleak factory 'ΔΝΟμΙΚΟΙ, 1922' with a single, tall, black chimney.
This is not derelict as may appear but is only wound into operation for the summer tomato
canning season. On the factory wall a painted sign proclaims 'Rooms To Let'. Striding out
beneath the roof overhang along the wall to the rear of the factory leads to dry gulch
countryside with a number of single-storey houses untidily scattered about. None of these
appear to let Rooms.

To the left (*Fsw*), beyond the rocky mole, a sandy track curves on past oil tanker mooring
buoys and some industry along a narrow shore. This is edged, on the land side, by a
porous, sandstone larva cliff, wind and sea tortured, with the occasional dwelling let into
the face of the rock. The rather kelpy sea-shore curves on in a series of small coves to a
tree planted headland after which the path becomes a bit rocky. After about 1½ km there is
a small untidy taverna where the track heads inland to the village of Karterados.

Back on the Main Road to Akrotiri from Mesaria, after about ¾ km a left-hand turning
spurs off and up towards the coastal resort of Kamari, passing by:-

EXO GONIA (5 km from Thira Town) A little Village piled up and spread over the
hillside. The road is in a thoroughly bad state hereabouts and down the steep decline
leads to:-

EPISKOPI (Mesa) GONIAS Episkopi has a rather unique 11th century Byzantine
Church, Panagia Episkopi, in which the faith has alternated over the years between
Orthodox and Catholic. The Venetians whilst masters of the Island changed the religious
aspect to Catholic only for the Turks to allow it to revert to the Orthodox. It is also here that
the Islands largest Panayieri is celebrated on 15th August.

The route from Kamari to the Mesaria - Monolithos connection is only metres away.
Turning right leads along a pleasantly Gum tree-lined avenue, similar to a Dordogne

country road, past a Wine-Factory on the right offering samplings, all the way to:-

KAMARI (10 km from Thira Town) The site of the port of 'Ancient Thira' which City topped the 370m mountain closing off the right-hand side of the bay.

The road terminates at the right-hand end of the seaside Village where a fleet of about 12 small fishing boats and caiques pull up on the beach. The development edges the broad, black sandy beach as it stretches away to the left (*Fsw*) and is based on a previously small fishing hamlet that has grown and grown and.... The concrete water front road is planted with Arethemusa trees and there are also beach-mounted rubbish bins! The Esplanade is lined with taverna/restaurants, gift shops, travel offices, discos as well as hotels, pensions and **Rooms**. Next door to the very expensive 'C' class *Hotel Kamari* is the well run **Kamari Tours** (Tel 31455), who represent 'Sun Med', operate a book exchange library and change travellers cheques and currency. Referring back to the *Hotel Kamari* when I write expensive, I mean expensive with a single room en suite starting off an 1900 drs and a double room 2400 drs. (Ouch!).

The **National Bank of Greece** opens Monday, Wednesday and Thursday between 0900 - 1300 hrs. Other seafront hotels include the 'B' class *Sunshine* and 'E' class *Nikolina*. There are scooters for hire as there are some pedaloes.

Kamari might not prove a bad spot for the ferry-boat traveller looking for some action, even if there are now a number of package-holiday hotels. But it would be best to approach say Georgio and Gisella of **Nomikos Travel** to locate inexpensive Rooms.

On a closing note aircraft swing close by on their approach to the runway, panning from left to right (*Sbo*).

ANCIENT THIRA (2 km) From the right-hand side of Kamari bay a very steep, winding hairpin ascent on a mainly flint road, ends in a roundabout on the saddle of a ridge. A mountain path sets off to the right prior to the roundabout for Pyrgos; another track crosses over the ridge down to the seaside Village of Perissa, whilst the other path climbs steeply up on the spine of the ridge towards the Ancient City passing through an entrance gate. Admission is free and the site is open Monday to Saturday between 0845 - 1500 hrs and Sundays and holidays, 0930 -1430 hrs.

From the mountain top there are magnificent views and on a clear day... it is possible to see as far as the mountain tops of Crete to the south and naturally the island of Anafi. The site which dates back to the 9th century BC was excavated in the 1890s by a German archaeologist. The remains are the usual 'Greek village reduced to ground level stones'. Apart from the more scholarly matters one of the houses bore a phallus in relief inscribed 'To my friends'! A terrace exhibits carvings of nude boys dancing and scratched graffiti, expressing admiration in verse. Do not attempt the walk from Kamari at the height of the mid-day sun if there is not a strong Cycladean wind blowing nor without wearing good, strong shoes.

Back on the Thira Town to Akrotiri Main Road, from Vothonas the road snakes along the mountain side to the turning off to the left to:-

PYRGOS (8 km from Thira Town) A very pleasant hillside Village badly knocked about by the 1956 earthquake. The surfaced road peters out on an irregular square to one side of the pretty houses and alleys that climb up the steep slopes. To the immediate left of the square is a very convenient taverna and patio up a few stone steps from the road. There is a baker, mini-market, Post Office, scooter rental, tourist shop and once a Venetian Castle, now disappeared but recorded in a quarter of Pyrgos, called Kastelli.

From Pyrgos Village the road strikes out and up to:-

Monastery Profitis Ilias (10 km from Thira Town) The 560 m mountain top is not only the province of the Monastery but television and radio masts and a radar station, but that's progress. The Monastery, built in the early 1700s, makes a worthwhile visit having a fine exhibition of icons, manuscripts, paintings and relics as well as a Museum. Visitors may visit the old cells and workshops as well as the main building. Weekday admission is between 0800 - 1300 hrs and 1500 - 1800 hrs and costs 100 drs. Magnificent views but the Monastery is on the Excursion Bus trips so you won't be alone.

It makes a lovely 2½ hour walk to keep going along the path to the seaside Villages of Kamari or Perissa.

A little further on from the Pyrgos turning, back on the Main Road, is the tortuous, steeply descending road down to Athinos Port (*See* **Arrival by Ferry**). After 1½ km or so, a left-hand thoroughfare heads off through Ag Nikitas to:-

EMPORIO (9 km from Thira Town) A large, provincial, rural, Village with many Churches, low and high. The Main Square is the bus turn-round point and a taxi rank. On the far side, the *Hotel Archea Elefsina Adenauer* (D class) has single rooms from 660 drs and a double room from 955 drs, both en suite, rising respectively to 765 drs and 1270 drs (1st July - 15th September).

To the right of Emporio there is a line of 'dead' windmills scaling the heights whilst after 6 kms the road ends at:-

PERISSA (15 km from Thira Town) The long, straight avenue to the Village passes through an unsightly scattering of new building sprawl in amongst which are many *Rooms*, a *Youth Hostel* on the right, several discos as well as a large campsite to the right, alongside the beach. Almost a 'mirror image' of Kamari with the headland and main village to the left and the black, coarse, sandy beach curving away 'for ever' to the right. But note that there the similarities end for Perissa is a Clacton to Kamari's Frinton. One writes village but as there must be 12 small hotels it is almost a town, towered over, to the left, by mountain cliff faces, topped off by radio beacons and dominated at beach level by a large Church. Beyond the Church, to the left (*Fsw*), is the Main Square on which the buses park up and our good friends **Nomikos Travel** open an office at the height of the summer. The centre of Perissa sports a cinema, 'crazy-golf' course (Ugh), mini-markets, *Restaurant Popeye Grill* (Double Ugh!) and scooter hire.

The sea edge is cleanish, pedaloes are to be found and the development peters out in a scrubby, messy sprawl. Keeping to the left (*Fsw*) and starting out on the rough, wide track towards Ancient Thira, leads to a number of houses with *Rooms* and the *Hotels Marianna* and *Artemis*, all in unlovely surroundings.

A friend let me into the secret of one out-of-the way spot that helps to alleviate Perissa's shortcomings. About ¾ km on up the road back to Emporio and there is a track across the fields to the left just before a Church on the right. This leads, after a kilometre or two, to the *Taverna* and *Hotel Georgios*. Highly recommended and has a seawater pool.

Back on the Main Road at Ag Nikitas, a surfaced lane to the left cuts off a larger corner, passing through gently undulating agricultural countryside planted with the low vines typical of the Island with the occasional small Chapel dotted about. Just after the Main Road is rejoined there is an isolated pension to the left, absolutely in the middle of nowhere.

AKROTIRI (14 km from Thira Town) An old Village built round and up a rocky spur around the edge of which more modern development is spreading along the road. There are several houses with *Rooms*, a mini-market, doctor, and the *Hotel Paradise*.

A further kilometre on the left is the site of the:-

Akrotiri Excavations My general lack of enthusiasm for piles of archaeological this or that may have percolated through to readers of the **Candid Guides**. But here and there a particular site captures my obviously pedestrian imagination and make no mistake about it, Akrotiri is an emperor of archaeological remains, nay a God. Enough to say that if a visitor came blindfolded to Santorini and only saw these remains, then that would be enough.

Another prejudice involves Guides (the human type) or more correctly evading paying for a Guide. I prefer to enjoy my own pottering about with one of the coloured brochures, usually imprecisely translated into English, and customarily available at the admission point. Well forget it, and stump up and hope you are lucky enough to join a group with young, bespectacled Nena as your mentor.

The discovery of this Ancient Town provided undeniable proof of the Island's close connection with Crete and, as with Pompeii, the larvae and ash preserved many buildings, even multi-storey ones, in their originally constructed shape. Furthermore many of the door and window frames, fireplaces, even lavatory systems were preserved in place. Of course the most dramatic finds were the frescoes and murals. Worryingly for the inhabitants of Santorini, Athens has got its grasping hands on these as well as much of the best pottery and jars keeping them safe supposedly until Santorini gets its own new Museum! Other islands have heard that story. The Greek Father of the Akrotiri excavations, Professor Marinatos who commenced his dig as recently as 1967, must be spinning his grave.

It would appear that the original inhabitants had sufficient warning of the impending disaster to remove nearly all their personal items and almost every living thing because to date none have been found — an archaeological 'Marie Celeste'. Chillingly, the Guide Books written before or at the time of the discovery of this site, refer to the locals vivid description of ghosts observed in the area over the years.

The site is open daily 0800 - 1445 hrs and on Sundays between 0930 - 1430 hrs. Admission costs 150 drs. A last word of advice is to arrive early as the site is covered by Dexion supported, semi-translucent roofing beneath which, by midday, it gets very hot.

Down the slope from the excavations and the road runs out on a backshore of large black boulders and pebbles and set in a wide bay. Besides the shore is the:-

Hotel Akrotiri (Class C)   Tel 31295

Extremely expensive with en suite rates for a single room of 1700 drs and a double room, 2200 drs.

From the 'Dig' it is possible to take the 500 m dirt road to the:-

Red Beach Taverna

This is run by Loule, a friendly islander who spent 20 years as a steelworker in Indiana, U.S.A.

A path leads off by a small Chapel up a rocky hill to another cove with, on the far side, (I am reliably advised), a splendid and 'accommodating' cave.

ROUTE TWO

To Ia (10km) and back to Thira Town via Vourvoulos The Main Road to

Ia climbs quite steeply from the Thira Town Bus Square (*Tmr* 1.C4/5) through Firostephani, now a suburb of Thira Town, on to:-

IMEROVIGLI (Merovigli) (1 km from Thira Town) To one side of the Main Road a very steep, short, country lane climbs to this unexceptional, dusty but pleasant village. A taverna, mini-market, scooter hire and the large E class *Hotel Katerina* wherein a single room sharing a bathroom costs 1000 drs and a double room 1510 drs for the months of July to September. The Church at the entrance to the Village is a convent (Irish, yes. . .).

It is a pity that the poorly surfaced road to Ia is, on the west, caldera side, hemmed in by the mountain range which blanks off the incredible view. This is compensated for, to some extent, by the dramatic drop to the flat, fertile plain way below to the right.

There is a way of enjoying the western views and scenery which is to make the 2½ hour

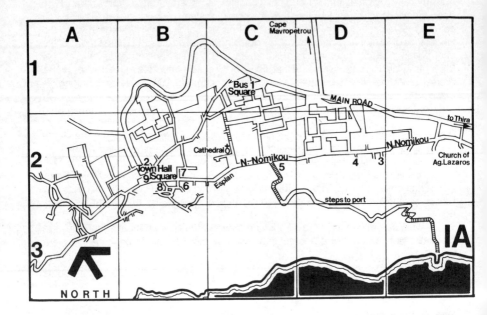

KEY

1	Bus Square	C1
2	Town Hall Square	B2
3	Hotel Fregada	D2
4	Hotel Anemones	D2
5	Rooms – Lauda	C2
6	Post Office	B2
7	Maritime Museum	B2
8	N.T.O.G.	B2
9	Clinic	B2

Illustration 28

walk on the path from Imerovigli that edges the precipitous drop. To the left of Imerovigli (facing north), on a promontory below the Village, was the Venetian Island Capital of Tourlos and a Castle.

The advent of Ia is signalled by, to the right, the little hamlet of:-

FOINIKIA (9 km from Thira Town) Immediately beyond the Foinikia turning a signpost indicates the presence of a *Youth Hostel* to the right, after which, on the left, a blue sign with white lettering advertises 'Traditional Houses'. A short scramble up a steep country path leads to a sensational, cliff-hanging clustering of dazzlingly white apartments converted from old dwellings. Admittedly the position and view is magnificent. Ia is draped over the dark brown streaked, sheer drop to the right, Thirasia Island is across the incredibly deep blue bay and, to the left, the west coast of Santorini curves away in a series of rocky inlets. Magnificent it may be, but so it should be at 4200 drs per night for a double bed apartment.

IA (Oia) (10 km from Thira Town) (Illustration 28). The Village evinces a slow, leisurely pace but is on the Day-Trip Excursion circuit leaving those remaining here in a similar situation to those staying on small offshore islands where trip-boats flood and ebb every day, leaving the place almost deserted overnight.

The pedestrian-only Esplanade road, N. Nomikou edges the precipice of this cliff-hanging Village while the Main Road is a bypass that curves around to the right past the Bus Square (*Tmr* 1.C1) ending up on the Town Hall Plateia (*Tmr* 2.B2). The diversion of the two roads happens alongside the large, cobalt blue domed Church of Ag Lazaros. Incidentally, one item Ia is not short of is Churches and at the last count there were some 40 crammed into the Village. An arrowed sign on the wall of the Church points along the Esplanade Odhos N Nomikou, to the **National Bank of Greece** 'Tues - Friday 0900 - 1300 hrs'. The first 100 m or so of the Esplanade is bland, rather like an Eastbourne suburb(!), after which the surrounds become 'standard', that is extremely picturesque which definition does not allow for the startling drop to the left. Ia suffered far more than Thira in the 1956 earthquake, resulting in a number of ruined buildings with wired off roof terraces still drunkenly clinging to the cliff-face terraces.

A sign to the left indicates the whereabouts of the Baker followed by:

Rooms For Rent Delfini
Splendidly situated and cliff-hanging with a nice terrace. The young proprietor speaks English. A double room en suite costs 1150 drs.

Hotel Fregada (*Tmr* 3.D2) (Class D)   Tel 71221
Directions: 50 m further on, almost opposite a souvenir shop and alongside the *Hotel/ Cafe-Bar Marinos.*

A double room is expensive starting at 1500 drs, sharing or with en suite bathroom, and rising to 1800 drs (July - September).

A few paces further on is the:-

Hotel Anemones (*Tmr* 4.D2) (Class E)   Tel 71220
A single sharing the bathroom, starts at 600 drs, rising to 780 drs (July - September), whilst a double room sharing starts at 850 drs, rising to 1120 drs. En suite prices are 1100 drs and 1440 drs respectively.

A taxi rank is signposted off to the right (fare to Thira Town about 350 drs, the Airport 500 drs) and there is a general store on the left. From hereabouts the tavernas and restaurants straddle the road in earnest.

A green sign pointing down steps to the left points a way to:-

Christo Foros Houses (Rooms For Rent Lauda) (*Tmr* 5.C2) (Class B)   Tel 71204
Actually a pension not a hotel. Rather spartan with single rooms sharing the bathroom at a cost of 850 drs, a double room sharing for 1120 drs and en suite for 1440 drs.

Twenty metres beyond *Pension Lauda* and the street is straddled by **Nikos/Zorbas** disco/cocktail bar and video music joints, followed by a couple of gift shops, opposite which are more steps leading to *Pension Lauda.* On the right is the Panagia Platsani Cathedral (*Tmr* C2) behind which steps lead to the Bus Square (*Tmr* 1.C1).

Beyond the Cathedral, on the right, is the folksy:-

Karvounis Tour Office   Tel 71209/71205
Book-exchange and trips to the Island of Thirasia.

As elsewhere on Santorini it is a plus point to have inside seating and many restaurants advertise seats in the building so clients can get out of the howling wind.

Continuing on to the left is the:-

Post Office (*Tmr* 6.B2)
Complete with two telephone booths.

Thirty metres further on, opposite the *Pub Sphinx,* to the right is the small:-

Maritime Museum (*Tmr* 7.B2)
Open daily 1100 - 1200 hrs and 1630 - 1730 hrs.

Beyond the Museum, on the left, up a short lane is a:-

NTOG Office (*Tmr* 8.B2) Tel 71234. Located in a plain, bare wooden floored room an efficient lady dispenses information, somewhat grudgingly. The lists available include interesting details of *Traditional Settlements* available in Ia. These vary from a double bed studio with bathroom, to a 9 bed apartment complete with a fully equipped kitchen. For those contemplating a week in a charming location the following will give an idea of prices. Per night charges for a 2 bed studio are 1000 drs, a 2 bed/flat and kitchen costing 2100 drs, while a 4 bed 'pad' is 2050 drs, 6 beds from 3600 drs and 9 beds 5150 drs. For further details of this interesting scheme write to **EOT, Paradosiakos Oikismos, Ois, Santorini Island, Greece.**

Beyond the **NTOG** office there are a few gift shops on the left followed by the **National Bank of Greece Exchange Office** across an arch from the Clinic (*Tmr* 9.B2), both on the right. A short stride or two along an alley on this side of the Esplanade leads to the Town Hall Square (*Tmr* 2.B2).

To the right is an old fashioned store followed by:-

Trident Travel A tiny, provincial office advertising, on signboards, tickets to almost everywhere. The owner is a larger than life 'Fix-it'.

An intriguing feature of Ia is that the various shops, similar to Nisiros in the Dodecanese, display painted signs depicting the purveyors trade.

Hereabouts the Main Street becomes a lane and a left fork tumbles down to the remains of the Castle and what is left of the Old Town. A misleading and long defunct sign still points to an extinct NTOG office on the Castle lane.

There are smelly public lavatories at each end of the Town and a 'squatty' on the edge of the dusty Bus Square (*Tmr* 1.C1). As in Karterados Village many of the streets are painted with whitewashed flower outlines.

From the vicinity of the Bus Square a surfaced track makes off in a northerly direction to curve round the eastern coastline which makes a most interesting alternative route back to Thira Town.

Once adjacent to Cape Mavropetrou the road as far as Cape Kouloumbo becomes a track. This undulates through scrub and Gorse moorland backed by terraced landscapes with low volcanic cliffs bordering a coarse, sandy beach and sea-shore. The clean beaches which are almost deserted, only accommodating the occasionally isolated sun worshipper here and there, narrow down, become rather kelpy with black boulders and shingle, fringed by low sandstone cliffs.

From Cape Kouloumbo the only sign of life is an infrequent Chapel or house set in undulating countryside but the track as far as the hamlet of Pori can be very dangerous in places for two-wheeled powered vehicles, so beware. The surface is often thick, shifting sand which makes for spills and accidents.

PORI (5 km from Thira Town) The enterprise exhibited in originally opening *Panaghia Rooms for Rent, Restaurant Low Prices*, seems to have been wasted. The establishment may open up at the height of the summer but cannot otherwise be relied on as a 'way-station'.

VOURVOULOS (2 km from Thira Town) A truly agricultural settlement from which a wide path makes down to the sea, an inland track forks to the right back to Thira Town, via Kontochori, whilst the left track staggers off to the hamlet of:-

KATIKIES (1 km from Thira Town) Some Island Maps propose all sorts or roads here and there in this area with connections to the Karterados coast roadway but ignore them. There is a track to the sea, signposted 'Beach', but actuality is only a small mole and sheltern with crude doors cut into the cliff-face by fishermen.

From Katikies the road rejoins the Vourvoulos route to the outskirts of Thira Town.

EXCURSION TO THIRASIA ISLAND

Ia is the best point of departure for an Excursion boat to Manolas Port, Thirasia Island. The trip takes about ½ hr and the Port Village is, as are the western towns of its bigger brother, reached by mounting 300 odd steps up a cliff face.

It is a pity more tourists do not stay overnight on Thirasia but should a visitor decide to stop-over first ask for Rooms at one of the two dockside tavernas. The Town is a jumble of starkly white small cubes, haphazardly muddled together. For a better beach than the pebbles of the harbour it is necessary to cross the Island by the reasonable track to the inland Villages of either Agrilia or Potamos and then strike out to the coast.

EXCURSION TO ANAFI ISLAND (Anaphi, Anaphe)

FIRST IMPRESSIONS Golly gosh — am I getting off here. Barren.

RELIGIOUS HOLIDAYS & FESTIVALS include: 15th August — Festival, Panagia Kalamiotissa Monastery.

VITAL STATISTICS Approximately circular in shape and 28 sq km in area with about 300 inhabitants.

HISTORY & MYTHOLOGY Fable has it that the island emerged from the sea at the command of Apollo in order to shelter Jason and the Argonauts who were beset by a storm. Quite possibly this legend relates to the Santorini 'big bang'. The Gods, Apollo and Artemis were worshipped here and their Temples were located close by an original, Ancient Town.

One of the Dukes of Naxos had his brother fortify the island with a Castle. The Russians are supposed to have removed a number of archaeological finds to their museums during their short period of stewardship.

GENERAL Anafi really would be an 'ideal get-away-from-it-all' for travellers if it were not for the effect of adverse weather on the schedules of the few Ferries that make the trip. Added to this it would appear that only the ferry-boat operators really requiring the subsidy make this out-of-the-way trip. For instance in 1985 the two craft calling on a regular basis were my old 'favourites', the Ferries '**Miaoulis**' and '**Kyklades**'. The sea time from Santorini is about 1 hour. The only other caveats must be the general water shortage and paucity of fresh vegetables on occasions.

The Island is in effect a ring of rock with the Port Village, Ag Nicholas (or Skala) on the south coast. Apart from the small harbour quay there are several tavernas, a couple of shops and a grouping of private homes.

The Chora is above the Port and reached up a steep, very steep path. Oddly enough there are more tavernas and kafenion in the Port. Combined with the Santorini habit of sitting inside this gives an initial impression of desertion and unfriendliness, soon dispelled once a visitor has made his number. The Chora has a baker and Post Office.

There are a number of sandy beaches around to the east of the south coast, one quite close, another some 5 kms distant.

The Monastery of Panaghia Kalamiotissa, site of early Temples and a Venetian Castle, is about an 1 ½ hr walk to the south-east of the Chora.

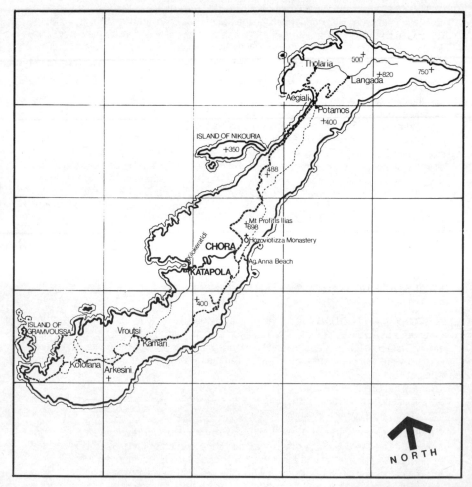

AMORGOS

Illustration 29

18 Amorgos (& Donoussa, Koufonissi, Shinoussa, Iraklia) Cyclades Islands — Eastern chain

*****

FIRST IMPRESSIONS
Splendid sea cliff vistas; parched mountainous countryside; sea-mine casings; the flies bite.

SPECIALITIES
None.

RELIGIOUS HOLIDAYS & FESTIVALS
include: 15th August — Festival, Panagia Ag Epanochori.

VITAL STATISTICS
Tel prefix 0285. The elongated Island lies obliquely in the Aegean, north-east to south-west, and is approximately 29 km in length and up to 11 km in width with an area of 177 sq km. The population numbers about 1,500.

HISTORY
It seems unlikely now but the island in days of antiquity sported three City States, 'Minoa' on a hill to the south of and close by Katapola Port; 'Arkesini' to the north of the modern day hamlet of the same name and 'Aegiali' situated where today is the Port of Aegiali. Excavations at Aegiali in 1888 revealed a Gymnasium, Stadium and a Temple dedicated to Apollo, not a lot of which is now discernible.

The Romans used the Island for the incarceration of exiles which rather set the tone for the future. The usual bunch of savage marauders mauled the island and inhabitants over the years. The Dukes of Naxos took Amorgos under his wing in 1209 and a Castle was built alongside the Chora. During the Turkish occupation the Island women are supposed to have contributed significantly to the wealth of Amorgos by dint of their embroidery output, the fame of which spread throughout Europe.

GENERAL
The most easterly of the islands accepted by the authorities as part of the Cyclades grouping although it will have been noted that I consider Astipalaia should be included in Cyclades islands (*See* **Chapter 19**). The far-flung position of Amorgos and the lack of daily ferry-boat connections results in the Island receiving less visitors than its more popular and accessible western neighbours.

The Government is making efforts to encourage tourists by offering a certain amount of free travel prior to the 1st June and after the end of September. Despite these official blandishments, the residents, certainly of Katapola, seem unable to make up their mind if they really want to join in the Western European holiday 'dream-machine' and tend to present a diffident countenance to visitors. This is best exemplified by their reluctance to advertise accommodation at all, let alone the usual rash of billboards and scrawlings. Additionally prospective landlords can be very selective.

The Island is rugged and the two major coastal settlements, (the southern main Port of Katapola and the northern Port of Aegiali), are only linked by a rough road, wrested from the unyielding terrain. The sole bus will not trespass beyond the scheduled route from

Katapola Port to the Chora. Nor will the lone taxi venture forth, so the choice rests between a 4-5 hour walk or the connecting Ferry-boats that call at both Ports.

As Katapola Port is reserved and quiet (to the point that the arrival of a bus is an event), so Aegiali Port is rather more thrusting. Aegiali not only boasts beaches (which Katapola does not), but more forthcoming accommodation and possibly the cheapest taverna and restaurant food in the Cyclades. Both Ports offer, either side of the busiest summer months, that peace, calm and tranquillity that must have been the mark of most Greek islands before the tourist boom really took off.

KATAPOLA: main port (Illustration 30)

I have read the occasional Guide Book that refers to the towering cliffs edging the Bay of Katapola — well there must have been some rapid erosion because this Port lies in an indented 'U' shaped Bay edged by comparatively soft, gentle, rolling hillsides. The location is rather evocative of Vathi Port, Ithaca.

Really the Port Town is two, no three village/hamlets with Katapola the Ferry-boat Port to the right of the bay (*Sbo*); Rachidi, the rather drab central settlement set back from the bottom of the bay and dominated by a twin tower Church and Xilokeratidi, a small fishing boat hamlet to the left of the bay, with some lovely, aged, flower bestrewn buildings and remnants of an Old Quarter.

It is difficult to describe, and as difficult to understand, why Katapola Port 'feels low' as if a visitor is stepping down or docking at a development where height has been diminished. I think the effect comes about at those ports where the houses do not climb the hillside and or they are not hemmed in by mountains. Over to you reader.

An unusual architectural feature, is the large number of doors sporting Roman style door lintels or, more correctly, pediments.

ARRIVAL BY FERRY

Ferry-boats pull up at the quay (*Tmr* 1.A/B3), a pace or two prior to the Port Main Square (*Tmr* 2.B4). It is a problem that Amorgos is more often than not a late night stop for those inter-island ferries that include the Island in their schedules. Combine this with the 'reluctance' of Room owners to proclaim themselves and it may well be, if the boat's arrival is very late at night, that the convenient park benches close by the tree dominating the Main Square will prove a convenient place to rest one's head. Late night visitors should ensure they don't fall into the large goldfish pond between the (Main Square) tree and the 'dead' Periptero.

The residents wake early and go to bed early, most tavernas are shut by 2300 hrs and siesta is rigidly kept with a total shut-down from 1300 - 1700 hrs.

The local fishermen communicate across the wide bay with blasts on a conch shell which can sound very like a Ferry-boat's hooter.

THE ACCOMMODATION & EATING OUT

The Accommodation There is a Hotel (*Tmr* 3.C4) in the Port, along the quay on the way round the bay, but it seems not to have a name. A double room, if anybody can be bothered to attend to prospective clients, costs from 1200 drs.

The few streets and the quay road radiate off the Main Square (*Tmr* 2.B4), from the right-hand corner (*Sbo*) off which a narrow lane leads past the Port Police office (*Tmr* 4.B4). Where the lane bends sharp right there is, on the left:-

Rooms Voula Beach (*Tmr* 5.B4)
Directions: As above, next door to a large butchers shop and up a few broad steps.
A very neat set-up with a row of cabins.

Pension Tassia (*Tmr* 6.A4)
Directions: Proceed on up the steps, around to the right, then left and on the left, up against the hillside.

George Simidalas (*Tmr* 7.A/B4)   Tel. 71291
Directions: Follow the lane round a short distance and on the right, opposite the Church.

A quiet, family man, George served in the Merchant Navy and speaks some English. The large, ground floor bedrooms share a bathroom and the rates include a hot shower. They are a bit mean with the lavatory paper which runs out by mid-afternoon but the bathroom is kept spotlessly clean.

George whose pleasure is to fish from his little benzina, is selective and will not take the 'great unwashed'. Despite this the roof terrace has a bamboo-shaded area where mattresses can be laid out to cope with the height-of-season influx. Additionally, there is a washing line, access being by a flight of steps to one side of the house. A double room costs 800 drs mid season.

Standing on the Main Square (*Sbo*) and across a 'look-alike' for a builders yard and a building displays the sign:-

Pension Minos (*Tmr* 8.D4) No 75
Directions: To get to the establishment it is necessary to walk along the lane, one back and parallel to the quay road, take the first alley to the right, which breaks into steps, and then the first right again. The wrought iron gate to No 75 is let into a stone arch and gives access to a lovely garden.

The owner speaks no English and is rather 'laid back' — (okay, is not too bothered). A double room mid season costs 1000 drs, sharing the bathroom.

Pension Amorgos (*Tmr* 9.B4)   Tel 71214
Directions: Left along the quay road from the Main Square (*Sbo*), and on the right, behind the Baker.

Quite acceptable with a double room sharing the bathroom costing 1000 drs.

Around the bottom of the bay, across a little bridge and on the right is a large area of waste ground. A rough track winds off to the right cutting off the corner to Rachidi, (the 'middle' village) and ends up opposite:-

Rooms (*Tmr* 10.D3)
Directions: As above or turn right off the Esplanade alongside the Public Gardens (*Tmr* 11.C3) and keep right along the track. A young Scottish couple recommended these 'digs' in which use of a kitchen is included. A double room sharing the bathroom can cost as little as 500 drs but is more usually 700 drs, mid season.

The Esplanade along the bottom of the bay skirts the tree-lined, narrow, grey, scrubbly beach on the left and the waste ground to the right. On the right, alongside the Public Gardens and to one side of a Municipal building, is:-

Rooms (*Tmr* 12.C3)
Directions: As above, over the Electric Company office. The front garden is full of bamboos which almost eclipse two statues.

A large first floor balcony but rather basic accommodation.

Towards the far side of the bottom of the bay, prior to a second bridge, and a road advances along to the heart of the 'middle' village which is dominated by a large Church. The road 'trifurcates' (if there is no such word to describe dividing into three, there should be). The right-hand track leads off to already described **Rooms** (*Tmr* 10.D3) whilst straight on up a comparatively broad street rises to:-

Rooms (*Tmr* 13.D3)
Directions: As above, on the left, behind a black wall and well maintained garden.

Back on the Esplanade, proceeding along the bottom of the bay, towards the far Village of Xilokeratidi and, on the right, a private road crosses some tree-edged farmland to the:-

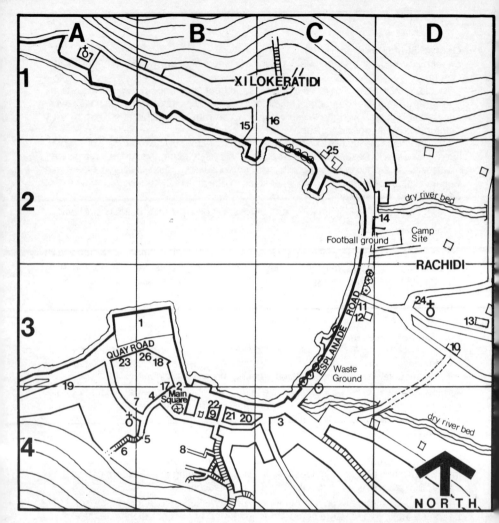

KATAPOLA

KEY

1 Ferry-boat Quay — A/B3
2 Main Square — B4
3 Hotel — C4
4 Port Police — B4
5 Rooms –
  Voula Beach — B4
6 Pension Tassia — A4
7 George Simidalas — A/B4
8 Pension Minos — B4
9 Pension Amorgos — B4
10 Rooms — D3

11 Public Gardens — C3
12 Rooms — C3
13 Rooms — D3
14 Rooms — D2
15 Pension — B1
16 Pension — C1
17 Taverna
  To Akroyiali — B3/4
18 Taverna
  To Mourayo — B3
19 Cafe-Pub –
  Diogenis — A3/4

20 Ferry-boat Ticket
  Office — B4
21 General Store — B4
22 Baker — B4
23 Dairy & Grocers
  Shop — A3
24 General Store — D3
25 General Store — C2
26 Chemists — B3

Illustration 30

246

Camp Site
Complete with a shower/toilet block facility with a site costing 100 drs per head.

Prior to the Esplanade turning the far corner of the bay, and beyond the Campsite track, the beach is (still) narrow, grey, scrubbly and pebbly but enlivened by a resident family of ducks. To the right is a stone littered football ground and a tree or two to the side of the (dead?) **Navy Bar Disco Pub**, behind which is the skeleton of a large building, beyond which is:-

Rooms (*Tmr* 14.D2)
Directions: As above.

A very pleasant choice with rooms and cabins 'out the back'. A double room with en suite bathroom for 700 drs a night. Can't be bad.

The bay and quay road now turns abruptly left and, beyond the narrow, stony, scrubbly foreshore, on which a number of local boats are pulled up, breaks into an irregular square, on either side of which are the:-

Pensions Psaki & Prekag (*Tmr* 15.B1 & 16.C1)
Directions: As above.

A double room in this pleasant locality, sharing a bathroom, costs 700 drs mid-season.

The Eating Out Despite being a 'Flotilla Port' the comparatively small number of yachts that visit do not upset the balance as they so often do elsewhere in the Aegean. A number of excellent tavernas. Possibly the most convenient is:-

To Akroyiali (*Tmr* 17.B3/4)
Directions: On the edge of the Main Square.

In the main, the wife runs the Taverna whilst her husband runs a small fishing boat. A small, nervously busy, balding man, he is usually to be seen early in the morning wearing wet weather gear, with his crew on the quay edge opposite the Taverna, sorting out the fish from the nets. They are surrounded by a semi-circle of stray cats, crouched at a respectful distance, who dash in and out to grab the wasted bits and bobs thrown in their direction. The wife starts early to prepare much of the food served up during the day, baking some in large stainless steel lined units half boxed in beneath the verandah. Goodies include loukoumades (50 drs), and probably the best cheese pies I have ever tasted (50 drs), but for the life of me, I cannot understand why they consistently serve up stale bread.

After early afternoon, much that has been on offer disappears and or gets 'tired'. Offerings range from a traditional breakfast of yoghurt, honey, loukoumades and coffee as well as a plate of eggs and bacon, popularised by the flotilla yachts. A lunch of 2 small omelettes, (70 drs, yes small but 70 drs), a plate of green beans (90 drs), a bottle of beer (60 drs), and (stale) bread (10 drs), all for 230 drs. Two helpings of kalamares, a plate of giant beans, a Greek salad, a plate of chips, a bottle of retsina, a bread for two cost 628 drs. More traditional offerings include moussaka 130 drs and stuffed tomatoes 90 drs.

A good all round base.

Further along the quay away from the Square (in the direction of the open sea) and opposite the Ferry-boat quay (*Tmr* 1.A/B3) is:-

To Mourayo (*Tmr* 18.B3)
Directions: As above.

The Taverna appears rather shabby and the patron is usually stern faced, but I have seen him smile when lobster goes on the menu. In the evening this establishment is very popular with the flotilla crews, especially when the aforementioned lobster is available — now you realise why the proprietor smiles. The attendance is not surprising as he only charges 600 drs, while other meals are similarly priced to the *Akroyiali Taverna*. His drinks are reasonable with a beer 60 drs, a Metaxa 30 drs and a bottle of Fanta 40 drs. The establishment's other and very real claim to fame is that it is the possessor of Katapola's sole public telephone that can be used for International calls. Added to this the owner only charges 3 drs per unit, not a great deal more than the OTE fees. But I should add that Amorgos is famed for the unreliability of its telephone service.

Cafe Pub Diogenis (*Tmr* 19.A3/4)
Directions: At the far, sea-end of the quay road, beyond and almost chair by table with the *Minoa Restaurant.*

I hope for visitors in future years that the young chef, with haltingly good English, and in partnership as late as 1985, stays on. The standard of food and service are almost second to none. Particularly noteworthy are the green beans (100 drs) served hot or cold (but he prefers to dish them up cold) and the Greek salad (130 drs) which includes olives, onions, peppers and quartered boiled eggs. Additionally the 'dish of the day' are remarkably good in quality and value. I don't say that George on Syros will have to watch his laurels but .... Certainly an establishment where a client can order meat balls. A very good meal, leisurely served course by course costs about 800 drs. Oh yes, he also serves up reasonably priced fish with a mackerel type dish for 200 drs.

Before closing off this section the Bar, to the front and one side of which is the Ferry-boat ticket office (*Tmr* 20.B4), is well worth patronising being a traditional turn-of-the-century Greek 'watering-hole'.

THE A TO Z OF USEFUL INFORMATION

BANKS Yes, well there's the rub. The Island is rather short of banks, in fact there are none. Change facilities are operated by the rude, surly man in the General Store (*Tmr* 21.B4) opposite the charter yacht portion of the quay (who I wouldn't use on principle) and the polite gentleman (gentleman in the old sense of the word) who operates the Ferry-boat ticket-hatch and changes money, that is foreign notes only. Note the Chora has a Bank but it does not even change travellers cheques let along Eurocheques.

BEACHES The bottom of the bay between Katapola and Xilokeratidi has two narrow strips of dirty, grey coarse sand and pebble beach but ....

On the Katapola side, walk to the open sea end of the quay road beyond the *Cafe Pub Diogenes* and take the track behind the last of the houses to a very narrow, scrubbly sliver of beach in front of a walled garden. Unfortunately the sea bottom pebbles are slimy and weedy, there are sea-urchins and some tar. Further along the track there is a statue facing into the bay followed by a large Chapel, with a tripod-hung bell, after which there are two very tiny thumb-nail sized beaches.

On the Xilokeratidi side it is necessary to take the track uphill past the cemetery and the small statue set on a flat rock in the sea, on to a low headland. This juts into the sea and is surmounted by a Chapel with a few small coves on the near side. The first is a thin strip, with donkey droppings and some tar, and the next, a small cove with flat rocks beneath the Chapel. To get down to them keep to the track until a path bends down a small valley to the foreshore. The quicker route is to take the angled zig-zag track to the left, beside the fallen signboard down to the first narrow foreshore.

BREAD SHOPS (*Tmr* 22.B4) Left along the quay from the Main Square (*Sbo*), past *To Kamari Taverna* and on the far side of the narrow Square in which is mounted a very large, incongruous tower of a water fountain. The Baker, unusually, opens on Sunday mornings as well as Mondays to Saturdays.

BUSES Apart from 'shanks pony' and a 'may-be' taxi, the small, old Dodge bus is the only transport available. The sole route is the approximate 6 km main road that the bus puffs and strains up to the Chora. The timetable is impossible to work out but the bus ties in with Ferry-boat arrivals until the late evening. Departures from the Port would appear to include

0945/1000, 1330/1345, 1835 and 1935 hrs. The fare is 40 drs collected at the end of the journey.

CHEMISTS & PHARMACIES *See* **Medical Care.**

COMMERCIAL SHOPPING AREA In the narrow alley off the Main Square, alongside *To Akroyiali Taverna*, is a Mini-Market on the right and further along, on the opposite side, a large Butchers shop. Mark you on may last visit I saw him unload a delivery of frozen(!) boxes of chicken and meat labelled Hungary, (the country, not a state of physical deprivation).

There is a Dairy and Grocer's Shop (*Tmr* 23.A3) opposite the Ferry-boat quay and, on the Main Square is a thoroughly 'dead' Periptero. As already indicated the owner of the General Store (*Tmr* 21.B4) is surly and uncouth.

The 'middle' Village also has a General Store (*Tmr* 24.D3) and there is a little Grocer's shop, (entrance to the rear of the building) (*Tmr* 25.C2) in Xilokeratidl.

FERRY-BOATS The classy **CF Naxos** connects from Piraeus as does the **CF Nireus**. The Ferry **Miaoulis** clatters in to port but this craft almost requires a chapter on its own and some details are recorded in **Chapter 3**.

The only other Ferry-boat is a local affair, the **FB Marianna**, and Amorgos is its home port. I have chosen to discourse upon this 'unique' vessel in the Naxos island chapter. The Marianna journey time from Naxos to Amorgos (Aegiali Port) takes about 7 hours and don't forget that the first port of call is Aegiali NOT Katapola Port. Perhaps this would be the point at which to discuss the matter of Port identification. A number of visitors on their first visit can disembark at the wrong place as night-time recognition is difficult. A general rule when approaching from the west is that Aegiali is the first port of call while from the east, it is Katapola. Secondary pointers are that Aegiali's quay is an enormous finger pier, while at Katapola the quay is a small affair, and the Ferry-boats lie alongside, dominating the waterfront quite close to the Port's Main Square. One last word is to remind travellers proceeding along the coast north of Aegiali not to miss the wonderfully dramatic and mountainous coastline, which the Ferry-boats hug.

Ferry-boat timetables
Unless stated otherwise Ferries call at both Ports.

Day	Departure time	Ferry-boat	Ports/Islands of Call
Monday	0630 hrs	Marianna	Aegiali (Amorgos), Donoussa, Koufonissi, Shinoussa, Iraklia, Naxos.
Tuesday	0600 hrs	Miaoulis	Aegiali (Amorgos), Astipalaia, Nisiros, Tilos, Simi, Rhodes.
Wednesday	0400 hrs	Nireus	Aegiali (Amorgos), Astipalaia, Kalimnos, Kos, Nisiros, Tilos, Simi, Rhodes, Crete.
Thursday	0330 hrs	Miaoulis	Paros, Piraeus (M).
	0630 hrs	Marianna	Aegiali (Amorgos), Donoussa, Koufonissi, Shinoussa, Iraklia, Naxos.
Friday	0530 hrs	Naxos*	Koufonissi, Shinoussa, Iraklia, Naxos, Paros, Syros, Piraeus (M).
	2100 hrs	Nireus	Paros, Piraeus (M).
Sunday	0800 hrs	Nireus	Aegiali (Amorgos), Astipalaia.
	1600 hrs	Nireus	Donoussa, Koufonissi, Shinoussa, Iraklia, Naxos, Paros, Syros, Piraeus (M).

*Does not call at Aegiali.

Note that the long distance Ferry **Nireus** and the local boat **Marianna** can be up to 5 hours late.

FERRY-BOAT TICKET OFFICES (*Tmr* 20.B4) The gentleman who runs this pokey little hut is friendly and kindly. The office is positioned to the left of the covered verandah in front of a magnificently rustic Bar. Open every day including Saturday and Sunday but closes for the 1300 - 1700 hr siesta.

MEDICAL CARE
Chemist (*Tmr* 26.B3) There is one close by the *To Mourayo Taverna* on the quay.
Clinic *See* **the Chora.**

OPENING HOURS Strictly traditional.

OTE *See To Mourayo Taverna,* **The Eating Out.**

PLACES OF INTEREST *See* **Introduction.**

POLICE
Port (*Tmr* 4.B4) In the narrow lane off the Main Square.
Town They are there, somewhere.

POST OFFICE *See* the **Chora**, but there is a post box on the wall of the Main Square, alongside *To Akroyiali Taverna.*

TAXIS The taxi rolls up to and down from the Chora but is difficult to locate.

THE CHORA (Amorgos): capital

The choice of whether to stay in Katapola or the Chora is very much a personal decision. Certainly the Chora is closer to the Greek ethos but on the other hand is rather cut off from beaches.

At the journeys end at the small irregular Square where the bus parks up, there is, on the left, a Clinic and an OTE office in which there are two booths. The OTE is open Monday - Friday between 0730 - 1510 hrs and there are *Rooms* over the office. The Main Street wanders through the Village in which there are several *Rooms*, a taverna, two general shops, a grocers, a baker, a bank (which does not change any money) on a stepped Square and diagonally across from which is a Post Office. This office may well exchange travellers cheques in future years as the practice spreads throughout Greece. Still proceeding eastwards (towards the rising sun in the early morning) and the street crosses the rather strange area of 'The Wells', a grouping of water holes where 'Camping is Forbidden'. Between 'The Wells' and the telephone dish mast is a large Kafenion. *Rooms* in the village are simple and cost about 600 drs for a double bed with the use of a shower.

The Village is dominated by the indistinct remains of the Castle. This was built on top of the curious rock outcrop (similar to the Chora of Ios), and is overlooked by a hilltop row of windmills in various states of decay and disfigured by a complex 'Meccano-like' radio mast and reflector.

If a traveller has taken the bus up to the Chora it could make a pleasant alternative to return on foot making the 15 - 20 minute walk down the rubbly donkey path.

Excursion to Hozoviotizza Monastery This is about a 20 - 30 minute walk east

from the Chora, beyond the area of 'The Wells', and past the large square building that serves as a School on the left. Turn right beyond the Helicopter pad marked with a large 'H', leaving the stone wall enclosed area to the left. Note that to keep straight on and bear round to the left proceeds on to the wide stony track to the northern Port of Aegiali.

Almost immediately the landscape falls sharply away and the traveller is clinging to a steep amphitheatre of rocky mountain-side similar to being located on a saucer almost tilted in the upright position. Way down below is the sea with the mountains encircling the saucers edge. Follow the steeply descending goat track as it zig-zags down the hillside until it crosses a dirt track road. Here, turn left along the track, and keep on round the cliff edge to the wrought iron gates let into a modern rock slab wall. The white, cliff-hugging Monastery stands out even more starkly (if that is possible), because it is hung like a limpet to the drab brown, grey and orange mountain rock-face. A steep, stepped path climbs to the Monastery.

There are a number of legends regarding the *raison d'etre* of the institution, most revolving around an icon miraculously found washed up on the shores of Amorgos. Quite honestly the Mediterranean in the Medieval Ages must have almost been awash with unmanned rowing boats ferrying icons hither and thither. Be that as it may the monks own pamphlet sets the scene and raw anger of the few remaining monks at the State grab of 1952.

Obviously the brothers were pretty 'cheesed off' with the Greek Government's latter day Dissolution of the Monasteries.

Visitors MUST of course ensure they are dressed properly, that is to the standard demanded here and elsewhere in Religious Houses throughout Greece. There is no fudging the issue at this Monastery and visitors arriving in shorts and or without a respectable shirt/blouse will be turned away. One of the three monks will, after a short guided tour in Greek, refresh those who have made the journey with a cup of Greek coffee, a glass of water and a Turkish delight served in a little upper anteroom. Incidentally, beneath a cloth and rather out of place in this Medieval atmosphere, is a telephone. Open daily between 0800 and 1400 hrs. Admission is free but donations are welcome, nay obligatory.

Excursion to Ag Anna Beach From the area described for the **Excursion to Hozoviotizza Monastery** either follow the track to the right (as opposed to the left for the Monastery), or zig-zag down the hillside goat path for another 20 minutes or so.

The pebble beach is clean and startlingly white. To the right is another, larger beach with a rock face spring, a certain amount of nudity and *ad hoc* camping.

AEGIALI (Aigiali, Agiali, Egiali): port (Illustration 31)

This northern and only other inhabited Port is as different from Katapola as say an olive and a glass of retsina. Vacationeers tend to cover a wide ranging spectrum of cultures and class, with a fair proportion of 'Hippy-style' Europeans.

Aegiali has several distinct advantages over Katapola. It has several beaches, and the eating out is not only cheaper but possibly the most inexpensive anywhere in the Cyclades.

ARRIVAL BY FERRY

The bay in which Aegiali snuggles is very large and dramatic. The Port Village is on the right-hand corner of the broad 'U' (*Sbo*), the bottom of which is a long tree-edged beach. On the left-hand side a number of small coves are backed by steep, rocky mountain sides. High in the encircling mountains is the Upper Port Village of Potamos as well as the other Villages of Langada and Tholaria.

The quay is massive for a Port of this size. It marks the right-hand boundary of the Village which spreads out straight up the hill and to the left around the waterfront. At the bottom right-hand of the boulder edged quay is a small phallic shaped 'I-know-not-what'. The local fishing boat fleet of caiques moor up inside the quay which forms the harbour. Part of the quay is taken up with nets which are stretched out daily and left to dry. The Ferry-boats are met by the few Room, Pension and Hotel owners who are far more forthcoming here than at Katapola.

THE ACCOMMODATION & EATING OUT

The Accommodation Whatever time the Ferries dock, disembarking visitors will be offered Rooms, even if, due to the spread out nature of the Village's layout round the

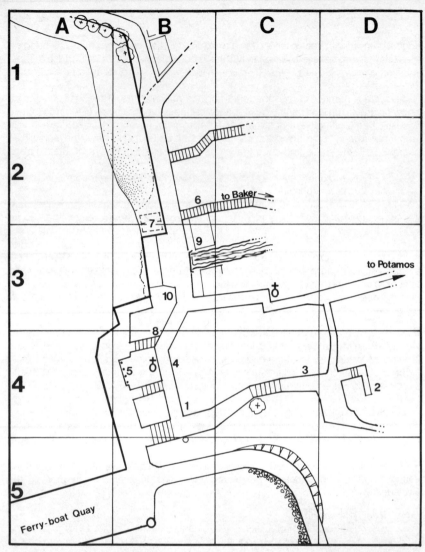

AEGIALI PORT

Illustration 31

bottom of the bay, it may involve a long walk.

Cafe-Bar/Restaurant O'Kphtiko∑ (*Tmr* 1.B4)
Directions: From the bottom of the quay straight ahead, rising up the hillside is a wide, steep, stepped street on the corner of which is an old bright blue painted mine casing. The Cafe-bar is on the left.

The patroness has a friend with **Rooms** on the narrow street, between her establishment and the *Taverna/Restaurant To Nimani*. Mid-season a double room sharing the bathroom costs 600 drs.

At the top end of the stepped street is a pleasant house with **Rooms** (*Tmr* 2.D4).

Before striking out for the middle of the bay area of the Village it is worth popping in to enquire at **Ormos Souvenirs** (*See* **'Information Office', A to Z**). Ignore the road, skirt the first messy bit of beach and walk along the wide, concrete path skirting the main beach until reaching a large flat bridge. Beyond this is a cylindrical old buoy set in the shore and a run-down, faded Cafe-bar complex with **Rooms** on the far right backshore. To the right is an irregular path over some waste ground which connects with the rough track from the Village. Turn left, past a 'dead' disco and on the left is:-

Lakki Rooms To Rent
Directions: As above, with a large water-tower close by.

Michael Gavalas is the proprietor and a double bed costs about 1000 drs in mid-season.

Hotel Askas
Directions: Further on along and on the right of the track.

Not really a Hotel but a modern, nicely equipped, elongated single storey Pension with the rooms off the long corridor. The owners, Lefteras and Costas Sinodinos, are very pleasant and willing to please, but with limited English. To understand anything more than a simple request the owner sends off to the fields from whence a relation emerges to translate. The very pleasant, spacious en suite double rooms in mid season cost 800 drs per night. A brother runs the catering side of the team and a very reasonably priced breakfast is available on a shingle covered area surrounded by orchard trees. Coffee, bread, honey and jam for one costs 75 drs.

The Eating Out As previously indicated, probably the most inexpensive place in which to eat out in the Cyclades, if not the Aegean. The referred to street climbing the hillside from the bottom of the quay possesses two excellent establishments.

Cafe-Bar/Restaurant O'Kphtiko∑ (*Tmr* 1.B4)
Directions: On the left of the stepped lane, almost opposite the old sea-mine casing, with tables spread out on the surrounds.

Good value with a splendid view of the bay, even if the bread has been known to have weevils. The price of breakfast is reduced if the butter-pats suplied are not all used. Two chicken (200 drs), chips (60 drs), bread (15 drs), a bottle of beer (60 drs), and a bottle of retsina (30 drs), all for 415 drs. An extra brandy 25 drs, a 'limon' 30 drs and a black Nescafe 35 drs.

Almost at the top of the same street, on the left, is the:-

Restaurant/Taverna To Kopaλi (*Tmr* 3.C4)
Directions: As above with tables both sides of the pedestrian path.

This really is a first-rate Taverna and a wonderful spot from which to watch the evening sun setting over the slope of Cape Akrotiri, diagonally across the bay. A meal for two of kalamares, a Greek salad (100 drs), 2 large 'open' retsinas (120 drs) and bread (15 drs) costs 435 drs. Admittedly the kalamares should have cost 200 drs each but as the patron explained, they were small portions so he only charged 100 drs! The reason for 2 large carafes of retsina on this occasion must have been that we spent so long over the meal! Stuffed tomatoes and courgettes for two, a plate of chips, 2 Greek salads, a large retsina and bread for 480 drs.

Another good news, 'all day and night' Restaurant/Taverna is:-

To Nimani (*Tmr* 4.B4)
Directions: In the narrow lane parallel to the waterfront, above and opposite the Church.

'We serve on the Roof too'. The *To Nimani* has a cavernous dining room with a few tables across the lane. The Taverna substitutes for an evening club and meeting place. The atmosphere is that of a French bistro and Greeks and tourists inter-mix, gathered round the tables in animated conversation. A varied menu, with meat balls (piled up like profiteroles) a speciality but as they are fast moving (no not that sort of 'fast moving'!) there is no problem. A large bottle of 'open' retsina costs 60 drs; 2 coffees and a small bottle of retsina 110 drs. Through the bar, up a step or two, are clean lavatories complete with a shower head.

The Restaurant conveniently stays open for the arrival of late night/early morning Ferries. Although the quay is blinded from the taverna by buildings the boats announce their presence with a strong blast of the horn. Due to the distance to the end of the quay and the chance that it might be quite a rush, it is a good notion to dump one's bags at the top of the quay prior to ambling off for the evening's entertainment.

There are a number of other establishments including a Taverna on the waterfront, below the Church; the *Cafe Asteria* (*Tmr* 6.B2) beyond George Vassalos' Souvenir shop, and a *Kafenion*, almost side by side with the *Asteria.*

THE A TO Z OF USEFUL INFORMATION
BANKS None but *See* **Information Office.**

BEACHES The whole stretch of the bottom of the bay is a long shoreline which is a mixture of flat horizontal rocks and large pebbles.

Beyond the roofless boat sheds (*Tmr* 7.B2/3) is a small, sandy beach on which the locals pull up the occasional boat. Despite the sign 'Forbidden Public Nudity & Camping on the Beach', a number of visitors camp out in the thick trees edging the first part of the bay.

At the far side of the bay are a number of coves, the first of which has a large, sandy beach, the second rough sand and shingle and the third is rocky.

BOOKSELLERS None but *See* **Information Office.**

BICYCLE, SCOOTER & CAR HIRE None, which is not surprising — there's no where to go.

BREAD SHOPS There is a Baker up the steps alongside the *Cafe Asteria* (*Tmr* 6.B2). He is often to be observed with large cooking trays containing various taverna 'meals of the day' which he bakes.

CHEMISTS & PHARMACIES Bring everything, but there is a Clinic, *See* **Medical Care.**

COMMERCIAL SHOPPING AREA Yes, well, there is a small, cramped, rather primitive and unfriendly Store (*Tmr* 8.B3/4) beyond the Church on the left. This Aegean 'Harrods' doubles up as a very 'doo-hickey' telephone exchange. Okay, it possesses a primitive telephone box and an old fashioned switchboard but the system here is even more unreliable that at Katapola.

FERRY-BOATS *See* **Katapola** and George at the **Information Office.**

INFORMATION OFFICE (*Tmr* 9.B3)   Tel 71252/71346
Really George Vassalos' Souvenir Shop but as the sign loudly proclaims
'EXCHANGE
RENT ROOMS
STAMPS — FILMS
BUY & SELL BOOKS HERE
GENERAL INFORMATION
RENT A DONKEY NOT A MOTORBYKE'
George, the owner, is a most helpful young man and a mine of information, some inconsequential, some extremely useful. . . 'don't buy bottled water, the tap in the Main Town Square is excellent'. Mind you the small area he referred to across the way was more a building materials yard. Usually assisted by a male friend, the pair of them often sit on the shops verandah dispensing advice and the odd drink.

The shop has some pleasant souvenirs including an interesting island map drafted by a German Professor. The preponderance of 'other' Europeans, or possibly the few English speaking people that visit, results in their being few English books for exchange A 50 drs charge is made for book swop.

LUGGAGE STORE *See* **Information Office.**

MEDICAL CARE There is a Clinic half-way up the steep, wide, unmade road to the Upper Village of Potamos, on the right.

OPENING HOURS Hardly applies but the few shops operate strict siesta hours.

OTE Well hardly but *See* **Commercial Shopping Area.**

PLACES OF INTEREST *See* The **Introducton** and **Excursions.**

POST OFFICE *See* George at the **Information Office.**

Excursion to Potamos The upper Village of Aegiali is up the steep hillside, on the track that starts out as a lane opposite the old Kafenion (*Tmr* 10.B3), jinks around the Church and widens out into a broad, unsurfaced road.

Potamos is an 'up and down' hillside Village with a Town Hall and School. In the right-hand part (*Sbo*) there is a post box on the wall close by the Village Shop which shop is only recognizable by a pile of empty crates outside. The owner lives next door.

Excursion to Langada (Lagada) & Tholaria To make the 30 - 40 minute journey to Langada, rather than taking the zig-zag unsurfaced Main Road, proceed to the minor crossroads on the way to the Upper Village of Potamos. Take the left-hand turning and clamber through the Olive grove to reach this lovely, picturesque Village which has a worthwhile taverna.

Although the conventional route to Tholaria is to advance to the far end of the bay and wind up the rough path or take the unsurfaced road, a better alternative is to proceed along the track from the bottom of Langada Village. The journey takes another 30 minutes, and, whilst Tholaria is not so pretty as Langada, there are great views of the Island.

There are four inhabited, small Islands (and two uninhabited) lying between Naxos and Amorgos. They are little visited and share (with Sikinos) the ability to reflect the older ways and values of the Greece of yester-year. Don't expect a bank or even a change office, an OTE, Post Office or mains electricity. Do expect shortages, including scarcity of water and provisions and take a phrase book.

For Ferry-boat connections *See* **Katapola Port, Amorgos** or **Naxos Island, Chapter 15.**

EXCURSION TO DONOUSSA ISLAND (Dhenoussa, Dhonoussa)
The Ferry docks at the south coast Dhendro Bay. The small jetty, usually cluttered with

drums, sacks and boxes is to the left of the Hamlet Port (*Sbo*) which spreads up the low hillside. There is a very handy Cafe-bar/Taverna to the right of the jetty. A friendly island with a splendid, sandy beach curving round to the right backed by a bamboo grove and solitary palm tree.

EXCURSION TO KOUFONISSI ISLAND (Koufonisia, Koufonisi)

Actually two Islands, Lower Koufonissi and Upper Koufonissi. The Ferry-boat Port is to the south of Upper Koufonissi above the northern point of Lower Koufonissi (still with it?).

The most developed of these rarely visited islands. The largish, untidy quay is to the left of the expanding Village Port set in an arid, low hillside, with a wide road to the right. There are quite a number of small craft lying at anchor.

To the left and right of the quay are some pale blue signboards proclaiming that 'Nudity/ Camping not permitted' in four languages.

Across from the left-hand corner of the quay, a road arrows up the hillside between low stone walls with, away to the left, a solitary windmill almost on the top of the hill. A number of buildings are going up here and there, many remaining in a skeltal state, and the fairly substantial Village is a little back and to the right. There is a Pension to supplement the usual *Rooms*.

To the right of the quay the shoreline curves sharply round and in the corner there is a stretch of sandy beach backed again by a low hillside with a collection of even larger two-storey buildings concentrated in the centre.

EXCURSION TO SHINOUSSA ISLAND (Skhinoussa)

Ferries dock at the large quay to the right of the almost land locked and lovely Myrseni Bay set in enveloping, gently sloping hills. The donkeys gather by a large stone built shed and the quay is often heaped high with piles of building materials. To the left of the quay, the bottom of the small bay has two small, narrow, shingle beaches and, in the crook of the inland track, behind the first beach, is a Taverna/Restaurant.

The track winds up the hillside in front of the Ferry-boats bow, to the delightfully unspoilt, chaste village Chora tucked away behind the hill. The Chora boasts a couple of tavernas, one of which has *Rooms* for rent.

EXCURSION TO IRAKLIA ISLAND

The Ferry steams in to the ever narrowing, high-hill enveloped, rocky Bay of Ag Georgis at the north-east of the Island with the quay to the left and close by the bottom of the bay. A good, unsurfaced road curves round past a number of small, anchored fishing boats, along the scrubbly beach to the Main Road. This gently rises through the Village, to the right of a blue domed Church that dominates the upper village and on to the hillside Chora, about an hour inland. To the right of the bay there is a certain amount of new building taking place. There are no beachside tavernas.

To the south-east is Pegadi Beach set in a deepening fjord-like inlet.

19 Astipalaia (Astypalaia, Astypalea, Astipalea) *****
(I say) Cyclades Islands — Eastern chain
(others say Dodecanese)

FIRST IMPRESSIONS
Water wells 'dressed up' as Chapels; colourful, purposeful fishing fleet; well looked after cats — so much so they even have the energy to fight, most of the night; fishing with dynamite; steps and more steps; 'yassou' becomes 'ya'.

SPECIALITIES
No snakes; curiously elaborate females traditional costume; hares and rabbits; 'Gasosa' lemonade.

RELIGIOUS HOLIDAYS & FESTIVALS
include: 2nd February— Candlemas; 21st May— Saints Constantine & Helen; 2nd July — St Panteleimon; 20th July— Prophet Elijah; 15th August— Dormition of the Virgin; 29th - 31st August — Festival and feast, Monastery of St John the Beheaded (west of island).

VITAL STATISTICS
Tel prefix 0242. This island is popularly described as being shaped like a pair of butterfly wings because two land areas are linked by a narrow neck of land, thinning to less than say 300 m. The overall length (or width in this case) is 18 km, greatest width (or depth) is 24 km with an area of some 99 sq km. The population numbers about 1,100 of whom 700 - 800 or so live in Skala Port and or the Chora.

HISTORY
Possibly the Island's most famous citizen of history and mythology was the disgraced Olympian athlete Kleomedes who, during a wrestling competition in the 71st Olympiad, killed a competitor with a foul blow. Disgraced and deprived of his victory, the one-time hero returned home and, probably goaded on by the lads in the Public Bar, charged off to the local school and gave the supporting columns a bear hug pulling the roof down and killing 60 or 70 pupils. The incensed parents sought him out to exact revenge only to be advised by the Delphic Oracle that Kleomedes had been immortalised.

The Minoan Cretans had an outpost here and the Island was written about in glowing terms regarding its fertility. The Romans allowed Astipalaia autonomy in exchange for the right to take advantage of its strategic position, using the numerous coves to anchor up whilst waiting in ambush for marauding pirates. The Venetians ran affairs during the Middle-Ages followed by the Turks between about 1540 and 1912, when the Italians took over and used Astipalaia as a launching pad for the assault of Rhodes and domination of the Dodecanese. Mark you the islanders were no pushover and twice during Turkish occupation, managed to free their oppressors yoke for several years at a time, including a period during the War of Independence.

GENERAL
The Island is administratively incorporated in the Dodecanese but surely this can only be by the stroke of a mandarins pen, for Astipalaia is in many ways more Cycladean than the other Cyclades islands. Or put another way, rather in the nature of a religious convert, it is more typical than its unadopted brethren. The Port corkscrews up to a dramatic Chora,

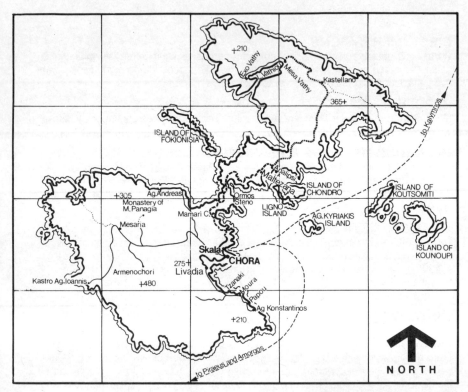

ASTIPALAIA

Illustration 32

topped off with a splendid Venetian Castle. The Island is, in the main, arid and the Ferry-boat connections from the Cycladean outposts are far more frequent than those from the Dodecanese islands. Admittedly there is the mandatory Dodecanese Italianesque Municipal collonaded building, even if it is rather insignificant, and the Italian overlords restored the hilltop Castle but there all similarity with its administratively co-related bretheren ends.

Certainly Astipalaia stays firmly rooted in the Greek past and many of the now lost Hellenique niceties are still to be found there.

The few beaches are not golden sand, more grey pebble and often dirty but this short-coming is more than compensated for by the contented and intrinsically Greek nature of the islanders and their environment. Beneath the everyday comings and goings beats a throbbing pulse of island life, rich in characters and those daily happenings that weave the rich pattern of everyday Greek life A touching example of the islanders disposition Is illustrated by the Grandfather of the family that runs the beach Taverna (*Tmr* 10.B1), *To Akpoyiaλ*. A Simiot fisherman, he rowed single-handed all the way to Astipalaia to marry his sweetheart, a distance of some 130 kms.

A reserved nature is balanced by an overwhelming friendliness that blossoms after the first few days of acquaintance. A mark of islands that have been isolated and outside of the main stream is the occurrence of a particular physical peculiarity. Astipalaia's own abnormality is hereditary deafness and it is not uncommon to observe lip-reading natives.

A visitors first impression may initially be of some disappointment for there are few of the manifestations expected by many hedonistic holiday-makers nourished on a diet of discos and Fast Food. But perservere and the natural charm of the people and the location will surely weave a spell that will hold the true Greekophile tightly in its untidy, somewhat messy, but lively bonds.

If the natives of Amorgos go to bed early, Astipalaians make up for it as they rise late but don't seem to stop until early next morning. Visitors should note that Astipalaia does not really come to life until the end of June.

Certainly it is one of the few islands on which I have had to exercise all my will-power to break the spell and get on the Ferry-boat (others include Paxos and Lefkas (Ionian islands) and the Dodecanese island of Karpathos.

SKALA: main port (Illustration 33)
Dominated by the Kastro topped Chora to which the buildings stretch all the way up from the pleasantly scruffy and intimate Port which exhibits few concessions to tourism. In fact the Skala is bustling and noisy, with goats 'baaing', cats fighting, people ambling home late and fishermen rising early. The Electricity Generation Station (*Tmr* 1.C5) would dominate the left-hand side of the port (*Sbo*) if it were not for the preponderance of fishing boats and the Meccano-like OTE reflector tower that almost brushes the corner of the *Hotel Paradissos* (*Tmr* 2.B4). The Hotel itself fronts up this corner of the Esplanade, if that is not too smart a descriptive word for the Skala waterfront.

It is rather as if the squashed up Port, set in arid hillsides and surprisingly undevelopd, was an after-thought, a dropping from the Chora's table that splashed into the pebble shale beach. Perhaps the most telling sight is the Italian constructed Municipal Building which, on many islands, would be neatly smartened up, perhaps even gleaming. Not here, everyone is too busy for that sort of bull — the despondent structure moulders and peels.

ARRIVAL BY AIR
Laurel, of whom more later, on being questioned regarding the Island Map detailing an Airport in the area of Maltezana, advised us that there is one man, his donkey and a wheelbarrow engaged in the construction work, that he had been thus preoccupied for

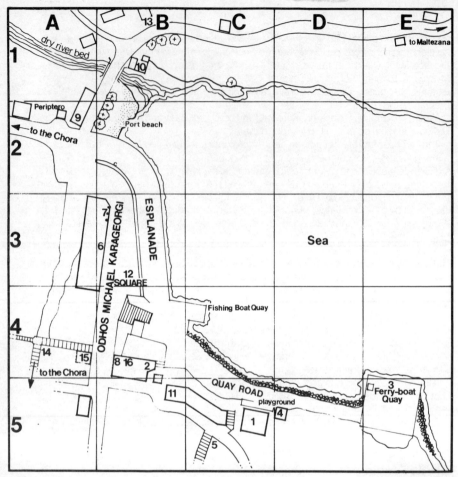

KEY

1 Electricity Generating
   Station   C5
2 Hotel Paradissos   B4
3 Ferry-boat Quay   E5
4 Public Toilets   D5
5 H. Monaεia – Rooms
   & Restaurant   C5
6 Hotel Astynea   A/B3
7 Municipal Administrative
   Building   B3
8 Cafe-bar Estapion B4
9 Cafe-bar   A2
10 Taverna
   To Ακρογιαλι   B1
11 Baker   B5
12 Port Square   B3
13 General Store/
   Grocers   B1
14 Butcher   A4
15 A. Economou
   Ferry-boat Office A4
16 O.T.E.   B4

SKALA PORT

Illustration 33

some years and will be so for some years to come. . . .

ARRIVAL BY FERRY

The comparatively infrequent Ferries are met any time of day and night by Hotel and Room owners, including some from Livadia. The Ferry-boat quay has been enlarged and now travellers have quite a few strides along the broad concrete road to get to the Esplanade.

There are sufficient Hotels, Pensions and Rooms to cope with the comparative dribble of mid-season visitors but the height-of-Season influx could swamp the available facilities.

THE ACCOMMODATION & EATING OUT

The Accommodation The walk along the quay from the Ferry-boat landing stage (*Tmr* 3.E5) passes the Public Toilets (*Tmr* 4.D5), the Generating Station (*Tmr* 1.C5) with playground to the fore, after which a flight of steps climb to the :-

H Mona ia (*Tmr* 5.C5) Tel 61290
Directions: As above.

Advertises 'Rooms to Rent & Restaurant' but I'm afraid the position almost on top of the constantly throbbing Generating Station, would possibly preclude any but the heaviest sleeper enjoying an undisturbed night. It is said that the locals get accustomed to the noise.

Hotel Paradissos (*Tmr* 2.B4) (Class D) 24 Michael Karageorgi Tel 61224
Directions: Continue on along the quay and directly to the forefront.

The owner Frank, short for Franciscos, and his family run this 1930s style Hotel which is in the process of being refurbished. Although the public corridors, surrounds and lobby are a bit of a shambles, the position must be one of the finest on any Greek island that I have stayed on, being comparable with *The Brothers Dracos* at Milopotamos Beach, Ios island. (Naturally, this comment excludes the upper end, purpose built holiday hotel centres). Furthermore the rooms have been excellently modernised and already possess panoramic balconies allowing a splendid view of the Port's activity. The renovation has included a shower head hanging point and an extractor fan in the en suite bathrooms. Mark you 'not all that is revamped glitters', if you take my meaning. The retaining box frame of the very comfortable spring mattress's have been left with sharp edges that bite into unwary sleepers. . . and the loose brass button mattress holders rise up like soldiers, with fixed bayonets, marching across the night. But this is nitpicking, unwarrantable, carping criticisms, the cavils of a regimental sergeant major not the measured, objective, value-judgement expected of a level headed observer!

In mid-season a double room en suite costs 850 drs (and the rooms have lampshades!).

Hotel Astynea (*Tmr* 6.A/B3) (Class D) 21, Michael Karageorgi Tel 61209
Directions: Further to the centre of the Port, towards the Municipal Administrative Block (*Tmr* 7.B3).

Only opens up (if at all) during the height-of-the-season months of July to September.

Where the quay road joins Odhos Michael Karageorgi a surfaced road starts on the steep, winding journey to the Chora. Prior to the first, sharp bend, there are three Hotels, but the *Viva Mare*, on the right, is in actuality apartments, so does not count.

Hotel Aegean (Class D) Tel 61236
Directions: As above and further up the road, on the left.

Average accommodation at average prices.

Hotel de France
Directions: In the apex of the first bend of the rapidly rising road. Such is the climb that the

1st storey, prior to the bend, becomes the ground floor round the corner.

An English lady born in Chile and married to a French banker assured me that the rooms were very small cubes (and between you and I they moved to the *Paradissos*). As the owner is an expatriate baker from Marseilles, clients can have croissants for breakfast.

There are **Rooms** to either side of the steps from the Port to the Chora.

The Eating Out
Cafe-Bar Estapion (*Tmr* 8.B4)
Directions: In the same block as the *Hotel Paradissos*.

Young Marcos, and his wife, run the place for his mother. Even if the bar is rather 'down-at-the-heel', Marcos maintains equable composure despite the crippling hours he has to work. Prices are reasonable even if, in common with the rest of the island, a bottle of beer is a few drachmae more expensive than some other islands, at 70 drs. A Metaxa costs 25 drs, coffee with milk 38 drs and quite often a small bowl of fruit appears. Moreover Marcos will, if asked, cook a tasty omelette, breakfast, kalamares or, on request and with some notice, lobster, accompanying all meals with a Greek salad.

Cafe-Bar (*Tmr* 9.A2)
Directions: The first of a number of 'dead', 'half-dead' and alive Cafe-bars that are hunched side by side along the opposite side of the slip-shod Esplanade road to the tree-lined beach. A few chairs and tables are scattered about beneath the trees.

But to keep the best to last is to now detail the:-

To Akpoγiaλi (*Tmr* 10.B1)
Directions: Further along the Esplanade, roughly where the tree cover ends, a small oblique flight of steps angles down on to the beach. At the far end, across a dried up river bed, is this delightful beach edge Taverna. There is a sign over the door proclaiming 'RAKA Yachts welcome'.

A very 'smiley' lady and her family run the Taverna. Apart from the narrow verandah, tables and chairs are also put out on the pebbly back-shore. In addition to the standard menu there is a fresh and often out-of-the-ordinary 'meal of the day'. The food is excellently prepared, portions are generous and the prices are very reasonable. Why eat anywhere else? Examples of the cuisine (and cost) include, 2 potato omelettes (75 drs each), 2 plates of fried zucchini (45 drs each), bread (20 drs), and a bottle of retsina 50 drs; 'filet fish' (really battered fillets at 160 drs each), a garlic sauce dip and bread for 390 drs; pistachio pie (an enormous helping), Greek salad, chips, 2 bottles of retsina, a (free) mezes, all for 550 drs and lastly a meal for two of meat loaf and potatoes, aubergines cooked in oil, a bottle of retsina and bread — a super meal for 550 drs. Rosemary, the dear girl, commented that the food is served up on nice china as well.

If the cooking were not good enough, their charming, simple wish to please combined with the *au naturel* atmosphere marks this as a truly memorable taverna. I hope visitors will agree.

Other establishments stretch up the hill of the Maltezana road, that hugs the bay hillside, and include the *Restaurant Australia Cafeteria* (slick, gushy ice-creams) and another very smart Restaurant prior to the **Disco Faros.**

Back in the centre of the Skala, almost alongside, the Generating Station are two perhaps three, 'eateries'.

The closest to the 'power source' is the seemingly 'dead' *Sea Food O'Nikodas*, next to which is the *Cafe OpγanakhΣ* followed by the *Restaurant Astipalea*, a rather lively establishment.

THE A TO Z OF USEFUL INFORMATION

BANKS None, but the proprietor of the *Hotel Paradissos* (*Tmr* 2.B4) offers a lousy rate of exchange with about 10/15 drs spread, but can beggars be selective. . . .?

Another change facility is offered in the small store that 'lurks' beneath the *Hotel Aegean*, open between 0900 - 1300 hrs, and sometimes in the evenings.

BEACHES The Port beach is adequate if rather small and scrubbly, consisting of shale and grey pebble. The locals careen their smaller fishing boats which adds to the general mess but the sea is excellent for a swim even if the beach is not ideal for comfortable sunbathing. A refreshing sight is the number of Greek mothers and children who disport themselves, including the older, usually ample ladies, who often bathe fully clothed, wearing a straw hat and when finished wrap a loose shift over everything.

BICYCLE, SCOOTER & CAR HIRE. None.

BREAD SHOPS (*Tmr* 11.B5) Excellent crusty loaves dispensed from the Bakers along from the *Hotel Paradissos* (*Tmr* 2.B4).

BUSES The very small, modern bus parks up on the Port Square (*Tmr* 12.B3) above the sweep of the road to the Ferry-boat quay.

Bus timetable There is a timetable pinned up on the Square but as a sighting shot the following may help.

Skala to Livadia
Daily   0900, 1030, 1530 hrs
Skala to Maltezana
Daily   1130 hrs
Return journey
Daily   1500 hrs

I consider the fares expensive, a one-way ticket to Maltezana costing 70 drs.

My last visit unfortunately coincided with the regular driver having incurred an eye injury. Five months later the islanders were still awaiting the arrival of a man from Athens to fill in, so schedules were definitely astray.

CHEMISTS & PHARMACIES *See* **Medical Care.**

COMMERCIAL SHOPPING AREA None but there are just enough outlets to keep the wolf from the. . . . On the other hand a certain amount of steep walking is necessary because complete shopping cover is only available by including the Chora.

There is a small but useful General Store/Grocers (*Tmr* 13.B1) on the far corner of the cove, a Butcher (*Tmr* 14.A4) close to the onset of the Chora steps, a Periptero close by the crossroads and the *Hotel Paradissos* has a dark, cavernous and cluttered single room store. For other shops, *See* **the Chora.**

A closing note must be made in testament to the unknown salesman/men who one day descended on the unsuspecting shopkeepers and, no doubt with a very smooth line of patter, flogged the shopkeepers not only unquantified numbers of cans of flykiller but also innumerable Japanese porcelain figures. The flykiller they need but the ceramics. . .?

DISCO There is the **Disco Faros** on the cliff top road to Maltezana.

FERRY-BOATS As has been pointed out the Cyclades connection is more frequent than the Dodecanese link — not a lot but just a little, with only the **CF Miaoulis** and **Nireus** calling.

Ferry-boat timetables Best ask Laurel but *See* **Amorgos, Chapter 18** and add or deduct 3½ hours.

It must be hoped for the continuing welfare of travellers that Laurel, an 'English rose', continues to run the Ferry-boat ticket office of **A Economou** (*Tmr* 15.A4). Not only is she most charmingly helpful but very knowledgeable and will help with even the most tedious enquiry. (I should know, I must have tried her patience very dear. . .).

The simple single room office which Laurel operates is conveniently located close by the **Cafe-bar Estapion** (*Tmr* 8.B4) where a prospective client can sip away while waiting for her to open up. Office hours vary to tie in with the Ferry-boat arrivals but as a guide are, or more correctly were, Monday 1800 - 2000 hrs; Tuesday 0700 - 0800 hrs, and 1800 - 2000 hrs; Wednesday 0700 - 0800 hrs and 1300 - 1400 hrs; Thursday 1800 - 2000 hrs; Friday 1500 -1700 hrs; Saturday 1800 - 2000 hrs and Sunday 0800 - 1000 hrs.

HOSPITAL *See* **Medical Care.**

MEDICAL CARE Oh, ho, ho. *See* **The Chora.**

NTOG No. Best to enquire at **A Economou,** the Ferry-boat ticket office.

OPENING HOURS Cafe-bars and tavernas seem to stay open most of the day and night. Otherwise strict siesta hours apply.

OTE (*Tmr* 16.B4) Oh, yes. An interesting office beneath the *Hotel Paradissos*, run by a couple of engaging fellows who have distinct ideas of what should happen when duty and pleasure clash! The office is frankly faded (uncared for), although the lads have encouraged some large pot plants to flourish. The opening hours are Monday and Friday 0730 - 1510 hrs but there is a bench seat outside and an intending client may well need it.

The *Hotel Paradissos* has a metered phone for which they only charge 3 drs a unit but it is rather public and a bit of a crush being located in the General Store.

PLACES OF INTEREST *See* **the Chora.** Really the sub-heading might well have read 'Characters of Interest' but it cannot be surprising in this mildly frontier-town atmosphere that the place should support more than its fair share of 'personalities'.

There are a number of small offshore islets which can be reached by trip boat or as it is quaintly called, 'Sea-Taxi'. Two skippers run excursions from Skala harbour, 'anytime - anywhere' and no more totally disparate characters can be imagined.

Captain Roussos is a slight, one-eyed and one handed Greek fisherman. The story goes that these injuries happened when Roussos, planning another dynamiting trip, decided in order to double his 'bait', to saw one of his grenades in half. . . ! Captain Pete, the Welshman, is a piratical but very friendly expatriate of rather wild looking and 'lived-in' appearance. His craft, shared with a German friend, is recognizable by the stylised eyes painted on the bows even if his St David's Welsh flag has disintegrated (well in 1985 it had). The boat suffered a burst engine in 1984 which may delay operations. Rumour, only rumour, has it that Pete drives the craft rather hard which may, or may not, have something to do with the occasional breakdown. . . . Trips are very reasonably priced with 3 or 4 people ferried to the nearest island for about 400 drs (one-way).

Whilst writing about characters, it is worth mentioning Captain Nicolis from the Dodecanese who drives a grey-hulled, sponge and sword-fish boat and is a frequent visitor to the Island in the season. Your luck will be in if you are here when he visits, as he sings and dances superbly and will be found livening up proceedings in one of the Chora bars on most nights. Try *Mikalis's* or *Manoulis.*

When the fisherman have landed their catch in mid-afternoon they have a habit of spending the siesta spreadeagled on their nets in the lee of the *Hotel Paradissos.*

POLICE The Port and Town police are located in the Municipal block (*Tmr* 7.B3).

POST OFFICE *See* **the Chora.**

TAXIS A car or three slink on to the Port Square (*Tmr* 12.B3) but they strike me as being on the expensive side with the Livadia journey costing 200 drs and Maltezana 500 drs.

TOILETS There is an absolutely 'mind boggling' facility (*Tmr* 4.D5) close by the Ferry-boat quay. I write 'boggling' for the two cubicles of this squatty are in such an indescribable condition that I hope the flies can't make it down to the waterfront tavernas!

TRAVEL AGENTS *See* **Ferry-boat timetables.**

THE CHORA: capital (Illustration 34)

Really the top end of the Port (or is the Port the bottom of the Chora?). The Chora itself is split into two, the Middle or saddle level and the Upper Castle level.

The Middle level wherein the Town Hall and Library Squares, a Post Office (*Tmr* 1.A1) on the side of the road down to the Skala; a small, tidy Store (*Tmr* 2.A/B2) on the corner of the Livadia road; a Taverna (*Tmr* 3.A3) on the edge of the Library Square; the Library; a Periptero and a local bar with a balcony (*Tmr* 4.D2) on the junction of the Town Hall Square and steps to the Port. The 'Self-Service' (*Tmr* 5.C2), which is actually a hole-in-the-wall General Store, owned by a cuddly Australian speaking Greek lady, is at the top of the Skala steps. Alongside (actually the far side and to the rear) of the Town Hall is a Clinic. The English speaking doctor, Vassilis is said to stay on Astipalaia from choice which is rare as island duty appears to be considered a punishment.

The road towards Livadia is dominated by windmills, eight in fairly good condition and one ruin.

The Upper Castle level, reached along either of two steep uphill traverses, possesses a heavily restored Venetian Castle circled by a very pretty parade with an Oleander littered walk on the far (Livadia) side of the Castle. There are masses of Churches, higgledy-piddledy Medieval private houses and innumerable, but discreet bars. These include *Manoulis Cafe-bar* owned by two pleasantly crazy Greeks, one who dances, one who sings, and the *Castle Bar* in an alley beside a Church almost to the front of the Castle promontory. The strange thing is that the Chora has no tavernas, only Kafenions and bars, therefore to eat it is necessary to descend to the Skala. Perhaps this is the reason that the bars do not open before late evening and stay open until early morning.

The 13th century Castle has a Church over the vaulted entrance and contains a mass of part covered alleys, old houses and Ag Georgios Church built on the site of an Ancient City/Temple settlement. To one side of the Castle, to the east of the bluff, stands the large Church, Panagia Portaitissa, founded in 1764.

Excursion to Kastro Ag Ioannis (10 km) On the west coast. The path from the Chora divides after 2 km, the right fork leading off to the cove of Ag Andreas on the north coast from whence it is sometimes possible to catch small boats to Exo Vathy (*See* **Maltezana**).

The main path proceeds westwards. After another 8 km it progresses past the right-hand fork to the Monastery M Panagia (Flevariotissas). The main left-hand track advances past the few scattered houses of Armenchori (where incidentally the referred to archaeological remains are no longer visible) and the farm or two of Mesaria to the coastal site of:-

KASTRO AG IOANNIS (10 km from the Chora) Only the ruins of the Venetian Castle and one house now remain. In the Spring there are a number of waterfalls. The story of the Castle's original despoilation by the Turks is that an old lady was left outside the walls to tend the goats. The Turks found and 'persuaded her to tell'. She did and the marauders found their way in, slaughtering her and everybody else.

Close by is the Monastery Ag Ioannis with splendid views.

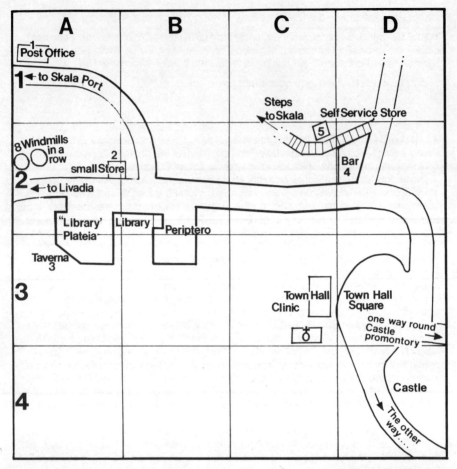

KEY
1 Post Office   A1
2 Store   A/B2
3 Taverna   A3
4 Bar   D2
5 'Self-Service' Store C2

CHORA
DIAGRAMMATIC LAYOUT

Illustration 34

ROUTE ONE

To Livadia (2 km) From the Chora the surfaced road wanders over the crest of the mountain bringing into view a very green, cultivated valley, with homesteads dotted throughout, set in dry mountain sides. To the left a wide swathe cuts down the cliff-edge to the near side of the bay. The Main Road circles to the back of the valley plain and wanders through walled groves of agriculture to the main 'Highway' — an unmade, stony river-bed. This is similarly walled right up to the beach backshore which forms the tree-lined and shaded, grey, rough sand and pebble surfaced 'Esplanade'! On the left of the 'Highway', prior to the 'Esplanade', are **Rooms**.

The messy beach is made up of light brown shale and pebbles and edges a clear sea in which a number of small boats are anchored. The beach is fringed by a continuous, narrow but comparatively thick stand of trees. Nude bathing.

To the right, along the 'Esplanade', are **Rooms** as well as a number of tavernas set in amongst the trees and squalor. A Periptero-cum tiny Store is located in the remains of a half demolished public toilet block and there is a post box fixed to one of the remaining walls.

To the left, along the 'Esplanade', from the 'Highway' is similar to the right-hand but more so. Beneath the trees are piles of rubble with goats, hens and other assorted domestic animals scratching and fighting it out. The extensive tree cover almost camouflages the concrete block houses and a Taverna, the owner of which is a rather surly roly-poly. He serves the very nice 'Gasosa' island lemonade.

It appears that many Chora residents shut up shop for the summer months and migrate to Livadia, opening up other little shops. In general a double room is cheaper here than in Skala Port averaging out at 500 drs mid-season. BUT cold water showers are the order of the day which, added to the abundance of flies and mosquitoes, just might deter the less hardy souls. . . .

Recommended **Rooms** include *Nicolas Pension*, owned by a smiley Greek Australian who meets the Ferries, as does the early and mid morning Livadia bus. The *Galigadia Taverna* comes 'mentioned in dispatches' as the food is excellent, not expensive and local specialities are included on the menu. Dishes include garlic sauce, dolmades, egg soup and fresh yoghurt.

ROUTE TWO

To Maltezana (9 km) & beyond This is a two hour walk, in dry shelterless countryside for those not prepared to wait for the bus or to pay the taxi fare. The road climbs up the side of the Port cove, past the rubbish dump, and after 1 km, becomes unsurfaced dropping down to the first of a series of bays. This is pleasant and marked 'Marmari B' on the maps which show a cluster of houses. No signs of dwellings but there is a 'dead' Generating Station. Closer examination gives a lie to this immediate impression, as the building is obviously new but appears to be bereft of the necessary machinery. The story goes that after years of debate it was agreed that the power plant at Skala Port was incapable of coping with future demand. The new station was built and the machinery ordered. So far so good. The delay in completion appears to centre round the fact that the manufacturers can prove dispatch but the relevant Greek authorities are not sure where the generators are. . . . Meanwhile the men allocated to complete the job have had to go elsewhere. Official fingers are kept crossed that the present equipment's output will continue to meet the increasing requirements. . . .

The next bay is marked on the map as 'Marmari C' with the almost obligatory indication of a cluster of dwellings which boil down to one solitary farmhouse, set in a pleasant valley at the far end of the bay. This has the look of an early settlement and my 'Minoan senses' twitched. The steeply shelving, narrow 'beach' is made up of big pebbles and both sides of the track are lined with small trees. On the left is the rustic:-

Campsite Anatoli
Signposted from both the Chora and Skala from which it is some 2 km in distance.

Further round the curve of the bay the beach becomes a broad swathe of pebble with the sea bottom mainly comprised of shelving 'biscuit rock'.

The road now climbs towards the narrowest neck of land marked on the map as the Hamlet of Stavros but this settlement is non-existent. Despite the configuration and lie of the ground it is just possible to glimpse both sides of the sea. The lovely, rocky, indented coast on the left is unfortunately despoiled by dumped rubbish.

The next portion of the southern coastline, skirted by the rough road is a series of coves which make up Ormos Steno. The middle cove is clean with some kelp, a sandy sea-bed, a fairly broad beach and a pleasantly tree planted backshore, set in which are a couple of water wells. The others have narrow shore lines and all are tar polluted.

From the hillside at the far side of this bay are lovely views of, in one direction, the Chora, spiralling up its Castle topped hillside and with about 120° of swivel, the inshore islands settled into the surrounding sea rather like the exposed backs of giant semi-submerged whales.

MALTEZANA (9 km from Skala) Both young and old villagers are very smiley and friendly but any traveller who expects a substantial development will be disappointed. Upper Maltezana smacks of a Mexican adobe village and is an untidy sprawl. In actuallity most of the village is set in a verdant oasis with a widespread farming community. The approach is along a concrete surfaced, bamboo lined road which curves round to the waterfront of the bay.

Panayiotis Taverna
Directions: Prior to the sharp bend of the final, slight downhill run to the quay and on the left.

A modern, smart Taverna (but don't be put off) with very nicely appointed, clean chalet Rooms to the rear.

Panayiotis, once an engineer, is very welcoming, friendly and a mine of information. The food served is good and reasonably priced with 4 omelettes and a cucumber salad costing 290 drs and a double room starts at 500 drs rising to 800 drs.

Ask him for directions to the 'Chapel Mosaics', some 10 minutes walk into the countryside. Okay I will direct. Back along the road towards Skala Port and a straight track makes off towards an off-white Chapel-like building, set in an enclosure of prickly pears. Keep to the left and head over the rise in the ground towards a startlingly white Chapel, through a rustic gate, across a cacti littered gorge, past a stone walled enclosure, to the right of a large bread oven, past the face of a dwelling to the low stone wall of the Chapel on the left. Lo and behold, ones own archaeological discovery. There, to one side of a small agricultural building and forming a backyard, are mosaics and column bases with the columns lying on the ground with the capitals. All this and no Guided Tour or Museum fee. Oh Greece of yester-year.

For the antithesis to *Panayiotis Taverna*, it is only necessary to stop off at the small, thoroughly rustic Kafenion around the bend in the road. It is on the right, immediately prior to the Municipal looking buildings where the bus pulls up. The Kafenion has the date 1956 set in the wall but the old, jolly lady and her nearly blind husband look as if they have been here a century or two. The vine shaded bench seat outside in a narrow alley is backed by green painted, beaten out olive oil drums.

At the bottom of the road, the quay is inordinately large and set in a smallish, tree-edged bay with a semblance of a narrow beach to the left (*Fsw*) and a stony and weedy seabed. The sea-bottom, clearly visible, is not only weedy but is littered with bits and bobs and home to a lot of sea urchins. It was rumoured that there was a sunken City in the harbour area. Be that as it may I was not going to chance the sea urchins.

The track to the left circles round the horn of the bay, past a new, small Public Toilet block set in the trees, and on, towards the headland bluff whereon there is the occasional dwelling close by the waters edge.

Over the headland the track becomes a pedestrian way to another scrubbly cove with a grey, stony beach.

This path winds on up through the centre of this blob of land around and up to the Kafenion at Mesa Vathy and on to the Taverna at Exo Vathy. Both hamlets are set on the fjord-like inlet of Limin Vathiou. There are occasional caique connections to Ag Andreas (*See* **Chora Excursion**).

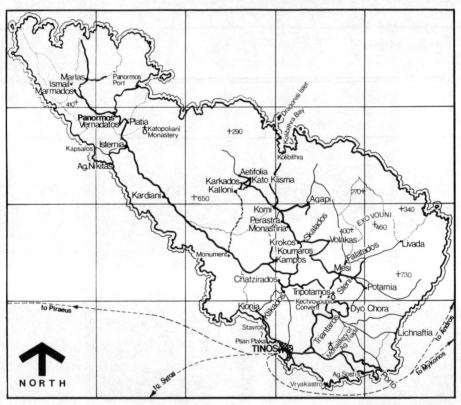

TINOS

Illustration 35

FIRST IMPRESSIONS

Pilgrims; sick children; black-clothed crones; candles; votives; driving schools; Venetian dovecotes; (distinctive) Church bell towers; mules; green rocks; wild passion flowers; ouzeries.

SPECIALITIES

Religion; loukoumades; frontalia omelettes; Greek tourists and pilgrims; red American-style fire hydrants; green marble.

RELIGIOUS HOLIDAYS & FESTIVALS

include: 30th January — Festival, the Discovery, Panagia Evangelistria (or Church of Megalochari); 25th March* — Festival, the Annunciation, Panagia Evangelistria; 23rd July — Festival, Ag Pelegia, Panagia Evangelistria; 26th July— Festival, Isternia; 15th August* — Festival, the Assumption, Panagia Evangelistria; 31st August — Festival, Isternia; 8th September —Festival, Kardiani; 14th September — Festival, Isternia; 11th November — Festival, Kardiani.

*The most important days around which is it is simply not worth travelling to or from the island.

VITAL STATISTICS

Tel prefix 0283. The Island is 34½ km in (diagonal) length, up to 15 km wide with an area of 194 sq km and, some say, 64 villages but certainly between 50 and 60. Estimates of population vary between 9,000 and 12,000 of which between 3,000 and 4,000 live in the Capital. Another rumour suggests there are up to 750 Chapels, Churches and Monasteries and as many dovecotes, but I have not counted them.

HISTORY

For a change, an individual historical background compared to the other Cyclades islands. The Venetians took the island over in 1207 and managed to beat off the Turks, not succumbing to the general sweep of the middle 1500s, till 1714. This extra period of stubborn resistance included repulsing nine or so specific assaults. This defiance owed not a little to the impregnability of the now, all but vanished, Exobourgo Castle, built by the Venetians close by an Ancient City. The 500 years occupation by Catholic worshipping overlords resulted in nearly all the inhabitants being of this religious persuasion. Even today a fifth or more islanders are still of the Catholic faith.

The Islands supreme moment came when a nun, Sister Pelagia, now Saint, of the Convent Kechrovounio had a dream and vision in July 1822 in which the Virgin Mary revealed where an icon depicting her and the Archangel was to be found, in a field. Sister Pelagia's conviction must have been persuasive because excavations soon started but it was not until early the next year the buried treasure came to light close to the ruins of an old Byzantine Church. It was a propitious moment to have a Sign from the Almighty, two years into the War of Independence, added to which the icon appeared to possess healing powers.

Building of the Church of Megalochari (Blessed Virgin) or Panagia Evangelistria (Good tidings or Annunciation, take your pick) commenced in 1823 and things never looked back, the Island becoming the 'Aegean Lourdes'. If this were not enough on one of the Holiest Days, the 15th August 1940, the **Elli** a Greek ship, variously described as a Cruise Liner, Cruiser, Destroyer and Warship, dressed overall and joining in the religious celebrations was torpedoed. Although never conclusively established it was assumed that this dastardly attack was made on the instructions of the 'fascist swine Mussolini and his murderous blackshirted thugs'. And this was prior to War being declared between the two countries. Golly, gosh, the bounders! To the Greeks a Hellenic Pearl Harbour with religious overtones, if you see what I mean!

The Island not only conceived and was famous for its stone masons but achieved an artistic renown. Amongst its famous artist sons were Giannoulis Halapas, N Gyzis and N Lytras.

GENERAL

Guides in general tend to refer to the Holy status of the island and the consequential quiet, dignified religious milieu that presents itself to a visitor. Holy, Tinos island may be, but quiet and dignified, no. The Main Town and Port of Tinos is an appealing mix of old and new. The 40 or so villages of the hard working agricultural communities are attractively spread amongst the neat country hillsides. There are a number of extremely inviting beaches and sufficient spots in which to hide away, as the urban Greek is not a great explorer. This probably accounts for the almost deserted nature of one or two seaside beauty spots, even in high season.

The islanders are very friendly people which, combined with their pleasant surroundings, would lend one to think that they should be carefree, 'happy-go-lucky' and generally satisfied with their lot. Well, they are outwardly but there is a psychotic discontent, an almost paranoic distrust of their near neighbours, Mykonos. For instance the Delos/Mykonos link and the thought of all those tourists going 'astray' really gets beneath the average Tiniots skin. Certainly there is a story regarding the Mykonos pelican being kidnapped by the islanders of Tinos, a matter that became so serious that it is rumoured to have reached Prime Minister level. Not to be outdone by Mykonos, Tinos Town now has its own resident pelican which is to be found in and about restaurants on the waterfront. Furthermore day trips are available to Delos! But the hostility goes back further than that for a Tiniot will woefully repeat the 100 year old folklore story regarding the devious Mykonots stealing copious quantities of beach sand, yes a 100 years ago. The obsessive religious beliefs of the older islanders have had interesting social consequences in respect of the tourists. Certainly until recent years negroes were considered by the elderly ladies to be children of the devil. Well there you go.

This most agreeable Island is a cross between Patmos in the Dodecanese and Paros, its close Cycladean cousin. The countryside has just the right mixture of soft mountains, hills and verdant plains with golden green, verdant fields of hay and rivers of Olive trees. Churches and Chapels vie with Venetian Gothic dovecotes for the available space. These undoubted attributes should make it a prime target for both package and backpacking holiday-makers. Fortunately, for the time being, the Island has remained outside the mainstream of the overseas summer onrush. (For how long I wonder?). That is not to say that the Island is not invaded but the majority of the tourists are Greek and apart from the height-of-the-season most of the resorts are nigh on empty.

TINOS: capital & main port (Illustration 36)

A bustling, busy Town which greets the disembarking traveller with a Grecian bazaar, strident and swarming even on Sundays. Perhaps 'even' is a misnomer, for it is more active on Saturday and Sundays due to the high percentage of Greeks who spend their weekends on the Island. So much so that it is best to arrive at any other time than a Friday, depart any other day than Sunday and avoid weekends if possible.

ARRIVAL BY FERRY

The mainland Port for Tinos is Rafina (*See* **Chapter 10**) from whence daily inter-island connections are made by the **FB Eptanissos** which also calls at Andros, Mykonos and Syros. Piraeus also operates a daily ferry-boat. The ferries conveniently dock (*Tmr* 1.C3) almost at the bottom of the High St, Leoforos Megalocharis, that rises up to Panagia Evangelistria Church.

THE ACCOMMODATION & EATING OUT

The Accommodation Accommodation, though plentiful, tends to be expensive due in the main to the all-year round number of Greek pilgrims, tourists and sick searching for a cure. This influx is in addition to holiday-making Athenians who traditionally visit those Cyclades islands most adjacent to the mainland including Andros, Tinos, Kea and Kithnos. Even mid-season 'C' class Hotels average about 1600 drs for a double room.

Radiating out from the Band Stand (*Tmr* 2.C3) at the bottom of the Ferry-boat quay (*Tmr* 1.C3) facing up the High St, Leoforos Megalocharis, towards the Church Panagia Evangelistria.

Hotel Aigli (*Tmr* 3.C3) (Class D) 7 El Venizelou   Tel 22240
Directions: To the left in amongst and over a gaggle of taverna/restaurants that line this stretch of the Esplanade.

Well I said they were expensive and here a single and double bed sharing a bathroom costs 1250 drs and 1500 drs respectively and en suite 1560 drs and 1860 drs.

On up the High St gives access to the:-

Hotel Meltemi (*Tmr* 4.C2) (Class C) T.D. Philippoti   Tel 22881
Directions: The turning to the right prior to the OTE/Post Office (*Tmr* 6.D2) and on the right.

A newish Hotel with a double room and bathroom en suite costing 1360 drs or 1600 drs.

Hotel Theoxenia (*Tmr* 5.C2) (Class B) 2 Leoforos Megalocharis   Tel 22274
Directions: On the left of the High St, opposite the OTE/Post Office (*Tmr* 6.D2). Modern and expensive with double rooms starting from 945 drs and rising to 2400 drs with differing charges for season and with or without a bathroom.

Rooms (*Tmr* 7.C2)
Directions: Down the side street alongside the *Hotel Theoxenia* and on the left.

Continuing along this street advances to a small Square in the Old Quarter with an impressive Fountain (*Tmr* 8.C2) dated 1797, on the near side of which a left turning drops down in a crescent curving back round to the High St.

Rooms (*Tmr* 7.C2)
Directions: As above, following the paved way down from the fountain and on the left, about a third of the way round.

From the Band Stand (*Tmr* 2.C3) the narrow 'Bazaar Alley', Odhos Evangelistrias, climbs towards the Church Panagia Evangelistria but has to struggle through a maze of stalls, shops and cafe-bars.

Rooms Stratis (*Tmr* 9.C2) 37 Evangelistrias   Tel 23166
Directions: Up 'Bazaar Alley' beyond the large fountain in a narrow alley to the left, on the near side of the Herb Shop and opposite a Cake and Bread Shop. The steps to this first storey pension are on the right.

Stratis, the helpful, smooth-talking, English speaking owner is a young man of outwardly supreme confidence in not only his own judgement but in the excellence of his establishment. His judgment remains, to my knowledge, unsurpassed but the rooms. . . ! The steps decant onto a narrow, dirty balcony with unwatered flowers, the pots of which are filled up with cigarette ends and bottle tops. A corridor with bedrooms on both sides, runs the length of the building from a small reception area peppered with information and a tiny kitchen which can be used by guests. The conversion of the old building has been carried out at minimal cost, the bedroom walls are paper-thin and the corridor acts as a sounding box. The bathroom facilities are at the end of the corridor and do not let us down. There is no lock on the gentlemens toilet and the general washroom water tap misses the washbasin (unless the flow is a dribble). To be fair Stratis could not be more friendly and the rooms are clean. A double room costs 800 drs mid-season.

Stratis also owns some modern Bungalows, close by the campsite *Camping Tinos*, in which room rates seem to be inexpensive.

There are **Rooms** (*Tmr* 7.C2 & 7.D2) to the left and right of the crossroads next Street up Odhos Evangelistrias from *Rooms Stratis*.

Hotel Poseidonion (*Tmr* 10.C3) (Class C) 4 Paralias   Tel 23123
Directions: Along the Esplanade to the right (*Sbo*) and over an expensive Cafe-Restaurant and the *Pizza Spaggetti*.

A single room en suite costs 1520 drs and a double room 1860 drs. Well they would, wouldn't they.

Hotel Delfinia (*Tmr* 11.C3) (Class C) Paralia   Tel 22289
Directions: Further along the Esplanade, across the side lane, on which is the 'Bus ticket office' (*Tmr* 12.C3) and there are a row of expensive cafe/restaurants above one of which is the Hotel.

Considering the position, surprisingly not over expensive with a single room en suite 1150 drs and a double room 1560 drs.

Still proceeding along the Esplanade crosses an initially wide Street to the left by a Taxi Rank which street leads up to the Church Ag Ioannou.

Rooms
Directions: As above and over the Bakers shop (*Tmr* 13.D3) on the right-hand side of the street.

Hotel Eleana (*Tmr* 14.D3) (Class D)   Tel 22561
Directions: On up the street to the pretty little Church Ag Ioannou, around which the road splits. Take the right lane hugging the side of the Church.

Very well spoken of by those who have stayed here, although on the expensive side, with a double room sharing a bathroom costing 1600 drs and en suite 1700 drs.

Further on round the corner and right along the lane of Odhos Anton Mosxatoy breaks out into an irregular Square on which are two **Rooms** (*Tmr* 7.D3).

Hotel Avra (*Tmr* 15.D3) (Class C) Paralia   Tel 22242
Directions: Right along the Esplanade (*Sbo*), beyond the Port police office (*Tmr* 16.D3), opposite that smelly part of the waterfront where the benzina's are moored, and on the left.

Has the appearance of an English Country Town Hotel. A single room en suite costs 1300 drs and a double room, 1800 drs.

Beyond the *Hotel Avra*, the next turning left is the Main Road east out of the Town. The Esplanade end is a Rent-a-Bike and Car Hire stretch. A Street to the left divides round a small triangular island. Close by the corner are two separate **Rooms**.

About ½ km further along the Main Road uphill and on the left, just before the last Scooter Hire Firm on the opposite side of the road, are:-

Rooms
Directions: As above and over a Greengrocers Shop, distinguishable by the yellow shutters.

Hotel Tinion (*Tmr* 17.D4) (Class B) 1 C Alavanou   Tel 22261
Directions: From the Main Road turning, instead of following the Esplanade road, keep up

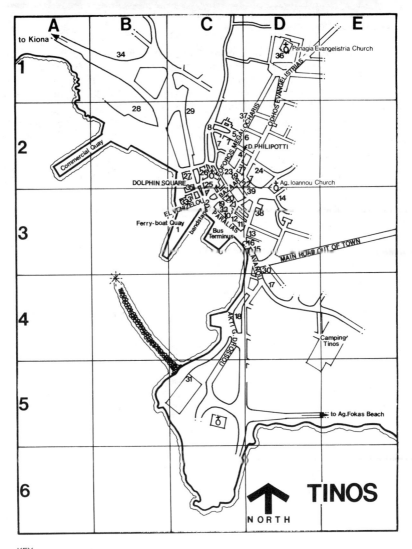

KEY

1	Ferry-boat Quay	C3
2	Band-stand	C3
3	Hotel Aigli	C3
4	Hotel Meltemi	C2
5	Hotel Theoxenia	C2
6	O.T.E./Post Office	D2
7	Rooms	
8	Fountain	C2
9	Rooms – Stratis	C2
10	Hotel Poseidonian	C3
11	Hotel Delfinia	C3
12	Bus Office	C3
13	Bakers	D3
14	Hotel Eleana	D3
15	Hotel Avra	D3

16	Port Police	D3
17	Hotel Tinion	D4
18	Rooms – not expensive	C4
19	Souvlaki Pita	C3
20	Taverna To Koytoyki	C3
21	Taverna Michalis	C3
22	Cake Shop	C/D2
23	Restaurant Toxinari	C2
24	Taverna – Good Heart	D2
25	Greengrocer/Fruit Shops	C2
26	Taverna – Dionisos	C2
27	Bakers	C2

28	Childrens Playground	B2
29	Cafeteria – Pizza	C2
30	Estiatopion Ozefiros	D3
31	Taverna – Vintsi	C5
32	Commercial Bank	C3
33	National Bank	C3
34	Moto Mike	B1
35	Market	C2/3
36	Panagia Evangelistra Church	D1
37	Museum	C/D2
38	Galerie Cybele	D3
39	Town Police	D2/3

Illustration 36

275

the lane, (that proceeds on to *Camping Tinos*) and on the left.

Comparatively reasonably priced and unusually (for Tinos that is) with seasonal differentials. A single room sharing a bathroom starts off at 640 drs rising to 800 drs (July, August and early September). A double sharing starts off at 1060 drs and en suite 1310 drs, rising to 1150 drs and 1700 drs respectively.

This lane widens out and runs out in scrubby, new development and waste ground.

Camping Tinos (*Tmr* E4)   Tel 22344
Directions: On the right behind a stand of trees.

Well laid out to a very high specification complete with a cafeteria, mini-market, kitchen and toilet block with hot water available all day. Charges are 100 drs per head per day and the hire of tent also costs 100 drs. The sea is only 100 m walk away.

Rooms Not Expensive (*Tmr* 18.C4) Akti G Drossou
Directions: Almost round the corner along the waterfront at the far right-hand end of the Esplanade, here named Akti G Drossou.

Hotel Oceanis (Class C) 3 Akti G Drossou   Tel 22452
Directions: Next door to *Rooms Not Expensive*. A double room with bathroom costs 1600 drs.

For further accommodation *See* **Beaches, A to Z**.

The Eating Out
The continuous flow of Greeks has kept prices high and the establishments stylised in the Town. Generally there are few low price snack-bars, some reasonable priced tavernas but a great many expensive cafe-bars and waterfront taverna/restaurants. Certainly meal prices are kept more expensive by the taxes being charged as an extra. Wines tend to be dear, more so as retsina is not always available. This I am sure will not worry some readers. Additionally the competition does not result in lower prices but much 'schlepping', shouting and 'encouragement'. The widest choice of eating places is in the area of the Port, and it is worth noting that a number of Kafenions off the waterfront only serve Greek coffee.

On, and to one side of Odhos Evangelistrias, are a number of widely differing establishments including:-

Souvlaki Pita Stall (*Tmr* 19.C3) Odhos Evangelistrios
Directions: Almost immediately on the right in the awning covered section of 'Bazaar Alley'. A good value 'handful' at 55 drs.

The first turning off to the right of Odhos Evangelistrias is a narrow alley in which:-

To Koytoyki (*Tmr* 20.C3)
Directions: As above and on the left.

A rather run-down, ramshackle, oddly festooned Cafe-bar/Taverna advertised 'OK Boy You Satisfied 100 Per-Ent' (sic). The contents of the pots and pans were 'thought provoking'. The character who runs the place dresses in white, sports a chefs hat and obviously once enjoyed a popular following but I cannot do more than make a mention.

Taverna Michalis (*Tmr* 21.C3)
Directions: A few metres further up the lane, on the left, with some tables lining the pavement.

Not particularly noticeable at first but to be recommended, if possibly on the expensive side. The young couple who run the Taverna work hard. A dinner for two of kalamares, a plate of chips, a good Greek salad, a bottle of retsina and bread cost 754 drs.

On the other side of the lane, back a bit towards 'Bazaar Alley', on the corner of a side lane, is:-

Kafenion
Super loukoumades and passable, if rather Greek tasting, Nes. (Okay, not so passable)

but what the coffee lacks is more than compensated for by the price differentials with the waterfront chaps. Two black Nes, an ouzo and a plate of loukoumades (65 drs) cost 160 drs while on the Esplanade two Nes with milk and an ouzo costs in excess of 200 drs. The waterfront has one saving grace, the *Self Service Cafeteria* for details of which read on.

Two side streets further up the 'Bazaar Alley', Odhos Evangelistrias, and on the right is:-

Cake Shop (*Tmr* 22.C/D2)

The lively owner not only stocks a range of drinks but serves tasty pies, cakes, ice-creams and bread.

Almost opposite, a narrow lane, on which are *Stratis's Rooms*, jinks on to a Square edging the High St, Leoforos Megalocharis, and on the left is:-

To Xinari (*Tmr* 23.C2)

Directions: As above.

A pizza Restaurant pleasantly located but the prices reflect the linen table-cloths and Spanish style, high-backed chairs.

Back to Odhos Evangelistrias, climbing beyond the crossroads and the next turning right leads to:-

The Good Heart (*Tmr* 24.D2)

Directions: As above, and on the right.

'Cleanliness, Good Care' and clean, with the interior dominated by a rather out-of-place snow-capped mountain scene. Worth a try, serving a good value, house speciality, a frontalia omelette containing nearly everything including the kitchen sink. A meal for a couple of 2 'Special' omelettes including salami, zucchini and potatoes (500 drs), a salad (small, but only 50 drs), ½ bottle of demestica (100 drs), bread (30 drs) and taxes (34 drs) all for 704 drs.

Back on the Esplanade waterfront, at the outset of Leoforos Megalocharis, almost immediately on the right, is a small triangular piece of pavement on which is:-

Kostas Cafe-Bar Ouzerie

Directions: As above

Specialises in octopus mezes which naturally, accompany glasses of ouzo.

On the other side of Leoforos Megalocharis, an alley (at the start of which are two Greengrocer/Fruit Shops side by side — *Tmr* 25.C2), sallys forth opening out on to an irregular Church Square, an Old Quarter and a maze of streets.

Dionisos Taverna (*Tmr* 26.C2)

Directions: As above, on the Square with tables prettily spread about.

Average fare at average prices.

The Esplanade to the left (*Sbo*) from the bottom of the Ferry-boat quay (*Tmr* 1.C3) has to jink round the end of a row of restaurant/tavernas. Around the corner and on the right is a Square dominated by an sculpture of a dolphin, 'Dolphin Plateia', edged on two sides by tavernas, as is the alley towards the Bakers (*Tmr* 27.C2).

Further on, the Esplanade widens out and curves left around the back of a large childrens playground (*Tmr* 28.B2), *Tinos Mariner* Cafe-bar and *Adonis Yacht Club* — (no, not quite like a British yacht club). In front of this island site a massive concrete way leads to an equally large expanse of commercial quay. Before the playground, across some public gardens are a row of restaurants one of which is the:-

Pizza Cafeteria (*Tmr* 29.C2).

Along the Esplanade to the right (*F-bqbo*) is one establishment which may not be a 'jewel in the crown' but is a good hedge against the almost outrageous cost of most of the other waterfront cafe-bar/restaurants, the:-

Pizza Spagetti (sic)
Directions: Beneath the *Hotel Poseidonion (Tmr* 10.C3).

Now I am no great devotee, no worshipper at the altar of self-service whilst in Greece, but.... At least it is reasonably priced with a milky coffee at 58 drs, a Greek salad 74 drs, an omelette 110 drs, a bottle of retsina 102 drs. Sitting out on the awning covered patio is rather spoilt by the management failing to empty the flower boxes of cigarette ends, old bits of food and other odds and sods that get deposited there.. Oh well, we can't have everything can we....? Don't forget that next door in the *Poseidon* two coffees and an ouzo cost 208 drs.!

Further on around the Esplanade, beyond the Main Road out of Town and the *Camping Tinos* street, there are two Restaurants/Tavernas side by side.

Estiatopion O'Zefiros (*Tmr* 30.D3)
Directions: As above.

A little cheaper than the other, more central competitors but similar style of service. Two spaghetti bolognese (218 drs each), a plate of fassolakia freska (green beans) (100 drs), open retsina and bread for 697 drs.

Next door is the *Coffee shop Euripidus.*

Before leaving the subject, at the far right-hand end (*Sbo*) of the Esplanade is the:-

Vintsi Taverna (*Tmr* 31.C5)
Directions: As above.

More an up-market, Northern Working Mans Club style of building than a taverna.

Advertises 'live' bouzouki music and only opens its doors late evening. Reputedly excellent value for a night-out.

THE A TO Z OF USEFUL INFORMATION

BANKS Two banks which cash Eurocheques:-

The Commercial Bank (*Tmr* 32.C3) Alongside the steps on the small Esplanade Plateia 'Cathedral Steps' Square which lead up to the Catholic Cathedral and the:-

National Bank (*Tmr* 33.C3) Let into the row of restaurant/tavernas to the left of the Ferry-boat quay (*Sbo*). Pleasant and efficient service.

Both operate the usual hours.

BEACHES Two town beaches, both rather unsatisfactory, include:-

Beach 1. West (or left (*Sbo*)) beyond, and around the corner from the Commercial Quay (*Tmr* A2). Large pebbly cove.

Beach 2. Ag Fokas beach, south-east (or right (*Sbo*)) along Akti G Drossou and up the slope to the left of the ruined Church. After 100 m or so the road drops to the left of the headland along a narrow tree-shaded, pebbly beach.

For those prepared to strike out, hire a taxi or in possession of transport there is:-

Beach 3. The beach above (No 2) edges the sea until a rocky outcrop after which the surfaced road runs out by the side of two cafe-bars. The first cafe-bar doubles up as a disco at night and there is another disco a little further on, at the commencement of this beach. Less shaded than Beach No. 2, with small Arethemusa trees scattered about, this very long stretch of beach runs all the way along to the large headland of Vryokastro. There are many more people here than on the other beaches mentioned. This is not surprising as despite the beach being initially pebbly, the sea bottom is pleasantly sandy after a metre or so and about a third of the way along it widens out and the foreshore also becomes sandy with a gently shelving sea bed. Half-way along there is the:-

Golden Beach Cafe-Bar   Tel 22579
The cafe has Bungalows to Let, alongside which is:-

Furnished Rooms to Let
Really a self-contained Cabin complete with a fully equipped kitchen containing a cooker, sink and fridge. The breakfast bar divides off the 3 beds (new) and there is an en suite bathroom with shower. The cost is 1500 drs a day reducing for a weeks rent, and a goat is thrown in! Super value for a family in a splendid location.

From here on there is only about one person per 100 m of beach which finally peters out on the nearside of the conical Vryokastro headland. A track progresses over the headland to a very small, quiet cove with a kelpy beach and stony sea bottom. A number of nude bathers may be found discreetly lounging on the odd, 'pocket handkerchief' sized bits of shore.

BICYCLE, SCOOTER & CAR HIRE 'Rental Alley' is on the Main Road east out of the Town, with establishments on either side of the road. Scooter hire is on the costly side, with the daily rate averaging 1000 drs. Petrol is extra with a litre of 2 stroke-mix costing 70 drs.
   My own favourite outfit, at the other (west) end of Town is:-

Moto Mike (*Tmr* 34.B1)
Situated at the west end of the Esplanade, across a small triangular garden from the childrens playground. Costas is a cousin of Stratis, who has the Pension on Odhos Evangelistrias, and is a very friendly, helpful young man speaking excellent English. His scooters are in good condition and the office/repair shed, in which there is a useful, wall-mounted town map, opens up at 0800 hrs, closing mid evening. Despite his admirable traits, the hire rates are still 1000 drs a day.

BOOKSHOP Apart from a scattering of shops that keep a selection of tourist guides, foreign newspapers and magazines ranged in a semi-circle around the Esplanade Band Stand (*Tmr* 2.C3), there is a Bookshop half-way up Leoforos Megalocharis, on the left. *See* **'Galerie Cybele', Places of Interest**, for details of second-hand books.

BREAD SHOPS There is a baker (*Tmr* 27.C2) on the far side of the building block that edges the 'Dolphin Plateia' (*Tmr* C2); a shop selling bread (*Tmr* 22.C/D2) about a third of the way up 'Bazaar Alley', Odhos Evangelistrias; a Baker in the second Street off to the left of the High St, I enforms Megalocharis, with a ***Rooms*** sign in the window and a Baker (*Tmr* 13.D3) on the right of the Street up to Ag Ioannou, with ***Rooms*** over the top.

BUSES The Bus Terminus (*Tmr* C3) is on a rectangular extension to the Esplanade which juts out into the harbour, right of the Ferry-boat quay (*Sbo*).
   The bus ticket office (*Tmr* 12.C3) is across the Esplanade from the terminus, in a short alley, the other side to the *Hotel Poseidonion*. The timetable is chalked up on a board outside the office.

Bus timetable

Tinos Town to Panormos (Pyrgos) NW of the island)		Bus A
Daily	0630, 1100, 1400, 1630 hrs	
Tinos Town to Steni (NNE, middle of the island)		Bus B
Daily	0700, 0720 (and on to Falatados), 0930, 1100, 1400, 1545, 1800 hrs	
Tinos Town to Kalloni (NW, middle of the island)		Bus Γ
Daily	0630, 1100, 1400, 1630 hrs	
Tinos Town to Kampos (NW, south of middle of the island)		Bus Δ
Daily	0630, 1400 hrs	
Tinos Town to Porto (Ag Ioanni, SE coast)		Bus E
Daily	0800, 1230, 1600, 1830 hrs	
Tinos Town to Kionia (S coast, W of Tinos Town)		Bus Z
Daily	0900, 1000, 1100, 1200, 1300, 1400, 1600, 1700, 1800 hrs	

CHEMISTS *See* **Medical Care.**

COMMERCIAL SHOPPING AREA Do not think that the religious overtones blanketing the island result in a Sunday shut-down. No way. In fact if anything the activity is more frenzied, with even the siesta swept to one side so the shopkeepers can take advantage of the exodus of weekenders on the **CF Eptanissos**, late Sunday afternoon.

Odhos Evangelistrias ('Bazaar Alley'), is a narrow lane,jam-packed with stalls and shops selling souvenirs, meat, fruit and vegetables, cakes and drink, pictures and religious items including candles. In the first lane off to the right is a Cigarette Kiosk and in the second side street up from the Souvlaki pita stall there is a splendid fruit and vegetable shop.

On the kerb edge of the 'Cathedral Steps' Plateia a morning display of produce appears. There is a small Market building (*Tmr* 35.C2/3) on the edge of 'Dolphin Square' and the whole of this Square is taken up by traders in the early morning. To one side, and to the back of the Square, is a well organised Supermarket and there are others scattered about.

To one side of the High St (Leoforos Megalocharis), are two Fruit and Vegetable Shops (*Tmr* 25.C2) side by side in the first alley on the left. Lastly but not least there are two Peripteros, one on the 'Cathedral Steps' Square, to the right of the Band Stand, and another to the front of *Kostas Cafe-Bar Ouzerie* at the outset of Leoforos Megalocharis.

DISCOS None in the inner Town but elsewhere the situation is as normal. To make up for the lack of discos there are a number of cocktail music bars on the periphery of the 'Old Quarter' (not a lot to do with Greece, but there you go). These include **Georges Place**, open until 0300 hrs, and the **Seagull Bar** run by Anna, a large, blonde, Dutch girl who speaks 5 languages.

FERRY BOATS The craft moor up at the large quay (*Tmr* 1.C3) from which the Town conveniently radiates. The biggest influx occurs on Friday/Saturday with a mass departure on Sunday afternoon. One of the popular craft, the **CF Eptanissos**, that runs between Tinos Port and Rafina on the mainland, is extensively used by the Greeks, but has an expensive one-fare price structure.

Nowhere is the hardiness of the old, black-dressed Greek 'ladies' better exemplified than when boarding this ferry. They rush the boat, sweeping everything before them and, on the last occasion I travelled this route they actually swept me off my feet, all 16½ stone of me plus my heavily laden back-pack. The disadvantage for inter-island travel is that Tinos, in common with Andros, is rather off the well-worn Piraeus Port/Cyclades Ferry-boat lanes. This should not come as an unexpected shock as the Island is on an easterly wing. It is sometimes necessary to connect between the mainland ports of Piraeus and Rafina via Athens, using the buses.

Ferry-boat timetable

Day	Departure time	Ferry-boat	Ports/Islands of Call
Daily	1530 hrs	Naias	Piraeus (M, arrive 2000 hrs)
	1550 hrs	Panagia Tinou	Piraeus (M, arrive 2100 hrs)
One-way fare 1100 drs.			
Monday	1205 hrs	Eptanissos	Syros.
	1435 hrs (possibly)	Eptanissos	Gavrion (Andros), Rafina (M, arrive 1930 hrs)
	2400 hrs	Atlas II	Mykonos
Tuesday	1205 hrs	Eptanissos	Mykonos
Wednesday & Thursday	1430 hrs	Eptanissos	Gavrion (Andros), Rafina (M, arrive 1930 hrs)

Wednesday	(possibly) 2400 hrs	Atlas II	Mykonos
Friday & Saturday	1205 hrs	Eptanissos	Gavrion (Andros), Rafina (M, arrive 1640 hrs)
	2205 hrs	Eptanissos	Mykonos, Rafina (M, arrive 0345 hrs next day)
Friday	(possibly) 2400 hrs	Atlas II	Mykonos
Saturday	(possibly) 1230 hrs	Atlas II	Mykonos
Sunday	1205 hrs	Eptanissos	Mykonos
	1430 hrs	Eptanissos	Gavrion (Andros), Rafina (M, arrive 1930 hrs)

One-way fare to Andros 475 drs, Rafina 850 drs.

FERRY-BOAT TICKET OFFICES Spread about the waterfront and thickest in the area of the Band Stand (*Tmr* 2.C3).

HAIRDRESSERS Both gents and ladies.

LAUNDRY A dry-cleaners alongside the *Taverna Dionisos* (*Tmr* 26.C2).

MEDICAL CARE
Chemists & Pharmacies One close by the **Commercial Bank** (*Tmr* 32.C3) on the 'Cathedral Steps' Square and another opposite the Baker in the side street to the left of the High St.

NTOG None, so the Ferry-Boat Ticket Offices have to be used for information, as do the various friendly sources.

OPENING HOURS A varied and unexpected mixture of traditional and holiday island, seven-day 'free-for-all'.

OTE (*Tmr* 6.D2) On the right, half-way up Leoforos Megalocharis. The office is open on weekdays between 0730 - 2400 hrs and at weekends from 0730 - 1510 hrs.

PETROL (GASOLINE) There are three petrol stations almost side by side about 1 km east out of Town on the Main Road

PHARMACIES *See* **Medical Care.**

PLACES OF INTEREST
Cathedrals & Churches
The Panagia Evangelistria (*Tmr* 36.D1) This Church dominates and overshadows the Port Town, sitting on top of the hill which is approached up the quite steeply climbing Leoforos Megalocharis. The history of the Church has been briefly outlined. *See* **History**.

Once through the principal wrought iron gates, the main Church is reached across the colourful pebble mosaic courtyard and up a majestic flight of marble steps. The dark interior is festooned with icons, masses of suspended lamps, candle holders and hanging votives, some of which depict the miraculous reason for their being donated. An outstanding example is the trading ship modelled in silver with a fish attached to the hull. This is in thanksgiving from the captain of a boat which was holed beneath the waterline and foundering in a storm, only to be saved by a large fish filling the breach, thus saving the ship and crew.

The miraculous icon is mounted inside and on the left. Continuous streams of pilgrims place candles in a battery of candle holders After seemingly only a few minutes they are snatched away to be reduced in the candle incinerator. I hope the pious communicant is not aware of the apparently callous commercial disregard for his or her Act of Worship or contrition.

CI-S

Beneath the main Church is a Chapel in which is the excavated hole where the icon was originally found and the fountain which started up soon after the discovery.

Close by the Chapel, in an aisle, is a ritualistic pile of stones, on which the icon was supposed to have been found and now covered with candles. Also in this area is the 'Elli Mausoleum' containing a portion of the torpedo that sank the ship in 1940.

Other buildings include a Museum dedicated to Island artists, hung with their pictures and displaying various sculptures, a Byzantine Museum exhibiting mainly 18th and 19th century icons and a Picture Gallery.

Day-Trips Local trip-boats ply daily to the Islands of Delos and Mykonos, leaving the harbour at 0900 hrs, spending 2½ hrs on Delos and 5 hrs on Mykonos, and returning at 1800 hrs at a cost of 1000 drs.

See **Chapter 13** for full details in respect of Delos and Mykonos islands.

Fountains There are two particularly large and interesting fountains, one on Odhos Evangelistrias and the other, dated 1797, at the upper end of the Old Quarter (*Tmr* 8.C2). From the small, paved Square on the side of which is situated the last mentioned fountain, a narrow, walled lane makes up the hillside through lovely gardens on either side. This pretty, stepped way finishes up above and to the left of Panagia Evangelistria.

Galerie Cybele (*Tmr* 38.D3) Worthy of a mention, although this type of establishment would not usually be included in this category. Next door to a very old building on the right-hand side of the Street leading up to the Church Ag Ioannou.

A very nice old lady, who speaks some French, presides over a shop full of antiques and, more importantly, second-hand books. These include some English language publications priced between 50 and 150 drs. She also sells 5 drs postcards and often gives purchasers a painted pebble as a memento.

On Sunday evenings the Town Brass Band slumps around the edge of the band-stand rotunda and unharmoniously thump their way through a routine.

Museum (*Tmr* 37.C/D2) A modern building on the way up Leoforos Megalocharis, on the left. Exhibits include a collection of the usual mix.

POLICE No Tourist police.

Port (*Tmr* 16.D3) Situated in a block to the side of the Esplanade along to the right (*Sbo*).

Town (*Tmr* 39.D2/3) Crammed into a large building in a narrow lane off Odhos Evangelistrias.

POST OFFICE (*Tmr* 6.D2) Shares the same building as the OTE, on the right of Leoforos Megalocharis. Open the usual weekday hours.

TAXIS Two main ranks on the Esplanade to the right of the Ferry-boat quay (*Sbo*), one on the Bus Terminal Square (*Tmr* C3) and the other further on on the corner of Ag Ioannou Street.

TELEPHONE NUMBERS & ADDRESSES

First Aid Centre	Tel 22210
Police	Tel 22234
Taxi Rank	Tel 22470

TOILETS On the edge of the 'Dolphin Square' alongside the Market building (*Tmr* 35.C2/3).

TRAVEL AGENTS See **Ferry-Boat Ticket Offices.**

ROUTE ONE

Tinos Town to Kionia (5 km) This coastal road curves up past the Commercial Quay (*Tmr* A/B2), leaving the *Hotel Asteria* on the right, the small stony beach on the left and then cuts inland of the Psari Plaka headland before dropping down to:-

STAVROS (2½ km from Tinos Town) A Chapel on the hillside of the cove overlooks a small harbour with the possible remains of an ancient Stoa stretching into the sea. It now incongruously doubles up as benzina moorings.

Further on towards Kionia, on the right alongside the road, is a field in which there are a scattering of remains including a Temple, an altar and a well. This is an Ancient Pilgrimage site dating back to the 4th century BC.

KIONIA (5 km from Tinos Town) A small settlement that has 'benefited' from plush hotel development. The beach starts out sandy with a pebble seashore but beyond a low, small, rocky promontory (alongside which is a very smart hotel), towards the far end, both beach and sea bottom are sandy.

The road encourages to deceive, turning sharply at a particularly grand Hotel on to a concreted water-course, only to run out on a rocky river-bed.

ROUTE TWO
Tinos Town to the South-East Coastal Villages The Main Road out of
Tinos Town climbs up to a fork around which are three petrol stations.

The right hand turning sallys forth and, after about 2 km, passes the:-

Monastery Agia Triada Not only a very old, picturesque Monastery with a Church, a handicraft Museum, Library, a fountain and a mausoleum but also, during the Turkish occupation, a secret, forbidden School for children ('Kryfo Schofo Scholio').

Not much further on, another right turning at the next fork (4 km) leads to:-

AG SOSTIS (7 km from Tinos Town) A lovely, sweeping, sandy beach set in low-rise hills. The backshore edge of the beach are low dunes, supporting small, sparse Arethemusa trees. A small outcrop of rocks divides the beach in two.

Over the low headland is:-

PORTO (7½ km from Tinos Town) To reach this dignified, new low rise 'Costa' development it is necessary to return to the last mentioned fork in the road.

The very smart *Rafael Bungalows* epitomises the quality of the new building taking place. Despite this 'up-market' attention, the beach close to the 'Bungalows' is rather scrubbly with some kelp heaped about. The sea bottom is sandy and the low backshore dunes are being sorted out, and the beach extended around the curve of the low headland. No taverna.

It is possible to make a cross-country run to the last south-east coast village to be detailed, which is good news as some cartographers slip in a non-existent road back to the inland village of Triantaros. The initial section of the existing track is poorly surfaced but improves, emerging above the village of:-

LICHNAFTIA (11 km from Tinos Town) The track to this very North Welsh 'look-a-like', ends above the Village. It is necessary to scramble down the path and keep to the right along the near side property wall. This emerges at the far right-hand edge of a tree and property lined, pebble and sand beach. Do not turn left parallel to the shore past the rustic fountain and up and down the slate steps of the 'High St', which runs with water. The path simply peters out.

The sea bottom is large pebbles, the foreshore fine pebbles, with very fine shingle in amongst the right-hand rocky headland. And that is that. Visitors are not encouraged. No smiling Greeks here and possibly the only sight of a local will be the disappearing view of a back. No taverna, kafenion, 'knocking shop' (whoops — wrong book) but this spot does offer secluded, perfect peace.

To return to Tinos it is possible to climb the long, wide, snaking unsurfaced road to

Triantoros and wander around the fascinating hill and mountainside Villages of, for instance, Steni, Mesi, Skalados, Tripotamos and *ad infinitum.*

If I have not already rambled on about it, there is no doubt that Tinos is a fascinating Island on which to spend several weeks walking from village to village.

ROUTE THREE

Tinos Town to Panormos Port via Panormos (35 km) Repeat the climb out of Tinos Town to the petrol stations as described in Route Two and take the left sweep at the fork which proceeds on up to the mountaineous interior. After about 5 km a right fork leads to:-

Kechrovounio Convent Built in the 12th century on the site of a Religious establishment reputably founded in the 8th/9th century. Its most famous celibate was of course St Pelagia who, in 1822, had the vision revealing the existence and location of the miraculous icon.

The Main Road winds around the hillsides dotted with Chapels and dovecotes (in about equal numbers), to the Village of:-

KAMPOS (14 km from Tinos Town) The Church Ag Aikaterini was built in 1771, during the brief Russian occupation. The Village was the birthplace of Loukia Negreponti, later to become Sister Pelagia (yes she) and marks one of the points from which it is possible to make the fascinating Excursion to:-

KOLIBITHRA (Kolympithra) 22 km from Tinos Town) From Kampos after 4 km the track reaches the spread out Village of:-

KOMI Set in a lovely, rich agricultural valley. By the bridge, and the Kolibithra junction, is the eccentrically named *Garage Pub* after which the route runs on to Kolibithra.

The other more adventurous route to Kolibithra is from the Main Road 3½ km beyond Kampos village. The junction of the unsurfaced turning off is marked by an old quarry, abandoned machinery and, on the left, a flat stone Monument in the style of a dovecote, commemorating I know not what. This track descends through the Villages of Kalloni, Karkados and Kato Klisma, on the north-west edge of the fertile valley.

The final approach is a drive along the flat valley bottom to a large, broad, glorious, sandy beach. This stretches away to the left with a swampy river to the right-hand side (*Fsw*), which runs into the rocky edged Bay of Kolibithra. The sea entrance to the bay almost seems to be blocked off by an islet. Around a bluff to the right is a deep-set, small, sandy beach cove, spoiled by some tar I'm afraid. Above the cove, to the right, are six terraced-house Apartments, a Restaurant/Cafe-bar and, on the far side, overlooking the edge of the beach is the admirable, rustic:-

Drakonisi Taverna Run by a smiling, round-faced man who will rustle up omelettes and Greek salad, in addition to coffees and liquid refreshment. Opposite the Taverna, back across the cove, on the beach edge is a toilet and shower block but cross your legs as its usually locked.

A lovely spot unless, as my reader pointed out, you are dying to use the toilets!

A map maker, who shall remain nameless, has depicted a secondary track from the Village of Aetofolia across to Isternia which would be jolly useful if it existed. Path, yes but certainly not negotiable by wheeled vehicles. I shall say no more. . . .

Back on the Main Road, at the dovecote Monument, the stretch of mountainside road to Kardiani village allows here and there, tantalising glimpses of pleasant looking coves, and the occasional hamlet, way down below to the left. They are only accessible by donkey or boat, more's the pity. Out to sea, in the distance, Syros Island basks in the Aegean Sea.

ISTERNIA (28 km from Tinos Town) A picturesque, 'hanging garden', Village off to the right of the Main Road and a convenient crossroads to various other villages. Close by is a saddle ridge lined with substantial old windmills. One has been quaintly converted and adjacent to which are some rather strange, Romanesque buildings, both to the left facing Panormos Village.

The left turning leads steeply down to the port of:-

AGIOS NIKITAS (30 km from Tinos Town) There is still the old paved way down the steep hillside to this lovely small seaside hamlet. I imagine the Port was once destined for greater things in the sphere of tourism, but the one Hotel passed on the way into the Village, is now deserted and closed, but things do change very quickly. . . . I am fairly certain that Ag Nikitas, also known as Ormos Isternian, was historically the Port to the Upper Village as far back as the Roman occupation.

Out of the height-of-season hardly a tourist in sight other than a few Greeks. To the right (*Fsw*) is a rather oversize commercial quay, probably a relic of the days when marble exporting was a viable proposition. To the left, the unmade track shambles on parallel to the narrow, pebbly beach on which are drawn up a number of benzinas. On the waterfront is the:-

Kafe, Ouzerie, Restaurant Ormos
Owned by a large, friendly, ex-Merchant Seaman who speaks some English. A limited fare is available.

Continuing up and over a small bluff leads to a lovely, sandy cove to the left of the bay (*Fsw*). A sandy sea bottom and upwards curving sand backshore, newly planted out with tree saplings. Well worth the trek.

On the way down (or up depending. . .) the steep mountainside to Ag Nikitas, a track turns off to the right, becomes a stony donkey path and leads to Kapsalos (30 km from Tinos Town). A lovely deserted cove with sandy beach and seabed.

On the Main Road close by the Isternia ridge, a track makes off to:-

Katapoliani Monastery Built in 1786 and guarded by an unfriendly dog kept within the bounds of the Monastery by wire mesh. A track rises steeply past the building but becomes impassable except on foot.

The Main Road winds down the mountain side to the Island's largest Village or more correctly Town of:-

PANORMOS (Pyrgos, Pirgos) (33 km from Tinos Town) The Main Road, still descending, bypasses Panormos circling around the left side. Where the bus pulls up on the bypass there is a large shelter and wall mounted Town Plan. A paved pedestrian way ascends past a small Museum, on the left, to the pretty, profusely flower and tree planted, higgledy-piggledy Town which is in effect a Chora.

To the left at the top of the pedestrian way is a Baker (nice bread) and General Store across from which are **Rooms** with a double room sharing the bathroom costing 785 drs.

To the right of the pedestrian way the winding 'High St' passes a rustic Post Office (change and telephones) and opens out on to a very interesting, irregular Plateia. The far side of this tree shaded Square is edged by a rather 'OTT' fountain, the doubled arched structure of which would not disgrace a Town Hall. One of the two sources of sustenance is a Kafenion advertising 'vegetarian seafood' whilst the other, a Cafe-bar seems more conventional.

Famous for sculptures and ikons, a number of small businesses keep the traditions alive.

The north-western end of the Island is mountainous with a number of hamlets and villages nestling here and there. The most renowned is Marlas, famed for its marble quarries and stone masons.

A further 3½ km on and the road from Panormos runs out in:-

PANORMOS PORT (36½ km from Tinos Town) A 'seedy' port with a very large quay at the end of an equally large concrete Quay Road skirting the right-hand side of the harbour. A number of benzinas moor up in shallow water close to the quay road which one hesitates to name an Esplanade. The reason for the inordinately big port facility is that a lot of marble used to be shipped from Panormos, reputably the safest port of Tinos Island. To the left is a small, scrubbly beach.

There are a Restaurant and a Coffee-bar side by side, both on the expensive side, a couple of stores and one gift shop. There are two houses with **Rooms** available but they fill up very quickly, when vacancies occur, despite being costly with a double room, in mid season, charged at 1250 drs — (whow!).

21 Andros
Cyclades Islands — Eastern wing

***

FIRST IMPRESSIONS
Verdant island; space and breadth; flowers; prosperity; Greeks on holiday; red roofs; neat villages; unplastered walls.

SPECIALITIES
Mineral water; unique walls; 'frontalia' omelette (includes potatoes, sausage and bacon or pork — scrumptious)

RELIGIOUS HOLIDAYS & FESTIVALS
include: 27th July — Feast of Ag Panteleimon, the Monastery of Panachrantos; 6th December — Feast of Ag Nikolaos, the Monastery of Agios Nikolaos.

VITAL STATISTICS
Tel prefix 0282. Most northern, and second largest of the Cyclades islands (to Naxos). Up to 39½ km from NW to SE, up to 16 km in width with an area of about 373 sq km. The population numbers approximately 10,000 of which about 1,800 live in the capital, Andros Town.

HISTORY
The average historical mix although the Andriots appear to have caused their various overlords rather more difficulties than most other Cycladean islands. This may have been due to the large number of Albanians who settled on the Island during the Middle-Ages.

Andros experienced an Axis troops fall-out (as did for example Cephalonia in the Ionian) with the Germans bombing the resident Italian soldiers into submission in 1943.

GENERAL
Geographically a very large Island, but despite this massive physical presence Andros somehow gives the impression of being much smaller. In part this is not surprising considering the comparatively small size of the main centres. The scruffy port of Gavrion would be more suitable for one of the small island, off-the-cuff, ferry-boat calls. The villa holiday resort of Vatsi (Batsi) could be swallowed by many other popular locations without a hiccup. Andros Town, the capital, is a disappointment lacking a Cycladian Chora and masquerading more as a seaside beach development than the main town. On the other hand nothing can detract from the soft, awesome beauty of the Islands rolling mountains which are divided by large fertile plains. Wealthy Athenians have developed many of the villages into neat, red tile roofed, tidy, bi-annual commuter settlements, nestling in the tree-clad hill and mountain sides. Moreover the plenteous supply of water supports not only rich agricultural vistas, but Cypress tree plantations that march up the hillside amphitheatres. Mind you the south-eastern fishing port of Ormos Korthion does not let us down, for here emerges a hint, a suggestion of the Greece we know and love. That messy beauty of chickens, goats and donkeys rooting and grazing in unkempt backyards; unmade, pot-holed streets; lanes that run out in the tumbling stones of summer-dry river-beds; old, graceful houses deteriorating in amongst new, stark, skeletal concrete frames and fishing nets draped wherever. Other true evocations of the Greek islands of yester-

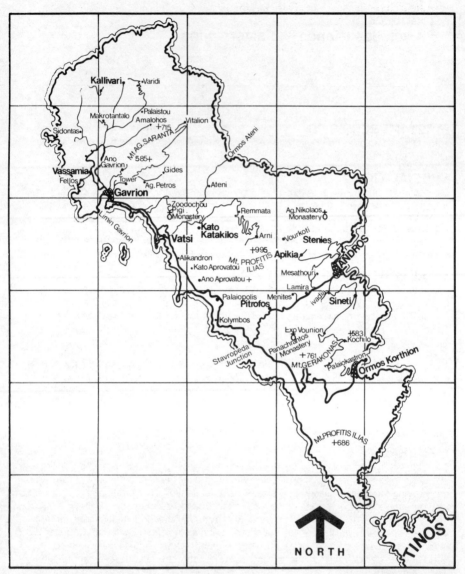

ANDROS

Illustration 37

year are also present at nearby Palaiokastron, where there is even dilapidated property, and the untidy port of Gavrion.

Although Venetian dovecotes are not so numerous as on Tinos, the Andriots have their own countryside quirk — the unique walling in which a large, triangulated plate of stone is placed sideways in to the wall.

The present, comparatively low numbers of package holiday-makers combined with the continuing, but now meaningless, rumour that Andros is a rich Greeks preserve has kept ferry-boat island hoppers to a low level and helped maintain some of the islands spirit and traditions. If all this were not enough there are lovely, relatively empty beaches, so is it any wonder that Andros is a favourite holiday and weekend stop-off for mainland travellers?

Travellers should note that signposting, especially off the main roads, is very poor but the islanders, if not the commuter mainlanders, are very friendly and will be more than helpful.

If the Meltemi is blowing, stay on the south-west, not the east coast.

GAVRION: main port (Illustration 38)
Not a prepossessing place, although it may well grow on one if allowed the time to weave its spell. The appearance is certainly not improved by the expansion of the car and lorry parking which has created an untidy, ugly waste ground, south (or to the right) of the Ferry-boat quay (*Sbo*). The Port and Village is to the right of the encircling bay (*Sbo*) with a small, haphazard, shanty bungalow development on the backshore of the beach at the bottom of the bay. Almost the whole Port is lined up on the 'High St-cum-Esplanade' reminiscent and not dissimilar to a Yukon mining town.

ARRIVAL BY FERRY
Rather out of the ordinary, the Ferry-boat Port of Gavrion is not the capital, a main town or even an important holiday resort.

Another relatively unusual, and unwelcome practice is that the boats are not met even by a handful of Room owners. However the local buses, up to 12 taxis and the *Camping Andros* van attend a Ferry's docking.

All the above leaves a disembarking traveller with a dilemma — to stay in Gavrion or make for Vatsi (Batsi) or Andros Town. My own preference is to make an immediate base and, bearing in mind my views on the general unattractiveness of Andros Town, plump for either Gavrion or possibly Vatsi as the first stop-off.

An important point to bear in mind when planning itineraries is that Andros is a mainland Greeks weekend resort. You have been warned.

THE ACCOMMODATION & EATING OUT
The Accommodation As intimated there is not a superabundance and it is best to get a move on and grab what is on offer. Fortunately one of the best places to stay is almost opposite the Ferry-boat quay (*Tmr* 1.C3).

The Hotel Galaxy (*Tmr* 2.C/D2) (Class D)   Tel 71228
Directions: Half-left from the bottom of the Ferry-boat quay and across the Esplanade.

Mikali, the proprietor, is almost shy and does not push himself forward to procure clients so it is necessary to take the Hotel by the horns, as it were. Fortunately, and mistakenly, the smart look of the place tends to put off waverer's so the fleet of foot and mind will ensure themselves accommodation. The rooms are comfortable and, naturally, those positioned to the front overlook much of the Port activities. A single room en suite starts off at 800 drs rising to 1000 drs (June and September) and a double room en suite 1000 drs, rising to 1300 drs, and the water is hot.

The ground floor is most conveniently taken up by a spacious Cafe-bar Restaurant. The friendly waiters speak some English and Mikali the amicable owner allows luggage to be

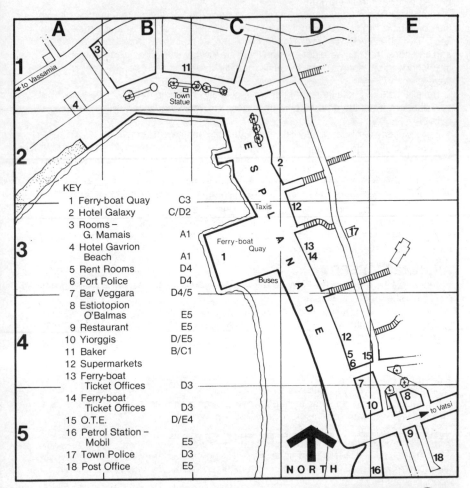

KEY

1	Ferry-boat Quay	C3
2	Hotel Galaxy	C/D2
3	Rooms – G. Mamais	A1
4	Hotel Gavrion Beach	A1
5	Rent Rooms	D4
6	Port Police	D4
7	Bar Veggara	D4/5
8	Estiotopion O'Balmas	E5
9	Restaurant	E5
10	Yiorggis	D/E5
11	Baker	B/C1
12	Supermarkets	
13	Ferry-boat Ticket Offices	D3
14	Ferry-boat Ticket Offices	D3
15	O.T.E.	D/E4
16	Petrol Station – Mobil	E5
17	Town Police	D3
18	Post Office	E5

GAVRION PORT

Illustration 38

stored in his mezzanine office. Two coffees and an ouzo cost 160 drs.

Radiating out from this hotel are:-

Rooms G Mamais (*Tmr* 3.A1)   Tel 71219
Directions: Left from the Ferry-boat quay (*Sbo*) past the Town statue and right down the side street on the nearside of the building containing the smart *Hotel Gavrion Beach* (*Tmr* 4.A1). At the bottom of this short road, on the right-hand corner.

A Mama runs the neat accommodation with a double room sharing the bathroom costing (mid-season) from 900 drs.

The Hotel Gavrion Beach (*Tmr* 4.A1) (Class C)   Tel 71312
Directions: As above.

Smart and expensive with a double room costing 1600 drs.

In the other direction from the Ferry-boat quay, to the right (*Sbo*) is:-

Rent Rooms (*Tmr* 5.D4)
Directions: The waterfront side of the building is situated over a shop, next door to the Port police (*Tmr* 6.D4). To the rear of the building the back lane is level with the first-floor. A bit of a 'doss house'.

Hotel Aphrodite (Class B)   Tel 71209
Directions: To the left of and about 150 m up the Vatsi Road out of Gavrion, towards the top of the rise.

Actually classified as a Pension with a double room en suite costing some 1600 drs.

Bearing in mind the general lack of available Rooms, although I do not as a rule strongly advocate camping, the site near Gavrion must be a good proposition.

Camping Andros   Tel (Athens) 8228549
Directions: From the Ferry-boat quay (*Tmr* 1.C3) turn left (*Sbo*) along the waterfront as far as the *Sea Star Kafenion* and turn down the lane on the far side. This makes a junction with the back road at which turn right for the site, which is about a couple kilometres distant.

A super set-up with good facilities and a cafeteria at which a number of locals eat — there can be no better recommendation. The attentive owner lived in America for a time and is mindful of satisfying his clients. A varied and good menu with a meal for two of say a plate of roast-beef and peas, a plate of meat and rice, fried zucchinis, a portion of chips, bread and a bottle of retsina costs 600 drs. Last orders for a meal is 2200 hrs.

The Campsite van meets the Ferries.

The Eating Out Although there is not a great deal of choice, Gavrion has at least one excellent Taverna, able to stand against all but the very best the Cyclades has to offer.

Εστiατopion O'Balmas (*Tmr* 8.E5)
Directions: Turn down the alley alongside *Bar Veggara* (*Tmr* 7.D4/5). This opens out on to a pleasant, tree shaded irregular square and the Taverna is on the far right-hand side.

A number of unusual dishes with a meal for two of liver (yes liver), (404 drs). A plate of briami (a 'sort of' ratatouille), chips, a tomato and cucumber salad, 2 'open' retsinas (of an 'interestingly' rich familiar consistency and flavour) and bread cost 660 drs.

See **Andros Camping, The Accommodation.**

Naturally there are a number of other establishments, including:-

Restaurant (*Tmr* 9.E5)
Directions: On the right at the start of the Main Road to Vatsi.

THE A TO Z OF USEFUL INFORMATION
BANKS No.

BEACHES The flat, narrow, Port beach at the bottom of the bay is around to the left (*Sbo*) of the Ferry-boat quay. Local benzinas are anchored in the shallow water for the first half of its length and there is a small, rustic Kafenion on the backshore. It will do as a standby.

BICYCLE, SCOOTER & CAR HIRE I suppose my favourite outfit (in the year 1985) must be

Yiorggis (*Tmr* 10.D/E5). At the far right-hand end of the Esplanade (*F-bqbo*). Don't misunderstand me, his vehicles are on the 'ropey' side but.... In his middle 30s, round faced, moustachioed, excellent English and an absolute mine of information. But steady girls, Amanda, his pretty English wife is usually nearby. Yiorggis hires out a rather motley selection of scooters, from a narrow garage of bomb-site appearance. Hire rates are on the expensive side considering the general state of the machines but his smiling, happy nature will charm customers from any misdirected thoughts of complaining!

He might well return to his occupation as a Merchant-Navy radio officer. If he does, a far less *simpatico* compatriot runs a more bland outfit, seemingly from the patio tables of *Bar Veggara.*

Whatever is written elsewhere regarding the availability of petrol, it is a problem on Andros so insist that whichever firm you select guarantees to supply the 'propellant'. (*See* **Petrol**).

BREAD SHOPS (*Tmr* 11.B/C1) There is a Baker to the left of the Ferry-boat quay (*Sbo*), immediately behind the Town Statue. The Baker sells pies and doughnuts.

BUSES Pull up alongside the Ferry-boat quay on the waste ground. The fleet of four buses are rather old but a new one arrived in 1985.

Bus timetable Yes well! *See* **Andros Town** but there is a regular service which ties into the Ferry-boat arrivals.

COMMERCIAL SHOPPING AREA There are two Supermarkets (*Tmr* 12.D3 & 12.D4). Another interesting outfit sells honey from the back of an orange Volkswagon van occasionally parked up to the left of the *Hotel Galaxy* (*Sbo*). Inside the van are a few pictorial details of the process and some examples of old island beehives.

FERRY-BOATS Rafina is the only Mainland Port serving the Island, there being no direct Piraeus connection.

Ferry-boat timetable

Day	Departure time	Ferry-boat	Ports/Islands of Call
Monday	1000 hrs	Eptanissos	Tinos, Syros
	1130 hrs	Nisos Andros	Rafina (M)
	1645 hrs	Eptanissos	Rafina (M, 1930 hrs)
Tuesday,	1000 hrs	Eptanissos	Tinos, Mykonos
Wednesday	1130 hrs	Nisos Andros	Rafina (M)
	1645 hrs	Nisos Andros	Rafina (M)
Thursday	1000 hrs	Eptanissos	Tinos, Mykonos
	1130 hrs	Nisos Andros	Rafina (M)
	1645 hrs	Eptanissos	Rafina (M)
	1930 hrs	Nisos Andros	Rafina (M)
Friday	1000 hrs	Eptanissos	Tinos
	1130 hrs	Nisos Andros	Rafina (M)
	1415 hrs	Eptanissos	Rafina (M)
	1930 hrs	Nisos Andros	Rafina (M)
	2010 hrs	Eptanissos	Tinos, Mykonos, Rafina (M, 0345 hrs next day)

Saturday	1000 hrs	Eptanissos	Tinos
	1130 hrs	Nisos Andros	Rafina (M)
	1415 hrs	Eptanissos	Rafina (M)
	2010 hrs	Eptanissos	Tinos, Mykonos, Rafina (M, 0345 hrs next day)
Sunday	1000 hrs	Eptanissos	Tinos, Mykonos
	1200 hrs	Nisos Andros	Rafina (M)
	1645 hrs	Eptanissos	Rafina (M)
	1930 hrs	Nisos Andros	Rafina (M)
	2210 hrs	Eptanissos	Rafina (M, 0040 hrs next day)

One-way fare 550 drs, duration 3 hrs (to Rafina).

FERRY-BOAT TICKET OFFICES Two side by side (*Tmr* 13.D3 & 14.D3), opposite the Ferry-boat quay.

OTE (*Tmr* 15.D/E4) To the far right-hand end of the Esplanade, down the lane alongside the *Bar Veggaria*. It is often difficult to make an international connection from this office which only opens weekdays from 0800 - 2100 hrs.

PETROL (GASOLINE) There is a Mobil petrol station (*Tmr* 16.F5) to the far right of the waterfront(*F-bqbo*) but for most of 1985 it was 'dead'. The elderly owner was ill and his son-in-law was supposed to be arriving from Athens (as is everybody who is filling in for someone else anywhere on the Cyclades — a sort of end of the rainbow place). But, as already stated, petrol on the Island is very difficult to come by, the Andros Town area, being the best source. In fact as Yiorggis said "it's as difficult to obtain as rocking-horse 'big potty' ".

POLICE
Port (*Tmr* 6.D4).
Town (*Tmr* 17.D3).

POST OFFICE (*Tmr* 18.E5) In the street alongside the Restaurant (*Tmr* 9.E5) on the Main Road out of Gavrion Port.

TAXIS Queue up to the left of the Ferry-boat quay (*Sbo*). Up to 12 meet the Ferry-boats.

TELEPHONE NUMBERS & ADDRESSES
First Aid   Tel 71210
Town police   Tel 71220

ROUTE ONE
Gavrion Port to Vassamia, Fellos & beyond The route to the north of the
Island runs off round the bottom of the bay and along the road behind the *Hotel Gavrion Beach*. Once at the far side of the flat agricultural plain backing the bay, the road starts to climb and the rural country lane leads on up into massive, rounded mountains with gentle valleys cuddled in their curves.

From the village of Vassamia (4½ km) a track meanders off left, by an abandoned bulldozer, tumbling down to a couple of very pleasant seaside coves set in rather 'moth-eaten' hills. The first is the larger of the two, both have sandy beaches and discreetly set in the surrounding hillsides are the bungalows of affluent foreigners.

On this northern coastline there are other 'secret' coves but travellers will require a strong conveyance or very long legs. . . . One of the spots recommended by the locals is Zorko Beach reached via Kallivari Village but you will have to ask the way. The signposting to the little hamlets up here, as elsewhere on the Island, is very poor and mainly non-existent excepting that to Amolohos which, for some reason. . . .!

ROUTE TWO

Gavrion Port to Andros Town (35 km) The Main Road to Andros Town climbs up from the right-hand side of the Port (*Sbo*) and across the headland that forms one side of Limin Gavriou, from whence a pleasant view to seaward of a group of inshore islets. The road descends to sea level where there is a very small cove which is hardly worth a mention in the light of the others to come.

Hereabouts a dusty track makes off into the hillside and the left fork leads to *Andros Camping* (*See* **The Accommodation, Gavrion Port**). The right-hand, surfaced road, initially signposted Ag Petros and then confusingly Vitalion, leads to the:-

Tower of Ag Petros (St Peter) Frankly not so dramatic as the pre-publicity would suggest and quite the most outstanding feature is the neatness of the workmanlike masonry. The structure is the subject of much conjecture as to the date and reason of its construction. Was it a fort, store or signalling tower?

A little further on the sea level Main Road is a lovely, shade-less sandy beach with two tavernas at the far end. Over a low, small headland is another attractive, shallow shelving, sheltered, small, sandy beach cove backed by dunes. Beyond a rocky outcrop is a longer, very sandy beach on the near edge of which is the **Pell Mell Disco** and a taverna complex with the *Hotel Perrakis* across the road.

A track into the interior from this cove snakes up to:-

Zoodochou Pigi Monastery (10 km from Gavrion Port) There are a number of Island Monasteries worthy of a visit including Panachrantos, south-west of Andros Town, and Agios Nikolaos, north of Andros Town, but Zoodochou Pigi is the most accessible. Originally a Monastery but more correctly, since the 1920s, a Convent. The date of foundation wavers between the 9th and 14th century AD so it seems a pity that the celibates are now down to about 5 or 6. This loss in numbers has unfortunately put a stop to the weaving once practiced and for which the Monastery was famed. Visitors should call before 1100 hrs and although the views are excellent the buildings are drab.

VATSI (Batsi) (8 km from Gavrion Port) (Illustration 39)

The Main Road bypasses this 'Greek St Ives', part port, part summer resort, with the resort aspect becoming increasingly dominant. There are plenty of Rooms, the package holiday firms have a toe-hold and there are a few souls sleeping at the far end of the beach (from the Port).

The Streets parallel to the Esplanade rise up the contoured hillside and are progressively one storey higher than the last.

THE ACCOMMODATION & EATING OUT

The Accommodation Described in a clockwise direction starting from the north-west (Gavrion end) of the harbour bay round to the south.

Hotel Skouna (*Tmr* 1.B/C1) (Class C)   Tel 41315
A combination of hotel, cafeteria and bar. A single room en suite costs either 825 drs or 1100 drs rising to 1060 drs or 1300 drs (July - August). A double room similarly costs 1060/1350 drs and 1350/1600 drs.

In the area behind the *Hotel Glari* (*Tmr* B2), a package-holiday Hotel, there are a number of **Rooms** and 5 Villas to let.

Hotel H Karanasos (*Tmr* 3.C1)
No details, sorry.

Hotel Lykion (*Tmr* 4.C1) (Class B)   Tel 41214
Actually a Pension with a double room sharing a bathroom, costing 1000 drs.

Hotel Chryssi Akti (*Tmr* 5.D2) (Class C)   41236
A 'look-alike' for a 'Spanish Costa' block in which an en suite double room rises from 1350

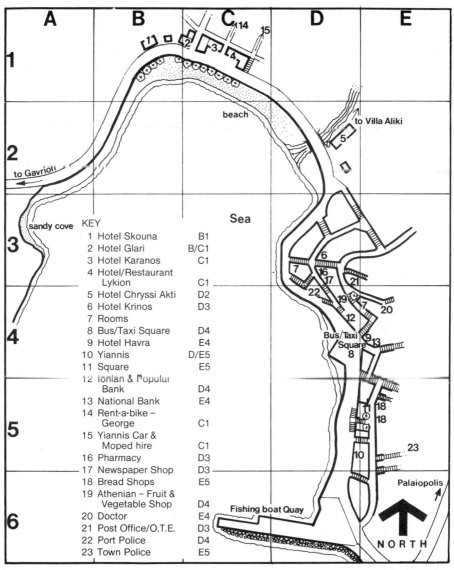

KEY

1	Hotel Skouna	B1
2	Hotel Glari	B/C1
3	Hotel Karanos	C1
4	Hotel/Restaurant Lykion	C1
5	Hotel Chryssi Akti	D2
6	Hotel Krinos	D3
7	Rooms	
8	Bus/Taxi Square	D4
9	Hotel Havra	E4
10	Yiannis	D/E5
11	Square	E5
12	Ionian & Popular Bank	D4
13	National Bank	E4
14	Rent-a-bike – George	C1
15	Yiannis Car & Moped hire	C1
16	Pharmacy	D3
17	Newspaper Shop	D3
18	Bread Shops	E5
19	Athenian – Fruit & Vegetable Shop	D4
20	Doctor	E4
21	Post Office/O.T.E.	D3
22	Port Police	D4
23	Town Police	E5

VATSI

Illustration 39

drs to 1600 drs. Alongside there is a small, beach-shower prefab but for the use of hotel clients only. . . .!

To the side of the Hotel a sign points along an unmade track, indicating the:-

Villa Aliki — Rooms to Rent 30 m

The Esplanade makes a sharp right turn and then curves round to the left. A flight of steps climbs up to the:-

Hotel Krinos (*Tmr* 6.D3) (Class D)   Tel 41232

'Provincial'. A single room sharing the bathroom starts at 660 drs rising to 750 drs (15th June - 15th September). A double room costs 1000 drs and 1100 drs respectively.

To the right of the same steps are:-

Rooms (*Tmr* 7.D3)

Further around the Esplanade on the 'Bus/Taxi' Square (*Tmr* 8.D4), opposite a small quay is the:-

Hotel H'Avra (*Tmr* 9.E4) (Class D)   Tel 41216

Same rates as for the *Hotel Krinos*.

The Eating Out Similarly clockwise from the north-west to the south of the harbour.

The Hotel Lykion Restaurant (*Tmr* 4.C1)

A busy establishment. In amongst more expensive offerings they serve up an extremely reasonably priced macaroni cheese dish — well spaghetti really but should one quarrel about the particular brand of pasta? Two plates of a (small) tomato and cucumber salad, and bread for 250 drs.

In the area of the 'Bus/Taxi' Sq (*Tmr* 8.D4) there are divers restaurants, including a row edging the square but the most highly recommended in Vatsi is:-

Yiannis (*Tmr* 10.D/E5)

Directions: South of the 'Bus/Taxi' Sq, along the Esplanade towards the fishing boat quay.

Yiannis keeps his own animals, some of which, not unnaturally, finish up on his taverna tables (cooked of course) and enjoys a reputation for the best meat on the Island. A fillet steak costs 500 drs (I remember fillet steak) but the menu also includes 'prawns in curry sauce'. Ugh!

Prior to *Yiannis* two flights of steps leads up to a pretty, small Square (*Tmr* 11.E5) around and off which are at least four restaurants.

THE A TO Z OF USEFUL INFORMATION

BANKS Two exchange offices.

Ionian & Popular (*Tmr* 12.D4) Boxed in by restaurants that line the 'Bus/Taxi' Square. Open Monday, Tuesday and Thursday 0900 - 1300 hrs.

National Bank (*Tmr* 13.E4) Almost lost in the tree filled corner of the 'Bus/Taxi' Square, to the far side of the *Hotel H'Avra*. Open Monday, Wednesday and Friday between 0900 - 1300 hrs.

BEACHES Again clockwise from the north.

Beach 1. Across the bay, opposite the fishing boat quay. A small sandy cove.

Beach 2. The main beach stretches from close by the *Hotel Skouna* (*Tmr* 1.B1) all the way round to the *Hotel Chryssi Akti* (*Tmr* 5.D2). Mainly coarse sand with a scattering of large pebbles. A shingly foreshore and sea bottom. There are pedaloes and wind-surfers at the north end.

Beach 3. A lovely looking, small, sandy outcrop around the quay, on the edge of the 'Bus/Taxi' Square but smelly. I suspect sewage outfalls here!

A small 'taxi boat' ferries clients to beaches north and south of Vatsi. To walk south to the sandy beaches of Delevoyas and Ag Marina, takes about 25 minutes along the coastal track. The path starts out from the Memorial on the side of the acute bend in the Andros road, south out of Vatsi.

BICYCLE, SCOOTER & CAR HIRE
Rent-A-Byke George (*Tmr* 14.C1) On the left behind the *Hotel Karanasos* in the basement of a large villa.

Yiannis Car & Moped Hire (*Tmr* 15.C1) Down the side street to the south side of the *Hotel Lykion* (*Tmr* 4.C1).

Average rates are about 1000 drs a day for scooters.

BOOKSELLERS (*Tmr* 17.D3) More a purveyor of foreign newspapers. Climb up the angled flight of steps to the 'Athenian Fruit & Vegetable' shop and left up the inclined and stepped alley. On the right, to the near side of the Pharmacy (*Tmr* 16.D3).

BREAD SHOPS (*Tmr* 18.E5) Actually two, one of which is a Bakery, and only separated from each other by a restaurant. South of the 'Bus/Taxi' Sq and up the pair of stone steps to the tree-shaded mini-Square (*Tmr* 11.E5).

BUSES They park up on the side of the 'Bus/Taxi' Square. I have to own up (here, as elsewhere) that I found the Andros Island bus timetables complicated and those stuck up in Andros Town Bus terminal absolutely unfathomable.

Daily services to Gavrion, Andros Town and Ormos Korthion.

CHEMISTS *See* Medical Care.

CINEMA A local, open-air job, behind the *Hotel Glari* (*Tmr* 2.B/C1). Shows start at 2110 hrs and entrance costs 120 drs.

COMMERCIAL SHOPPING AREA No Central Market but for a Village this size it is amply provided with shops. These include 'Athenian Fruit & Vegetable' (*Tmr* 19.D4), reputably housed in one of the oldest dwellings in Vatsi. There is a Periptero on the edge of the 'Bus/Taxi' Square.

DENTISTS & DOCTORS *See* Medical Care.

DISCOS Yes, 3, including the '**Chaf**', which advertises 'Wet T-Shirt Partys'. (Golly gosh. I've dreamt of. . .).

FERRY-BOAT TICKET OFFICES *See* Travel Agents.

MEDICAL CARE
Chemists & Pharmacies (*Tmr* 16.D3) On the lane, one back and approximately parallel to the Esplanade, quite close to the *Hotel Krinos*. Weekday opening hours, 0830 - 1330 hrs and 1800 - 2130 hrs.

Dentist Telephone Mr Vastardis on 41450 for surgery, Monday, Wednesday and Friday.

Doctor (*Tmr* 20.E4) In the alley that angles off to the left, standing with the Post Office (*Tmr* 21.D3) on your left. The notice requests clients to telephone and the telephone number is 41326.

OTE (*Tmr* 21.D3) Shares the building with the 'doo-hickey' Post Office and is most easily reached up the flight of steps alongside the *Hotel Avra*. Opens daily 0800 - 1300 hrs and 1700 - 2200 hrs except Sundays when the OTE is open 0900 - 1200 hrs and 1700 - 1900 hrs. Closed holidays. The Post Office hours are the standard weekday opening hours.

PETROL There is a petrol station on the Main Road that bypasses Vatsi, on the Andros Town side.

PHARMACIES *See* **Medical Care.**

POLICE
Port (*Tmr* 22.D4) In a small, modern block.

Town (*Tmr* 23.E5) The police station is up a steep flight of steps at the south end of the Port. Tel 41204.

POST OFFICE (*Tmr* 21.D3) *See* **OTE.**

TAXIS Not surprisingly park up on the waterside of the 'Bus/Taxi' Square (*Tmr* 8.D4).

TOILETS None (so hold on).

TRAVEL AGENTS Not so much Travel Agents, more ticket offices combined with souvenir shops, side by side on the south-east side of the 'Bus/Taxi' Square.

From the Vatsi bypass, a surfaced road of about 4½ km in length heads inland for:-

KATO KATAKILOS The Ateni stream runs through the Village. The three tavernas not only serve reasonable food at acceptable prices but put on a show of music and dancing in the evenings. If transport is not available the 1½ hr walk is most agreeable (if you must). On Saturday nights, in the summer, they roast a pig.
    From Kato Katakilos the upper Hamlet Village of Ano Katakilos is only a hop, skip and a jump (perhaps a little bit further than that) as is:-

ATENI (16½ km from Gavrion Port) The small Village unfurls down the river valley to the sea and some splendid sandy beaches (set in the Ormos Ateni) which are almost empty throughout the summer, even at the height-of-the season. No refreshments.
    Almost from Kato Katakilos the track winds up the sides of Mt Profitis Ilias, through the Hamlet of Remmata, to the lovely, lush, near mountain top Village of:-

ARNI (20 km from Gavrion Port) Well worth the journey although even at the height of the summer it can be cloud-bound. There is a cafe-bar. Current construction work indicates that a connecting road to Vourkoti, around the mountain side, is on the drawing board. There is a restaurant/taverna in the Village— why not make the trek before there are coach parties and a hamburger bar?

Continuing on towards Andros Town, the Main Road rises up from Vatsi Port to skirt the steep mountain side. On the way, to the left, are the villages of:-

KATO & ANO APROVATOU Both possess tavernas and Kato has *Rooms* and a cafe-bar. A path from the Kato part of the Main Road descends to an attractive and peaceful beach.
    On a beautiful, giant curve in the lush mountainside which is sprinkled with stately Cypress trees, is the clean and neat, hillside 'hanging' Village of:-

PALAIOPOLIS (17 km from Gavrion Port) The terraced hillsides are kept verdant by the numerous springs from high up the steep sides of Mt Kouvara. No wonder the ancients chose this area for their Capital which was possibly destroyed in the 4th century AD. Part of the remains are supposed to lie beneath the sea below the Village, in the long, straight edged cove bordered by a stony foreshore and beach. As is often the way, the most notable find, a statue, the 'Hermes of Andros', is on display in Athens.
    The stepped path down to the beach starts out from the Main Road, opposite the little Shrine with a Kafenion one side and a taverna the other. On the way down, turn right along the first path into which the steps run, over a bridge and keep straight on past the fountain (on the right) beyond the steps that run off to the left. After the next bridge, and further steps down, at the cross paths keep almost straight on down the path, leaving steps to left and

right. Where the path breaks into another flight of steps, keep straight on leaving a flight off to the left. Okay. Don't blame me if you make a false move. . . .

After another 7½ km of Main Road, at a windswept, exposed, scruffy ridge, is the 'T-junction turning for Andros Town. The left-hand road descends along the natural cleft in the mountains to left and right (whilst the road straight on skirts Mt Gerakonas and then tumbles down to Ormos Korthion). Incidentally, the highways are poorly surfaced in patches from the junction to both Andros Town and Ormos Korthion.

Frankly, the road and its immediate surrounds down the valley to Andros Town are messy, as are the villages of Koumani, Messaria and Messa Chorio. Furthermore, they are almost sprawling, urban outposts of Andros Town. Admittedly the dramatic hillside surrounds are Samos-like in their verdancy with masses of trees including Cypresses. Out of these, to the left, peek the neat, almost densely populated, red tile roofed Villages of Menites, Lamira, Strapouries and Mesathouri which parallel the road. Many of the houses in these Villages are owned by Athenian commuters who winter on the mainland and spend summer on the Island.

MENITES (28½ km from Gavrion Port) Famous for its mineral springs.

ANDROS TOWN (35 km from Gavrion Port): capital (Illustration 40)

This is no Chora, and the Town is more a Greek 'Eastbourne or Weymouth' and disappointing, although I have seen and heard it described as attractive. Oh well, beauty is in the eye. . . . Maybe I suffer from vision defects.

Many of the official buildings are imposing 19th century 'Municipal' and a notable feature is that the long Main Street is a marble paved pedestrian way. The Town is built on a high headland or promontory that juts out and divides Kastrou Bay into two, leaving a beach down below on either side.

The worthy citizens make little or no attempt to accommodate tourists and those lodgings available are usually taken up by Greeks. Because of this, and the layout of the Town I propose to stray from the usual arrangement and progress from the inland end of the Main Street, towards the Castle topped islet at the sea-tip end of the promontory.

The Police station (Tel 22300) is followed by the Post Office and the OTE (*Tmr* 1.A4). Where the Square-like, wide avenue narrows down to the pedestrian way High Street, there is a Taxi rank.

To the right, a side turning leads on to the very scruffy, sloping 'Bus Terminus' Square (Plateia Olga, *Tmr* 2.A/B4). At the far side of this Square is the messy Bus office building (*Tmr* 3.B4) on the wall of which is a timetable I found difficult, nay impossible to decipher. Sufficient to say that there are daily connections to, amongst other Villages, Ormos Korthion, Stenies, Menites, Sineti, Pitrofos Apikia (Apoikia) as well as half a dozen a day to Vatsi and Gavrion. On Saturdays there are few less services and Sunday they are very restricted. On the right of Olga Square is a Restaurant (*Tmr* 4.B4), although I am not sure that to use that all encompassing word may be unnecessarily derogatory to other establishments using the same appellation. From the High Street a sign pointing the way proclaims:- 'The *Stations Restaurant* in Olga Square, Bus Station offers fine Foos [sic] at fair prices. Only the freshest local produce is u-sed in our kitchen, we also do take-away service'. In reality it is a greasy shack.

From Olga Square a lane winds along and up and down the side of the headland to Plateia Kairis, the Main Square, passing on the way the Public Tolets (*Tmr* 5.B3).

Back on the High Street, there are a brace of Chemists, and on the right the Ionian and Popular Bank (*Tmr* 6.A/B3). Prior to the Bank is a Baker who sells sausage pies (more a sausage roll) for 45 drs, and a Green Grocer in the basement. On the right of the Street opposite the Bank, that falls rapidly towards the left-hand beach, is a Galaktopoleio that sells fresh yoghurt. On the far side of the Ionian and Popular Bank, a flight of steps rises steeply to the:-

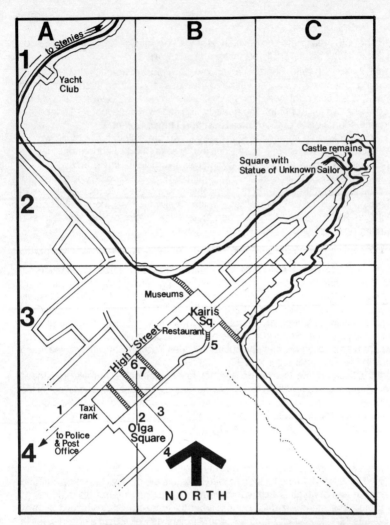

Town of ANDROS

Illustration 40

Hotel Aegli (*Tmr* 7.B3) (Class C) Tel 22303
If one is available, a single bed, sharing the bathroom, starts at 650 drs rising to 750 drs
(1st July-15th September). A double room rises from 880 drs sharing, or en suite 1140 drs,
to 1070 drs and 1370 drs respectively. Opposite the steps up to the *Hotel Aegli* is
the:-

Bar Sofrita A sign announces:- 'Information Upstairs Hotel Rooms for Rent This is... Old
Old Andros Saloon. The best Snakbar with lovely view and good music'.
The High Street ends on Plateia Kairis with, on the left, the Archaeological and Modern
Art Museums, straight ahead a covered archway and couple of cafe-bars and, round to
the right, a well situated Restaurant with views over the broad, right hand beach.
By the way, the Museum summer time hours are: Archaeological daily 0845 - 1500 hrs
and 0930 - 1430 hrs on Sundays and holidays with entrance costing 50 drs; and the
Modern Art, daily 1000 - 1400 hrs and 1600 - 1800 hrs. Both are closed on
Tuesdays.
On the right of the covered way is a Bookshop selling foreign newspapers and the neat
lane proceeds down through the Old Quarter. There are alleys branching off to either side
and on the right, a path down to a few, very small fishing boat quays. The lane passes a
Naval Museum and peters out on a rather barren paved Square at the end of the bluff. This
Plateia is dominated by a large statue of an 'Unknown Sailor' peering seawards, with a
ditty-bag slung over his shoulder, and commemorates all Andriot seamen lost at sea.
The narrow headland, hemmed in by a rocky sealine, is tipped by the ruins of a Venetian
Castle on a tiny rock islet. The Castle's state of repair was not helped by being subject to
German bombing in 1943 in order to quell the resident Italian Occupation Troops. On the
way back to the Plateia Kairis, a lane branches off to the right (Castle behind one) through
what is left of an Old Chora, which is not yet overwhelmed by new development.
The beach to the right of Andros Town promontory (*Fsw*) is an expansive stretch of
sandy shore. To the left, is a narrow beach with an Esplanade road edging the bay and
leading past a heavily tree-shaded seaside development with a number of restaurants
and two houses with **Rooms**. The road circles to the right, round a Yacht Club, the very
smart 'Naval Club', incorporating a lido, followed by a small craft harbour opposite which
is the 'Disco Romadzo'. The owners of this establishment must have friends in high places
as the place is officially signposted from many kilometres away.

ROUTE THREE
Andros Town to Stenies (5 km) From the left-hand Town beach, the surfaced
road proceeds to Ormos Yialia, a pebbly, small beach hemmed in by towering cliff
headlands and large trees to landward. There is a cafe-bar restaurant as well as wind-
surfers and pedaloes for hire.
From the seafront the road winds up the hillside to a fork in the road from which the right-
hand route advances to the Village of:-

STENIES (5 km) The road ends prior to this neat, red tile roofed, rich mans 'Roman Villa'
Village and the only access is on foot or donkey.
The left-hand turning, at the fork, leads to the wealthy Village of Apikia (Apoikia), famous
for its mineral springs.

ROUTE FOUR
Andros Town to Ormos Korthion (20 km) The shortest route is across a
pleasantly tree-shaded, agricultural plain via the hamlet of Livadia and on to the Village of
Sineti. From here the road climbs up the extremities of Mt Gerakonas and down again to
wind along the mountain side past:-

PALAIOKASTRON A pleasantly older, almost dilapidated, more typically Cycladean

Village with flat roofed houses (some of which are actually dilapidated. Goodness me). The site is graced with the remains of a Venetian Castle. The story of the downfall of the beleaguered defenders is the familiar one of an old crone betraying them to the besieging Turkish forces.

And so to:-

ORMOS KORTHION (20 km): port

A messy, 'rustic', 'provincial', spread out Village Port but a very pleasant spot for which to head. The attentions of the wealthy Mainlanders appears to have bypassed this more traditional mixture of old and new, neat and dilapidated, surfaced roads and potholed streets.

The large Main Square and immediate grid layout of streets contain most services including a Post Office, OTE, National Bank, Bus office and terminus and Taxis. The local Police Station telephone number is 61211. There are two Bakers selling very edible bread, a Supermarket and Snackbar serving souvlaki pita. Goody.

The Esplanade, if that is not too smart a word, edges the gently curving bay. There is a splendid, small, square Kafenion/Taverna with a ridged and tiled roof opposite the first, small jetty going left along the sea road (*Fsw*). It is well patronised by local fishermen which is no surprise, as an enormous, mixed omelette for two, a salad, beer and bread costs as little as 378 drs.

Accommodation includes the 'C' class *Hotel Korthion*, to the right of the Palaiokastron road into Ormos Korthion, on the backshore of the beach. Across the road from the *Korthion,* and slightly to one side, is the *Villa Korthion* with Apartments to Rent.

Rainbow Rooms For Rent   Tel 61344
Directions: Almost the first side street off to the left of the Palaiokastron road into the Port.

This smart, modern building is at the far end, on the right and to one side of a spacious, scruffy garden/backyard. Stellios, a friendly, chunky, young man, who speaks excellent American, runs this very pleasantly decorated accommodation. His personality infuses the place and the entrance hall reflects the atmosphere. A double room en suite costs 1300 drs for one night and less for more than one day.

The 30 km Main Route back to Andros Town, via the Stavropeda junction, crosses a patchy, agricultural plain prior to climbing up and through the mountains towards the high escarpment road edging the west coast.

22 Sikinos
Cyclades Islands

*****

FIRST IMPRESSIONS
No cats; dry, but comparitively verdant countryside; plentiful water wells but slimy water; donkey and mule trains; no vehicles (yet!); a handful of tourists — 10 - 12 at any one time; no clothes or tourist shops, just some postcards; few flies; partridges.

SPECIALITIES
There are rumours of a highly resinated wine not often found other than on Sikinos   I'm not surprised (*See* **The Accommodation & Eating Out**).

RELIGIOUS HOLIDAYS & FESTIVALS
None out of the ordinary, of which I am aware.

VITAL STATISTICS
Tel prefix 0286. An area of about 40 sq km, with a population of some 300 spread between the Port and Chora.

HISTORY
Settled in ancient times. About 4 km south-west of the Chora is a 5th century AD Church built over a 2nd century BC temple of Apollo, whilst to the north of the Chora, on the coast at Palaiokastro, are the remains of an Ancient Sanctuary.

GENERAL
There used to be trip-boats from Ios but it is my theory that the Niots in charge of tourism have cunningly decided not to promote the delights of Sikinos or for that matter the sister island of Folegandros **(Chapter 23)**.

All enquiries made on Ios are met by hints and innuendos, if not 'open' advice, cataloguing the dubious nature of the proposed venture, the general unsuitability of the island, the undesirable nature of visitors and, as if to scotch the whole matter, the impossibility of docking. Bearing in mind the otherwise general soundness of one of the principle deprecators Andreas (yes he of **Acteon Tours & Travel** *See* **Chapter 16**), I can only surmise he has not visited Sikinos for some years!

There are occasionally suggestions of or illusions to a 'conspiracy of silence' in respect of this or that island by those in the know. Presumably this is to keep the delights to themselves, and others sharing the secret. Surely an almost impossible task unless all map makers expunge the particular island from their maps and Ferry-boat operators remember to leave the details off their schedules. On the other hand those 'in the know' at Ios tend to actively discourage potential visitors by talk of the 'great unwashed', lack of Rooms, stony beaches and lastly the unpredictability of the Ferry-boats ability to stop off in inclement weather. This last is the only pertinent negative factor as, due to the lack of a suitable quay at Sikinos, transference of pasengers and freight takes place in the mouth of the harbour. This is an operation of uncertain nature,without allowing for the natural Greek ability to make any act or sequence of events infinitely more difficult than it need be. But the lack of a suitable landing place at which even charter yachts can easily berth has preserved Sikinos as one of those finds, a 'jewel of island uniqueness' set in the Cycladean sea beset by tourist hordes.

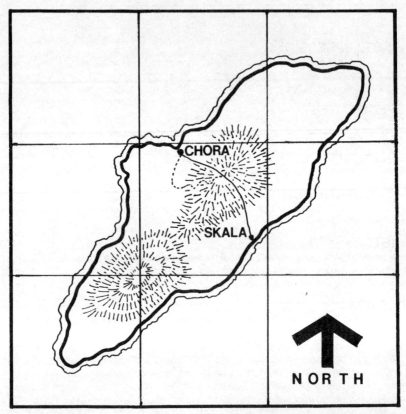

Illustration 41

The symmetry of the Port and its accompanying bathing beach set in a lovely cove is complimented by the bewitching, 'old world' Chora of outstanding, simple, agricultural beauty. And there are no buses, only one paved narrow road from the Port to the Chora, an ever upward climb which will take about an hour.

There is a hint, a suggestion, a rumour of a taxi or of course the chance of a ride on one of the many, many donkey and mule trains that ply their way up and down. The lack of any vehicles requires quadrupeds to transport all normal loads which includes drinking water to those houses without a well, all and every day.

A colourful, almost verdant, dramatic landscape with a surprising amount of agriculture. There are water wells everywhere which are constantly replenished by spring water trickling from the surrounding hillsides. Once a 'resort' for exiled Communists, the isolation and interbreeding of the Island has resulted in a physical hereditary deformity, the Sikinos jaw, akin to the deafness of Aotipalians.

THE SKALA: harbour (Illustration 42)

Also known as Alopronia and really only a semi-circular cove with a caique quay and a small settlement to the left (*Sbo*), a broad, sandy beach to the centre and a thin ribbon of development to the right. Prior to the preoccupation of the Colonels Junta with tourism and the inception of widespread development of the islands, Sikinos was regarded as a rather uninteresting, forced port of call. Mind you this was when Ios was described as 'lesser-known', quiet and off the beaten-track.

ARRIVAL BY FERRY

The quayside is too small for the smallest Ferry (even if the cove was deep enough), so the inter-island Ferry-boats anchor up in the bay and passengers board two 'pass-boats' to complete the journey to the harbour quay. It certainly needs to be calm to make the transfer and those of a nervous disposition should try to ascertain the particular method of exit. For instance the **MV Georgios Express** tends to push passengers out of side ports in the car hold which requires a short climb down a rope ladder into one of the waiting but bucking boats. If wearing a backpack, unshoulder it prior to disembarking. On the other hand the **CF Santorini** lowers the stern car ramp to effect the change over. In this method the shore boats bump and scrunch against the ramp while the transfer takes place of packages of almost every conceivable commodity, bundles of black dressed, old Greek ladies, small children with young mothers, string-tied suitcases and cardboard boxes, as well as the odd domestic animal. This part of the journey costs 70 drs a head but I'm not sure who should pay whom? One plus point is that accommodation is proffered by Room owners, even whilst waiting to disembark from the inter-island Ferry and a traveller will certainly be approached on the 'pass-boat' trip to the harbour quay.

THE ACCOMMODATION & EATING OUT

Naturally not a very wide choice but quality makes up for the lack of quantity. On the other hand there are far more Rooms on offer than there are eating establishments.

The Accommodation

Pension Kountouris (*Tmr* 5.D2)   Tel 51232
Directions: From the shore-boat landing point (*Tmr* 1.B2/3), turn right along the quay past the local Kafenion (*I.N. Xaλkea, Tmr* 2.C2), the water fountain and mount the steps between, on the left, a small *Cafe-bar/Loykas Rooms* (*Tmr* 3.D2) and on the right *Rooms* (*Tmr* 4.D2/3). The rising, stepped alley turns sharp left around the back of the buildings.

In the very unlikely event of not already being accosted it is best to make enquiries in the Taverna on the ground floor of the Pension and the near side of the steps up to the accommodation. The owner, genial Panayotis Kountouris is no fool and he and his son-in-law accost the incoming Ferries, gathering prospective clients under their wing, like

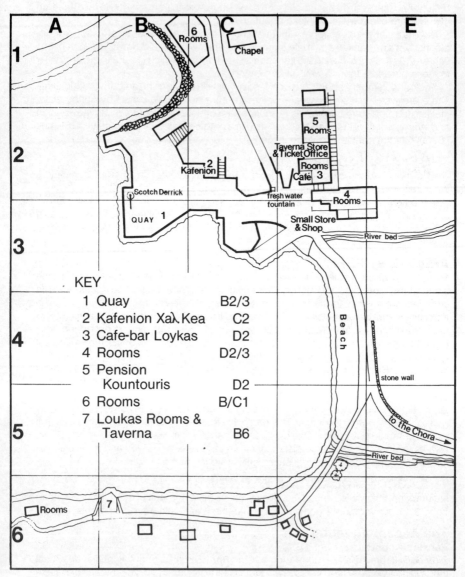

KEY

1 Quay   B2/3
2 Kafenion Χαλ Kea   C2
3 Cafe-bar Loykas   D2
4 Rooms   D2/3
5 Pension
   Kountouris   D2
6 Rooms   B/C1
7 Loukas Rooms &
   Taverna   B6

SKALA

Illustration 42

mother hens. He invites his 'chicks' to a coffee in the taverna whilst the rooms are made ready and to introduce himself and the family. A double room, mid-season costs 700 drs a night, sharing the simple bathroom facility which does not enjoy the luxury of hot water.

The Taverna unfortunately does not possess a patio or terrace but the food is reasonable as are the prices. (Incidentally this is the case for all of Sikinos, that is lack of terraces and inexpensive meals). The house retsina (an island brewed, 'little killer'), is served up in a look-a-like for the British milk bottle, with a pear-shaped fruit stone acting as a stopper. Certainly less cloudy than the Kartarados (Santorini) retsina, it has a similar consistency to the Gavrion (Andros) and Siphnos variations. Cutlets with aubergines for two, a Greek salad with a local curd cheese, bread, a bottle of 'open' retsina, 1 Greek and 3 Nes coffees costs 910 drs, while 2 plates of stuffed tomatoes, a Greek salad, bread and a beer works out at 475 drs. A local meatball dish and lemon soup are included on the menu.

Papa Panayotis runs a store from a corner of his taverna, as he does the sole Ferry-boat ticket office. Additionally he changes travellers cheques (he juggles as well!). Panayotis and his family own quite a lot of land to the west of the Island which can only easily be reached by boat.

Apart from the accommodation referred to above (and passed on the way to Panayotis's) there are:-

Rooms To Let (*Tmr* 6.B/C1)
Directions: At the water fountain, where the donkey and mule trains 'park up' for the drivers to fill the water containers, turn left up the lane, which is initially cobbled. The modern, single storey building is opposite a Chapel and, on the sea side of the path, overlooks a small harbour around the corner from the main quay. A lovely situation on the low hill with distant views of Santorini Island.

On the other side of the bay is:-

Loukas Rooms & Taverna (*Tmr* 7.B6)
Directions: Follow the quay round to the right (*Sbo*) along the concrete path, with a stone wall on the left and the beach to the right. The Chora road swings off to the left but it is necessary to keep right, hugging the beach backshore. In the area of the dry, rocky river bed the surface of the path has broken up beyond which a road climbs behind the houses along this side of the bay. The prettily situated building overhangs the sea with a very pleasant first storey terrace and is approximately opposite the main quay, across the cove.

Run by father and son Loukas and well recommended but does not really open up until July.

About ½ km up the Chora road, on the left, is the surprisingly large restaurant-

N Eytyxia EΣtiatopio
Directions: As above.
There are **Rooms** over the Restaurant.

For other accommodation *See* **The Chora,** but it is a long trudge. . . .

The Eating Out Most places are referred to in The Accommodation. It is worthy of note that there are no food price tariffs here or in the Chora. Order, smile and pay up, you will not be 'turned over'.

I.N. XaλkeaKafenion (*Tmr* 2.C2)
A locals haunt and the handsome, dark skinned man (and his family), eye up newcomers with a hard, disinterested stare. A beer costs 55 drs. . . The family might, no will, unbend in time. The fishermen sort out their nets on the quay in front of the Kafenion.

I'm not sure but surely the patron is related to the similarly good-looking, swarthy, Cretan featured muleteer who doubles up as a shore to ferry boatman.

There is another small Cafe in the corner of the building in which is situated *Loykas Rooms* (*Tmr* 3.D2).

THE A TO Z OF USEFUL INFORMATION

BANKS No but Panayotis, he of *Pension Kountouris* (*See* **The Accommodation**) changes travellers cheques. Naturally the rate reflects the less rigid constraints experienced outside the conventional banking system. . . .

BEACHES The Port beach, which fills the bottom of the cove is splendid with a comparatively generous sweep of sand and a backshore of pebbly sand on which are scattered some small boats, boat trailers and beer crates. The backshore is backed by the narrow, stone laid path that sweeps up to the Chora (after a long, steep climb). Beyond this is a dry river bed on the side of which is an incongruously sited, abandoned, squatty Toilet Block. Beyond the river-bed is a small, flat, grass field which has a marshy appearance. On the far side of the cove the sea bottom is rocky, and the narrow foreshore is made up of big pebbles with a pleasant grove of trees on the backshore.

Some years previously a 'Hippy' population discovered the Island and the convenient camping area behind and to the far side of the beach. The residents erected the 'squatty' but must have decided in the end that it was best to exclude the 'Great Unwashed'.

BREAD SHOPS The bread is baked in the Chora and brought down by mule train daily.

DISCO Believe it or not, yes. *See* ROUTE ONE.

FERRY-BOATS As described they anchor up in the mouth of the bay.

Ferry-boat timetable

Day	Departure time	Ferry-boat	Ports/Islands of Call
Monday	0500 hrs	Georgios Express	Ios, Santorini
	1000 hrs		Folegandros, Paros, Syros, Piraeus (M)
Tuesday	1800 hrs	Santorini	Folegandros, Santorini
Wednesday	1000 hrs	Santorini	Ios, Naxos, Paros, Syros, Piraeus (M)
Friday	1800 hrs	Lemnos	Folegandros, Santorini
Saturday	1000 hrs	Lemnos	Ios, Naxos, Paros, Syros, Piraeus (M)

FERRY-BOAT TICKET OFFICES As detailed, Papa Panayotis operates the only ticket office from the store part of his Pension/Taverna (*Tmr* 5.D2). The relevant timetables are stuck up on the walls of the Taverna.

MEDICAL CARE Best not to be ill, but there is a Clinic on the Chora Town Hall Square.

OPENING HOURS Strict siesta.

POLICE & POST OFFICE *See* **the Chora.**

ROUTE ONE (& only route)
The Port to the Chora (1 hour uphill) From the backshore of the beach the pleasant rock-slab surfaced, narrow street steadily and steeply climbs up the mountainside to the Chora. Unfortunately, and obviously to take motorised transport, there is extensive road widening work taking place. I suppose it is easy for a transient visitor to regret this steady progress into the 20th century but it does seem a pity. Incidentally, some two thirds of the way up the road are the remnants of the original, very old, stepped path that curves off left down into the valley only to rise steeply to emerge in the Chora

alongside the Town Hall. Apart from the road diggers, the only traffic are the loaded donkey and mule trains that wind up and down the mountain.

Back at the Port,the Chora road passes the 'squatty toilet block' to the right, an extensive private house on the left and, a little further on, the Generating Station beyond which almost immediately is the **Disco Sikinos**. I think I am correct to say that the founders of this (surely unnecessary) facility were refugees from the Ios Disco scene. Certainly the delights of this unexpected entertainment centre were advertised at the *Far Out Cafe*, Milopotamos Beach, Ios Island.

Beyond the Disco building, at about that part of the route where the upward climb is becoming serious, is the surprisingly large Restaurant *N Eytxia EΣtiatopio*, above which are **Rooms**.

At about the halfway stage there is a small, shady spinney, a very convenient spring and a water well. Travellers in need of a rest, can shelter beneath the low, spreading branches of the trees.

Until the work on the road is finished the resultant powdered rock-dust, up to 50 mm thick in places, makes a mess of anyone who wears anything but workmanlike footwear.

THE CHORA

Truly, this must be one of the loveliest examples of a 'working' town. I stress working because agricultural pursuits are taking place almost to the core of the Chora. Few concessions to whitewash here. Behind stone walls, hidden by rises in the ground, clouds of chaff indicate when the crops are being winnowed. There are a number of now defunct windmills stretched along the ridge of the Chora, facing out over and high above the sea, beyond the tumbling, brown, parched mountainside.

Almost the first building that the 'new' road passes, as it flattens out on the approach to the Chora, is the Post Office, after which it joins the right-hand part of the Village. To explain, the approximate centre of the Chora is on the sunken part of the saddle ridge, to the left above and beyond which is the left-hand segment of the Village which rises up the hillside.

To the right (of this right hand portion of the Village) is:-

To Kaμivia This signposted Taverna is run by a smiley, friendly mama who has to call her grown-up daughter to calculate the mathematics of any bill and to translate. There is no patio or terrace and entrance is through a curtain.

Two omelettes, a salad with local olives and curd cheese, bread and a beer costs about 330 drs. The beer is charged at 65 drs and a Fanta or orange 35 drs.

Behind Mamas is:-

Loukas Rooms A clean looking Pension.

To the left, prior to Mamas, is Odhos ZΘOΔOXOY MHΓHC the name of which is neatly carved on a marble plaque conveniently attached to the side of the a house. The path leads up the remainder of the mountain to the once fortified :–

Monastery Zoodochos Pigi The last part of the track across the rocky surface is indicated by whorls of whitewash and passes a rough hewn grave, presumably that of a long departed monk.

The high walls of the building encloses a very pretty, flower planted courtyard in front of the attractive campaniled Chapel. There is extensive restoration underway but the locked gates necessitate climbing up through the yet unrestored ruins of the monks living quarters, to the right of the building. There are marvellous all-round views over the sea to the north, the Chora and, to the south, down the tumbling valley to the distant Port.

The 'left-hand' Chora is connected to the central 'Town Hall Plateia' by a long flight of steps. These rise from close by a Chapel, on the one side, and the Clinic and a flour miller's on the left. The faded, rather dilapidated Town Hall seems disproportionately large for the possible administrative duties. Mind you the Athenian who caused the Municipal Building to be erected also owns the large private house just up from the Port at the outset of the Chora road. Perhaps he just likes large buildings! The old steps connecting the Chora to Port head off down the hillside from the side of the Town Hall.

Close by the 'Town Hall' Square are a shop, Kafenion and, in a narrow street overhung by a grape vine trellis, a Cafe-bar Taverna with comfortable, orange coloured, plastic chairs, scattered about. A beer here is very inexpensive at 50 drs.

The overriding impressions of the 'left-hand' Chora are of donkeys in trains, donkeys corralled in various old buildings (for that matter any nook and cranny) as well as of Jasmine and Cactii. Quite frankly one expects the 'Dirty Dozen' to come riding in at any moment. Apart from donkeys the 'left-hand' Chora houses the Police Station, opposite which is a Butchers. There are many dilapidated buildings and tiny alleys wander off here and there in a higgledy-piggledly network of lanes.

As part of the 'right-hand' Port (*Sbo*) is owned by wealthy citizens of Piraeus, a number of Chora houses are being purchased by (*cognisent*) foreigners.

I am reliably informed that the Chora and Port inhabitants are currently at loggerheads, as they have been for years.

23 Folegandros (Pholegandros, Polycandros) ****
Cyclades Islands

FIRST IMPRESSIONS
Arid; terraced mountain slopes; water short; Danish holidaymakers; lack of flies; shops open late; few cats; no taxis; a 'Santorini' Chora.

SPECIALITIES
Koukoulas, distinctive womens hats.

RELIGIOUS HOLIDAYS & FESTIVALS
include: None that are only relevant to the Island.

VITAL STATISTICS
Tel prefix 0286. Some 12 km long orientated NW/SE, up to 4 km at the widest and under 1 km at the narrowest, with an area of about 35 sq km. The population numbers some 700, spread between the Port, the Chora and northern settlement of Ano Meria.

HISTORY
The usual mixture of Dorians, Cretans, Romans (who used the Island as a place of exile), Venetians and Turks.

GENERAL
Folegandros is usually lumped together with Sikinos at the tail-end of an Ios chapter. This is to sweep both islands under the same carpet of anonymity but they are almost totally dissimilar. To start with the comparitively recently built Ferry-boat quay at Karavostasis Port has resulted in a more sophisticated location than Sikinos. For instance there is a Bus service between the Port and Chora complemented by a private enterprise venture. Both travel the few donkey-wide roads, even if they are rather mystical in respect of timetables. There are several hotels in the Chora even if it would appear that the owners are disinterested in procuring guests. There are a number of tavernas in the Port, even if the patrons appear luke-warm to tourists. Perhaps the arid nature of the land imparts some of its stern, unyielding characteristics to the islanders for they are, in general, reserved and appear at first to lack the traditional Greek warmth. But have no fears, for only a slight scratch to the surface reveals a very rural, rustic, old-world, Greek island charm.

The 'mains' drinking water, which is necessary as many of the wells dish up slimy water, is only turned on for a few hours in the morning. Once away from the simply beautiful and verdant Chora the remaining countryside and few villages are delightful, agricultural backwoods. The lack of other than generally inferior beaches is, I would like to think, more than adequately offset by the Island's other attractions. These include the stunning 'Santorini-like' scenery to one side of the Chora, perched close to the edge of the precipitous east coast mountain sides that plunge steeply into the surrounding sea; by the simple, fishing Hamlet of Agkali, nestling at the foot of an almost dry river gorge as well as by the quiet, unsophisticated northern cluster of inland agrarian Hamlets that make up Ano Meria, strung along the spine of the mountain range.

It could be considered a pity that the now substantial Ferry-boat quay has resulted in an increase in the number of tourists. In addition some Danes run a series of teaching holiday-courses on the Island during the months of June to August, which has resulted in

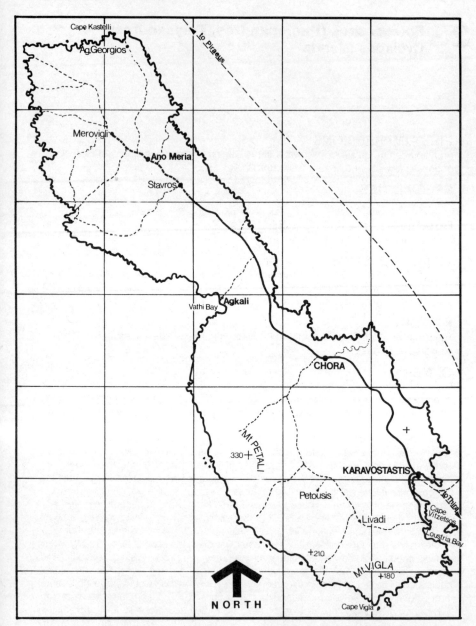

FOLEGANDROS

Illustration 43

a hefty increase in prices over the last couple of years. Despite these irritating and minor shortcomings Folegandros must still rate as one of the more idyllic Cyclades islands.

KARAVOSTASIS: port (Illustration 44)
The approach to the Port from Sikinos Island is marked by a number of rocky outcrops. The Ferry-boat quay is set in a craggy inlet of the large bay imparting an impression of claustrophobia and clutter.

There are no shops, one taverna, a cafe-bar taverna, a Kafenion, a 'canteen' periptero and everything closes for the siesta.

The Port bay is generally untidy with most of the development crammed into a stretch on the right (*Sbo*). There is a certain amount of creeping infill round the near side of the beach.

ARRIVAL BY FERRY
The quay (*Tmr* 1.E1), situated on the extreme right of the harbour (*Sbo*), is surprisingly large. The waterfront leads quickly into the heart of the tiny Port development, with all the impression of a messy, hot 'Yukon' development, especially the area rising up the hilloido to the right of the Ferry-boat quay.

Due to the lack of choice and disinterest of local Room owners, who do not even bother to meet the Ferry-boats, it is one of the few Islands where I can whole-heartedly endorse heading for the Chora. It is not entirely true to say that visitors disembarking are not met, as some Room owners do sidle up to stragglers in the street. Maybe the newly constructed Hotel/Pension (*Tmr* 2.A3/4), to the left of centre of the beach, will alter this detached attitude — unless it is to be block-booked.

Both the Buses meet Ferry-boat arrivals (*See* **Buses, A to Z).**

THE ACCOMMODATION & EATING OUT
The Port does not suffer from a surfeit of either accommodation or eating places and the presence of the Danes in disproportionate numbers has hardened up prices especially in the Chora. It may be of interest to know their classes include 'body consciousness' and 'dream interpretation'.

The Accommodation
Rooms (*Tmr* 3.C6)
Directions: Probably one of the best Rooms available is around the bay, on the road towards *Camping Livadia* (of which more later). Walk along the quay from the Ferry-boat disembarkation point, past the fishermans 'bus shelter' (*Tmr* 4.D1) (where lines and hooks are daily baited), up the 'Esplanade' chicane, beyond the Chapel to the left, the Bus stop/turn round point to the right (*Tmr* 5.C1), left along the tree-shaded, stony backshore track, past the *Restaurant Kati Aλλo* (*Tmr* 6.A3) on the right, and the probably now completed Hotel also on the right. Following the curve of the bay on a now concrete sectioned surface, past the little Shrine on the right (*Tmr* 7.B5), behind which are a few buildings — one probably uncompleted **Rooms**, on to a laid stone road surface and the chalet is on the right (Phew!).

The Papa, a 'Sancho Panza', unsmiling, middle-aged man is recognisable by his small scooter which has a box fixed behind the pillion seat and without which he is rarely seen. I'm not sure he doesn't also wear one of those Italian Colonial pith helmets seen extensively on the Dodecanese islands. A smiley Mama. Oh yes, the framed, glass-screened shower is outside in the garden. Well, there you go. Rates average at about 800 drs for a double bedroom sharing the bathroom.

Rooms (*Tmr* 8.B1)
Directions: Fronting the 'High Street'. The bungalow is the last building on the right, the far side of which are a rock wall and fields.

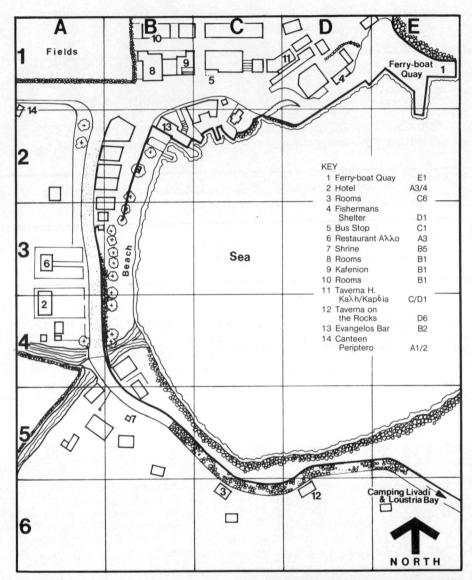

KEY

1	Ferry-boat Quay	E1
2	Hotel	A3/4
3	Rooms	C6
4	Fishermans Shelter	D1
5	Bus Stop	C1
6	Restaurant Αλλο	A3
7	Shrine	B5
8	Rooms	B1
9	Kafenion	B1
10	Rooms	B1
11	Taverna H. Καλh/Καρδia	C/D1
12	Taverna on the Rocks	D6
13	Evangelos Bar	B2
14	Canteen Periptero	A1/2

KARAVOSTASTIS

Illustration 44

The old lady demands 800 drs for a double room but will not entertain less than three days stay. The bathroom and washbasin is an open air affair!

Rooms (*Tmr* 10.B1)
Directions: A street behind the Rooms above. Wander up the fairly steep, unmade road, between the Bus stop and a Kafenion (*Tmr* 9.B1), set on the edge of a municipal shelter and terrace. Turn left, along an equally unmade street and the house is on the right, beyond a small square of wasteland. The house is noticeable by the garishly yellow and blue painted patio concrete columns.

The extremely basic accommodaton at the rear of the house is owned by 'Henry and Minnie Crun' — to those of you old enough to recall the 'Goon Show'. I suspect the primitive, raftered room is their spare bedroom, but the bed is board-like. The bathroom is an external shed abutting on to the house, and contains a very low pressure, cold water shower, the dribble of which is controlled by a single gate valve. This drains away into the street through a 'mouse-hole' in the wall and why not? It is quite on the cards that whilst walking to and from the 'bathroom' a guest will be nuzzled by one of the local mules hobbled near the street. The double room, mid-season, costs 700 drs.

One of the drinking water hydrants is across the way, but note they are only turned on at certain times of the day, so it is necessary to fill up the water bottles for the day. (*See* **Commercial Shopping Area, A to Z**). Another point to note is that this is a 'cold shower water' island.

In keeping with the general reticence regarding accommodation, across the rough surfaced street at the rear there is a substantial house with **Rooms**. The owner makes no effort to advertise the fact.

Camping Livadia   Tel 41203
Directions: See ROUTE ONE, but for those not prepared to turn a page or two it is a 2 km walk round the left-hand curve of the harbour bay (*Sbo*).

Where an island is as short of accommodation as Folegandros, a campsite is a possible option. However this particular location means being rather cut off from 'Town life' and the surrounding,unlovely countryside does not compensate. On the other hand their grey van does meet the Ferries, parking up by the Bus terminal. The site, on the side of an arid hill, is fairly new and rather exposed to the elements with no shade although young trees have been planted and there are covered areas for some tents. Site amenities include a shower/toilet block, kitchen, cafe-bar and a small mini-market. The cafe-bar prices are reasonable and the menu includes breakfast (80 drs), moussaka (170 drs), meat balls (180 drs), green beans (80 drs) and salad (55 drs). The fees are 150 drs per head a night and tent hire costs 100 drs but the site is only open from June to the middle of September.

The Eating Out
Cafe-Bar Taverna H Καλh Καρδia (*Tmr* 11.C/D1)
Directions: From the quay through the Esplanade chicane and immediately right, almost back on oneself. A few outside tables almost fill the alley.

The patron is rather taciturn and dour but his wife is very friendly but there are house-rules. Do not insult the status of the establishment by asking for ice-cream, cigarettes or even a pure orange juice — "This is a Kafenion." Oh and don't queue at the 'bar', even if in a pressing hurry, it does upset mine host. Counter-loungers are dismissed. As the time of a Ferry-boat arrival approaches, the taverna fills up despite which our Patron keeps up his slow, measured pace but with an underlying sense of panic. Certainly one of the cleanest tavernas at which I have ever sat down, I once observed him order out a group who were accompanied by their dogs. Two 'Proyevma' (breakfast) of bread, butter, jam and coffee, yoghurt and honey costs about 250 drs. I write 'about' because his addition is suspect, (often to the advantage of the customer I hasten to add), and this bill should have totalled 300 drs! The food is excellent and some prior notice can result in various fish and meat dishes being available. Another pleasant thing is to see mezes served with an ouzo. A meal of 2 spaghetti bolognese, 1 tomato and cucumber salad, 1 plate of patatas (sliced, fried potatoes), bread, 2 bottles of retsina (110 drs), and a metaxa brandy all for 520 drs. Damn good value but I have been charged 75 drs for a bottle of the same retsina and a coffee can vary between 40 and 55 drs. An omelette plus a tomato and cucumber salad costs as little as 100 drs and a beer 65 drs.

The Kafenion (*Tmr* 9.B1)
Further along the High Street but diffident service.

Restaurant Kati Aλλo (*Tmr* 6.A3)
Directions: Along the stony backshore beach track.

A well organised restaurant, with large patio terrace, serving the usual fare at reasonable prices. Lamb is often on the menu and a meal (of lamb) for two (560 drs, nicely cooked but served cold), a plate of giant beans (120 drs), briami (80 drs, a type of ratatouille) bread and a bottle of retsina (59 drs) for 827 drs.

Taverna Xakia On The Rocks (*Tmr* 12.D6)
Directions: The far side of the bay. A simple hut-like building in a pleasant situation affording a wonderful view when the sun sets, the last of the rays brightly illuminating Sikinos Island. Even the Port looks pretty from the terrace of *The Rocks*!

I am a great one for dishing out travel rules and principles but often am to be found wanting in their execution. No better example than here at '... *on The Rocks*', which you certainly will be if you do not establish their menu prices before ordering! I only applied my mind to cost when I overhead some Danes complaining — need one say any more. A spread including, 2 plates of Greek sausage and sliced potatoes, an indifferent Greek salad, 1 briami (stale), bread, a bottle of retsina, 2 brandies and 2 Portakalidos (orange juice) costs 900 drs.

No find but a pleasant change. Perhaps the lady owner's handsome son might spend a little more time attending to the clients and a little less steaming up the inside of his eyelids over, around and up against clean-cut, almost clinically good-looking, free-moving Danish girls. And I am not jealous!

Evangelos Bar (*Tmr* 13.B2)
Directions: Along the road up from the quay, and down narrow steps to the left. The nicely situated bar is set in a converted boat shed with the wide, shallow slipway now doubling up as a terrace. 'Chatty' setting and a 'chatty' proprietor, who speaks good English, the whole overlaid by taped music all of which results in 'chatty' prices. Two coffees and an ouzo 195 drs. Gosh! There are sea urchins in the shallows.

THE A TO Z OF USEFUL INFORMATION
BANK *See* **Chora.**

BEACHES The main beach fills the bottom of the small cove, is tree-edged and rather scrubbly with a shore made up of big pebbles. The first metre or so of the sea bottom is made up of rather slimy stones after which the whole of the bay is sandy and the water very clear. The elements are so propitious, that for a strong swimmer, Dio Adelfia, the nearest of the two Islets set down in the bay, makes a pleasant swim.

Over the headland to the left of the quay (*Fsw*) are two beaches on the adjoining, large bay. The far one is a coarse sand cove crowded in by quite high cliffs but almost impossible to reach. The closer, another coarse sand beach with a sea bottom of big stones is just over the neck of the headland but is a very difficult scramble, added to which the Port's rubbish is tipped over the low cliff-edge to the left of the cove. On the Port side of the headland, half-left of the quay, is a very small cove with a broad, shingly sand beach.

For other beaches *See* ROUTE ONE.

BUSES Apart from the official services, there is a 'Pirate' 12 seater, bright green Mercedes Benz bus (similar to a 'Transit Van' with windows). This parks up close by the *Cafe-bar Taverna H Καλh Καρδια (Tmr* 11.C/D1), whilst the 'Bus bus' parking spot is close to the Port bus stop *(Tmr* 5.C1). Both buses meet the Ferries and, if they cannot cope with the number of passengers, return for stragglers. The owner/driver of the 'Pirate' bus is a member of one of the two families who own most of the Chora.

The timetables are complicated by the differing methods of operation. The official State buses run between the Port and the near side of the Chora and operate a separate service from the far side of the Chora to Ano Meria (with a stop-off at the top of the track down to Agkali).

The 'Pirate bus' runs from the Port, turning off on a narrow lane that circumnavigates the pedestrian Chora. This lane emerges at the far end of the Chora and then proceeds on to Ano Meria. Being an owner-driver he really crams them in, so much so that the 'Guiness Book of Records' would probably like to monitor his activities.

Bus timetable
STATE BUS
Karavostasis Port to the Chora
Daily   0745, 1115, 1315, 1815, 1915, 2115 hrs.
Return journey
Daily   0730, 1100, 1300, 1500, 1800, 1900, 2100, 2300 hrs.
Chora to Ano Meria via a roadside stop for Agkali track
Daily   0900, 1045 (to Agkali stop off) 1215, 1500, 1840, 2100 hrs.
Return journey
Daily   0645, 0945, 1100 (From Agkali stop off), 1300, 1800 (Agkali), 1915 hrs.
'PIRATE' BUS
Karavostasis Port to Ano Meria via the Chora (far side) and Agkali track
Daily   0845, 1030, 1200, 1445, 2045 hrs.
Return journey
Daily   0945, 1130, 1300, 1545, 2145 hrs.
Fare to the Chora, 40 drs one-way, to Ano Meria 60 drs; duration to Ano Meria ¾ hr.

COMMERCIAL SHOPPING AREA Yes, well There is an important contribution to the Ports trading in the shape of a 'Canteen' (*Tmr* 14.A1/2). A concrete box Periptero on the edge of some waste ground on the left at the start of the Chora road. Sells cigarettes, beer, ice-cream, cheese-puffs, chocolate, orange drinks and bottled water.

The last item brings me to the matter of the Island's drinking water which is available from water taps here and there, but these are only turned on between 0930 - 1100 hrs. It is therefore not a bad idea to obtain one or two bottles of mineral waters.

FERRY-BOATS (& timetables)
Monday	0400 hrs	Santorini
	1100 hrs	Paros, Syros, Piraeus (M)
Tuesday	2000 hrs	Santorini
Wednesday	0900 hrs	Sikinos, Ios, Naxos, Paros, Syros, Piraeus (M)
Friday	1900 hrs	Santorini
Saturday	0900 hrs	Sikinos, Ios, Naxos, Paros, Syros, Piraeus (M)

FERRY-BOAT TICKET OFFICES *See* **Chora**. A lady sets up a stool at the start of the quay prior to a Ferry-boats arrival.

OPENING HOURS Strict siesta.

OTE, POST OFFICE, POLICE & TRAVEL AGENTS *See* **Chora.**

TAXIS None.

EXCURSION TO LOUSTRIA BAY (2 km)

The track curves round the far end of the bay, past Cape Vitzetzos, to the south of which are, down below, two rather inaccessible and tiny coves with grey, coarse sand beaches. The track peters out on the nearside of a vaguely scrubbly, unlovely, grey sand and shingle beach alongside a grove of Arethemusa bush trees. These groves spread along and shelter the backshore of the beach. Some hardier souls camp out in amongst them. The sea bottom is weedy with a tendency to being slimy and the far end consists of slate stones, pebbles and biscuit rock. Nude bathing.

Camping Livadi is set back from the far end of the beach on the lower, shade-less slopes of the hillside but at least the last part of the trek, no track, is concrete surfaced. (*See* **The Accommodation**).

ROUTE ONE

To the Chora (2½ km) A winding climb up through the mountains of stone to a fairly flat, gently undulating, rock surfaced plain with fields broken up by stone walls. Note the private bus turns off before the Chora alongside a building that was once a 'Souvenir' shop. Surely a strange place for such a business, well into the barren countryside.

THE CHORA: capital (Illustration 45)

A Chora of water wells and Churches.

The Main Road ends at the south-east side of the Chora on the sloping 'Bus' Square (*Tmr* 1.E4), the far side of which is edged by pleasant, two storey houses. To the left, across an undulation in the lie of the land on a low hillside, is a maze of stone walls, enclosures, and old stone dwellings reminiscent of a Minoan settlement — it probably was. An acute angled path climbs up the hillside on the right to a Monastery and further on to the Chrissospilia Cave on the coast (for which a guide is recommended). In the angle formed by the Plateia wall and the Monastery path is a Monument. This wall edges the cliffs which fall sharply away to the sea and from this high point there are marvellous views. The 'State' bus 'terminuses' on this Square.

This Chora may well be one of the most beautiful in the Cyclades and certainly the Old Quarter/Kastro is much photographed. There are the usual Chora features of whitewashed buildings and Churches, but unusually this Village is spread out, not being confined by the restrictions of a crowded hillside. Added to which there are two, not one, large Squares, both shaded by the canopy of branches of the numerous trees. Naturally there are also the mandatory interconnecting lanes, wells, fountains, tavernas, Kafenions and shops of all shapes and sizes.

From the 'Bus' Square a lane leads off the top left-hand corner, past a Church, to the bottom right-hand corner of a very large, profusely tree shaded irregular square with a number of water wells (the 'Water-Wells' Sq, (*Tmr* 2.D3/4)) and a large oval, wall-enclosed, Public Garden. The left-hand side of this Square is shut off by two Churches and the dark right-hand side by the medieval Castle wall which encloses the Old Quarter.

The extremely picturesque Old Quarter consists essentially of two paved streets that, with the remainder of the Castle wall, form a rectangle enclosing some of the Chora's oldest houses. These are two storey buildings with external stone staircases to the upper floor front doors. Next door to the 'Water-Wells' Sq, on the other side of the two Churches, is a smaller Plateia, the 'Kafenion Square' (*Tmr* 3.D3/4) with a pretty, mature, tree-planted, semi-circular terrace. From the top left-hand side of this Square, a street leads into yet another small Square from the far side of which a lane curves round to the left and runs into the stone wall edged road to Ano Meria.

There are a number of vantage points on the north side of the Chora from which to behold the lovely 'Santorini-like' views over the very steep, terraced slopes that tumble into the sea way, way below.

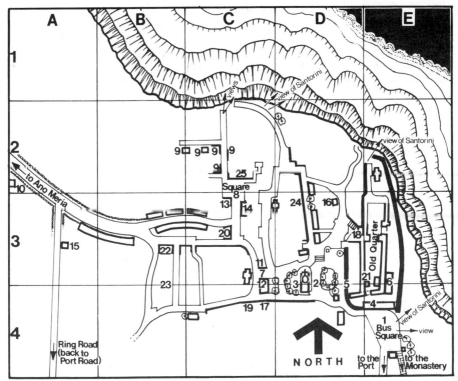

CHORA

KEY

Illustration 45

THE ACCOMMODATION & EATING OUT

The Accommodation A fair number of Rooms and even a hotel or two. 'Oveh'!

Rooms (*Tmr* 4.E4)
Directions: On the edge of the 'Bus' Square.

Rooms (*Tmr* 5.D3/4)
Directions: On the right-hand side of the 'Water-Wells' Sq, close to the 'tunnel' into the Old Quarter.

The long, low, raftered bedrooms reflect the property's age for these houses originally formed part of the Venetian Castle walls. A double room for 800 drs.

Hotel Danassis (*Tmr* 6.E3/4) (Class E)   Tel 41230
Directions: Up the 'tunnel' from the 'Water-Wells' Sq (*Tmr* 2.D3/4) along the alley through another covered archway and the Hotel is in the far corner. A splendid example of a walled Cycladean Hotel and or Pension (what do you mean 'a splendid example of a walled Cycladean. . . .!'?).

There are third party reports of rats on the ground floor but. . . . The owner keeps the showers locked against payment of extra drachmae. Only double rooms, sharing a bathroom which cost 1000 drs.

Rooms (*Tmr* 9.C2)
Directions: At the far end of the Chora. From the third, small Square (*Tmr* 7.C3), the lane from the top left-hand corner curves left into a wider street which leads off at a right angle and runs up to the 'Post Office' Square (*Tmr* 8.C2/3). A Street runs straight and slightly downhill from the top left corner and the **Rooms** are to either side.

The pleasant buildings hereabouts are more modern and rates for a double room, sharing a bathroom (and with a cold shower), are about 900/950 drs.

A little further on the Street runs out. There are more splendid views over the terraced, sloping mountain side that plunges precipitously into the sea. A road to the left has new developments on the nearside including:-

Rooms (*Tmr* 9.B/C2)
Directions: As above.

At least two houses have Rooms and the first is separated from the *Rent Rooms OΔγΣεαΣ* by some waste ground, probably a potential building plot.

Hotel Γani-Vevis (*Tmr* 10.A2) (Class B)   Tel 41237
Directions: On the Ano Meria road just beyond the stop for the 'Pirate' bus at the junction with the 'ring road'.

Actually a Pension not a Hotel. Whatever, it is a substantial, smartly refurbished old building in an excellent situation. No single rooms and double rooms are available sharing a bathroom, or en suite starting at 1100 drs and 1350 drs rising to 1350 drs and 1550 drs respectively for the height of the summer months.

The Eating Out A number of excellent Kafenions, Cafe-bar restaurants and a couple of tavernas including:-

Cafe/Restaurant Okritikos (*Tmr* 11.C3)
Directions: Spanning the third Square. I say spanning because the Restaurant proper is one side of the Plateia but operates in conjunction with a Butcher (*Tmr* 12.C3/4) opposite. This is a strange Butchers shop selling ice-cream and has a kitchen in the back but as to the working arrangement. . . ?

The tables and chairs are pleasantly spread about against the Church wall side of the Square but the service is rather 'laid back', well all right, off-hand and some of the food below par. A meal of stuffed tomatoes (160 drs), Greek salad (100 drs — rancid tasting oil), bread (30 drs, yes 30 drs and stale) and a bottle of beer (60 drs) costs 350 drs.

Cafe-Bar Nikos 'with Garden' Restaurant (*Tmr* 13.C3)

Directions: Diagonally opposite the Post Office, across the Square.

No tables and chairs in front of the Taverna, but a pleasant if rather low, heavily shaded and walled garden patio at the back. This very pleasant establishment is run by a friendly family and opens between 0900 - 1500 hrs and 1800 - 2300 hrs.

Inside the Cafe-bar is a very good, interesting picture of the Port dated 1977, as well as some other excellent black and white photos of old Folegandros. The menu is only in Greek but the smiley Mama is very helpful. Nescafe is reasonably priced at 38 drs. A meal for two of moussaka (170 drs each), a plate of briami (80 drs) and fassolakia freska (80 drs), 2 bottles of retsina (55 drs each), one (tired) Greek salad (100 drs) and bread (20 drs) costs 730 drs. 2 plain omelettes (60 drs each), a Greek salad (100 drs), 2 beers (50 drs each) and bread (20 drs), totals 340 drs.

Opposite is a neat:-

Cafe-Bar (*Tmr* 14.C3)

Equipped with bench seats and serves a reasonably priced breakfast for 80 drs and a boiled egg for 20 drs. Oh, by the way the butter is actually butter, if you see what I mean.

At the far, west-end of the Chora, at the start of the Chora 'ring road', on the left is a:-

Cafe-Bar (*Tmr* 15.A3)

Interesting because the young, pleasant Greek, married to a Danish girl, is very knowledgeable and erudite in respect of Greek classical music.

THE A TO Z OF USEFUL INFORMATION

BANKS No but *See* **Ferry-boat Ticket Office.**

BREAD SHOPS (*Tmr* 16.D3) Actually a Baker, across the lane from the Castle Wall on the Street up from the 'Water-Wells' Sq, and distinguishable by the piles of Gorse brush stacked outside.

BUSES *See* **Karavostasis Port.**

COMMERCIAL SHOPPING AREA No central conglomeration but a rather pleasant sprinkling of shops to satisfy most needs including a Grocer (*Tmr* 17.C4), who sells a fairly wide range of 'goodies' and a General Store (*Tmr* 18.D3), hard up against the Castle wall, access to which is up an angled stone flight of steps. This shop sells hats, shoes and bedding amongst other things, rather similar to the British haberdashers in days of yore. There are, rather surprisingly, a number of souvenir shops, with a small Gift Shop (*Tmr* 19.C4) and tasteful Tourist Shop (*Tmr* 20.C3). There seems to be an excess of Butchers but this is often the way in the older Greek towns. Maybe this is the reason for the Butcher in the small Square (*Tmr* 7.C3) going over to the restaurant trade?

DISCOS I only list the matter because there are innumerable signs directing prospective clients towards the 'Music Bar Deaf Seagull' (sic) but I never found it but why deaf? Maybe the intensity of sound resulted in the loss of hearing!

FERRY-BOAT TICKET OFFICE (*Tmr* 21.D/E3/4)   Tel 41273

In the Old Quarter, with pretentions to being a NTOG.

The very helpful lady, Maraki Lizardoy, with passable English, changes travellers cheques and foreign currency (notes only) in addition to dispensing a wide range of information. The office is definitely open between 1800 and 2100 hrs (with a hint that during the summer rush there could be 'morning surgery').

On the left side of the lane, heading towards the Ano Meria road is a 'dead ticket-office' (*Tmr* 22.B3) of a Ferry-boat no longer calling at the Island but who knows. . . ?

MEDICAL CARE

Chemists & Pharmacies The shops stock the basic necessities.

Clinic (*Tmr* 23.B3/4) At the west side of the Chora.

OPENING HOURS Strict siesta.

OTE (*Tmr* 24.D3) A small, cell block of a single storey building on the left of the narrow alley branching off the top left-hand corner of the 'Water-Wells' Plateia (*Tmr* 2.D3/4). To help distinguish the otherwise totally inconspicuous office there is a large black sign painted with an arrow almost opposite the building. A friendly lady gives a personal service but it is hardly an OTE, more a 'front-room', open weekdays, after 1800 hrs. Sometimes open in the mornings but the patroness closes the doors if there is no business.

POST OFFICE (*Tmr* 25.C2) A 'doo-hickey' office in a row of houses on the edge of the irregular shaped 'Post Office' Square. Usual hours but there are also some phones here.

ROUTE TWO

To Ano Meria (5 km) A narrow, concrete road rises and falls along the high spine of the mountain range which falls away either side towards the coast. After 2½ km there is a pedestrian track to the seaside settlement of:-

AGKALI The buses pull up at the top of the path, the start of which is distinguishable by an ugly concrete box of a building, on the edge of a large water-well catchment.

The steep 1 km, 20 minute walk down the valley cleft is initially on a laid stone path which alternates with an unmade track. The lower reaches course along a river-bed, dry except for a seeping spring and one or two crude wells. The final descent is through massed Oleanders, before breaking out on to the scrubbly, coarse sand, pebble littered backshore of the cove, hemmed in by steep hillsides set in Vathi Bay. At the bottom of the path there is drinking water cistern with two taps but the water is 'soapy'.

Houses, tavernas and **Rooms** are let into both hillsides. On the right-hand side (*Fsw*), at beach level, is a concrete block built shed, humourously labelled OTE, which does in truth contain a telephone (of sorts). There is also a Taverna, run by a nice man who serves good mezes with a drink (2 beers with mezes 120 drs) and who will knock up a meal. Also to the right is the concrete fishing boat quay.

Above the beach taverna is a Restaurant with **Rooms**, where the owner allows sleeping on the roof terrace. A double room costs about 500/600 drs and eating out is inexpensive.

To the left of the cove is the hamlet's concrete Toilet Block, set on a plinth of rock. Around the projecting cliff rock, behind the toilet facility is a very small cove and at this end, the beach and sea-bottom consists of small pebbles. It is often rather windy here and the water rough, but the beach and sea are clean, with a coarse sand foreshore and a sea bottom made up of biscuit rock and pebbles.

A half-hour cliff walk to the west or right (*Fsw*) leads to:-

AG NIKOLAOS A nice sandy beach with a taverna that opens up at the height-of-the-season.

Back on the Main Road and after another 2½ km the route spills out into the Village of:-

ANO MERIA In actuality a string of connected, neat agricultural Hamlets, made up of huddles of dwellings, spread out and straggling along the rounded and extensively terraced, dry range of mountain tops. The road becomes track almost as soon as the first outpost is reached. Cattle, donkeys and goats are very much in evidence, herds of which appear to ebb and flow through the Village with women and children tending the flocks. There is a Baker and the Bus conveniently parks up for ¼ hour by a prominent taverna.

24 Milos (Melos, Milo) & Kimolos
Cyclades Islands — Western chain

Milos	★★
Kimolos	★★★★★

FIRST IMPRESSIONS
Attractive sea approach; the Island appears to be under reconstruction (ie mining and quarrying); saline water, old men's attire includes a cummerbund.

SPECIALITIES
Venus de. . . . . ; mineral mining; hot water thermal springs.

RELIGIOUS HOLIDAYS & FESTIVALS
include: 7th May — Feast and Festival, Church Ag Ioannis Theologos (south-west of Island); 8th September — Feast of Birth of Virgin Mary, Church Panagia Korfiatissa (Plaka).

VITAL STATISTICS
Tel prefix 0287. The Island has an area of about 160 sq km, is roughly 20 km wide, 13 km deep and would resemble a flattened circle if it were not for the huge horseshoe bay that almost divides the island in two. The population numbers between 4500 and 5000.

HISTORY
The volcanic nature of the rocks and the 'apple like bite-of-a-bay', points to an ancient volcanic eruption that tore out the centre of the Island.

The Island served as an important Minoan outpost and has been mined and quarried throughout the centuries. Has anybody considered the prediliction for Minoans to select sites associated with volcanic action? The obsidian, a glassy, volcanic stone, was used for all manner of implements (including knives, spear and arrow heads) prior to perfection of the treatment of metal ore. Apart from the mining activities the history of the Island has tended to follow the Cycladean historical 'norm'.

Admittedly the Athenians cut-up pretty rough in about 450 BC, when the islanders refused to side with them in the Persian wars and an example had to be made to discourage this backsliding. All the males were slaughtered, the women carried away and the Island colonised with mainland settlers. The Turks, during their rule, did not physically occupy the Island, only extracting taxes by envoy. The population of the main Port of Adamas was supposedly stiffened by the large influx of Cretans during the War of Independence, in 1924.

During the First World War the Bay of Adamas was used as a harbour by large numbers of Allied warships.

GENERAL
The association with Venus (and for the less sophisticated of our American cousins such as one young Robert, Venus de Milo, now of the Louvre) often convinces visitors to believe that this most southerly island of the Western Cyclades will be another jewel set in the Aegean Sea. If you prefer to be let down slowly do not read on, for Milos is not everyone's dream, more a disturbed sleep. Milos, probably not wildly attractive to start with, has been (and still is) under constant 'reconstruction' by the mining industry for thousands of years resulting in a chewed look to the scenery.

The dusty, unattractive main Port and Town of Adamas lies on the edge of a huge bay,

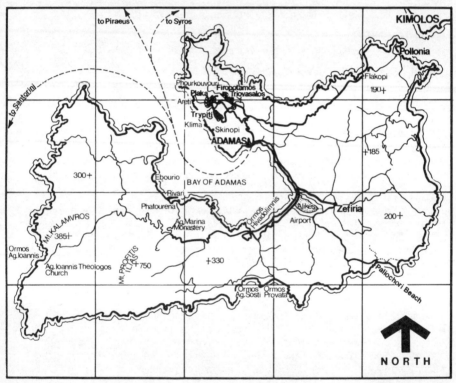

MILOS

Illustration 46

but just the islands luck, not a pretty bay. Certainly the various concentrations of ore moving machinery dotted around the periphery exacerbates the lack of charm. To add insult to injury, the Plaka (or Chora) is an unattractive jumble of four settlements, muddlingly draped out over the surrounding hillsides. If this were not enough, the best beach (Paliochori) is a comparatively long bus ride across the Island. Perhaps the best feature of Milos is the not unattractive northern fishing Port of Pollonia which can be used to visit the adjacent Island of Kimolos.

Now there's a different 'cup of retsina'. How the beautifully simple, lovely Island of Kimolos can have remained unsung for so long is a mystery to me. Even the local Guide which comments on all the neighbouring islets declines to give Kimolos more than a passing mention. Perhaps its larger neighbour has kept the wraps firmly on the undeniable attractions of Kimolos in case it should detract from the 'delights' of Milos. If so it is quite understandable for Kimolos must be the rose amongst the thorns of Milos.

Many visitors leave Milos almost as fast as they can catch the next convenient boat, and who am I to argue.

ADAMAS: main port (Illustration 47)
A dusty, unattractive mish-mash of a Port with a large Ferry-boat quay and the main development of the Town sprawling away to the right (*Sbo*). Set in a ring of hills and with a southerly aspect, if there is no wind the Port gets very hot and sticky. This, combined with the dust resulting from the continuing mining activity, makes it necessary for the streets to be watered down every day — by tanker. With so much waterfront it would be nice if there were glorious beaches but. . . .

ARRIVAL BY AIR
The small, dusty airstrip lies to the south of a large working salt bed about 4½ km from Adamas Port. The term Airport is rather grand for this collection of 'large garden sheds' and I hope the eager expectations of arrivals are slowly deflated. Certainly if the Airport lives up to passengers hopes the drive along the huge Bay of Milos will probably allow doubts to intrude. But some may like what they see. . . .

ARRIVAL BY FERRY
The approach to the Port flatters to deceive as the Ferry-boats run down the lip or east shoreline of the very large Bay of Adamas. To the right, about 8 km offshore is the comparatively large, uninhabited Island of Anti Milos, a sanctuary for chamois. The boats cut in between the untenanted inshore islets of Akradies and the Island. They steam past some fascinating geological formations and the colourful, picturesque 'Venetian' summer fishing Hamlets of Phourkovouni, Areti, Klima and Skinopi. The buildings cling to the waters edge so low that it appears that the wash of the larger boats will swamp the dwellings which are only inhabited in the summer months, the citizens returning to the Plaka for the winter.

Even the last sandy headland, around which the Ferry sweeps, flatters to deceive, keeping a travellers hopes high but. . . . The Ferries dock at the large, prominent quay (*Tmr* 1.C4) and are met by any number of Hotel and Room owners.

On a warning note, it is worth bearing in mind that the Ferry-boats often sound their hooters rather too early, before rounding the headland, which masks the notice of their impending arrival.

THE ACCOMMODATION & EATING OUT
Accommodation, except possibly at the height of the season, does not pose a problem, on the other hand eating out does.

The Accommodation It rather depends on a travellers sensibilities. Around to the left of the quay (*Tmr* 1.C4) (*Sbo*) is the pleasant, cosy, package holiday style cove, and hotel

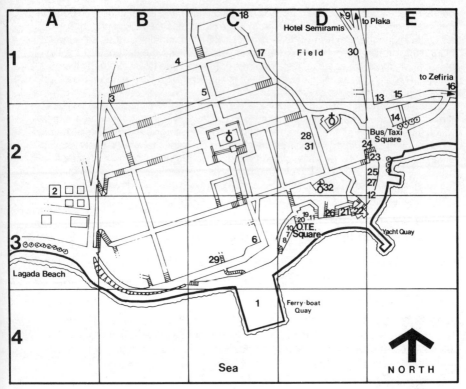

ADAMAS

KEY

1	Ferry-boat Quay	C4
2	Hotel Delfini	A2
3	Rooms	B1/2
4	Kanaris Rooms	B1
5	Hotel Corali	C1
6	Hotel Adamas	C3
7	Rooms	D3
8	O.T.E.	D3
9	Olympic Office	D1
10	Milos Tours	D3
11	'Tourist' Office	D3
12	Averkios Tours	E2/3
13	Hotel Georgantas	E1/2
14	Cafe-bar Restaurant	E2
15	Hotel Meltemi	E1
16	Hotel Milos	E1
17	Rooms	C1
18	Antonios Rooms	C1
19	Cavo D'Amore	D3
20	Post Office	D3
21	Restaurant O'Φλοισbος	D3
22	Kafenion	D3
23	Cafeteria Milos	E2
24	Charcoal Taverna	D/E2
25	Commercial Bank	E2
26	National Bank	D3
27	Newspapers	E2
28	Baker	D2
29	Unisex Hairdresser	C3
30	Pharmacy	D1
31	Clinic	D2
32	Catholic Church	D2

Illustration 47

development at Lagada Beach (*Tmr* A3). Of the 3 or 4 hotels at least one has **Rooms**, the:-

Hotel Delfini Rooms (*Tmr* 2.A2) (Class D)   Tel 22001
Directions: From the end of the quay, follow the waterfront track, hemmed in by a cliff-face, around to the left which leads to a small beach cove. The modern Hotel is third block back and one building in from the road as it heads up the valley.

Up to 31st May and after 30th September a single room sharing a bathroom costs 685 drs, and a double 790 drs while en suite costs 1110 drs. During the month of June and period 16th to 30th September a single costs 725 drs and doubles 870 and 1220 drs respectively, while the height of season rates are 820 drs for a single and 1035 and 1445 drs for a double room (sharing a bathroom and en suite).

Further along the valley from the *Hotel Delfini*, on the right of the road, on the junction with a backward angled street that climbs steeply up the 'Chora Hill', are:

Rooms (*Tmr* 3.B1/2)

A little further on, a flight of steps to the right rises up to the:-

Kanaris Rooms (*Tmr* 4.B1)
Directions: As above and on the left, but note this area may well be approached in an anti-clockwise direction.

Another hotel, easily accessible if you have come this far round, is the:-.

Hotel Corali (*Tmr* 5.C1) (Class C)   Tel 22204
Directions: As above, the next turning right and on the right.
No single rooms but doubles en suite cost 1200 drs rising to 1550 drs (1st July - 15th September).

Back at the Ferry-boat quay (*Tmr* 1.C4), and close by, is the:-

Hotel Adamas (*Tmr* 6.C3)
Directions: Up on the crest of the cliff overlooking the waterfront, but it was closed for much of 1985.

To the right (*F-bqbo*), the Esplanade widens out on to the lop-sided 'OTE' Square and on the left is:-

Rooms (*Tmr* 7.D3)
Directions: As above, next door to the OTE office (*Tmr* 8.D3) and over a small office, up a flight of external steps. There are only two double rooms available (starting off at 800 drs mid season, rising to 900 drs), so stake them out as they are much in demand.

Unfortunately the owner lives at the far end of the Town, off the Plaka Main Road, along the narrow lane that branches off to the left prior to the Olympic Office (*Tmr* 9.D1), beyond the *Hotel Semiramis*.

Both Tour Offices (*Tmr* 10.D3 & 11.D3) lining the 'OTE' Square offer accommodation advice, as will **Averkios** (*Tmr* 12.E2/3) on round the corner.

This waterfront Esplanade opens out on to the main or 'Bus/Taxi' Square (*Tmr* E2) to the right of which both buses and taxis park up.

Hotel Georgantas (*Tmr* 13.E1/2) (Class D)   Tel 41636
Directions: On the far side of the 'Bus/Taxi' Sq (*Tmr* E2), on the corner of the Plaka and Bay waterfront roads.
Part of the ground floor is occupied by *Maggie Fast Food Self-Service Restaurant* which opens up for the height of the season. A single room sharing a bathroom starts off at 620 drs rising to 700 drs (June - September) while double rooms sharing a bathroom or en suite cost 920 drs/1200 drs rising to 1000 drs/1400 drs.

A few metres further along the east road, that circles round the bay, separated from the waterfront by a Coffee-Bar Restaurant (*Tmr* 14.E2) and a grubby lorry-park, are the:-

Hotel Meltemi (*Tmr* 15.E1) (Class C)   Tel 22284
Directions: As above but only a step or two to the side of the 'Bus/Taxi' Sq. Neat, but rather pricey with doubles en suite rising from 1400 drs to 1700 drs.

and the:–

Hotel Milos (*Tmr* 16.E1) (Class C)   Tel 22087
Directions: As above, but further along the road.

Pleasant looking but the situation behind an old warehouse, in the lorry park area, leaves something to be desired. The en suite-double room rates also leave something to be desired, rising from 1550 drs to 1750 drs (July - August).

Hotel Popi (Class B)   Tel 22301
Directions: A 'room or so' further along the waterfront as it starts to curve around the bay.

Actually rated as a Pension and may be referred to as the *Adamas*. Jolly expensive with en suite singles rising from 1000 drs to 1500 drs and doubles 1500 drs to 2000 drs.

Proceeding along the Plaka Main Road, the previously referred to lane that angles off to the left, beyond the *Cafeteria Pub Dream* (sic), advances to the:–

Hotel Semiramis (Class D)   Tel 41617
Directions: As above and on the left.

A single room costs 667 drs, sharing a bathroom, and 1023 drs en suite rising to 889 drs/1334 drs (16th June to 25th September). Double rooms start at 889 drs or 1067 drs rising to 1067 drs/1378 drs.

From the main, 'Bus/Taxi' Sq a narrowing lane climbs and curves off from the left-hand side (facing up the Main Road to Plaka) skirting a field on the right. Beyond the second flight of steps to the left, at a kink in the road, and on the right is a house with:–

Rooms (*Tmr* 17.C1)
Directions: As above.

Pleasant surroundings with a single room from 400 drs and a double room starting at 800 drs.

Keeping along this Street from the house above, prior to descending, a turning to the left leads to *Kanaris Rooms* (*Tmr* 4.B1). Carrying on down the dip, almost to the outskirts of the development leads to:–

Antonios Rooms (*Tmr* 18.C1)   Tel 22002
Directions: As above, on the right.

A large, purpose built, recently 'uncompleted' Pension displaying a number of unique features in addition to the more usual failings. The plumbing must have been subject to last minute adjustments as several pipe runs are laid over the floors of the corridors with resultant bumps and humps. The walls are so thin that guests in rooms next door to the bathroom are party to the most intimate and shared moments. The cavernous bathrooms contain conveniently large waste-bins, which I'm afraid to report are rarely emptied. For some reason the corridors echo loudly and the pleasant rooms are devoid of cupboards, hanging capacity being furnished by one those 'sassy', sagging material covered frames. Prospective 'roomers' must not get the impression that *Antonios Pension* is not a solidly, well constructed building. For instance the window and balcony door units are very expensive, aluminium framed modules — which, incidentally, don't lock.

The Eating Out The use of the Port by a fairly small-time, Swiss yacht organisation has not resulted in such a diversity of choice as one would expect if the experience of other islands is anything to go by. Prices are generally on the high side.

On the way round from the Ferry-boat quay, where the Esplanade widens out on to the 'OTE' Square, close to the small yacht quay (*Tmr* E3), is the:–

Cavo D'Amore (*Tmr* 19.D3)
Directions: Next door to the Post Office (*Tmr* 20.D3) with a double awning stretching out into the road.

Chatty and expensive with beer served in large glass mugs! Pizzas, toast, ice-creams, a fast food menu but prices are almost double those of the main 'Bus/Taxi' Sq *Cafeteria Milos*. Say no more.

Further along the Esplanade, side by side, are two similar restaurants with much the same offerings, the:-

Restaurant O' ΦλοιΣboς (*Tmr* 21.D3)
Directions: As above.

The owner is smooth and attentive enough until a clients order is taken, after which interest and memory fails. Every so often a dish ordered is forgotten but the food is fresh, even if the portions are small. A plate of chicken (174 drs), spaghetti bolognese (180 drs), a Greek salad (130 drs), a bottle of retsina (60 drs), and bread (20 drs), for 550 drs.

The other is the:-

Restaurant Mariana — take your choice.

On the corner, where the waterfront Esplanade road bends sharply around to the left, is a local Kafenion (*Tmr* 22.D3). Alongside the 'Bus/Taxi' Sq is possibly the best value in the Port, the:-

Cafeteria Milos (*Tmr* 23.E2)
Directions: As above, on the left. There are tables and chairs the other side of this wide section of the Esplanade, by the waterside.

The (rather deaf, slow moving) husband and (striking, driving force) wife team keep the Cafe-bar Taverna open all day, and quite a lot of the night. Her English is peppered with the catch-phrase "Bravo darling, sit down". A breakfast of a boiled egg, bread, jam and coffee costs 100 drs; a coffee 'meh ghala' 40 drs, an ouzo with mezes 30 drs, a bottle of retsina 70 drs and they will rustle up an omelette any time during the day. Prices seem to vary from day to day. A 'cave-like' toilet.

Next door is the:-

Cafe-Bar Aktaion
Directions: As above.

A politer, smarter, more expensive variation of the *Milos* and serves beer in cans. Need one say more?

Still on the same side of the road, towards the crossroads of the 'Bus/Taxi' Sq, and there is a small, sandy, rectangular yard off to the left. This is empty in the day, edged on the far side by a dusty chandlers. Lo and behold, at night there opens up the:-

Charcoal Taverna (*Tmr* 24.D/E2)
Directions: As above.

The limited menu is only written in Greek but let neither caveat put a prospective diner off, for this is where the best value meals are served in Adamas.

Naturally, only charcoal cooked food. The dishes on offer include individual dishes of souvlaki (at 40 drs a stick — clients ordering so many sticks), beef steak (in actuality minced beef) and large pork cutlets. To accompany the meat dishes there are very good Greek salads, large helping of chips and big plates of correctly prepared tzatziki (I'm salivating whilst writing!). One drawback is the lack of retsina (although some would regard this as a plus point or two), only Demestica being available. A meal for two of tzaztiki, 8 souvlaki sticks, Greek salad, chips, bread and a ½ bottle of wine costs 645 drs. Oh, by the way, the beef steaks cost 180 drs each.

A number of imported Fast Food establishments appear to be closed, including *Fast Food Snoopys*. Good!

Cafe-Bar Restaurant (*Tmr* 14.E2)
Directions: Alongside the taxi rank and well shaded by mature trees, with tables and chairs pleasantly spread about. Sophisticated, but should be avoided at all costs if cost is a primary concern. The patron is a vast, profusely bearded man in his middle 30s. Waiter service only with 500 gm tin of beer costing 100 drs.

THE A TO Z OF USEFUL INFORMATION
AIRLINE OFFICES & TERMINUS The office (*Tmr* 9.D1) is to the left of the Plaka Main Road and is open daily 0900 - 1300 hrs except Sundays.

Airline timetables
Milos to Athens
Daily 1745 hrs. From 1st May additionally daily 0815 hrs. From 23rd June additionally Tuesday and Saturday 1515 hrs.
One-way fare 1900 drs, duration ¾ hr.
Athens to Milos
Daily 1640 hrs. From 1st May additionally daily 0710 hrs. From 23rd June additionally Tuesday and Saturday 1410 hrs.

BANKS
Commercial Bank (*Tmr* 25.E2) Fairly close to the 'Bus/Taxi' Sq. Usual hours. They change personal cheques but manage to combine off-hand service with requiring every conceivable document and a minimum of three people to effect the transaction.
National Bank (*Tmr* 26.D3)

BEACHES
Beach 1: Around from the Ferry-boat quay to the left (*Sbo*) is a small cove, behind which is a patch of new hotels. The backshore of the coarse sand beach is pleasantly tree-shaded but the sea bottom, at depth, becomes rather weedy. There are a number of fishing boats anchored in-shore and windsurfing to the nearside of the beach.

It is possible to walk on past a tiny cove to the lighthouse headland, some hot water springs and a sandy foreshore.

Beach 2: Almost a 'bayful' really with a tree-lined Main Road, east from Adamas Port edging the bay most of the way round to the Zefiria turn off with a representative stretch close by the Petrol Station.

BICYCLE, SCOOTER & CAR HIRE Two Tourist/Ticket/Travel offices have scooters for hire (*Tmr* 10.D3 & 11.D3) but the most active is:-
Averkios Tourist Office (*Tmr* 12.E2/3)   Tel 22191
Directions: On the left of the Esplanade, half-way between the private yacht quay and the Main Square.

When I write the most active, Averkios, a pleasant, 'street-wise', young man, with very good English, is not too bothered about hiring out his machines. A Vespa costs 1000 drs a day, but the extensive number of rough tracks created by the mining companies makes for extremely difficult navigation, once off the few surfaced roads. It is possible to spend hours and hours, lost, wandering about the scarred, chewed, dusty, loose-surfaced hill and mountain paths. In fact it must be a moot point if it is worth hiring a powered conveyance because not only are the number of attainable destinations limited but, due to the appalling road and track surfaces, there are even more accidents on Milos island than is usual on the islands.

BOOKSELLERS (*Tmr* 27.E2) More a vendor of foreign language newspapers. I have no doubt that this unprepossessing man will, on high-days, change his vest. Maybe not!

BREAD SHOPS (*Tmr* 28.D2) A Baker who sells cheese pies. To reach his premises either climb the steps alongside the *Cafeteria Milos* (*Tmr* 23.E2) and take the first Street on the right or climb the half-left lane from the Main Square and cut down the first left, almost acutely back on oneself.

BUSES A reasonably widespread, efficient service with an 'interesting', cross-country journey to Paliochori. The buses gather on the side of the Main Square (*Tmr* E2) where there is displayed an up-to-date timetable. Not only do the buses run on time but, the drivers are very helpful indeed.

To make the return journey to Kimolos Island in one day it is essential to catch the first bus to Pollonia (0645 hrs). Conveniently the smart *Hotel Meltemi* Cafe-bar opens up early enough to enjoy a life-reviving coffee before mounting the bus. The coffee is reasonably priced and hot but otherwise the Cafeteria is rather expensive.

Bus timetables
Adamas Port to Plaka (& some buses on to Trypiti*)
Daily   0730, 0830, 0930, 1030, 1130, 1230, 1330, 1500, 1630, 1730, 1830, 1930, 2030, 2130, 2230 hrs
*Now the Catacombs are closed these buses are not so vital, although there is a good swimming beach at Kilima
One-way fare (to either destination) 30 drs.

Adamas Port to Pollonia Port
Daily   0645, 0930, 1215, 1415, 1615, 2015 hrs
Return journey
Daily   0715, 1000, 1245, 1445, 1645, 2045 hrs
One-way fare 60 drs, duration 25 minutes.

Adamas Port to Paliochori Beach
Daily   1020, 1120, 1520, 1620 hrs
One-way fare 60 drs, duration 20 minutes.

CHEMISTS *See* **Medical Care.**

COMMERCIAL SHOPPING AREA No particular Market, but a number of shops are concentrated on the entrance to the narrowing lane that climbs off to the left of the Main Square (*Tmr* E2). Here are 3 General Stores as well as a Fruit and Vegetable 'Importers' and a Butcher). There is a shack-like Greengrocers on the Esplanade, close by the Commercial Bank, but the quality is not very good. There are a considerable number of 'back of donkey' sales pitches.

DISCOS
Disco Milos is adequately signposted from the quay area and **Cocktails Pub 82** does its best to be heard on the neighbouring islands from its eyrie above the area of the *Charcoal Taverna* (*Tmr* 24.D/E2).

FERRY-BOATS The only main-line Ferry for much of 1985 was the **CF Kimolos** but the **CF Ionian** was supposed to be making scheduled stops here and other islands on the western chain.

One of the Travel Agents, **Averkios** (*Tmr* 12.E2/3) has a daily cruise motor yacht, that at the 'height-of-season', purports to make a number of other Cycladian islands connections but these inter-island joy rides only take place, if at all, during the months of July and August.

Ferry-boat timetable

Day	Departure time	Ferry-boat	Ports/Islands of Call
Tuesday	2200 hrs	Kimolos	Kimolos, Syros.
Wednesday	0945 hrs	Kimolos	Siphnos, Serifos, Kithnos, Piraeus (M).
	1730 hrs	Ionian	Siphnos, Serifos, Kithnos, Piraeus (M, 0230 hrs next day).

Friday	2400 hrs	Kimolos	Piraeus (M)
Saturday	1600 hrs	Kimolos	Kimolos, Ios, Santorini
Sunday	0830 hrs	Ionian	Siphnos, Serifos, Kithnos, Piraeus (M, 1700 hrs).
	1200 hrs	Kimolos	Kimolos, Siphnos, Serifos, Kithnos, Piraeus (M).

FERRY-BOAT TICKET OFFICES

Milos Tours (*Tmr* 10.D3) On the 'OTE' Sq and acts for the **CF Kimolos** which is unfortunate as the proprietor is a rather unpleasant, surly man. Open 0830 - 1330 hrs and 1730 - 2200 hrs.

The Tourist Office (*Tmr* 11.D3) Also on 'OTE' Sq, sells tickets for the **FB Ionian**, when it runs.

HAIRDRESSERS

Hope (*Tmr* 29.C3) A Unisex Hairstylist, (what's that?). On the hill in front of the Ferry-boat quay, accessible up some steep, rickety concrete steps that scale the cliff-face.

MEDICAL CARE

Chemists & Pharmacies (*Tmr* 30.D1) On the left of the Main Plaka Road.

Clinic (*Tmr* 31.D2) In the same Street as the Baker.

OPENING HOURS Traditional siesta, with Sunday shutdown for some services including Petrol Stations.

OTE (*Tmr* 8.D3) One of the first buildings at the start of the waterfront Esplanade road round from the Ferry-boat quay (*Tmr* 1.C4). A small office, open weekdays, between 0730 and 2100 hrs.

PETROL There is a Petrol Station on the bay encircling road, about 450 m east out of the Port. Closes on Sunday.

PHARMACIES *See* **Medical Care.**

PLACES OF INTEREST

The Catholic Church (*Tmr* 32.D2) A date 1827 is inscribed in the plaster. The building lies obliquely to the Street and is neatly snuggled in and around by surrounding buildings.

Out on the navigation light point, Bombarda, west of the Port, is a monument to French sailors killed in the Crimean War.

POLICE

Port Over an office on the 'OTE' Sq between the Ferry-boat and the private yacht quays.

POST OFFICE (*Tmr* 20.D3) On the waterfront 'OTE' Sq, alongside which a wide flight of steps climbs up to the Old Quarter hillside. Above the Post Office is the Customs office.

TAXIS They rank on the Main Square and a board lists the 'going rate' charges including
Plaka 200 drs, Pollonia 380 drs, Paliochori 450 drs and Voudia 450 drs.

TELEPHONE NUMBERS & ADDRESSES

| Doctor | Tel 41703 |
| Taxi | Tel 41833 |

TRAVEL AGENTS *See* **Ferry-Boat Ticket Offices.**

ROUTE ONE
To the Plaka (6 km) Although I lump together the various hill-top Villages under the one, all encompassing name Plaka, in fact the Plaka is the Chora Village close by the now disappeared, Kastro. The other settlements include Pera Triovasalos (where a Petrol Station), Triovasalos, Firopotamos, Plakes, Trypiti and Mili that distantly circle a rather weed infested modern day stadium.

At Trypiti there are windmills, an Ancient Theatre and very early Christian Catacombs, which are unfortunately closed. It would appear the Catacombs date back to the 1st century AD, the islanders possibly being converted to Christianity by St Paul on a voyage from Crete. The burial site was probably the final resting place for between 2,000 and 5,000. It was at Trypiti, in a field, that a farmer found the 'Venus de Milo'. It is possible that the French broke the hands off in their haste to remove the statue, as a contemporary report refers to their position.

The bus pulls up at a 'T' junction with the main body of the Plaka Village to the left and a Clinic (Tel 21222) to the right, on the edge of the small, unsatisfactory Main Square. From the Square a signposted track leads down to Phourkouvouni and Areti.

The confusing bus timetable includes the following detail:-

Plaka Town to Adamas Port
Daily   0630, 0750, 0850, 0950, 1050, 1150, 1250, 1400, 1500, 1530, 1650,
                                      1750, 1850, 1950, 2050 hrs.

Plaka Town to Pollonia Port (via Adamas Port)*
Daily   0630, 0900, 1150, 1400, 1550 drs.

Plaka Town to Paliochori Beach
Daily   1020, 1120, 1520, 1620 (via Adamas Port)*
*Doubtful.

The Town police station (Tel 21378) is close to the bus turnround and taxi rank on the Square.

Around the edge of the Plaka are **Rooms**. There is an OTE and Post Office (which changes Travellers Cheques). The Plaka is an absolute pedestrian maze with a couple of friendly cafe-bar tavernas and a disturbing number of pharmacies (do they know something we don't?). The Folk Museum is very difficult to locate as the signs run out. So do the signs to the Baker which is down steep steps to the left, after climbing to a very pretty view of the north coast and the Bay of Firopotamos.

The signs for the Archaeological Museum also disappear but best to ignore them in any case, it is located just below the Post Office. The spacious, well laid out, but sparse Museum has the best lavatories on the Island. There are a minimum of three staff to run this delightfully air conditioned building.

From the part marbled terrace of the Church of Panagia i Korfiatissa (a repository for various icons and treasures), is one of the loveliest views out over the bay and western part of the Island. The site of the Old Kastro is marked by a rock hilltop Church.

ROUTE TWO
To Paliochori Beach (9½ km) The Main Road east skirts the huge bay at sea level. Stretches of the fairly narrow foreshore are suitable for bathing, if rather scrubbly, with the backshore and edge of the road irregularly planted with trees. Inland of the road mainly resembles a lunar landscape with mines and machinery littered all over the place, the occasional foray being made from the workings by a pierhead projecting into the bay. Furthermore there is not a taverna in sight.

Opposite the very large ΔEH, Electricity Generating plant (3 km), is a pleasant little beach and remarkably hot water, possibly from the Electricity plant outflow, and not a thermal spring.

The inland road curves off alongside the Generating plant to:-

ZEFIRIA ((and Palaiochori) 5 km from Adamas Port) Now a small, almost insignificant, Village set in an agricultural plain, but once the Islands capital with a population of about 5,000, 17 Churches and two bishops, one Orthodox and one Catholic. In fact from the 8th century AD to 1793, much of the prosperity was derived from pirates who used the Island as a base, but earthquakes, pestilence and sulphurous fumes caused the inhabitants to abandon the site. Well that is all except the modern day *Taverna/Restaurant Madam Lulu — All information here* and Greek evenings as well!

The first time traveller can be forgiven for not noticing the Pachiochori Beach turn-off, which is in the Village prior to the prominent Church, because there are no signposts. The route to the beach now becomes nothing more than a narrow, unmade track which snakes through farmland and up over the hills to:-

PALIOCHORI BEACH How the Bus Company envisaged this as a scheduled route I'm not sure but. . . . The settlement is circled by extensive quarry-scarred countryside which, with the shack-like nature of some of the buildings, imparts a 'frontier feel' to the place.

There is a large, central, clean beach, with grey sand and pebble foreshore, and two wing coves. The steeply shelving beach results in small breakers when the wind is in a particular direction. Of the several tavernas, the one closest to the bus pull-up is the best value, the:-

Artemis Bixos   Tel 22101

The inordinately large building has a neat, gravel laid patio. Two omelettes (200 drs), fresh bread (20 drs), a large can of beer — all right a can but at least a large one (100 drs), and a plate of chips (55 drs) for 375 drs.

Not inexpensive, I hear readers say, but compared to the Restaurant/Bar on the edge of the beach, to the right of the bay (*Fsw*), the prices are reasonable. This smart and expensive establishment caters for the trip boats, has canned music, linen table-cloths and a 330 gm tin of beer costs 70 drs.

There are **Rooms** available (Tel: summer 22101, winter 21788).

The beach is on the Day Trip Boat Excursion schedule which, if it is the 'Round the Island' cruise, costs 1000 drs and takes up to 9½ hrs.

To reach the cove to the right-hand (*Fsw*), it is necessary to clamber through a low rock tunnel. The smell of sulphur is very strong and the cliffs are stained a dirty yellow. There is some 'camping out', a little more litter (surely the two are connected) and some nude bathing.

The small, rather lovely cove to the left is only accessible by climbing over a pile of rocks edging and tumbled into the sea. The low cliffs hem in the narrow, pebble beach and there are rocks in the deep, dark coloured sea-water.

ROUTE THREE

As for ROUTE TWO until the Electricity Generating Station, where the Main Road continues to curve round the bay. Very soon after the turning off to Zefiria is a very large Alikes or salt works. At the far end of the salt pans is, after some 4 km, a track along to the 'doo-hickey' Airport — a shack or two and a small runway.

ORMOS HIVADOLIMNIS (6 km from Adamas Port) Tucked into the near side of a promontory and perhaps one of the finest beaches on the Island, with a clean, small cove and a big sweep of sand.

The road turns slightly inland and makes a junction with a cross-country track to the south coast, across an agricultural plain (yes agriculture, not mining) to either:-

ORMOS PROVATA (8.5 km from Adamas Port) A lovely sandy cove, with a steeply shelving shore, some kelp and six little boat-houses. Or:-

ORMOS AG SOSTI (8.5 km from Adamas Port) Two small coves with tiny, sandy beaches bounded by rocks, both set in low, crumbling hills and connected by a track.

The Main Road now climbs steeply up into the ugly mountaineous area surrounding Mt Profitis Ilias to:-

AG MARINA MONASTERY (11 km from Adamas Port) In the proximity of this Middle Ages Monastery, set in a pleasant, lush garden, the road becomes an unsurfaced track and there is some cultivation. A very steep path drops down from the side of the Monastery to the edge of the great bay and perhaps the prettiest area of the island, more especially:-

PHATOURENA (12½ km from Adamas Port) Along with the other locations north from here this nice sweep of sandy beach is not only attractive, but also rather inaccessible except by trip boat from Adamas Port. This is a pity because adjacent Rivari, the lagoon, Ag Nicholaos, and further up the coast, the sandy beach and scattered houses of Ebourio are well worth a visit, or two. Further along the bay, to the north, are two small, sheltered sandy beaches and the Church of Ag Dimitris set on a small headland.

A 7 km trek circling Mt Profitis Ilias to the north and then cutting through a cleft between Mt Kalamavros leads to the:-

Church of Ag Ioannis Theologos (Siderianos) The Church overlooks a bay of the same name and is the site of great celebrations. The story goes that when miscreants attacked the Church, the worthy worshippers begged St Theologos to intercede. He caused the door to harden as iron and when an assailant on the roof attempted to shoot at those sheltering inside the Church, the pistol seemed to explode in the man's hand, both pistol and severed limb falling into the church. These grisly reminders of the fortuituous salvation were preserved as was a tatter of cloth affixed to the front of the door, supposedly that of a womans dress torn as she scrambled inside, in the face of the pirates onslaught.

ROUTE FOUR

To Pollonia (9½ km) On the way to the north eastern fishing Port, the route passes:-

FLAKOPI (Phylakopi) (7½ km from Adamas Port) This important archaeological location, once the site of 3 Cities, overlooks the pleasant beach of Papafranga and the Bay of Flakopis. It comes as no surprise, considering the location, that one of the city civilisations was Minoan. With the decline of Flakopi, about 1100 BC, Klima, to the west of Trypoti, assumed the mantle of Island capital. Off the coast are the islets of Glaronissia.

POLLONIA (9½ km from Adamas Port) A pretty, typical, quiet fishing Port set in a small, semi-circular bay with (*Fsw*), the Hamlet and quay to the right. Centre is a narrow tree-lined, sandy beach running around to the left of the bay and on the far horn of which are a surprising number of Greek villas and holiday homes.

The bus parks up at the start of the Port Hamlet, close by a fork in the road. A street makes off to the right (whereon scooter hire), and the waterfront road to the left, which is edged by buildings, runs out on the quay.

Rooms and several restaurant/tavernas.

EXCURSION TO KIMOLOS ISLAND

Area 36 sq km and a population of about 1,000

As long as the weather is clement a caique makes the ½ hr duration sea crossing from Pollonia to Kimolos Island. The boat departs from Pollonia quay daily at about 0715 hrs, returning the same day at 1400 hrs, again connecting with the return bus to Adamas. The return boat fare costs 200 drs.

The boat trip passes by a couple of islets with cargo ships lurking at anchor here and there and, in the middle distance to the right, the large uninhabited Island of Paliegos. Probably a more reliable method to reach the island in indifferent weather conditions is to catch the inter-island **CF Kimolos** (*See* **Ferry-boat timetables, the A to Z, Adamas Port**).

The Island has been the scene of much mining activity in the past, but somehow less intrusively than Milos. The low, chalky white cliff faces of Kimolos evince the occasional evidence of quarrying and shore to ship loading gear. Originally chalk was the deposit extracted but a crushed stone used for chemical purposes is still excavated.

At Palaiokastro, on the west coast side of the Island, on a 430 m hilltop, are the remains of a Venetian Castle and a very old Church. To the north-east is the Hamlet of Klima, a beach and further on sulphur springs at Prassa (about 6½ km).

I have written before that a Guide Book author experiences a certain amount of conflict when a 'find' is made — to tell or not to tell. Now of course it all depends on what constitutes a find. Readers should by now have sorted out my foibles, prejudices, idiosyncrasies (or bigotry? take your choice). Taking all these into account I must nominate Kimolos as one of the slowly decreasing circle of islands on which I would wish to be landed in order to enjoy peace, a lack of modern day 'necessities' and unaffected, old fashioned, Greek island charm.

PSATHI: port
The Port is set in comparatively gentle hills, the middle of which are crowned by the Chora. To the right of centre, the crown of the hills are spotted with windmills.

Ferry-boats land at the end of the small quay, to the extreme right of the lovely harbour cove (*Sbo*), and are met by a swarming mass of humanity who dash helter-skelter to and from the ship. The inter-island caique berths up at about the middle of the quayside.

Stretching along the rest of the bay to the left is a pebble beach backed by a scattering of trees and buildings. The first quarter of the backshore has a narrow concrete track up against which is a combined Kafenion-cum-simple-Store. The proprietor is a smiley, gold toothed man. No food served here, just drinks.

Fifty yards to the right (sea still behind one) at the end of the boat quay is the:-

Kafenion O Tzakiσ
The owner is surly but his wife is friendly and they serve an excellent meal. For example a splendid meal of small sardine-like fish for two, an omelette, a plate of very tasty beans with lemon (no sauce), a Greek salad and 2 bottles of retsina cost 650 drs. Fish soup is also on the menu. There is a telephone but. . . .

About 3 hours to the west of the Port is a long sweeping beach but the Port seems sufficient to me and is in reach of a taverna or two. . . .

ROUTE ONE
To the Chora The steep uphill path to the Chora passes a really very large private house, which it is rumoured belongs to the owner of the **CF Kimolos**. One hundred and fifty metres up the hill are:-

Rooms for Rent Σmeλanith
Tel 51392

A nice looking, single storey block gathered round a patio. But no hot water and a double room is rather expensive, costing 1100 drs.

Other Rooms are charged out at about the same price.

The walk up to the Chora takes about 20 minutes and on the way there is, off to the right, a sight of a large cemetery and a glimpse of a fishing village (*See* **Oupa**).

CHORA (Kimolos)

A crumbling, twisting maze of lanes and alleys which often end above a ruin or in a backyard animal enclosure. A number of lovely old Churches and one Kafenion. Alongside the large Cathedral is a Clinic and Police station.

From the Chora left around a hillside gorge, leads to:-

OUPA A stunningly beautiful, simple, fishing Village built into and around the rocky hillsides. The boatsheds and stores are cut into the rock with the living accommodation above. The community spreads out over the rocks and cliff, spanning and bridging voids and fissures with makeshift bridge spans. To the right, (*Fsw*), is a small, semi-circular bay edged by a pebbly beach, on the far side of which are a row of surprisingly large 'lock-up' style boat sheds. The rather stony sea bottom of the cove is riven by a narrow band of sand enabling bathers to walk painlessly into the sea. No taverna, not even a Kafenion, but what a delightful spot to while away a part of the day.

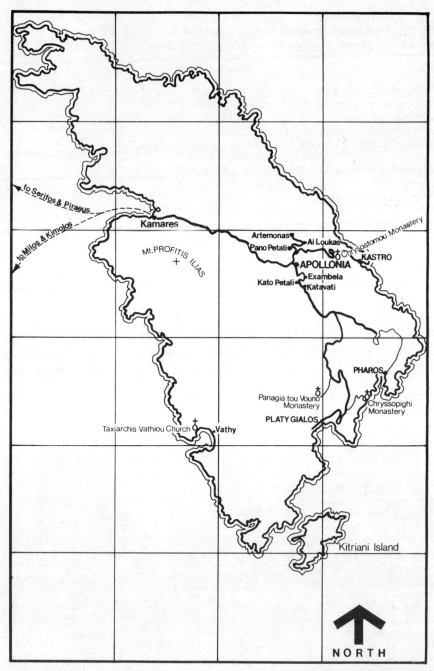

to Serifos & Piraeus

to Milos & Kimolos

Kamares

Mt.PROFITIS ILIAS

Artemonas
Pano Petali
Ai Loukas
Chryssostomou Monastery
APOLLONIA
KASTRO
Kato Petali
Exambela
Katavati

PHAROS

Panagia tou Vouno
Monastery
Chryssopighi
Monastery

PLATY GIALOS

Taxiarchis Vathiou Church
Vathy

Kitriani Island

NORTH

Illustration 48

SIPHNOS

25 Siphnos (Sifnos)
Cyclades Islands — Western chain

****

FIRST IMPRESSIONS
Greek holiday resort; few flies; cats and dogs look well fed; neat countryside; fanciful ceramic chimney pots; clean, neat, almost smug; green and cultivated; relatively unspoilt.

SPECIALITIES
Pottery.

RELIGIOUS HOLIDAYS & FESTIVALS
include: 6th September — Feast and Festival, Taxiarchis Vathiou, Vathy.

VITAL STATISTICS
Tel prefix 0284. Up to 20 km from top to bottom and up to 10 km wide with an area of some 74 sq km. The population numbers about 2,000 of which 1,600 or so live in the Capital of Apollonia and its satellite villages.

HISTORY
Gold and silver mines gave the island great wealth in antiquity and resulted in Siphnos being the largest contributors to the mainland Delphi Treasury. It is rumoured that this tribute to Apollo irked the islanders not a little so, instead of sending a golden ball equivalent to a tenth of their production, they conceived the wheeze of producing a gold leaf wrapped replacement. When found out they incurred the Gods wrath and he caused the mines to sink out of sight. The Siphniots cup of woe overflowed when the Samos tyrant Polycrates attacked the Island and levied an enormous tribute. Otherwise the Island generally followed the average 'run-of-the-mill' history of the rest of the Cyclades.

GENERAL
The approach around the north-west coast to the Port of Kamares leads the visitor to expect an arid Island. Not so, for in the main inhabited areas the agriculture is neat and intense with many field stone walls. The valleys and river gorges are perhaps most impressive with the intense cultivation sprinkled with dwellings and magnificent castellated dovecotes between which cascade 'rivers' of flowering Oleander.

The initial impression of tidiness is reinforced throughout the Island and even the cats, dogs and ducks look well fed. On an island frequented by Greeks for their own holiday jaunts, it would be unseemly of either the animals or tourists to intrude AND they don't! What a delightful change from the sweltering hordes of blistering holiday-makers, on say, Paros.

The beaches that the publicity blurb lauds are worthy of praise, if not quite so wonderful in actuality, as the more glowing and poetic descriptions. They certainly are profusely signposted with messages urging the 'hordes' to behave themselves.

Even the buses run on time in this well ordered and pleasant land, added to which the service is extensive and inexpensive. For those who prefer 'shanks pony' the Island is fertile ground for 'super walkies'. Although I have drawn readers attention to the matter, I shall not elaborate as I try to keep my pedestrian activities to that absolutely necessary for authorship. Okay.

KAMARES: main port (Illustration 49)

The clean, orderly Port and fishing Village of Kamares (resembling a hot, sunny Frinton-on-Sea) and with an aura, a milieu of wealth, is impressively positioned in an amphitheatre of mountains inevitably crowned here and there by the occasional Chapel. The horse-shoe bay is bordered by the tree-lined Esplanade of the Port, on the right, backed by the range of which Mt Profitis Ilias climbs to a height of 893 m; an impressive, sandy beach fills out the bottom centre of the bay and there are rocky cliff faces to the left.

The provision of accommodation is not allowed to encroach on this peaceful, 'vicars-tea-party' atmosphere and is discreetly unobtrusive. Unfortunately accommodation costs comparatively more (for less), and eating out is expensive.

ARRIVAL BY FERRY

The Ferry-boat quay (*Tmr* 1.A4) is at the very top end of the right-hand side of the Port. The boats are met by Room owners but mainly those with expensive accommodation, so it may well be best to locate one's own. The buses also await disembarking travellers, even the late night boat, as do the taxis and most of the Village. The bus gets very, very crowded despite which the cognoscente might well travel directly to say the seaside Village of Pharos.

THE ACCOMMODATION & EATING OUT

Apart from the introductory comments it is worth noting that the bathrooms are, in general, on the basic side and the showers are cold water only.

The Accommodation At the bottom of the Ferry-boat quay (*Tmr* 1.A4) there are quite possibly **Rooms** up the track to the right.

Rooms
Directions: Left from the bottom of the Ferry-boat quay, along the Esplanade and on the right, across the road from the small fishing boat quay (*Tmr* B4). Over **Katsoulakis Tourist Agency** (*Tmr* 2.B5).

Rooms
Directions: Three buildings down from **Katsoulakis Tourist Agency**, to the nearside of a flight of steps, over the cafe-bar *EΣtiatopion H'Mεροπh* (*Tmr* 3.B5).

Rooms (*Tmr*4.B5) No. 47
Directions: Just beyond the flight of steps from the Cafe-bar above.
Expensive with a double room costing 1200 drs mid-season which is 300 drs more than other middle priced rooms.

Rooms No 46
Directions: Next door to No 47 and above a Cafe-bar.
A double room sharing the bathroom for 900 drs.

Hotel Stavros (*Tmr* 5.C5) (Class C)   Tel 31641
Directions: Further on along the Esplanade, beyond the large Church, a flight of steps and on the right above the family owned **Food Market.**
Neat with brown paint everywhere. Single rooms start at 700 drs and double rooms from 800 drs. Double bedrooms vary from those sharing the rather ethnic bathroom (cold-shower), those with no windows, those with a balcony view of the Esplanade (900 drs) and bedrooms en suite (1000 drs). The period between 1st July and 15th September adds about another 300 drs.

From close by the area of *The Old Captain Bar* (*Tmr* 6.D5), the beach starts off along the bottom of the bay. About one third to halfway along the beach and a grove of trees, on the backshore, is the locality of an unofficial Campsite.

Further on, almost at the far end of the bay, the wide, dry river bed of the Livadas

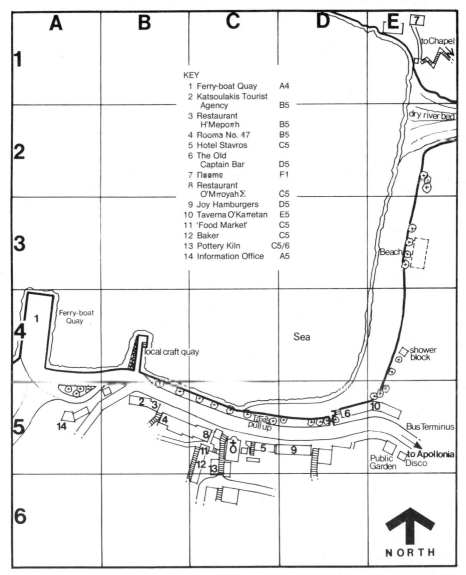

KEY
1 Ferry-boat Quay — A4
2 Katsoulakis Tourist Agency — B5
3 Restaurant H'Μεροπh — B5
4 Rooms No. 47 — B5
5 Hotel Stavros — C5
6 The Old Captain Bar — D5
7 Πooμe — F1
8 Restaurant O'ΜπroγαhΣ — C5
9 Joy Hamburgers — D5
10 Taverna O'Καπetan — E5
11 'Food Market' — C5
12 Baker — C5
13 Pottery Kiln — C5/6
14 Information Office — A5

NORTH

KAMARES

Illustration 49

meanders down from the mountain gorge. To one side is a taverna and an official Campsite.

At the far end of the beach, where the bay turns the corner and rocks take over, is:-

Rooms (*Tmr* 7.E1)
Directions: As above, in a cluster of buildings.

A double room en suite, in this new but provincial block, costs 1000 drs. The old peasant couple who manage the accommodation speak no English at all.

Hotel Kamari (Class B)   Tel 31641
Directions: On the right of the Apollonia road out of Kamares Port, beyond the Bus turn-round area.

A modern three storey Pension (that's the official classification). A double room en suite, starts at 1150 drs, rising to 1495 drs (1st July - 15th September).

The Eating Out As with the accommodation, the introduction has covered a few general aspects. The layout of the Port Village is easy to follow, as the waterfront Esplanade is lined by the various establishments. All over the Island a bottle of beer is pricey, at 70 drs.

Εστiatopion H Μεροπh (*Tmr* 3.B5)
A pleasant little Cafe-bar, mainly used by the locals. The cheapest Nes 'meh ghala' (48 drs) in the Port and a 'mind-blocking', cloudy, 'open' retsina costing 30 drs a carafe. Ouzo is served with mezes.

Εστiatopion Ο'ΜπογαηΣ (*Tmr* 8.C5)
The taverna tables line the waterside across the Esplanade, beneath a scattering of mature trees. In fact most of the waterfront is cluttered with chairs and tables set in amongst the trees. The prices are, as are most in the Port, above average and a meal of moussaka, ratatouille, Greek salad, bread and a Rotunda wine costs about 440 drs per head. The service is leisurely. Inside the building is an interesting picture of Old Kamares — have a look.

Joy Hamburgers (*Tmr* 9.D5)
Beyond the *Hotel Stavros* and surprise, surprise, serves up a range of hamburgers and ice-creams. I am sad that there is no souvlaki pita instead of this glossy, milk-shake, 'hand-me-down' from North America.

Ψapotabebpna Ο'Καπetan (*Tmr* 10.E5)
Bordered by the road to Apollonia on one side and the beach on the other. The tables and chairs are set out on the curve of the backshore, amongst the shelter of some trees.

Somehow the menu and cooking put me in mind of the French Mediterranean, as do the prices, which are on the expensive side.

THE A TO Z OF USEFUL INFORMATION

BANKS None. *See* **Apollonia** but note there are only Change offices.

BEACHES The fine sandy beach which fills the bottom of the very long bay, has only one shortcoming, the extremely slow gradient of the seabed. It is a long wade to achieve more than knee-height — ideal for 'littlies'. It has to be admitted that the foreshore gets a little messy towards the far end of the great sweep. None-the-less a beautiful beach and clean sea, second only to Milopotamos Beach, Ios island. At the near end there is a small block of beach showers.

BICYCLE, SCOOTER & CAR HIRE
Sifnos Car   Tel 31793/31661
Beyond the wasteground Bus terminal on the left-hand side of the Apollonia Main Road. A two seater moped costs 1000 drs and a car 2400 drs a day. Do not forget that the bus service is excellent, so much so that vehicle hire is rather unnecessary.

BREAD SHOPS There is a Baker (*Tmr* 12.C5) through the archway alongside the *Restaurant ΕΣtiatopion O'ΜπογahΣ* and round to the right, behind the '**Food Market**'.

BUSES The main turn-round area is at the start of the Apollonia Road and only buses connecting with a Ferry-boats arrival carry on down to the quay. Lots of horn on arrival and prior to departure.

Bus timetables Timetables are stuck up everywhere.

Kamares Port to Apollonia Town
Daily   0730, 0930 and every hour to 2230 hrs.

Return journey
Daily   0700, 0830, 0900 and every hour to 2200 hrs.
One-way fare 30 drs, duration 10 minutes.

Some buses proceed on from Apollonia, after a ½ hr stop over, to Platic Yialos but for most connections, it is necessary to change buses at Apollonia.

COMMERCIAL SHOPPING AREA None, but there is a Food Market (actually a food-cum-gift shop) on the ground floor of the *Hotel Stavros* (*Tmr* 5.C5) as well as a Food Market (*Tmr* 11.C5) (actually an old fashioned store) through the archway alongside the *Restaurant O'ΜπογahΣ*.

A ceramics pottery kiln workshop (*Tmr* 13.C5/6) can be found by climbing the steps alongside the large Esplanade Church.

DISCO One beyond the Public Garden at the start of the road to Apollonia.

FERRY-BOATS Well served and connected to the Eastern chain by the **FB Kimolos**. The **FB Ionian** (out of action for much of 1985) sails the more traditional north-south route.

As least two small excursion boats make the all important transverse connection with the pivotal Cycladean Ferry-boat island of Paros. The **MV Yiannis Latsos II**, for example, has a clean top-deck, well appointed main through deck and cabin, very clean toilets, a small bar and a change office. She does roll a bit BUT compare with a description of the more traditional **MV Marianna** (*See* **Naxos, Chapter 15**).

Ferry-boat timetable

Day	Departure time	Ferry-boat	Ports/Islands of Call
Daily*	1500 hrs	Yiannis Latsos II	Paros
*	1130 hrs	Magarita	Paros

*These craft only operate on a daily basis between June and September.

Day	Departure time	Ferry-boat	Ports/Islands of Call
Monday	1330 hrs	Kimolos	Ios, Santorini
	2230 hrs	Kimolos	Serifos, Piraeus (M)
Tuesday	2000 hrs	Kimolos	Milos, Kimolos, Syros
Wednesday	1100 hrs	Kimolos	Serifos, Kithnos, Piraeus (M)
	1500 hrs	Ionian	Milos
	1900 hrs	Ionian	Serifos, Kithnos, Piraeus (M)
Thursday	1330 hrs	Kimolos	Ios, Santorini
	2230 hrs	Kimolos	Kithnos, Piraeus (M)
Friday	2200 hrs	Kimolos	Milos, Piraeus (M)
Saturday	1400 hrs	Ionian	Milos
	1500 hrs	Kimolos	Milos, Kimolos, Ios, Santorini
Sunday	0945 hrs	Ionian	Serifos, Kithnos, Piraeus (M)
	1400 hrs	Kimolos	Serifos, Kithnos, Piraeus (M)

FERRY-BOAT TICKET OFFICES Almost every other shop in Kamares appears to sell tickets for the **CF Kimolos**, but, in 1985 at least, it was necessary to go to Apollonia to buy a ticket for the **CF Ionian**. This arrangement may change when the **Ionian** or a sister ship actually runs.

Katsoulakis Tourist & Travel Agency (*Tmr* 2.B5)   Tel 31700
The most professional outfit but the young women assistant is rather sour-faced. 'Authorised AGENGY (sic) Olympic'.

OPENING HOURS Although the mid afternoon siesta is complied with, shops stay open late into the evening.

PLACES OF INTEREST Trip boat excursions to the south-western harbour of Vathy depart every day at 1030 hrs, from the inland side of the Ferry-boat quay. They leave Vathy at 1430 hrs and, at the height-of-the-season, there are up to three boats a day.
   Vathy, which is only accessible by sea, is reputably the most scenic of all the Islands seaside resorts. The harbour and sandy beach of this fishing boat and pottery Port are set in a decanter shaped inlet. There are *Rooms*, two tavernas and unofficial backshore camping as well as a 16th century Byzantine Church, Taxiarchis Vathiou. The Church celebrates on 6th September and the 8th November.

TAXIS Two ranks, one, at the bottom of the Ferry-boat quay and the other on the water's edge opposite the *Hotel Stavros* (*Tmr 5.C5*).

TRAVEL AGENTS Apart from the Ferry-Boat Ticket Offices there is an:-
Information Office (*Tmr* 14.A5)
Conveniently situated behind a small Public Garden on a layby not far from the end of the Ferry-boat quay. Inaugurated in 1985, the office opens daily 0900 - 2100 hrs, except Friday when the hours are 1030 - 2330 hrs. It is planned to be open all year round, with another office in Apollonia. The staff are enthusiastic and speak excellent English, so one hopes the constant bombardment of tourist hordes will not blunt their keenness.

ROUTE ONE
To Apollonia (6 km) The road climbs the mountainside beside an intensely cultivated valley gorge. The stone wall bordered, dry river-bed is awash with Oleanders in and amongst which are the occasional small dwelling and dovecote. At Pano Petali, on the outskirts of Apollonia, there is a petrol station.

APOLLONIA: capital (Illustration 50)
The Capital Town and centre of a cruciform development of Villages spread across the ridge and saddle of the busy, neat agricultural hills which are enclosed by tidy terraces. Apollonia encompasses, from north to south, the villages of Artemonas, Ai Loukas, Pano Petali, Katavati and Exambela. Busy, active and more a Town than a Greek island Chora.

THE ACCOMMODATION & EATING OUT
The Accommodation There is not as much as one might hope for. The Port bus parks up on 'Museum' Square (*Tmr* 1.B4), on the far side of which is a convenient Kafenion (*Tmr* 2.B4), even if the old boy is a bit surly. On the Post Office (*Tmr* 3.B4) side of the Square (facing it), and to the left, is a counter selling souvlakis, in the window of which is a card advertising *Rooms*.
   Along the narrow street connecting 'Museum' Sq (*Tmr* 1.B4) with the 'OTE' Sq (*Tmr* 4.B4), there is the:-
Hotel Sophia (*Tmr* 5.B4) (Class C)   Tel 31238
Directions: On the left with a restaurant on the ground floor.
   A well travelled friend maintained that the Hotel room was amongst the best he had ever stayed in, even if the only time to ensure a hot water shower was 3 o'clock in the morning! A

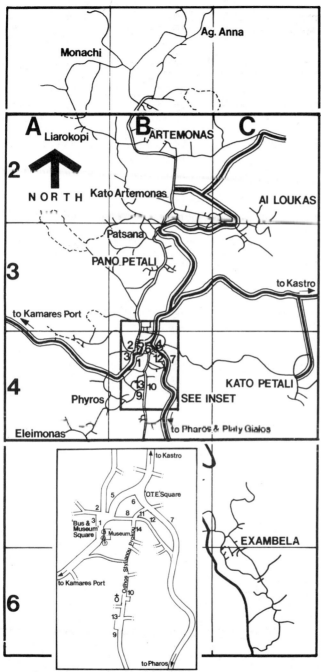

KEY

1	'Museum' Square	B4
2	Kafenion	B4
3	Post Office	B4
4	'O.T.E.' Square	B4
5	Hotel Sophia	B4
6	O.T.E.	B4
7	Pension Apollonia	B4
8	Police Station	B4
9	Hotel Sifnos	B4
10	Restaurant Krevatina	B4
11	Store/Change Office	B4
12	Rent-A-Bike	B4
13	Baker	B4
14	Katsoulakis Travel Agency	B4

APOLLONIA

Illustration 50

single room en suite costs 720 drs rising to 845 drs (1st July - 10th September) and a double 1060 drs and 1245 drs respectively.

Hotel Anthoussa (Class C)   Tel 31431
Directions: Next door to the OTE (*Tmr* 6.B4), over a famous Patisserie.

A modern building with single room rates en suite costing 720 drs, rising to 1100 drs and a double room 1060 drs increasing to 1335 drs (July - August).

South, along the Main Road to Pharos and Platy Gialos, is the:-

Pension Apollonia (*Tmr* 7.B4) (Class B)   Tel 31490
Directions: On the left.

A long, single storey *Auberge* style building, close by the side of the road. Despite the Youth Hostel look to the place, the Room rates reflect the Pension's B class classification. Rooms share the bathrooms with singles rising from 620 drs to 720 drs and double rooms 750 drs to 1050 drs.

There are **Rooms** almost opposite the *Pension Apollonia.*

From the top of the 'Museum' Sq (*Tmr* 1.B4), opposite the Post Office, a narrow alley bears off alongside the elongated tree planted and seat scattered Public Garden. After about 30 m, across the way from the Town police station (*Tmr* 8.B4), another narrow lane, Odhos Stylianou Prokou, sets off at right angles climbing and snaking upwards. On the right, alongside a small Plateia is the:-

Hotel Sifnos (*Tmr* 9.B4) (Class C)   Tel 31624
Directions: As above.

Single and double rooms en suite are respectively 800 drs/960 drs and 1200/1400 drs (high season July and August).

Rooms   Tel 31459/31255
A chance meeting with an amply proportioned lady, Madame Aliopi Nicolou, failed to give me any more than the phone number. Nonetheless double rooms in her house cost 1000 drs. It may help out.

The Eating Out Apart from the Kafenion (*Tmr* 2.B4) and Souvlaki Snackbar on 'Museum' Sq (referred to under **The Accommodation**), the best value Taverna/ Restaurant must be:-

Restaurant Krevatina (*Tmr* 10.B4), Odhos Stylianou Prokou
Directions: See the directions for the *Hotel Sifnos*. The establishment is on the left, alongside a small Square, which the seats of the Restaurant fill, beyond the *Argo Cocktail Bar* on the right, opposite a Church and prior to the Hotel.

The Patron, Nicolaos Lantsis, presides over a not inexpensive (well actually expensive) but varied menu. This includes swordfish but unfortunately only a large, costly bottle of retsina. A meal for two of swordfish, ratatouille, a plate of green beans, Greek salad, potatoes and a bottle of retsina costs about 1200 drs. Despite the prices the establishment is well patronised and closes in the afternoon from 1400 hrs until early evening. A notice proclaims further 'goodies' namely 'Sundays Special Live Greek Music 10 - 12 pm. A surprise'. Yes I'm sure!

On the 'OTE' Sq, in fact next door to the OTE (*Tmr* 6.B4), the tables of a smart Patisserie, located in the ground floor of the *Hotel Anthoussa*, spread across the terrace and the OTE office front.

On the 'Museum' Sq (*Tmr* 1.B4), between the Post Office and the Souvlaki stall, is the:-

Restaurant Cyprus
Directions: As above.

Average menu but the Spanish style tables and chairs and linen table-cloths tend to blunt my interest as the cost of these luxuries usually translates itself into higher than average prices. Nod, nod, wink, wink.

THE A TO Z OF USEFUL INFORMATION

BANKS None, only Change offices, two of which are almost side by side, close to the Police station (*Tmr* 8.B4). One (*Tmr* 11.B4) is straight on (and to the left) from the Police station, set in a large shop which not only sells dairy products, sliced meats, and some ironmongery but also operates the Ticket office for the **FB Ionian**. It has to be admitted that the owner gets very stroppy and off-hand when questioned about this Ferry, which is not really surprising as the boat ". . . has been broken" (for much of 1985).

The other Change office (and gift shop), the:-

Metro Life Hellas
Is up Odhos Stylianou Prokou from the Police station, almost immediately to the left. Both offer fair rates.

BICYCLE, SCOOTER & CAR HIRE
Rent-A-Moto-Bicycle (*Tmr* 12.B4) situated between the 'OTE' Sq (*Tmr* 4.B4) and *Pension Apollonia* (*Tmr* 7.B4) on the right.

BOOKSELLERS
'Boomerang' International Agency On the 'Museum' Sq (*Tmr* 1.B4) between the Post Office and the Souvlaki stall. They stock a wide range of foreign newspapers and magazines.

The gift and haberdashery shop on the left of the road connecting 'Museum' and 'OTE' Squares has a number of useful maps including a gem written and illustrated by a John Barkett Smith of England, in respect of the Kastro.

BREAD SHOPS There is a Baker (*Tmr* 13.B4) along Odhos Stylianou Prokou, on the other side of the small Square to the *Hotel Sifnos* (*Tmr* 9.B4).

BUSES Park up on both 'Museum' and 'OTE' Squares.

The service, as has been written, is first class, added to which some routes connect-up. For instance the Pharos to Apollonia connection, after a dawdle of ½ hour, proceeds to Kastro.

Bus timetable
Apollonia Town to Platy Gialos (Plati Yelos)
Daily   0700, 0900, then every hour to 2200 hrs.

Return journey
Daily   0730, 0930 and every hour to 2230 hrs.
One-way fare 50 drs.

Apollonia Town to Pharos (Faros)
Daily   0700, 0900, 1030, 1215, 1345, 1615, 1800, 1945, 2115 hrs.

Return journey
Daily   0730, 0930, 1100, 1245, 1400, 1700, 1830, 2015, 2200 hrs.
One-way fare 35 drs.

Apollonia to Kastro
Daily   0800, 1000, 1130, 1315, 1430, 1545, 1730, 1900, 2045, 2230 hrs.

Return journey
Daily   0815, 1015, 1200, 1330, 1445, 1600, 1745, 1815, 1915, 2100, 2245 hrs.
One-way fare 30 drs.

CHEMISTS *See* **Medical Care.**

COMMERCIAL SHOPPING AREA North from 'OTE' Sq, towards the Hamlet of Artemonas, is an excellent 'provincial' supermarket, on the right.

One of the aforementioned Money Change and Ferry-boat ticket offices (*Tmr* 11.B4) is a General Store with a dairy and sliced meats counter. On the right of the road connecting the two main Squares at the 'Museum' Sq end is a Butcher and shop and opposite the Souvlaki stall is a Periptero.

MEDICAL CARE
Chemists & Pharmacies There is a Pharmacy on the left of the narrow lane which heads off alongside the Kafenion (*Tmr* 2.B4) in a northerly direction from 'Museum' Sq.

Clinic On the left of Odhos Vassalopoulou which connects 'OTE' Sq with the Hamlet of Artemonas.

OTE (*Tmr* 6.B4) Open weekdays only, 0730 - 1500 hrs.

PETROL On the left of the road south from 'OTE' Sq in the direction of Pharos and Platy Gialos.

PHARMACIES *See* **Medical Care.**

PLACES OF INTEREST Naturally a plethora of Churches and the Museum but one of the big attractions of Siphnos island is the opportunity to walk the many paths and tracks. I am aware that I rarely laud the delights of marching about the countryside but.... This is an Island where 'walkies' pays off, especially as no particular trek is of inordinate length and nearly every route passes at least one, if not two, interesting Churches and or Monasteries.

POLICE The Police station (*Tmr* 8.B4) is on the left of the alley branching off at right angles from the north end of 'Museum' Sq. The small hut-like office is open Saturday as well as weekdays and the officers will help in a search for Rooms, but they do not speak very much English.

POST OFFICE (*Tmr* 3.B4) On the left of 'Museum' Sq, facing north.

TAXIS They park up on both Main Squares.

TELEPHONE NUMBERS & ADDRESSES
Clinic	Tel 31315
Police	31210

TRAVEL AGENTS Apart from the Office (*Tmr* 11.B4) detailed under Banks, there is the:-

Katsoulakis Travel Agency (*Tmr* 14.B4)   Tel 31004
On the left of Odhos Stylianou Prokou. The friendly, young lady speaks clear English.

ROUTE TWO
To Pharos (7 km) The surfaced road strikes south from Apollonia through the outlying Village of Katavati and, after some 2 km, forks left off the Platy Gialos Main Road. Despite the usual island map detail, the road is paved for another 2 km, after which the surface becomes rather bad and rough, especially for the bus. The last section of the route is paralleled by a lovely river gorge full of Oleanders, set in farming country.

PHAROS (Faros) (7 km from Apollonia) A small, busy, bustling one-time Port, now an *ad hoc* holiday resort and certainly where I would head for if not staying in Kamares Port.
    The buses pull up to the left of the Hamlet, on the edge of the fishing boat quay which not only frames this side of the bay, but is at right angles to the waterfront.
    On the left of the quay (*Fsw*) are the rather rustic:-

Rooms   Tel 31822
and a small basement gift shop that sells inexpensive, second-hand English language

books.

Proceeding along the waterfront to the right are:-

Rooms

With mid-season doubles sharing a bathroom costing 735 drs and 945 drs en suite; a Chalet owner (Tel 31989) with double rooms at 1115 drs and the:-

Restaurant Mesimeriatis

The bright, young owner, serves up a 'Euro Breakfast' — coffee or tea, fruit juice, bread, butter and honey or a 'Super Breakfast' as above with eggs, bacon and chocolate cake (sic). A plate of stuffed tomatoes, bread and a beer cost about 266 drs which is not cheap.

Beyond the Restaurant are two beaches. This first is small and sandy with a coarse sand sea bed and a pebbly backshore on to which a dried up river bed expires.

From the far end of this beach, steps rise up to a pocket-sized and pretty 'Old Quarter' draped over a prominent headland. Several rudimentary **Rooms**, and one simple tourist shop. The double rooms overlooking the sea, on the tip of the promontory, cost 900 drs en suite but the shower water is cold.

Beyond the bluff is another small, very sandy beach with some kelp at the centre and backed by a stone wall and bullrushes at the far end. A certain amount of informal camping takes place close by the wall. Nude bathing, despite the sign prohibiting the same.

ROUTE THREE

To Platy Gialos (10 km) From the Pharos fork the Main Road loops past the Monastery Panagia tou Vouno, built in 1813, and the track to the beautifully sited:-

MONASTERY PANAGIA CHRYSSOPIGHI Built in 1650 on a rocky cape and founded because of the discovery of a glowing icon in the sea, which makes a change from the usual rowing boat legends. The fissure twixt Monastery and the shore is attributed to Holy intervention. The story goes that three local women were set on by pirates, who no doubt had other thoughts in their minds than ballroom dancing. The ladies prayed to the Virgin Mary who caused an earthquake and the cleft, which understandably shook the pirates no end.

The Main Road drops down the surrounding hills to:-

PLATY GIALOS (Plati Yelos) The road parallels the long, flat sea-shore. The landward side of the road is edged by stone-walled fields of Olive trees. The plain is ringed by hills. The road passes the occasional apartment or private house.

The sea side of the road is fringed by a row of single storey dwellings, the occasional taverna, restaurant, snackbar, tourist shop and a two storey Hotel, the D class *Panorama*.

The far left-hand side of the bay *(Fsw)* is bordered by a gathering of fishermans cottages with benzinas and a fishing caique or two anchored in the shallow water. The beach at this end is stony with some kelp whilst the central section is comparatively narrow and made up of coarse sand, flecked with pebbles. The sea bottom has some biscuit rock and large pebbles. There are two small, low quays between which a flock of ducks and drakes swim back and forth. About centre is a fascinating jumble of low buildings. To the left *(Fsw)* is a ceramic kiln with all the paraphernalia necessary to produce the pottery. To the right is a simple terrace, conspicuous by a solitary shower head, backed by some very rudimentary **Rooms**. These are complete with elemental beds and shallow stone washbasins — quite reminiscent of Cycladean accommodation of years gone by, but the prices are not. The old lady tries to charge up to 1100 drs for a double bed despite the fact that the rate card on the back of the door says 780 drs! Oh and the shower head on the edge of the terrace is the washing facility! To the right the beach becomes progressively more stony as does the sea bottom and ends by the:-

Hotel Platis Gialos (Class B)   Tel 31224
Directions: As above.

Simple construction, nice looking three storey building let into the rock that edges the bay. Single rooms sharing the bathroom cost 900 drs and en suite 1300 drs rising to 1250 drs and 1600 drs respectively. The double room prices are 1300/1600 drs and 1650/2100 drs.

The bus pulls up right of centre of the bay, opposite a small Campsite enclosed by a stone wall.

The backshore has occasional clumps of trees and signs 'Do Not Swim Naked In The Crowded Beaches. Withdraw To Isolated Places' and 'Please Keep Sifnos Clean. Cleanliness Means Health And Civilisation'. Despite this last admonishment the beach is a little messy. There are windsurfer boards for hire at 400 drs an hour.

ROUTE FOUR

To Kastro (5½ km) Why not save the best to last (unless you've experienced the prized tit-bit being swiped off your plate). As nobody can take the Kastro away, reserve it for a treat.

The bus makes the short journey along the road which drops steeply down to a saddle bordered by some windmills and pulls up on the right flank of the massive headland, which is swathed by the Medieval fortress.

The Kastro is a really very beautiful, clean, whitewashed Chora, dramatically positioned on the promontory that falls away sharply on either side into the sea, way below. The streets are in terraced tiers, climbing up the side of the hilltop in the fashion of a layered cake.

The antiquity, and continous development of the site is no better evidenced than by the bits and pieces of ancient columns and headless busts incorporated, here and there, into the facades of various houses. A plentiful supply of Churches and an Archaeological Museum,. The original Castle walls have almost all but disappeared.

There are very few concessions to tourists apart from *Zorbas Taverna, Rooms Helen Lempesi,* 'Green Grocery and Snack, The Star' and a post box scattered about the alleys and lanes. Some of these pedestrian-only ways form bridges to the top floors of the lower houses while some are arched and covered by buildings whose first floors connect overhead.

The approach road to the Kastro dips on to a 'bridge-like' hillside saddle, on the left of which are three remaining windmills. These are interesting in that they are constructed in the style of the Cretan models with a rounded front, elongated main body and flat back instead of the archetypal circular Cycladean pattern. A Snackbar has been set into the side wall of one of two of the mills that stand almost side by side.

To the right of the Main Road as it approaches the side of the Kastro, is the steep mountain side drop to a small, stony, beautiful cove. A rocky track winds and wanders down to Ormos Seralias, the narrowing and dimunitive backshore and dry valley river-bed which are almost crowded out by a clutter of buildings. One of these was once a tannery, another is a domed Church alongside which is a Restaurant.

On the other side of the mountain to the Kastro and high above Seralias Bay is the:-

MONASTERY CHRYSOSTOMOU Founded in 1550 and once a Convent. Its claim to fame is that it served as headquarters of the Island opposition to the Turkish overlords, including an illegal school to educate children in traditional Greek customs.

To the left of the Main Road, just before the windmills, an unsurfaced, short track ends abruptly overlooking the craggy, sea edged, cliff-face. On a small blob of headland, almost at sea-level, is the blue domed Church of the Seven Martyrs. On the side of this track are the foundations of what may be a projected Hotel. If this is so why not visit the Kastro before the delights and demands of 20th century holiday-makers ruin this lovely Capital City of Antiquity and manage what 3,500 years of turbulent island history have failed to inflict — its despoilation.

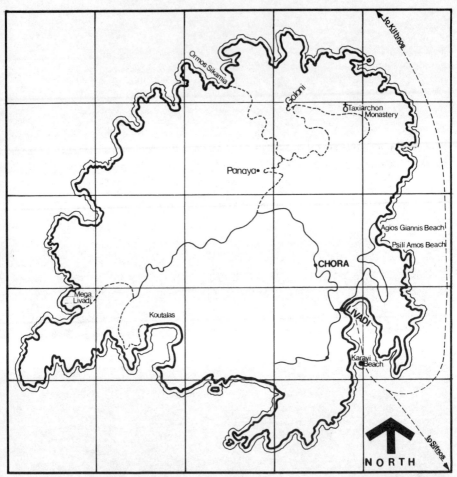

Ilustration 51

SERIFOS

FIRST IMPRESSIONS

Womens bonnets (koukoula); intrusive pop music; unhelpful bus drivers; rather secretive, unfriendly islanders; beautiful butterflies; wild buddleia; fine mules; unsurfaced roads; charter caiques and yachts; Greek holiday island; winnowing.

SPECIALITIES

None that I know of.

RELIGIOUS HOLIDAYS & FESTIVALS

include: 5th May — Festival, Ag Irenes, Koutalas; 6th August, Ag Sotiras, Kalo Amebli (south coast); 15th August, Panagia, Ramos; 15 - 16th August — Feast and Festival, Pirgos; 7th November — Festival, Monastery of Taxiarchon.

There is a pleasant, local folk-tale that at the Panagia Festival, the first couple to dance around an Olive tree close to the Church would get married very, very soon. Naturally fights broke out amongst pairs who wished to be first to the tree. The weapon of attack was traditionally a branch and it is said that 'it was best to be stabbed by a Turk, rather than a Serifiot wielding a staff. . . or words to that effect.

VITAL STATISTICS

Tel prefix 0281. The almost circular island is up to 8 km from side to side and top to bottom with an area of 70 sq km. The population numbers about 1,200.

HISTORY

Mythology informs us that Princess Danae and her son Perseus landed on Serifos after being set adrift by her father. It was Perseus that killed Medusa, the ghastly gorgon, at the request of the King of Serifos who really wanted the lad out of the way in order to have his wicked way with mother. Unfortunately for these lecherous intentions, Perseus returned home early and, enraged, held up the dead head of Medusa, turning the King and his court to stone. Historically the Island has been rather humdrum, following the usual Cycladean succession of overlords. The Romans sent exiles here, as they did to a number of other unprepossessing islands.

GENERAL

For an island to be so close to Siphnos and yet be so totally different should be almost impossible, but then that is the joy of discovering and travelling the Greek islands. The mountains seem rather massive, old and rounded. The peaks are centrally located which, combined with the almost circular shape of the outline, gives a blob-like appearance to the Island.

The name is supposed to designate dry, which is probably why the map makers are so keen to detail a plethora of massive (and non-existent) rivers.

It is as if the worthy citizens of Serifos do not want tourists and or are unable to overcome their secretive nature. No one meets the Ferries, so accommodation has to be ferreted out and what there is available is expensive. Eating out is rather prohibitive and often unrewarding; the best beach to the port, oft sought, remains unsignposted; the scenically picturesque Chora makes little attempt to welcome visitors and the bus service only travels betwen Livadi Port and the Chora which does not aid connection with the two or three extremely rewarding seaside Hamlets. Admittedly the roads are nothing more than fearsome tracks through the interior. Even the bus drivers, so often a source of useful information on other islands, are uncommunicative. If only the so-helpful citizens of Milos could have some of the attractions of Serifos island, they would probably be very grateful.

But perhaps I have painted too dismal a picture. Livadi Port is situated in an extensive bay, with every possible attraction dotted about its periphery. Within fairly easy reach of the Port are one or two exceptional beaches; the Chora is an acceptable example of its genre and the seaside Hamlets of Mega Livadi, Koutalas and Sikamia are each unique in their style and type.

LIVADI: port (Illustration 52)

Originally a small-time fishing Village, fortuitously sited on a lovely sweeping beach at the end of a horseshoe bay, and now attempting to be a 'big-time' holiday resort. The result is a disjointed 'mishmash' circling the water's edge.

On the left (*Sbo*) is the massive Ferry-boat quay (*Tmr* 1.D/E4/5) followed by a concrete walk towards the caique and yacht quay (*Tmr* 2.B4), on the landward side of which is the Village. From hereon, all the way round to the far edge of the bay is a spread-out ribbon of development skirting the waters edge, including tavernas, restaurants, hotels, private homes, discos, pensions, rooms, cafe-bars and a few shops that slowly thin out as one progresses. But the disparate growth is rather scrubby and 'tacky', which may be the result, in part, of the high incidence of cruise caiques and charter yachts.

The Main Road from the quay to the centre of the almost modern Village runs out by the turning off for the Chora. The rest of the 'Esplanade' is a dirt track only enhanced by the number of mature trees spread along the backshore. Almost one of the only islands where pop music (not Greek) is intrusive.

Strange that such a pretty location has grown or developed (if that is the word) as it has. Livadi has its resident 'character', the grizzled, small, lean man who masterminds the Port's rubbish. Easily recognisable by the oversize Wellington boots into which are tucked tight jeans, into which is tucked a check shirt. A large pair of dark glasses perch on the end of his dew-drop nose, and his chin sports several days 'pepper and salt stubble', all topped off by a grimy yachting hat. He totters back and forth with ever larger boxes of rubbish, that is when he is not lavishing attention on his possibly eternally land-bound, small benzina fishing boat fitted with an impossibly oil begrimed engine.

ARRIVAL BY FERRY

Quite a hike to the Village centre and Ferries are not met by the owners of Rooms. As there is little accommodation in the Chora it is important to locate accommodation quickly in Livadi. The bus and taxis meet some Ferries.

THE ACCOMMODATION & EATING OUT

Rooms, at the height-of-season, are in short supply and meals are expensive, probably as a result of the large numbers of charter yachts and cruise caiques that call.

The Accommodation From the Ferry-boat quay in a clockwise direction:-

Apeth Guest House
Directions: From the side of the *Skorpios Restaurant* (*Tmr* 3.C5), a flight of steps climbs the hillside. The Pension is on the left. A double room 1200 drs.

Pension Cristi
Directions: On the other side, the right side, of the steps to the *Apeth*, with similar rates.

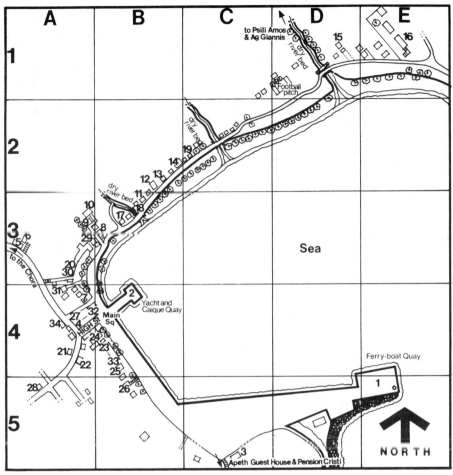

LIVADI

Illustration 52

355

Alongside the caique and yacht quay (*Tmr* 2.B4), the 'Esplanade' is wide enough to form an 'unofficial' Main Square where the buses park up. A short 'High St', at right angles to the waterfront, leads off left to a 'T' junction where the right-hand turning makes off for the Chora.

'Bakery' Rooms (*Tmr* 4.A4) Tel 51277/51484
Directions: As above, on the right, on the corner over the Bakery.

Anna, mother of Mikalis, runs the rooms over her sons Bakery. Both are characters in their own right and Anna must have been a very good looking woman in her youth, which is not to say she is not now, despite her rather severe countenance. Mikalis, likeable and in his 40s, is just the right side of being a smooth-talking 'trapper'. He was a ships Radio Officer for 5 years (which explains his excellent English), and has a degree in mathematics which he teaches in Athens during the winter months. The entrance is on the Chora Road and the situation can be on the noisy side, as the Pension fronts the 'High St'. The rooms are rather 'cell-like' and don't have lampshades. Our own room had to be entered by negotiating a structural pillar that just happened to be almost smack in front of the door. The top window wouldn't shut, due to a rusted fitting. Rooms share the separate, rather smelly 'just' toilet and shower. I write 'just' because everything just works and care must be taken when using the shower, not to flood the corridor, or else.... The first floor corridor has some substantial hooks but they hang off the wall. But as a double room only costs 750 drs in mid-season, these trifling criticisms must be regarded as carping and nit-picking, musn't they?

Further on along the Chora Road, steps by the modern building, containing the Port police (*Tmr* 5.A3) drop down to:–

Rooms (*Tmr* 6.A3)

From the 'High St', along the unsurfaced waterfront 'Esplanade' and, on the left, beside a narrow alley that emerges on the Chora Road, is:-

Captain George Rented Rooms (*Tmr* 7.A4) Tel 51274
Directions: As above.

A double room with an en suite bathroom in this lively area, costs from 1450 drs.

Beyond Froggies Pub (sic), a cul-de-sac leads past-

Hotel Cavo d'Oro (*Tmr* 8.B3) (Class E)
Directions: As above, on the right. A smart new block in the ground floor of which is the Self-Service *Restaurant Cavo d'Oro.* A double room starts off at about 1200 drs rising to 1650 drs.

Hotel Serifos Beach (*Tmr* 9.A3) (Class C) Tel 51209
Directions: As above. Another new building shutting off the end of the cul-de-sac.

They accept American Express and Diners credit cards which 'benefits' are reflected in the room rate charges. Single rooms en suite cost 1160 drs mid-season and double rooms 1420 drs rising 1420 drs and 1780 drs respectively (July - September).

Perhaps more in the budget of readers pockets is the:-

Pension K Potas (*Tmr* 10.A3)
Directions: This delightful Pension is hidden away in charming surroundings behind the *Hotel Serifos Beach.* Slide down the alley to the right of the Hotel and turn left along the back wall.

Hotel Perseus (*Tmr* 11.B3) (Class B) Tel 51273
Directions: Continue along the waterfront 'Esplanade' round the bay, over a summer-dry river-bed spanned by a footbridge, and on the far side of the *Restaurant Perseus.* Actually classified as a Pension.

Hotel Maistrali (*Tmr* 12.B2/3) (Class C) Tel 51381
Directions: From the *Hotel Perseus* the next building beyond the *Pizzeria Restaurant.*

Double rooms en suite start at 1490/1760 drs and rise to 1700/2000 drs (July - August).

Albatross Rooms (*Tmr* 13.B2)
Directions: Almost next door to the *Hotel Maistrali.*
Cell-like rooms but a very pleasant looking building in a nice position with an Oleander bush-tree to the fore. A double room sharing the bathroom costs 1000 drs mid-season.

Rooms (*Tmr* 14.B/C2)
Directions: The rooms are on the near side of an Ouzerie/Snack-bar from which emanate waves of loud rock music. A forked tree prominent.
Beyond the river-bed path to Psili Amos and Giannis Beach, at the far end of the bay are;-

Pension Erotas (*Tmr* 15.D1)
Directions: As above, at the back of a long plot.

Rooms
Directions: Next site along but may only open up for the height-of-season months.

Rooms (*Tmr* 16.E1) No 119
Directions: In the corner of a track that bends back from the waterfront in the shadow of the hillside that blocks off this end of the bay.
Rather spaced out with a 'cabin-like' hut end on. There is a large tree towards the back corner of the yard.
The beach here is rather scrubbly consisting of sand and pebbles with a few small boats anchored up in the shallow water.

The Eating Out I am advised that the reason for the expensive restaurant meals is that the owners do not work the establishments themselves, but let them out on short term leases to managers. This makes for costly overheads. . . .

Kafenion (*Tmr* 17.B3) No 46
Directions: A simple, square building with a raised patio about a quarter of the way round the bay.
The best value coffee in town but the owner and his wife close for the siesta and fairly early in the evening. 2 Nes 'meh ghala' costs 76 drs and 1 frappé coffee and a bottle of beer 96 drs.

Perseus Restaurant (*Tmr* 18.B3)
Directions: A little bit further on round the bay from the Kafenion above. Smarty, very expensive and run by, in 1985, a neat Belgian, often ever-so-slightly 'awash'! The pricing is probably not all his fault but a result of the referred to system of leases, but that does not make the meals any cheaper.

EΣstiatopion O'ΣtamathΣ (*Tmr* 19.C2)
Directions: On towards the dried up river-bed/road at the centre of the bay.
Looks as if it should be satisfactory, with reasonable prices, but the food may well be served up very cold, that is the whole meal. Two spaghetti bolognese (150 drs each), a tomato and cucumber salad (67 drs), a (battered, tired) plate of zucchini (60 drs), bread for 2 (20 drs), and a bottle of retsina (58 drs), totalling 505 drs.

The Restaurant (*Tmr* 20.A3)
Directions: Back towards the Village and next door to the 'Kovaki Gift Shop', which is itself alongside the 'Rock Cocktail Bar'.
Possibly, on average, the best food served up in Livadi Port although the *Restaurant Pizza* (*Tmr* 21.A4) might have cause to object. A meal for two of kalamares (230 drs each), a plate of briami (or ratatouille) (150 drs), and fassolaka freska (125 drs), bread (16 drs each) and a bottle of retsina (59 drs) for 826 drs. The small plate of briami is very expensive, the

bread is pricey at 16 drs and the appallingly costly list of wines is only saved by the availability of a bottled retsina (an oversight?). Added to the expense, the manager has a rather patronising and superior air, but there you go.

Tootsie Fast Food Hamburgers (*Tmr* 22.A4)
Directions: Along the 'High St', left (not right towards the Chora) up the steep slope and on the left.

Normally I do not list establishments which are inspired by say a North American counterpart and serve such unrepresentative offerings as hamburger with potatoes (150 drs) and hot-dog with potatoes (185 drs). But they do serve up a souvlaki pita for 46 drs.

Almost directly across the road is:-

Restaurant Pizza (*Tmr* 21.A4)
Directions: As above.

The only reason I have not sampled the menu is that the establishment is on the caique and cruise yacht itinery with the resultant exuberant courier at the top of the table leading the communal jollities. Sorry, I cannot bring myself to rejoice with them.

Zacharoplasteion ΜεδογΣa (*Tmr* 23.B4)
Directions: On the waterfront, the Ferry-boat quay side of the 'Main Square', in a row of breakfast/cake shop/bars. A reasonable breakfast and changes money (*See* **Banks**).

Central Kafenion (*Tmr* 24.A/B4)
Directions: In a block alongside an 'up-market' gift shop (which accepts American Express and Diners credit cards).

A good Cafe-bar for an evening post-prandial. Two brandies and 2 oranges cost 120 drs; 2 coffees and 1 ouzo 150 drs — a rather pricey ouzo though on another occasion the same drinkies costs 130 drs!

Two other smart restaurants, that cater for the affluent 'yachties' on the way round to the Ferry-boat quay, are the:-

Kafe-Bar Fish Taverna O' Mokkas (*Tmr* 25.B4) and the **Restaurant International** (*Tmr* 26.B5)

An alternative is the 3-wheeler pop-corn cart that sets up on the 'Main Sq'.

THE A TO Z OF USEFUL INFORMATION

BANKS None but there are one or two offices that change foreign notes and travellers cheques including:-

Serifos Travel (*Tmr* 27.A4)   Tel 84005
They change travellers cheques, locate Rooms and offer tours and. . . .

Zacharoplasteion ΜεδογΣa (*Tmr* 23.B4) This cake shop/cafe-bar, is a bank agent and changes foreign currency (notes only) and travellers cheques.

BEACHES

Beach 1. Well really one big beach, from left to right, almost all the way round the bay. The beach proper commences approximately opposite the *Perseus Restaurant* (*Tmr* 18.B3) and keeps on to the far right-hand edge (*Sbo*) of the bay. The near side is sand and fine shingle whilst the middle section is very pebbly sand becoming coarse sand in the area of the track to Psili Amos. For the far end beach make-up *See* **Rooms** (*Tmr* 16.E1), **The Accommodation.**

Beach 2. Ormos Livadakia can be reached from the track close by the Ferry-boat quay, up the steps adjacent to *Skorpios Restaurant* (*Tmr* 3.C5) or along the Street to the left at the top of the 'High St'. A once 'sweet' bay edged by a tree-lined, narrow, sandy beach, there is now a Windsurfing School to the near side and the 'Great Unwashed' extensively and unofficially camping out in the summer.

Beach 3. Karavi beach can be reached along a path beyond Ormos Livadakia and is comparatively deserted with a few holiday homes on the backshore slopes. About 40 minutes walk from the Port.

BICYCLE, SCOOTER & CAR HIRE
Rent-Bykes (*Tmr* 28.A5) A friendly firm, the owner of which speaks good English. He operates well maintained scooters costing 1300 drs a day, complete with a full tank of fuel. Office hours 0830 - 1930 hrs.

BREAD SHOPS (*Tmr* 4.A4) *See* **Bakery Rooms, The Accommodation.**

BUSES Two conveyances, one manufactured in the 1930s which runs when it 'feels well'. No, all right, only when spare parts are available. I must admit to initially allowing the Serifiots usual secrecy to overwhelm me in respect of the bus timetables but, after days of carrying on beneath my breath, a summer schedule appeared. As explained in the Introduction, the service only connects the Port and Chora, although with the amount of road reconstruction taking place in the stretch between Panaya, Pirgos and Galani it may only be a matter of time before the coverage is expanded.

The Port turnround point is on the 'Main Sq' alongside the caique and yacht quay (*Tmr* 2.B4).

Livadi Port to Chora

Daily	0730, 1000, 1130, 1230, 1330, 1430, 1500, 1730, 1830, 1930, 2030, 2130, 2300 hrs.

Return journey

Daily	0700, 0930, 1000, 1100, 1200, 1300, 1400, 1500, 1700, 1800, 1900, 2000, 2100, 2200 hrs.

One-way fare 40 drs.

CHEMISTS *See* **Medical Care.**

COMMERCIAL SHOPPING AREA None, but some stores are in unexpected locations. For example there is a self-service store 'O ΜαρίνοΣ' in a large building curiously situated behind the *Kafenion No 46* (*Tmr* 17.B3) to one side of which is a small general shop.

A little closer to the centre of the village is a Butchers and Gift shop side by side (*Tmr* 29.A/B3).

Alongside the 'Rock Cocktail Bar' (*Tmr* 30.A3), a narrow lane, which joins up with the main Chora Road, has a Butchers shop. The next short alley, a cul-de-sac, ends up by a Shop (*Tmr* 31.A4) which has a metered overseas telephone.

On the corner of the 'High St' and the waterfront is Peters-Shop (*Tmr* 32.A/B4) selling gifts, foreign papers and magazines, alongside which is a Periptero. Across the road is a Supermarket, more a disorganised store, which also sells tickets for the **FB Ionian**. Separated from this store, by a Cafe-bar, is an up-market gift shop who accept American Express and Diners credit cards.

Further on along the quay is a well stocked Mini-Market (*Tmr* 33.B4). On the left of the Chora Road is a Grocery Shop/Store (*Tmr* 34.A4) where tickets for the **CF Kimolos** are also sold.

DISCOS A remarkable collection probably as a result of the port calls of the aforementioned caique and charter yachts. They include **Froggies Pub, Heaven Can Wait - Bar to Discs**. Away from the bay is the **Nyktelia** Disco, beyond the Scooter Hire Business (*Tmr* 28.A5) and home-in on the noise.

FERRY-BOATS Quite well connected with the other Cyclades islands if travellers are prepared to chop and change boats and bear in mind the daily excursion boat connections between Siphnos and Paros.

Ferry-boat timetable

Day	Departure time	Ferry-boat	Ports/Islands of Call
Monday	1200 hrs	Kimolos	Siphnos, Ios, Athinos (Santorini)
	2330 hrs	Kimolos	Piraeus (M)
Tuesday	1900 hrs	Kimolos	Siphnos, Milos, Kimolos, Syros
Wednesday	1215 hrs	Kimolos	Kithnos, Piraeus (M)
	1345 hrs	Ionian	Siphnos, Milos
	2130 hrs	Ionian	Kithnos, Piraeus (M)
Friday	2100 hrs	Kimolos	Siphnos, Milos, Piraeus (M)
Saturday	1330 hrs	Kimolos	Siphnos, Kimolos, Milos, Ios, Athinos (Santorini)
	1330 hrs	Ionian	Siphnos, Milos
Sunday	1130 hrs	Ionian	Kithnos, Piraeus (M)
	1530 hrs	Kimolos	Kithnos, Piraeus (M)

FERRY-BOAT TICKET OFFICES Not so much Ticket offices more stores with a niche from which tickets are sold. These include the Grocery Store (*Tmr* 34.A4) on the Chora Road alongside the tiny Church, agent for the **FB Kimolos** and the Supermarket on the corner of the 'High St' and the 'Main Sq', selling tickets for the **FB Ionian.**

MEDICAL CARE Not a lot. For pharmacy items try the various stores. There is a Clinic up in the Chora.

OPENING HOURS Normal hours with strict siesta.

OTE There is a metered overseas telephone in a small store (*Tmr* 31.A4), a short way along the unsurfaced waterfront. (*See* **Commercial Shopping Area**).

POLICE
Port (*Tmr* 5.A3) On the right of the Chora Road.

POST OFFICE Up in the Chora. There is a post box mounted on the wall, almost opposite the Buses turn round, between the smart gift shop and the money-changing Zacharoplasteion.

TAXIS When available park up on the 'Main Sq'.

TRAVEL AGENTS
Serifos Travel (*Tmr* 27.A4)   Tel 51488
In a small office on the right of the Chora Road, opposite a tiny Church beyond the *Bakery Rooms*. The sign says 'You ask, we've got it'. Certainly they are very helpful and offer details of accommodation apart from a number of Excursions. The office is open daily 1000 - 1200 hrs and 1800 - 2100 hrs.

Excursion to Psili Amos & Agios Giannis Beaches
The unsignposted path starts up the stony river-bed, hedged in and overgrown by Oleanders and Bamboos, beyond the football pitch (*Tmr* D1). I have not written dry because even as late as June the river still flows, just, and water lies in pools. It is about a ¾ hr walk up and over the hillsides to:-

PSILI AMOS BEACH The rough track passes by above the lovely, clean, golden sand cove with small Arethemusa trees planted out on the edge of the low sand dune backshore. The sea is delightfully clean and there is one solitary Taverna which hosts daytime visitors. Between the taverna and the track, on the steeply sloping hillside, a house appears to have been built in direct line with the winter storm culvert — some erosion has already taken place.

Taxis make the trip as do small caiques from which it is a 'leap into the shallow water' disembarkation. Oh, by the way, the taverna only sells beer in small cans (60 drs).

AGIOS GIANNIS Another 15 minutes walk on from, and larger than Psili Amos. The coarse sand beach at the near side, blends into large pebbles backed by a grove of trees. There are a number of private dwellings.

ROUTE ONE

Livadi Port to the Chora (2 km) The road progresses up the very fertile and profusely tree-planted plain that backs the Port. This runs out in an ever narrowing valley against the side of the mountains.

Half-way up the snaking road and the 'Marco Polo' cocktail bar is on the right of an acute bend (one of many hairpin bends). Only indicated by a small sign but distinguishable by a bamboo shelter.

THE CHORA

If the ascent is made by bus, and readers will understand my preference for motorised transport, it circles round at the top, far end of the Chora which spreads over a precipitous hilltop, spilling over and down its flanks.

I think the Chora looks most picturesque from the Port.

Immediately prior to where the Chora bus pulls up, there is a Public Toilet on the side of the road with separate men and womens cubicles, clean squatties and urinals. Opposite is an OTE office.

Of the three or four ridge mounted windmills, one is in a good state of repair. To the side of the small 'Bus Square' are two Cafe-bar Kafenions.

Climbing the steps from the right of the 'Bus Square' (with the Square behind one) gives access to a large, marble paved Square on which stands an impressive Town Hall, alongside a Church. The ochre tinted Town Hall, built in 1908, has a distinctive roof balcony with cast iron railings of sculpted swans. There is a general store with dark interior on the edge of this Square.

From the terrace of another Church, below the Castle walls, facing south out over Ormos Livadi are some impressive views including those over Livadi Port. Descending from the Chora 'Bus Sq', the Main Road passes a Clinic, Post Office, (which changes money), the Police Station, a number of Kafenions and a few tavernas including, along a lane to the left alongside a blue domed Church, the:

Restaurant Bar Remezzo

It would be very pleasant to be able to recommend readers to catch the bus up the hill to the Chora, have a meal here and then ramble back down to the Port, replete and full of good cheer BUT. . . .

The dimunitive patroness and her equally small assistant work hard but the quality of the food often leaves something to be desired and some of the charges are absolutely astronomical. As an example, 2 plates of kalamares (inexpensive at 260 drs but gritty), an average Greek salad (185 drs), a plate of chips (60 drs), bread for two (40 drs, an almost stratospheric price) and 2 small bottles of retsina (260 drs — Ouch). I am reluctant to write favourably. Close by to the Restaurant are two shops.

It makes a pleasant alternative to walk back to the Port via the wide steps that cross and re-cross the serpentine windings of the Main Road. It takes between ½ and ¾ hour down. Incidentally, if readers feel the need for excessive exercise, it is a ¾ to 1 hr hard climb up.

A path also makes off from the Chora to join up with the track between Livadi Port and Psili Amos Beach.

ROUTE TWO

The Chora to Ormos Sikamia (6 km) & Taxiarchon Monastery (7⅓ km) From the Chora to beyond the junction (2 km) of the Mega Livadi and Sikamia roads is a steep climb up the mountainside. At the junction the road for Sikamia climbs on up to the right for a short distance to a crest marked by an ugly Chapel. From here there are glorious views down the mountain side to the Bay of Sikamia.

The maps mark various villages, including Panaya and Galani, as being on the roadside, but they are off to one side, down steep access tracks. Whilst berating the cartographers, it is best to totally ignore the roads marked in yellow and, note that, as late as 1985, the Main Road was subject to extensive rebuilding. Signposting is very poor. The Church in the Village Panaya dates back to the 10th century. After another 2 km, between the villages of Panaya and Pirgos, a left-hand turning tumbles very roughly down a lovely, intensively farmed valley to:-

ORMOS SIKAMIA (6 km from the Chora) The lovely and unspoilt bay is backed by groves of Bamboos, set on the extensive dunes with some plastic litter scattered about. The beach is sandy, the sea clear and clean and the backshore mixed sand and pebbles, planted with occasional clumps of trees.

There is no taverna, 'no nothing' apart from some new buildings spread out amongst abandoned, older dwellings. The 'High Street' is a sandy track, winding between the dunes and outcrops of Bamboo. A delightful spot with donkeys and mules in the ascendancy. A final word of warning in respect of the track surface to Sikamia must be 'TAKE CARE' and if at all unsure of riding a scooter, do not attempt the journey, it is tricky.

By keeping round to the right at the turning down to Sikamia, the poorly surfaced track loops round a further 3⅓ km to:-

TAXIARCHON MONASTERY (7⅓ km from the Chora) A fortified Monastery built in the 16th century and possessing Byzantine manuscripts and 18th century icons.

It is possible, on foot, to double back to the Chora, a distance of a further 3 km, by continuing on beyond the Monastery through the very pretty Village of Kallistos (¾ km) which is set in a lush valley.

ROUTE THREE
The Chora to Mega Livadi (7 km) and Koutalas (7¼ km) A turning
off to the left from the road to Ormos Sikamia, at about 2 km, is well signposted. The route is actually a rough surfaced track which descends to a fork in the road (5⅓ km). The right-hand turning bears off down to:-

MEGA LIVADI (7 km from the Chora) The track runs up the side of a widening agricultural plain, hesitating by some building ruins and remnants of ore wagon tracks, for this was a mining Town and Port. Vestiges of the erstwhile activity still litter the area including the lattice framework of a freighter loading span projecting out over the water.

The path then tumbles down on to the near or left side (*Fsw*) of the rather closed-in, small bay. The stony backshore of the mature tree-lined beach runs parallel to the sea's edge taking in a stony football pitch. The beach is made up of a scrubbly foreshore and a broad sandy strip. The landward side of the track is edged by a hotch-potch of buildings including a Kafenion, store and a Taverna where they serve up a very nice omelette. The omelette, bread, an ice-cream and bottle of beer costs 180 drs.

The locals are delighted to welcome visitors to this once thriving Town that 'died' some 35 years ago. Vivid reminders of the glorious past remain at the far end of the waterfront where there is an amazing old colonial house in ruins, fronted by Palm trees and a scattering of Oleanders. . . very South American.

On the far, cliff side of the bay is a big cave and a Monument which appears to commemorate the dead of a 1916 strike. Were they shot?

The left-hand turning back at the fork in the road loops around a large headland and runs along the near right-hand side (*Sbo*) of the very large bay of:-

KOUTALAS (7¼ km from the Chora)

The track passes rusting reminders of erstwhile quarrying activity, for Koutalas was once another mining Town.

The very spacious bay is divided up by a large Church topped bluff in the middle distance. A scattering of buildings now perch on the gentle mountain slope, that hems in the narrow tree-lined, shingle beach and small pebble foreshore. The scant community of fishermen support a 'Hillbilly Taverna', the owners of which are delighted to minister to travellers requirements. Two bottles of Carlsberg and a small Greek salad, served with a separate plate of 'scrummy', local, very curdy feta cheese, cost 230 drs.

Both the seaside Hamlets of Mega Livadi and Koutalas are delightful places in which to while away a day but **Rooms** are not ordinarily available.

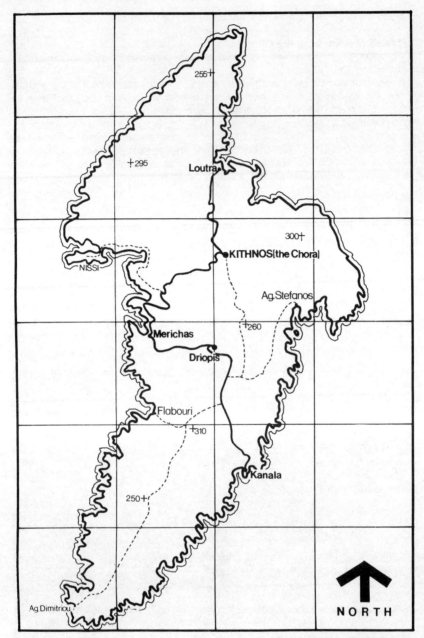

KITHNOS

Illustration 53

FIRST IMPRESSIONS
Greek holiday island; friendly inhabitants.

SPECIALITIES
Basket weaving; cheese.

RELIGIOUS HOLIDAYS & FESTIVALS
include: 0th Coptombor — Festival, Monastery Panagia, Kanala (SE coast).

VITAL STATISTICS
Tel prefix 0281. Kithnos is 22½ km from top to bottom and, at the widest part, 11¼ km across with an area of 86 sq km. The population numbers about 1,500.

HISTORY
Apart from the usual Cycladean story, nothing outstanding although the Island was once infamous for snake infestation. Additionally Kithnos was supposedly one of the original Island City States.

GENERAL
A comparatively small, dry, arid Island, all but for the winter river-beds and valleys, possessing no outstanding features or out-of-the-ordinary beauty other than that associated with most Cycladic islands — if that were not enough.

In common with a number of other islands close to the mainland, Kithnos is almost solely the preserve of holiday-making Greeks. This presents accommodation problems for other visitors in the peak summer period and more especially weekends.

The Port of Merchas was once a small hamlet with a few older red-tile roofed buildings. I write once, for now it is almost crowded out by small, round edge cubes and is dominated by a six storey Hotel at the far right-hand (*Sbo*) side of the bay. Despite this, the Port still manages to radiate a 'frontier settlement' milieu with only a section of the beach edging 'Esplanade' track being concrete surfaced.

The other Island Villages include the very attractive fishing Port of Loutra, the small residential beach resort of Kanala as well as the undistinguished inland settlements of the Chora — Kithnos and Driopis.

For reasons that are difficult to pin down with more than hunches, the Island is not a location that excites the imagination, or conversely lulls visitors to contentedly drift into a lazy, *laissez-faire*. Perhaps the most intriguing pastime is to guess, or try to divine, how the bus service works. Mark you, the Island has been selected for experiments in solar and wind power generation.

The friendly inhabitants do not appear yet to have made up their minds if this tourism fad will last, or is even worth the candle. There are two pleasant, unofficial Camping beaches, one only 5 minutes from the Port.

The Island is water-short but the times and places officially listed, when the hydrants are turned on, do not seem to tie up with any of the Island locations!

MERICHAS: port (Illustration 54)
The rather frontier town atmosphere described above is accentuated by the makeshift

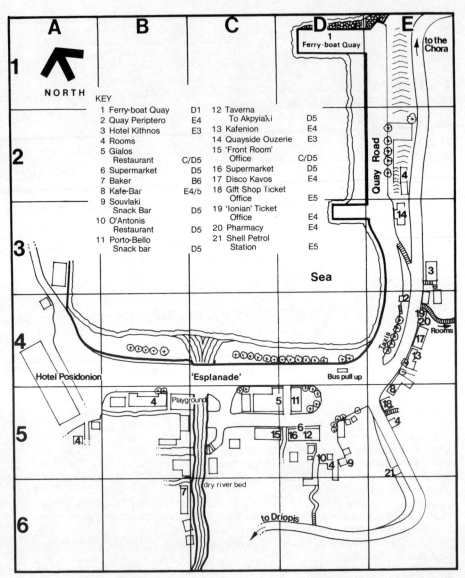

KEY

1 Ferry-boat Quay	D1	12 Taverna
2 Quay Periptero	E4	To Akpyiaλi	D5
3 Hotel Kithnos	E3	13 Kafenion	E4
4 Rooms		14 Quayside Ouzerie	E3
5 Gialos		15 'Front Room'
Restaurant	C/D5	Office	C/D5
6 Supermarket	D5	16 Supermarket	D5
7 Baker	B6	17 Disco Kavos	E4
8 Kafe-Bar	E4/5	18 Gift Shop Ticket
9 Souvlaki		Office	E5
Snack Bar	D5	19 'Ionian' Ticket
10 O'Antonis		Office	E4
Restaurant	D5	20 Pharmacy	E4
11 Porto-Bello		21 Shell Petrol
Snack bar	D5	Station	E5

NORTH

to the Chora

Ferry-boat Quay

Quay Road

Sea

Hotel Posidonion

'Esplanade'

Bus pull up

Playground

Rooms

Taxis

dry river bed

to Driopis

MERICHAS

Illustration 54

character of the unsurfaced tracks that spread out from the middle to the far side of the bay. In fact the 'Esplanade', that borders the backshore, is in danger of being completed and tidied up despite being in part, nothing more than a cleared swathe.

ARRIVAL BY FERRY

In common with other of the smaller Cyclades islands, the recently enlarged Ferry-boat quay is very large. The boats are not met with offers of accommodation (despite most of the population appearing to turn out), but luggage-laden travellers wandering down the quay may well be 'accosted'. On the other hand the bus drives up to the quay-side to await the arrival of the larger Ferry-boats. This alludes to the fact that a small Ferry connects with the mainland Port of Lavrio, whilst in recent years one or two of the inter-island Ferries include Kithnos on their itinerary.

Certainly arrivals might consider making directly for the delightful fishing Port of Loutra.

THE ACCOMMODATION & EATING OUT

The Accommodation Even the Greeks are asked to vacate their rooms over weekends, so consider stopping off during the week. The problem is that accommodation is often booked by long standing holiday-makers from one year to the next. Visitors intending to stay in the Port should move quickly.

One convenient aspect is that most of the available accommodation is on the left-hand side of the bay (*Sbo*) from the Ferry-boat quay (*Tmr* 1.D1). Two-thirds of the way along, prior to a Periptero (*Tmr* 2.E4), about which more later, and a flight of steps leads up to the higher level Main Chora Road. Opposite the top of the steps, across the road is the:-

Kithnos Hotel (*Tmr* 3.E3)   Tel 31247
Directions: As above.

A very pleasant Hotel, the excellent rooms of which are complete with sensibly sized, nicely fitted en suite bathrooms. If possible get a front room facing over the bay but more importantly just get a room, back or front. A double room en suite in mid-season costs 1000 drs. There was once a restaurant on the ground floor, now only a *Cafe-bar/ Zachroplasteion O'Merlxas*, which is a pity as good eating places are at a premium. Mind you they serve up a good standard breakfast plus some cheese for 100 drs and a boiled egg costs an extra 30 drs. A bottle of beer (Lowenbrau) costs 50 drs and a frappé coffee 45 drs.

The Periptero (*Tmr* 2.E4) on the left of the quay-side road is run by a very friendly man with some English. A sign proclaims **Rooms** which in fact refers to the *Hotel Kithnos*. The periptero owner ascertains the up-to-date position regarding accommodation by simply bellowing up the stone retaining wall.

Rooms (*Tmr* 4.E2)
Directions: A private house up along the Chora Road from the *Hotel Kithnos*, on the left overlooking the waterfront.
Average room rates.

Rooms
Directions: Down the slope of the road from the *Hotel Kithnos*. On the left, between a pharmacy and a motor-bike hire firm, a narrow flight of steps scales the steep hillside to a cliff-hugging house on the right.
A double room, sharing the bathroom, costs 1000 drs a night.

Rooms (*Tmr* 4.E5)   Tel 31243/31425
Directions: At the start of the Esplanade where the quay and the Chora roads join, the road to Driopis takes off to encircle this end of the Village. Almost immediately to the left.
A private house charging the going rates.

Rooms (*Tmr* 4.D5)
Directions: Off the first small Square along the 'Esplanade' from the Ferry-boat quay, opposite the Souvlaki snackbar.
Rooms
Directions: Over the *Gialos Restaurant* (*Tmr* 5.C/D5) on the 'Esplanade'.
Rooms
Directions: In the Street parallel to the waterfront and over the first Supermarket (*Tmr* 6.D5) on the left.
Rooms
Directions: Further along the 'Esplanade' a wide, dry river-bed, leads off at right angles. The accommodation is on the right, over the Baker (*Tmr* 7.D6).
Rooms (*Tmr* 4.B5)
Directions: Still in a southerly direction, towards the *Hotel Posidonion*, and on the left, two buildings before *The Sunshine Cafe-Pub* (Ugh).
Rooms (*Tmr* 4.A5)
Directions: To the left and in the shadow of the massive 6 storey *Hotel Posidonion*.

The Eating Out Frankly no one establishment redeems the Ports lack of any gastronomic excellence. Young children have to supplement the output of the more usual staff and a number of the restaurants close for the afternoon.

Kafe-Bar (*Tmr* 8.E4/5)
Directions: Close by the junction of the Driopis and Chora Roads and the waterfront. A low, shed-like building, with a 'laid-back' atmosphere. The young proprietor speaks tolerable English and serves a good bacon omelette (150 drs) and Greek salad (curd cheese but small) (100 drs). A bottle of beer costs 50 drs.

Snackbar (*Tmr* 9.D5)
Directions: To one side of the 'Souvlaki Sq' at the start of the 'Esplanade'.
The souvlaki pita is not 'giro' cooked but inexpensive at 40 drs.

O'Antonis Restaurant (*Tmr* 10.D5)
Directions: The other side of the Square above with an attractive trellis, plant covered patio but.
One can only brand the food tired and lukewarm and the prices do not assuage these shortcomings. A plate of (worn out and chilly) pistachio (200 drs), a plate of (similarly afflicted) stuffed tomatoes (200 drs), 1 helping of giant beans (cold, weary and with a feeble sauce, 100 drs), an (old) tomato and cucumber salad (56 drs) with bread and service costing 30 drs. After a bit of a grumble a Likori retsina, (56 drs), not listed on the menu, was made available.
The waterfront 'Esplanade' is paralleled by a Street one block back which runs out in the river-bed.

Porto-Bello Snackbar (*Tmr* 11.D5)
Directions: In a singularly ugly building, spanning the two streets described above.
The establishment's speciality is lobster but I usually manage to turn a deaf ear to the siren calls of this costly dish. The sloppy service epitomises the general shortcomings of eating out in the Port. A meal of 2 cheese spaghetti milanaise (a good helping but salty and expensive at 150 drs each), a very good Greek salad (130 drs), ½ bottle of Demestica (95 drs) and bread (20 drs) totals 545 drs.
On the other hand. . . .

Taverna To Ακρογιαλι (*Tmr* 12.D5)
Directions: Squeezed in between the forgettable *Cafe-Snackbar Byzantio* and a busy supermarket, in the Street parallel to the waterfront.

Papa cooks the grills and his 10 year old son takes the ordes and serves. In essence a Souvlaki Taverna and jolly good value at that. Eight sticks of souvlaki (280 drs), 2 plates of patatas (80 drs), a Greek salad (80 drs), and bread (10 drs) all for 450 drs. Unfortunately only open in the evening and arrive early because the Greeks know about the place!

Two Kafenions deserve a mention:-

One is at the outset of the Chora Road (*Tmr* 13.E4), with tables across in the trees dividing the road from the Ferry-boat quay.

The other, an Ouzerie (*Tmr* 14.E3), is on the side of the approach to the Ferry-boat quay, built over and round a fishermans shelter. Serves retsina, inexpensive ouzo with good mezes and stays open until late into the evening. An excellent position from which to survey the Ferry-boat quay.

THE A TO Z OF USEFUL INFORMATION

BANKS None. But a 'Front-Room office' (*Tmr* 15.C/D5), in the street behind the Gialos Restaurant, 'trebles up' as a local Ferry-boat ticket office, cigarette wholesaler and change office.

BEACHES The narrow, tree-edged, dirty, grey coarse sand beach is frankly scrubbly, even unacceptable. Restaurant tables encroach on the stony backshore. That is the bits of the backshore that are not piled high with building materials, surface shale and lumps of concrete. Additionally the sea bottom is made up of slimy pebbles covered with weeds.

A number of fjord-like bays with beaches lie to the north of the Port to which a small, red-hulled 'Express' cabin boat runs a water-taxi service.

The first beach is 5 minutes walk along the Chora Road and round the first headland from which a path and steps angle down to the very pleasant, narrow, coarse sand cove set at the end of a fertile valley. To the right-hand side of the path down are **Rooms** in a house set into the hillside.

There is a Church at the far side of this cove and the beach is planted with small Arethemusa trees in amongst which there is a certain amount of unofficial camping. The grey, coarse sand beach is in surprisingly good condition, considering the campers. The sea edge is biscuit rock, except at the far side, but the steeply shelving seabed is sandy. Disadvantages include biting flies and the location does fill up. A Taverna fulfills most of the bodily requirements, having an accessible toilet and the usual fare but no menu is available. To the right, the small islet of Ag Loika is attractively connected to the mainland by a narrow neck of sand and is a worthwhile destination using the water-taxi.

BICYCLE, SCOOTER & CAR HIRE Another Island on which the admittedly erratic, and at times baffling, bus service and convenient taxis invalidate the need to hire transport.

There is a motor-bike firm in the large building on the right of the Chora Road, mid-way between the waterfront and the *Kithnos Hotel* (*Tmr* 3.E3).

BREAD SHOPS A Baker (*Tmr* 7.B6) is on the right of the 'River-Bed Road', halfway round the bay.

BUSES The buses park up on the broad stretch of concrete where the waterfront and quay Road run into each other. Despite the timetable being stuck up all over the place it is a confusing service, so much so that even(!) the Greeks get excitable about it.

For what it is worth, here are my notes:-

Merichas Port to Kanala via Driopis
Daily   0700, 0945, 1200, 1345, 1700, 1930 hrs.
Return journey
Daily   0730, 1020, 1230, 1415, 1730, 2000 hrs.
One-way fare to Driopis 40 drs, to Kanala 80 drs.

Merichas Port to Loutra (via Kithnos — the Chora*)
Daily   0815 hrs.
One-way fare 80 drs.

*There appears to be a Port to Chora bus (and vice-versa, costing 40 drs), that ties in with the Ferry-boats, but which operates throughout the day. Additionally there is a Loutra to Chora bus (40 drs). A point to note is that the Loutra bus does not enter the Chora but stops up at the junction just outside the Town.

The wise Villagers use the taxis which operate on a share-basis and cost 150 drs for 2 from the Chora to Port (or vice-versa). One or two of the drivers think they are at the wheel of a Porsche, especially the dark, handsome driver in his mid 30s, and the Loutra journey is accompanied by many a blast on the horn, which is programmed to produce a 'Colonel Boogie' effect. Oh goody!

Mind you I must admire the gall of the Greek garage owner from Piraeus. He addressed himself to one driver of a bus on which we were passengers saying he had left his purse at the hotel and would he, the driver, mind lending him 2000 drs. . . and the driver did just that.

CHEMISTS *See* **Medical Care.**

COMMERCIAL SHOPPING AREA None but well served by two Supermarkets (*Tmr* 6.D5 & 16.D5) side-by-side in the Street one back from and parallel to the waterfront. Both display a public telephone sign and one (*Tmr* 6.D5), has **Rooms** above.

Incidentally, there are no Island Guide Books, only two fairly simple maps one costing 25 drs, the other 50 drs.

DISCO (*Tmr* 17.E4) I have not sampled the delights but the **Kavos** is conveniently situated.

FERRY-BOATS An interesting situation where, apart from the 'mega'-inter-island Ferry-boats connecting with Piraeus, there is a smaller connection to the mainland Port of Lavrio. This little ex-Merseyside craft, the **FB Ioulis Keas II**, does not, repeat does not, connect the Islands of Kea and Kithnos whatever they say at the NTOG office in Athens. I cannot understand why, but it is necessary to return to Lavrio to connect between the two Islands, but this cock-eyed arangement, it is rumoured, may be amended in 1986.

Ferry-boat timetable

Day	Departure time	Ferry-boats	Ports/Islands of Call
Monday	2400 hrs	Kimolos	Piraeus (M)
Tuesday	1500 hrs	Ioulis Keas II	Lavrio (M)
	1730 hrs	Kimolos	Serifos, Siphnos, Milos, Kimolos, Syros
Wednesday	1200 hrs	Ionian	Serifos, Siphnos
	1400 hrs	Kimolos	Piraeus (M)
	2300 hrs	Ionian	Piraeus (M)*

* A separate note advises passengers that as this boat arrives at 0330 hrs passengers may stay on board the rest of the night free of charge. (Just try to stop them!)

Thursday	1130 hrs	Kimolos	Serifos, Siphnos, Milos, Ios
	2400 hrs	Kimolos	Piraeus (M)
Friday	1115 hrs	Ioulis Keas II	Lavrio (M)
Saturday	1130 hrs	Ionian	Serifos, Siphnos, Milos
	1530 hrs	Ioulis Keas II	Lavrio (M)
Saturday	1130 hrs	Ionian	Serifos, Siphnos, Milos
	1530 hrs	Ioulis Keas II	Lavrio (M)
Sunday	1330 hrs	Ionian	Piraeus (M)
	1730 hrs	Kimolos	Piraeus (M)

The Kithnos-Lavrio one-way fare is 650 drs compared to the Kithnos Piraeus fare of 692 drs.

FERRY-BOAT TICKET OFFICES The **CF Kimolos** is represented by the Gift Shop (*Tmr* 18.E5) tucked in the corner of the Driopis Road. Tickets for the **CF Ionian** are sold from the small office (*Tmr* 19.E4) on the right of the Chora Road, before the *Kithnos Hotel*. The 'Front-Room' office (*Tmr* 15.C/D5) in the Streets behind the *Gialos Restaurant* represents the **FB Ioulis Keas II.**

MEDICAL CARE
Chemists & Pharmacies There is a Pharmacy (*Tmr* 20.E4) on the right of the Chora road, next door to the **CF Ionian** ticket office.

Clinic *See* **The Chora.**

OTE & POST OFFICE *See* **The Chora.**

PETROL A Shell otation (*Tmr* 21.F5) on the right of the Driopis Road.

PHARMACY *See* **Medical Care.**

TAXIS Bunch up on the start of the Ferry-boat quay. *See* **Buses** for further details.

ROUTE ONE
Merichas Port to Loutra (8 km) via the Chora Apart from the valley bottoms, the countryside is arid with multi-terraced hillsides. The road from the Port winds up a fertile valley, the summer dry river-bed of which is prettily and profusely flowered with Oleanders and Buddleia.

KITHNOS VILLAGE (The Chora) (5 km from Merichas Port) Set in a high, agricultural, rolling plain, but lacking the traditional whitewashed hill-capping beauty associated with the 'standard model' Chora. This is not to say Kithnos does not lack appeal.
  There are no Rooms that I could find but the Village is well resourced with a bread shop, general stores, clinic, butcher, several Kafenions, smart taverna, greengrocers, Post Office and OTE, all widely spread throughout the Village.
  The buses park up on a Square at the entrance to the Chora. The OTE is off round to the right, and right again alongside a clock tower. The Post Office changes travellers cheques, Eurocheques and foreign currency notes.

The road from the Chora snakes down to the large plain backing:-

LOUTRA (8 km from Merichas Port) Situated on an attractive bay at the end of a wide river valley, this is a truly lovely, working fishing Port Village, inhabited by friendly people. Note the beauty is not that of poets and artists.
  The site has been a Spa since ancient times, hence the name Loutra derived from the word for bath, 'Lutra'. The thermal waters are delivered to the baths at two temperatures, 40° and 70°F, the one suitable for rheumatism and the other for ladies wishing to have babies, but I cannot remember which is for whom!
  The left-hand horn of the bay (*Fsw*) has a bluff dominated by a white wall enclosed Church, an old mining jetty and the ruins of a Castle beyond which is a small cove.
  To the right-hand side of the bay is a very low concrete edging that contains the wide swathe of a continually running warm, brown stream that bubbles over the stony river-bed. Across this stream, in an English moorland setting, is, incongruously, a Bakers in a low, square white building to which there is a path that fords the bed of the stream.
  The final approach to the spread out Village is dominated by the very large:-

Xenia-Anagenissis (Class C)   Tel 31217
In the front and to the side are various outbuildings, including a Church and the thermal baths for which the Hotel must have been created. A double room, en suite, costs 1550 drs, if accommodation is available.
  The Main Road approaches the Village down the right-hand side (*Fsw*) and turns sharp

371

left along the front of the *Xenia,* leaving to the right, a spindly tree fringed, large square of wasteland. The far edge of this area is bordered by the backshore of the coarse sand and pebble beach and the left-hand by the back of the buildings lining the 'High' Street. The road traverses to the far left cliff-face bordering the Village and turns right into the 'High' St which runs out on the left of the beach.

The 'High' St has *Rooms* on both left and right. The left-hand buildings are set into and on top of the steep hillside that edges this side of the development.

Rooms To Rent Delfini Tel 31464/31468
Directions: On the right of the Street. There is a sign in the hall 'Please dont let the doors to hit and generally dont make a noise at the times. . .'.

A double room with en suite bathroom costs 1440 drs,

Next door to the Hotel is a Gift Shop. The grand-papa of the proprietors chatters to passers-by and, if they are English, calls them in to the shop in order to proudly display his personal letter from the Field Marshall Lord Alexander. This commends him for assistance rendered to the Allies during the Second World War. All the time the conversation is punctuated by his repetitious phrase "Bad business", his English being rather rudimentary, despite 6 years spent in London.

The 'High' St also contains a supermarket, two Ferry-boat ticket offices, a Kafenion, a small store and the bus parks up on an earth surfaced square on the left of the street.

From the bottom, sea-end of the 'High' St, the beach stretches away to the right, backed by the large area of wasteground in amongst the trees of which are pulled up a number of caiques, small fishing boats and a small block of changing room cubicles. As late as 1985 a local Priest seemed to have quite a large job on his hands (if you see what I mean) refitting a caique including some replanking. Maybe he will still be thus engaged in 1986 and 1987? The centre portion of the beach is made up of fine pebbles at the sea's edge and the sea bottom is sandy, whilst at the far end, by the stream outfall, the beach is coarse sand and pebbles. To the left of the bottom of the 'High' St, the clean, fine sand 'Beach Road' curves round past a Restaurant, *Rooms* and another Restaurant. A surfaced Street angles off up the hillside to a supermarket and more *Rooms* whilst the beach runs out on the edge of a small, concrete fishing boat quay. When the boats land there are a swarm of villagers surrounding the fishermen who sell their catch from the quay. The 'Beach Road' and the main beach are kept very clean by a 'council workman'.

Despite the mention of Rooms this is an unusual location, in that some enquiries regarding accommodation are met with the advice that they are only available to Greeks. Of course it is a very popular holiday resort with the Greeks so why does it not get more than a mention in most Guide Books? In conclusion, Loutra is 'a find'.

ROUTE TWO
Merichas Port to Kanala (8 km) via Driopis A similar road to ROUTE ONE
makes its way up to the Village of:-

DRIOPIS (4 km from Merichas Port) More spaciously laid out than Kithnos Village and more representative of a Chora, with pleasantly tiled roofs and over-looked by old windmills on the hillside, to one side. There is a Baker who prepares awful looking bread.

As with Kithnos Village, the Main Road bypasses the village despite the detail on the official maps.

After the large Byzantine Church of Ag Kostodinos, the road winds steeply downhill to the seaside development of:-

KANALA (8 km from Merichas Port) Not at all typical, this neat, verdant, mainly modern holiday resort, with a few *Rooms*, sits on top of a tongue of headland, flanked by a bay to either side. Flowers, trees and roses bedeck the gardens.

The bus pulls up in the widened road end, to the right of the Village (*Fsw*). There is a water tap to one side and bread is sold here daily, from the back of a van.

To reach the left-hand, small cove, climb the steps by the bus pull-up, step between the houses, over a wall, and down the track. The beach is coarse sand and pebbles, with biscuit rock at the sea's edge and a sandy sea bottom. No taverna but a pleasant spot nevertheless.

To the right-hand is a very small, generally crowded cove, with a tiny, rock edged, sandy beach reached through the gates at the entrance to the 'Bus' Square. Beyond a rocky outcrop is the large, main bay, access to which is through the large gates, at the front or sea end of the 'Bus' Sq. These lead through a sloping Public Garden (on a zig-zag stone path, sheltered from the sun and closely packed with Fir and Pine trees), down to a concrete fishing boat quay. The lower path leads to the small cove described above. The upper path continues on and over the low hillside to the spread-out bay with a narrow, sandy, fine shingle beach and some buildings behind the wall-lined backshore. These include a Pension, cafe-bar and breakfast restaurant. Some unofficial camping in the shade of the few spindly Arethemusa trees.

The large, centre-of-beach Taverna serves up a limited, but excellent menu. A large, well cooked spaghetti bolognese with plenty of meat (190 drs), a simple 'no embellishments' Greek salad but with plenty of curd cheese (110 drs) and bread (20 drs) for 450 drs. A bottle of beer costs 65 drs.

373

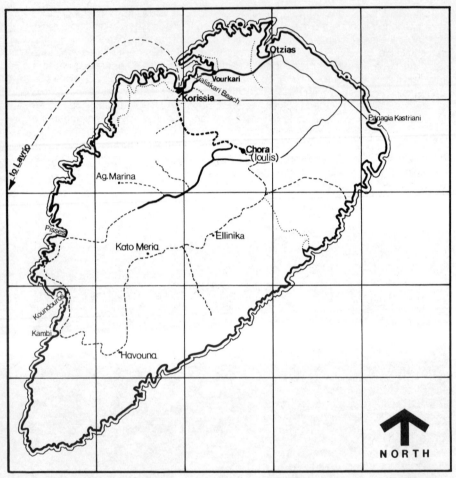

NORTH

KEA

Illustration 55

FIRST IMPRESSIONS

Expensive accommodation impossible at weekends; generally unhelpful natives; butterflies; low mountains; buddleia; mules & cows; oak trees.

SPECIALITIES

Pasteli (bars of sesame seeds and honey).

RELIGIOUS HOLIDAYS & FESTIVALS

include: 17th July — Festival, Ag Marina, above Pisses; 7th September — Festival, Ag Sostis, Otzias.

VITAL STATISTICS

Tel prefix 0288. The pear shaped Island is 19 km from top to bottom, up to 9½ km wide with an area of 121 sq km, and a population of between 1,600 and 1,700 people.

HISTORY

In vivid contrast to its close neighbour Kithnos, which has little history of outstanding note, Kea has a rich and vivid past with a number of Ancient City sites. On the small headland of Ag Irini, opposite the fishing Port Village of Vourkari, excavations have uncovered a Bronze Age settlement and Minoan palace. Apart from poets, a philosopher, a politician and an anatomist of note, the Keans were famous for their athletes. They were also renowned by reason of a simple cure for old-age — citizens aged 60 took a dose of hemlock!

Later, much later, a Greek warship Captain wrought havoc against the Turkish Navy. When boxed into the large bay on which are sited the Ports of Korissia and Vourkari he is supposed to have escaped to the open sea again by dragging his fleet over a shallow neck of land. The Turks were rather 'miffed' and 'terse' about the affair and promptly burnt Korissia to the ground.

Korissia yielded up a Kouros which is now in Athens Archaeological Museum. What isn't?. Much of the islands wealth was based on mineral exploitation.

GENERAL

A lovely Island and, in terms of geographical make-up, a smaller version of Andros.

Kea, in common with Kithnos, Andros and Tinos, lying as it does to one side of the main Ferry-boat routes, remained remote from the hordes of overseas tourists of the last two decades. In fact, in common with the aforementioned islands, Kea became a preserve of the Greek holiday-maker. And this is not only for summer vacations, but for weekends as well, which is the rub. Nowadays, during the summer month weekends, the Island is crowded, bursting at the limited seams, with all the paltry 230 beds available taken. So bad is the situation that even the Greeks have to resort to the Port beach. This pressure is reflected in the ambivalence of the islanders attitudes to foreign visitors, for they are, in the main, disinterested, with a tendency to rudeness. During the week Kea reverts to a sleepy, none too busy Island.

The cost of rooms is very high, shopping is expensive, scooter hire pricey and eating out is in the price brackets experienced on some of the more tourist packed islands. But despite the foregoing, do not be put off as the Island is extremely attractive. The Port of Korissia is endearing, even if the adjacent beach is not of a high quality. One cove further on, there is a splendid beach, followed by the pleasant, seaside, private yacht and fishing boat Hamlet of Vourkari. The Chora or Main Town of Ioulis is no whitewashed show-piece, but a fine example of a working Island Centre. Additionally, there are a number of other, if rather far-flung beaches and the most lovely agricultural hillside routes running the length of the Island.

A further word or two of caution. Lavrio, the mainland Port servicing Kea, is unlovely, the Ferry rates are expensive and lastly but not least, try not to time arrival on the Island at a weekend for the reasons detailed above.

KORISSIA: port (Illustration 56)

A pleasant enough harbour Village, rather reminiscent of, and similar in layout to Katapola Port, Amorgas. The setting sun lighting up the hillsides across the bay is a lovely sight, which can be watched in perfect comfort from one of the quayside Kafenions.

ARRIVAL BY FERRY

The point on the quay at which the Ferry backs up (*Tmr* 1.B4) is rather narrow and claustrophobic, being hemmed in by the hillside which rises steeply from the quay road and on which is an eye-catching, green pavilion type building.

Frankly, bearing in mind the shortage of accommodation between Friday and Monday, it is best to get a sharp move on and locate a Room. The boats are rarely, if ever met by Room owners added to which there is an additional twist to the plot, namely that the proprietors operate through a co-operative. *See* **The Accommodation**, for more (frightening) details! Despite all this, after the weekend when everyone has gone home to the mainland, the Island simply 'dies', even in July.

THE ACCOMMODATION & EATING OUT

The Accommodation As prefaced in **Arrival by Ferry**, most of the available Rooms are part of a collaborative association which is handled by the:-

Tourist Office (*Tmr* 2.C5)   Tel 31256
Directions: On the waterfront quay, where it widens out, opposite the taxi-rank.

The Room owners leave the letting in their hands and the basement office is down a few steps of the square, low building. Although it was rumoured that the office might be moving further along the quay, closer to the Ferry-boat landing point, my correspondent thinks not, at least for 1986. Not only is the renting of accommodation centralised, but the prices are structured, so much so that the door of the office exhibits a price guide.

	One Bed		Two Beds		Three Beds	
	'simple'	with shower	'simple'	with shower	'simple'	with shower
Class A	773 drs	976 drs	1017 drs	1437 drs	1464 drs	1709 drs
Class B	664 drs	895 drs	963 drs	1153 drs	1315 drs	1397 drs
Class C	570 drs	759 drs	814 drs	1139 drs	1139 drs	1207 drs

The standards are not outstanding and 'C' class is in effect 'village rustic'.

The owner has sensibly employed a young man 'Periclis' who speaks excellent English and is really most helpful. But when the Rooms run out I'm afraid there is little even he can do. The shoulders are shrugged and that is that. Best to ring up and book in advance. The office hours are Monday 0730 - 2130 hrs; Tuesday 0900 - 1200, 1700 - 2100 hrs; Wednesday 0730 - 2130 hrs; Thursday as Tuesday; Friday as Monday; Saturday as Friday; Sunday 0900 - 2300 hrs.

One or two establishments appear to be outside the organisation and these include:-

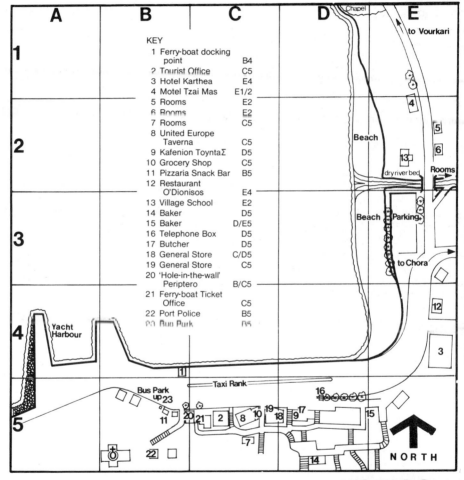

KEY
1	Ferry-boat docking point	B4
2	Tourist Office	C5
3	Hotel Karthea	E4
4	Motel Tzai Mas	E1/2
5	Rooms	E2
6	Rooms	E2
7	Rooms	C5
8	United Europe Taverna	C5
9	Kafenion ToyntaΣ	D5
10	Grocery Shop	C5
11	Pizzaria Snack Bar	B5
12	Restaurant O'Dionisos	E4
13	Village School	E2
14	Baker	D5
15	Baker	D/E5
16	Telephone Box	D5
17	Butcher	D5
18	General Store	C/D5
19	General Store	C5
20	'Hole-in-the-wall' Periptero	B/C5
21	Ferry-boat Ticket Office	C5
22	Port Police	B5
23	Bus Park	B5

KORISSIA

Illustration 56

Hotel Karthea (*Tmr* 3.E4) (Class C)   Tel 31222
Directions: At the far end of the quay where the road bends round to the left, as does the
bottom of the bay. A large modern building.

Despite the official double room en suite rate of 1500 drs between 1st July - 15th
September, the owners quote 1684 drs. A single room en suite should cost 1000 drs. The
rest of the year the respective rates are supposed to be 900 and 1200 drs.

The only other hotel is the:-

Motel Tzai Mas (*Tmr* 4.E1/2) (Class B)   Tel 31305/31223
Directions: Along the beach road and on the left, beyond the school, set in a tree shaded
position backing on to the beach. A low rise modern hotel.

The management also 'amend' the official prices. The published high season rates for a
double room with en suite bathroom is 1600 drs, charged out at 2000 drs plus a
mandatory breakfast. This should cost another 150 drs.

Incidentally, across the road are two private houses wherein are:-

Rooms (*Tmr* 5.E2 & 6.E2)
The one closest to the Port has the Tel No 31358/22206.

Back towards the Port, left up the river-bed road and on the right is:-

Rooms
Directions: As above.

This is the house of the lady who advertises her accommodation on a fence close by the
ticket office, at the mainland Port of Lavrio. 'Rooms for Rent with Bathrooms *Kopissia* Tel
0288 31355'. Not cheap though at 1500 drs for a double room.

From the *Hotel Karthea* (*Tmr* 3.E4), proceeding along the waterfront towards the Ferry-
boat part of the main quay and a sign nailed to some trees proclaims **Rooms** which may
lift the spirit but it is a 'dead' notice.

The key to the Port map indicates the position of various **Rooms** but do not expect too
much from the direct approach. On my last visit we stayed in a ladies house (*Tmr* 7.C5)
behind the *United Europe Taverna* (*Tmr* 8.C5). This was 'C' class accommodation with an
en suite bathroom. Well, yes! The ceiling of the bedroom was untreated hardboard, there
was no lampshade, the bathroom door would not shut, the shower control was 'iffy' and it
would have been difficult to swing a wet flannel. But it was a bed and I had spent the night
before on the beach and it had rained. Say no more.

Even the Greeks have to sleep out beneath their motorbikes, or in their cars so a few
pointers are discussed, for which **See Beaches, A to Z.**

The Eating Out Generally prices are medium to expensive, with establishments
varying from one of the most enjoyable tavernas I have eaten at to the rudest service I have
ever experienced — and that's a lot of experience.

Kafenion ΔΚ. ΤοyntaΣ (*Tmr* 9.D5)
Directions: Central quay, flanked by a butcher and steps.

The owner is no 'smiler' but opens early and serves good coffee with 2 Nes 'meh ghala'
and an ouzo (sketo or without mezes) costing 140 drs.

Taverna/Restaurant United Europe (*Tmr* 8.C5)
Directions: A quarter of the way along the quay from the Ferry-boat berth with steps to the
right of the building (*Sbo*) and a squashed up grocery shop to the left (*Tmr* 10.C5).

Fast, friendly, disorganised service, with good meals served in a pleasant atmosphere
of controlled chaos, overseen by the middle-aged, rather disinterested owner who masterminds the bills. Bags of shouting. Closes for siesta but serves food up to, if not after,
midnight.

Good the food is but perhaps a little expensive with prices for two averaging out at about
850 drs. A typical evening meal could be two plates of stuffed egg plants — filling and

ungreasy (250 drs), 1 giant beans (112 drs), a (small) Greek salad (110 drs), 2 bottles of retsina (very reasonably priced at 56 drs), bread and cover charge (11 drs each). Rosemary reminds me that the excellent menu choice included succulent grilled liver at 237 drs a plateful. And if you think it took time to be served wait until you ask for the bill. . . .

Oh, by the way, the owner has **Rooms** to let but he is in the co-operative.

Pizzaria Snackbar (*Tmr* 11.B5)
Directions: Beyond the Ferry-boat berth, next door to the friendly Kafenion (which is especially popular around boat arrival times).

I should have obeyed my basic instincts and allowed the raised hairs on the back of my neck to dictate departure prior to ordering. The reasons for my initial antipathy included draught pressurised lager and a menu that declared 'Sundays and Holidays prices are 10% higher'. Well the signs were there, the spoor was clear.

The establishment serves up pre-made pizzas from white boxes despite which it is very popular with the Greeks, who receive preference in the matter of order taking and meal presentation. Pizza prices range between 354 drs and 389 drs for a wide range of fillings including the house speciality. Unless forewarned, up to 2 hours can pass before the realisation that the food ordered quite simply is not going to be served. The young waiter expresses dissatisfaction about the state of affairs but his equally young, sharp-looking employers override any attempt on his part to make amends. After this inordinate delay disgruntled clients may be offered an alternative such as antipasti, good but expensive at 400 drs for two. This was not only my own, but also the experience of two other couples on different weekend nights. I can assure readers that the thought that the pen was mightier than their pizzas did not assuage my nagging hunger and final fury.

Restaurant Cafeteria Pizzeria O'Dionisos (*Tmr* 12.E4)
Directions: Across the unsurfaced street from the *Hotel Karthea.*

A surprisingly large establishment with a spacious terrace patio. They serve up a jolly good breakfast, and there are acceptable toilets, both of which may be necessities to those who have over-nighted on the beach. Eggs and bacon, bread, butter and marmalade for two costs 420 drs. Open 0700 - 2400 hrs.

THE A TO Z OF USEFUL INFORMATION

BANKS No. *See* **The Chora.**

BEACHES The unattractive Port beach occupies the bottom of the bay and is dominated by the red tiled, white walled School. At the near side, in amongst the scrubbly backshore of grassy, low dunes, small boats are beached. Some attempt is made to bulldoze the sand about.

From the middle to the far side of the beach, where a small Chapel tops a sea hugging rocky outcrop, the indifferent, fairly clean beach of sand mixed with pebbles is not very wide. The foreshore and immediate sea bottom is weedy and pebbly whilst the road edge is lined with Arethemusa trees. As the far side is approached the surface becomes almost entirely pebbles. There are some almost derelict changing cubicles and a concrete pad. A number of tubular frame, bamboo roofed shelters are dotted about. These give some overnight shelter, but my own favourite location, if there can be such a thing, is the porch of the Village School (*Tmr* 13.E2).

BICYCLE, SCOOTER & CAR HIRE Only one establishment, **Moto Kea**, on the right of the Chora Road out of the Port. No chance at the weekend and only motorbikes for hire at 1500 drs a day, including petrol. A rather bandit-like atmosphere and no telephone, so do not breakdown at too great a distance.

BREAD SHOP There is a Baker (*Tmr* 14.D5) on a small irregular Square reached by the steps alongside the Kafenion (*Tmr* 9.D5) and another at the bottom of the quay road, over which is the Police station (*Tmr* 15.D/E5)

BUSES A good service but a limited number of destinations. A timetable is stuck to the glass pane of the waterfront public telephone box (*Tmr* 16.D5) as is a Ferry-boat schedule.

On Wednesday, Thursday and Sunday the service expands its horizons making for far-flung desinations (marked with asterisks*). The timetable details an 'AX' followed by a number. This is the registration number of the particular bus.

Bus timetable

Monday

Ioulis (Chora) to Korissia	0515 hrs
Korissia to Ioulis	0930 hrs
Otzias, Vourkari, Korissia, Ioulis	0930 hrs
Ioulis, Korissia, Vourkari, Otzias	1045 hrs
Ioulis, Korissia, Vourkari	1045 hrs
Otzias, Vourkari, Korissia, Ioulis	1300 hrs
Vourkari, Korissia, Ioulis	1300 hrs
Ioulis, Korissia, Vourkari, Otzias	1545 hrs
Korissia, Ioulis	1630 hrs
Otzias, Vourkari, Korissia, Ioulis	1830 hrs
Korissia, Ioulis	2030 hrs
Ioulis, Korissia	2130 hrs

Tuesday

Ioulis, Korissia	0715 hrs
Korissia, Ioulis	0800 hrs
Otzias, Vourkari, Korissia, Ioulis	0930 hrs
Ioulis, Korissia, Vourkari, Otzias	1015 hrs
Otzias, Vourkari, Ioulis	1300 hrs
Ioulis, Korissia, Vourkari, Otzias	1545 hrs
Otzias, Vourkari, Korissia	1900 hrs
Korissia, Ioulis	1930 hrs
Ioulis, Korissia	2100 hrs
Korissia, Ioulis	2130 hrs

Wednesday

Ioulis, Korissia	0515 hrs
Korissia, Ioulis	0800 hrs
Otzias, Vourkari, Korissia, Ioulis	0930 hrs
Ioulis, Korissia	0945 hrs
Korissia, Ioulis	1030 hrs
Ioulis, Pisses*	1100 hrs
Otzias, Vourkari, Korissia, Ioulis	1300 hrs
Pisses*, Ioulis	1430 hrs
Ioulis, Korissia	1515 hrs
Ioulis, Korissia, Vourkari, Otzias	1600 hrs
Otzias, Vourkari, Korissia, Ioulis	1800 hrs
Korissia, Ioulis	1930 hrs
Ioulis, Korissia	2100 hrs

Thursday

Ioulis, Korissia	0715 hrs
Korissia, Ioulis	0800 hrs
Otzias, Vourkari, Korissia, Ioulis	0930 hrs
Ioulis, Korissia, Vourkari, Otzias	1015 hrs
Ioulis, Korissia, Vourkari	1010 hrs
Otzias, Vourkari, Korissia, Ioulis	1300 hrs
Ioulis, Korissia, Vourkari, Kastriani*	1600 hrs

Kastriani*, Vourkari, Korissia, Ioulis	1830 hrs
Korissia, Ioulis	1930 hrs
Ioulis, Korissia	2100 hrs

Friday: As Monday but the 1045 hrs bus departs at 1015 hrs, the 1630 hrs at 1600 hrs and the 2130 hrs at 2100 hrs.

Saturday

Ioulis, Korissia, Vourkari, Otzias, Kastriani*	0915 hrs
Vourkari, Korissia, Ioulis	0930 hrs
Korissia, Ioulis	1030 hrs
Ioulis, Korissia, Vourkari, Otzias	1030 hrs
Otzias, Vourkari, Korissia, Ioulis	1230 hrs
Otzias, Vourkari, Korissia, Ioulis	1300 hrs
Ioulis, Korissia, Vourkari	1600 hrs
Vourkari, Korissia, Ioulis	1830 hrs
Korissia, Ioulis	2100 hrs
Ioulis, Korissia	2130 hrs

Sunday

Ioulis, Ellinika*, Katomeria*, Havouna*	0630 hrs
Havouna*, Katomeria*, Ellinika*, Ioulis	0800 hrs
Otzias, Vourkari, Korissia	0930 hrs
Ioulis, Korissia, Vourkari, Otzias, Kastriani*	1000 hrs
Korissia, Ioulis	1030 hrs
Kastriani*, Otzias, Vourkari, Korissia, Ioulis	1200 hrs
Ioulis, Korissia	1445 drs
Ioulis, Ellinika*, Katomeria*, Havouna*	1530 hrs
Korissia, Ioulis	1900 hrs
Ioulis, Korissia	1915 hrs
Korissia, Ioulis	2100 hrs

Incidentally, the buses park up (*Tmr* 23.B5) at the far end of the quay, towards the yacht harbour.

CHEMISTS *See* **Medical Care.**

COMMERCIAL SHOPPING AREA None, but a Grocery Shop (*Tmr* 10.C5), Butcher (*Tmr* 17.D5), two General Stores (*Tmr* 18.C/D5 & 19.C5) and a small, 'hole-in-the-wall Periptero' (*Tmr* 20.B/C5). Fruit and vegetable vans ply their trade daily, including Sundays. This reminds me to mention that Sunday does not deter the island worthies from trading, and even the Baker opens in the morning.

DISCOS
Disco Kea On the Chora Road beyond the Olive oil factory, possibly as much as 1½ km distant.

FERRY-BOATS The Island is not on the large inter-island Ferry-boat itineraries. The year round connection is with the mainland Port of Lavrio on an ex-Merseyside Ferry, 'The Royal Daffodil', which was purchased by the Greek company in 1977 and renamed the **Ioulis Keas II.**

In the height-of-season months a 'look-alike' to the **Ioulis Keas II**, the **CF Papadiamadis** connects the mainland Port of Rafina with the Island but I am not sure of the times, frequency or if it goes onto Kithnos.

Ferry-boat timetable

Day	Departure time	Ferry-boat	Port/Island of Call
Monday	0600 hrs	Ioulis Keas II	Lavrio (M)
	1645 hrs	"	Lavrio (M)
Tuesday	0600 hrs	"	Lavrio (M)

Wednesday	0700 hrs	"	Lavrio (M)
	1530 hrs	"	Lavrio (M)
Thursday	0700 hrs	"	Lavrio (M)
	1530 hrs	"	Lavrio (M)
Friday	0600 hrs	"	Lavrio (M)
	1645 hrs	"	Lavrio (M)
Saturday	0600 hrs	"	Lavrio (M)
	1030 hrs	"	Lavrio (M)
Sunday	0600 hrs	"	Lavrio (M)
	1500 hrs	"	Lavrio (M)
	1930 hrs	"	Lavrio (M)

One-way fare 430 drs.

It will be noted, that as things stand, it is necessary to return to Lavrio to connect with Kithnos but there are rumours, innuendo and hints at changes for the better, in 1986.

FERRY-BOAT TICKET OFFICES Only one (*Tmr* 21.C5) close to the Ferry-boat docking point and slightly set back. The unsmiling, uncommunicative man also runs the Grocery shop (*Tmr* 10.C5). The office opens up prior to a Ferry-boats departure but allow ½ hr to purchase tickets, as no one is allowed on board without one and a queue forms at the office with the occasional native holding up matters for agonisingly long periods.

Do not miss the marvellous panoramic photo of the Port and surrounding area hanging in the office.

MEDICAL CARE *See* **The Chora** for both Clinic and Pharmacy.

OPENING HOURS Siesta but on Sunday many shops open.

PETROL A Shell petrol pump beyond the Ferry-boat docking point.

OTE & POST OFFICE *See* **The Chora.**

POLICE
Port (*Tmr* 22.B5) Up on the hillside, directly opposite the Ferry-boat docking point.
Town At the bottom end of the waterfront quay above a Bakers (*Tmr* 15.D/E5). No help in finding accommodation.

PHARMACY *See* **Medical Care** (which says *See* **The Chora**).

POST OFFICE
Well more a post box on the wall, close by the 'Tourist Office' (*Tmr* 2.C5).

TAXIS The rank is opposite the 'Tourist Office' (*Tmr* 2.C5).

TELEPHONE NUMBERS & ADDRESSES
Police   Tel 22300

TRAVEL AGENTS
Tourist Office (*Tmr* 2.C5). Apart from the detailed discourse (and adulation) under **The Accommodation**, the office sells maps and a Guide Book.

ROUTE ONE
From Korissia Port to Panagia Kastriani (10½ km) The surfaced road
borders the Port beach and curves round the edge of the bay and the small headland to dive down to:-

YIALISKARI BEACH (1 km from Korissia Port) A very pleasant, popular, small, sandy beach cove backed by verdant groves of Gum and Tamarisk trees. The foreshore does sport some green weed. On the nearside is a beach taverna and there is a Public Toilet and tap water. Despite the signs forbidding the same there is some unofficial Camping at the far end of the beach.

Beyond Yialiskari the road parallels the sea but a little up the slope of the hill. To seaward I'm sure there is an indistinct, but underlying smell of Olive oil dross, but I could be wrong.

On the far horn of land that encircles the bay, set close to the shore, are the abandoned but sturdy buildings of a once thriving industrial activity but I am not sure if it was an Olive oil or tanning factory (for which last process the prolific Island Oak trees were a necessary growth). Keep an eye open for some Andros Island style walling. The wall bordered road curves sharply right and down past a Public Toilet to the busy waterfront of:-

VOURKARI (2½ km from Korissia Port) Once a fishing Port but now host to a multitude of motor boats, yachts and a few, very large private caiques all lying at moorings bow or stern-on with some at anchor on the left-hand side of the quay. The waterfront, which forms the through road, is busy and the Port smart, as one would expect with this amount of money swilling about. Bench seats, street lights and 'no swimming' signs. Not very Greek really.

On the right-hand side, lining the quay road are the buildings, businesses and homes of Vourkari. The taverna/restaurants include, according to the signs displayed by one of the proprietors, the world famous *Taverna Aristos*. The menu prices seem a little more expensive than those of Korissia. There is a supermarket.

Across the bay is the Chapel topped promontory of Ag Irini whence a number of archaeological finds referred to in the Introduction. At the end of the Port quay, the bay is very shallow and speed boats, inflatables and small power boats are moored. The **Disco Medusa** is 300 m beyond Vourkari.

The road now climbs and leads inland across to:-

OTZIAS (5½ km from Korissia Port) A very pleasant, deeply inset, circular bottomed bay with, along the right-hand edge, a narrow, sandy beach, edged by young Tamarisk trees. To the left is a wide, coarse sand, rather scrubbly beach with a few rocks dotted about and some beach shelters (as there are at Korrissia Port beach). On the right of the road is a taverna and just beyond a fresh water tap, opposite which is a Toilet block. Unofficial Camping in the groves of trees.

From the edge of the bay the now unsurfaced track zig-zags steeply up (and down) very dry, arid, stony hillsides to a final saddle connecting to:-

PANAGIA KASTRIANI (10½ km from Korissia Port) Naturally enough, from this Church and Monastery topped Kastri Hill, the views are splendid. The original Church was erected in 1708 at the site where an icon of the Madonna was found by shepherds attracted to the strange glow. A larger Church was added to the site in 1910.

The last 5 km from Otzias to Kastriani can prove an unpleasantly hot walk at the height of the day.

ROUTE TWO

Korissia Port to the Chora (Ioulis) (5 km)
The road to the Chora is very pleasant, passing through lovely countryside, even if the road surface is appalling. To make the steep climb the road serpentines through old terraced hillsides (similar to Siphnos) and the buses really labour up the last section. By keeping to the left the road spills out on to a small Plateia of the:-

CHORA (Ioulis) (5 km from Korissia Port)
The smart Square is edged by a Post Office, a pharmacy, a hardware-cum-general-cum-drink store and the chic *Restaurant Piazza Delia Pizza*. The buses and taxis pull up here, but be careful not to park illegally as the police are prone to turn up and levy on-the-spot

fines! A sign directs those in need of medical care the odd 50 m to the Clinic.

The covered way from the Square (the right-hand of wall of which is muralled and behind which is an art antique shop), leads to a Kafenion cluttered junction with the 'High' Street. To the left up the lane (or 'High' St), steps, more steps and left again through remnants of the old Kastro walls, an archway and then right progresses to the:-

Hotel Ioulis (Class B)   Tel 22177
Directions: As above.

Actually classified as a Pension, the building is faded 1930s provincial in style, with an impressive tree-shaded patio. From here the view looks out over the mountain slopes, Korissia Port, the sea and, in the distance, the Island of Makronissos that lies between Kea and the mainland. To the side of the patio is the 'imaginatively' named *Bar Panorama.*

A single room sharing a bathroom costs 900 drs rising to 1000 drs (1st July - 15th September). A double room sharing a bathroom costs respectively 1125 drs and 1350 drs, with an en suite bathroom 1500 and 1650 drs.

Back at the 'Archway Junction', the turning to the right leads up the steeply rising 'High' St past the very large, three storey island Museum— which in common with many other Island Museums was closed in 1985. I cannot believe that it is always for restoration. Perhaps the Greek Government has been slowly selling the exhibits, without telling the populace, maybe to pay for the 'Parthenon Marbles'. Well it's a thought.

Beyond the Museum, still rising up the 'High' St, on the same right-hand side is the OTE (weekdays 0730 - 1510 hrs) as are bakers and butchers, and, on the left, the impressive 'Toy-Town' Town Hall, in the basement approach side of which is a Kafenion. The Town Hall really is an extraordinary building with the roof top balcony pedestals topped off by statues.

The 'High' St keeps on rising, curving to the left from the Town Hall tree-planted Square past a 'doo-hickey' dress shop into a musty, narrow Street. On either side are various legal offices with a papershop on the right, which is also an agent for the National Bank, and the *Hotel Filoxenia* (about which unfortunately I know nothing). Opposite the Hotel, in a covered way, is another baker and further along the lane, on the left side of a slow right-hand curve is a building with a 1930s British Railway Station style fretwork canopy which looks just like a Waiting Room.

This Street, now a path, leaves the outskirts of the Chora, and stutters to an end in fits and starts. Opposite a Church Cemetery and a dovecote, across a small valley ravine, set in heavily terraced hillsides is the famed Lion of Kea, supposed to date back to the 6th century BC. Frankly it looks like a Cheshire cat to me. Rosemary reminds me that, assuming the season is correct, a stolen fig from this stone walled path is a treat.

Glancing back the Chora tumbles down the hillside and across a wide saddle to a pinnacle of rock. The red tile roofed houses belong to a working Town, not a whitewashed monument to life and a world long disappeared to be gawked at by neck-craning tourists. Incidentally a number of the building facades incorporate bits and pieces of ancient masonry in the door uprights and jambs.

ROUTE THREE
Chora (Ioulis) to Ellinika via Pisses, Koundouros, Kambi, Havouna & Kato Meria
A circular route out and back to the Chora, in this case in an anti-clockwise direction, but the reader can always travel the other way round.

Initially taking the route back towards the Port, the surfaced road branches off quickly to the left in the shadow of the Chora mounted, steep cliff face. In common with much of this route it climbs to 'contour' at a comfortable height.

A left-hand turning cuts round above the Chora, joins up with the return track of this circular route and is signposted OTE leading, as it does, to the southerly mountain top mounted dish reflector. After about 4 km a path stretches away to the right towards the ruined tower in which nestles the Chapel of Ag Marina.

Another ½ km or so and the road surface deteriorates to a rough track and dips down a verdant valley, planted with Cyrpesses and Olive trees to:-

PISSES (8 km from the Chora) A sandy, fairly clean beach with, at the left-hand, a taverna/cafeteria possibly with **Rooms**. The owner is Basilis Denegas Tel 22122.

KOUNDOUROS (11 km from the Chora) It is with mixed feelings that this resort (yes a resort) is described. The developers of the Kea Beach Holiday Complex, have built a series of windmills in classical style, in addition to the Hotel, for accommodation and there are at least four swimming pools and a tennis court. If this were not enough, on the second of a series of small coves, on a beautifully sandy beach, are organised fun and games! Oh and don't let me forget the plastic matting laid down to save the hedonists feet from getting sandy.

The third cove appears to be private and the fourth, with a kelpy beach, has a taverna, the **Manos Taverna**. It is difficult to get served as assorted distractions, including a table tennis table, side track the staff from other than desultory interest in clients. The fifth cove is stony while the sixth and last is:-

KAMBI A lovely, lonely situation with a coarse sand and pebble strip of beach and a sandy strip of foreshore. A summer dry river-bed, lined with Buddleia is set in very neat agricultural holdings and runs out on the backshore. Two tidy, wide stone paths make off inland, one to a Chapel and, on the north side, are a few stone fishermens cottages that have been tastefully converted to private homes.

One other attractive looking cove is passed to the right as the track winds up from the coastal strip but access could only be by boat, foot or donkey.

HAVOUNA (17 km from the Chora) More a widespread collection of agricultural, stone-walled houses and farm buildings. Here a rocky path heads off across craggy hillsides to the most southerly point of the Island. The immediate landscape (or more correctly the mountain top), is dominated by the OTE reflector and mast. The tracks are rather confusing hereabouts with no signposts but they join up on the other side of the Hamlet. Away down to the right, on the edge of Poles Bay are the remains of the Ancient City of Karthea, but I am not sure where the path takes off to make the 3 km or so excursion.

The rest of the 12 km journey, high up on the mountainside, passes through beautiful, neat agricultural countryside, interspersed by profuse groves of Olive and Oak trees.

In common with many of the Islands countryside dwellings, the external plastered stone walls are not whitewashed, often making them difficult to see, melding as they do with the surrounding rock bestrewn land.

The track finishes up overlooking the lovely Chora with distant views of the Port, a fitting point at which to conclude.

INDEX

Artwork by Ted Spittles.

Typeset by:
Barbara James
Monitor Business Magazine

Printed in Great Britain by A. Wheaton & Co., Ltd., Exeter